Prentice Hall Health

complete review of Dental Hygiene

Jacqueline N. Brian, LDH, MS
Division of Dental Education
Indiana University–Purdue University
Fort Wayne, Indiana

Mary Danusis Cooper, LDH, MSEd
Division of Dental Education
Indiana University–Purdue University
Fort Wayne, Indiana

Upper Saddle River, New Jersey 07458

Library of Congress Cataloging-in-Publication Data
Prentice Hall complete outline review of dental hygiene/ [edited by] Jacqueline Brian and Mary Cooper.
p. ; cm—(Prentice Hall health review series)
Includes bibliographical references and index.
ISBN 0-13-083328-2
1. Dental hygienists—Examinations, questions, etc. 2. Dental hygiene—Examinations, questions, etc. 3. Dentistry—Examinations, questions. etc. I. Title: Health outline review of dental hygiene. II. Brian, Jacqueline. III. Cooper, Mary (Mary D.) IV. Series.
[DNLM: 1. Oral Hygiene—Examination Questions. 2. Dental Hygienists—education. WU 18.2 P532 2001]
RK60.5 .P47 2001
617.6'01'076–dc21

00065252

Publisher: Julie Alexander
Acquisitions Editor: Mark Cohen
Managing Development Editor: Marilyn Meserve
Director of Production and Manufacturing: Bruce Johnson
Managing Production Editor: Patrick Walsh
Production Editor: Jessica Balch, Pine Tree Composition
Production Liaison: Danielle Newhouse
Manufacturing Buyer: Pat Brown
Design Director: Cheryl Asherman
Design Coordinator: Maria Guglielmo
Cover and Interior Designer: Janice Bielawa
Marketing Manager: David Hough
Product Information Manager: Rachele Triano
Editorial Assistants: Melissa Kerian and Mary Ellen Ruitenberg
Composition: Pine Tree Composition
Printing and Binding: Banta Book Group

Pearson Education, Ltd., *London*
Pearson Education Australia Pty. Limited, *Sydney*
Pearson Education Singapore Pte. Ltd.
Pearson Education North Asia Ltd., *Hong Kong*
Pearson Education Canada, Ltd., *Toronto*
Pearson Educación de Mexico, S.A. de C.V.
Pearson Education—Japan, *Tokyo*
Pearson Education Malaysia, Pte. Ltd.
Pearson Education, Upper Saddle River, New Jersey

Notice: The authors and the publisher of this volume have taken care that the information and technical recommendations contained herein are based on research and expert consultation, and are accurate and compatible with the standards generally accepted at the time of publication. Nevertheless, as new information becomes available, changes in clinical and technical practices become necessary. The reader is advised to carefully consult manufacturers' instructions and information material for all supplies and equipment before use, and to consult with a health care professional as necessary. This advice is especially important when using new supplies or equipment for clinical purposes. The authors and publisher disclaim all responsibility for any liability, loss, or damage incurred as a consequence, directly or indirectly, of the use and application of any of the contents of this volume.

This book is dedicated in memory of my father, Paul Nusbaumer, and in honor of my mother, Kathryn, who taught me that if you believe in yourself, you can accomplish anything.

To my daughter, Diedre, for her encouragement and words of wisdom. To my husband, Michael, for his unfailing support, understanding, and gift of spirit. You are a great blessing.

J.N.B.

In loving memory of my father, Dimitrios Danusis, who instilled in me that all things are possible, and to my mother, Afrodhiti, who continues to unconditionally give her love.

And to the Georges in my life, my husband and son, I thank you eternally for your love, patience, and support.

M.D.C.

10 9 8 7 6 5 4 3 2
ISBN 0-13-083328-2

Contents

Preface

For a dental hygiene student to become a quality oral health care professional, it is essential to master the basic concepts offered in the dental hygiene curriculum. The intent of this text is to review those basic concepts in a clear, concise manner, using an outline format. This review is not intended to be the sole body of knowledge for dental hygiene, but rather to emphasize the fundamental aspects of dental hygiene education.

To introduce the process of National Board Examination testing, our introductory chapter addresses practical information about study strategies and methods to develop a positive attitude and overcome test anxiety.

Several important features support the strength of this review. The variety of multiple choice questions provides typical stand-alone and case-based questions, as well as more in-depth, thought-provoking questions that allow readers to demonstrate learning and understanding. Rationales are provided, explaining both correct and incorrect answers. In addition, references for each chapter are provided at the end of the book.

Using a different approach to address special needs patients, we have included this subject material in most of the chapters, as well as in the case studies. In addition, we combined the subjects Patient Assessment and Preventive Dentistry. This will enhance learning and develop perspectives by combining disciplines and capturing the interrelationships of these subjects.

As an added feature, the companion CD-ROM embellishes the text by offering additional cases and enough stand-alone questions to simulate a mock National Board Examination. A glossary is also included in the CD-ROM as a quick reference to key words and their meanings.

We hope that this text benefits the readers by helping them to successfully complete a major milestone in their lives—passing National Boards and starting a professional career in dental hygiene.

Jacqueline Brian
Mary Cooper

Acknowledgments

We would like to thank all of the contributing authors for their understanding, patience, time, and expertise in this laborious project. Also, to Mark Cohen, Acquisitions Editor, Allied Health, and Robin Lazrus, Development Editor, we thank you for your support. To Bobbie Shadle, from our Learning Resource Center, we give gratitude for your creative work. A very special thank you to Julie Yoder, who so unselfishly gave of her time and computer knowledge to help meet the deadlines and pull this manuscript together.

In memory of Dr. Phillip E. O'Shaughnessy, author of Chapter 3 on Head and Neck Anatomy. We remember him as a brilliant educator who loved teaching, and as a mentor and colleague of good spirit and humor.

Contributors

Marsha L. Baltes, PhD
Adjunct Associate Professor
Indiana University School of Medicine
Instructor
Department of Dental Hygiene
Indiana University–Purdue University
Fort Wayne, Indiana
Chapter 2: Anatomy and Physiology

Joseph E. Baughman, DDS
Supervising Dentist
Department of Dental Hygiene
West Central College
Douglasville, Georgia
Chapter 7: Oral Pathology

Barbara L. Bennett, CDA, RDH, MS
Chair
Department of Dental Hygiene
Texas State Technical College
Harlingen, Texas
Chapter 6: Microbiology and Infection Control

Linda D. Boyd, RDH, MS, RD
Clinical Faculty
Department of Periodontology
Oregon Health Sciences
University School of Dentistry
Portland, Oregon
Chapter 5: Nutrition and Oral Health

Charlene C. Goodwin, RDH, MSEd, MS
Assistant Professor
Department of Dental Hygiene
Macon State College
Macon, Georgia
Chapter 4: Oral Anatomy and Histology

Emma Henderson, RDH, BS
Associate Faculty
Department of Dental Hygiene
Indiana University–Purdue University
Fort Wayne, Indiana
Chapter 4: Oral Anatomy and Histology

Heather O. Mapp, RDH, MEd
Program Director
Department of Dental Hygiene
Lanier Technical Institute/Gainsville College
Gainsville, Georgia
Chapter 1: Introduction to the National Board Examination: Preparation, Format and Strategies

Patricia J. Nunn, RDH, MS
Chair and Associate Professor
Department of Dental Hygiene
University of Oklahoma Health Sciences Center
College of Dentistry
Oklahoma City, Oklahoma
Chapter 13: Medical Emergencies

Phillip E. O'Shaughnessy, DDS, MSD
Assistant Professor Emeritus
Indiana University School of Dentistry
Adjunct Associate Professor, emeritus
Indiana University School of Medicine
Indiana University–Purdue University
Coroner, Allen County
Fort Wayne, Indiana
Chapter 3: Head and Neck Anatomy

Carol A. Palmer, EdD, RD
Professor and Co-head
Division of Nutrition and Preventive Dentistry
Tufts University School of Dental Medicine
Boston, Massachusetts
Chapter 5: Nutrition and Oral Health

Jeffrey A. Platt, DDS, MS
Assistant Professor
Department of Restorative Dentistry
Indiana University School of Dentistry
Indianapolis, Indiana
Chapter 14: Dental Materials

Frieda Atherton Pickett, RDH, MS
Adjunct Associate Professor
Department of Dental Hygiene
East Tennessee State University
Johnson City, Tennessee
Chapter 8: Pharmacology

Betsy Reynolds, RDH, MS
Associate Clinical Professor
University of Colorado
Denver, Colorado
Chapter 15: Community Dental Health

Marilyn J. Stolberg, DDS
Director
Dental Hygiene Program and Clinical Education
Ferris State University
Big Rapids, Michigan
Chapter 12: Clinical Periodontology

Barbara J. Stubbs, RDH, MS
Assistant Professor
Department of Dental Hygiene
Armstrong Atlantic State University
Savannah, Georgia
Chapter 10: Periodontal Instrumentation

Ruth Fearing Tornwall, RDH, MS
Instructor IV
Dental Hygiene Program
Lamar Institute of Technology
Beaumont, Texas
Chapter 8: Pharmacology

Lauri Weichmann, RDH, MPA
Coordinator
Dental Hygiene Program
Carl Sandburg College
Galesburg, Illinois
Chapter 9: Patient Assessment and Preventive Dentistry

Gail F. Williamson, RDH, MS
Professor, Dental Diagnostic Sciences
Oral and Maxillofacial Imaging
Department of Oral Surgery, Medicine and Pathology
Indiana University School of Dentistry
Indianapolis, Indiana
Chapter 11: Oral and Maxillofacial Radiology

Reviewers

Marianne Belles, RDH, MS
Assistant Professor
Department of Dental Hygiene
Hudson Valley Community College
Troy, New York

Wanda Cloet, RDH, MS
Supervisor
Department of Dental Hygiene
Central Community College
Hastings, Nebraska

Elena Bablenis Haveles, PharmD.
Adjunct Associate Professor of Pharmacology
Old Dominion University
Norfolk, Virginia

Laura Jansen, RDH, MS
Clinical Associate Professor
School of Dentistry
The University of North Carolina at Chapel Hill
Chapel Hill, North Carolina

William W. Johnson, DDS, MS
University of Nebraska Medical Center
Section of Operative Dentistry
Lincoln, Nebraska

C. Merry LeBlond, RDH, MS
Coordinator and Acting Chair
Department of Dental Auxiliaries Education
Middlesex County College
Edison, New Jersey

Leah MacPherson, RDH, BS, MHP
Assistant Professor
Forsyth School for Dental Hygienists
Boston, Massachusetts

Elizabeth C. Reynolds, RDH, MS
Oral Biologist
Denver, Colorado

Barbara Ringle, RDH, MEd
Assistant Professor
Cuyahoga Community College
Cleveland, Ohio

Elaine Satin, RDH, MS
Program Coordinator
Associate Professor
Dental Hygiene Department
Bergen Community College
Paramus, New Jersey

Mary Jo Saxe, RDH, MHA
Associate Professor
Program Coordinator
Pennsylvania College of Technology
Williamsport, Pennsylvania

Cynthia R. Veach
Associate Professor
Dental Hygiene Program
Chattanooga State Technical College
Chattanooga, Tennessee

Introduction

SUCCESS ACROSS THE BOARDS: THE PRENTICE HALL HEALTH REVIEW SERIES

Prentice Hall Health is pleased to present ***Success Across the Boards,*** our new review series. These authoritative texts give you expert help in preparing for certifying examinations. Each title in the series comes with its own technology package, including a CD-ROM and a Companion Website. You will find that this powerful combination of text and media provides you with expert help and guidance for achieving success across the boards. This outline review for the dental hygienist provides help for preparing for the National Board Examination.

COMPONENTS OF THE SERIES

The series is made up of two separate books and CD combinations, as well as a Companion Website that support both books.

About the Book

Complete Review of Dental Hygiene **by Jacqueline N. Brian and Mary Danusis Cooper**

- *Outline Content Review:* Key topics that may be covered on the board examination are included in this book. With the easy-to-use outline format, you can quickly identify the important ideas, concepts, and facts that are presented. Important terms are defined where necessary, and illustrations are included where they will help illuminate and clarify information. The concept of the review book is to make it easier to understand information you have learned elsewhere—in courses, from textbooks, in the field. The purpose of the outline format is to help you focus your review on the most important information and use your study time most effectively.
- *Study Questions:* Multiple choice questions at the end of each chapter follow the format of questions that appear on the examination. Working through these questions after reviewing each chapter outline will help you assess your strengths and weaknesses in each topic of study. Correct answers and comprehensive rationales are included.
- *Case Studies:* Full-color case studies similar to those you will find on the board examination are included in the final chapter.

About the CD-ROM

A CD-ROM is included in the back of this book. The CD provides additional practice multiple choice questions, additional full-color case studies, and an audio glossary.

- *Practice Questions:* The accompanying CD includes 200 stand-alone questions and 150 questions based on case studies with full-color art. The software was designed so that you can practice by topic or through simulated exams. Correct answers and comprehensive rationales follow all questions. You will receive immediate feedback to identify your strengths and weaknesses in each topic covered.
- *Audio Glossary:* Over 150 words are pronounced and definitions provided to help you review and practice the all-important terms you need to know.

Companion Website for Dental Hygiene Review

Visit the companion website at **www.prenhall.com/review** for additional practice, information about the exam, and links to related resources. Designed as a supplement to both books in the series, you will want to bookmark this site and return frequently for the most current information on your path to success.

Companion Book

Question & Answer Review for Dental Hygiene by Caren Barnes and Michelle Sensat (0-8385-0342-X)

Once you are comfortable with the topics on the exam and want multiple opportunities to practice your skills, this is the perfect book. The 5th edition of this review book includes over 1,500 exam-type questions with answers, comprehensive rationales, and references. By combining quick content reviews with practice questions in print, on a CD, or on the Web, you will increase your likelihood of success on the exam.

CERTIFICATION

Licensure is the responsibility of the government at the state or district level. State legislatures adopt laws that determine the specific requirements for each individual state. Those requirements include educational, written examination, and clinical requirements. The agency within the state government that is directed to administer licensure is the state board of dental examiners.

ABOUT THE EXAMS

National Board Dental Hygiene Exam

The National Board Dental Hygiene Examination is used to fulfill or partially fulfill the written examination requirements for licensure. The exam is comprehensive and consists of 350 multiple-choice items. There are two components of this exam: Component A, which consists of 200 items, and Component B, which consists of 150 case-based items. This examination is given three times a year throughout the United States. Additional information about the test may be obtained by contacting the Joint Commission on National Dental Examinations, American Dental Association, 211 East Chicago Avenue, Suite 1846, Chicago, Illinois 60611-2678, or by calling (312) 440-2678.

Clinical Exams

To fulfill the clinical requirements for licensure, Clinical Exams may be conducted by each individual state. However, some states jointly administer clinical examinations. The states that combine to administer boards are considered to be part of groups that are called regional boards. They must be contacted individually for examination information. Not all states are part of a regional board. Regional boards are testing agencies, not licensing authorities.

There are four regional boards:

Central Regional Dental Testing Service (CRDTS)
Northeast Regional Board of Dental Examiners (NERB)
Southern Regional Testing Agency (SRTA)
Western Regional Examining Board (WREB)

The addresses for the individual states as well as the regional boards can be found in the ADHA pamphlet, *The Dental Hygienist's Resource Booklet.*

STUDY TIPS

Review Materials

Choose review materials that contain the information you need to study. Save time by making sure you aren't studying anything needlessly. For preparation before the exam, the best study preparation would be to use both the Outline Review Book and Question & Answer Review Book. Use the references in these books to easily find related textbooks if additional study is required. We strongly encourage all exam candidates to obtain a copy of the Candidate's Guide.

Set a Study Schedule

Use your time-management skills to set a schedule that will help you feel as prepared as you can be. Consider all the relevant factors—the materials you need to study, how many months, weeks, or days until the test date, and how much time you can study each day. If you establish your schedule ahead of time and write it in your date book, you will be much more likely to follow it.

Take Practice Tests

Practice as much as possible, using the questions at the end of each chapter in this book, along with over 1,500 more questions available in the companion Question & Answer book, the accompanying CD, and the Companion Website. These questions were designed to follow the format of the exam, so the more you practice with these questions, the better prepared you will be on test day.

The practice tests on the CDs will give you a chance to experience the exam before you actually have to take it and will also let you know how you're doing and where you need to do better. For best results, we recommend you take a practice test 2 to 3 weeks before you are scheduled to take the actual exam. Spend the next weeks targeting those areas in which you performed poorly by reviewing the Outline and practicing additional questions in those areas.

Practice under test-like conditions—in a quiet room, with no books or notes to help you, and with a clock to monitor the time limit. Try to come as close as you can to duplicating the actual test situation.

TAKING THE EXAMINATION

Prepare Physically

When taking the examination, you need to work efficiently under time pressure. If your body is tired or under stress, you might not think as clearly or perform as well as you usually do. If you can, avoid staying up all night. Get some sleep so you wake up rested and alert.

Eating right is also important. The best advice is to eat a light, well-balanced meal before a test. When time is short, grab a quick-energy snack such as a banana, orange juice, or a granola bar.

The Examination Site

The examination site should be located prior to the required examination time. One suggestion is to find the site and parking facilities the day before the test. Parking fee information should be obtained so sufficient money can be taken along on the examination day.

Allow plenty of time for travel to the site in case of unexpected mishaps such as traffic snarls. During travel, think positive thoughts (e.g. "My preparation for the exam was thorough, so I'll be able to answer the questions easily"). Maintain a confident attitude to prevent unnecessary stress.

Materials

Be sure to take all required identification materials, registration forms, and any other items required by the testing organization or center. Read information and instructions supplied by the testing organizations thoroughly to be sure you have all necessary materials before the day of the exam.

Read Test Directions

Read the examination directions thoroughly! Because some board examinations have different test sections with different question formats, it is important to be aware of changes in directions. Read each set of directions completely before starting a new section of questions.

Machine-scored tests require you use a special pencil to fill in a small box on a computerized answer sheet. Use the right pencil (usually a number 2), and mark your answers in the correct space. Neatness counts on these tests, because the computer can misread stray pencil marks or partially erased answers. Periodically, check the answer number against the question number to make sure they match. One question skipped can cause every answer following it to be marked incorrectly.

Selecting the Right Answer

Keep in mind only one answer is correct. First read the stem of the question with *each* possible choice provided and eliminate choices that are obviously incorrect. Be cautious about choosing the first answer that *might* be correct; all possibilities should be considered before the final choice is made; the best answer should be selected.

If a question is complicated, try to break it down into small sections that are easy to understand. Pay special attention to qualifiers such as *only*, *except*, etc. For example, negative words in a question can confuse your understanding of what the question asks ("Which of the following is *not*…").

Intelligent Guessing

If you don't know the answer, eliminate those answers that you know or suspect are wrong. Your goal is to narrow down your choices. Here are some questions to ask yourself:

- Is the choice accurate in its own terms? If there's an error in the choice, for example, a term that is incorrectly defined—the answer is wrong.
- Is the choice relevant? An answer may be accurate, but it may not relate to the essence of the question.
- Are there any distractors, such as *always, never, all, none,* or *every*? Qualifiers make it easy to find an exception that makes a choice incorrect.

Mark answers you aren't sure of, and go back to them at the end of the test.

Ask yourself whether you would make the same guesses again. Chances are you will leave your answers alone, but you may notice something that will make you change your mind—a qualifier that affects meaning or a remembered fact that will enable you to answer the question without guessing.

Watch the Clock

Keep track of how much time is left and how you are progressing. Wearing a watch may be helpful. You will be notified by the test proctor throughout the examination when you are at the halfway point, as well as how much time is remaining. Some students are so concerned about time, they rush through the exam and have time left over. In such situations, it's easy to leave early. The best approach, however, is to take your time. Stay until the end so that you can check your answers.

KEYS TO SUCCESS ACROSS THE BOARDS

- Study, Review, and Practice
- Keep a positive, confident attitude
- Follow all directions on the examination
- Do your best

Good luck!

You are encouraged to visit* http://www.prenhall.com/success *for additional tips on studying, test-taking and other keys to success. At this stage of your education and career you will find these tips helpful.

Some of the study and test-taking tips were adapted from Keys to Effective Learning, Second Edition, by Carol Carter, Joyce Bishop, and Sarah Lyman Kravits.

CHAPTER

1 Introduction to the National Board Examination

Preparation, Format, and Strategies

Heather O. Mapp, RDH, MEd

contents

Three of the most stressful times for students pursuing a career in dental hygiene are waiting for confirmation that they have been accepted into a dental hygiene program, preparing to take the National Board Examination, and then waiting for confirmation that they have "passed" the examination.

This chapter is intended for dental hygiene students who are preparing to take the National Board Examination, as well as licensed hygienists who are faced with the formidable task of retaking the examination. Reasons for the latter include dental hygienists who have not practiced for a period of time or have moved to an area that requires passing scores from a current National Board Examination.

A major component of success for passing any examination is familiarity with the test itself. This chapter—Preparing for the National Board Examination—presents the reader with practical information about the examination, as well as helpful study hints, methods to develop a positive attitude, and strategies for overcoming test anxiety. All of these elements are essential to successfully passing the National Board.

➤ ADMINISTRATION OF THE EXAMINATION

The National Board Dental Hygiene Examination is administered by the Joint Commission on National Dental Examinations. This Commission is composed of fifteen members who include representatives from dental schools, dental practice, state dental examining boards, dental hygienists, and the public. The examination is given to determine qualifications of dental hygienists who seek licensure for the practice of dental hygiene by assessing their ability to recall information from biomedical, dental, and dental hygiene sciences, as well as their ability to apply critical thinking skills in a problem-solving context.

➤ ELIGIBILITY REQUIREMENTS

To take the National Board Dental Hygiene Examination, a candidate must qualify as a dental hygiene student or graduate of an accredited dental hygiene program. A dental hygiene student is eligible for examination when the dental hygiene program director certifies the student is within 4 months of anticipated graduation. Further information on eligibility requirements can be obtained in the *National Board Dental Hygiene Examination Candidate's Guide,* which is available from the Joint Commission on National Dental Examinations, 211 E. Chicago Avenue, Suite 1846, Chicago, Illinois 60611-2678 (312/440-2678).

➤ TESTING CANDIDATES WITH A DISABILITY CONDITION

At the discretion of the Joint Commission, special arrangements may be made to enable a candidate with a disabling condition to be examined. To request special arrangements, the candidate must submit a request by the application deadline for the testing date the applicant has chosen. It is advised to make the request at least 90 days before the testing date, which will provide time to make special arrangements or provide additional information.

The applicant must provide with the request documentation of the disability and its effect on the candidate's ability to participate in National Board Examination under normal conditions. If the candidate is a student in an accredited dental hygiene program, a letter from a school official fulfills this requirement. Otherwise, a letter from a physician or other appropriate professional is required. The candidate should propose in the request the type of special arrangement needed. Special arrangements are approved to give the candidate an opportunity equivalent to other candidates, but not to provide an advantage over other candidates.

➤ TESTING SCHEDULE

The testing schedule for the Dental Hygiene National Board Examination is listed in the *Candidate's Guide*. The examination is given three times a year. A deadline for application precedes each examination by 5 weeks. Seven and one half hours are allocated for the test. Candidates report to the testing center at 8:00 a.m., at which time instructions are given and the test materials distributed. The morning session begins at 8:30 a.m. and ends at 12:00 noon. One hour is allocated for lunch. The afternoon session begins at 1:00 p.m. and the examination concludes at 5:00 p.m.

➤ EXAMINATION FORMAT

The morning session of the examination, Component A, is composed of 200 stand-alone, multiple-choice items. The afternoon session, Component B, consists of 150 multiple-choice items that refer to case-based studies. All of the questions consist of a stem, which poses the problem, and a set of possible answers. There can be as few as three possible answers, or as many as eight options. There is only one *best* answer, although there may be several options that might also be correct. It is the candidate's responsibility to determine which choice answers the question in most cases, under most circumstances. Often detractors are given as choices, but are not the *best* selections. The topics are interspersed throughout the examination, with the exceptions of items pertaining to Community Dental Health. Those questions are included at the end of the morning session and are based on community dental scenerios, which the Commission refers to as testlets.

➤ DISTRIBUTION OF ITEMS

Component A contains 200 items that include the Scientific Basis for Dental Hygiene Practice, Provision of Clinical Dental Hygiene Services, and Community Health. Five percent of the test items simultaneously address behavioral science; another 5% addresses professional responsibility, including ethics and risk management. The distribution of items is approximately as outlined below:

I. SCIENTIFIC BASIS FOR DENTAL HYGIENE PRACTICE (60)

- A. Anatomic sciences (17)
  1. Anatomy (12)
     - a) Head and neck anatomy (6)
     - b) Dental anatomy—Includes tooth morphology, eruption sequence, and occlusion (6)
  2. Histology and embryology (5)
- B. Physiology—This content area can contain information on *anything* related to human physiology (5)
- C. Biochemistry and nutrition (6)
- D. Microbiology and immunology (10)
- E. Pharmacology (10)
- F. Pathology (12)
  1. General (5)
  2. Oral (7)

II. PROVISION OF CLINICAL DENTAL HYGIENE SERVICES (120)

- A. Assessing patient characteristics (23)
  1. Medical and dental history (5)
  2. Head and neck examination (4)
  3. Periodontal evaluation, including stains and deposits (9)
  4. Oral evaluation (3)
  5. Occlusal evaluation (1)
  6. Clinical testing (1)
- B. Obtaining and interpreting radiographs (19)
  1. Principles of radiophysics and biology (4)
  2. Principles of radiologic health (5)
  3. Technique (5)
  4. Recognition of normal and abnormal (5)
- C. Planning and managing dental hygiene care (30)
  1. Infection control (6)
  2. Emergency situations and care (5)
  3. Individualized patient education—Includes instruction, caries, periodontal disease, and oral conditions (13)
  4. Anxiety and pain control (3)
  5. Recognition and management of compromised patients (3)
- D. Performing periodontal procedures (27)
  1. Etiology (7)
  2. Therapy (15)
  3. Reassessment and maintenance—i.e., implant care (5)

E. Preventive agents (12)
   1. Fluoride (7)
   2. Sealants (4)
   3. Other (1)

F. Providing supportive treatment—i.e., dental materials (9)
   1. Properties and manipulation of materials (3)
   2. Polishing teeth (2)
   3. Impressions and study casts (2)
   4. Other (2)

III. COMMUNITY HEALTH—INCLUDES 4 TESTLETS (20)

A. Promoting health and preventing periodontal disease in groups (4)

B. Community programs (8)

C. Analyzing scientific information and applying research results (8)

Each testlet presents a short scenario. The body includes two to three paragraphs. There are at least five multiple-choice questions based on each scenario, which are dependent on the main body. Each question has four to five responses, with one correct *best* response. The testlet topics may include, but are not limited to, a wide range of populations such as:

1. Geriatric
2. Medically compromised
3. Special needs
4. Preschoolers
5. Grade schoolers
6. Adolescents
7. Veterans and the military
8. Ethnic populations
9. Immigrant populations

Component B is composed of 150 items based on dental hygiene cases. There are between ten and fifteen items per case. The examination may include a case study of one of the following types of patients:

1. Geriatric
2. Adult-periodontal
3. Pediatric
4. Special needs
5. Medically compromised

The case studies address knowledge and skills required in assessing patient characteristics, obtaining and interpreting radiographs, planning and managing dental hygiene care, performing periodontal procedures, preventive agents, and supportive treatment.

➤ TYPES OF QUESTIONS

Nine question formats are used in the National Board Examination. These question types are interspersed throughout the examination and vary in difficulty. The question formats include:

1. Completion. These questions pose a problem in the stem and the correct answer will complete the statement.
   Example: Carbohydrates may be stored in the body as
   A. fiber.
   B. glucose.
   C. glycogen.
   D. adipose tissue.
   E. polysaccharides.
2. Question type. This is composed of a question as the stem, followed by possible answers.
   Example: Which of the following are thick-walled vessels that are predominately elastic in nature?
   A. veins
   B. venules
   C. arteries
   D. arterioles
   E. capillaries
3. Negative items. These questions will be given in a negative format. They will contain such words as EXCEPT, NOT, or LEAST in the stem. These words will be listed in bold capital letters in the test booklet.
   Example: Each of the following is affected by saliva EXCEPT one. Which one is the EXCEPTION?
   A. swallowing
   B. dental caries
   C. oral microflora
   D. protein digestion
   E. carbohydrate breakdown

Hint: Underline or circle the negative words in the test booklet when you come to them.

4. Paired true/false. These questions contain two sentences relating to the same topic. The candidate must decide whether each statement is true or false.
   Example: Protection from excessive exposure to radiation is aided by use of aluminum filters and a lead diaphragm. The filters reduce the soft radiation reaching the patient's face, and the diaphragm controls the area exposed.
   A. Both statements are TRUE.

Hint: Write T or F above each sentence in the test booklet. THEN select your answer. Avoid trying to answer the entire question before you determine the validity of each sentence.

B. Both statements are FALSE.
C. The first statement is TRUE, the second is FALSE.
D. The first statement is FALSE, the second is TRUE.

5. Cause and effect. The stem contains a statement and a reason, which are written as a single sentence and connected by the word "because." The candidate must decide if the statement and reason are correct, and whether there is a causal relationship between them.
Example: A tooth whose sealant has worn away requires an immediate restoration because this tooth is more susceptible to decay than a tooth that has never been sealed.
A. Both statement and reason are correct and related.
B. Both statement and reason are correct but not related.
C. The statement is correct but the reason is not.
D. The statement is NOT correct but the reason is an accurate statement.
E. Neither the statement nor the reason is correct.

Hint: Underline or circle the word "because" in the test booklet. Determine if the statement (the first part of the question) is correct or incorrect; then determine if the reason (the part of the question that follows "because") is correct or incorrect. Write a T or F over each part of the question in the test booklet. THEN determine if the statements are related to each other and choose the correct answer.

6. Combination answers. These questions present a dual-part answer in a table or column form. Your answer is based on the combination of the items presented.
Example: Which of the following combinations is MOST likely to cause moderate fluorosis (without systemic toxicity)?

	Concentration of Fluoride in Water (in ppm)	*Age of Individuals (in years)*
A.	0.5	2
B.	2	4
C.	3	6
D.	8	7
E.	10	8

Hint: Determine what the question is asking (i.e., What concentration of fluoride will cause moderate fluorosis without systemic toxicity?) Use only the information you need. Avoid extraneous material. It can be confusing.

7. Sequencing questions. These items ask you to place steps in a procedure or chronology in the proper sequence.
Example: What are the stages of learning (from lower to higher) as depicted in the "Learning Ladder"?
1. self-interest
2. habit
3. awareness
4. unawareness
5. involvement
6. action

A. 4, 3, 1, 5, 6, 2
B. 4, 3, 5, 1, 6, 2
D. 1, 3, 4, 5, 6, 2
D. 1, 3, 5, 4, 6, 2

Hint: Write the number of each step, starting with #1 and continue to the end. THEN select the answer by matching your order with the choices given.

Hint: Determine WHAT the question is asking (What type of study is the hygienist using?). Use only material presented which is needed to answer the question. Avoid being confused by the other information given.

8. Testlet (Community Dental Health). These test items give a brief case study, or scenario, and base the question on the information presented.
   Example: As she examines four classrooms of children, a dental hygienist uses an index designed to assess past and present dental caries. She notices that many of the children either presently have caries, or have had them in the past. These findings far exceed those reported by other researchers—both for the population being examined and for similar groups. Which of the following types of epidemiological investigations is the hygienist conducting?
   A. Analytical
   B. Descriptive
   C. Prospective
   D. Experimental
   E. Cross-sectional

   Key to sample questions 1–8:

1. c	5. e
2. c	6. c
3. d	7. a
4. a	8. b

9. Case-based items. A case study of a patient is given with a synopsis of the patient's history, a clinical examination chart, radiographs, and clinical photographs. The patient's history will include the following information:
   - Synopsis of patient's history including age, gender, height, weight, and vital signs.
   - Medical history: Under care of physician, hospitalizations, medical conditions, current medications, and pregnancy status.
   - Dental history: Gingival bleeding, oral hygiene care, dental care, and dental concerns.
   - Social history: Tobacco and alcohol use, unusual weight loss or gain, occupational and recreational information.
   - Patient's chief complaint.

The clinical examination chart represents the patient's clinical findings. Restorations are not charted, but carious lesions may be charted. Periodontal probing depths and furcations are listed. Supplemental oral examination findings may include attrition, recession, plaque, and calculus deposits.

Radiographs presented may be a complete mouth series, bitewings, or a panoramic film. The radiographs are labeled Right and Left and are of good quality. In addition to radiographs, photographs of study models may be given. Color photographs are utilized when needed.

➤ TIPS FOR TAKING MULTIPLE CHOICE TESTS

1. Read the stem of the question carefully and completely before looking at the answers. Determine what the question is asking. Identify key words and then try to formulate the answer in your mind before looking at the answers.
   - Read each answer carefully and determine whether it is an appropriate response to the question and gives as complete an answer as possible.
   - Immediately eliminate any answers that are obviously incorrect and attempt to narrow the choices down to not more than two.
   - When the choices have been narrowed as much as possible and the correct answer is still not clear, make an educated guess.
   - Avoid selecting an answer because of complex choices or words and/or phrases that are unfamiliar to you.
2. Avoid selecting any answer that contains such words as "always," "never," "none," "all," or "every." There are seldom any conditions that are absolute in the health field, and unconditional responses are usually incorrect answers.
3. Watch for the words "not," "least," or "except" in the question. Make note of these words by circling or underlining them in the test booklet. If an item does not make sense, reread it carefully to be sure a key word has not been overlooked.
4. Look for the answer that best applies to the conditions presented in the question. An option may be partially true or may apply under certain conditions. Select the best answer that will generally apply under most conditions and specifically is applicable to the question. If several options might be true, but one option would incorporate all possibilities, that option should be the best answer. Avoid selecting answers that are based on isolated rules or are applicable only to certain locales or regions, or refer to procedures and techniques that are not broadly practiced.
5. Be alert for grammatical clues. A well-edited question will offer options that are all grammatically correct with the stem.
6. The pattern of numbers for correct answers should be fairly random. Do not be overly concerned if the same numbered answer is selected repeatedly. It is not advisable to base answers on a pattern of numbers.
7. Be careful to mark the correct space on the answer sheet that relates to the item. Periodically review the answer sheet to make sure you have not inadvertently marked in the wrong space. After every ten questions, check to make sure you are on the same question in the test booklet as you are on the answer sheet.

8. The space on the answer sheet should be completely marked with a dark line, but no marks should extend outside the lines. Listen carefully when instructions are given for marking the answer sheet. Do not assume it is just like others you may have used.
9. Use the test booklet to write helpful learning aids such as key phrases, tooth numbering systems, and mnemonics. Refer to them when needed.
10. Avoid making any stray marks on the answer sheet. It may be read as an answer.
11. Keep your answer sheet on a hard surface when recording your answers. Do not place it on top of the test booklet, as it may prevent your marks from being dark enough to be recorded.
12. NEVER leave a question blank. There are no penalties for incorrect answers. By leaving a question blank, you may also increase your chances of marking the wrong space.
13. Utilize all *positive* resources—1996 Pilot examination, instructors, mock boards, form study groups, and/or past graduates.
14. RELAX—Remember, you wouldn't be taking this test if you hadn't shown proficiency in knowledge.

Test Anxiety

It is impossible not to experience some anxiety when preparing to take the National Board Examination. Knowing the format of the Board will help reduce some of that anxiety. One method of reducing stress is to take practice tests to determine your individual strengths and weaknesses.

Practice Tests

Many dental hygiene programs administer a "mock Board" to help students prepare for taking the National Board. It is important to remember when taking a mock examination, the test needs to be realistic and comparable to the "real thing." This means that the mock board should be taken within the same time parameters, have the same number of questions, follow the same format, and be given in a similar setting that the actual examination will be given (i.e., classroom or auditorium). It is ideal to take the mock examination in the same room that the Board will be given.

No National Board Examinations have been released since 1988, which means no examinations are available that follow the new format. There are several ways, however, to construct a viable, realistic, mock Board examination. The American Dental Association has released copies of the 1996 Pilot National Board Examination. This test is available to dental hygiene programs. The pilot examination was given to senior dental hygiene students nationwide to determine the validity and reliability of the examination. It is an abbreviated version of the actual examination, and is composed of 100 stand-alone multiple choice items, and 75 multiple choice questions on the case-based studies. The pilot examination, therefore, is exactly half the length of the National Board. To make a mock Board examination totally realistic, it is necessary to add 100 stand-alone items and 75 more items for the case-based portion of the test. Representative-type questions to add might include those from previous course examinations that have been replaced. Case-based items can be found in some textbooks and compact disc case studies (i.e., the Proctor and Gamble [P&G] case studies available on the Internet, or provided by P&G at no charge to dental hygiene programs). These additional questions can be added to the Pilot examination to complete the requisite number of items that appear on the National Board.

When taking a practice test or mock examination, it is imperative that the student have a complete 8 1/2-hour day without interruptions to complete the test. This will enable the student to experience not only the questions presented on the examination, but also the physical aspect of an examination of this caliber.

After the practice test has been taken, it should be graded with a key to determine the student's performance. It can then be determined which subjects are the student's strong or weak areas, and hence additional study time can be allocated based on the student's needs. It is also important to understand how the examination will be graded, using a conversion scale for final test scores.

Before the Examination

The day before the examination should be spent doing something enjoyable and calming. *This is not the time to cram for the examination.* Studying at the last minute may only confuse and panic the candidate. If possible, try to keep physically and mentally occupied. Try to get a good night's rest before the examination. On the morning of the examination, plan to eat a light, healthy breakfast. Surround yourself with *positive* thoughts and people before the test. Avoid being around any negative people. You need to be positive and enthusiastic as you take the test. Arriving at the test site in a relaxed, calm mood will help tremendously when taking the test as well. Your attitude, positive or negative, will be reflected in your test scores!

Scoring the Examination

Two factors affect a candidate's scores—the number of items answered correctly and the conversion scale for the examination. In addition, if a test item is found to be defective, the Joint Commission will exclude the test item from scoring. Also, up to 15% of the items included in the test determine the standards of quality for the examination. These pretest items are not included in the scoring process and do not contribute to the candidate's scores. The conversion scale is based on the performance of a reference group. This group consists of all students enrolled in accredited dental hygiene programs who are examined for the first time.

A score of 75 is used as a passing score for the National Board Examination. This is not a raw score. This means that a candidate does not need to correctly answer 75% of all of the questions to pass the examination. The number of correct answers required is determined by the conversion scale. An average *raw score* of approximately 65% converts to a *standard score* of 80 to 85. Typically, less than 10% of all first-time candidates score below a 75. Over 90% pass!

Adequately preparing for the National Board Examination will enable the candidate to think positively, reduce anxiety, and become confident in test-taking. Remember, positive expectations bring positive results. All things come to those who go after them. If you can dream it, you can do it! Good luck!

CHAPTER

2 Anatomy and Physiology

Marsha L. Baltes, PhD

contents

Anatomy is the study of form and arrangement of body parts. Physiology deals with the study of body functions.

➤ SKELETAL SYSTEM

I. FUNCTIONS

A. Supports the body against the pull of gravity

B. Protects soft parts of the body (thoracic cage protects the lungs and heart)

C. Produces blood cells (hematopoesis) in the marrow of certain bones

D. Stores mineral salts, such as calcium

E. Provides a site for muscle attachments

II. ANATOMY

A. Bones (Figure 2-1)

1. Types
   a) Long bones—covered on the outside by *periosteum*
      (1) Parts
         (a) *Epiphyses*—growing ends
         (b) *Diaphysis*—shaft
         (c) *Bone marrow*—inside cavity
         (d) *Articular cartilage*—covers ends that articulate with other bones
      (2) Composition
         (a) Compact bone is dense with *osteocytes* (bone cells)
         (b) Cancellous bone (spongy bone) is less dense, but very strong
         (c) *Osteoblasts*—develop new bone
         (d) *Osteoclasts*—resorb bone
         (e) Bone is living and constantly being resorbed and reformed
   b) Skull—*cranium* (protects brain) and facial bones
      (1) Cranial bones include frontal, parietal, occipital, temporal, sphenoid, and ethmoid
      (2) Facial bones
         (a) Consist of maxillae, palatine, zygomatic, lacrimal, nasal, vomer, inferior nasal conchae, and mandible
         (b) Hyoid bone—only bone that does not articulate with another bone
      (3) Sutures—separate bones (fuse with age)
      (4) Some bones contain *paranasal sinuses;* they are lined with mucous membrane and make bones of skull lighter; sinuses drain into nasal cavity
   c) *Vertebral column*—consists of 7 cervical, 12 thoracic, 5 lumbar, 5 (fused) sacral vertebrae, and 1 coccyx
      (1) Intervertebral discs—fibrocartilaginous material that separates vertebrae
      (2) Atlas—first cervical vertebrae; articulates with occipital bone of cranium

(3) Axis—second cervical vertebrae
(4) Exhibits four curvatures

d) *Thoracic cage*
(1) 12 pairs of ribs
(2) Sternum—anterior bone for attachment for upper ribs
(3) Thoracic vertebrae—where all ribs articulate
(4) Function—protects heart and lungs

e) *Pectoral girdle*—connects upper limb to axial skeleton
(1) Clavicles (collarbones)
(2) Scapulae (shoulder blades)

f) Upper limbs
(1) Humerus—upper arm
(2) Ulna and radius—located in forearm

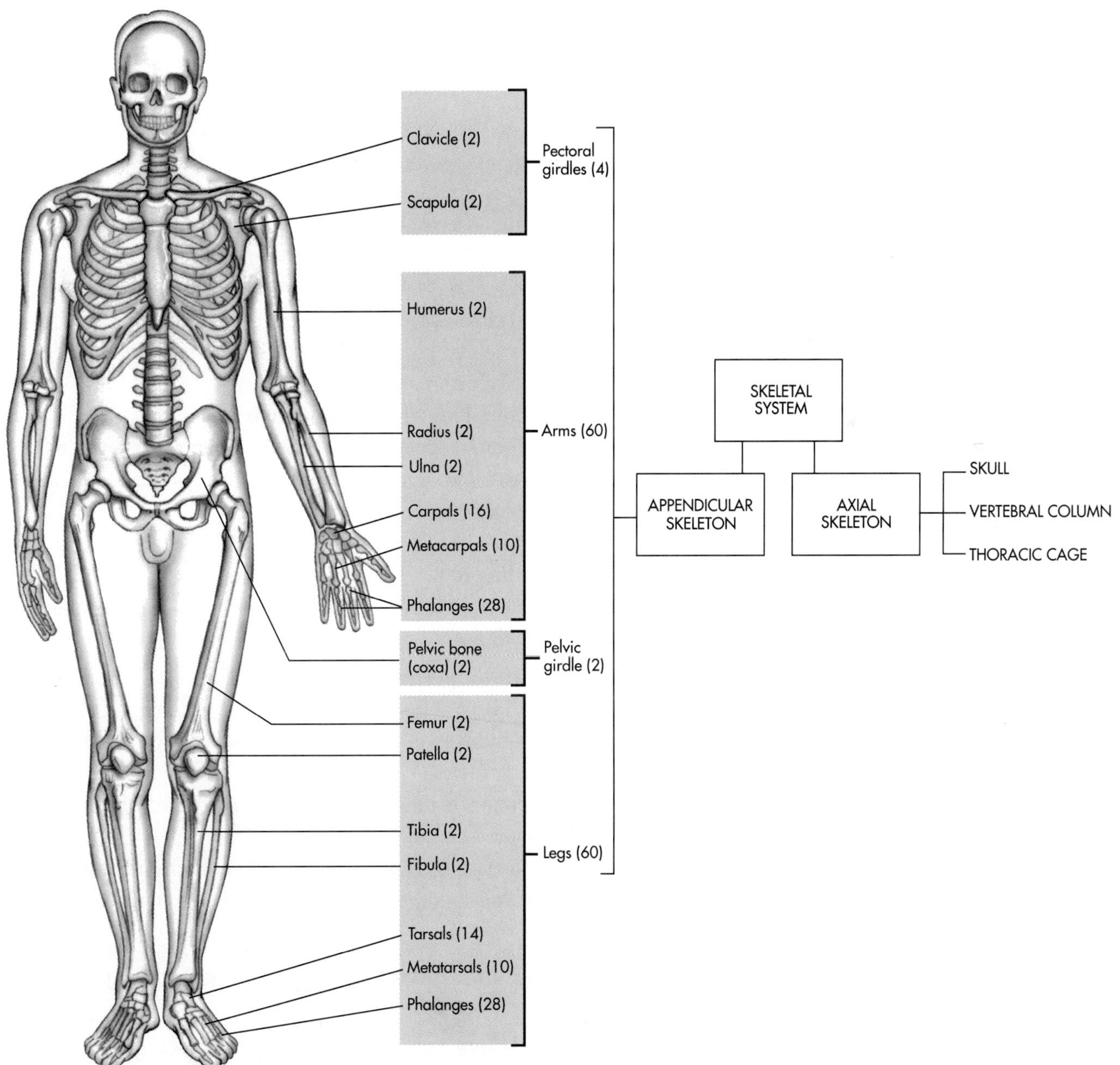

FIGURE 2-1. Major bones of the skeleton.

(3) Carpals—located in wrist
(4) Metacarpals and phalanges—located in hand

g) *Pelvic girdle*—forms attachment for lower limb with axial skeleton; female pelvis is shallower and wider than male pelvis
(1) Coxal bone—consists of two ilium, two ischium, and one pubis
(2) Sacrum
(3) Coccyx

h) Lower limbs
(1) Femur—located in thigh; top is defined by a greater trochanter and articulating head and neck
(2) Tibia and fibula—comprise lower leg
(3) Patella—kneecap
(4) Tarsal bones—make up ankles; calcaneus—bone of heel
(5) Metatarsals and phalanges—make up foot

B. Joints

1. Types
   a) *Synarthroses*—found in the cranium; immovable
   b) *Amphiarthroses*—connected by hyaline cartilage or fibrocartilage; slightly moveable
      (1) Vertebrae—separated by intervertebral discs
      (2) Pubic symphysis—located between pubic bones
   c) Diarthroses
      (1) Contain *synovial joints* (articular cartilage with synovial membrane that produces synovial fluid; see Figure 2-2)
      (2) Types of diarthroses
         (a) Saddle joint—located in thumb
         (b) Ball-and-socket joint—located in hip and shoulder
         (c) Pivot joint—located between radius and ulna, and atlas and axis
         (d) Hinge joint—located in elbow and knee
         (e) Gliding joint—located in wrist and ankle
         (f) Condyloid joint—located between metacarpals and phalanges

C. Connective tissue

1. Types
   a) *Ligament*—binds two bones together; made up of fibrous connective tissue
   b) *Tendon*—connects muscles to bones; made up of fibrous connective tissue; helps stabilize joints
   c) *Bursae*—consists of fluid-filled sac; eases friction between moving tendons and ligaments over fixed structures

III. PHYSIOLOGY

A. Bones are living structures that are constantly being remodeled

B. *Marrow* is very active tissue, constantly producing blood cells

C. Movements by synovial joints

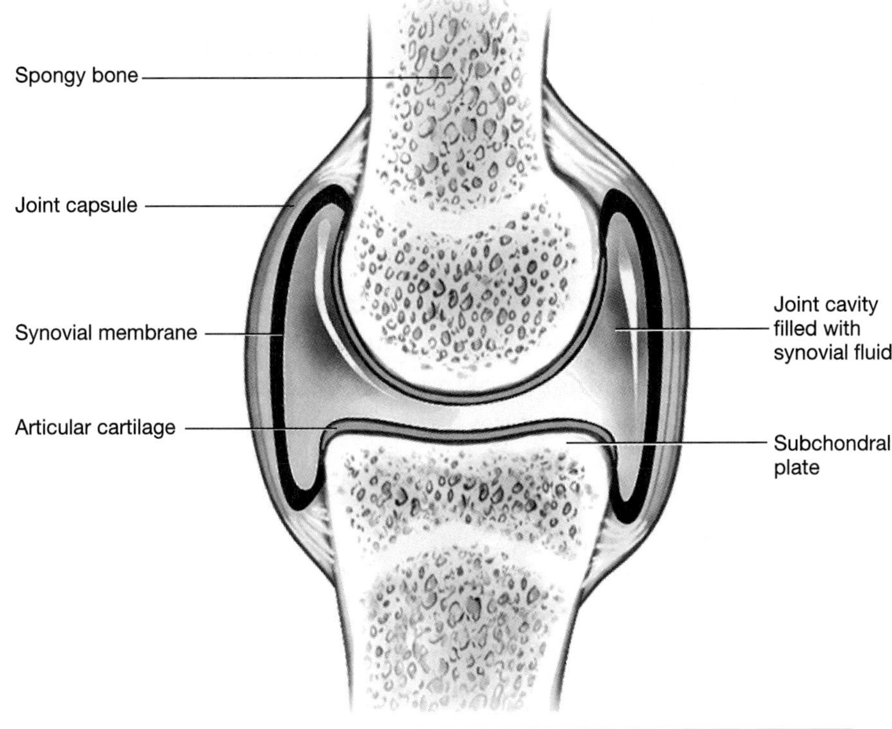

FIGURE 2-2. Freely movable joint.

1. *Flexion*
   a) Decreases joint angle
   b) Example—bending the knee
   c) *Dorsiflexion*—flexes foot upward
   d) *Plantar flexion*—flexes foot downward
2. *Extension*
   a) Increases joint angle
   b) Example—straightening the knee
3. *Abduction*
   a) Moves body part laterally, away from the midline
   b) Example—swinging arm out to the side
4. *Adduction*
   a) Moves body part toward midline
   b) Example—pulling arm in to the side
5. *Rotation*
   a) Moves body part around its own axis
   b) Example—turning head back and forth
6. Supination—rotates lower arm so palm faces upward
7. Pronation—rotates lower arm so palm faces downward
8. Circumduction—moving body part in wide circles; example—moving arms in large circles
9. Inversion—turns foot so the sole is facing midline
10. Eversion—turns foot so the sole is facing outward
11. Elevation—lifts body part, such as shrugging the shoulders
12. Depression—drops body part such as dropping shoulders or opening jaw

IV. HOMEOSTASIS—produces elements of the blood that carry oxygen and helps to maintain pH

➤ MUSCULAR SYSTEM

I. FUNCTIONS

A. Stabilization—tendons of muscles cross joints and give them stability

B. Oppose force of gravity—solid structure of bones allows us to remain upright; muscle contraction opposes force of gravity

C. Movement—contraction of muscle produces movement

1. *Skeletal muscle*—produces movement of skeletal system, eyeball, soft tissue of the face, and breathing
2. *Smooth muscle*—produces movement of digestive tract and blood vessels
3. *Cardiac muscle*—produces movement of heart (contraction)

D. Heat—biochemical process of muscle contraction gives off heat as a by-product, which maintains body temperature

II. ANATOMY

A. Skeletal muscle (striated muscle)

1. Microscopic anatomy
   a) Myofibrils—contractile elements made up of smaller myofilaments, which are made up of actin and myosin
      (1) Actin and myosin
         (a) Give skeletal muscle its striated appearance
         (b) Slide past each other, causing myofibrils to shorten (contract)
2. Innervation of skeletal muscle
   a) *Motor unit*—consists of motor neuron, which goes to several muscle fibers
   b) *Neuromuscular junction*—point where motor neuron innervates muscle fiber
   c) Contraction—requires energy (adenosine triphosphate, ATP) and calcium
3. Muscle contraction
   a) *Origin of muscle*—attaches to end of stationary bone
   b) *Insertion of muscle*—attaches to end of moving bone
   c) Functions
      (1) Can only shorten during contraction
      (2) For every movement, there is usually an opposite movement; therefore muscles work in pairs as *antagonistic muscles*
         (a) Example—flexors and extensors (biceps and triceps brachii acting at the elbow; see Figure 2-3)
      (3) Several muscles may be involved in one movement
         (a) *Prime mover muscle*—does most of the work of a movement
         (b) *Synergist muscle*—assists in movement

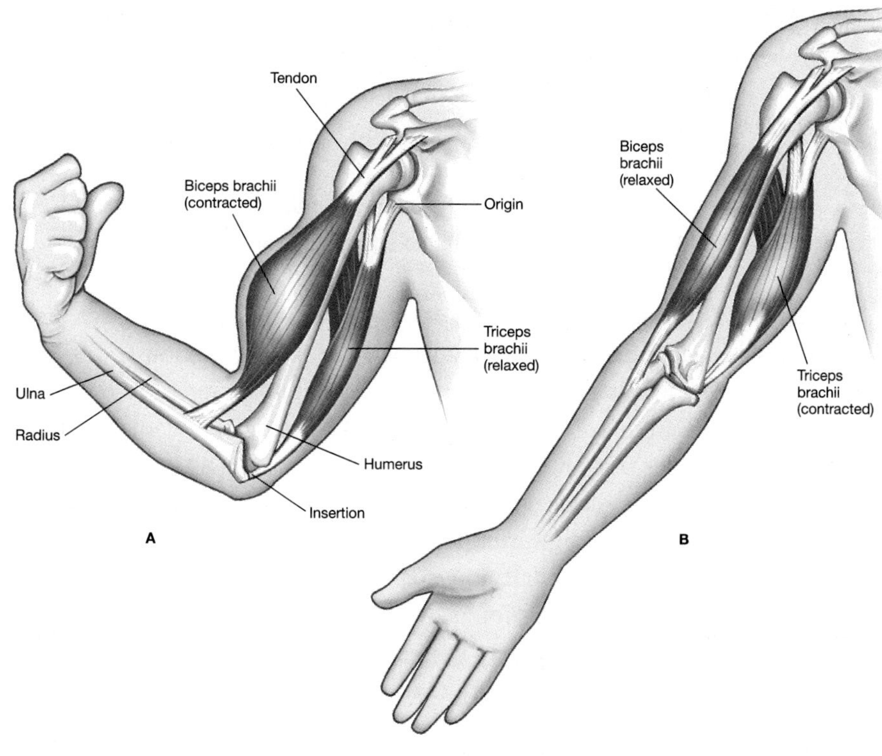

FIGURE 2-3. Antagonistic muscle.

- d) Types of contractions
  - (1) *Isotonic contraction*—muscle shortens and movement occurs
  - (2) *Isometric contraction*—muscle contracts, but does not shorten or produce movement
  - (3) *Muscle tone*—even at rest, some fibers are always contracting to keep muscle from being flaccid

4. Specific skeletal muscles
   - a) Muscles of facial expression—supplied by cranial nerve VII
   - b) Muscles of mastication—supplied by cranial nerve V
   - c) Muscles of head, neck, and trunk—include antagonists sternocleidomastoid and trapezius
   - d) Abdominal muscles—contain contents of abdominal cavity; assist in maintaining upright posture; include external and internal obliques, transversus abdominus, and rectus abdominus
   - e) Muscles of pectoral girdle—help hold upper arm in socket; provide movement at shoulder; include deltoids, pectoralis majors and minors, lastissimus dorsi, and serratus anterior
   - f) Muscles of forearm—include antagonists triceps brachii, brachialis, and biceps brachii
   - g) Muscles of wrist (also move the hand)—include flexor carpi ulnaris, extensor carpi ulnaris, flexor carpi radialis, and extensor carpi radialis
   - h) Muscles of hand—include flexor digitorum and extensor digitorum

(1) Iliopsoas—flexes thigh
(2) Gluteus maximus—extends thigh
(3) Gluteus medius—abducts thigh
(4) Adductor group—adducts thigh

j) Muscles of leg
(1) Quadriceps femoris group—extends lower leg
(2) Hamstring group—flexes lower leg and extends hip

k) Muscles of ankle
(1) Gastrocnemius and soleus—form Achilles tendon, which attaches to calcaneus of the heel; plantar flexion
(2) Tibialis anterior—dorsiflexion and inversion
(3) Peroneus (fibularis) muscles—eversion and plantar flexion

l) Muscles of foot
(1) Flexor digitorum longus—flexes toes
(2) Extensor digitorum longus—extends toes

m) Extraocular (eyeball) muscles—movement of the eyes; origin is in bony orbit, insertion is on eye

n) Diaphragm—separates thoracic from abdominal cavity; contracts during inspiration, relaxes during expiration

B. Smooth muscle

1. Located in walls of hollow internal organs (gastrointestinal tract and blood vessels)
2. Involuntary—controlled by autonomic nervous system
3. Contains no striations
4. Slower to contract than striated muscle
5. Maintains contraction longer than striated muscle
6. Does not fatigue easily

C. Cardiac muscle

1. Involuntary muscle found only in heart
2. Striated
3. Relaxes completely between contractions

III. PHYSIOLOGY (Figure 2-4)

A. All-or-none law

1. Only applies to muscle fiber, not to entire muscle
2. Stimulation of muscle fiber either causes it to or not to contract—strength of muscle contraction is dependent on total number of fibers contracting

B. *Muscle twitch*—single stimulus causes muscle to contract and then relax

C. *Summation*—muscle fibers contract in rapid succession

D. *Tetanus*—sustained maximum contraction

E. *Fatigued muscle*—can no longer contract because of lack of ATP

F. *Oxygen debt*—continued need for oxygen after vigorous exercise; lactic acid accumulates during exercise because oxygen is necessary for its metabolism

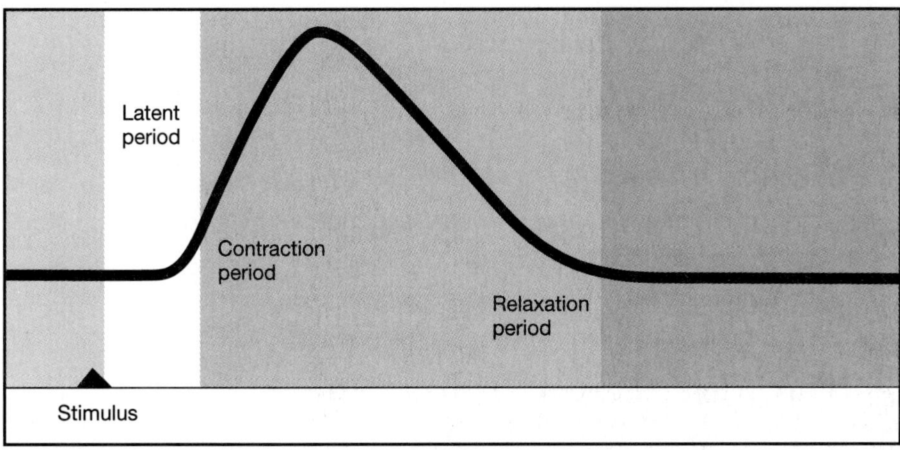

A Simple muscle twitch

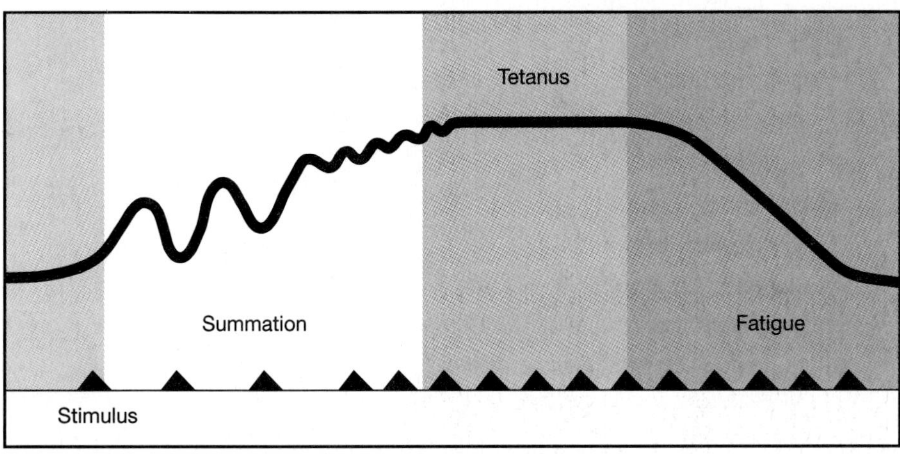

B Summation, tetanus, fatigue

FIGURE 2-4. Physiology of a skeletal muscle contraction.

IV. HOMEOSTASIS—muscular activity helps to maintain body temperature (37°C)

➤ NERVOUS SYSTEM

I. FUNCTION

A. Regulates systems of the body

B. Coordinates systems of the body

C. Maintains *homeostasis*

D. Responds to stimuli, both internal and external

1. Permits sensory input
2. Integrates input into central nervous system (CNS)
3. Stimulates motor output

II. ANATOMY

A. Divisions

1. Central nervous system (Figure 2-5)
   a) Brain
      (1) Contains unmyelinated gray matter and myelinated white matter

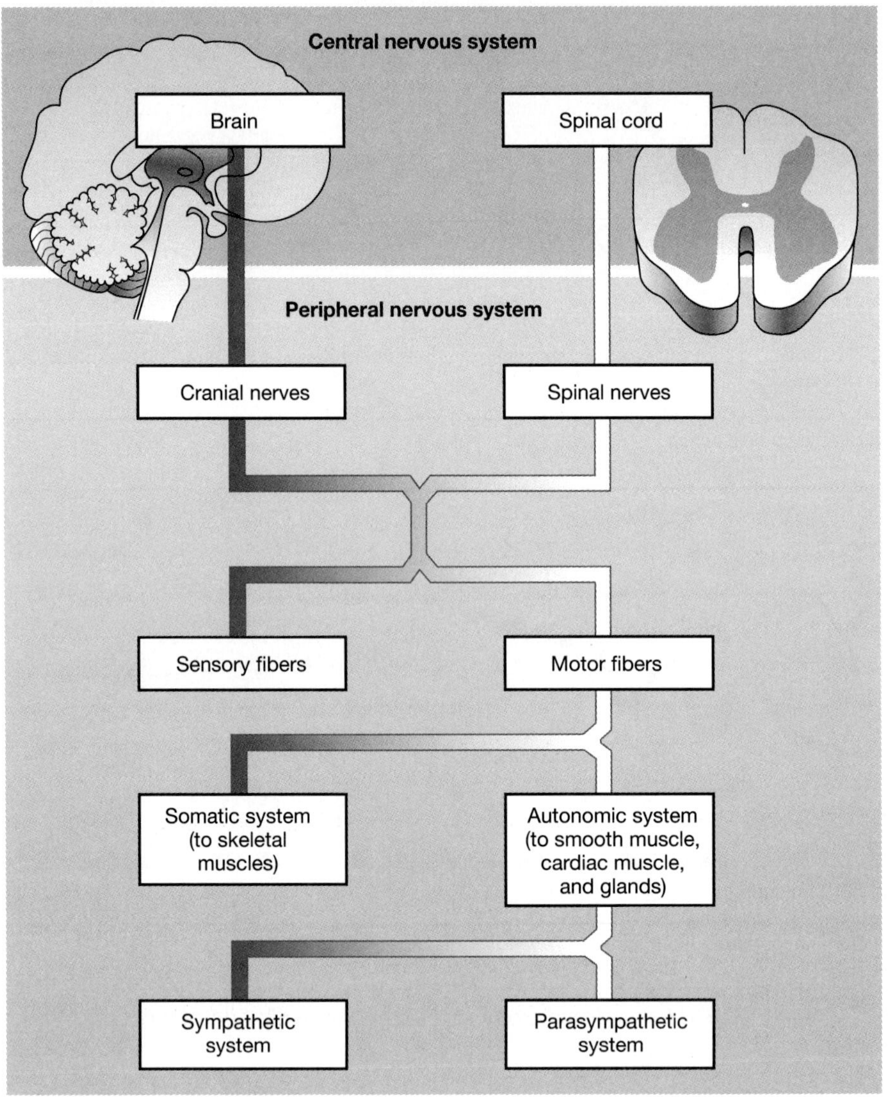

FIGURE 2-5. Central nervous system and peripheral nervous system.

(2) Contains four ventricles that are filled with *cerebrospinal fluid* (CSF)

(3) Brainstem
- (a) *Medulla oblongata*—controls and regulates heartbeat, breathing, and blood pressure
- (b) *Pons*—also regulates breathing; connects cerebellum with CNS
- (c) *Midbrain*—tracts to and from other parts of the CNS

(4) *Diencephalon*
- (a) *Hypothalamus*
  - (i) Maintains homeostasis
  - (ii) Regulates hunger, thirst, body temperature, sleep, blood pressure, and water balance
  - (iii) Works with pituitary gland
  - (iv) Functions in conjunction with endocrine system

(b) *Thalamus*—central relay station for afferent impulses into brain

(5) *Cerebellum*

(a) Functions in muscle coordination to produce smooth motion

(b) Maintains muscle tone

(c) Maintains and restores balance

(6) *Cerebrum*—site of consciousness and reasoning

(a) Functions

i) Controls interpretation of sensory imput

ii) Initiates muscular movement

(b) Parts

i) Right and left *cerebral hemispheres*—lobes include frontal, parietal, occipital, and temporal

ii) *Corpus callosum*—bridge of fibers that joins right and left hemispheres

iii) *Basal ganglia*—clusters of gray matter involved in movement; dysfunction associated with Parkinson's disease

iv) *Limbic system*—involved in learning and memory; site of generation of emotions

b) *Spinal cord*—center for reflex activity

(1) Contains unmyelinated gray matter and myelinated white matter

(2) Ascending tracts carry sensory input to brain

(3) Descending tracts carry motor output from brain and cord to muscles

c) *Meninges*—three membranes that cover brain and spinal cord

(1) Dura mater—tough, outermost cover

(2) Arachnoid mater—consists of middle layer; CSF circulates in subarachoid space

(3) Pia mater—involves innermost layer

d) CSF—made up of clear fluid, which is produced inside brain

(1) Supplies CNS with nutrients

(2) Acts as cushion for the CNS

(3) Circulates around brain and cord

(4) Blockage in system leads to hydrocephalus

2. *Peripheral nervous system* (PNS)

a) *Cranial nerves*—all 12 pairs are concerned with head and neck, except for vagus (X), which also innervates viscera in thorax and abdomen

b) *Spinal nerves*—consists of 31 pairs, innervate segmentally, carry impulses to and from spinal cord

c) *Autonomic nervous system* (motor division of PNS)

(1) Function—innervates smooth and cardiac muscles and glands

(2) Consists of a two neuron system: preganglionic and postganglionic

(3) Is not under conscious control
(4) Two divisions
(a) Sympathetic nervous system
i) Arises from thoracic and lumbar parts of spinal cord
ii) Uses neurotransmitter norepinephrine
iii) Involved in "fight or flight" response
iv) Inhibits digestion
v) Dilates pupils
vi) Increases heart and respiratory rates
(b) Parasympathetic nervous system
i) Arises from cranial (some cranial nerves have parasympathetic components) and sacral parts of cord
ii) Uses the neurotransmitter acetylcholine
iii) Promotes functions of body during a relaxed state
iv) Constricts pupils
v) Digestion of food takes place
vi) Normal, resting heart rate—heartbeat is not fast or forceful

B. Nervous tissue

1. *Neurons*—conduct nerve impulses
   a) *Dendrites*—receive information from other neurons and send impulse toward cell body
   b) *Axons*—send impulses away from cell body
   c) *Cell body*—contains cell nucleus
   d) *Myelin*
      (1) Formed by Schwann cells
      (2) Wraps around some fibers giving a white appearance ("white matter")
      (3) Acts as insulation and increases transmission speed
   e) Types
      (1) Motor (efferent)—long axon; conducts impulses from CNS to muscles
      (2) Sensory (afferent)—conducts impulses from body to CNS
      (3) Interneurons—connects neurons within CNS
2. Neuroglial cells—located within CNS to nourish, support, and protect neurons

III. PHYSIOLOGY

A. Nerve impulse

1. Involves change in polarity in axonal membrane
2. Utilizes sodium and potassium

B. Synapse

1. Location where an axon of one neuron meets dendrites on another neuron
2. Axon and dendrites do not touch
3. Chemical messengers, *neurotransmitters,* relay nerve impulse across synapse

4. Some neurotransmitters are *acetylcholine, norepinephrine, dopamine,* and *serotonin*
5. Diseases associated with imbalance of neurotransmitters are *Parkinson's disease* (dopamine) and depression (norepinephrine and/or serotonin)

C. Reflexes and reflex arc

1. *Reflex*—involuntary, automatic response to an external or internal stimulus
2. Examples—changes in heart rate, sneezing, gagging, vomiting, swallowing, and urination
3. Reflex arc—sensory neuron synapses with an interneuron in spinal cord; the interneuron synapses with motor neuron to muscle, which will cause reaction to the stimulus (e.g., knee-jerk; see Figure 2-6)

IV. HOMEOSTASIS—whole nervous system, especially neurotransmitters and reflexes, works with the endocrine system to maintain homeostasis of the body

A. Blood glucose at 0.1%

B. pH of the blood at 7.4

C. Blood pressure at 120/80

D. Blood temperature at 37°C (98.6°F)

➤ ENDOCRINE SYSTEM

I. FUNCTIONS

A. Composed of glands that release hormones

B. Works with nervous system, which is fast-acting, to coordinate functioning of all parts of body

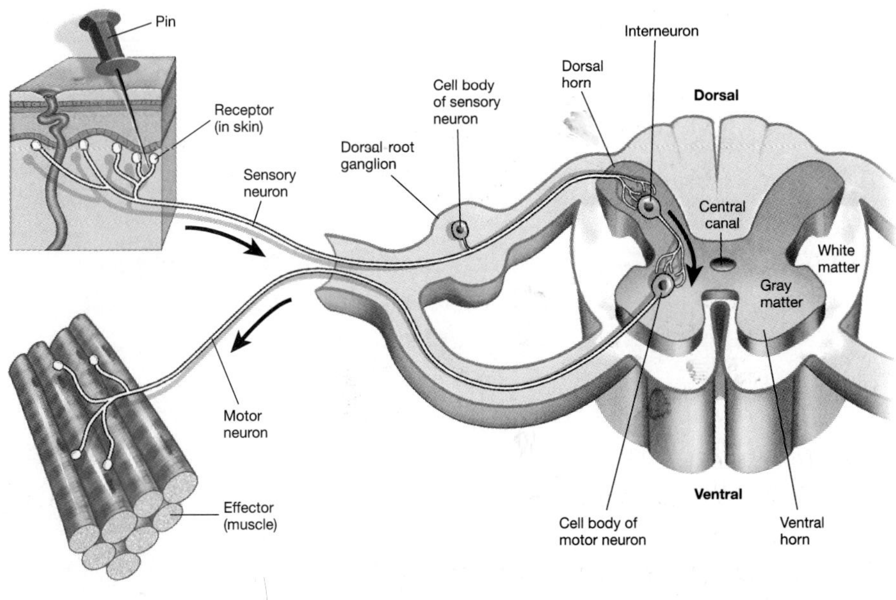

FIGURE 2-6. Reflex arc.

C. Slow-acting endocrine glands release hormones into blood that have a specific function on target tissue

II. ANATOMY

A. Hypothalamus—part of brain that controls heart rate, body temperature, and water balance; contains the pituitary gland

1. *Pituitary gland*—connected to hypothalamus by a stalk
2. Produces releasing factors and hormones that travel down stalk to pituitary gland (Figure 2-7)

B. Posterior pituitary gland—releases two hormones that are produced in hypothalmus

1. *Antidiuretic hormone* (ADH)—also called vasopressin
    a) Induces reabsorption of water from the kidneys, preventing dehydration
    b) Deficiency causes diabetes insipidus
2. *Oxytocin*—target organs are breast and smooth muscle in uterus; causes uterus to contract during labor and milk to be released when baby nurses

C. Anterior pituitary gland—production of hormones is regulated by factors from hypothalamus (Figure 2-8)

1. *Growth hormone* (GH)—affects overall growth of individual, especially epiphyseal plates of long bones
    a) *Pituitary dwarf*—results from deficiency in GH during childhood
    b) *Giant*—results from having too much GH during childhood
    c) *Acromegaly*—results from too much GH in adulthood
2. *Prolactin* (PRL)—produced after childbirth; causes mammary glands to produce milk
3. Melanocyte-stimulating hormone (MSH)—active in frogs; human concentration very low
4. *Thyroid-stimulating hormone* (TSH)—stimulates thyroid to produce thyroid hormones; release is determined by blood concentration of thyroid hormones; when thyroid hormones are low, TSH is released (negative feedback)
5. *Adrenocorticotropic hormone* (ACTH)—stimulates adrenal cortex to secrete cortisol and aldosterone
6. *Gonadotropic hormone*—stimulates ovaries in females and testes in males to secrete sex hormones

D. Thyroid gland—secretes calcitonin, which helps regulate body calcium level; TSH causes thyroid gland to secrete thyroid hormones, which controls metabolic rate

1. Iodine
    a) Required for production of thyroid hormones
    b) *Goiter* (an enlargement of the gland)—caused by lack of iodine
2. *Cretinism*—in children, caused by insufficient production of thyroid hormones
3. *Myxedema*—in adults, caused by insufficient production of thyroid hormones
4. *Graves' disease*—caused by too much thyroid hormones

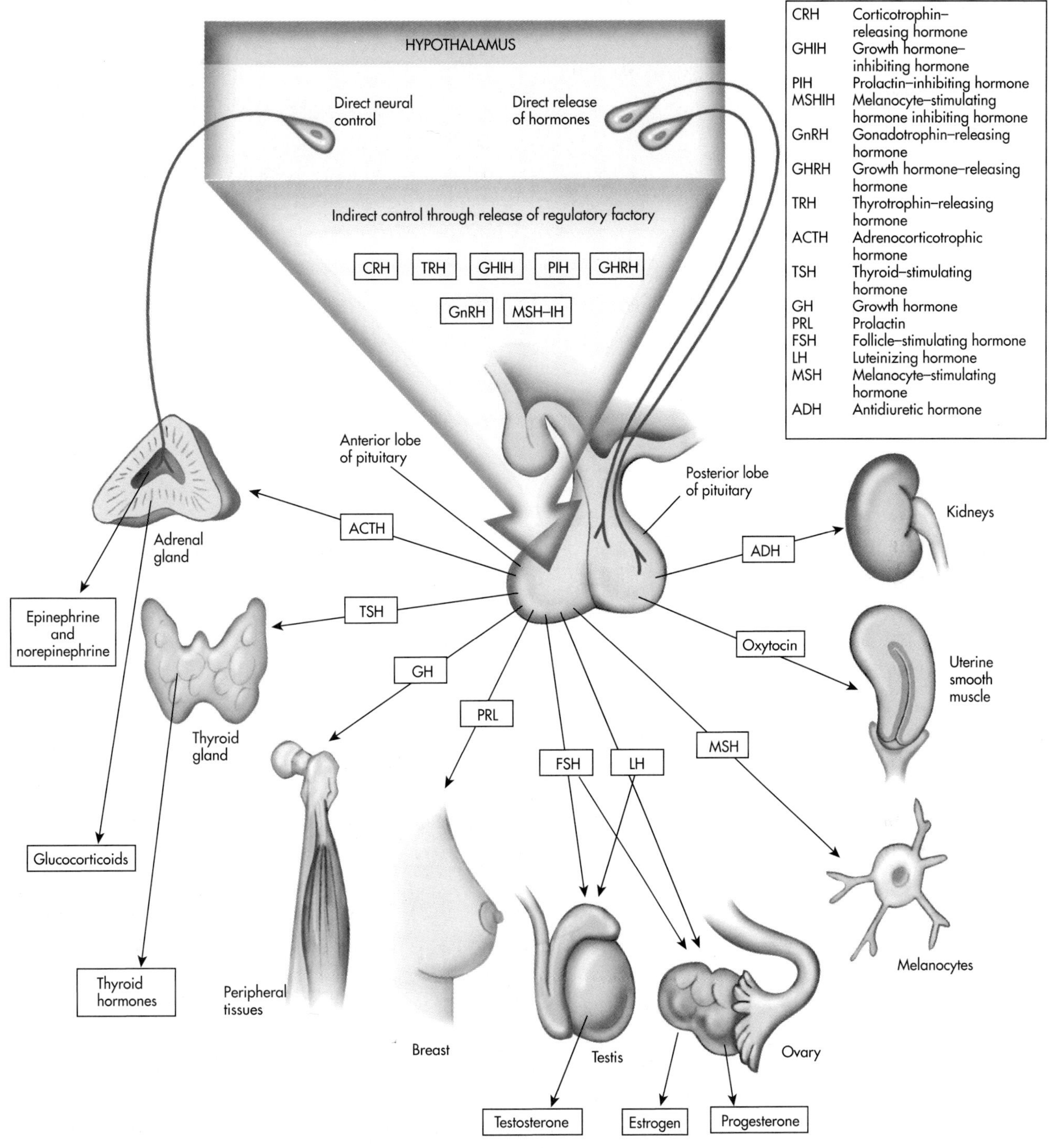

FIGURE 2-7. Hormones excreted by the pituitary.

E. *Parathyroid glands*—located behind the thyroid glands

1. Produce *parathyroid hormone* (PTH), which also regulates calcium level in the body
2. Tetany occurs when blood calcium level becomes too low

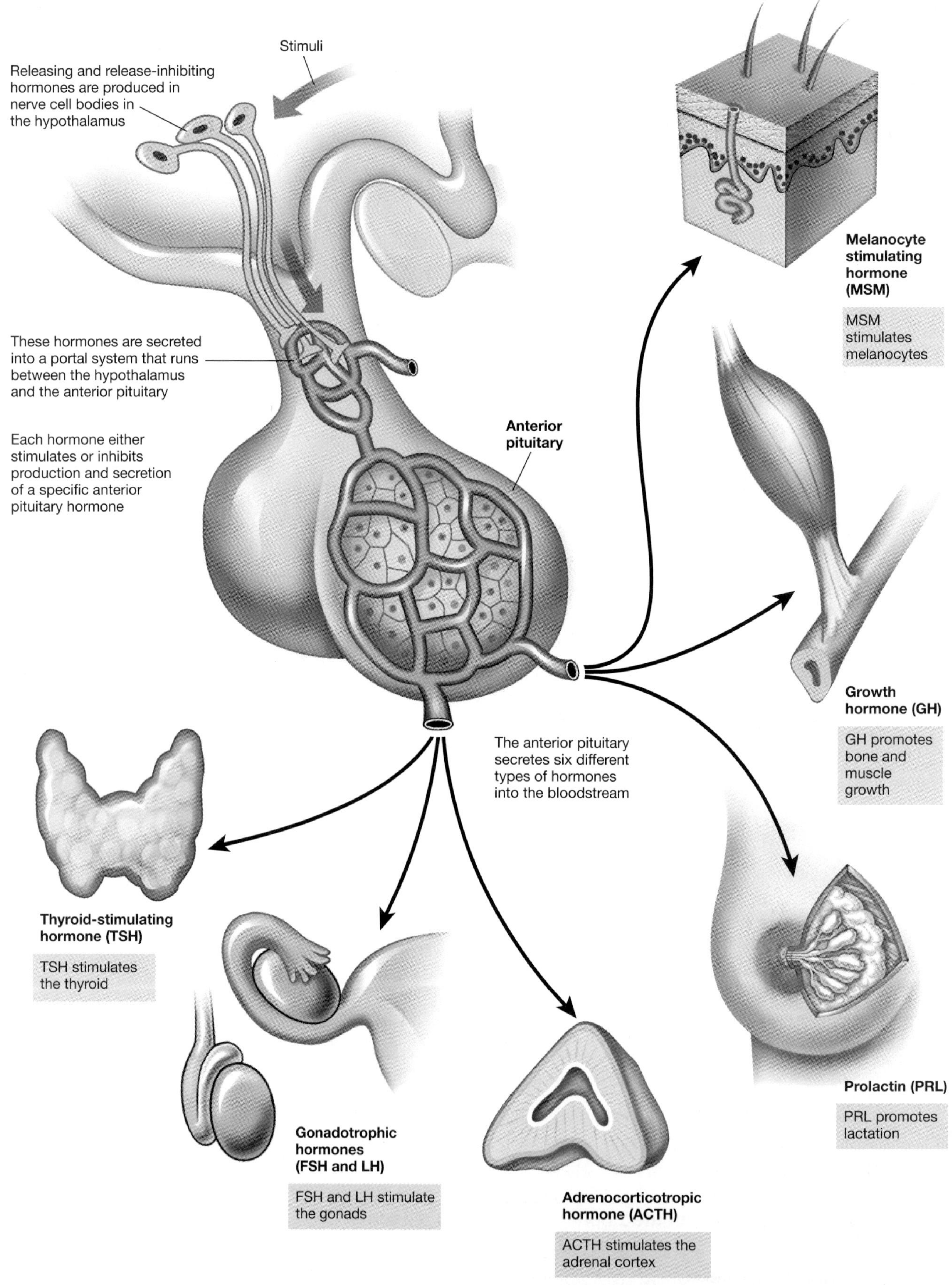

FIGURE 2-8. Hormones of the anterior pituitary.

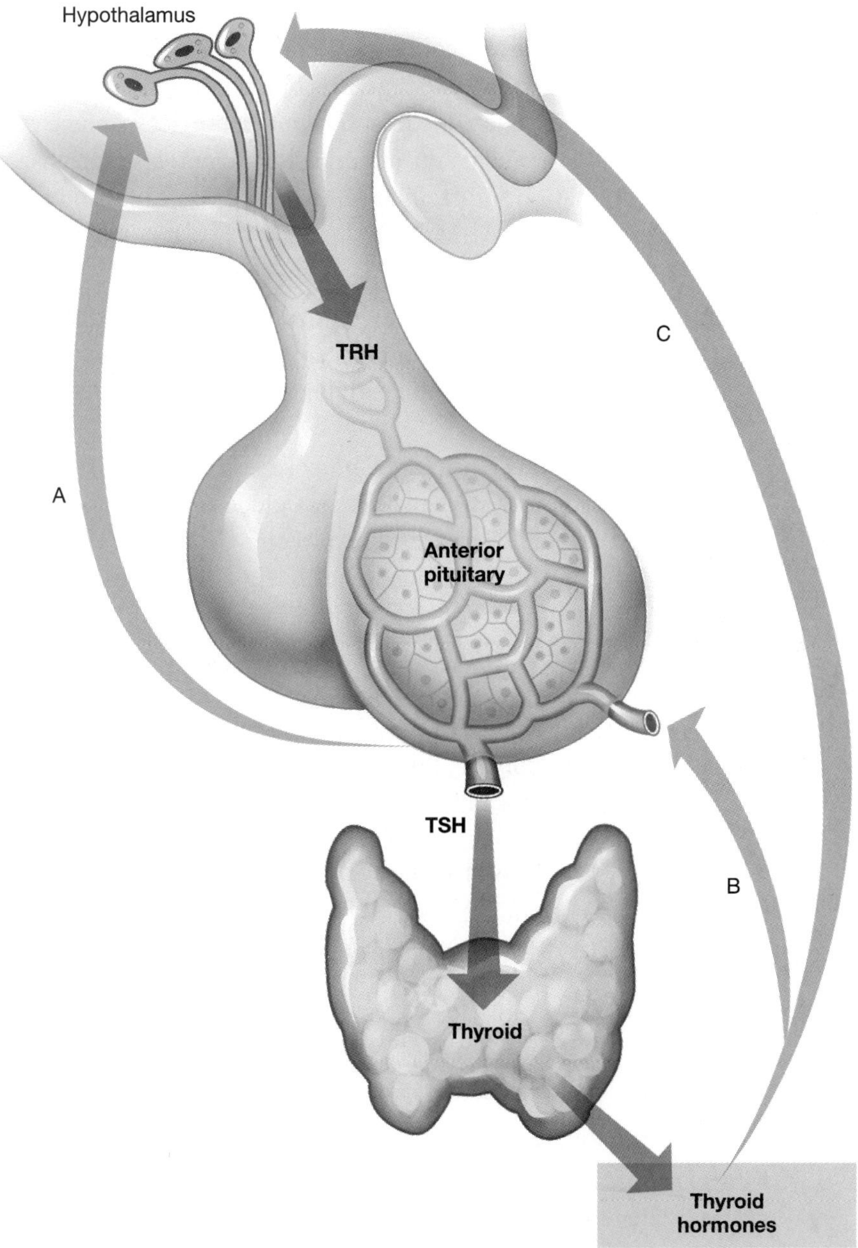

FIGURE 2-9. Regulation of the hypothalamus, anterior pituitary, and thyroid. A, B, and C are feedback mechanisms. A) The level of TSH in the blood controls the release of TRH from the hypothalamus. B) The blood level of thyroid homones regulates the release of TSH from the anterior pituitary. C) The blood level of thyroid hormones regulates the release of TRH from the hypothalamus.

F. *Adrenal medulla*—controlled by sympathetic division of autonomic nervous system; produces *epinephrine* and *norepinephrine,* which causes following results

1. Increases blood glucose level, breathing, and metabolic and heart rates
2. Dilates bronchioles and increases breathing rate
3. Dilates blood vessels to skeletal muscle
4. Constricts blood flow to gastrointestinal tract
5. Increases heart rate and force of contraction

G. **Adrenal cortex**

1. Produces mineralocorticoid, aldosterone, which controls levels of sodium and potassium and regulates blood pressure
2. Produces glucocorticoid, cortisol, which depresses immune responses and is a potent anti-inflammatory agent; also increases glucose formation and facilitates the breakdown of fat and protein

H. **Pancreas**

1. Parts
   a) Exocrine—produces digestive juices that flow into duodenum
   b) Endocrine—islets of Langerhans (islands of tissue within the pancreas) produce insulin and glucagon
      (1) *Insulin*
         (a) Secreted when blood glucose level is high
         (b) Promotes storage of excess glucose as glycogen in liver and buildup of fats and proteins
         (c) Lowers blood glucose level
         (d) Disorders associated with insulin
            i) Diabetes mellitus—due to insufficient insulin production or cell response
               - Symptoms—polyphagia (excessive eating), polyuria (excessive urination), polydipsia (excessive thirst), weakness, itching, and hyperglycemia (too high of blood glucose level)
               - Type 1 diabetes—islet cells do not produce enough insulin
               - Type 2 diabetes—cell receptors do not respond to insulin
      (2) *Glucagon*
         (a) Secretes when blood glucose level is low
         (b) Promotes breakdown of glycogen into glucose
         (c) Raises blood glucose levels

I. ***Pineal gland*—produces melatonin, which regulates the sleep–wake cycle**

J. ***Thymus gland*—(sometimes still called a gland, but primarily a lymphatic organ) produces hormones called thymosins, which are used in development of immunity; important in maturation of T lymphocytes; active in childhood**

K. ***Testes***

1. Produce testosterone and secondary sex characteristics
2. Promote development of sperm and are responsible for male aggression

L. ***Ovaries*—produce secondary sex characteristics, estrogen, and progesterone—necessary for egg maturation**

III. **PHYSIOLOGY—most hormones are regulated by a system of negative feedback with the pituitary gland; blood level of the hormone turns off the releasing factor of the pituitary, thereby slowing or shutting off the production of the hormone (see Figure 2-9)**

IV. HOMEOSTASIS—endocrine system works with nervous system to regulate blood glucose, blood pressure, blood pH, and temperature

➤ CIRCULATORY SYSTEM

I. FUNCTION

A. Blood carries everything needed for cellular metabolism to cells and unwanted by-products away from the cells, to lungs and kidneys

B. Blood vessels—means by which blood gains proximity to cells

C. Heart—maintains constant movement of blood in blood vessels

II. ANATOMIC STRUCTURES

A. Vascular system (blood vessels)

1. Arteries
   a) Characteristics
      (1) Made up of thick walls with elastic fibers; needed because arterial blood has high pressure
   b) Functions
      (1) Transport (oxygenated) blood away from heart
      (2) Lead to smaller arterioles
2. Capillaries
   a) Characteristics
      (1) Made up of thin walls so oxygen and nutrients can diffuse through to cells
      (2) Arterioles—branch into capillaries
      (3) Venules—lead away from capillaries
3. Veins
   a) Characteristics
      (1) thin-walled; some contain valves to prevent blood from flowing backwards since venous blood has low pressure
   b) Functions
      (1) Venules—drain capillary beds that flow into veins
      (2) Most carry unoxygenated blood (carbon dioxide) and wastes away from cells
      (3) Once returned to the right side of the heart, venous blood is pumped to lungs

B. Heart—muscular organ in thorax

1. Characteristics
   a) Contains specialized cardiac muscle tissue
   b) Enclosed in a pericardial sac
   c) Consists of *myocardium* (muscular layer) and *endocardium* (internal lining)
   d) Has its own internal electrical conduction system
      (1) *Sinoatrial node* (pacemaker of the heart)—sends out impulses for atria to contract approximately 72 beats/minute and sends signals to atrioventricular node

(2) *Atrioventricular node*—receives signals from sinoatrial node and causes ventricles to contract

2. Parts—composed of four pumping chambers
   a) Right atrium—receives venous blood from body (superior and inferior vena cavae); opens into right ventricle through tricuspid valve; thin-walled
   b) Right ventricle—pumps venous blood through pulmonary valve into pulmonary artery, which leads to lungs; thick-walled
   c) Left atrium—receives arterial (oxygenated) blood from lungs through four pulmonary veins; opens into left ventricle though mitral valve; thin-walled
   d) Left ventricle—pumps arterial blood to entire body; blood flows from left ventricle through aortic valve and into aorta; contains thickest walls of all the chambers

III. PHYSIOLOGY

A. Blood flow (Figure 2-10)

1. Venous blood—flows through right side of heart to lungs
2. Arterial blood—flows through left side of heart to body
3. Structural order of blood flow (into and out of heart)
   a) Inferior and superior vena cavae
   b) Right atrium
   c) Tricuspid valve
   d) Right ventricle
   e) Pulmonary valve
   f) Pulmonary trunk and arteries
   g) Lungs
   h) Pulmonary veins
   i) Left atrium
   j) Mitral valve
   k) Left ventricle
   l) Aortic valve
   m) Aorta

B. Heartbeat (pulse—approximately 72 beats/minute at rest)

1. Stroke volume—amount of blood pumped by ventricle during one heartbeat
2. Cardiac output—amount of blood pumped by ventricle during one minute

C. Cardiac cycle—contains three phases (Figure 2-11)

1. Both atria contract
2. Both ventricles contract
3. Heart rests

D. Blood pressure (average normal is 120/80)

1. *Systole*—measured during ventricular contraction
2. *Diastole*—measured during heart relaxation
3. Hypertension (high blood pressure) affected by:
   a) Increased cardiac output (heart rate and/or blood volume increases)

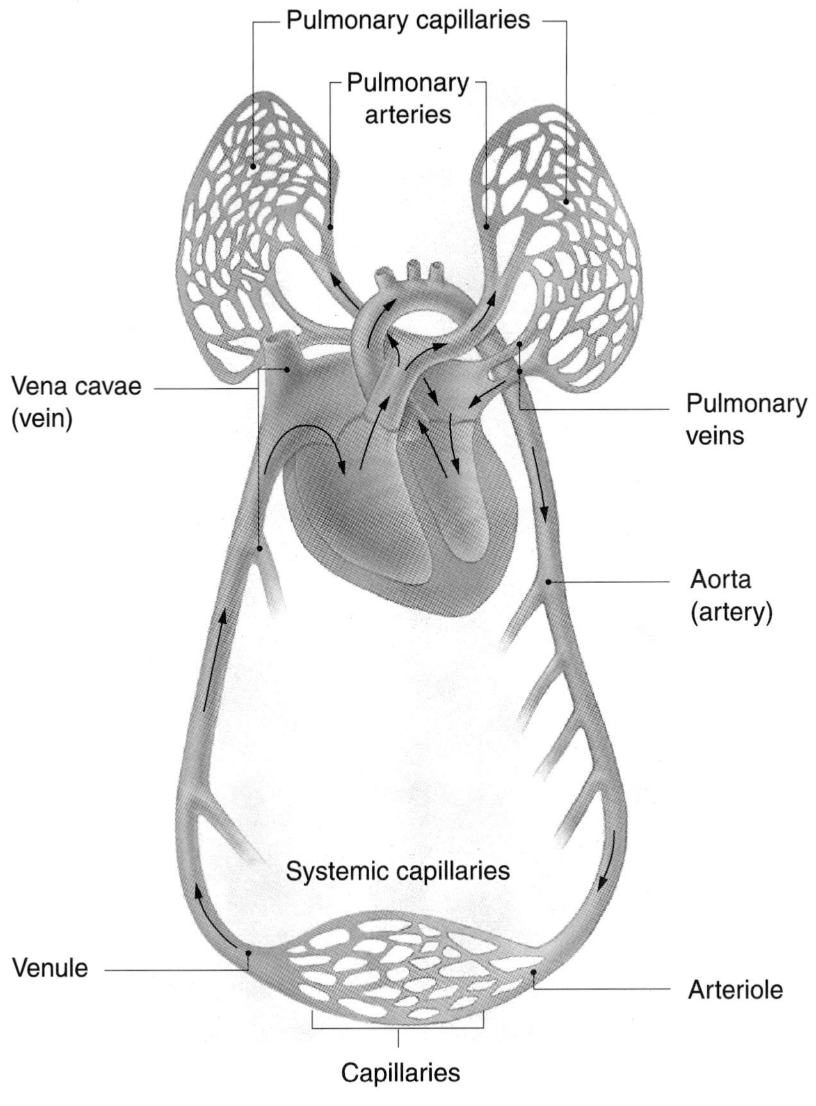

FIGURE 2-10. Pulmonary and systemic circulation.

b) Increased peripheral resistance (arterial constriction)
c) Hormones epinephrine, norepinephrine, aldosterone, and ADH (an antidiuretic hormone) cause a rise in blood pressure
d) Arteries—elevated blood pressure due to blood leaving the forceful contracting left ventricle
e) Veins—blood pressure is lower; muscular contraction assists in moving the venous blood

E. Blood supply of the heart

1. *Coronary arteries*—early branches off the aorta; provides a rich supply of blood to the continual muscular contraction of the myocardium
2. *Myocardial infarction* (heart attack)—caused by occlusion of coronary arteries from atherosclerotic plaque or clots

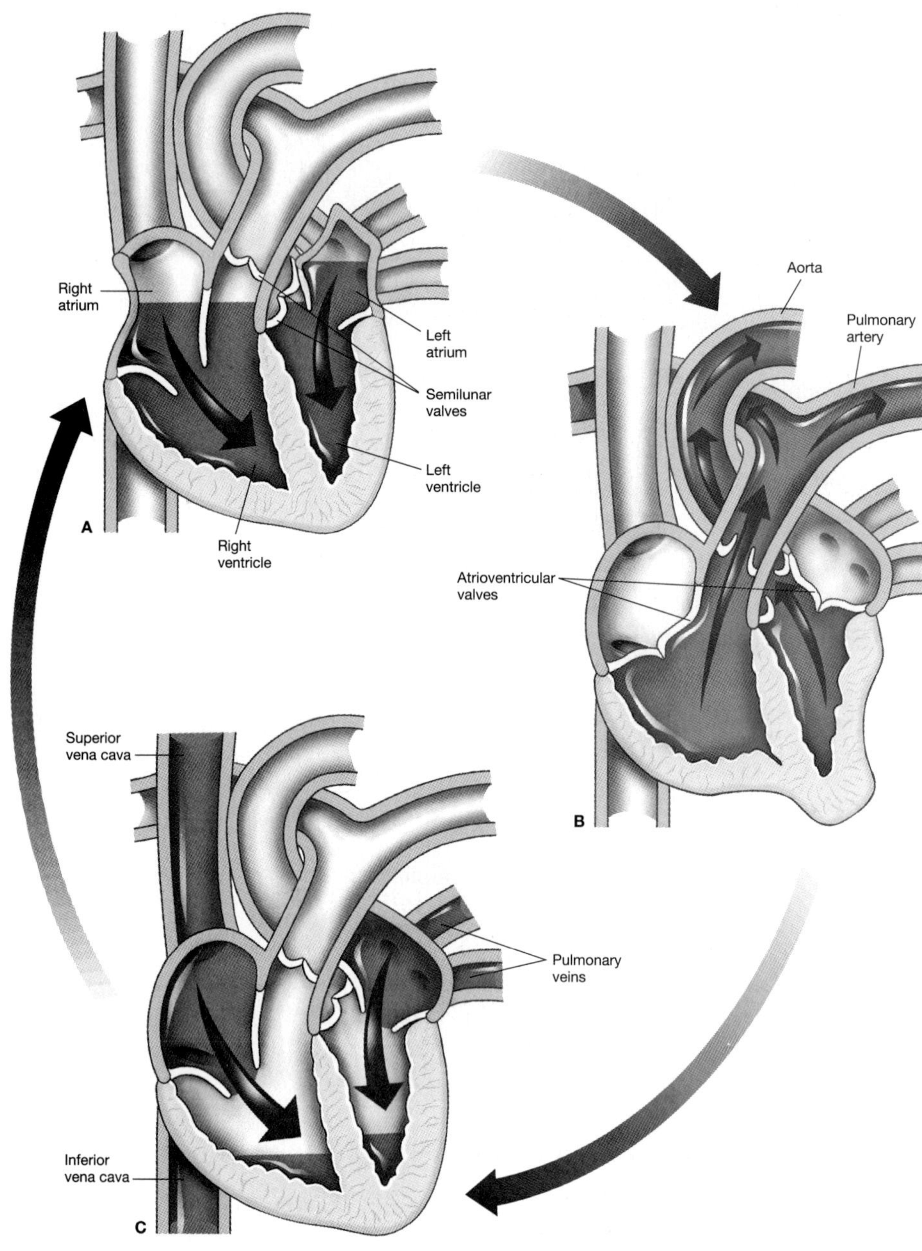

FIGURE 2-11. Stages in the cardiac cycle. A) During atrial systole the atria contract. B) During ventricular systole the ventricles contract. C) During diastole the heart rests.

F. **Blood supply to the brain—brain requires constant supply of glucose and oxygen; supplied by four arteries—two carotids and two vertebrals**

IV. **HOMEOSTASIS—heart and blood vessels are responsible for the blood pressure of 120/80; glucose concentration 0.1%, pH 7.4, and temperature 98.6°F are possible because of the circulation of the blood through vessels and organs. This circulation is propelled by contractions of the heart.**

➤ BLOOD

I. FUNCTIONS

A. Transports

1. Oxygen to and carbon dioxide away from cells
2. Nutrients to and wastes away from cells
3. White blood cells to fight infectious invaders
4. Hormones to target organs
5. Clotting elements to breaks in the vascular system
6. Heat away from areas of high cellular metabolism (contracting muscles)

II. ANATOMICAL STRUCTURES

A. Form elements (45% hematocrit)

1. Red blood cells (RBCs)—erythrocytes
   a) Contain *hemoglobin*—protein carrier for oxygen
   b) Formed in red bone marrow
   c) 4 to 6 million per cubic mm of blood
2. White blood cells (WBCs)—leukocytes
   a) Fight infections
   b) Formed in red bone marrow
   c) 5,000 to 11,000 per cubic mm of blood
   d) Types
      (1) *Granular leukocytes*
         (a) *Neutrophils*—engage in phagocytosis (engulf bacteria); most numerous
         (b) *Eosinophils*
         (c) *Basophils*
      (2) *Agranular leukocytes*
         (a) Monocytes—engage in phagocytosis; largest of the WBCs
         (b) Lymphocytes—responsible for immunity
            i) B cells—mature in bone marrow and produce antibodies
            ii) T cells—mature in thymus; some regulate the immune response, while others attack antigen-bearing cells
      (3) *Platelets*—used in clotting; amount is 150,000 to 300,000 per cubic mm of blood

B. Plasma

1. Consists of liquid part of blood
2. Accounts for about 55% of whole blood
3. Composed mostly of water
4. Includes substances such as hormones, gasses, plasma proteins, salts, and nutrients

III. PHYSIOLOGY

A. Clotting—includes many factors in addition to platelets, prothrombin, and fibrinogen; creates tangle of threadlike structures that incorporate red blood cells to form clot

B. Types of blood groups—A, B, AB, and O; type O is universal donor because it contains neither A nor B antigens

C. Exchange between blood and tissue fluid

1. Occurs in capillaries and is dependent on osmotic pressure
2. Moves water, glucose, oxygen, and amino acids out of blood
3. Moves water, carbon dioxide, and waste molecules into blood

IV. HOMEOSTASIS—vital in regulating blood pressure

A. Regulates body temperature by shunting blood to skin or internal organs

B. Transports oxygen and carbon dioxide, which assists in maintaining pH

C. Transports nutrients to and wastes away from cells

➤ RESPIRATORY SYSTEM

I. FUNCTION—external respiration, which involves exchange of gasses (oxygen and carbon dioxide) between air in alveoli and blood in lungs

II. ANATOMY (Figure 2-12)

A. Nose

1. Filters, warms, and humidifies the air
2. *Concha*—increases surface area through projections in lateral wall
3. *Nasolacrimal duct*—eyes drain into nose via this duct
4. *Paranasal sinuses* (air-filled cavities in cranial bones) drain into nose

B. *Pharynx* (throat)

1. Opening for nose and mouth
2. Divided into three parts: nasopharynx, oropharynx, and laryngopharynx

C. *Larynx* (voice box)—consists of

1. Glottis—top opening of larynx
2. Epiglottis—flap protects larynx when food is swallowed
3. Vocal cords—contain folds of tissue for speech

D. *Trachea*

1. Extends from larynx to thoracic cavity where it splits into bronchi
2. Aperture is held open with C-shaped rings of cartilage

E. Bronchi

1. *Bronchus* (right and left)—one main stem goes to each lung
2. Contains cartilage to hold lumen open
3. Continue dividing until there is a tertiary bronchus to each bronchopulmonary segment of lung

F. *Bronchioles*

1. Result from branching of tertiary bronchi; lead to alveoli
2. Contain smooth muscle that can contract and constrict airways (i.e., asthma)

G. *Alveoli*

1. Consist of terminal structures of bronchial tree; elastic epithelial sacs
2. Where external respiration takes place

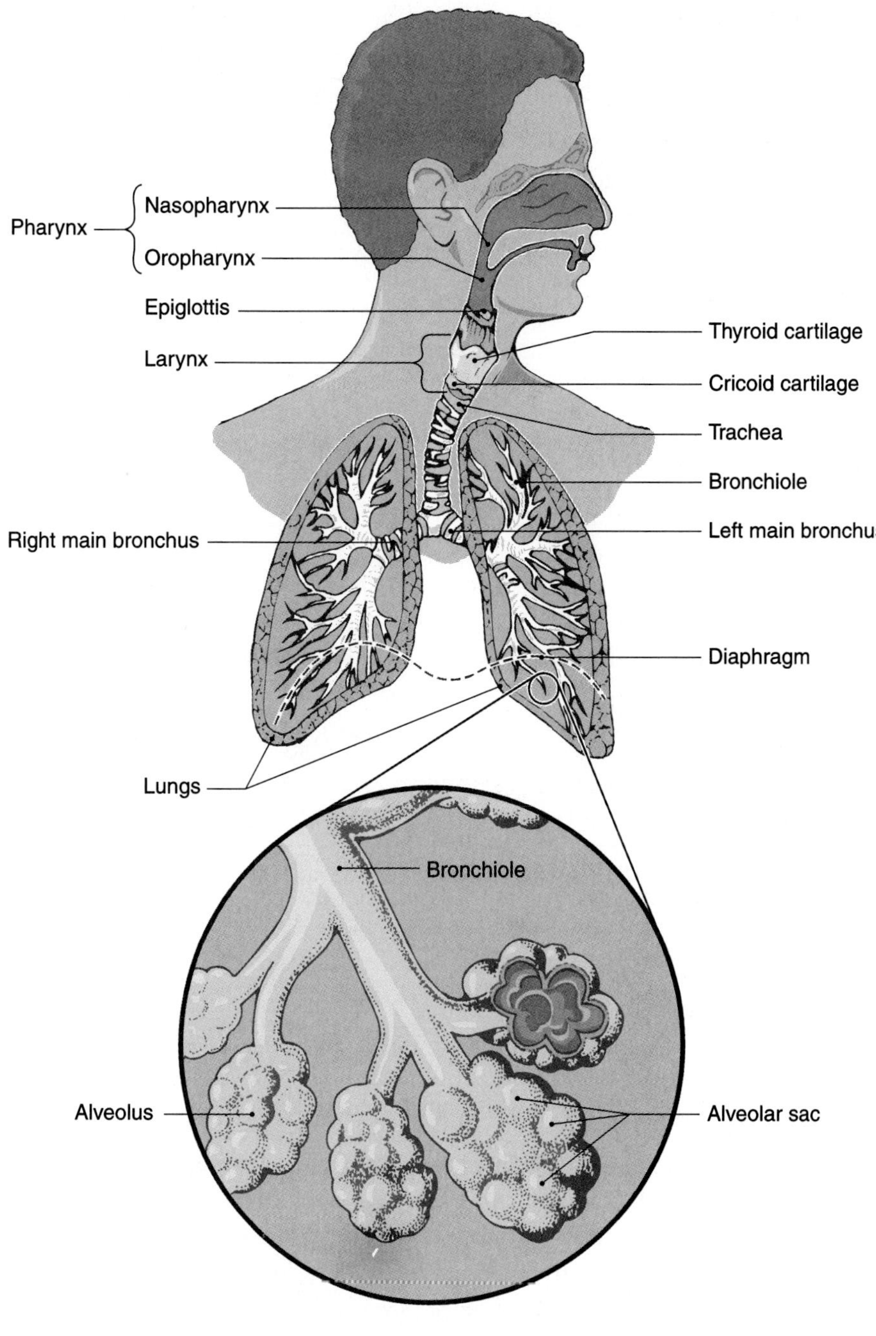

FIGURE 2-12. Respiratory organs.

H. Lungs

1. Organs that contain bronchial tree, bronchioles, and alveoli
2. Surrounded by pleural sac
3. Rich in blood supply for gas exchange

I. *Diaphragm*—separates thoracic and abdominal cavities

1. During inspiration—contracts and moves downward, creating negative pressure in thoracic cavity and causing air to rush in
2. During expiration—relaxes, and elastic tissue of lungs contracts, allowing air to be exhaled
3. Supplied by phrenic nerve, which comes down from neck

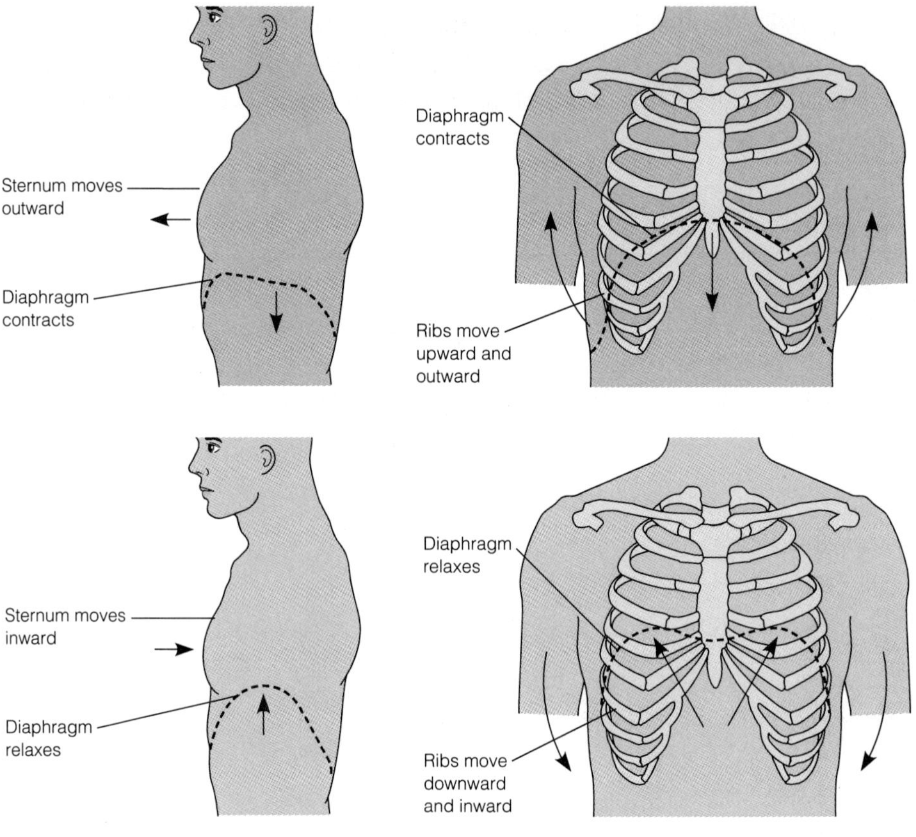

FIGURE 2-13. Inspiration vs. expiration.

III. PHYSIOLOGY

A. Oxygen—passes from air in an alveolus across respiratory membrane to enter capillaries surrounding alveolus, where it is picked up by hemoglobin in an RBC and carried to tissue capillaries in body

B. *Ventilation*—involves movement of air in and out of lungs (Figure 2-13)

1. Diaphragm—most important muscle involved in ventilation
2. Rib cage—also involved in moving air; during inspiration, the ribs move up and increase size of thoracic cavity

C. Function—can be determined by tests that measure lung capacity

1. *Tidal volume* (TV)—measures amount of air moving in and out with each breath
2. *Vital capacity* (VC)—measures total amount of air that can be moved in and out of lungs with a single breath
3. Inspiratory reserve (IRV)—measures increase inspired beyond tidal volume
4. Expiratory reserve (ERV)—measures amount forcefully expired beyond tidal volume
5. Vital capacity = tidal volume + IRV + ERV
6. Residual volume—amount of air that remains in lungs, even after forceful expiration

IV. HOMEOSTASIS—respiratory system maintains oxygen content of blood; helps maintain temperature by releasing excess heat and regulates pH of blood by exhaling carbon dioxide

➤ LYMPHATIC SYSTEM

I. FUNCTIONS

A. Returns extracellular tissue fluid (*lymph*) to bloodstream

B. Lymphatic capillaries in gastrointestinal tract absorb fat molecules and transport them to bloodstream

C. Helps defend body against disease

II. ANATOMY

A. Lymph vessels (Figure 2-14)

1. One-way system of vessels, which carry lymph back to bloodstream
2. Vessels come from all parts of body
3. Contain lymph nodes (LN) through which lymph passes: LNs contain many white blood cells that destroy infectious agents

B. *Spleen*—abdominal organ

1. Acts as a filter of the blood, much as a lymph node
2. Filters out broken red blood cells

C. *Thymus*—thoracic organ; produces thymosins (hormones); active during childhood; decreases in size in adults; site of maturation of T lymphocytes

D. *Red bone marrow*—site where all blood cells (red and white) are produced

III. PHYSIOLOGY

A. *Inflammatory response*

1. Reaction to an injury
2. Releases *histamine,* which causes capillary dilatation and permeability
3. Swelling occurs
4. White blood cells migrate to site
5. *Pus* forms as a result of dead WBCs and bacteria

B. Immune response

1. *Antigen*—any substance (microbe, food, pollen, cell) that immune system recognizes as foreign
2. Non-self-recognition of antigen by body
3. Body response—activates B and T (lymphocytes); B cells produce antibodies, which are proteins that can inactivate antigens; some cells attach to antigen-bearing cells, while others regulate the immune response

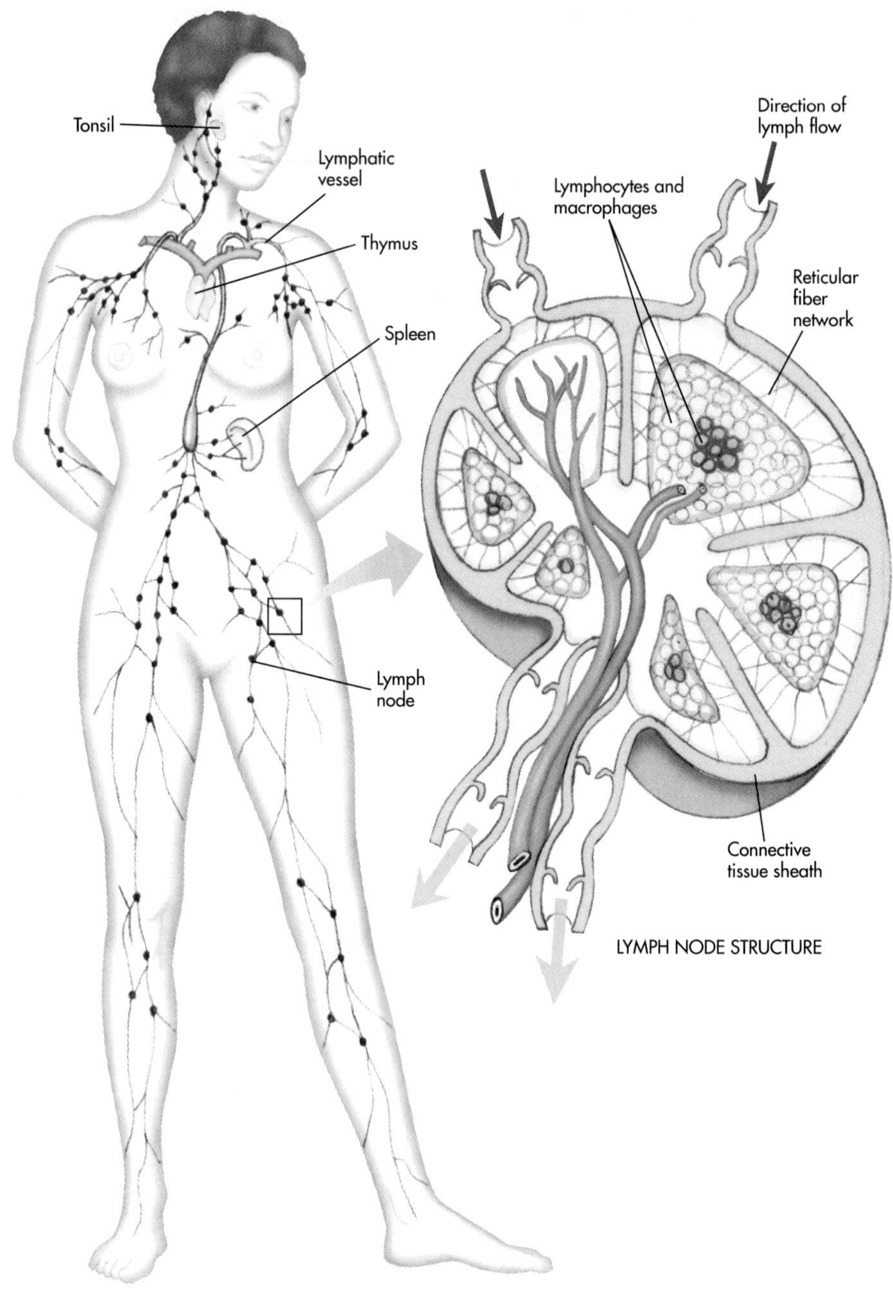

FIGURE 2-14. Lymphatic system.

4. System is responsible for developing immunity to diseases and immunity rendered by vaccination; results in *active immunity* (can last a lifetime; *passive immunity* occurs when immunoglobulins are received from another individual [short-lived])

IV. HOMEOSTASIS—by keeping the body free of infectious agents and their effects on the body, the lymphatic system plays a vital role in maintaining homeostasis (i.e., body temperature is often elevated in infections)

➤ DIGESTIVE SYSTEM

I. FUNCTIONS

A. Ingests food

B. Breaks down food into molecules that can be absorbed across plasma membrane

1. Proteins—break down into amino acids
2. Carbohydrates—break down into glucose
3. Fats—break down into glycerol and fatty acids

C. Absorbs amino acids, glucose, glycerol, and fatty acids

D. Eliminates nondigestible foods

II. ANATOMIC STRUCTURES (Figure 2-15)

A. Mouth—food is chewed (masticated) in oral cavity

1. Teeth
2. Tongue
3. Hard and soft palates
4. Salivary glands—secrete saliva that moisten bolus of food and contain salivary amylase—enzyme that begins breakdown of starch

B. Tongue—propels bolus to back of throat, the pharynx, where it moves down into esophagus

C. Esophagus—muscular tube that passes through diaphragm to reach stomach

D. Stomach—stores food and starts digestion of proteins

1. Lined with glands that secrete hydrochloric acid and the enzyme pepsin
2. *Gastroesophageal sphincter*—prevents food from refluxing into esophagus
3. Food leaves stomach as chyme and passes through *pyloric sphincter* into duodenum of small intestine

E. Small intestine—approximately 10 feet long

1. Functions
   a) Mechanically and chemically breaks down chyme so nutrients can be absorbed through finger-like projections called *villi*
      (1) Glucose and amino acids—absorbed into capillaries and then enter liver via portal vein
      (2) Fats—enter a lacteal, small vessel of lymphatic system
2. Parts
   a) *Duodenum*—makes up first 10 inches of small intestine
      (1) Receives bile from liver to emulsify fats
      (2) Receives pancreatic juice from pancreas
      (3) Produces intestinal juice that contains enzymes to chemically break down chyme
   b) *Jejunum*—makes up next 3 feet of small intestine
   c) *Ileum*—makes up last 6 to 7 feet of small intestine

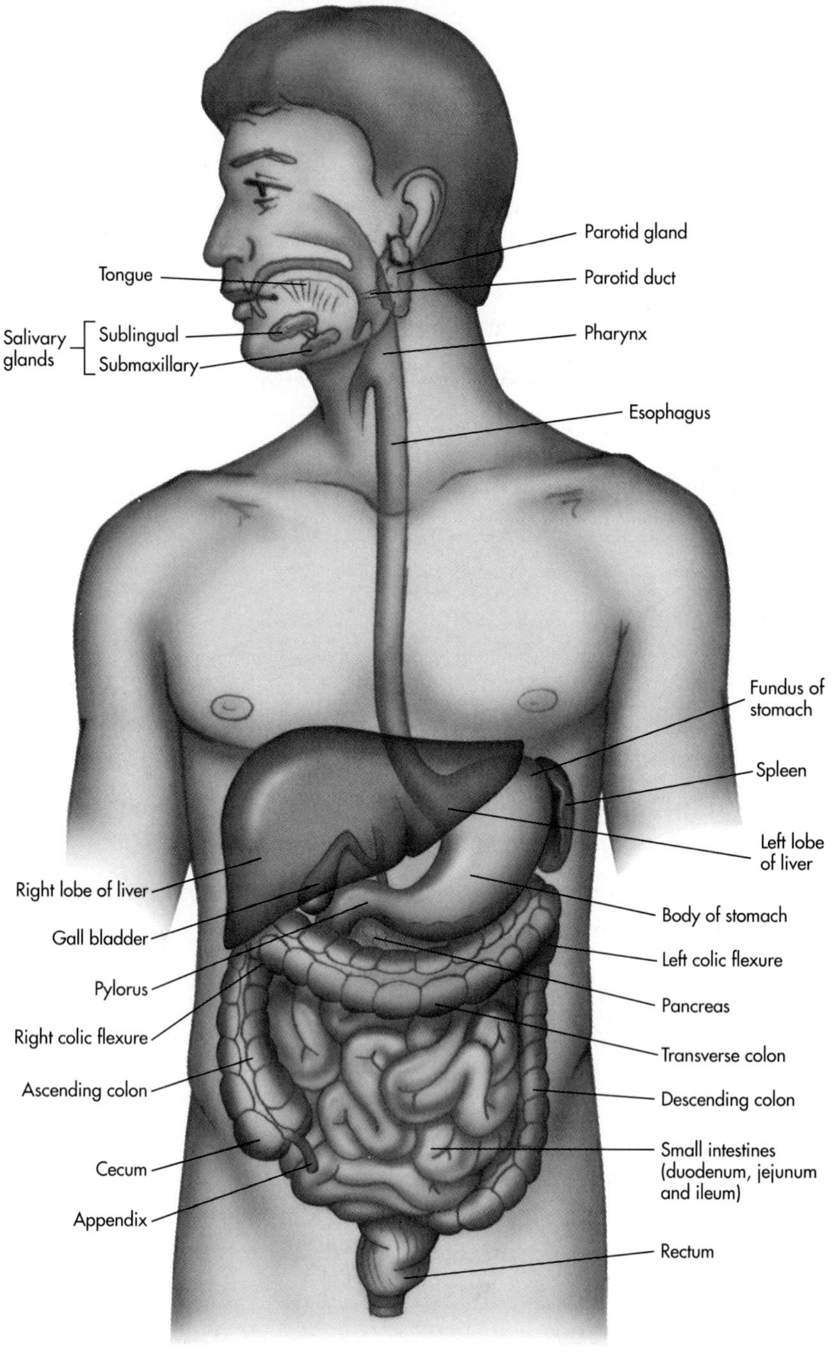

FIGURE 2-15. Digestive system.

F. Large intestine—approximately 5 feet long

1. Functions
   a) Absorbs water and electrolytes
   b) Stores feces and nondigestible food until they can be eliminated
2. Parts
   a) *Cecum* (through the ileocecal valve)—ileum of small intestine opens into this part of large intestine
   b) *Vermiform appendix*—projects off cecum

c) *Ascending colon*—located on right side of abdomen into which cecum opens
d) *Transverse colon*—extends from right to left side of abdomen
e) *Descending colon*—opens into sigmoid colon; located on left side of abdomen
f) *Sigmoid colon* (S-shaped segment)—opens into rectum, which ends in the anus, an external opening

G. Pancreas—an abdominal organ that produces exocrine digestive enzymes and bicarbonate and endocrine hormones, insulin and glucagon

H. Liver

1. Produces bile that flows via bile duct into duodenum; extra bile is stored in gall bladder, a pouch hanging down from liver
2. Receives nutrients absorbed through portal vein
3. Removes and stores iron
4. Stores fat-soluble vitamins A, D, E, and K
5. Removes and detoxifies poisons
6. Stores glucose as glycogen
7. Destroys old red blood cells
8. Produces plasma proteins

III. PHYSIOLOGY

A. *Peristalsis*—rhythmic movements that begin in esophagus and propel food through digestive system

B. *Chemical digestion*—breaks down carbohydrates into glucose, proteins into amino acids, and fats into fatty acids and glycerol; all these molecules are small enough to pass through plasma membrane of digestive system

C. Provide nutrition

1. Glucose—used for immediate energy or stored as glycogen in liver
2. Amino acids—used for protein synthesis
3. Fats—reserved as a long-term energy source
4. Vitamins—essential for cellular metabolism
5. Minerals—inorganic elements necessary for some metabolism

IV. HOMEOSTASIS

A. Water is absorbed in stomach and large intestine to maintain blood volume that helps to regulate a normal blood pressure

B. Liver—assists in controlling glucose concentration (0.1%)

C. Pancreas—produces bicarbonate, which assists in proper pH (7.4) of the blood and produces insulin and glucagon, which regulate glucose concentration

D. Absorption of nutrients to nourish cells and maintain function

➤ URINARY SYSTEM

I. FUNCTIONS

A. Remove *nitrogenous wastes* (by-products of protein metabolism) from blood and excretes them; nitrogenous wastes are in the form of urea, uric acid, creatinine, and ammonium

B. Maintain blood volume—regulates amount of water excreted and/or reabsorbed

C. Regulate electrolyte balance in blood, i.e., sodium (Na+), potassium (K+), bicarbonate (HCO_3-), and calcium (Ca+)

D. Regulate blood pH by excreting hydrogen (H+) ions

E. Secrete erythropoietin—stimulates production of RBCs

F. Secrete renin—helps maintain blood pressure

II. ANATOMICAL STRUCTURES (Figure 2-16)

A. Kidneys—paired organs in retroperitoneal space (Figure 2-17)

B. *Nephrons*—functional unit of kidneys; over 1 million per kidney; each nephron contains

1. *Glomerulus*—capillary cluster through which fluid part of blood flows

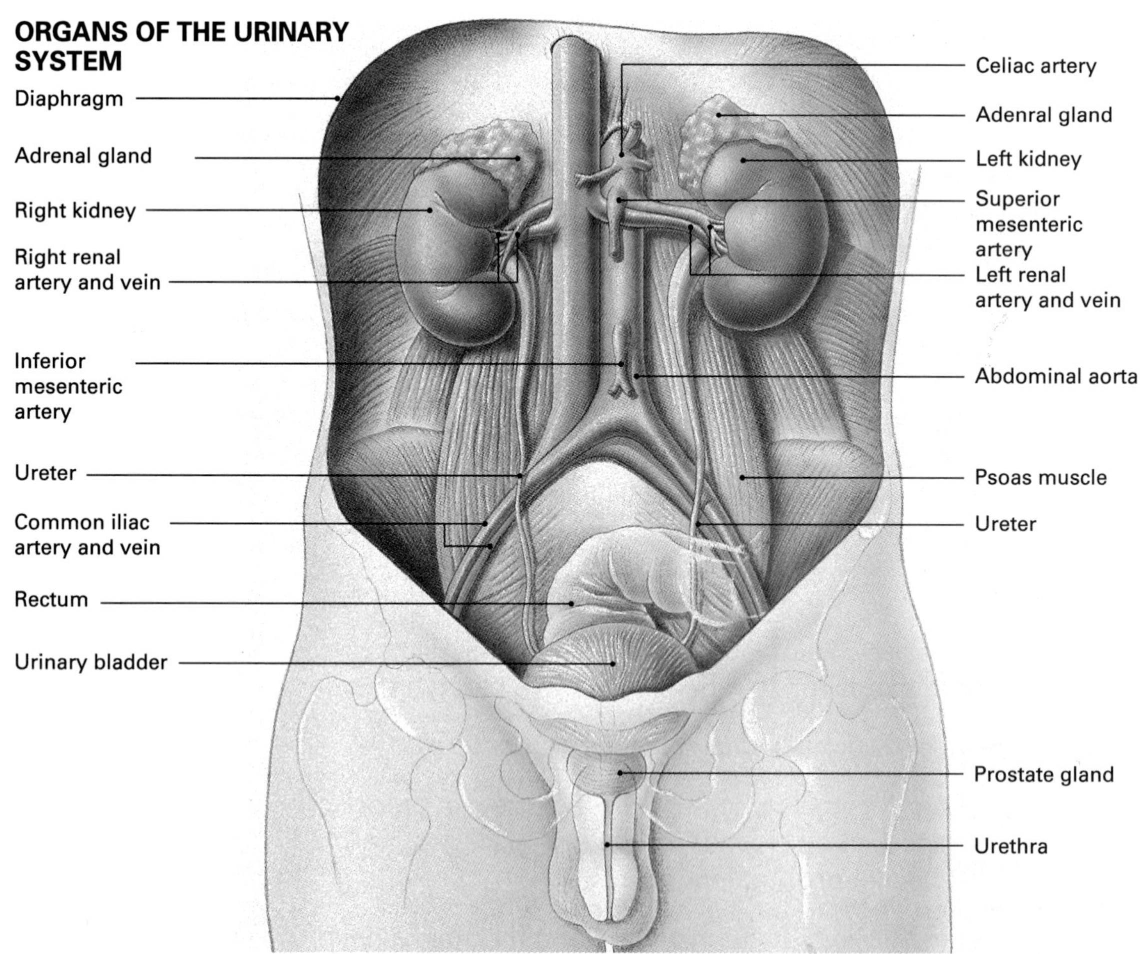

FIGURE 2-16. The urinary system.

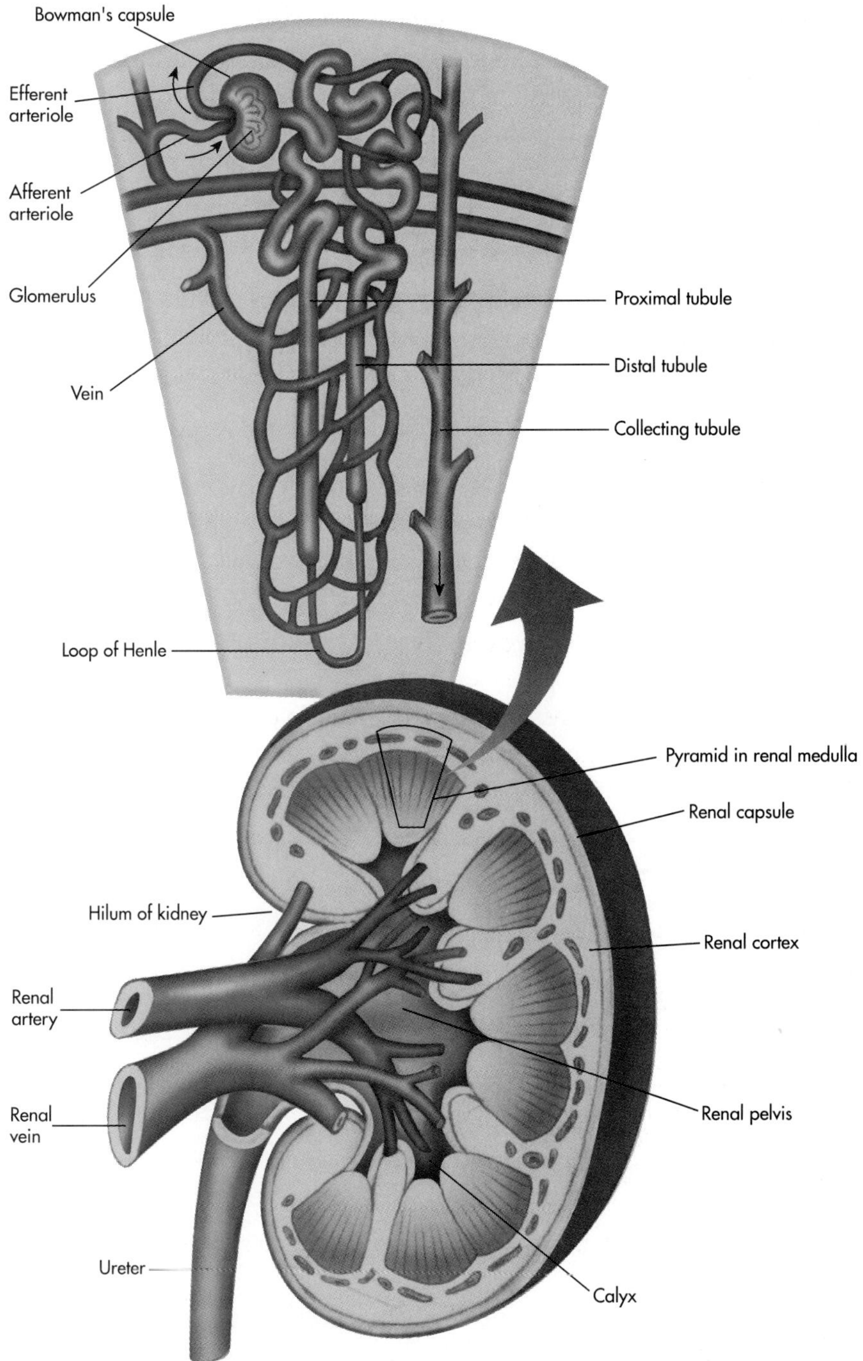

FIGURE 2-17. Structure of a nephron and anatomy of kidneys.

2. Glomerular capsule—leads to tubular system
3. *Tubular system*—secretes electrolytes and reabsorbs water
4. *Collecting ducts*—urine leaves nephron system and flows into these ducts, which all empty into renal pelvis

C. *Ureters*—paired tubes leading from kidneys to urinary bladder

D. *Urinary bladder*—pelvic organ used for storage of urine

E. *Urethra*—tube leading from urinary bladder to outside; short in females, long in males

F. Urination (micturition)—emptying of bladder through urethra

G. Renal arteries—since kidneys regulate blood volume and composition, they have a rich supply of blood from large renal arteries that come directly off descending aorta

III. PHYSIOLOGY

A. Kidney—function is regulated by the following hormones

1. *Aldosterone*
   a) Secreted by adrenal cortex and regulates sodium (Na+) and potassium (K+)
   b) Regulates blood pressure and blood volume with help of enzyme, renin, secreted by kidney
2. *ADH* (antidiuretic hormone)
   a) Secreted by posterior lobe of pituitary gland when body is dehydrated to conserve water
   b) Regulates blood pressure and blood volume, which are elevated by actions of aldosterone and ADH

B. Electrolytes—dissolved in the plasma of blood and regulated by kidneys

1. Sodium and potassium—used in muscle contraction and nerve impulse conduction
2. Bicarbonate ion (HCO_3)—maintains pH of blood

IV. HOMEOSTASIS—maintained by regulating blood volume and pH

➤ REPRODUCTIVE SYSTEM

I. FUNCTION

A. Males

1. Produce sperm within the testes—nurture and transport sperm until they exit the penis
2. Produce sex hormones

B. Females

1. Release eggs from ovary—nurture and transport egg in uterine tube until it reaches uterus
2. Nurture and house fetus in uterus during pregnancy
3. Produce sex hormones

II. ANATOMY

A. Male

1. *Testes*—contained in scrotum, outside of abdominal cavity
   a) Produce sperm and sex hormones
   b) Must be kept cooler than body temperature for viable sperm
   c) Seminiferous tubules—where spermatogenesis occurs
   d) Interstitial cells—produce male sex hormones, androgens
2. *Epididymis*—stores maturing sperm
3. *Vas deferens*—connects epididymis with urethra; portion cut during a vasectomy (for birth control)
4. Seminal fluid
   a) Secretion that contains sperm during ejaculation

b) Produced by three glands: seminal vesicles, prostate gland, and bulbourethral glands

5. Penis—tip is covered by flap of skin, foreskin, which may be removed (circumcision)
   a) Penetrates vagina during sexual intercourse
   b) Contains erectile tissue that fills with blood to cause an erection
6. *Testosterone*
   a) Production is regulated by pituitary gland and is necessary for production and maturation of sperm
   b) Responsible for secondary sex characteristics

B. Female

1. Ovaries
   a) Release eggs and produce sex hormones
   b) Graafian follicle—maturing egg in follicle tissue
   c) *Ovulation*—time at which egg is released from follicle
   d) *Corpus luteum*—formed by an empty follicle
      (1) If pregnancy does not occur, corpus luteum degenerates 10 days after ovulation
      (2) If pregnancy occurs, corpus luteum persists up to six months to produce hormones that maintain pregnancy
2. *Uterine tube* (fallopian tube)—where fertilization usually occurs; transports egg to uterus; egg begins dividing while in uterine tube (several days)
3. *Uterus*—thick-walled, muscular organ
   a) Enlarges to accommodate growing fetus
   b) *Myometrium*—composes muscular layer
   c) *Endometrium*—composes lining; rich in blood vessels to supply the placenta
4. Vagina—fibromuscular organ; also functions as birth canal during parturition (childbirth)
5. External genitalia (vulva)
   a) Labia majora and labia minora—folds of skin around vaginal opening
   b) Clitoris—female counterpart of the penis, but much smaller; contains erectile tissue for sexual excitation and climax

III. PHYSIOLOGY

A. Orgasm

1. Physiological and psychological climax of sexual stimulation
   a) In males, results in ejaculation, release of semen and relaxation of muscular tension
   b) In females, is preceded by lubrication of vagina and followed by relaxation of muscular tension

B. Regulation of female hormones

1. Controlled by the hypothalamus, which secretes gonadotropic-releasing factor to pituitary gland
2. Anterior pituitary gland—secretes follicle stimulating hormone (FSH) and luteinizing hormone (LH), which target ovaries
3. Ovaries secrete estrogen and progesterone

4. Estrogen
   a) Necessary for egg maturation
   b) Responsible for secondary sex characteristics
   c) Predominates during first half of menstrual cycle
5. Progesterone
   a) Secreted by corpus luteum
   b) Prepares endometrium to receive a fertilized egg
   c) Predominates during second half of menstrual cycle
6. Menstruation
   a) Occurs if egg is not fertilized and does not implant in uterus
   b) Endometrium is sloughed off
   c) Menstrual cycle is usually 28 days
      (1) Menstruation occurs during first 5 days
      (2) Ovulation occurs about day 14
      (3) Period of fertility is approximately from day 10 to 18

C. Pregnancy

1. Occurs when sperm and egg (gametes) unite to form an embryo
2. Placenta transfers nutrients from maternal bloodstream to fetus
3. Embryonic membranes produce hormone human chorionic gonadotropic hormone (HCG)
4. Full-term pregnancy lasts 40 weeks

III. HOMEOSTASIS—sex hormones help to maintain a robust and youthful body, capable of adjusting to stimuli and maintaining homeostasis

review questions

DIRECTIONS Each of the questions or incomplete statements below is followed by suggested answers or completions. Select the **one** answer that is best in each case.

1. Which of the following blood components is necessary for clotting?
   A. plasma
   B. platelets
   C. neutrophils
   D. hemoglobin

2. Which of the following heart chambers pumps with the greatest force?
   A. right atrium
   B. right ventricle
   C. left atrium
   D. left ventricle

3. Diastole occurs when the
   A. ventricles contract.
   B. ventricles fill.
   C. heart rests.
   D. atria contract.

4. All of the following nutrients can be absorbed by the gastrointestinal system EXCEPT one. Which one is the EXCEPTION?
   A. fatty acids
   B. glucose
   C. proteins
   D. glycerol

5. Which of the following BEST describes the large intestine?
   A. Possesses villi for absorption.
   B. Secretes acid and digestive juice.
   C. Receives bile from the liver and pancreatic juice from the pancreas.
   D. Absorbs water and electrolytes.

6. All of the following are functions of the liver EXCEPT one. Which one is the EXCEPTION?
   A. Secretes glucagon.
   B. Stores vitamins A, D, E, and K.
   C. Removes and detoxifies poisons.
   D. Produces bile.

7. Which of the following glands BEST regulates blood glucose level?
   A. thyroid
   B. pituitary
   C. pancreas
   D. adrenal medulla

8. During inflammation, histamine is released and causes
   A. swelling.
   B. clotting.
   C. bleeding.
   D. pus formation.

9. Which of the following systems produces heat, which helps maintain body temperature at 37°C?
   A. skeletal
   B. lymphatic
   C. digestive
   D. muscular

10. Which of the following BEST describes a striated (skeletal) muscle?
    A. Contracts slower than smooth muscle.
    B. Fatigues more quickly than smooth muscle.
    C. Controlled by the autonomic nervous system.
    D. Found in hollow organs, such as the intestine.

11. Which part of the brain controls respiration?
    A. medulla
    B. thalamus
    C. cerebellum
    D. cerebrum

12. A synapse is
    A. the place where an axon of one neuron meets the dendrites of another neuron.
    B. where the nucleus and organelles of a neuron are located.
    C. the insulation surrounding the axon.
    D. a sensory receptor.

13. Sperm are produced in the
    A. testes.
    B. epididymis.
    C. vas deferens.
    D. prostate gland.

14. Fertilization of the egg MOST commonly occurs in the
    A. ovary.
    B. fallopian tube.
    C. uterus.
    D. vagina.

15. During a normal human mentrual cycle of 28 days, the period of human fertility occurs in day(s)
    A. 1–5 of the menstrual cycle.
    B. 14 only.
    C. 10–18.
    D. 18–28.

16. During respiration, gas exchange occurs in the
    A. trachae.
    B. bronchi.
    C. bronchioles.
    D. alveoli.

17. The diaphragm
    A. contracts during inspiration.
    B. contracts during expiration.
    C. is an abdominal structure.
    D. is located superior to the lungs.

18. All of the following are functions of the skeletal system EXCEPT one. Which one is the EXCEPTION?
    A. Protects the soft parts of the body.
    B. Produces blood cells.
    C. Holds joints together.
    D. Stores mineral salts, such as calcium.

19. Ribs attach to which of the following vertebrae?
    A. cervical
    B. thoracic
    C. lumbar
    D. sacral

20. The action of flexion
    A. increases the joint angle (straightens it).
    B. moves the body part laterally away from the midline.
    C. moves the body part towards the midline.
    D. decreases the joint angle (bends it).

21. All of the following are functions of the urinary system EXCEPT one. Which one is the EXCEPTION?
    A. Absorbs glucose.
    B. Removes nitrogenous wastes.
    C. Maintains blood volume.
    D. Regulates electrolytes.

22. Which of the following structures provides the opening to the outside for the urinary system?
    A. nephron
    B. ureter
    C. urinary bladder
    D. urethra

23. Which of the following heart valves separates the right atrium from the right ventricle?
    A. bicuspid
    B. tricuspid
    C. mitral
    D. semilunar

24. Which of the following tissues lines the inner surface of the heart?
    A. pericardium
    B. pleura
    C. peritoneum
    D. endocardium

25. Which of the following valves separates the small intestines from the ascending colon?
    A. pyloric
    B. mitral
    C. semilunar
    D. ileocecal

26. Which of the following veins carry oxygenated blood?
    A. jugular
    B. facial
    C. pulmonary
    D. maxillary

answers & rationales

1.

B. Platelets are part of a complex cascade of reactions that causes clotting. Plasma is the fluid part of blood. Neutrophils are white blood cells used for fighting infection, and hemoglobin is the carrier for oxygen found in red blood cells.

2.

D. The left ventricle is the chamber that pumps blood to the entire body. This is why the left ventricular myocardium is the thickest. The right atrium is the chamber that pumps blood down into the right ventricle. The right ventricle is the chamber that pumps blood to the lungs and the left atrium only needs to pump blood down to the left ventricle.

3.

C. Diastole is the heart at rest. Systole is the highest reading in a blood pressure measurement and represents the force of the contraction of the ventricles. The ventricles are filling when the atria are contracting.

4.

C. Proteins must be broken down into amino acids before absorption can occur. Fatty acids, glycerol, and glucose are in the simplest state for absorption to occur.

5.

D. Fecal matter entering the cecum is watery; therefore it is the job of the large intestine to absorb water and electrolytes to give feces a solid consistency. The small intestine, which has villi for absorption, receives bile from the liver and pancreatic juice from the pancreas. The stomach is responsible for secreting acid and digestive juice.

6.

A. The pancreas secretes glucagon, not the liver. However, the liver stores fat-soluble vitamins A, D, E, and K; removes and detoxifies poisons; and produces bile.

7.

C. Pancreas secretes insulin and glucagon to maintain a fairly constant blood glucose level. The thyroid gland is involved in metabolic rate. Although the pituitary gland controls many glands, it does not control the pancreas. The adrenal medulla is part of the autonomic nervous system and produces epinephrine and norepinephrine.

8.

A. Histamine causes capillary dilatation and permeability, which leads to swelling. Histamine plays no part in the clotting mechanism. The fluids that leak out of the capillaries do not contain red blood cells. Pus formation is a late reaction to inflammation, formed by dead white blood cells and infectious agents.

9.

D. Heat is a by-product of the biochemical process of muscle contraction and helps to maintain body temperature. When muscles are very active, as in strenuous exercise, the body may become overheated. In the skeletal system, the metabolic activity is not great enough to produce enough heat to maintain temperature. The lymphatic system is involved in fighting disease and transports fat from the gastrointestinal tract. When blood is diverted to the digestive system during digestion, the body may actually experience a drop in temperature.

10.

B. Striated muscle is used for quick response, as in a reflex, but it cannot maintain contraction for a long time. Smooth muscle is controlled by the autonomic nervous system. Organs are controlled by the autonomic nervous system (we do not consciously think about it) and, therefore, contain smooth muscle.

11.

A. The medulla, or brainstem, controls functions such as breathing, heartbeat, and blood pressure, all of which maintain life. The thalamus is a relay station for afferent information. The cerebellum coordinates skeletal movement. The cerebrum is for higher cortical functioning, such as reasoning and thought processing. A person may live with a nonfunctional cerebrum and an intact medulla. This state is known as a vegatative state.

12.

A. Neurotransmitters conduct an impulse across a synapse from the axon of one neuron to the dendrites of another. The cell body of a neuron contains the nucleus and organelles. Some axons are wrapped in myelin that acts as an insulator, thus increasing conduction speed. A receptor is specialized to receive information from the environment (sight, touch, hearing) and generate nerve impulses from it.

13.

A. Sperm are produced in the testes. The epididymis is a highly convoluted tube in which sperm are stored. The vas deferens is a tube that connects the epididymis with the urethra. The prostate gland produces fluid that contributes to semen.

14.

B. While the egg is moving down the fallopian tube, sperm swim up the tube to fertilize it. The egg is released from the ovary unfertilized. The egg must be fertilized and ready to implant by the time it arrives in the uterus in order for pregnancy to occur. The vagina cannot support a placenta, and the egg cannot move back up into the uterus.

15.

C. Sperm can live for several days in the female reproductive tract. Likewise, the egg is viable for several days after ovulation, and may be fertilized for several days after ovulation. The lining is shed during days 1 to 5 of the menstrual cycle. Day 14 is the time of ovulation, but the period of fertility extends before and after this day. If the egg is not fertilized by day 18, it is usually no longer viable.

16.

D. The alveoli are thin-walled sacs through which oxygen diffuses into, and carbon dioxide out of, the surrounding capillaries. The trachea is a tube that leads to the bronchi of the lungs. Bronchi are too thick-walled (with cartilage) to allow gas exchange to occur. Bronchioles are small tubes, lined with smooth muscle that lead to the alveoli.

17.

A. When the diaphragm contracts it moves down, increasing the capacity of the thoracic cavity, which creates a negative pressure and draws in the air (inspiration). The diaphragm, which separates the abdomen from the thorax (inferior to the lungs), relaxes during expiration.

18.

C. The function of the muscles, and tendons of muscles and ligaments, is to hold the joints together. The skeletal system protects body parts, produces blood cells, and stores minerals.

19.

B. There are twelve thoracic vertebrae and one rib pair that attach to each vertebrae to form the thoracic cage. Cervical vertebrae are located in the neck and lumbar vertebrae are in the lower back, posterior to the abdomen. The sacrum articulates with the coxal bones to form the pelvic girdle.

20.

D. An example of flexion is bending (at the elbow). Straightening the joint angle is extension. Moving a body part laterally, away, is abduction. Moving a body part toward the midline is adduction.

21.

A. Absorption of glucose is the function of the digestive system. However, the urinary system removes nitrogenous wastes, maintains blood volume, and regulates electrolytes.

22.

D. The urethra is the tube that leads from the urinary bladder to the urethral opening for emptying the urinary bladder. Nephron is the functional unit of the kidneys. The ureter leads from the kidney to the urinary bladder. The urinary bladder stores the urine.

23.

B. The tricuspid is a three-leaf valve, which separates the right atrium from the right ventricle. The bicuspid or mitral valve separates the left atrium from the left ventricle. The semilunar valves are three-cusped valves in the aorta and the pulmonary artery.

24.

D. The endocardium lines the inner surface of the heart. It may become inflamed, which occurs in bacterial endocarditis. The pericardium is the outside lining of the heart. The pleura is the lining around the lung cavity, and the peritoneum lines the abdominal cavity.

25.

D. The ileocecal valve separates the ileum from the cecum, part of the ascending colon. The pyloric valve is located at the junction of the stomach and duodenum. The mitral valve is located between the left atrium and left ventricle. The semilunar valve is a three-cusped valve located within the pulmonary artery.

26.

C. The pulmonary vein is the only vein to carry freshly oxygenated blood from the lungs to the heart. The jugular, facial, and maxillary veins carry unoxygenated blood.

CHAPTER

3 Head and Neck Anatomy

Phillip E. O'Shaughnessy, DDS, MSD

contents

Head and neck anatomy studies the highly specialized, interrelated structures that occur in the compact area of the mouth and its associated structures—especially surrounding and including the oral cavity.

➤ SKULL

The skull contains separate bones, the majority of which are joined by synarthrosis joints (sutures). The single exception is the mandibular joint, which is a diarthrosis (synovial) joint.

I. BONES

A. Cranial bones—in adults, these bones are fused at the sutures to enclose and protect the brain

1. Occipital bone—single, large, heavy bone that forms the posterior, inferior portion of cranium; contains
   a) *Foramen magnum*—opening for the spinal cord that emerges from the brain
   b) *Occipital condyles (paired)*—located lateral to foramen magnum; forms a joint with the first cervical vertebra (atlas)
   c) *Hypoglossal canals*—transmits cranial nerve (CN) XII
   d) Portion of *jugular foramen*—forms with temporal bone
2. Frontal bone—single, large bone that forms the forehead and superior portion of the orbits; contains
   a) *Supraorbital ridges*—bony prominence under eyebrows
   b) *Zygomatic process of frontal bone*—articulates with zygoma
   c) *Glabella*—smooth elevation between eyebrows
   d) *Lacrimal fossa*—contains lacrimal gland
   e) Paired *frontal paranasal sinuses*
3. Parietal bones—superior, paired, flat bones that articulate with the frontal, occipital, temporal, and sphenoid bones
4. Temporal bones—paired bones that form the lateral wall of cranium; contain 3 portions
   a) *Squamous portion*—large, flat area of bone that forms cranial wall
      (1) *Articular fossa*—portion that articulates with mandibular condyle
      (2) *Articular eminence*—elevation located anterior to articular fossa
      (3) *Postglenoid process*—prevents mandibular condyle from displacing posteriorly
   b) *Tympanic portion*—forms external acoustic meatus
   c) *Petrous portion*—inferior and medial portion that contains organs of hearing and balance; contains
      (1) *Mastoid process and air cells*—process located posterior to external acoustic meatus; composed of air spaces that communicate with the middle ear
      (2) *Styloid process*—pointed projection that serves for attachment of muscles and ligaments
      (3) *Stylomastoid foramen*—opening through which CN VII exits cranium

5. Sphenoid bone—"keystone," single bone of the cranium that is centrally located; contains
   a) Two paranasal sinuses in the body
   b) *Sella turcica*—located superior to the body; contains pituitary gland
   c) *Greater wings*—form lateral wall of skull
      (1) *Foramen ovale*—where mandibular division of V leaves cranium
      (2) *Foramen spinosum*—where middle meningeal artery (branch of maxillary) gains access to interior portion of skull
   d) *Lesser wings*—form part of anterior cranial fossa
   e) *Medial and lateral pterygoid plates* (paired)—extend inferiorly; where some muscles attach
   f) *Superior orbital fissure*—connects the orbit with the cranial cavity; CNs III, IV, VI, and ophthalmic division (V_1) travel through it
   g) *Carotid foramen*—also includes part of temporal bone; where carotid arteries enter cranium

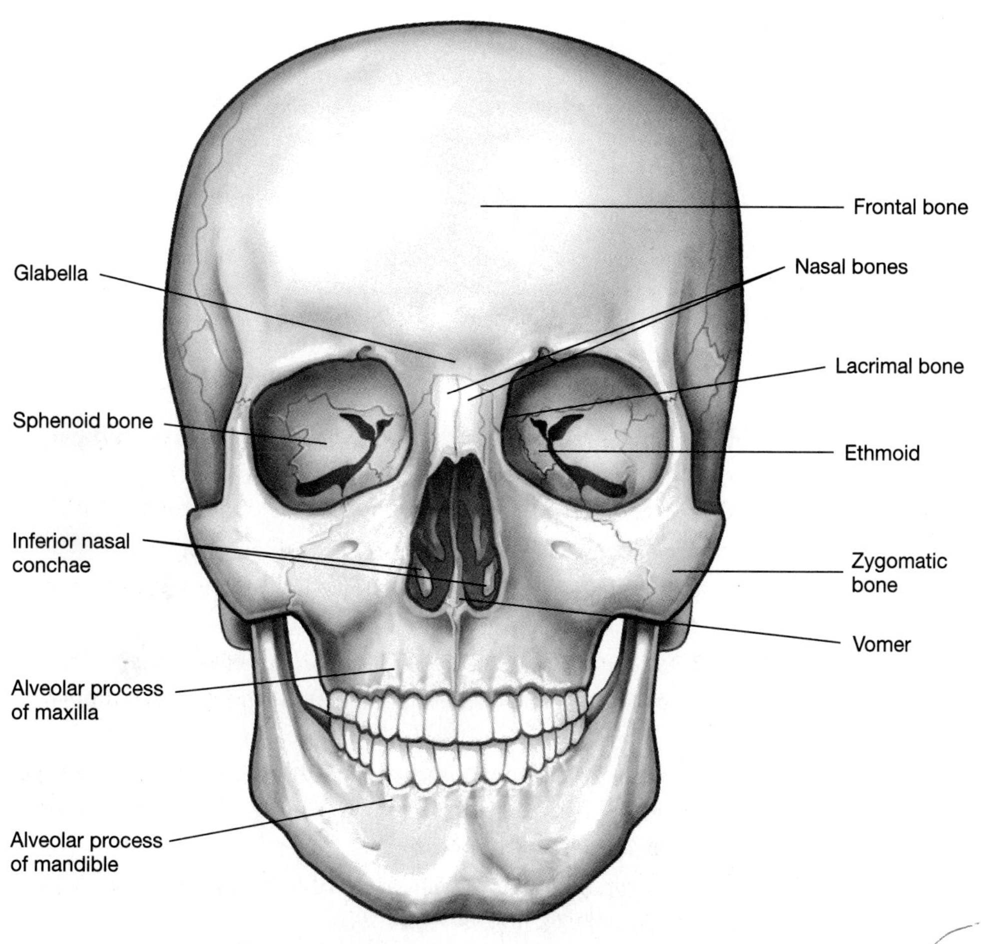

FIGURE 3-1. Bones of the skull.

6. Ethmoid—single, midline bone that forms posterior portion of nasal cavity and inferior, medial part of anterior cranial fossa
   a) Numerous sinuses or air cells
   b) *Cribriform plate*—perforated bone through which sensory nerves from nose ascend to olfactory bulbs of CN I
   c) *Perpendicular plate*—posterior, superior portion of nasal septum
   d) *Superior and middle nasal conchae*—bony projections in the lateral wall of the nasal cavity; increase mucous membrane surface area

➤ FACE

Bones of the face support facial features and provide dentition and movement of the jaw for speaking, swallowing, and eating.

I. FACIAL BONES

A. Maxillae—paired, fused, complex bones that comprise the upper jaw; contain

1. *Maxillary sinuses*—large space in body of each bone
2. *Frontal process*—articulates with frontal bone
3. *Zygomatic process*—articulates with zygoma to form cheek
4. *Palatine process*—forms anterior portion of hard palate
   a) *Median palatine suture*—located between the palatine processes of the maxillae
5. *Orbital process*—forms floor of orbit and infraorbital rim
6. *Alveolar process*—bone that surrounds and supports maxillary teeth
7. *Infraorbital foramen*—located inferior to orbit; opening for maxillary branch of CN V (V_2)
8. *Maxillary tuberosity*—located posterior to last molar; perforated by posterior superior alveolar foramina through which the posterior superior alveolar (PSA) nerves and blood vessels pass

B. Mandible—single, moveable bone of the lower jaw; *symphysis* is midline fusion of the right and left embryological processes

1. *Mental protuberance*—midline bony prominence of chin
2. *Mental foramen*—opening on exterior body where mental nerve enters to join inferior alveolar nerve
3. *Body of the mandible*—horizontal portion of heavy bone
4. *Alveolar process*—bone that surrounds and supports mandibular teeth
5. *Ramus*—vertical shaft that extends from body to condyle and coronoid process
6. *Angle*—corner where ramus and body meet
7. *Coronoid process*—sharp termination of anterior ramus; attachment for temporalis muscle
8. *Condyle*—connected to ramus by the neck; articulates with temporal bone as part of temporomandibular joint

9. *Coronoid notch*—concave area between coronoid process and mandibular condyle
10. *External oblique line*—anterior border of coronoid process that extends as a bony ridge on the body
11. *Genial tubercles*—small, raised roughened area on inner medial surface; where some muscles attach
12. *Mylohyoid line*—ridge on inner surface that separates sublingual from submandibular fossae
13. *Sublingual fossa*—shallow depression for sublingual salivary gland
14. *Submandibular fossa*—deeper depression for submandibular salivary gland
15. *Mandibular foramen*—opening of the mandibular canal on inner surface of ramus for the inferior alveolar artery, nerve, and vein
16. *Lingula*—spicule of bone that guards mandibular foramen
17. *Pterygoid fovea*—triangular depression below condyle; where lateral pterygoid muscle attaches

C. Zygomatic bones (zygoma)

1. Paired facial bones that form cheeks
2. Articulates with frontal, maxillary, and temporal bones

D. Vomer—single, midline bone that forms inferior, posterior part of nasal septum

E. Lacrimal bones—small, paired bones located in medial wall of orbit adjacent to nasolacrimal duct

F. Nasal bones—paired facial bones that form bridge of nose

G. Inferior nasal conchae—paired bones; third and inferior lateral wall projection in the nose; separate bone

H. Hyoid bone—only bone of the body that does not articulate with another bone; muscle attachment for hyoid muscles used in swallowing

II. JOINTS OF THE SKULL

A. Sutures—immoveable joints; bones are joined by fibrous tissue

1. *Coronal suture*—joins frontal bone anteriorly and parietal bones posteriorly
2. *Sagittal suture*—joins right and left parietal bones
3. *Lambdoidal suture*—joins occipital with parietal bones

B. Temporomandibular joint (TMJ)—moveable, synovial joint located between temporal bone and mandible

1. Contains a fibrous *meniscus* or disc
2. Reinforced by external ligaments
   a) Stylomandibular ligament—connects styloid process of temporal bone to posterior border of ramus of the mandible
   b) *Sphenomanbibular ligament*—connects angular spine of sphenoid bone with lingula of mandible; not an actual part of joint, but helps stabilize it
   c) *Temporomandibular joint ligament*—prevents excessive retraction of joint

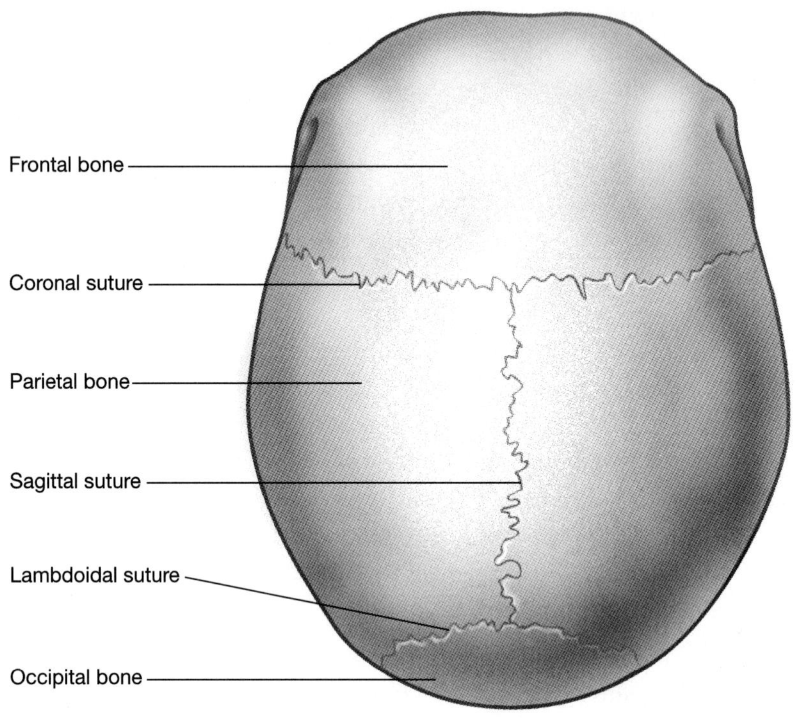

FIGURE 3-2. Sutures of the skull.

3. Movements of TMJ
   a) *Gliding*—condyles move forward or backward on articular eminence
      (1) *Protrusion*—forward movement of mandible
      (2) *Retraction*—backward movement of mandible
   b) *Rotation*—condyles rotate on meniscus
      (1) *Depression*—drops mandible and opens mouth
      (2) *Elevation*—elevates mandible and closes mouth
   c) *Lateral deviation*
      (1) Mandible protrudes to either right or left, as in chewing
      (2) Lateral pterygoid muscle will contract on the side opposite of deviation
4. Temporomandibular myofacial pain-dysfunction syndrome
   a) Conditions that may lead to syndrome
      (1) Malocclusions
      (2) Lack of coordination between meniscus and condylar movement, allowing head of condyle to slip off disc
      (3) Meniscus tears
      (4) Arthritis
      (5) Malformations
      (6) Tumors

III. CRANIAL FOSSAE

A. Anterior cranial fossa

1. Formed by cribriform plate of ethmoid bone, lesser wing of sphenoid bone, and frontal bone

2. Contains frontal lobe of cerebrum

B. Middle cranial fossa

1. Formed by greater wing of the sphenoid, temporal, and anterior portion of the occipital bones
2. Contains temporal lobe of cerebrum

C. Posterior cranial fossa

1. Formed by temporal and occipital bones
2. Contains cerebellum, pons, and medulla

IV. PARANASAL SINUSES

A. Paired air-filled cavities in bone, which make head lighter and easier to hold erect

B. Lined with mucous membrane

C. All communicate with nasal cavity and found in the following bones

1. Frontal
2. Sphenoid
3. Ethmoid
4. Maxillae

V. ORBIT

A. Composed of seven bones

B. Contains the eyeball and muscles that control its movements

C. *Superior orbital fissure*—transmits CN III, IV, and VI and ophthalmic branch of V (V_1)

D. *Optic foramen*—transmits optic nerve from eye to brain (CN II)

E. *Inferior orbital fissure*—contains mandibular branch V (V_3)

➤ MUSCLES

Muscles are divided into groups—muscles of mastication, muscles of facial expression, cervical muscles, suprahyoid muscles, infrahyoid muscles, muscles of the pharynx, pharyngeal muscles, palatine muscles, and tongue muscles. The innervation of each group of muscles reflects embryologic development from different branchial arches.

I. MUSCLES OF MASTICATION

A. Insertion—mandible, hence a common function—movement of mandible

B. Innervation—motor branch of trigeminal nerve, which follows mandibular division, V_3

C. Action—assist with speaking, swallowing, and mastication

D. Muscles include

1. Temporalis muscle—fan-shaped
   a) Origin—temporal fossa
   b) Insertion—coronoid process of mandible
   c) Innervation—mandibular branch of CN V
   d) Action—elevates and retracts mandible

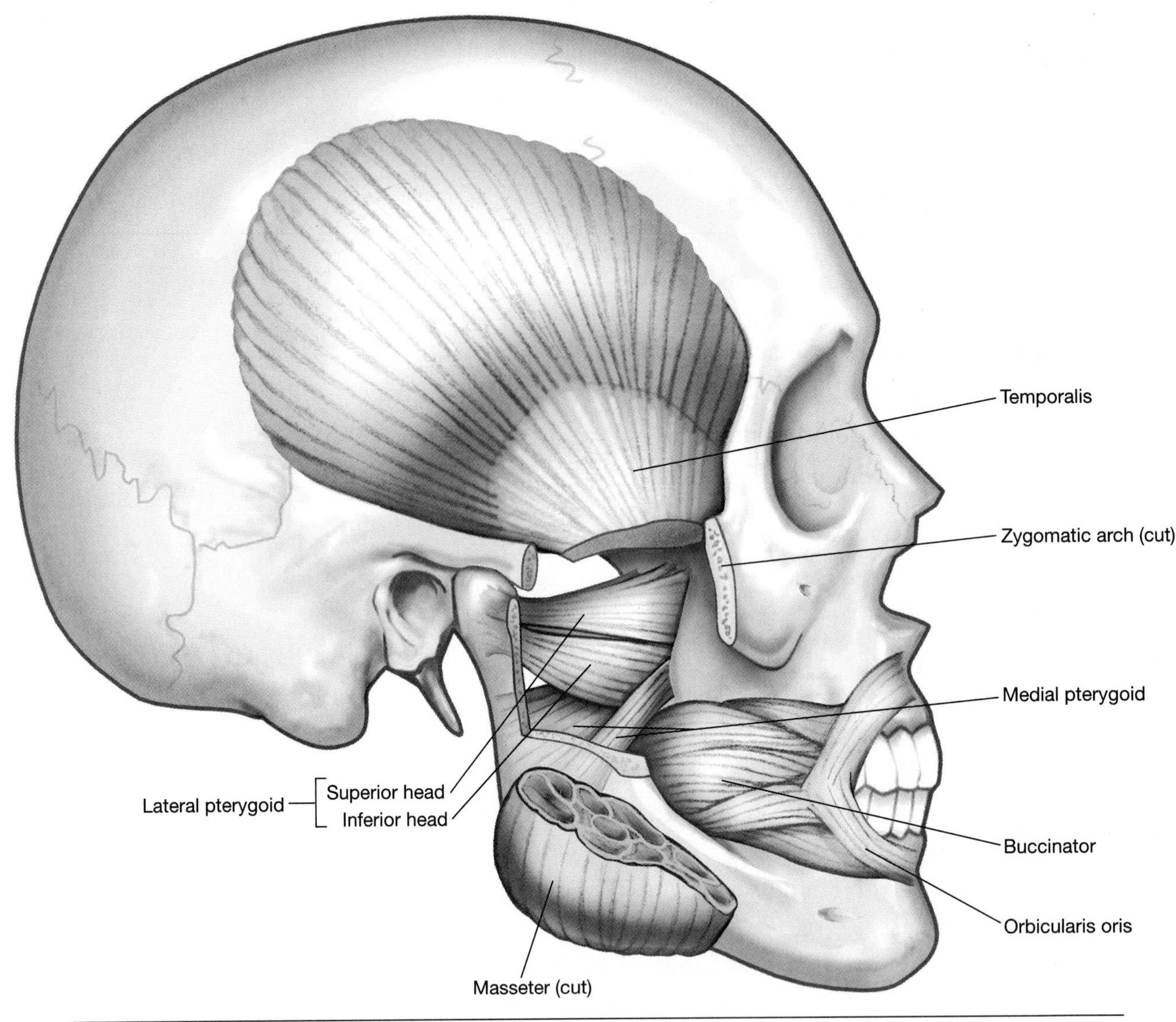

FIGURE 3-3. Muscles of mastication.

TABLE 3-1 MUSCLES OF MASTICATION

Muscle	Origin	Insertion	Function
Temporalis	Floor of temporal fossa	Coronoid process of the mandible	Elevates and retracts mandible
Masseter	Zygomatic arch	Angle and ramus of mandible	Elevates mandible
Medial pterygoid	Pterygoid fossa of sphenoid	Medial surface of the angle of mandible	Elevates mandible
Lateral pterygoid	Lateral surface of the lateral pterygoid plate; greater wing of the sphenoid bone	Pterygoid fovea of mandible	Depresses, protrudes, and laterally deviates mandible

Chewing

Chewing is a complex process in the mastication of food. If a point is placed on the chin while chewing, it revolves in a small circle. In addition to the superior/inferior movement of the mandible, there is a great deal of lateral movement brought about by the muscles of mastication. When the mandible is drawn to the right, for example, the right temporalis and masseter muscles contract along with the left medial pterygoid muscle. The remaining muscles of mastication must be relaxed. Moving to the left, the opposite muscles must contract and relax. While this is occurring, the mandible is moving up and down.

---

2. *Masseter muscle*—band-like muscle that forms a great portion of the cheek
   a) Origin—anterior and medial surfaces of zygomatic arch
   b) Insertion—angle and ramus of mandible
   c) Innervation—mandibular branch of CN V
   d) Action—elevates mandible
3. *Medial (Internal) pterygoid muscle*—deeper, yet similar to masseter muscle
   a) Origin—pterygoid fossa of sphenoid bone
   b) Insertion—medial surface of angle of mandible
   c) Innervation—mandibular branch of CN V
   d) Action—elevates mandible
4. *Lateral (External) pterygoid muscle*—horizontal muscle that attaches to medial surface of mandible
   a) Origin—superior head of greater wing of sphenoid bone; inferior head of lateral pterygoid plate of sphenoid bone
   b) Insertion—pterygoid fovea of mandible
   c) Innervation—mandibular branch of CN V
   d) Action
      (1) Both right and left sides protrude mandible
      (2) Use of one side allows lateral deviation of mandible
      (3) Inferior heads allows slight depression of mandible

II. MUSCLES OF FACIAL EXPRESSION

A. Origins—usually from bone, yet muscles insert into facial tissues; this allows for movement resulting in facial expression

B. Innervation—facial nerve, CN VII

C. Facial muscles that move mouth include

1. *Orbicularis oris muscle*—circular muscle around mouth; purses lips
2. *Depressor anguli oris muscle*—depresses corner of mouth
3. *Depressor labii inferioris muscle*—depresses lower lip
4. *Mentalis muscle*—draws chin to pucker

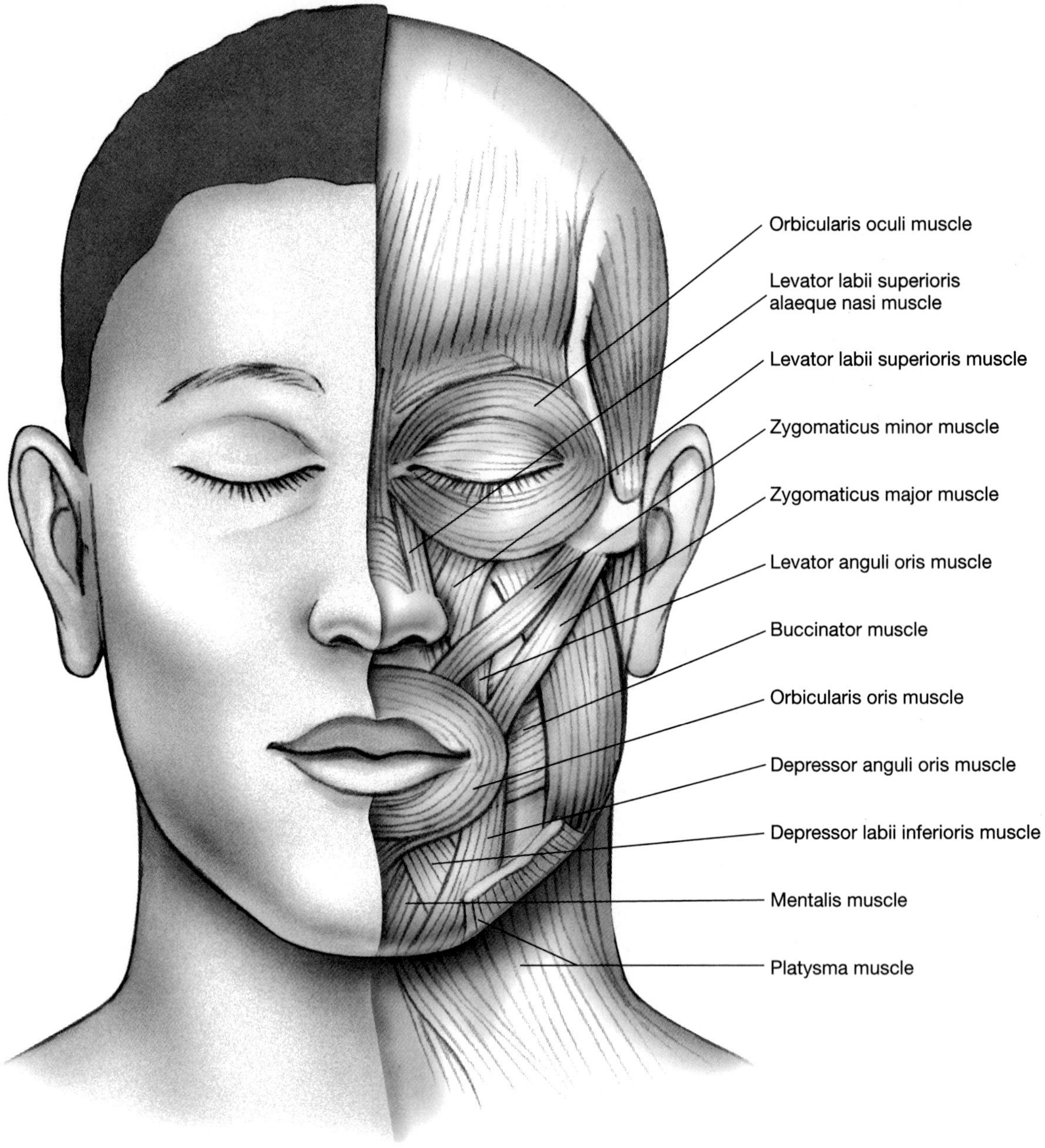

FIGURE 3-4. Muscles of facial expression.

5. *Buccinator muscle*—draws corner of lip laterally and helps form cheek; also keeps food pushed back on occlusal surface of teeth; assists in mastication
6. *Risorius muscle*—widens mouth
7. *Levator labii superioris muscle*—elevates upper lip
8. *Levator labii superioris alaeque nasi muscle*—elevates upper lip and ala of nose
9. *Zygomaticus major muscle*—elevates angle of mouth, as in smiling
10. *Zygomaticus minor muscle*—elevates upper lip
11. *Levator anguli oris muscle*—elevates angle of mouth, as in smiling
12. *Platysma muscle*—raises skin of neck and pulls down corners of mouth

B. Other muscles of facial expression

1. *Orbicularis oculi muscle*—closes eyelid
2. *Corrugator supercilii muscle*—causes frown lines between eyebrows
3. *Frontal belly of epicranius muscle*—raises eyebrows

III. CERVICAL MUSCLES—important as landmarks in the neck

A. Innervation—accessory nerve, CN XI

B. Muscles include

1. Sternocleidomastoid muscle—both muscles flex head, while a single muscle will turn head
2. Trapezius muscle—allows shrugging of shoulders and holds head erect

IV. SUPRAHYOID MUSCLES

A. Location—superior to hyoid bone

B. Insertion—hyoid bone

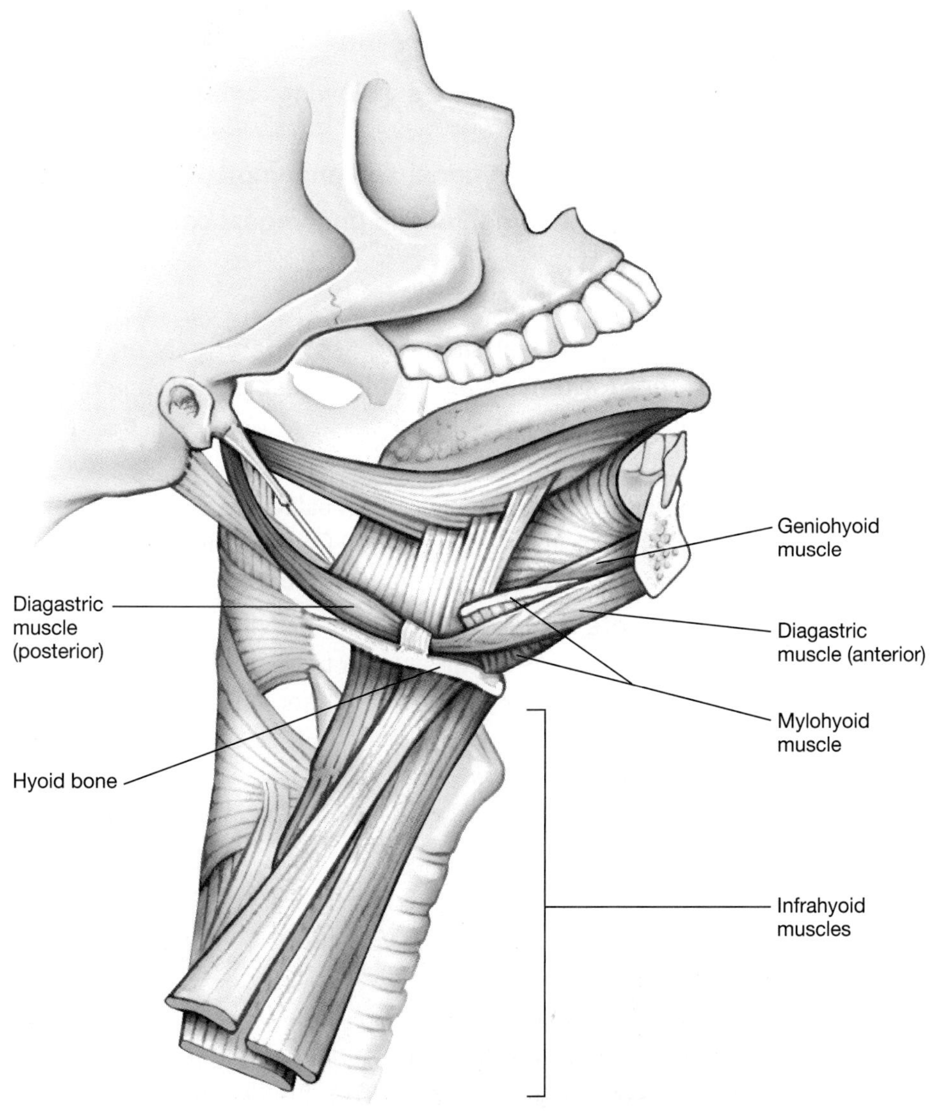

FIGURE 3-5. The suprahyoid and infrahyoid muscles.

C. Action—assist in chewing (contract to depress mandible) and swallowing (contract to lift hyoid and larynx, closing the glottis)

D. Muscles include

1. *Digastric muscle*—has two bellies
   a) Posterior belly—innervated by facial nerve, CN VII
   b) Anterior belly—innervated by mylohyoid nerve, branch of V_3
2. *Stylohyoid muscle*—innervated by facial nerve, CN VII
3. *Mylohoid muscle*—forms floor of mouth; innervated by mylohyoid nerve, branch of V_3
4. *Geniohyoid muscle*—innervated by branches of first cervical nerve

V. INFRAHYOID MUSCLES

A. Location—inferior to hyoid bone

B. Innervation—second and third cervical nerves

C. Action—depresses and stabilizes hyoid bone

D. Four pairs of hyoid muscles—include sternothyroid, sternohyoid, omohyoid, and thyrohyoid muscles

VI. MUSCLES OF THE PHARYNX

A. Action—involved in speaking, swallowing, and middle ear function

B. Innervation—glossopharyngeal and pharyngeal plexus (IX, X)

C. Includes the stylopharyngeus and pharyngeal constrictor muscles

VII. MUSCLES OF THE PALATE

A. Innervation—pharyngeal plexus (glossopharyngeal and vagus nerves) except for tensor veli palatini muscle, which is supplied by trigeminal nerve

B. Action

1. During swallowing, movement of soft palate separates nasopharynx from oropharynx preventing food from entering nasal cavity
2. Movement of soft palate is also used in speaking

C. Muscles of palate include

1. *Palatoglossus muscle*—forms anterior tonsillar pillar
2. *Palatopharyngeus muscle*—forms posterior tonsillar pillar
3. *Levator veli palatini muscle*—elevates soft palate
4. *Tensor veli palatini muscle*—stiffens soft palate
5. *Muscle of the uvula*—allows uvula to adapt in closing off nasopharynx

VIII. MUSCLES OF THE TONGUE

A. Innervation—hypoglossal nerve, CN XII

B. Muscles include

1. Intrinsic—located within the tongue
2. Extrinsic—have different origins, but all insert into tongue
   a) *Genioglossus muscle*
      (1) Origin—genial tubercles

Integrated Function of the Suprahyoid, Infrahyoid, and Masticatory Muscles

The muscles of mastication, suprahyoid muscles, and infrahyoid muscles act in a coordinated manner to perform mastication and chewing. To elevate the mandible (i.e., closing the mouth), the muscles of mastication must contract (except the external pterygoid). The suprahyoids and infrahyoid must relax. To depress the mandible (i.e., open the mouth), the muscles of mastication must relax, and the suprahyoids and infrahyoids must contract. In swallowing, the mandible must be fixed by contracting the muscles of mastication, the suprahyoids must be contracted to lift the hyoid and larynx to close the glottis, and the infrahyoids must be relaxed.

---

(2) Action—protrudes tongue and prevents it from falling back and obstructing the airway

b) *Styloglossus muscle*
   (1) Origin—styloid process
   (2) Action—retracts tongue

c) *Hyoglossus muscle*
   (1) Origin—hyoid bone
   (2) Action—depresses tongue

➤ CIRCULATORY SYSTEM

I. BLOOD SUPPLY TO THE HEAD AND NECK—provided through the three branches of the aorta

A. *Left subclavian artery*—carries blood to left arm; a branch, the left vertebral artery, delivers blood to brain

B. *Left common carotid artery*—splits into two branches; carries blood to most of head, neck, and brain by its two branches

1. Left internal carotid artery—to brain
2. Left external carotid artery—to head and neck

C. *Right brachiocephalic artery*—short branch of arch that immediately divides into two arteries

1. Right subclavian artery—gives rise to right vertebral artery to brain
2. Right common carotid artery—splits into
   a) Right internal carotid artery to brain
   b) Right external carotid artery to head and neck

II. BLOOD SUPPLY TO THE BRAIN—rich blood supply to the brain is provided by

A. Two anterior right and left internal carotid arteries that enter skull through carotid canals

B. Two posterior vertebral arteries that enter skull through foramen magnum

Blood Supply to the Brain

The brain and its coverings receive arterial blood from three main sources: the internal carotid, the vertebral arteries, and the meningeal arteries. The **internal carotid** enters the skull through the internal carotid canal, which is adjacent to the body of the sphenoid in the middle cranial fossa. The **vertebral arteries** arise off the subclavian arteries and enter the posterior cranial cavity through the foramen magnum. The branches of the vertebral and internal carotid join together at the **circle of Willis.** The middle meningeal arteries arise from the maxillary artery and reenter the middle cranial fossa via the foramen spinosum, carrying blood to the dura.

C. **These four arteries join and connect around the base of brain to form circle of Willis**

D. **Middle meningeal arteries—branches of maxillary arteries that enter cranium through foramen spinosum to supply blood to the meninges of the brain**

III. **BLOOD SUPPLY TO THE FACE (structures external to the skull)—comes from branches of external carotid arteries**

A. **Anterior branches of external carotid artery**

1. *Superior thyroid artery*—to superior portion of thyroid gland
2. *Lingual artery*—branches at level of hyoid bone; runs deep to suprahyoid muscles, supplying adjacent muscles, including floor of mouth through its branch—sublingual artery—and terminates by supplying the tongue
3. *Facial artery*—extends medial to mandible, then crosses mandible's lower border and travels to medial corner of eye, giving off numerous branches along the way
    a) *Submental artery*—to chin
    b) *Inferior labial artery*—to lower lip
    c) *Superior labial* artery—to upper lip
    d) *Lateral nasal artery*—to side of nose
    e) *Angular artery*—to medial corner of eye
    f) *Ascending palatine artery*—to nasopharyngeal area, especially the palatine tonsils

B. **Medial branch of external carotid artery—ascending pharyngeal artery supplies pharyngeal walls and soft palate**

C. **Posterior branches of external carotid artery include**

1. *Occipital artery*—supplies occipital region as well as sternocleidomastoid muscle
2. *Posterior auricular artery*—to posterior surface of ear, tympanic cavity, and adjacent scalp

D. **Terminal branches of external carotid artery include**

1. *Superficial temporal artery*—courses through parotid gland, supplying it and area around ear and temporal region

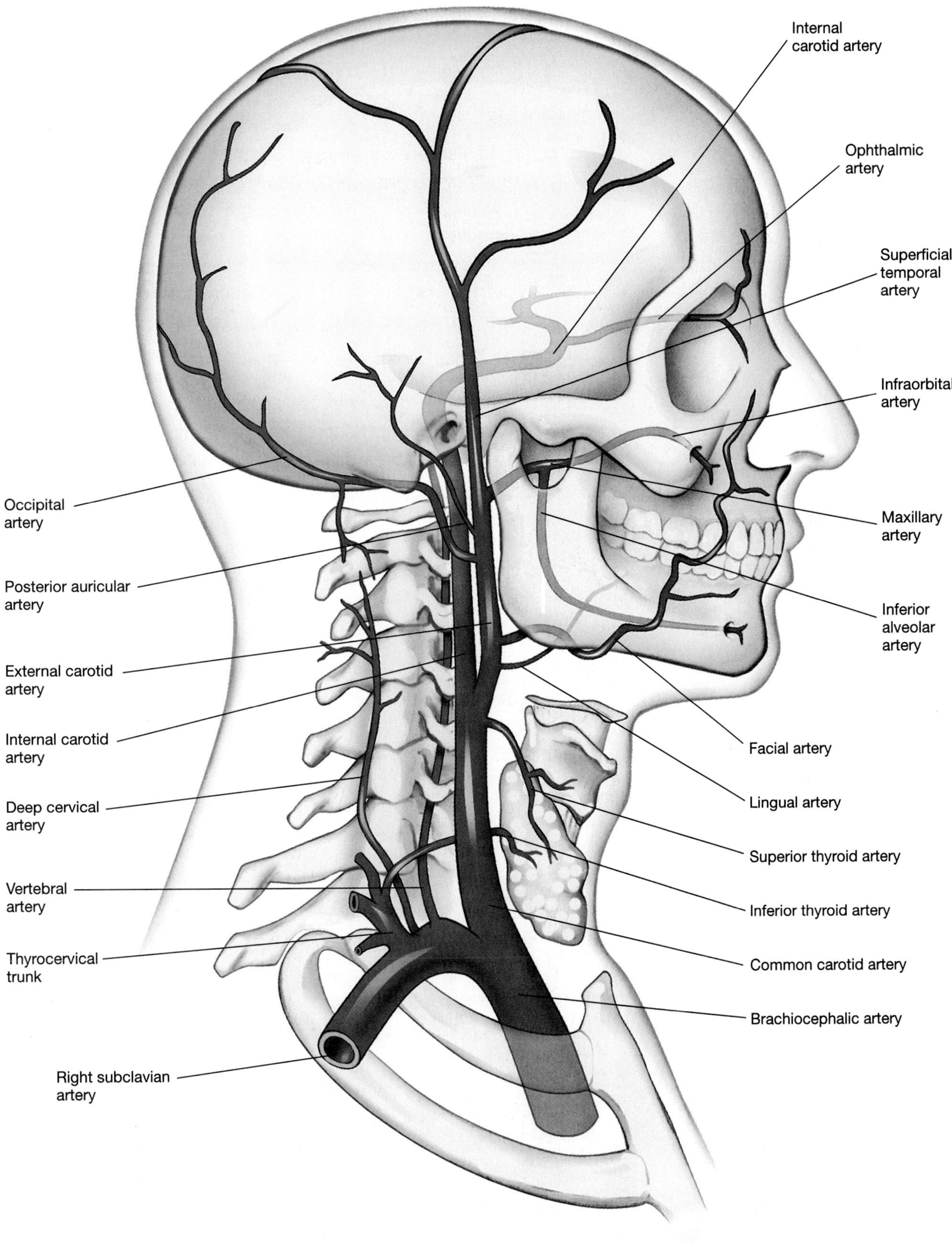

FIGURE 3-6. Anterior supply of the head and neck.

2. *Maxillary artery*—originates at level of neck of mandible and gives rise to following branches
   a) *Middle meningeal artery*—enters skull through foramen spinosum to supply the meninges of brain and bones of skull
   b) *Inferior alveolar artery*—enters mandibular canal through mandibular foramen and supplies mandible and mandibular teeth, floor of mouth, and mental region
      (1) *Mylohyoid artery*—supplies mylohyoid muscle and floor of mouth
      (2) *Mental artery*—exits mental foramen to supply chin region
      (3) *Incisive artery*—branches off inferior alveolar artery and divides into dental and alveolar branches to anterior teeth
   c) *Muscular branches*
      (1) Deep temporal arteries supply temporalis muscle
      (2) Pterygoid arteries supply medial and lateral pterygoid muscles
      (3) Masseteric artery supplies masseter muscle
      (4) Buccal artery supplies buccinator muscle and buccal region

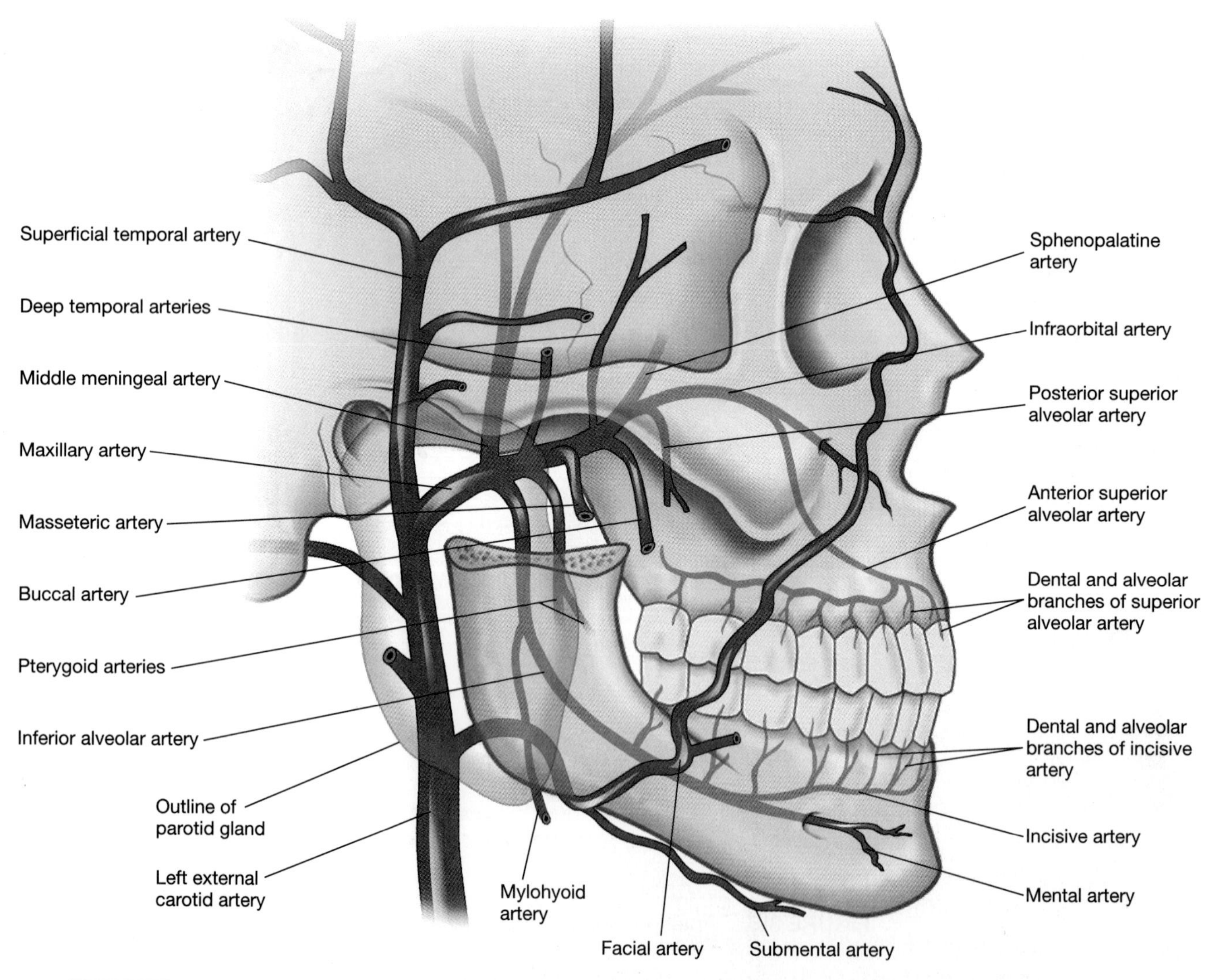

FIGURE 3-7. Maxillary artery.

d) *Posterior superior alveolar artery*—supplies posterior teeth and maxillary sinus
e) *Infraorbital artery*—travels in infraorbital canal
  (1) *Anterior superior alveolar artery*—arises from infraorbital artery and gives off to dental and alveolar branches to maxillary teeth; anastomoses with posterior superior alveolar artery
f) *Greater palatine artery and lesser palatine arteries*—descend in pterygopalatine canal to supply hard and soft palates, respectively
g) *Sphenopalatine artery*—termination point of maxillary artery; supplies nasal cavity; gives rise to the *nasopalatine artery* that accompanies nasopalatine nerve through incisive foramen of the maxilla

IV. VEINS OF THE HEAD AND NECK

A. Unlike veins in the rest of the body; valveless, which may contribute to spread of infection

B. Generally follow same path as arteries and share a common name, except for the following

1. Venous dural sinuses—intracranial structures formed by dura into which the brain, meninges, and skull drain
   a) Several external veins drain into this system creating potential for spread of infection
   b) System drains into internal jugular vein; some of named sinuses include
      (1) Superior sagittal sinus
      (2) Inferior sagittal sinus
      (3) Cavernous sinus
      (4) Transverse sinus
2. Pterygoid plexus—collection of anastomosing veins surrounding maxillary artery in infratemporal fossa
   a) Connects with facial and retromandibular veins
   b) Protects maxillary artery from compression during mastication
   c) Drained by maxillary vein
   d) Close proximity to maxillary tuberosity makes it vulnerable to accidents during dental procedures
3. Retromandibular vein—located posterior to ramus of mandible
   a) Formed by merger of superficial temporal and maxillary veins
   b) One branch forms external jugular vein; other branch flows into facial vein
   c) Travels through parotid gland
4. Internal jugular vein
   a) Drains most of tissues of head and neck
   b) Originates in cranial cavity; exits jugular foramen
   c) Found with internal carotid artery and vagus nerve in the neck
5. External jugular vein
   a) Usually smaller than internal jugular
   b) Located more laterally in the neck
   c) Receives much of outflow from the retromandibular vein
   d) Drains only extracranial tissues

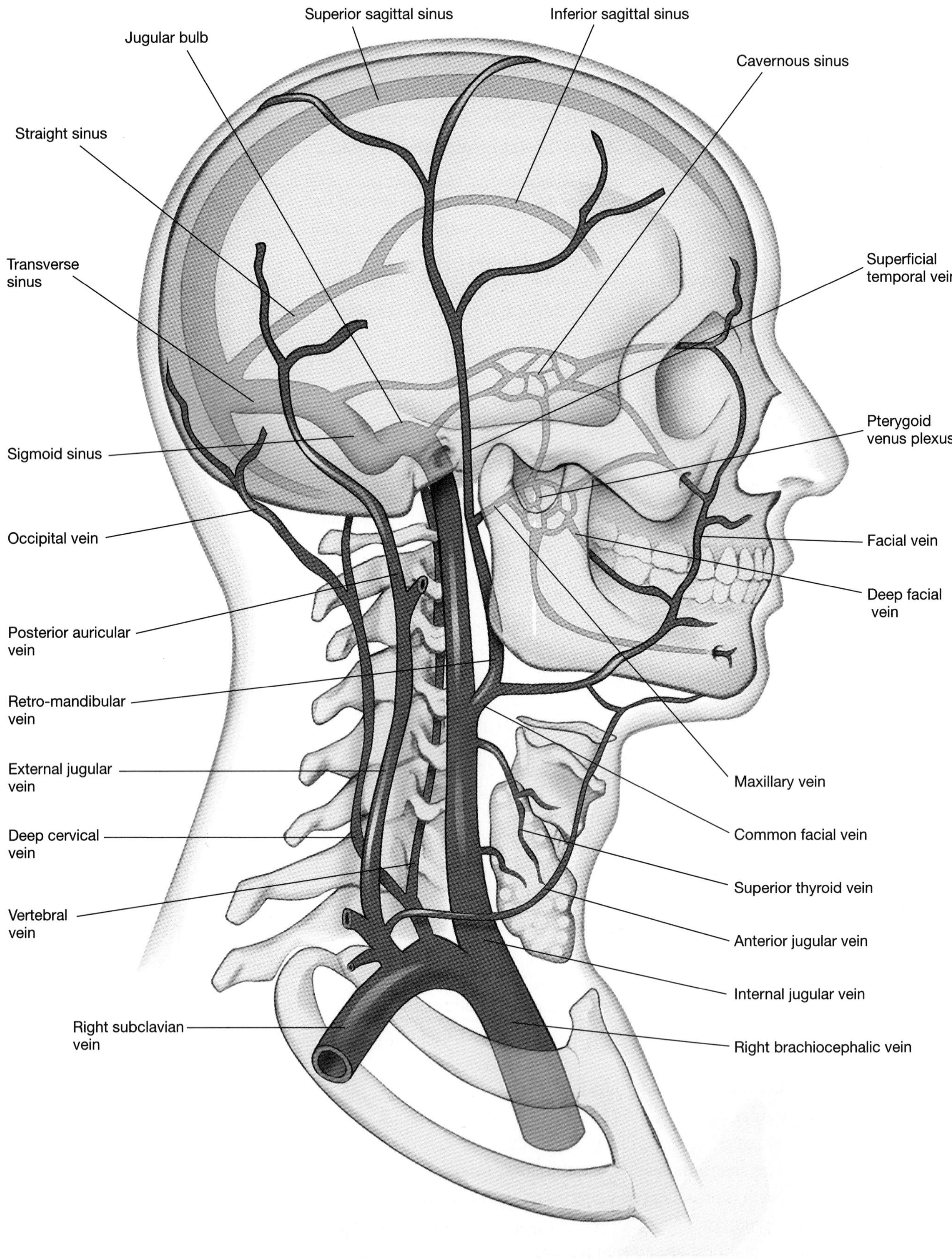

FIGURE 3-8. Venous drainage of the head and neck.

➤ NERVOUS SYSTEM

The nervous system causes muscles to contract, stimulates glands to secrete, regulates the blood system, and allows for sensation to be felt. It is made up of the central, peripheral, and autonomic nervous systems.

I. CENTRAL NERVOUS SYSTEM (CNS)—includes brain and spinal column

A. Brain

1. Divided into three areas
   a) Pair of cerebral hemispheres, which are divided into five lobes
      (1) Frontal—controls abstract thought and voluntary muscle control
      (2) Parietal—integrates incoming stimuli, contains center for speech and conscious sensations
      (3) Temporal—receives auditory perception
      (4) Occipital—contains vision center
      (5) Insula—function unknown
   b) Cerebellum is made up of two cerebellar hemispheres and controls muscle coordination
   c) Brainstem is divided into four areas
      (1) Diencephalon—contains thalamus and hypothalamus
      (2) Midbrain—function unknown; may be involved with basic instinctual reflexes
      (3) Pons—contains nuclei of various nerves including the facial and trigeminal
      (4) Medulla oblongata—contains center for certain vital functions such as breathing, vascular control, and heart rate

II. PERIPHERAL NERVOUS SYSTEM

A. Spinal Nerves

1. Contain 31 pair of nerves designated by spinal foramen from which they exit; C1 to C8, T1 to T12, L1 to L5, S1 to S5, and the coccygeal nerve

B. Cranial Nerves

1. 12 pairs of nerves designated by names and Roman numerals
   a) *Olfactory cranial nerve* (I)—receives sense of smell
   b) *Optic cranial nerve* (II)—receives sight
   c) *Oculomotor cranial nerve* (III)—eyeball movement and contains autonomic fibers for lens curvature and pupil size
   d) *Trochlear cranial nerve* (IV)—eyeball movement
   e) *Trigeminal cranial nerve* (V)—includes three divisions
      (1) *Ophthalmic division* (V_1)—sensory for upper one third of face
      (2) *Maxillary division* (V_2)—sensory for middle one third of face, including maxillary teeth, palate, and upper lip
      (3) *Mandibular division* (V_3)—sensory of lower one third of face, including mandibular teeth, tongue and lower lip; as a motor nerve, it serves the muscles of mastication and mylohyoid muscle

Perception

Generally, there are three main types of perception—exteroception, intraception, and proprioception. **Exteroception** receives stimuli from outside the body (e.g., pain, sight, hearing). **Intraception** receives stimuli from inside the body (e.g., thirst, hunger). **Proprioception** is muscle sense (e.g., knowing how many fingers are raised on one's hand without looking or touching). It is very important in coordination of movement.

---

f) *Abducens cranial nerve* (VI)—eyeball movement

g) *Facial cranial nerve* (VII)—muscles of facial expression and carries back taste sensation from anterior two thirds of tongue

(1) Contains fibers of the autonomic nervous system to submandibular and sublingual salivary glands via the chorda tympani nerve

(2) Innervates lacrimal gland and mucus glands in the nasal cavity (travels with branches of V)

h) Vestibulocochlear (auditory) cranial nerve (VIII)—receives sound stimuli via cochlear division and equilibrium via vestibular branch

i) Glossopharyngeal cranial nerve (IX)—receives taste sensation from posterior one third of tongue and motor control to a throat muscle; supplies autonomic fibers to parotid salivary gland

j) Vagus cranial nerve (X)—provides motor nerve to several laryngeal muscles, taste sensation from base of tongue, and autonomic control of many visceral organs (e.g., heart, lungs, and gastrointestinal tract)

k) Accessory cranial nerve (XI)—provides motor innervation to several neck and laryngeal muscles

l) Hypoglossal cranial nerve (XII)—provides motor nerve to several extrinsic and all intrinsic tongue muscles

2. Pathology associated with cranial nerves

a) Olfactory—damage may result in anosmia, which is total or partial loss of ability to smell

Chorda Tympani

The chorda tympani is a branch of the facial nerve that exits the skull via the **petrotympanic** fissure in the mandibular fossa. It passes inferiorly and joins the lingual nerve from which it branches to the salivary glands. It carries autonomic motor nerves to the submandibular and sublingual salivary glands and receives taste fibers from the anterior two thirds of the tongue.

TABLE 3-2 SUMMARY OF CRANIAL NERVES

Nerve	S/M	Area	Pathology
Olfactory (I)	Sensory	Sense of smell	Anosmia
Optic (II)	Sensory	Sight	Blindness
Oculomotor (III)	Motor & sensory; autonomic fibers	Muscle-eye; proprioception	Deviation of eyeball
Trochlear (IV)	Motor & sensory	Muscle-eye; proprioception	Deviation of eyeball
Trigeminal (V_1)	Sensory	Skin of face & scalp	Loss of general sensation
(V_2)	Sensory	Mucosa of mouth, nose, and maxillary teeth	Loss of general sensation
(V_3)	Motor	Muscles of mastication and myohyoid muscle	Paralysis of these muscles
(V_3)	Sensory	Proprioception, mandibular teeth, mucosa of floor of mouth, tongue	Loss of muscle coordination & sensation
Abducens (VI)	Motor Sensory	Muscle-eye Proprioception	Deviation of eyeball
Facial (VII)	Sensory Motor; autonomic fibers	Taste-tongue; proprioception Muscles of facial expression; submandibular, sublingual, and salivary glands	Loss of taste, affects anterior 2/3 of the tongue Bell's palsy
Vestibulocochlear (VIII)	Sensory	Hearing, balance	Deafness, dizziness
Glossopharyngeal (IX)	Sensory Motor; autonomic fibers	Posterior 1/3 of tongue, soft palate, pharynx; proprioception Pharyngeal muscles, parotid salivary gland	Loss of taste, posterior 1/3 of tongue Paralysis of pharyngeal muscles; difficulty in swallowing
Vagus (X)	Sensory Motor	Pharynx; proprioception Pharynx and larynx	Loss of some reflex (swallow) Loss of speech; difficulty in swallowing
Spinal accessory (XI)	Motor & sensory	Trapezius and sternocleidomasatoid muscles	Difficulty turning head and lifting shoulders
Hypoglossal (XII)	Motor	Intrinsic and extrinsic muscles of tongue	Paralysis of tongue

(1) Total loss—relatively uncommon; partial loss is quite common in aging process, with men generally losing more olfactory ability than women

(2) Temporary anosmia—quite common in people suffering from colds when mucus covers nerve endings

b) Optic—damage may result in partial or total sight loss in one or both eyes, depending on where the injury or affliction occurs

c) Oculomotor—damage may result in loss of certain eye movements

(1) Carries autonomic nerve fibers controlling pupil size and lens curvature

(2) Contains motor fibers to levator palpebrae superioris muscle, which raises upper eyelid

(3) Injury to this nerve may result in eye droop (ptosis)

d) Trochlear—injury results in loss of function of superior oblique muscle; lateral and downward movement of eyeball is lost
e) Trigeminal—damage is rare, but may occur when mandibular third molar is removed and inferior alveolar nerve (located in the inferior alveolar canal) may be damaged; results in temporary or permanent loss of sensation to lower lip; trigeminal neuralgia occurs when patient expresses excruciating pain in the distribution of maxillary or mandibular nerves
f) Abducens—damage results in loss of ability to move eyeball laterally; instead eyeball turns inward due to overreaction of medial rectus muscle
g) Facial—damage to the nerve in the skull, middle ear, stylomastoid foramen, or as it passes through parotid gland may result in Bell's palsy or facial paralysis (drooping of the lower eyelid, sagging of the mouth, and lack of expression on the affected side), loss of taste in anterior portion of tongue, and decrease production of tears
h) Vestibulocochlear—damage to the
   (1) Vestibular division results in loss of balance and dizziness (Ménière's disease); usually temporary
   (2) Cochlear division results in loss of hearing; associated with aging
i) Glossopharyngeal—damage to this nerve may result in loss of taste to posterior one third of tongue and secretion from parotid gland (parasympathetic fibers)
j) Vagus—damage of recurrent branch may result in partial loss of speech; hoarseness
k) Accessory—damage is rare; congenital spasticity of one sternocleidomastoid muscle results in the condition of wryneck, with permanent contracture and torsion of the neck
l) Hypoglossal—damage results in partial loss of tongue movement or deviation to one side

III. SPECIFIC INNERVATION OF DENTAL AND ORAL STRUCTURES FOR LOCAL ANESTHESIA

A. Maxillary nerve—branches used in dental anesthesia include

1. Posterior superior alveolar—nerves enter maxilla through the posterior superior alveolar foramina from
   a) Third molar and facial gingiva
   b) Second molar and facial gingiva
   c) First molar (except mesiobuccal root) and facial gingival
2. Middle superior alveolar—sensation received from
   a) Mesiobuccal root of first molar
   b) Second premolar
   c) First premolar
3. Anterior superior alveolar—sensation received from
   a) Canine
   b) Central and lateral incisors

4. Posterior palatine (greater palatine)—sensation received from
   a) Greater palatine—sensation received from
      (1) Lingual gingiva of molars and premolars
      (2) Posterior four fifths of hard palate
   b) Lesser palatine—soft palate
5. Anterior palatine (nasopalatine)—sensation received from lingual gingiva of anterior teeth

B. Mandibular nerve—branches include

1. Inferior alveolar nerve—receives general sensation from all mandibular teeth
   a) Mental nerve—receives general sensation from facial gingiva of mandibular anterior teeth, chin, lower lip, and labial mucosa
   b) Incisive nerve—branches from anterior mandibular teeth and surrounding periodontium
2. Long buccal nerve—receives general sensation from facial gingiva of molars and premolars
3. Lingual nerve—receives general sensation from all mandibular lingual gingiva, body of tongue, and floor of mouth

IV. TRIGEMINAL NERVE

A. *Ophthalmic division*—enters orbit by passing through superior fissure as sensory-only nerves

1. *Nasociliary*—sensory from nasal cavity and orbit
2. *Frontal*—sensory from forehead
3. *Lacrimal*—sensory from area adjacent to lacrimal gland

B. *Maxillary division*—passes into foramen rotundum via pterygopalatine fossa receiving numerous sensory branches thoughout maxillary region

1. *Meningeal nerve*
   a) Passes back into middle cranial fossa via foramen spinosum
   b) Carries sensory fibers from dura mater
2. *Posterior superior alveolar nerve*—branches off in the pterygopalatine fossa and passes through pterygomaxillary fissure; then enter the PSA foramina on posterior wall of maxillary tuberosity carrying sensation from molars and maxillary sinus, except for mesiobuccal root of maxillary first molar
3. *Zygomatic nerve*—branches carry sensation from malar (cheek) portion of face
4. *Greater and lesser palatine nerves*
   a) Pass through pterygopalatine fossa inferiorly entering oral cavity through greater and lesser palatine foramina
   b) Carry sensory fibers from the posterior four fifths of hard palate, soft palate, tonsillar area
5. *Nasopalatine (anterior palatine) nerve*
   a) Leaves pterygopalatine fossa via sphenopalatine foramen into nasal cavity, then passes anteriorly and inferiorly to nasopalatine foramen (incisive)
   b) Carries fibers from maxillary anterior teeth and tissues and nasal septum

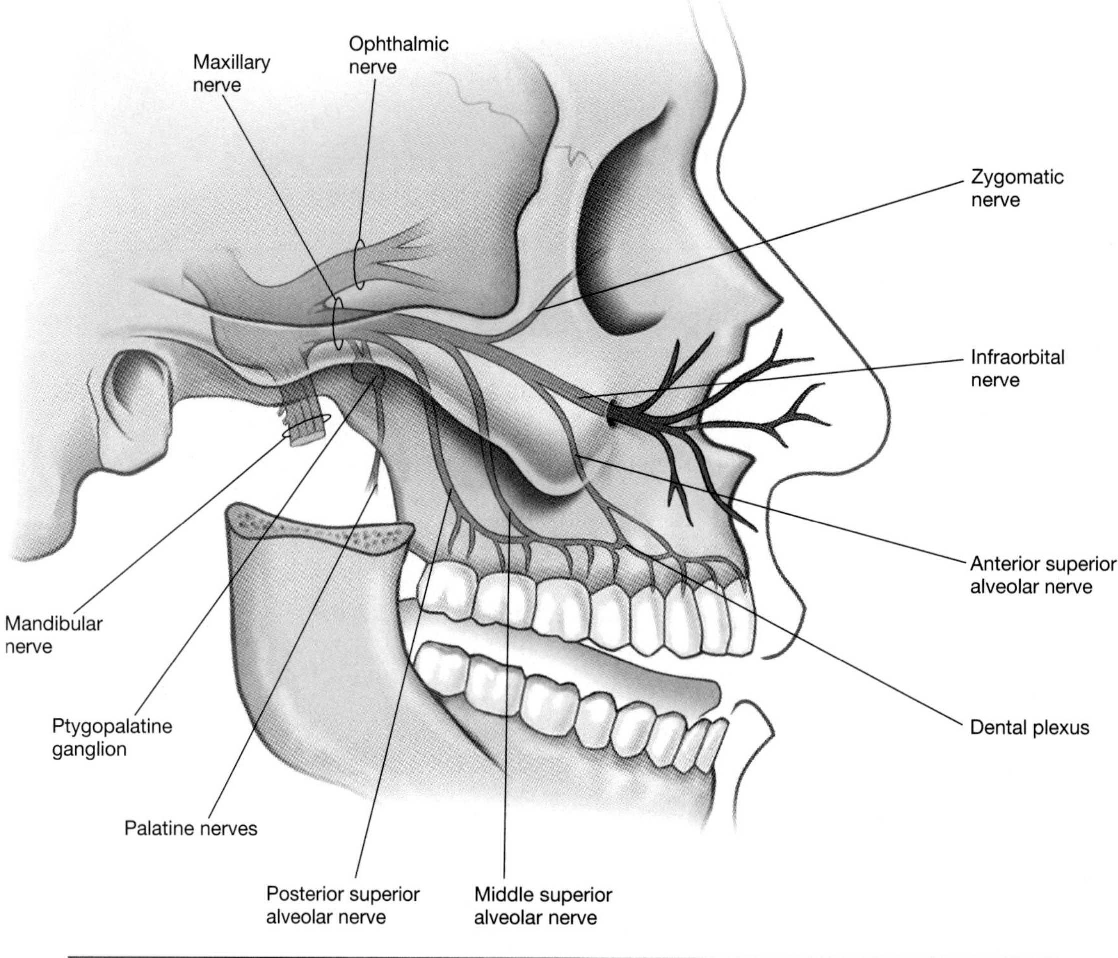

FIGURE 3-9. Maxillary division of the trigeminal nerve.

6. *Infraorbital nerve*—forward continuation of maxillary nerve
   a) Enters orbit via inferior orbital fissure, passing through infraorbital canal, and exits through infraorbital canal and foramen
   b) Carries sensory fibers from lower eyelid and adjacent tissue
7. *Middle superior alveolar nerve*—branch of infraorbital nerve and maxillary division; when present, carries sensory fibers from maxillary premolar teeth and mesiobuccal root of maxillary first molar and surrounding tissues, including buccal gingiva
8. *Anterior superior alveolar nerve*—branch of infraorbital nerve and maxillary division; carries sensory fibers from maxillary central and lateral incisors, canines, and associated tissues

C. Mandibular division

1. Only division that carries both sensory and motor fibers
2. Exits middle cranial fossa via foramen ovale
3. Main branches include
   a) Motor fibers—control muscles of mastication, and mylohyoid and anterior belly of digastric muscles
   b) *Auriculotemporal nerve*—carries sensation from area anterior to external ear

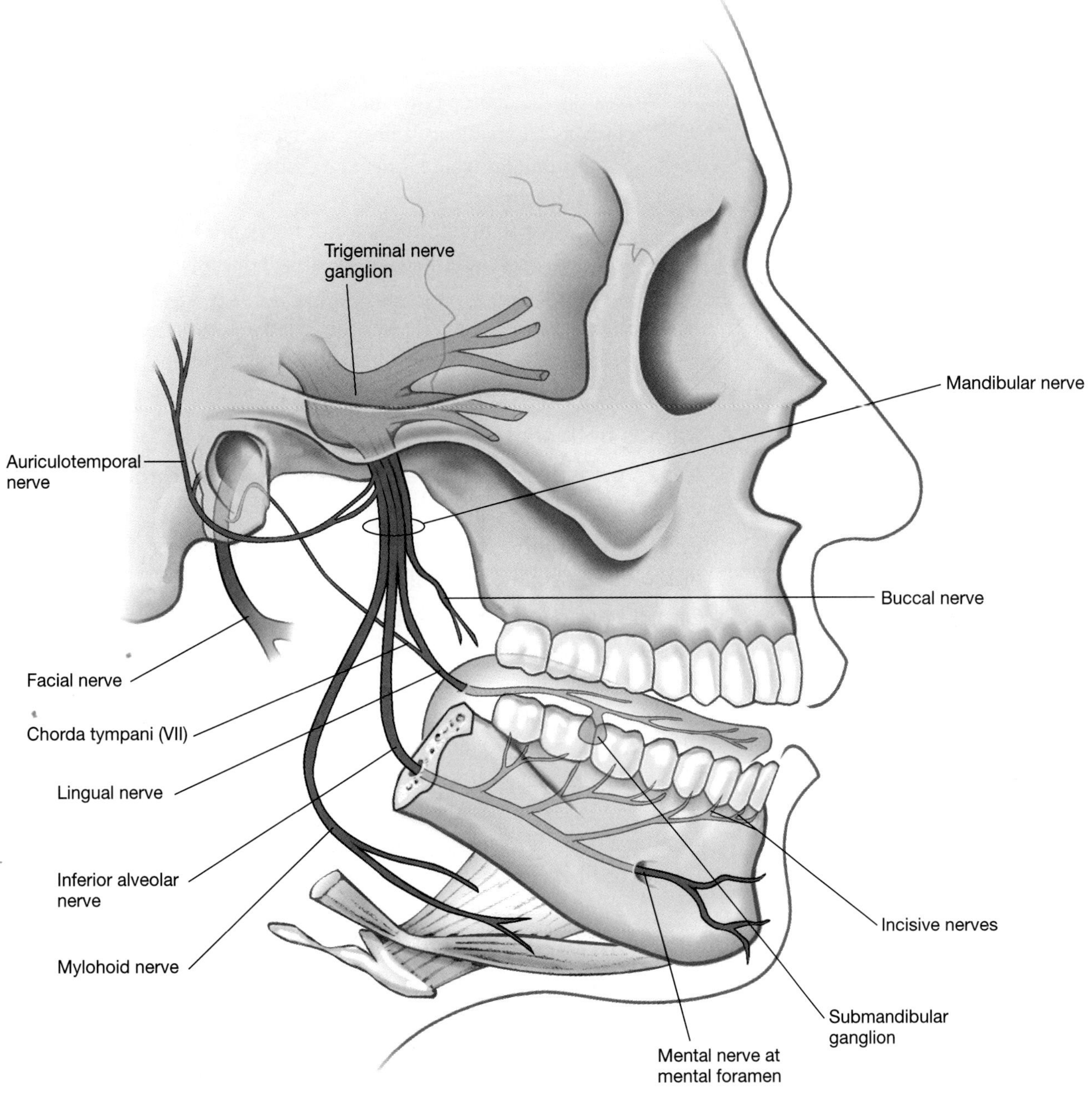

FIGURE 3-10. Mandibular division of the trigeminal nerve.

c) *Inferior alveolar nerve*—gives off the mylohyoid nerve (motor) before entering mandibular foramen
   (1) Enters inferior alveolar canal via mandibular foramen and carries sensory fibers from all mandibular teeth
   (2) Once in the canal, it divides into the mental nerve leaving the mandible via
      (a) Mental foramen, which carries sensation from lower lip and adjacent mucous membranes
      (b) Incisive nerve, which continues in the canal to anterior teeth

d) *Lingual nerve*—travels under tongue receiving general sensation from anterior two thirds of tongue, floor of mouth, lingual gingiva of mandibular teeth, and taste sensation from the same area via the chorda tympani (VII)
   (1) May be visible as it lies subcutaneously posterior to the third molar where it may be damaged by dental procedures in this area
   (2) Lies close to inferior alveolar nerve near mandibular foramen where it is also anesthestized during an inferior alveolar block

e) Buccal nerve—carries sensation from a portion of the cheek and mucous membrane adjacent to molars and premolars

V. FACIAL NERVE (VII)

A. Carries both sensory and motor fibers

B. Arises from pons and takes a circuitous route through middle ear

C. Exits through stylomastoid foramen as a pure motor nerve to muscles of facial expression

D. Chorda tympani nerve—branches off facial nerve as it transverses middle ear

1. Passes through petrotympanic fissure in mandibular fossa where it joins lingual nerve
2. Carries autonomic motor fibers to sublingual and submandibular salivary glands
3. Receives taste fibers from anterior two thirds of tongue
4. Some of its fibers join branches of V_1 and V_2 and carry autonomic motor fibers to the lacrimal gland and mucous glands of maxillary sinus and nasal cavity

VI. GLOSSOPHARYNGEAL NERVE

A. Arises from medulla and primarily supplies tongue and pharynx

Relationship of Parasympathetic Fibers with the Trigeminal Nerve

Pathways of the parasympathetic nerve fibers of cranial nerves III, VII, and IX are intricate and somewhat confusing. After the nerve leaves its point of origin in the brain, it goes to various branches of the trigeminal nerve. Nerve III gives parasympathetic fibers to V_1, which carries the autonomic fibers to the **ciliary ganglion** and lacrimal gland via the **nasociliary** branch of V_1. Nerve VII gives off branches to V_2, to the mucous glands of the nasal cavity, and a branch (**chorda tympani**) to the **lingual** branch of V_3, to carry parasympathetic stimulation to the sublingual and submandibular salivary glands. Nerve IX gives parasympathetic fiber to the auriculotemporal branch of V_3 carrying parasympathetic fibers to the parotid salivary gland.

The Autonomic Nervous System

The autonomic nervous system controls many organs at a subconscious level, such as heart rate, breathing rate, and salivary flow. The fibers of the system are found in various nerves of the peripheral nervous system. It is made up of two divisions, the craniosacral (parasympathetic) found in fibers of the III, VII, IX, and X cranial nerves and the thoracolumber found in spinal nerves thoracic 1 to lumbar 3 or 4. The sympathetic division produces effects that occur when one is fearful, fighting, or fleeing. The craniosacral division has the opposite effect.

B. Carries autonomic motor nerve fibers to parotid salivary gland via the auriculotemporal nerve and receives general sensory and taste fibers from posterior one third of tongue

C. Carries general motor fibers to a throat muscle and sensation from pharynx

D. Carries afferent fibers from carotid sinus that help control blood pressure

VII. AUTONOMIC NERVE FIBERS

A. Two neurons long

B. Fiber before synapse area (ganglion) is termed preganglionic and fibers after the synapse are termed postganglionic

C. Synapse area for all the sympathetic fibers is superior sympathetic ganglion, which is found in the neck

D. Parasympathetic ganglia—always found near organ they are controlling

1. *Pterygopalatine ganglion*—found in pterygopalatine fossa; serves nerve VII, lacrimal gland, and mucus glands
2. *Otic ganglion*—found just inferior to foramen ovale; serves nerve IX to parotid gland
3. *Submandibular ganglion*—serves chorda tympani branch of nerve VII to submandibular, sublingual, and minor salivary glands

➤ LYMPHATIC SYSTEM

The lymphatic system is a network of thin-walled vessels and lymph nodes returning fluid from the tissue spaces into the venous system. The presence of one-way valves ensures lymph flow back to the general circulation.

I. LYMPH NODES

A. Characteristics

1. Lymph nodes filter toxic products from tissue fluid (lymph) to prevent them from entering general circulation.
2. Lymph nodes and vessels are variable in location, and there is a great deal of overlapping coverage.

3. Lymph nodes are not normally palpable but, when infected, swell and become palpable, indicating the possible area of infection.
4. Lymph fluid from the head and neck ultimately drains into the right or left jugular lymphatic trunk, which empties into the venous system at the junction of the internal jugular and subclavian veins.
5. Lymph vessels have valves, similar to many veins in the body (but not in the head) that allow only a one-way flow of lymph through the vessels and nodes.

B. Lymph nodes of the head and neck

1. Occipital lymph nodes—superficial nodes that drain lymph fluid from base of skull
2. Retroauricular (posterior auricular) lymph nodes—superficial nodes that drain lymph fluid from posterior scalp and external ear
3. Anterior auricular lymph nodes—superficial nodes that drain lymph fluid from area anterior to external ear
4. Superficial parotid lymph nodes—superficial nodes that drain lymph from parotid gland and adjacent tissue
5. Facial lymph nodes—superficial nodes that follow path of facial vein and drain into submandibular lymph nodes
   a) Infraorbital (malar)—drains infraorbital area
   b) Nasolabial—drains area near nose and upper lip
   c) Buccal—drains area at corner of mouth
   d) Mandibular—drains mandibular area
6. Submental lymph nodes—located on the mylohyoid muscle and drain lymph fluid from chin, lower lip, cheeks, tip of tongue, and incisor teeth
7. Submandibular lymph nodes—located along inferior border of mandible and drain lymph fluid from chin, lips, nose, cheeks, anterior hard palate, sublingual and submandibular salivary glands, and all teeth except mandibular incisors and maxillary 3rd molars
8. External and anterior jugular lymph nodes—follow path of external jugular vein and drain lymph fluid from lower portion of ear and parotid gland
9. Superior deep cervical lymph nodes—located under sternocleidomastoid muscle superior to where omohyoid muscle crosses internal jugular vein
   a) Primary nodes for posterior nasal cavity, soft palate, posterior hard palate, base of tongue, and maxillary third molars
   b) Jugulodigastric lymph node (tonsillar node) is palpable when the pharynx or palatine tonsils are inflamed
10. Inferior deep cervical lymph nodes—located under sternocleidomastoid muscle, inferior to where omohyoid muscle crosses internal jugular vein
    a) Primary nodes for posterior scalp and neck and structures inferior to neck
    b) Jugulo-omohyoid lymph nodes occur at crossing of omohyoid muscle and internal jugular vein; drains tongue and submental region

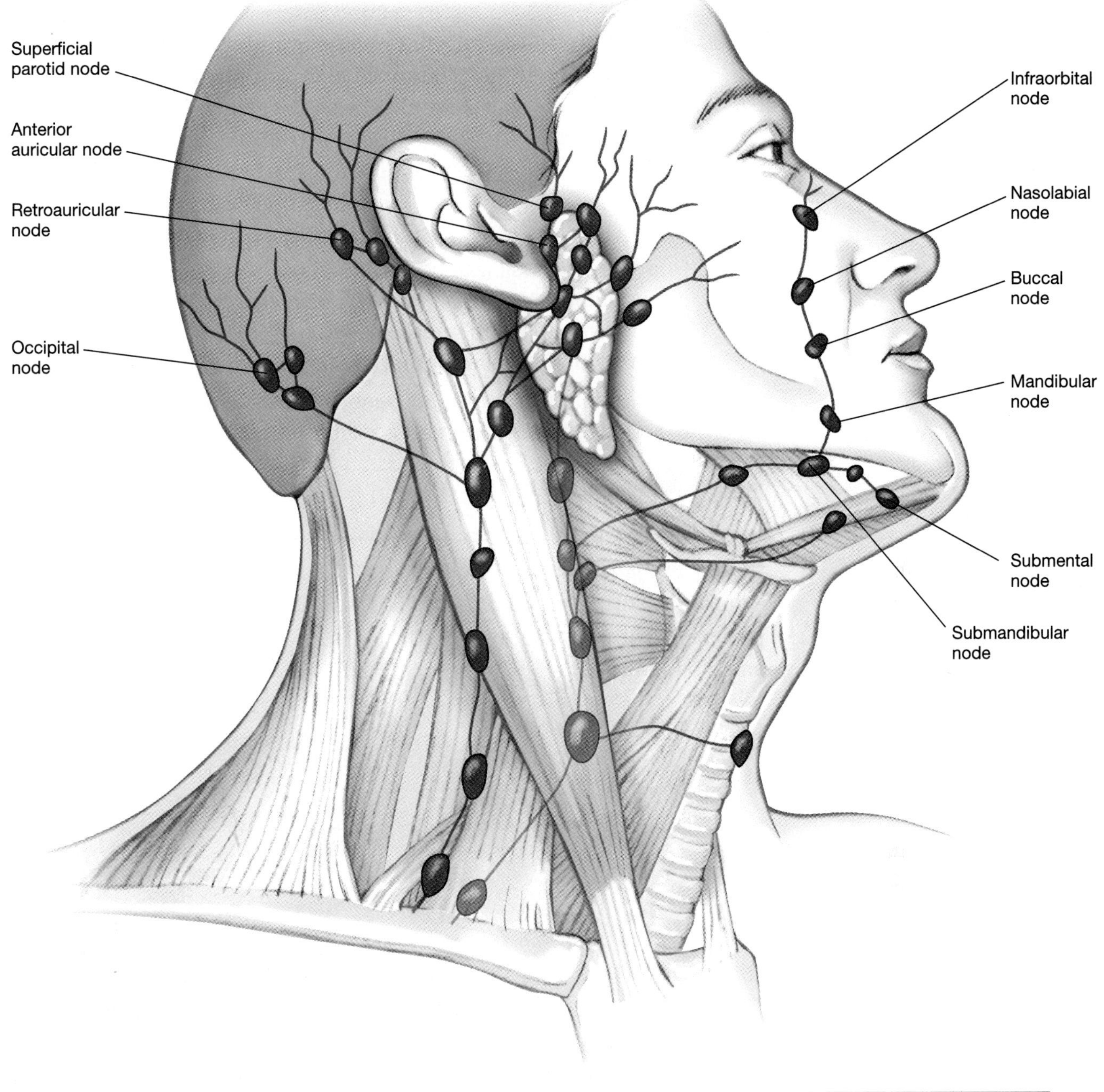

FIGURE 3-11. Lymph nodes.

➤ TONSILS

The tonsils are large masses of lymphoid tissue found around the opening to the pharynx. Their function is to protect the airway and help fight infection. The tonsils are quite large in youth, but tend to regress with age. When enlarged, pharyngeal tonsils may block the nasopharynx opening of the auditory tube, resulting in a nasal quality of speech and drainage from the middle ear. Palatine tonsils may block the oropharynx.

I. TYPES

A. Palatine tonsil—located at posterior lateral border of mouth at the border of the pharynx in a depression between palatopharyngeal fold and glossopharyngeal fold

1. *Palatopharyngeal fold* (*posterior tonsillar pillar*)—consists of a layer of mucous membrane covering palatopharyngeal muscle
2. *Palatoglossal fold* (*anterior tonsillar pillar*)—consists of a layer of mucous membrane covering palatoglossus muscle

B. Pharyngeal tonsil (adenoids)—located on posterior wall of the nasopharynx; may block the auditory (eustachian) tube, which runs from the middle ear to nasopharynx, thus decreasing drainage and complicating middle ear infections

C. Lingual tonsil—located at base of the dorsal surface of tongue; consists of a mass of lymphoid tissue

➤ SALIVARY GLANDS

Numerous accessory salivary and mucous glands, as well as the parotid, sublingual, and submandibular salivary glands, are controlled parasympathetically by cranial nerves VII and IX. All glands are controlled sympathetically by branches arising from the superior sympathetic ganglion in the neck.

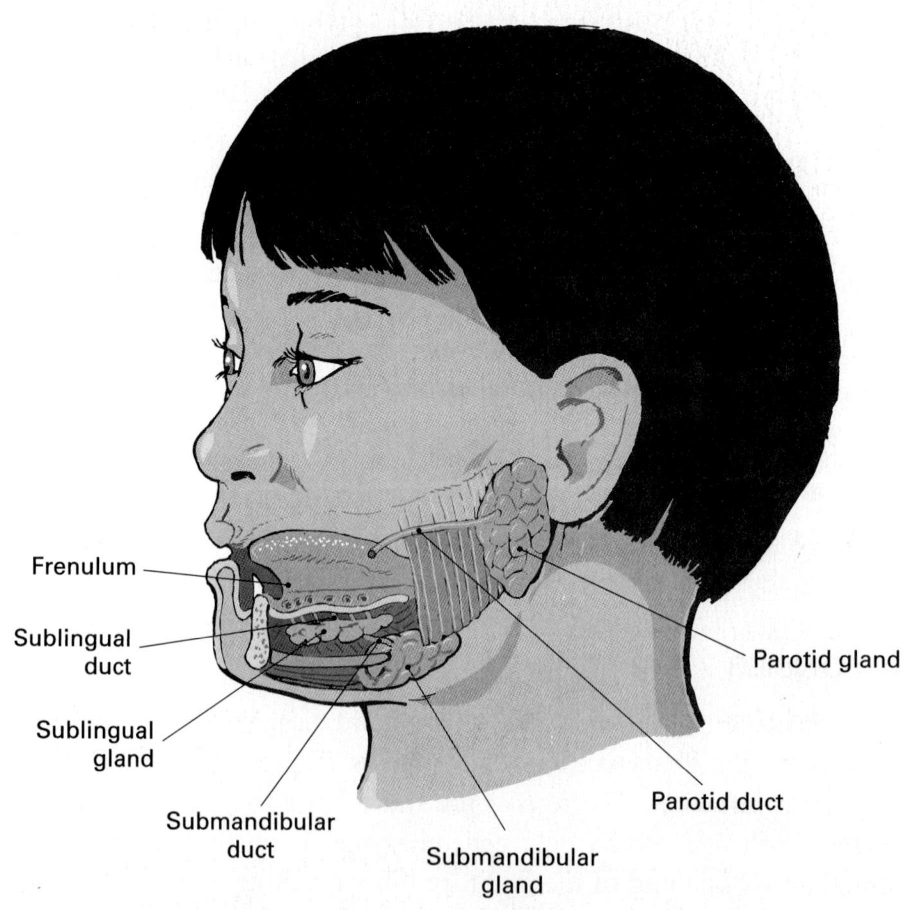

FIGURE 3-12. Salivary glands.

I. PAROTID GLAND

A. Largest gland

B. Located in front and below ear

C. Empties through parotid (Stensen's) duct

D. Secretes mostly serous fluid

E. Site of infection in viral disease, such as mumps

II. SUBMANDIBULAR GLAND

A. Located on lingual surface of mandible beneath posterior part of tongue

B. Empties through submandibular (Wharton's) duct

C. Secretes both serous and mucous fluid

III. SUBLINGUAL GLAND

A. Located anterior to submandibular gland

B. Ducts may open individually or unite to form the sublingual (Bartholin's) duct

C. Secretes both serous and mucous fluid

➤ TONGUE

The tongue is composed almost entirely of muscle, with mucous membrane covering the inferior surface and a specialized epithelium covering the superior surface.

Because the tongue forms from different branchial arches, it has different nerve supplies—the anterior two thirds of the tongue from the mandibular division of the trigeminal and facial nerves and the posterior one third is from the glossopharyngeal nerve.

I. MARKINGS ON THE SUPERIOR SURFACE (DORSUM)

A. Sulcus terminalis
1. Inverted V-shape, which points toward the throat
2. Marks division line between anterior and posterior portion of tongue

B. Foramen cecum
1. Pit located at posterior point of the sulcus terminalis
2. Marks site of origin for the thyroid gland before its migration to the neck

C. Median lingual sulcus—longitudinal depression down midline of tongue

D. Papillae—protrusions located on superior surface of tongue
1. *Circumvallate papillae*—flattened protrusions surrounded by a sulcus
   a) 8 to12 in number
   b) Located just anterior to the sulcus terminalis in a V-shape
   c) Serous glands (Ebner's salivary gland lies inferior to circumvallate papillae)
   d) Contain taste buds

2. *Fungiform papillae*
   a) Rounded, red protrusions primarily located on the apex and sides of tongue
   b) Contain taste buds
3. *Filiform papillae*
   a) Most numerous
   b) Conical shape
   c) Covers anterior two thirds of surface
   d) Only papillae not containing taste buds
4. *Foliate papillae*
   a) Located at lateral sides of base of tongue
   b) Few are present, if any
   c) Contain some taste buds

E. Lingual tonsil

II. INFERIOR SURFACE (VENTRAL)—covered by a thin and translucent mucous membrane, making the lingual vein very visible

A. Fimbriated fold

1. Plica fimbriatae run laterally to each deep lingual vein
2. Marks location of the deeper lingual artery, which runs anteriorly under it

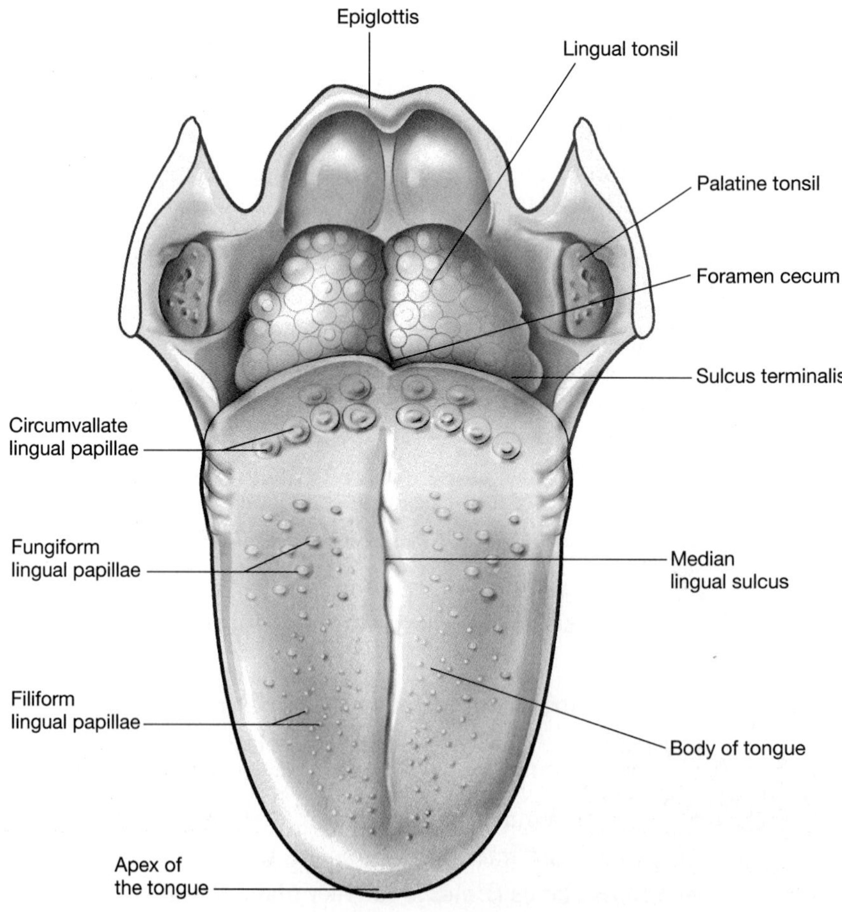

FIGURE 3-13. Tongue and tonsillar tissues.

B. Lingual frenum—fold of mucous membrane that attaches inferior surface of the tongue to genial tubercle area

III. MUSCLES OF THE TONGUE—divided into two groups

A. Intrinsic—determines shape; organized into vertical, horizontal, and longitudinal groups allowing tongue to make many intricate movements

B. Extrinsic—controls position; inserted on the body of tongue from outside locations

1. *Styloglossus muscle*—arises from the styloid process, inserts on the lateral side of the body of tongue, and is innervated by hypoglossal nerve (XII)
2. *Hyoglossus muscle*—arises from hyoid bone, inserts on the lateral side of the tongue, and is innervated by hypoglossal nerve (XII)
3. *Genioglossus muscle*—arises from genial tubercles of mandible, inserts on the posterior surface of tongue, and is innervated by hypoglossal nerve (XII)
4. *Palatoglossus muscle*—arises from the soft palate, inserts on the posterior portion of tongue, and is innervated by nerves of the pharyngeal plexus (IX and X)

IV. BLOOD SUPPLIED BY LINGUAL ARTERY—anterior branch of the external carotid artery

V. INNERVATION—mixed

A. General sensation

1. V_3—conveys sensory information from anterior two thirds of tongue
2. IX—conveys sensory information from posterior one third of tongue

B. Taste

1. Supplied by facial (VII) nerve—conveys taste from anterior one third of tongue
2. Glossopharyngeal (IX) nerve—conveys taste on posterior one third of tongue
3. Vagus (X) nerve—conveys taste on base of tongue

C. Motor control—supplied by hypoglossal (XII) nerve; motor fibers to the intrinsic and extrinsic muscles with exception of palatoglossus (IX and X)

Innervation of the Tongue

- General sensation—lingual branch of V_3 and IX
- Taste—includes VII, IX, and X
- Motor control—includes XII

VI. TYPES OF TASTE BUDS—differ in their perception to taste quality

A. Sour—located primarily along posterior border of tongue

B. Sweet—located primarily at apex of tongue

C. Salty—located primarily along anterior border of tongue

D. Bitter—located at base of tongue

➤ EMBRYOLOGY

I. CEPHALIC (HEAD) END

A. Stomodeum (primitive mouth)—invagination separated from the primitive gut by the buccopharyngeal membrane; located on ventral side; divides cephalic end into a superior frontal process and an inferior mandibular process

1. Buccopharyngeal membrane—ruptures at approximately fourth week of gestation; thin membrane
2. Pharyngeal pouches or clefts—form posterior to stomodeum during fourth and fifth weeks of gestation; form five branchial arches
   - a) Branchial arches—develop much of the face and neck; designated by Roman numerals I–V
     - (1) Arch I (mandibular)—innervated by trigeminal nerve (V); develops into some of the following structures
       - (a) Maxilla
       - (b) Mandible
       - (c) Sphenomandibular ligament
       - (d) Muscles of mastication
       - (e) Tensors veli palatini
       - (f) Anterior belly of digastric
       - (g) Mylohyoid
     - (2) Arch II (hyoid)—innervated by facial nerve (VII); develops into some of the following structures
       - (a) Part of hyoid bone
       - (b) Muscle of facial expression

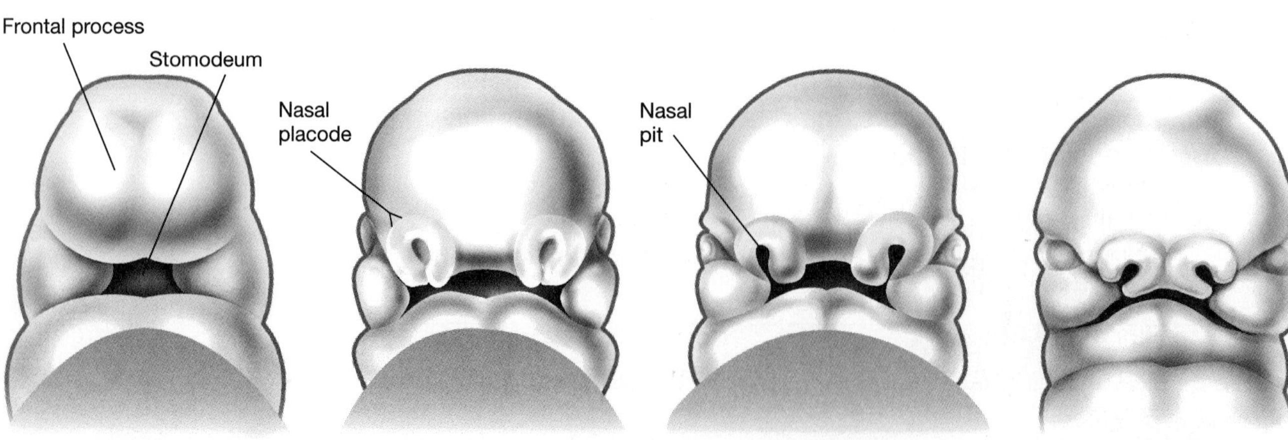

FIGURE 3-14. Developing face.

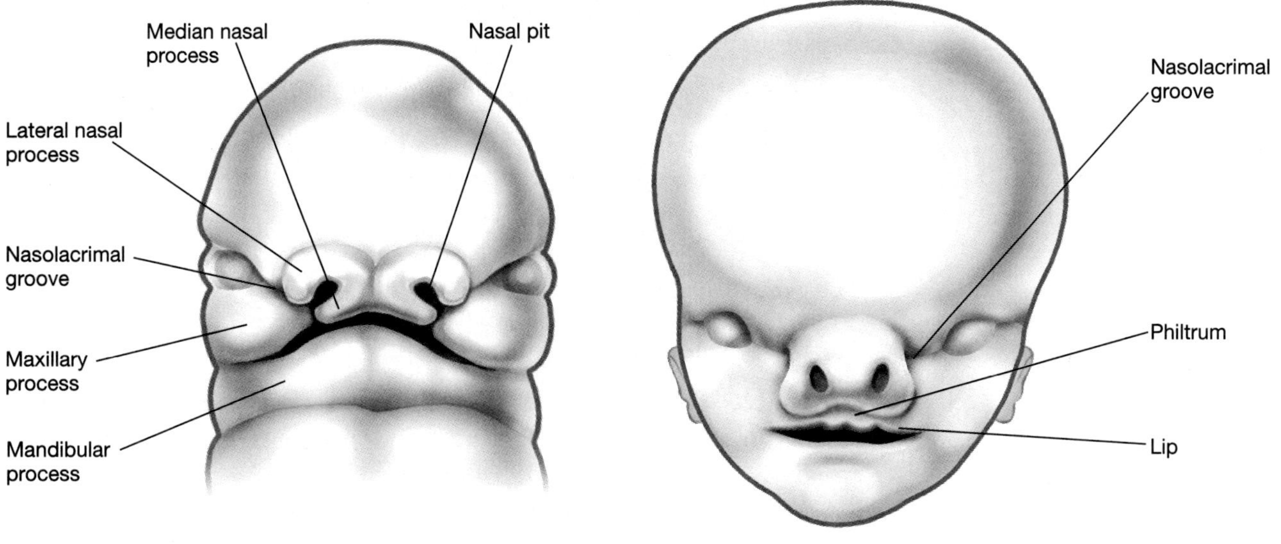

FIGURE 3-15. Face formation.

(c) Posterior belly of digastric
(d) Stylohyoid muscle

(3) Arch III—innervated by glossopharyngeal nerve (IX); develops into some hyoid and pharyngeal structures
(4) Arch IV—innervated by pharyngeal plexus (IX and X); develops into pharyngeal structures
(5) Arch V—innervated by vagus nerve (X); develops into laryngeal structures

II. FACIAL DEVELOPMENT—begins fourth week of gestation

A. Nasal placodes—two thick areas that form on frontal process, just superior to stomodeum

B. Nasal pits (invaginations)—forms from enlarged medial and lateral areas of nasal placodes

C. Lateral nasal processes—eventually form the ala of the nose

D. Medial nasal processes

1. Develops medial to nasal pit
2. Migrate towards each other where fusion occurs and becomes intermaxillary segment

E. Intermaxillary Segment

1. Formed by medial nasal process elongating inferiorly
2. Eventually becomes philtrum of upper lip and premaxilla
3. Intervenes between the maxillary processes and all three processes fuse to form maxilla

F. Maxillary processes (2)

1. Formed by two lateral growths that develop superior to mandibular process
2. Move anteriorly and medially toward each other with intermaxillary segment between

G. Mandibular processes (right and left)—fuse to form lower jaw

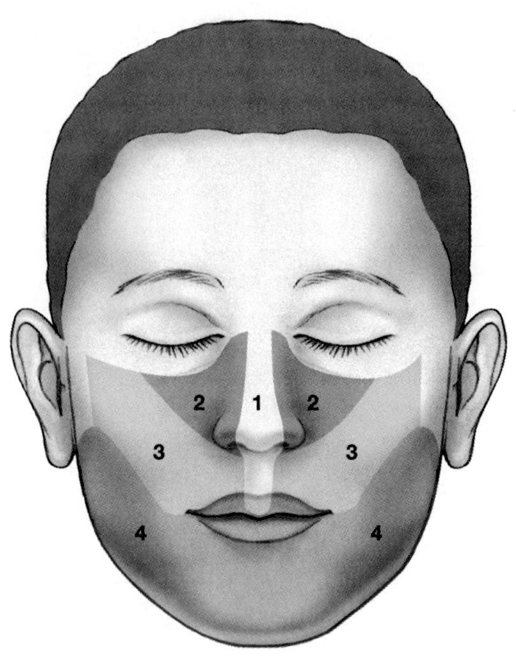

FIGURE 3-16. Development of face: 1) medial nasal process; 2) lateral nasal process; 3) maxillary process; 4) mandibular process.

III. TONGUE DEVELOPMENT

A. Foramen cecum (invagination)

1. Located at apex of V-shaped sulcus terminalis
2. Allows for down-growing area of ectoderm from which thyroid gland is derived

B. Tuberculum impar

1. Located cranial to foramen cecum
2. Forms mound of tissue that signifies beginning of tongue development

C. Lateral lingual swellings

1. Two lateral oval growths
2. Develop on each side of tuberculum impar
3. Grow rapidly and overgrow tuberculum impar
4. Form anterior two thirds of tongue
5. Median sulcus marks point of fusion

D. Copula

1. Mass of tissue formed just caudal to foramen cecum
2. Eventually forms posterior one third of tongue

E. *Sulcus terminalis*—notes line of demarcation of fusion of anterior two thirds and posterior one third of tongue

IV. PATHOLOGICAL CONSIDERATIONS OF MALDEVELOPMENT

A. Cysts and fistulas may develop at any point where embryonic parts fuse, trapping ectodermal cells deep within tissue

B. Cleft lip (unilateral or bilateral) and/or palatal cleft—results from lack of fusion of maxillary process with medial nasal processes

C. Cleft palate—results from failure of right and left palatine processes to close completely; closure begins anteriorly and progresses posteriorly; permits direct communication between oral and nasal cavities

D. Thyroglossal duct cyst—occurs when remnants of ectoderm begin to grow along the path of the downward migration of the thyroid gland

E. Ankyloglossia (tongue-tie)—common defect; shortening of lingual frenulum restricts movement of tip of tongue

F. Branchial cleft sacs/cysts—areas where the branchial arches do not fuse completely and may persist into adulthood as a pouch in neck

G. Micrognathia—serious defect of underdeveloped mandibular process; usually associated with microglossia (small tongue) and difficulty swallowing

review questions

DIRECTIONS Each of the questions or incomplete statements below is followed by suggested answers or completions. Select the **one** answer that is best in each case.

1. The inferior alveolar artery is a branch of which of the following arteries?
   A. maxillary
   B. temporal
   C. occipital
   D. facial

2. The left common carotid artery branches off the
   A. brachiocephalic artery.
   B. arch of the aorta.
   C. left subclavian artery.
   D. superior sagittal sinus.

3. The external auditory meatus is found in which of the following bones?
   A. sphenoid
   B. temporal
   C. occipital
   D. parietal

4. Within the mandibular canal, near the mental foramen, the inferior alveolar nerve is formed by the mental nerve and which other branch?
   A. incisive
   B. lingual
   C. mylohyoid
   D. buccal

5. The cribriform plate is a portion of which of the following bones?
   A. frontal
   B. sphenoid
   C. temporal
   D. ethmoid

6. Cleft lip results from lack of fusion of the
   A. mandibular process with the maxillary process.
   B. right mandibular process with the left mandibular process.
   C. maxillary process with the medial nasal elevations.
   D. right and left palatine processes.

7. The internal jugular vein empties into the
   A. subclavian artery.
   B. subclavian vein.
   C. arch of the aorta.
   D. thoracic duct.

8. Which of the following bones contains a paranasal sinus?
   A. sphenoid
   B. mandible
   C. occipital
   D. zygomatic

9. Which of the following muscles forms the anterior tonsillar pillar?
   A. palatopharyngeus
   B. mylohyoid
   C. stylohyoid
   D. palatoglossus

10. Which of the following muscles is NOT a suprahyoid muscle?
    A. geniohyoid
    B. stylohyoid

C. omohyoid
D. mylohyoid

11. Which of the following nerves innervates the buccinator muscle?
A. trigeminal
B. facial
C. glossopharyngeal
D. hypoglossal

12. Which of the following branches of the trigeminal nerve consists of motor and sensory fibers?
A. V_1
B. ophthalmic
C. V_2
D. mandibular

13. Which of the following muscles inserts on the coronoid process of the mandible?
A. masseter
B. lateral pterygoid
C. medial pterygoid
D. temporalis

14. Which of the following arteries exits the foramen apical to the mandibular premolars?
A. posterior superior alveolar
B. mental
C. lingual
D. incisive

15. Which of the following foramen is located on the medial aspect of the mandible and has the inferior alveolar nerve entering it?
A. infraorbital
B. ovale
C. supraorbital
D. mandibular

16. Which of the following bones is completely surrounded by soft tissue and does NOT articulate with any other bone?
A. vomer
B. hyoid
C. mandible
D. styloid

17. Which of the following sutures separates the occipital bone from the paired parietal bones?
A. coronal
B. sagittal
C. zygomaxillary
D. lambdoidal

18. Which of the following salivary glands is predominately serous in its secretory product?
A. submandibular
B. sublingual
C. parotid
D. minor salivary glands

19. Which of the following cranial nerves provides sensory taste innervation to the posterior one third of the tongue?
A. abducens
B. trigeminal
C. trochlear
D. glossopharyngeal

20. After a mandibular injection, a patient experiences paralysis of the muscles of facial expression on that side of the face. Which of the following nerves was MOST likely anesthetized?
A. V_1
B. V_3
C. IV
D. VII

21. Which of the following groups of lymph nodes provides primary lymphatic drainage for the mandibular incisors?
A. superficial parotid
B. submandibular
C. facial
D. submental

22. Which of the following processes in the skull is located immediately anterior to the mandibular fossa?
A. articular eminence
B. styloid
C. mental
D. mastoid

23. What is the movement of the mandible when the mandibular condyle moves forward on the articular eminence of the temporal bone?
    A. rotation
    B. protrusion
    C. depression
    D. elevation

24. Which of the following glands lies immediately inferior to the circumvallate papillae?
    A. parathyroid
    B. Ebner's
    C. thyroid
    D. parotid

25. Which of the following alveolar nerves innervates the mesiobuccal root of the maxillary first molar?
    A. anterior superior
    B. middle superior
    C. posterior superior
    D. inferior

26. Which of the following divisions of the trigeminal nerve enters through the superior orbital fissure?
    A. V_1
    B. V_2
    C. V_3
    D. all divisions

27. Which of the following factors ensures the flow of lymph in one direction?
    A. sphincters
    B. valves
    C. blood pressure
    D. hydrostatic pressure of lymph

28. Which of the following is a small projection of bone located on the medial surface of the ramus anterior to the mandibular foramen?
    A. lingula
    B. epiglottis
    C. vomer
    D. articular eminence

29. Which of the following organs is associated with the circle of Willis?
    A. heart
    B. liver
    C. brain
    D. spleen

30. Which lingual papillae are located just anterior to the sulcus terminalis?
    A. fungiform
    B. foliate
    C. filiform
    D. circumvallate

answers & rationales

1.

A. The inferior alveolar artery is a branch of the maxillary artery. The temporal, occipital, and facial arteries are branches of the external carotid artery.

2.

B. The left common carotid artery is a branch off the arch of the aorta. The brachiocephalic artery goes to the right arm and right side of the head, the left subclavian artery goes to the left arm, and the superior sagittal sinus is a dural venous sinus within the skull.

3.

B. The external auditory meatus is found in the temporal bone with the postglenoid process and articular fossa of the temporomandibular joint located anteriorly and the mastoid process located posteriorly. The sphenoid, occipital, and parietal bones are not associated with the hearing organ.

4.

A. The inferior alveolar nerve is formed by the merger of the incisive nerve, composed of dental branches from anterior mandibular teeth, and the mental nerve from the chin and lower lip. The lingual nerve arises from the body of the tongue to join the maxillary division of the trigeminal nerve. The mylohyoid nerve is efferent to the mylohyoid muscle and anterior belly of the digastric muscle and joins the inferior alveolar nerve posterior to the mandibular canal. The buccal nerve carries sensation from the cheek and buccal region of the oral cavity.

5.

D. The cribriform plate is the portion of the horizontal plate of the ethmoid that lies in the anterior cranial fossa and is the opening for the olfactory nerve to enter the superior aspects of the nasal cavity.

6.

C. Cleft lips usually develop slightly lateral to the midline due to a failure of the maxillary process to fuse with the medial nasal process. The mandibular and maxillary processes only meet at the angle of the mouth. The right and left mandibular processes fuse to form the single mandible. Failure of fusion of the palatine processes results in a cleft palate.

7.

B. The arch of the aorta and the subclavian artery are part of the arterial system and do not receive venous blood. The thoracic duct is a collection vessel of the lymphatic system.

8.

A. The sphenoid, frontal, maxilla, and ethmoid bones contain paranasal sinuses.

9.

D. The palatoglossus muscle forms the anterior tonsillar pillar and the palatopharyngear muscle forms the posterior tonsillar pillar—both structures found where the oral cavity opens into the oropharynx. The mylohyoid and stylohyoid muscles are suprahyoid muscles.

10.

C. The omohyoid muscle is an infrahyoid muscle that has an origin on the superior border of the scapula and inserts on the lateral border of the hyoid. The other three muscles are suprahyoid muscles inserting on the hyoid bone.

11.

B. The buccinator muscle is innervated by the facial nerve (VII) and is therefore not considered a muscle of mastication (innervated by V). The glossopharyngeal nerve innervates the pharynx and the hypoglossal muscles of the tongue.

12.

D. The mandibular branch carries sensory fibers from the teeth and supporting structures and motor fibers to muscles of mastication. V_1 is the ophthalmic division of the trigeminal. V_2 is the maxillary division of the trigeminal, both of which are only sensory.

13.

D. The masseter, temporalis, and lateral and medial pterygoid muscles are muscles of mastication. The temporalis muscle inserts on the coronoid process of the mandible, while the remaining three insert at the temporomandibular joint, ramus, angle, and body of the mandible.

14.

B. The mental artery exits the mental foramen on the anterior surface of the mandible. The posterior superior alveolar artery is located in the maxilla. The lingual artery is a branch from the maxillary artery providing the blood supply to the tongue and the floor of the mouth. The incisive artery is a continuation of the inferior alveolar artery distally and anteriorly within the mandible.

15.

D. The infraorbital foramen is in the maxilla, inferior to the orbit where the infraorbital nerve exits. The foramen ovale is in the base of the skull through which a portion of the trigeminal nerve exits the skull. The supraorbital foramen is superior to the orbital rim.

16.

B. The hyoid bone is a U-shaped bone in the upper neck that does not articulate with any other bone. The vomer bone forms a portion of the nasal septum, the mandible articulates with the temporal bone, and the styloid is a process projecting from the temporal bone at the base of the skull.

17.

D. The coronal suture separates the frontal bone from the paired parietal bones. The sagittal suture separates the paired parietal bones, and the zygomaxillary suture separates the maxilla from the zygomatic bone.

18.

C. The parotid is composed of mostly serous fluid. The submandibular gland is almost an even mixture of serous and mucinous secretory fluid. The sublingual gland is predominately mucous fluid and the minor salivary glands are mostly mucinous secretions.

19.

D. The glossopharyngeal nerve supplies taste to the posterior 1/3 of the tongue and the facial nerve supplies taste to the anterior 2/3 of the tongue via the chorda tympani. This is because developmentally the anterior and posterior parts of the tongue arose from two different branchial arches. The abducens (VI) provides motor fibers to a muscle of the eye. The trigeminal (V) provides motor and sensory to the teeth, sinus, gingiva, and muscles of mastication. The trochlear (IV), the smallest of the cranial nerves, provides motor to a muscle of the eye.

20.

D. The facial nerve (VII) courses through the capsule of the parotid gland where it divides into branches innervating the muscles of facial expression. It may become anesthetized with deep mandibular block injections. The ophthalmic division (V_1) of the trigeminal and is sensory only. The mandibular division (V_3) of the trigeminal provides both sensory and motor fibers. The trochlear nerve (IV) innervates a muscle of the eyeball.

21.

D. The superficial parotid nodes are too far superior for lymphatic drainage of the mandibular incisors, which drain into the submental nodes located just inferior to the mandibular incisors. The submandibular and facial nodes are the secondary group of nodes, which drain the submental nodes.

22.

A. The articular eminence is a protrusion of bone anterior to the mandibular fossa. The styloid process is a projection that is immediately inferior to the auditory canal. The mental process forms the anterior chin, and the mastoid process is a projection posterior to the mandibular auditory canal.

23.

B. Gliding movement involves protrusion, where the condyle moves forward on the articular eminence and retraction, where the condyle moves backwards. Elevation and depression are both forms of rotation, where the condyle rotates on the meniscus.

24.

B. Ebner's glands give serous secretions and aid in cleansing chemical stimulants from the taste buds. The parathyroids lie in the neck on the posterior surface of the thyroid. The thyroid lies in the neck inferior to the thyroid cartilage, and the parotids are major salivary glands that lie anterior to the ear.

25.

B. The middle superior alveolar nerve innervates the maxillary premolars and the mesiobuccal root of the maxillary first molar. The anterior superior alveolar nerve primarily innervates the maxillary anteriors. The posterior superior alveolar nerve primarily innervates the maxillary sinus and maxillary molars, except the mesiobuccal root of the maxillary first molar. The inferior alveolar nerve innervates the mandibular teeth, becoming the incisive nerve beyond the mental foramen.

26.

A. Cranial nerves V_1, along with III, IV, VI, and blood vessels travel within the superior orbital fissure. The foramen rotundum is the opening for the V_2 division, which later enters the infraorbital canal. The foramen ovale is the opening for the V_3 division.

27.

B. The lymphatic vessels contain valves to reduce backflow of lymph. Sphincters are absent in the lymphatic vessels. The blood pressure has no effect on lymphatic flow. There is little or no hydrostatic pressure present in lymphatic vessels.

28.

A. The lingula is anterior to the mandibular foramen and projects posteriorly to partially cover the foramen. The epiglottis is a flap of dense soft tissue, which covers the trachea during swallowing. The vomer is a vertical plate of bone that forms a portion of the nasal septum. The articular eminence is a projection of bone anterior to the mandibular fossa.

29.

C. The circle of Willis is an anastomoses of basilar and internal carotid arteries at the base of the brain. The heart, liver, and spleen do not contain intracerebral arteries.

30.

D. Circumvallate are 8 to 12 large papillae located just anterior to the sulcus terminalis. Fungiform papillae are mushroom-shaped and located on the apex and sides of the tongue. The numerous filiform papillae are found throughout the anterior portion of the tongue, while the foliate papillae are found at the lateral margins of the tongue.

CHAPTER

4 Oral Anatomy and Histology

Emma Henderson, RDH, BS
Charlene C. Goodwin, RDH, MSED, MS

contents

➤ MORPHOLOGY

Morphology is the study of form and structure.

I. DEFINITIONS

A. *Anatomic crown*—part of tooth covered by enamel (above the cementoenamel juntion [CEJ])

B. *Anatomic root*—part of tooth covered by cementum (below the CEJ)

C. Clinical crown—part of tooth visible above gingival margin

D. Clinical root—part of tooth attached to alveolar bone by periodontal ligament (begins at gingival line and ends at apex)

E. Cementoenamel junction—point where enamel of crown meets cementum of root (separates anatomic crown from anatomic root)

F. Longitudinal groove—groove (concavity) running longitudinally down root surface

II. GENERALIZATIONS RELATED TO PERMANENT TEETH

A. Facial surface, mesiodistally, is wider than lingual surface

B. Longitudinal grooves

1. Anterior teeth—may or may not be present; if present, they most likely will occur on distal surface
    a) Maxillary central incisor—LEAST likely to have longitudinal grooves on the mesial and distal surfaces than any other maxillary or mandibular tooth
2. Posterior teeth—more prominent and developed on mesial surface

C. Roots

1. Multi-rooted teeth—named for position they occupy in relation to crown surfaces and to each other
    a) Maxillary—trifurcated; include lingual (longest), mesiofacial, and distofacial roots
    b) Mandibular—bifurcated; mesial and distal roots
2. Deviate from norm more frequently than crowns
3. Apices diverge distally except for mandibular canine, which deviates mesially
4. All premolars exhibit single roots except for maxillary first, which usually is bifurcated

III. CHARACTERISTICS OF SPECIFIC TEETH

A. Maxillary central incisor

1. Exhibits longest crown in permanent dentition; greatest width is mesiodistally
2. Mesial and distal surfaces—converge lingually on a well-developed cingulum
3. Incisal edge—located in center of crown labiolingually
4. Root—cone-shaped with blunt apex; one root canal

B. Maxillary lateral incisor

1. Resembles central incisor, but narrower mesiodistally and faciolingually

2. Displays greatest variance in size and shape of all anterior teeth
3. Lingual fossa—more pronounced than central incisor
4. Root—longer than central incisor; blunt apex that bends distally; has one root canal

C. Mandibular central incisor

1. Smallest tooth in permanent dentition
2. Crown is bilaterally symmetrical
3. Lingual crown surface has no distinct anatomy
4. One root canal

D. Mandibular lateral incisor

1. Less symmetrical, yet slightly larger in all dimensions than mandibular central incisor
2. Incisal edge has a distinct distolingual twist
3. One root canal

E. Maxillary canine

1. Longest tooth in permanent dentition
2. Labial surface has distinct labial ridge
3. Lingual surface has large cingulum
4. Wide labiolingual dimension
5. Incisal has single cusp, which is centered over root
6. Distinct longitudinal depression located on distal root surface; one root canal

F. Mandibular canine

1. Crown is long and narrow compared with maxillary canine
2. Labial ridge is not as pronounced as maxillary canine
3. Cingulum is relatively small and off-centered toward distal
4. Incisal outline is more symmetrical than maxillary canine
5. Longitudinal depressions are on mesial and distal surfaces of root; one root canal

G. Maxillary first premolar

1. Crown is wide buccolingually with two cusps—one buccal and one lingual
2. Mesial surface has a longitudinal depression on cervical part of crown and root
3. Long central groove ends with mesial marginal groove, which crosses over mesial marginal ridge
4. Bifurcated root in apical one third; two root canals

H. Maxillary second premolar

1. Buccal and lingual cusps are similar in size
2. Occlusal surface has a short central groove with a pit at each end
3. Single root, which is longer than the maxillary first premolar; one or two root canals

I. Mandibular first premolar

1. Cusps
   a) Buccal cusp—long and sharp, centered over root axis
   b) Lingual cusp is small and nonfunctional
2. Lingual surface has mesiolingual groove that crosses mesial marginal ridge

3. Mesial marginal ridge more cervically located than distal marginal ridge, which is distinct to this tooth
4. Single rooted; one root canal

J. Mandibular second premolar

1. Two common types include
   a) Two-cusps—one buccal cusp and one lingual cusp; H-shaped occlusal pattern
   b) Three-cusps—one buccal cusp and two lingual cusps; Y-shaped occlusal pattern
2. Root is longer than mandibular first premolar; one root canal

K. Maxillary first molar

1. Largest tooth in maxillary arch with its greatest dimension buccolingually
2. Cusps—include five: four major and one minor (cusp of Carabelli), which is located on mesiolingual cusp
3. Exhibits oblique ridge on occlusal surface, which crosses from distobuccal cusp to mesiolingual cusp
4. Roots include
   a) Mesiobuccal (two canals)
   b) Distobuccal (one canal)
   c) Lingual root, longest (one canal)

L. Maxillary second molar

1. Overall size is smaller than maxillary first molar
2. Crown is similar to maxillary first molar except that cusp of Carabelli is absent
3. Exhibits three roots that are nearly parallel to one another; three root canals

M. Maxillary third molar

1. Size is generally smaller and poorly developed
2. Number of cusps can vary from one to eight
3. Often impacted
4. Roots are frequently fused; three root canals

N. Mandibular first molar

1. First permanent tooth to erupt into oral cavity (all primary teeth may still be present)
2. Largest tooth in mandibular arch with its greatest dimension mesiodistally
3. Cusps include five—two buccal, two lingual, and one distal cusp
4. Two buccal grooves—mesiobuccal, which frequently ends in a pit, and distobuccal
5. Occlusal surface has two transverse ridges
6. Bifurcated roots—mesial and distal; three root canals—mesial has two canals and distal has one canal

O. Mandibular second molar

1. Crown's greatest dimension is mesiobuccal with only one buccal groove
2. Distal cusp is absent
3. Roots are more parallel than mandibular first premolar; three root canals—mesial root has two canals and distal root has one canal

P. Mandibular third molar

1. Small and poorly developed
2. Most frequently impacted tooth
3. Roots are generally fused; three root canals—mesial root has two canals and distal root has one canal

IV. MORPHOLOGICAL DIFFERENCES BETWEEN PRIMARY AND PERMANENT DENTITION

A. Primary teeth are smaller, whiter in color, and less mineralized than permanent teeth

B. Primary teeth have constricted cervical area; cervical ridges are pronounced, especially on buccal aspect of first primary molar

C. Enamel and dentin are thin throughout entire crown

D. Pulp chambers are large; pulp horns extend close to occlusal surface

E. Developmental and supplemental grooves are less pronounced

F. Roots

1. Anterior teeth—long compared with the crown size; bend labially
2. Posterior teeth—widely spread—second molar roots are more widely spread than first molar roots, just opposite of permanent molars

➤ HISTOLOGY

Histology deals with the structure, functino, and composition of tissue.

I. TISSUE—group of cells that work together to perform special functions

A. Types—epithelium, connective, nervous, and muscle

1. Epithelial—tissue that covers outer body (skin) or lines mucous membranes (mouth, stomach, and intestine); gives rise to the enamel organ
   a) Surface tissue
      (1) Simple—single layer of epithelial cells; delicate tissue; lines blood vessels
      (2) Columnar—single layer of cells, but appear to be in layers; lines upper respiratory tract and intestines
      (3) Stratified—consists of several layers of epithelial cells; sturdier tissue; lines oral cavity, salivary glands, and most all surfaces of the body
   b) Glandular tissue—consists of surface epithelium that invaginates into underlying connective tissue (CT) to produce secretions
      (1) Exocrine or ducted glands—retains surface connection; i.e., salivary and sweat glands
      (2) Endocrine or ductless glands—loses surface connection; i.e., thyroid and pituitary glands
2. Connective—contains fewer cells and more intercellular substance (ICS); holds body parts together
   a) Types
      (1) Fibrous—underlies epithelium of skin and oral mucosa; makes up tendons and ligaments

(2) Bone—supports body
(3) Cartilage—gives support and allows for skeletal growth

3. Nerve—made up of nerve cells and tissue; classified as motor or sensory; react to stimuli and transmit impulses
   a) Central nervous system (somatic)—includes brain and spinal cord
   b) Peripheral nervous system (visceral)—involves nerves to and from brain and spinal cord; includes smooth muscle nerves (e.g., heart, liver, glands)
4. Muscle—responsible for contractions, movements
   a) Skeletal muscles—limbs, trunk, jaw, face
   b) Smooth muscles—digestive tract, eyes, blood vessels
   c) Cardiac muscles—heart

II. TISSUES OF THE TOOTH AND SURROUNDING PERIODONTIUM

A. Enamel—consists of 96% inorganic and 4% organic material; covers anatomic crown; forms from enamel organ

1. Amelogenesis—formation of enamel
   a) Ameloblasts—enamel forming cells; originate from ectodermal tissue
   b) Enamel matrix—organic matrix; consists of rods, rod sheath, and interrod substance
   c) Hydroxyapatite crystals—consists of calcium phosphate; found in enamel rods
2. Formations in enamel
   a) Hunter-Schreger bands—display curvature of enamel rods that run perpendicular to dentinoenamel junction (DEJ); viewed in cross section
   b) Lines (Striae) of Retzius—depressions that run from DEJ toward occlusal/incisal; viewed in cross section and lines appear brown
   c) Enamel tufts—undercalcified part of enamel rods; extend from DEJ outward into enamel; appear like "brushes"
   d) Enamel spindles—originate from odontoblasts; extend from dentinal fibers and cross over DEJ into enamel
   e) Enamel lamellae—defect in enamel that appear as fine lines on the facial surface
   f) Perikymata—horizontal ridges that appear on surface formed by lines of Retzius
   g) Nasmyth's membrane—consists of
      (1) Primary enamel cuticle—last product of ameloblasts
      (2) Secondary enamel cuticle—product of reduced enamel epithelium

B. Dentin

1. Consists of 70% inorganic and 30% organic material
2. Located in crown and root
3. Makes up bulk of tooth
4. First tissue to mineralize during tooth development

5. Forms from dental papilla
   a) Odontogenesis—formation of dentin
      (1) Odontoblast—cells that form organic matrix of dentin
         (a) Collagen fibers and ground substance—make up the 30% organic material
         (b) Hydroxyapatite crystals—make up the 70% inorganic material, which form mineralized matrix
      (2) Dentinal tubules—tubules that extend from dentinoenamel junction to pulp; contain cytoplasm of pulp cell
      (3) Dentinal fibers—nerve fibers located in tubules; transmit nerve impulses
      (4) Predentin—located next to pulp; consists of organic matrix that has not mineralized
      (5) Tomes granular layer—located in root portion just under cementum; an unmineralized area of dentin
      (6) Interglobular dentin—usually located in crown portion just under DEJ; an unmineralized area of dentin that occurs during tooth formation
      (7) Reparative or secondary dentin—produced throughout life of tooth, in response to stimuli such as caries or trauma; located next to pulp; modified type of dentin, usually found in older teeth
      (8) Sclerotic dentin—dentin tubules filled with calcuim salt because of degeneration of odontoblast
      (9) Dead tract—odontoblasts have degenerated, but tract is not filled with calcium salt

C. Cementum

1. Consists of 50% inorganic and 50% organic matters
2. Covers root dentin
3. Primary function is to provide medium for attachment of periodontal ligament
4. Forms from dental sac
   a) Cementogenesis—formation of cementum
      (1) Cementoblast—produces organic matrix of cementum; located in periodontal ligament
         (a) Collagen fibers—make up matrix
         (b) Hydroxyapatite crystals—consist of calcium phosphate; form mineralized matrix
      (2) Cementocytes—cementoblasts that become surrounded by organic matrix
         (a) Lacuna—"little space" occupied by cementocytes
         (b) Canaliculi—"little canal" area occupied by threadlike projections of cementocytes
      (3) Types
         (a) Acellular—without cells; located in apical half
         (b) Cellular—contains cells; located in cervical half
      (4) Cementoid—located on outer surface and is hypocalcified
      (5) Sharpey's fibers—bundles of fibers of periodontal ligament that embed into cementoid

D. Pulp

1. Noncalcified tissue that develops from dental papilla
2. Makes up vascular and nerve portion of tooth
   a) Formation of pulp—calcification does not occur
      (1) Fibroblasts—form and maintain pulp tissue; primary cell
      (2) Histocytes and undifferentiated mesenchymal cells—act as defense mechanism
      (3) Odontoblast—used in repair
      (4) Korff's fibers—important in formation of dentin matrix
      (5) Pulp stones (denticles)—mineralized bodies of irregular shape
   b) Functions
      (1) Formative—odontoblast produce dentin throughout life of tooth
      (2) Sensory—nerves bring sense of pain, heat, and cold
      (3) Nutritive—blood brings nutrients to pulp
      (4) Defensive—odontoblasts respond to injury or decay

E. Periodontal ligament (PDL)

1. Specialized connective tissue derived from fibers of the dental sac
2. Attaches tooth cementum to alveolus
3. Produces cementum and lamina dura
   a) Formation—does not calcify
      (1) Fibroblasts—form fibrils of ligament
      (2) Collagen—make up fibrils
      (3) Sharpey's fibers—ends of periodontal ligament become embedded in cementum and bone
         (a) Free gingival fibers—hold gingiva to tooth surface; extend from cementum to lamina propria of free gingiva
         (b) Transseptal fibers—extend from cementum of one tooth to cementum of an adjacent tooth; mesial and distal only
         (c) Alveolar crest fibers—extend from cementum to alveolar crest; help resist horizontal movement
         (d) Horizontal fibers—extend from cementum to bone; resist horizontal pressure
         (e) Oblique fibers—most numerous; extend from cementum obliquely to bone in a coronal direction; prevent apex from being "jammed" against base of socket
         (f) Apical fibers—extend from cementum at apex to bone; radiate around apex
         (g) Interradicular fibers—located between roots of multirooted teeth; help stabilize tooth

F. Alveolar bone

1. Part of the mandible and the maxilla that surrounds and supports teeth
2. Consists of 50% organic and 50% inorganic material
   a) Organ—compoased of bone tissue
      (1) *Compact bone* (cortical plate)—makes up outside wall of mandible/maxilla

(2) *Trabecular bone* (spongy)—makes up the inside wall of mandible/maxilla
(3) Bone marrow—projects into spaces around trabeculae
(a) Red—forms function of hemopoiesis (forms blood)
(b) Yellow—consists of adipose; contains no blood-producing function

b) Periosteum—consists of connective tissue that covers outside of bone
c) Endosteum—consists of connective tissue that covers inside of bone
d) Tissue
(1) Osteoblasts—cells that form bone
(2) Osteocytes—osteoblasts that are trapped in lacunae; osteocytic cell processes extend into canaliculi and maintain contact with adjacent osteocytes
(3) Lacunae—space in bone matrix that is occupied by osteocyte; "little space"
(4) Canaliculi—connect lacunae
(5) Lamellae—thin layers of mature bone
(a) Lamellar—lamellae that follow circumference of bone
i) Circumferential bone—makes up outer perimeter of adult bone
ii) Subendosteal—makes up surface of trabecular bone
(b) Haversian system—lamellae arranged in concentric circles around a central canal
i) Haversian canal—central canal that carries capillary-like blood vessels
ii) Volkmann's canal—canal through which blood vessels pass in and out of bone

G. Gingiva—specialized mucous membrane that firmly attaches to underlying bone

1. Composed of connective (fibrous) and epithelial tissues (stratified squamous)
2. Structure
a) Gingival sulcus—space between gingiva and tooth; encirles all around tooth
b) Free gingiva (marginal)—consists of gingiva not attached to tooth surface
c) Epithelial attachment (junctional)—point where epithelium attaches to tooth; located at base of sulcus; made up of stratified squamous epithelium
d) Free ginigval groove—depression located opposite alveolar crest and denotes sulcus depth
e) Attached gingiva—located beneath free gingival groove and attaches to bone
f) Mucogingival junction—point where attached gingiva ends; layer between gingiva and underlying bone

III. TOOTH DEVELOPMENT

A. Dental lamina—thickened oral epithelium (ectoderm) that will become occlusal border of mandible and maxilla

B. Tooth germ—invagination of dental lamina into the underlying connective tissue (mesoderm)

1. Enamel organ (dental organ)—forms enamel; first part of tooth germ to form; develops from dental amina
2. Dental papilla—forms dentin and pulp
3. Dental sac—forms periodontal ligament, cementum, lamina dura

C. Layers of enamel organ

1. Outer enamel epithelium—consists of low cuboidal cells
2. Stellate reticulum—consists of star-shaped epithelial cells
3. Stratum intermedium—consists of flat epithelial cells
4. Inner enamel epithelium—consists of cuboidal cells

D. Basement membrane

1. Separates enamel organ from underlying dental papilla
2. DEJ is located in this area as it develops

E. Reduced enamel epithelium

1. Results as the four cell layers of the enamel organ become compressed
2. Protects tooth until it erupts
3. Enamel cuticle
   a) Primary enamel cuticle—last product of ameloblast; mineralized
   b) Secondary enamel cuticle—product of reduced enamel epithelium; nonmineralized
4. *Hertwig epithelial root sheath*
   a) Strands of cells of the reduced enamel epithelium that bring about dentin formation
   b) Determines outline of root dentin and number of roots
5. *Epithelial rests* (*rests of Malassez*)—remnants of Hertwig's epithelial root sheath in periodontal ligament

IV. ORAL CAVITY

A. Oral mucous membrane

1. Categories
   a) Masticatory mucosa—keratinized; includes gingiva and hard palate
   b) Lining mucosa—nonkeratinized; includes nonmasticatory areas, such as cheeks, soft palate, and underside of tongue
   c) Specialized mucosa—applied to mucous membrane located on dorsum (top) of tongue; includes papillae
2. Functions
   a) Protect
   b) Secrete—e.g., nasal passages, salivary glands
   c) Absorb—has ability to take in solution; nutritive

DIRECTIONS Each of the questions or incomplete statements below is followed by suggested answers or completions. Select the **one** answer that is best in each case.

1. Compared with the permanent teeth, all of the following are characteristics of primary teeth EXCEPT one. Which one is the EXCEPTION?
   A. smaller pulp size
   B. whiter in color
   C. smaller in overall size
   D. less mineralized enamel
2. Which of the following tissues makes up the bulk of the tooth?
   A. enamel
   B. cementum
   C. dentin
   D. pulp
3. The number of roots a tooth will develop is determined by the
   A. dental sac.
   B. Hertwig's root sheath.
   C. periodontal ligament.
   D. cementum.
4. Which of the following components is the primary crystalline material of bone?
   A. magnesium
   B. carbonate
   C. potassium
   D. hydroxyapatite
5. Which of the following is the first mineralized tissue to appear in any developing tooth?
   A. enamel
   B. cementum
   C. dentin
   D. pulp
6. Rests of Malassez represent remnants of which of the following?
   A. outer enamel epithelium
   B. Hertwig's root sheath
   C. stratum intermedium
   D. stellate reticulum
7. Which of the following compositions represents normal enamel?
   A. 25% hydroxyapatite, 75% organic compounds
   B. 55% hydroxyapatite, 45% organic compounds
   C. 70% hydroxyapatite, 30% organic compounds
   D. 96% hydroxyapatite, 4% organic compounds
8. The attachment apparatus (cementum, PDL, and bone) originates from the
   A. inner enamel epithelium.
   B. outer enamel epithelium.
   C. stellate reticulum.
   D. dental sac.
9. Which of the following is a derivative of ectoderm?
   A. dentin
   B. enamel
   C. cementum
   D. alveolar bone

10. Which of the following BEST defines the lines of Retzius?
    A. Cracks in newly formed enamel.
    B. Defective enamel rods.
    C. Trapped odontoblastic processes.
    D. Incremental lines of enamel formation.

11. The last layer of enamel produced by ameloblasts, before tooth eruption, is the
    A. perikymata.
    B. imbrication line.
    C. primary cuticle.
    D. secondary cuticle.

12. Of the following permanent teeth, which is MOST likely to exhibit the cusp of Carabelli?
    A. mandibular right second premolar
    B. mandibular right first molar
    C. maxillary right canine
    D. maxillary right first molar

13. Which permanent premolar usually exhibits a bifurcated root?
    A. maxillary first
    B. maxillary second
    C. mandibular first
    D. mandibular second

14. Which permanent premolar has a functional buccal cusp and a nonfunctional lingual cusp?
    A. mandibular first
    B. maxillary first
    C. mandibular second
    D. maxillary second

15. A lingual groove is commonly found on the permanent premolar crown surface of the
    A. mandibular first.
    B. Y-type mandibular second.
    C. H-type mandibular second.
    D. maxillary first.

16. Maxillary permanent molars are the only group of teeth that normally exhibit
    A. a transverse ridge.
    B. two roots.
    C. an oblique ridge.
    D. a masticatory function of grinding.

17. A permanent molar, which exhibits four cusps and two roots, is MOST likely the
    A. maxillary first.
    B. maxillary second.
    C. mandibular first.
    D. mandibular second.

18. Which of the following roots is the longest on the permanent maxillary second molar?
    A. mesial
    B. mesiobuccal
    C. lingual
    D. distobuccal
    E. distal

19. A cingulum is normally located
    A. between two cusp ridges.
    B. on the same surface as the transverse ridge.
    C. on the lingual surface of anterior teeth.
    D. on the buccal surface of posterior teeth.

20. The periodontal ligament is located between the
    A. enamel and dentin.
    B. dentin and cementum.
    C. cementum and bone.
    D. bone and enamel.

21. One of the few anomalies associated with the permanent mandibular canine is
    A. a root bifurcation.
    B. a peg crown form.
    C. two cusps.
    D. a large cingulum.

answers & rationales

1.

A. The pulp chamber of deciduous teeth is proportionately larger than permanent teeth. Deciduous teeth are whiter in color, smaller in size, and have less mineralized enamel than permanent teeth.

2.

C. Dentin makes up the bulk of the tooth because it is located in both the crown and root portions. Enamel covers the outer covering of the anatomic crown and the cementum covers the anatomic root. The pulp decreases in size as the tooth ages.

3.

B. Hertwig's root sheath determines the number of roots a tooth will develop. The dental sac forms the periodontal ligament, cementum, and lamina dura.

4.

D. The primary crystalline mineral of bone, enamel, dentin, and cementum is hydroxyapatite.

5.

C. Dentin is the first mineralized tissue to develop. The production of enamel is stimulated by the presence of predentin and shortly follows dentin formation. Cementum and pulp develop later in the tooth development process.

6.

B. Rests of Malassez form Hertwig's root sheath.

7.

D. Enamel is made up of 96% hydroxyapatite and 4% organic material.

8.

D. The dental sac forms the attachment apparatus. The inner enamel epithelium leads to the development of preameloblasts. The outer enamel epithelium forms the outer layer of the enamel organ. The stellate reticulum is a layer of the enamel organ.

9.

B. The enamel organ develops from the basal layer of the oral epithelium—a derivative of ectoderm. Dentin, cementum, and alveolar bone are derivatives of mesoderm.

10.

D. The lines of Retzius represent enamel formed in increments.

11.

C. Perikymata (imbrication line) is a surface manifestation of the lines of Retzius. The secondary cuticle is Nasmyth's membrane.

12.

D. The permanent maxillary first molars exhibit the cusp of Carabelli on the mesiolingual cusp.

13.

A. The remaining premolars all have single roots.

14.

A. The remaining teeth have functional cusps.

15.

B. The Y-type mandibular second molar has three cusps—one buccal and two lingual, which are separated by the lingual groove.

16.

C. Maxillary permanent molars have an oblique ridge—characteristic of only these teeth. Transverse ridges are common on permanent premolars and mandibular molars. Maxillary molars have three roots, not two. The remaining permanent posterior teeth share the common masticatory function of grinding.

17.

D. The mandibular second molar displays two roots and four cusps. The maxillary first molar has three roots and may have five cusps. The maxillary second molar, has four cusps and three roots. The mandibular first molar has five cusps and two roots.

18.

C. The lingual root is the longest on the permanent maxillary molars.

19.

C. Cingulums are routinely located on the lingual surface of anterior teeth.

20.

C. The periodontal ligament is located between the cementum and bone. The dentinoenamel junction separates the enamel from the dentin. The Tomes' granular layer is located under the cementum. The bone and enamel do not connect.

21.

A. The mandibular canine may exhibit a bifurcated root. Mandibular canines have one cusp and generally do not have pronounced cingulums. A peg crown is associated with maxillary permanent lateral incisors.

CHAPTER

5 Nutrition and Oral Health

Linda D. Boyd, MS, RDH, RD
Carole A. Palmer, EdD, RD

contents

I. NUTRIENTS—used by the body to promote growth, maintenance, and repair. The six classes of nutrients, which are obtained from food, include carbohydrates, proteins, lipids, vitamins, minerals, and water.

A. Carbohydrates—Carbohydrates are made up of carbon, hydrogen, and oxygen. They are abundant in nature and provide a cheap source of energy—4 kcal/g. The three major classifications include monosaccharides, disaccharides, and complex polysaccharides.

1. Classifications
   a) Monosaccharides
      (1) Galactose—also known as milk sugar
         (a) Component of lactose; never found by itself in nature—always with glucose
         (b) Produced from glucose during lactation
      (2) Fructose—also known as fruit sugar or levulose
         (a) Sweetest of all sugars
         (b) Sources include honey, fruits, corn syrup, and vegetables
      (3) *Glucose*—also known as dextrose/blood sugar
         (a) Most important sugar; the final breakdown product of other carbohydrates; also the final form that circulates through the blood and is used by the tissues
         (b) Body uses this form best
         (c) Sources include honey, fruits, and corn syrup
      (4) *Sugar alcohols*—include sorbitol, mannitol, and xylitol; used as sweeteners
         (a) Poorly digested and inhibit rapid rises in blood sugar; often used by people limiting sugar intakes, such as diabetics
         (b) Poor absorption causes diarrhea
         (c) Xylitol cannot be metabolized by oral bacteria and is considered anticariogenic
            i) Chewing xylitol gum for 20 minutes after a meal causes a rise in salivary pH to > 5.5
            ii) Recommended dose is 10 g/day or two pieces of xylitol gum after each meal/snack containing fermentable carbohydrates
   b) *Disaccharides*—double sugars; vary in sweetness; digested to monosaccharides
      (1) Sucrose—table sugar
         (a) Made up of glucose and fructose
         (b) Sources include cane, beet, maple, brown, and table sugars, maple syrup, and fruits
      (2) Lactose—milk sugar
         (a) Made up of glucose and galactose
         (b) Unique to mammals
         (c) Least sweet of all simple sugars

- (3) Maltose—malt sugar
  - (a) Made up of two glucose molecules
  - (b) Exists in malt products (e.g., cereal and beer)
- c) Polysaccharides (Complex)
  - (1) Nondigestible (fiber)—resists digestion in gastrointestinal tract
    - (a) Insoluble
      - i) Cellulose—provides bulk/fiber for intestinal mobility
        - Sources include whole wheat flour, bran, and cabbage family
        - Physiological mechanism—increases fecal bulk
        - Clinical implication—may prevent constipation, hemorrhoids, and diverticulosis
      - ii) Hemicellulose
        - Sources include bran and whole grains
        - Physiological mechanism—increases fecal bulk
        - Clinical implication—may prevent constipation, hemorrhoids, and diverticulosis
      - iii) Lignin
        - Sources include fruits, mature vegetables, and whole grains
        - Physiological mechanism—decreases free radicals in gastrointestinal tract (GI) tract
        - Clinical implication—possibly anticariogenic
    - (b) Soluble—lowers blood cholesterol levels; slows glucose absorption
      - i) Pectins
        - Sources include apples and citrus fruits
        - Physiological mechanism—forms a gel with water
      - ii) Gums
        - Sources include oats, legumes, barley, and guar
        - Used as additivies, especially in dairy products (ice cream)
  - (2) Digestible
    - (a) Starch
      - i) Sources include legumes, rice, corn, potatoes, and other root vegetables
      - ii) Most important carbohydrate
    - (b) Glycogen
      - i) Animal equivalent to starch
      - ii) Storage sites—in muscle, it can supply glucose for muscle use; in liver, it helps regulate blood sugar
- d) Non-nutritive sweeteners—provide negligible calories and are noncariogenic
  - (1) Saccharin—found primarily in some soft drinks and tabletop sweeteners
  - (2) Aspartame—made from two amino acids—phenylalanine and aspartic acid
    - (a) Unstable in prolonged high heat

            (b) Sources include soft drinks, puddings, frozen desserts, and candies
        (3) Acesulfame K—can be used in baking, as well as in soft drinks
2. Functions
    a) Provide an energy source for all body tissues—source of energy for the brain and red blood cells (RBCs); yields 4 kcal/g
    b) Spares proteins so they can be used for tissue maintenance and repair instead of energy
    c) Needed for *oxidation* of fats—if diet is devoid of carbohydrates, body uses fat as energy, but not as efficiently as carbohydrates; ketone bodies are produced
    d) Regulates body processes (effect of bulk and fiber aids in *peristalsis*)
    e) Aids in palatability of diet (taste)
3. Cariogenic potential
    a) Cellulose and other fibrous carbohydrates are considered non-cariogenic
    b) Starches can be hydrolyzed to fermentable carbohydrates by the enzyme salivary amylase; breakdown begins in the mouth
        (1) Starch/sugar combinations are highly cariogenic
        (2) All monosaccharides and disaccharides are cariogenic under the *right* circumstances
        (3) Sucrose is the only carbohydrate used by *Streptococcus mutans* to form *glucans,* which permit bacterial colonies to adhere to tooth
    c) Many factors determine ultimate cariogenic potential—those specific to food include oral retention time, physical form, frequency of intake, and composition
4. Recommended intake: 55% to 60% of total calories primarily from complex carbohydrates and natural sugars
    a) Recommended fiber intake is 20 to 35 g/day
    b) Sources include
        (1) Complex carbohydrates—whole and enriched grains, cereals, pasta, rice, potatoes, legumes, and other root vegetables
        (2) Simple carbohydrates—fruits, dairy products, some vegetables (e.g., sweet corn and carrots), sweets, and soda
5. Disorders of carbohydrate metabolism
    a) Diabetes mellitus is characterized by high levels of blood glucose (hyperglycemia) resulting from insulin resistance by the body cells, impaired insulin secretion by the pancreas, and/or increased hepatic glucose production
        (1) Classifications
            (a) Insulin-dependent (Type 1; IDDM)—usually begins in childhood
            (b) Non-insulin-dependent (Type 2; NIDDM)—associated with older age, obesity, genetic component, environmental determinants, impaired glucose tolerance, physical inactivity, and race/ethnicity

(2) Symptoms
   (a) Type 1—acetone breath (fruity odor), *polyphagia, polydipsia, polyuria,* dehydration, fatigue, weight loss, and ketoacidosis
   (b) Type 2—may or may not exhibit the classic symptoms (polyphagia, polydipsia, and polyuria)
(3) Complications
   (a) Chronic complications—poor circulation, increased infections, blindness, kidney and heart disease, *neuropathy*
   (b) Oral complications—increase in periodontal disease and xerostomia
(4) Treatment goals—aimed at maintaining blood glucose levels (80 to 110 mg/dl) and glycocylated hemoglobin or hemoglobin A_1C (< 7%) as near normal as possible
   (a) Dietary control (for both Types 1 and 2)—self-monitor blood glucose 1 to 2x/week
      i) Eat a healthy, low-fat diet (20% protein, 50% carbohydrate, 30% fat)
      ii) Divide carbohydrate intake evenly throughout the day
      iii) Participate in regular physical activity
      iv) Restrict calorie intake if weight loss is needed
      v) Limit alcohol intake
   (b) Insulin—self-monitor blood glucose at least 2x/day
      i) Recommend frequent small meals to maintain blood glucose levels
      ii) Coordinate mealtimes and exercise with insulin
      iii) Schedule morning dental appointments to prevent hypoglycemic (blood glucose < 70 mg/dl) episodes
   (c) Oral medications—self-monitor blood glucose at least 1x/day

b) Hypoglycemia—low levels of blood glucose
   (1) Symptoms include mental confusion, blurred vision, weakness, agitation, shakiness, and anger
   (2) Treatment—administer treatment quickly to prevent *insulin shock*
      (a) Give 15 grams of rapidly absorbed sugar—such as orange juice or regular soda—3 glucose tablets or 1 tablespoon sugar
      (b) Wait 15 minutes and recheck blood glucose; if still not within the normal range, give another 15 grams of carbohydrate until levels are normal

c) Lactose Intolerance
   (1) Results from a deficiency of the enzyme lactase, which breaks down lactose in dairy products
   (2) Prevalent in Asians, North American blacks, and North American whites
   (3) Symptoms include abdominal cramping, flatulence, and diarrhea

(4) Diagnosis
(a) Use the "gold standard"—hydrogen breath test (the patient drinks a lactose load and then exhales into a machine, which will measure the hydrogen production. This indicates if the patient is digesting lactose)
(b) Most people self-diagnose the condition and avoid milk, results in an average calcium intake of 320 mg/day (25% of RDA); places patient at high risk of failing to achieve adequate levels of peak bone mass (risk of osteoporosis)
(5) Dietary recommendations—patient can consume
(a) Up to 1 cup of milk daily, in a divided dose with meals (as tolerated)
(b) Aged cheese (e.g., Swiss, colby, longhorn) and soft cheese (cream and cottage chesses and ricotta) because they are low in lactose
(c) Reduced lactose products
(d) Calcium-fortified products such as orange juice and cereals
(e) Nondairy sources such as broccoli, spinach, and legumes; however, they are relatively poor sources

B. Proteins—organic compounds synthesized from amino acids found in food and recirculated amino acids in the body. They are composed of carbon, hydrogen, oxygen, and nitrogen and provide 4 kcal/g.

1. Classification—all proteins are synthesized from 20 amino acids in two categories
   a) Essential amino acids—include 9
      (1) Needed for protein synthesis
      (2) Must be obtained directly from the diet
      (3) Cannot be synthesized from other amino acids
   b) Nonessential amino acids—include 11
      (1) Needed for protein synthesis
      (2) Can be synthesized in the liver from other amino acids
2. Types of proteins
   a) Complete proteins have all the essential amino acids present in the body
      (1) Can support tissue synthesis
      (2) Sources include animal and some plants, such as soy
   b) Incomplete proteins have one or more essential amino acids missing or have all amino acids, but in insufficient quantity to support tissue synthesis
      (1) *Deaminated* in liver; carbon fraction used for energy
      (2) Sources include plants, except soy
   c) Complementary proteins
      (1) Combine incomplete proteins with complementary amino acids to make complete protein (e.g., beans and rice)
      (2) Combine complete with incomplete proteins (e.g., cheeses and tortillas)

3. Functions
    a) Assist with synthesis of all body tissues
    b) Contribute to growth and maintenance
    c) Provide a source of energy if intake of fats and carbohydrates is insufficient
4. RDA—adults 0.8 g/kg
5. Food sources
    a) Complete—dairy products, meat, fish, and poultry
    b) Incomplete—whole grains, starchy vegetables, legumes, seeds, and nuts
6. Deficiency—results in abnormal growth, development, and synthesis of all tissues
    a) Protein-energy (calorie) malnutrition (PEM)
        (1) Kwashiorkor—severe protein deficiency; symptoms include delayed healing, decreased resistance to infection, skin lesions, loss of hair (alopecia) or change in hair color
        (2) Marasmus—chronic form of PEM in which the deficiency is primarily to protein energy; in advanced stages, it is characterized by muscle wasting and absence of subcutaneous fat
    b) Phenylketonuria (PKU)—inability to metabolize phenylalanine (essential amino acid); avoid aspartame found in products such as Nutrasweet and Equal

C. Lipids—insoluble in water, soluble in lipid solvents and composed of carbon, hydrogen, and oxygen. They provide 9 kcal/g of energy.

1. Classification
    a) Sterols—cholesterol is synthesized in the liver and available from the diet; needed for cell membranes and production of hormones
    b) Triglycerides are the primary form of lipids in food—in storage and blood; degree of saturation and length of carbon chain determine characteristics; made up of 1 glycerol and 3 fatty acids
        (1) Saturated fatty acids—contain only single bonds—each carbon atom has 2 hydrogen atoms attached
            (a) Usually solid at room temperature
            (b) Sources include animal fat and tropical oils
            (c) Examples: palmitic and stearic acids
            (d) High intake is associated with risk of cardiac disease
        (2) Monounsaturated fatty acids—contain one double bond
            (a) Associated with lowering serum cholesterol by lowering *low-density lipoprotein* (LDL); however, it does not lower *high-density lipoprotein* (HDL)
            (b) Sources include olive and canola oils, nuts, avocados
            (c) Example: oleic acid
        (3) Polyunsaturated fatty acids—contain more than one double bond
            (a) Lower LDL and HDL
            (b) Characteristics
                i) Usually liquid at room temperature
                ii) Sources include primarily vegetable oils

(4) Trans-fatty acids are from the *hydrogenation* of polyunsaturated oils
    (a) Can raise serum LDL levels, as do saturated fats, but may cause small lowering of HDL levels
    (b) Sources include stick margarine, shortening, commercial-frying fats, high-fat baked goods, and salty snack chips
(5) Essential fatty acids (EFA)—fatty acids the body needs, but cannot synthesize; two main EFAs are linoleic (omega-6) and linolenic (omega-3)
    (a) Precursors of eicosanoids (prostaglandins, thromboxanes, leukotrienes) and play a major role in retinal function and brain development
    (b) Sources include vegetable oils, walnuts, and wheat germ

c) Artificial fats or fat replacers—items that mimic fat in foods, but have different characteristics
   (1) Olestra®—approved by FDA in 1996
       (a) Made of sucrose with 6 to 8 fatty acids attached
       (b) Cannot be digested or absorbed; may cause excretion of fat-soluble vitamins, so products are fortified
       (c) Excess intake can cause diarrhea and gastrointestinal symptoms
   (2) Simplesse®—first fat substitute approved by the FDA
       (a) Formulated from egg white or milk protein
       (b) Provides 1 to 2 kcal/g
       (c) Cannot be used in cooking foods, because it coagulates and becomes rubbery when heated

2. Functions
   a) Provide a source of energy—9 kcal/g
   b) Act as a carrier of fat-soluble vitamins
   c) Provide a source of essential fatty acids
   d) Provide food with flavor, texture, palatability, and satiety
   e) Provide insulation and protection to body organs
3. Dietary recommendations—should not consume more than 30% of total calories; 10% of total calories should come from saturated fat
4. Food sources—animal fats, fish, poultry, vegetable oils, nuts, seeds, and dairy products
5. Diseases—overconsumption contributes to obesity, which is a major risk factor for many chronic diseases, including diabetes mellitus and cardiovascular disease

II. MICRONUTRIENTS (trace minerals)—inorganic substances required by humans in amounts less than 100 mg/day

A. Water-soluble vitamins (includes the B-complex and C vitamins)

1. Common characteristics
   a) Easily destroyed or lost during storage and cooking
   b) Absorbed through the portal system
   c) Stored in the body in very limited amounts, therefore required from the diet on a daily basis
   d) Excess is excreted in the urine and feces

2. Types
   a) Thiamin (vitamin B_1)—water-soluble; stable to dry heat; destroyed by moist heat and in the presence of alkali, such as baking soda, and by sulfur dioxide used in drying fruits
      (1) Functions as thiamin pyrophosphate (TPP)
         (a) Converts carbohydrates to fat
         (b) Converts two carbon units (transketolase reaction)
         (c) Converts amino acids, carbohydrates, and fats to energy (oxidative decarboxylation)
         (d) Converts glyoxylate to carbon dioxide
      (2) RDA—0.5 mg/1000 calories of energy intake, with a minimum intake of 1mg/day for adults
      (3) Food sources include whole/enriched grain products, legumes, and lean pork
      (4) Deficiency is no longer common in the United States
         (a) Types of thiamin deficiency diseases
            i) Beriberi ("I can't, I can't")—symptoms include mental confusion, muscular wasting and chronic poly-neuropathy, edema, anorexia, and foot and wrist drop
            (ii) Wernicke-Korsakoff syndrome—symptoms include disorientation, jerky movements of eyes, and a staggering gait
         (b) High-risk groups include alcoholics
         (c) Management is best accomplished with assistance from a professional and includes oral thiamin administration
   b) Riboflavin (vitamin B_2) is found in milk and is easily destroyed by light
      (1) Function—assists with metabolism of carbohydrates, protein, and fat as part of coenzymes flavin mononucleotide (FMN) and flavin adenine dinucleotide (FAD)
      (2) RDA is associated with protein consumption, energy intake, and body size (0.6mg/1000 calories for all ages) with a minimum of 1.2 mg/day for adults
      (3) Food sources—present in most plant and animal tissue such as eggs, lean meat, milk, broccoli, enriched breads, and cereals
      (4) Deficiency (ariboflavinosis) is rare and usually occurs concurrently with other B-complex vitamin deficiencies
         (a) Oral manifestations include edema of the pharyngeal and oral mucous membranes, *angular cheilosis, stomatitis,* and *glossitis*
         (b) High-risk groups include people with malabsorption syndromes
   c) Niacin is found in cells such as nicotimamide; can be converted from amino acid tryptophan; stable in heat
      (1) Functions
         (a) Coenzymes function as cofactors in tissue respiration, glycolysis, and other redox systems
         (b) Assists with structural repair of cells via DNA synthesis

(2) RDA is expressed as niacin equivalents because excess tryptophan (amino acid) can be broken down to produce niacin (1 niacin equivalent = 60 mg tryptophan); need is related to energy expenditure: 6.6 niacin equivalents/1000 calories
(3) Food sources include lean meats, poultry, fish, mushrooms, and peanuts
(4) Management of deficiency and/or diseases
(a) Pellegra—characterized by the 4 Ds (diarrhea, dementia, dermatitis, and death)
(b) Oral symptoms include glossitis, stomatitis, and burning mouth
(c) High-risk groups include alcoholics
(d) Treatment—provided by a physician with oral administration of 150-600 mg of nicotinic acid or nicotinamide

d) Pyroxidine (vitamin B_6) is found in 3 pyridine forms; pyridoxine, pyridoxal, and pyridoxamine; relatively heat stable in acid, but labile in alkaline
(1) Functions
(a) Assists with coenzymes involved in carbohydrate, fat, and protein metabolism
(b) Converts tryptophan to niacin
(c) Involved in heme biosynthesis
(d) Needed for neurotransmitter synthesis
(e) Helps clear blood of homocysteine
(2) RDA is 1.3 mg for adults
(3) Food sources include yeast, wheat germ, pork, glandular meats, whole-grain cereals, legumes, potatoes, bananas, and oatmeal
(4) Management of deficiency and/or disease
(a) High-risk groups include alcoholics and drug interactions (e.g., isoniazid, l-Dopa)
(b) Symptoms include hypochromic, microcytic anemia, neurologic disorders in infants and animals, stomatitis, cheilosis, glossitis, irritability, depression, and confusion
(c) Treatment involves 10 to 15 mg/day; prescribed and monitored by a medical professional
(5) Current issues
(a) Homocysteine—low intake of B_6 and folic acid are associated with high serum homocysteine which, in turn, is associated with increased risk of heart attack
(b) Deficiency is associated with decreased immunity in the elderly probably related to its function in protein synthesis

e) Folate/folic acid (pteroylglutamic acid) is readily soluble in water and destroyed when heated (50% to 90%) in neutral or alkaline media
(1) Functions
(a) Acts as a coenzyme for synthesis of purines and pyrimidines for DNA synthesis; needed for all cells that are replaced rapidly and need continuous DNA

(b) Involved in the interconversions of amino acids such as the conversion of homocysteine to methionine
(c) Interrelated with vitamin B_{12} (cobalamin); if either one is deficient, hematological changes occur
(d) Forms both red and white blood cells in the bone marrow

(2) RDA is 400 μg/day for adults
(3) Food sources include enriched breads and cereals, yeast, liver, organ meats, fresh green leafy vegetables, and legumes
(4) Management of deficiency and/or diseases

(a) Increased risk of neural tube defects (NTDs); risk can be reduced 60% with intakes of 400 micrograms for all women of childbearing age

i) Defect occurs in the first couple of weeks of pregnancy and may include cleft palate as well as spinal bifida
ii) Occurs in approximately 4000 pregnancies/year

(b) Megaloblastic anemia

i) High-risk groups include drug/nutrient interactions (e.g., methotrexate and dilantin), elderly, and alcoholics
ii) Clinical symptoms include poor growth and fainting
iii) Oral manifestations include burning tongue and oral mucosa, red and swollen tongue, and angular cheilosis
iv) Treatment should be provided and monitored by a physician

f) Vitamin B_{12} (cobalamin)

(1) Functions

(a) Essential for DNA synthesis
(b) Involved in the conversion of homocysteine to methionine

(2) Absorption

(a) Hydrochloric acid is necessary to release cobalamin from its peptide bonds
(b) Gastric secretions contain intrinsic factor, which is a protein carrier for vitamin B_{12}

(3) RDA is 2.4 μg/day for adults
(4) Food sources are found *only* in animal products such as meat, poultry, fish, and dairy products
(5) Management of deficiency and/or disease

(a) Pernicious anemia results from deficiency and causes megaloblastic anemia along with a red, beefy tongue; condition can progress to neurological damage with *paresthesia,* numbness and tingling in hands and feet, unsteadiness, *ataxia,* psychological disorders, and overt psychosis if left untreated
(b) High-risk groups include the elderly (secondary to *achlorhydria* or lack of intrinsic factor), vegetarians (lack extrinsic factor); those with resectioned stomachs or ileum

(c) Treatment is vitamin B_{12} given orally or intramuscularly (IM)

g) Pantothenic acid—widely distributed in food and deficiency is extremely rare
   (1) Functions as part of coenzyme A (CoA) which is involved in fatty acid metabolism and the TCA cycle
   (2) RDA/AI is 5 mg/day for adults

h) Biotin—synthesized by GI bacteria
   (1) Functions
      (a) Involved in gluconeogenesis, synthesis and oxidation of fatty acids, degradation of amino acids, and purine synthesis
   (2) RDA/AI is 30 μg for adults
   (3) Food sources include liver, egg yolk, soybean, and yeast
   (4) Deficiency is rare
      (a) High-risk groups include malabsorptions (biotinidase deficiency), long-term anticonvulsant therapy as in epilepsy, or diets high in raw egg whites (avidin binds biotin)
      (b) Symptoms include anorexia, nausea, mental changes, *myalgia,* localized paresthesia, squamous dermatitis of extremities, scaly seborrheic dermatitis, and sometimes alopecia (hair loss)

i) Vitamin C (ascorbic acid)—readily destroyed by heat, oxidation, and alkali
   (1) Functions
      (a) Acts as a powerful antioxidant-reducing agent
      (b) Involved as a cofactor in hydroxylation of proline and lysine in collagen formation
      (c) Participates in synthesis of tyrosine and adrenal hormones
      (d) Needed for folate metabolism and leukocyte function
      (e) Enhances iron absorption from non-animal food sources
   (2) RDA is 75 to 90 mg/day for adults
   (3) Food sources—green peppers, broccoli, strawberries, citrus fruits, tomatoes, melons, cabbage, and leafy greens
   (4) Management of deficiency and/or disease
      (a) Subclinical deficiency—symptoms include reduced enzyme activity and leukocyte function, and increased susceptibility to infection
      (b) Clinical deficiency results in scurvy—a defect in collagen synthesis
         i) Clinical symptoms include healing impairment, anemia, corkscrew hair, perifollicular petechiae (capillary hemorrhages surrounding hair follicles), bleeding in joints, joint pain, and defective skeletal calcification
         ii) Oral manifestations include hemorrhagic gingivitis with enlarged blue/red gingiva, spontaneous gingival bleeding on provocation, enlarged marginal

gingiva, interdental infarcts, loose teeth, and secondary gingival infections

(c) High-risk groups for marginal deficiency include people who consume no fruits or vegetables or discontinue massive doses of vitamin C, alcoholics, elderly people on limited diets, severely ill people under chronic stress, and infants consuming exclusively cow's milk

(d) Treatment—ingest 1 gm/day of ascorbic acid by mouth

B. Fat-soluble vitamins

1. Characteristics
   a) Soluble in organic solvents
   b) Absorbed and transported with lipids
   c) Require protein carriers
   d) Can be stored in the body tissues at toxic levels
2. Types
   a) Vitamin A (retinol, retinal, and the precursor forms: carotenes)
      (1) Functions
         (a) Required for rhodospin (for dark adaptation) and other photosensitive pigments
         (b) Maintains epithelial tissue (cornea, mucous membranes, GI lining, and skin)
         (c) Prevents infectious disease via role in epithelial tissue maintenance
         (d) Provides growth and modeling of bones and teeth
      (2) RDA
         (a) Male—900 µg/day
         (b) Female—700 µg/day
      (3) Food sources
         (a) Retinol (preformed vitamin A)—liver, butter, fish oil, egg yolk, whole milk, and fortified margarine
         (b) Carotene (provitamin A)—dark green, yellow, and orange fruits and vegetables
      (4) Management of deficiency and/or disease
         (a) Affects 1–5 million infants and preschool children in developing countries
         (b) High-risk groups include those with malabsorption and fat absorption disorders
         (c) Symptoms
            i) Clinical—includes follicular hyperkeratosis (keratin around hair follicles), night blindness, xerophthalmia (leads to blindness), Bitot's spots (dry patches on the conjunctiva)
            ii) Oral manifestations—*xerostomia,* impaired growth including teeth and bone, and reduced resistance to infection

iii) Treatment should be monitored by a physician and involves massive intermittent doses of vitamin A

(5) Prevention of toxicity

(a) Vitamin A is stored in the tissues and can reach toxic levels

i) Acute hypervitaminosis A can be induced by single doses of retinol ≥ 15,000 μg/day IU in adults

ii) Chronic hypervitaminosis A occurs with repeated intake of vitamin A in amounts at least 10 times the RDA (30,000 μg/day)

(b) High-risk groups include those with compromised liver function from drugs, hepatitis, or protein-energy malnutrition; pregnant women and children are also especially vulnerable

(c) Clinical symptoms include nausea, vomiting, fatigue, weakness, headache, bone pain, fragility, anorexia, and may cause birth defects if taken in high doses during pregnancy

(d) Oral manifestations include cheilosis and gingivitis

(e) Treatment involves discontinuing supplements; symptoms will usually disappear in weeks or months

b) Vitamin D is both a vitamin and a hormone

(1) Cholecalciferol is synthesized in the skin with exposure to sunlight and also found in animal food sources

(2) Ergocalciferol is found in plant food sources

(3) Functions

(a) Facilitates calcium absorption from intestine as well as remove and deposit bone mineral (remodeling)

(b) Maintains the blood homeostasis of calcium

(4) RDA for adults

(a) 0–50 years—5 μg

(b) 50–70 years—10 μg

(c) 70+ years—15 μg; this group has increased needs

i) Aging results in a fourfold decrease in capacity of the skin to produce vitamin D_3

ii) Many elderly have limited sun exposure

(5) Food sources include fish liver oils, *fortified* milk, margarine, and butter

(6) Management of deficiency and/or disease

(a) Rickets is a childhood disease associated with malformation of bones due to deficient mineralization of the organic matrix

i) High-risk groups include underprivileged children in northern latitudes; in the United States, black children are at higher risk because skin melanin shields conversion of 7-dehydrocholesterol to active vitamin D

(ii) Symptoms include bowlegs, knock-knees, pigeon breast, and frontal *bossing* of skull

(iii) Treatment
- Prevent by providing vitamin D supplementation to newborns until the child begins drinking fortified cow's milk at age one
- Rickets is rarely completely cured so prevention is essential

(b) Osteomalacia is a vitamin D deficiency in adulthood
i) High-risk groups include the elderly living alone, eating an inadequate diet, receiving little sunlight, and women of childbearing age who have been depleted of calcium after multiple pregnancies with inadequate diets
ii) Symptoms include softening of the bones of the extremities, spine, thorax, and pelvis, which leads to deformities, rheumatic-type pain, and general weakness
iii) Prevention
- Supply adequate dietary amounts of vitamin D, calcium, and phosphorus
- Increase exposure to ultraviolet light

iv) Treatment—provide 25–125 micrograms (1000–5000IU)/day of vitamin D along with calcium supplements under medical supervision

c) Vitamin E (tocopherol)
(1) Functions—acts as an antioxidant scavenging free radicals
(2) RDA is measured in milligrams of α-tocopherol equivalents (α-TE)
(a) Adult males—10mg α-TE
(b) Adult females—8mg α-TE
(3) Food sources include seed oils, wheat germ, fruits, vegetables, and animal fats
(4) Management of deficiency and/or disease
(a) Vitamin E deficiency is uncommon
(b) High-risk groups include those with malabsorption (e.g., cystic fibrosis and AIDS patients) or lipid transport abnormalities, and premature infants
(c) Symptoms include peripheral neuropathy
(d) Treatment is provided under medical supervision and may include water-soluble forms of the vitamin

d) Vitamin K
(1) Functions
(a) Essential as a cofactor in blood clotting
(b) Involved in bone crystalline formation
(2) RDA for men is 80 μg and for women, 65 μg
(3) Sources—microflora in the gut produces some vitamin K, the rest is obtained primarily from foods such as green leafy vegetables
(4) Management of deficiency and/or disease
(a) Deficiencies are rare

(b) High-risk groups include those with fat malabsorption problems (e.g., cystic fibrosis and celiac disease), destroyed intestinal flora through long-term antibiotic therapy, on anticoagulant therapy, and newborns

(c) Symptoms include abnormal bleeding

(d) Treatment needs vary:

i) Newborns receive vitamin K intramuscularly (IM) after delivery

ii) Those with fat malabsorption problems may require water-soluble forms

III. MACROMINERALS—Inorganic substances required by humans in amounts ≥ 100 mg/day.

A. Calcium—most abundant mineral in the body

1. Functions
   - a) Structural component of teeth and bones (99%)
   - b) Acts as a transport function in cell membranes
   - c) Assists with nerve transmission and regulation of heartbeat
   - d) Assists with blood clotting
2. Goals of DRI/AI
   - a) Build peak mass
   - b) Reduce bone loss and prevent osteoporosis
     - (1) 9 to 18 years—1300 mg/day
     - (2) 19 to 50 years—1000 mg/day
     - (3) 50+ years—1200 mg/day
3. Sources
   - a) Dairy products are best absorbed due to the presence of vitamin D and lactose; 1 cup milk = 300 mg calcium
   - b) Vegetable sources contain *phytates, oxalic acid,* and fiber, which *interfere* with absorption;
     - (1) 10 oz tofu
     - (2) 4 cups broccoli
     - (3) 6 cups cooked red beans
   - c) Fortified juices and cereals
   - d) Dietary supplements
     - (1) Calcium carbonate and malate are absorbed best; recommend sugar-free chewable tablets to reduce cariogencity
     - (2) Avoid oyster shell supplements due to possible lead contamination
4. Types of calcium deficiency diseases
   - a) Osteomalacia is associated with a vitamin D deficiency, resulting in a reduction in the mineral content of bone
   - b) Osteoporosis is loss of bone density without a change in the composition, fractures occur with minimal stress due to risk factors such as inadequate calcium and vitamin D intake, lack of weight-bearing exercise, estrogen depletion, family history, race (white or Asian), female gender, slight body build, alcohol and tobacco use, medications, and certain disease states
   - c) Management of deficiency and/or disease

(1) Encourage intake of 1000 to 1300 mg/day of calcium and 10 to 15 μg of vitamin D for those under 30 years of age to build adequate peak bone mass and to maintain bone mass in older adults

(2) Provide tobacco intervention and referral to an addiction medicine specialist for alcohol dependency/abuse

(3) Suggest to postmenopausal women not taking hormone replacement therapy to discuss the benefits and risks with their physician

(4) Encourage regular weight-bearing exercise (with a physician's approval)

B. Phosphorus—second most abundant mineral in the body

1. Functions
   a) Transfer and release of energy stored as adenosine triphosphate (ATP)
   b) Part of composition of phospholipids, DNA, and RNA
   c) Assists with metabolism of fats, carbohydrates, and proteins
   d) Acts as a buffering system
2. RDA
   a) 8 to 18 years—1250 mg/day
   b) 19 to 70+ years—700 mg/day
3. Food sources—widespread in foods, especially
   a) Proteins, such as meat, poultry, fish, eggs
   b) Milk and milk products
4. Management of deficiency and/or disease
   a) Hypophosphatemia rarely occurs in a healthy population
      (1) High-risk groups include those who excessively use phosphate-binding antacids, have *hyperparathyroidism,* alcoholism, renal insufficiency, and eating disorders
      (2) Symptoms include increased calcium excretion resulting in a negative calcium balance and bone loss
      (3) Treatment requires medial supervision

C. Magnesium—bones contain two-thirds of the body's magnesium

1. Functions
   a) Maintains calcium homeostasis and prevents skeletal abnormalities
      (1) Third most prevalent mineral found in teeth
      (2) Dentin contains two times the amount present in enamel
   b) Receives energy production from ATP
   c) Acts as a cofactor for more than 300 enzymes involved in metabolism
   d) Assists with calcium in neuromuscular transmission
2. RDA
   a) Women—320 mg/day
   b) Men—420 mg/day
3. Food sources—abundant in foods; general diet usually provides adequate amounts found in
   a) Whole grain products

b) Nuts and seeds
c) Legumes
d) Green leafy vegetables—magnesium is part of the chlorophyll molecule

4. Management of deficiency and/or disease
   a) Hypomagnesemia
      (1) High-risk groups include those undergoing renal disease, diuretic therapy, hyperthyroidism, diabetes, parathyroid gland disorders, and alcoholics
      (2) Symptoms include neuromuscular dysfunction, muscle spasm convulsions, tremors, anorexia, nausea, apathy, and cardiac arrhythmias
      (3) Treatment requires medical supervision

IV. MICROMINERALS (trace elements)—inorganic substances required by humans in amounts < 100 mg/day

A. Fluoride does not fit the strict definition of an essential nutrient because it has no known metabolic function

1. Functions
   a) Considered essential because of its beneficial effect on tooth enamel; replaces the hydroxyl ion in *hydroxyapatite* forming fluorapatite; less soluble and more resistant to acid demineralization
   b) Incorporated into the matrix of bone, improving strength and decreasing bone resorption
   c) Results in a systemic effect primarily when the teeth are forming; results in a topical effect after eruption
2. DRI/AI
   a) 6 mo. to 1 year—0.5 mg
   b) 1 to 3 years—0.7 mg
   c) 4 to 8 years—1.1 mg
   d) Adults—3.1 to 3.8 mg
3. Sources
   a) Fluoridated drinking water—62% of US water supplies are fluoridated; 1 cup of fluoridated water (1 ppm) provides approximately 0.2 mg of fluoride
   b) Fluoridated dental products—toothpaste, mouth rinses, and supplements; an average of 0.30 mg fluoride is ingested with each brushing by young children
   c) Food sources include tea, seafood, mechanically deboned poultry and food cooked in Teflon pans
      (1) Dietary intake of fluoride ranges from 0.3 to 1.0 mg/day for adults
      (2) Ready-to-feed infant formulas contain 0.1 to 0.2 mg/L of fluoride; fluoride content of powdered or liquid-concentrate formulas depends primarily on the fluoride concentration of the water used to reconstitute them and may range from 0.1 to 1.0 mg/day

4. Management of deficiency and/or disease
   a) Lack of fluoride results in an increased incidence of caries
   b) Treatment
      (1) Determine the total intake of fluoride from all sources
      (2) If below the AI, prescribe the appropriate level of supplementation
5. Tolerable upper intake levels (UL)
   a) Fluorosis—mottling of the enamel which results from excess fluoride intake during the preeruptive development of teeth
      (1) UL is 0.10 mg/kg/day for children 8 years old and younger
      (2) Fluorosis ranges from mild with whitish opaque flecks to severe with extrinsic, brownish discoloration, and varying degrees of enamel pitting depending on dose
   b) Skeletal fluorosis is characterized by dose-related calcification of ligaments, osteosclerosis, *exostosis,* osteoporosis of long bones, muscle wasting, and neurological defects due to hypercalcification of the vertebrae; UL for people 7 to 70+ years is 10 mg/day

B. Iron

1. Functions
   a) Acts as a component of hemoglobin which transports oxygen
   b) Acts as a catalyst for oxidative reactions in cells including ATP production
   c) Essential for normal immune function
   d) Critical for normal brain function
2. RDA—18 mg/day for adults
3. Food sources include meats, egg yolk, dark green vegetables, and enriched cereals
   a) Heme sources of iron found in animal products are absorbed with about 25% efficiency compared with nonheme sources absorbed at 5%
   b) Factors that enhance absorption include vitamin C, animal proteins, increased gastric acidity
   c) Factors that decrease absorption include the presence of phytates and oxalates, as well as coffee and tea consumption
4. Management of deficiency and/or disease
   a) Most common nutritional deficiency among children and women of childbearing age
   b) Iron deficiency anemia results in hypochromic, microcytic anemia
      (1) High-risk groups include infants less than 2 years of age, teenage girls, pregnant women, and elderly people
      (2) Clinical symptoms include fatigue, pale conjunctiva of eye, tachycardia, anorexia, pica (especially ice eating), koilonychia (spoon-shaped fingernails), and gastritis
      (3) Oral manifestations include atrophy of the lingual papillae, burning and redness of the tongue, angular stomatitis, and dysphagia
      (4) Treat with ferrous sulfate or ferrous gluconate supplements

5. Toxicity—iron overload results in oxidative damage to body cells/organs
   a) Hemochromatosis—genetic disease found in 1% of population
      (1) High-risk groups include men who have no mechanism for losing iron
      (2) Symptoms include fatigue, weakness, chronic abdominal pain, aching joints, *hepatomegaly*, skin pigmentation, diabetes mellitus, arthritis, cancer, and heart disease
      (3) Treatment includes drawing blood 2–3 times/week to remove excess iron and limiting heme sources of iron in the diet

C. Zinc

1. Functions
   a) Act as a cofactor in more than 120 enzymes involved in cell growth and reproduction
   b) Involved in fat, carbohydrate, and protein metabolism
   c) Stabilizes DNA and RNA in the cell nucleus
   d) Essential for bone growth including osteoblastic activity, formation of bone enzymes, and calcification
   e) Involved in collagen synthesis
   f) Supports immune function
   g) Enhances taste and appetite
2. RDA
   a) Women—8 mg/day
   b) Men—11 mg/day
3. Food sources include protein-rich foods
   a) Glucose, lactose, red wine, and soy protein enhance absorption
   b) High intakes of calcium, iron, copper, fiber, phytates, and phosphate salts interfere with absorption
4. Management of deficiency and/or disease
   a) High-risk groups include pregnant women, elderly, vegans, and alcoholics
   b) Symptoms include loss of taste acuity, poor appetite, impaired wound healing and growth, mild anemia, skin lesions, and hypogonadism
   c) Oral manifestations include changes to the epithelium of the tongue (such as thickening of the epithelium), an increase in cell numbers, and flattened filiform papillae
   d) Treatment should be monitored by a physician and registered dietitian
5. Toxicity
   a) Chronic ingestion of 100–300 mg/day may result in toxicity
   b) Symptoms include vomiting, diarrhea, epigastric pain, lethargy, fatigue, renal damage, and pancreatitis

D. Copper

1. Functions
   a) Forms red blood cells
   b) Acts as a catalyst in the formation of collagen; involved in the cross-linking of collagen necessary for tensile strength

c) Acts as a cofactor in oxidative reactions and production of neurotransmitters

2. RDA—900 µg/day
3. Food sources include shellfish, liver, nuts, sesame and sunflower seeds, legumes, and cocoa
4. Deficiency occurs rarely in genetic syndromes, such as *Menkes' syndrome* and malabsorption syndromes; symptoms include neutropenia, bone demineralization, hair and skin depigmentation; causes failure of iron absorption leading to anemia

E. Other Trace Minerals—iodine, chromium, cobalt, and selenium

1. Functions
    a) Iodine and selenium—involved in thyroid hormone activity
    b) Selenium—acts with antioxidants to reduce cell damage from free radicals
    c) Chromium—potentiate insulin action
    d) Cobalt—constituent of vitamin B_{12}
2. Food sources include seafood, liver, poultry, milk, grains, and iodized salt
3. Deficiencies are rare, except for iodine
    a) 1 billion people worldwide are at risk for iodine deficiency
    b) Symptoms include goiter, cretinism, shortened stature, and hypothyroidism

F. Electrolytes—compounds or ions that dissociate in solution

1. Sodium—major cation of extracellular fluid
    a) Functions
        (1) Regulates extracellular fluids
        (2) Aids in conduction of nerve impulses
        (3) Involved in control of muscle contraction
    b) Estimate of requirements for adults is 500 mg/day
    c) Food sources include table salt and protein-rich foods
    d) Deficiency—hyponatremia occurs when sodium losses exceed water losses
        (1) High-risk groups include those who use excessive diuretics, hyperglycemia in diabetics, and heat exhaustion
        (2) Symptoms include nausea, abdominal cramps, headache, confusion, lethargy, and coma
2. Chloride—principal anion in extracellular fluids
    a) Functions
        (1) Maintains water balance and osmotic pressure
        (2) Maintains acid-base balance in body fluids
    b) Estimate of requirements for adults is 750 mg/day
    c) Food source is primarily table salt
    d) Deficiency results in a loss of appetite, failure to thrive, muscle lethargy, and severe metabolic alkalosis
3. Potassium—major cation of intracellular fluid
    a) Functions
        (1) Maintains intracellular fluid levels
        (2) Regulates muscle contraction
        (3) Facilitates transmission of nerve impulses

(4) Regulates acid-base balance

b) Estimate of requirements of adults is 2000 mg/day

c) Food sources include fruits, vegetables, and fresh meats

d) Deficiency is rare

G. Water—accounts for 50–60% of body weight

1. Functions
   a) Acts as a solvent and medium for all reactions
   b) Participates as a substrate in metabolic reactions
   c) Essential as a structural component of cells
   d) Essential to the physiological processes of digestion, absorption, and excretion
   e) Transport medium for nutrients and body substances
   f) Involved in electrolyte balance and homeostasis
2. Recommended intake
   a) 1 ml per calorie for adults or about 2 to 3 quarts/day
   b) 1.5 ml per calorie for infants
3. Dehydration may occur due to
   a) Insufficient water intake—high risk groups include infants, elderly, the sick, and heavily exercising athletes
   b) Excessive water losses—causes include excess diuretic use, vomiting, blood loss, kidney disorders, and diarrhea

V. NUTRITION IN ORAL HEALTH

A. Systemic effects of nutrients

1. Hard tissues of the oral cavity
   a) Teeth and alveolar bone are made up of collagen fibers in which hydroxyapatite crystals are deposited
      (1) Collagen is a protein matrix synthesized by fibroblasts and is a component of the connective tissues of the gingiva and periodontal ligament, as well as the ground substance for the deposition of minerals to form teeth and bone
         (a) Vitamin C is required for hydroxylation of the amino acids proline and lysine, to form hydroxyproline and hydroxylysin, which are essential precursors of collagen biosynthesis
         (b) Copper is essential for the cross-linking of the collagen fibers and provides tensile strength
         (c) Other nutrients necessary for collagen synthesis and maintenance include zinc, vitamin A, silicon, and manganese
      (2) Odontoblasts and ameloblasts require the same nutrients involved in collagen biosynthesis to synthesize the protein matrix of the dentin and enamel; deficiency during the preeruptive stage may result in hypoplasia
      (3) Hydroxyapatite forms the calcified structure of the tooth/bone and requires calcium, phosphorus, magnesium, boron, manganese, vitamin K, and vitamin D; bone is constantly being remodeled by osteoblastic and osteoclastic activity and a constant supply of necessary nutrients is required to maintain bone and prevent bone loss

TABLE 5-1 OVERVIEW OF NUTRIENTS

Nutrient	Major Functions	Deficiency Symptoms	Oral Manifestations of Deficiency	Symptoms of Nutrient Excesses	Dietary Sources	Recommendations	Upper Tolerable Intake Levels
Macronutrients							
Carbohydrate	Energy source (4 kcal/g) Spares protein Needed for oxidation of fats			Dental caries	Complex CHOs: whole and enriched grains, cereals, pasta, and rice Simple CHOs: fruits, dairy, soda, baked goods	CHO: 55% to 60% of total calories Simple CHOs: ≤ 10% of total calories Fiber: 20 to 35 g/day	
(Fibers)	Facilitates normal peristalsis						
Protein	Synthesis of body tissues Growth and maintenance Source of energy w/↓ fat and ↓ CHO intake	Kwashiorkor Marasmus Abnormal growth, development, and synthesis of tissues	Lag period in initiation of wound healing Compromised antibacterial properties of saliva		Complete: dairy, meat, fish, eggs, soy, and poultry Incomplete: whole grains, legumes, nuts, and vegetables	Adults: 0.8 g/kg of body wt/day; 10% to 15% of total calories	
Fat	Source of energy (9 kcal/g) Carries fat-soluble vitamins Source of essential fatty acids Provides insulation and protection to body organs Satiety	Essential fatty acid deficiency symptoms: Scaly skin Hair loss Impaired wound healing		Obesity ↑ incidence of cardiovascular disease, Type 2 diabetes mellitus, hypertension, and some forms of cancer	Meats, fish, and poultry Vegetable oils, nuts, and seeds Dairy products	Fat ≤ 30% of total calories Saturated fat < 10% of total calories Essential fatty acids: Linoleic acid: 1% to 2% of total calories Linolenic acid: 3 to 6 g/day	
Micronutrients							
Water-Soluble Vitamins							
Thiamin (B_1)	Coenzyme in CHO metabolism	Beriberi Mental confusion Muscular wasting Chronic polyneuropathy			Lean pork Wheat germ Enriched breads and cereals Egg yolk Legumes	Males 14–70+ yr: 1.2 mg/day Females 19–70+ yr: 1.1 mg/day	None

(continued)

TABLE 5-1 OVERVIEW OF NUTRIENTS (*continued*)

Nutrient	Major Functions	Deficiency Symptoms	Oral Manifestations of Deficiency	Symptoms of Nutrient Excesses	Dietary Sources	Recommen-dations	Upper Tolerable Intake Levels
Thiamin (B_1)		Anorexia Wernicke-Korsakoff Disorientation Jerky movements of eyes Staggering gait			Whole grains		
Riboflavin (B_2)	Part of coenzyme CHO, fat, and protein metabolism	Photophobia Loss of visual acuity Burning and itching of the eyes Ariboflavinosis Oral symptoms Greasy eruption of the skin in the nasolabial fold	Soreness and burning of lips, mouth, and tongue Edema of pharyngeal and oral mucous membranes Angular cheilosis Stomatitis Glossitis—purple swollen tongue		Milk products Organ meats Lean meats Eggs Green leafy vegetables	Males 14–70+ yr: 1.3 mg/day Females 19–70+ yr: 1.1 mg/day	None
Niacin (B_3)	Part of coenzyme in release of energy from CHO, fat, and protein Structural repair of cells via DNA synthesis	Muscular weakness Anorexia Indigestion Skin eruptions Pellegra—the Ds Dermatitis Dementia Diarrhea	Irritation and inflammation of mucous membranes of the mouth Sore tongue (beefy tongue)	Liver toxicity "Flushing"	Lean meats, fish, and poultry Peanuts Enriched breads and cereals	Males 14–70+ yr: 16 mg/day Females 14–70+ yr: 14 mg/day	Adults: 30 mg/day
Pyroxidine (B_6)	Coenzyme in protein metabolism Conversion of tryptophan to niacin Neurotransmitter synthesis	Hypochromic, microcytic anemia Neurological disorders Confusion Irritability Depression	Stomatitis Cheilosis Glossitis	Severe sensory neuropathy	Yeast Wheat germ Pork Whole grain cereals Legumes Bananas	Males 14–50 yr: 1.7 mg/day Females 19–50 yr: 1.5 mg/day	Adults: 100 mg/day
Folate/Folic Acid	Coenzyme in DNA synthesis Interconversion of amino acids Formation of WBCs and RBCs	Alteration of DNA synthesis Megaloblastic anemia Poor growth GI disturbances Neural tube defects	Burning tongue and oral mucosa Red and swollen tongue Angular cheilosis		Liver Legumes Dark green leafy vegetables Lean Beef Potatoes	Adults 14–70+ yr: 400 μg/day	Adults: 1000 g/day

Folate/Folic Acid	Interrelationship with vitamin B_{12}				Enriched breads and cereals		
Cobalamin (B_{12})	Required for DNA synthesis	Pernicious anemia Megaloblastic anemia Neurological damage with paresthesia Numbness and tingling in hands and feet Unsteadiness Psychological disorders	Red, beefy tongue		Animal products *only* Meat, poultry, and fish Dairy products Eggs	Adults 14–70+ yr: 2.4 μg/day	None
Vitamin C (Ascorbic acid)	Antioxidant Cofactor in hydroxylation of proline and lysine in collagen formation Needed in folate metabolism Enhances iron absorption	Scurvy Healing impairment Defective skeletal calcification Joint pain Bruise easily Follicular hyperkeratosis	Swollen, hemorrhagic gingivitis Enlarged marginal gingivae Loose teeth Dryness of the mouth	Diarrhea "Rebound scurvy" after sudden discontinuation of massive doses of vitamin C	Citrus fruits Leafy green vegetables Green peppers Broccoli Tomatoes Potatoes Melons	Males: 90 mg/day Female: 75 mg/day	2000 mg/day
Fat-Soluble Vitamins							
Vitamin A (preformed: retinal and retinol) (precursor: carotenes)	Required for rhodopsin and other photosensitive pigments Cellular differentiation and proliferation Integrity of the immune system	Ocular changes from night blindness to xerophthalmia Increased susceptibility to infection Loss of appetite Hyperkeratosis	Xerostomia Impaired growth of teeth and bone Poor wound healing	Nausea and vomiting Fatigue Weakness Birth defects if taken in excess during pregnancy Bone pain and fragility	Retinol Liver Fish oil Fortified milk and margarine Carotene dark green, yellow, and orange fruits and vegetables	Males: 900 μg/day Females: 700 μg/day	3000 μg/day

(continued)

TABLE 5–1 OVERVIEW OF NUTRIENTS (*continued*)

Nutrient	Major Functions	Deficiency Symptoms	Oral Manifestations of Deficiency	Symptoms of Nutrient Excesses	Dietary Sources	Recommendations	Upper Tolerable Intake Levels
Vitamin D (cholecalciferol)	Facilitates calcium absorption Maintains blood homeostasis of calcium	Rickets (in children) Inadequate mineralization of the skeleton resulting in bowlegs, pigeon breast, and frontal bossing of the skull Osteomalacia (in adults) Softening of bones in the extremeties, spine, thorax, and pelvis General weakness		Hypercalcemia Hypercalciuria Deposition of calcium in soft tissues and irreversible renal and cardiovascular damage Death	Fish liver oils Fortified milk, margarine, and butter	0–50 yr: 5 μg/day 50–70 yr: 10 μg/day 70+ yr: 15 μg/day	Adults: 50 μg/day
Vitamin E (tocopherols)	Antioxidant scavenging free radicals	Peripheral neuropathy		Relatively nontoxic when taken by mouth High doses may interfere with blood clotting	Vegetable oils Wheat germ Nuts	Adults: 15 mg/day	Adults: 1000 mg/day
Vitamin K	Cofactor in blood clotting Involved in bone crystalline formation	Abnormal bleeding		Hemolytic anemia	Green leafy vegetables	Adults: Males 80 μg/day Females 65 μg/day	
Macrominerals							
Calcium	Component of teeth and bones (99%) Transport function in cell membranes Nerve transmission and regulation of heart beat Blood clotting	Osteoporosis Amount of bone ↓ and bone fractures with minimal stress	Possible association with alveolar bone loss	Constipation Possible ↑ risk of urinary stone formation Inhibition of absorption of iron and zinc	Dairy products Fortified juices and cereals Legumes Green, leafy vegetables	9–18 yr: 1300 mg/day 19–50 yr: 1000 mg/day 50+ yr: 1200 mg/day	Adults: 2500 mg/day

Phosphorus	Component of bone mineral Transfer of energy as ATP Component of phospholipids, DNA, and RNA Involved in metabolism of fats, CHOs, and proteins	Bone loss Weakness Anorexia Malaise Pain		↓ blood calcium level	Meat, poultry, and fish Eggs Dairy products	8–18 yr: 1250 mg/day 19–70+ yr: 700 mg/day	Adults: 4 g/day
Magnesium	Maintain calcium homeostasis Energy production from ATP Cofactor for over 300 enzymes involved in metabolism	Neuromuscular dysfunction Muscle spasms Convulsions Tremors Anorexia Cardiac arrhythmias		Nausea and vomiting Hypotension Bradycardia	Whole grains Nuts and seeds Legumes Green, leafy vegetables	Males 30–70+ yr: 420 mg/day Females 30–70+ yr: 320 mg/day	> 9 yr: 350 mg/day (nonfood Mg)
Trace Minerals							
Fluoride	Anticaries effect on tooth enamel Incorporated in bone matrix ↑ strength and ↓ bone resorption		↑ incidence of caries	Dental fluorosis Skeletal fluorosis	Flouridated water Flouridated dental products Tea Seafood Mechanically deboned poultry Food cooked in Teflon pans	6–12 mo: 0.5 mg/day 1–3 yr: 0.7 mg/day 4–8 yr: 1.1 mg/day	0–6 mo: 0.7 mg/day 6–12 mo: 0.9 mg/day 1–3 yr: 1.3 mg/day 4–8 yr: 2.2 mg/day 9–70 yr: 10 mg/day
Iron	Component of hemoglobin Catalyst cellular reactions Essential for immune function Critical for brain function	Microcytic, hypochromic anemia Fatigue Pale conjunctivae of eyes Anorexia Gastritis Koilonychia (spoon-shaped fingernails)	Atrophy of lingual papillae Burning, red tongue Angular stomatitis Dysphagia	Hemochromatosis Fatigue Weakness Chronic abdominal pain Skin pigmentation Aching joints ↑ risk of heart disease, diabetes mellitus, and cancer	Heme iron Meats, fish, and poultry Eggs Nonheme iron Enriched breads and cereals Dark green leafy vegetables	Adults: Males 8mg/day Females 15 mg/day 19–50 yr: 18 mg/day 50 yr: 8 mg/day	45 mg/day

(continued)

TABLE 5–1 OVERVIEW OF NUTRIENTS (*continued*)

Nutrient	Major Functions	Deficiency Symptoms	Oral Manifestations of Deficiency	Symptoms of Nutrient Excesses	Dietary Sources	Recommendations	Upper Tolerable Intake Levels
Zinc	Cofactor > 100 enzymes in cell growth Coenzyme energy metabolism Stabilizes DNA and RNA Involved in collagen synthesis Formation of bone enzymes and calcification Taste and appetite Immune function	Poor appetite Skin lesions Impaired growth and wound healing	Loss of taste acuity Flattened filiform papillae of the tongue Thickening of the epithelium of the tongue	Vomiting Diarrhea Epigastric pain Lethargy Fatigue Renal damage	Protein-rich foods	Adults: Males 11 mg/day Females 8 mg/day	40 mg/day
Copper	Formation of red blood cells Cross-linking of collagen	Neutropenia Bone demineralization Hair and skin depigmentation			Shellfish Liver Nuts and seeds Legumes Cocoa	Adults: 900 µg/day	10 mg/day
Electrolytes							
Sodium	Regulates extracellular fluids Aids in conduction of nerve impulses Control of muscle contraction	Hyponatremia Nausea Abdominal cramps Headache Confusion Lethargy Coma		Edema Hypertension	Table salt Protein-rich foods (meats and dairy)	Adults: 500 mg/day	
Chloride	Maintains water balance and osmotic pressure Maintains acid-base balance	Loss of appetite Failure to thrive Muscle lethargy Severe metabolic alkalosis			Table salt	Adults: 750 mg/day	

Potassium	Maintains intracellular fluid Regulation of muscle contraction Regulates acid-base balance Facilitates nerve transmission	Hypokalemia Weakness Nausea Listlessness Anorexia		Cardiac effects Death	Fruits Vegetables Meats	Adults: 2000 mg/day
Water	Universal solvent Medium for metabolic reactions Structural component of cells Transport medium for nutrients Involved in electrolyte balance and homeostasis	Dehydration Weight loss Hypotension Orthostatic hypotension Dry skin ↓ skin turgor ↓ urinary output	Xerostomia Shrinkage of mucous membranes	Water intoxication Headache Nausea and vomiting Muscle twitching Convulsion Blurring of vision	Drinking water Soft drinks Liquid milk Fruits and vegetables	1 ml/kcal or about 2–3 L

CHO, carbohydrate; WBC, white blood cell; RBC, red blood cell; RE, retinol equivalent; ATP, adenosine triphosphate.

(4) Fluoride added to the hydroxyapatite crystal reduces solubility of substance to acids, making it more caries-resistant

2. Soft tissues of the oral cavity
   a) Oral mucosa is made up of nonkeratinized tissues that line the oral cavity, except for the keratinized tissues found on the hard palate, gingiva, and dorsum of the tongue
      (1) Nutrients required for maintenance of tissues include the B-complex vitamins, iron, vitamins A and C, zinc, and protein
      (2) Oral cavity may be first site to exhibit signs and symptoms of systemic disease or nutritional deficiencies for several reasons
         (a) Rapid rate of cell turnover, every 3–7 days
         (b) Tissues are under constant attack by microorganisms
         (c) High risk of trauma to oral tissues
   b) Salivary glands
      (1) Functions of saliva
         (a) Lubricates the oral mucosa
         (b) Buffers to maintain a neutral pH
         (c) Contains minerals that aid in remineralization
         (d) Increases oral clearance of bacterial substrates
         (e) Possesses antimicrobial properties
      (2) Deficient intakes of protein, vitamin A, and iron may result in reduced salivary flow due to salivary gland dysfunction

B. Local effects of nutrients on dental caries

1. Dietary carbohydrates
   a) Caries process involves the hydrolyzing of mono- and disaccharides by enzyme salivary amylase to form sucrose, glucose, and fructose
      (1) These sugars are substrates for bacterial plaque, primarily *Streptococcus* and *Lactobacillus,* which produce acids (e.g., acetic, formic, lactic, carboxylic, propionic)
      (2) The critical pH for demineralization of enamel is 5.5 or less; pH remains low for 20 to 30 minutes after ingestion of fermentable carbohydrates
   b) Caries prevention must focus on modifying the causative factors
      (1) Remove plaque
      (2) Increase resistance of tooth to demineralization with topical fluorides
      (3) Modify cariogenic dietary factors
         (a) Evaluate oral retentiveness or length of time teeth are exposed to a lowered pH
            i) High sucrose foods deliver high sugar levels, but only for a short time and generally are not retained on tooth
            ii) Highly retentive, starchy foods (cookies, crackers, dry cereals, pretzels, and potato chips) are more cariogenic because they deliver a progressively increasing concentration of sugars over a prolonged

period as the starch particles, entrapped on the tooth, are hydrolyzed by the bacteria

(b) Frequency of eating meals and snacks; linear relationship between caries incidence and the number of snacks

(c) Physical form of the carbohydrate

i) Liquid forms are often found in acidic mediums such as soft and sports drinks and fruit drinks/juices that enhance demineralization

ii) Sticky carbohydrates, such as raisins and fruit leathers, are highly retentive and cariogenic

(d) Length of interval between meals/snacks

(e) Sequence of food consumption

i) *Anticariogenic* or cariostatic foods eaten at the end of a meal prevent the lowering of the pH

ii) Cariostatic foods such as meat are high in protein and fat

iii) Cheese is anticariogenic; when eaten after sucrose intake, it shortens the length of time the pH remains in the critical area from 15 to 20 minutes to 5 minutes

(f) Amount of fermentable carbohydrate consumed

i) In one study, the elderly (65–74 years of age) consumed 47% to 53% more sugar-containing foods than did 19–24 year olds

ii) Patients with root caries were found to consume twice the sugary liquids and 50% more cakes and cookies than a healthy control group

iii) A study group with root caries consumed 40% more sugar and 32% more starch than those without root caries

(g) Sugar concentration of the food or beverage

(h) Proximity of eating to bedtime—primarily a problem if thorough plaque removal does not occur; salivary secretions decrease during sleep

2. Topical fluoride—enhances the rate of remineralization of the enamel and dentin and reduces the acid production in dental plaque

C. Maintenance of periodontal health

1. Lack of nutrients does not cause periodontal disease, but it may be a modifying factor once the disease process has been initiated
2. Effects of nutrition in periodontal health and disease
   a) Healthy epithelial tissue prevents the penetration of bacterial endotoxins into the subgingival tissue; increased permeability of the gingival barrier at the gingival sulcus occurs with deficiencies of vitamin C, folate, and zinc
   b) Maintenance of the integrity of the host's immune response—important nutrients in the body's immune response include protein, iron, zinc, and vitamin E
   c) Calcification of the alveolar bone and cementum—for maintenance of the calcified tissues, good supplies of protein, calcium,

phosphorus, vitamin D, magnesium, vitamin K, and zinc are required

d) Stimulation of salivary flow to aid in oral clearance—may be enhanced by chewing firm, coarse, and fibrous foods

e) Repair and healing process—include protein, vitamins A and C, folate, calcium, iron, and zinc in diet

f) Amount and type of supragingival plaque—avoid sugar-rich foods, which enhance undesirable bacteria and use preventive measures to remove plaque from the teeth

VI. NUTRITION SCREENING

A. Purpose—to identify patients at nutritional risk

B. Methods

1. Nutrition Screening Initiative—developed to screen older adults for nutritional risk
   a) Forms are simple and can be completed by the patient
   b) Screening questions address a number of issues (medical, dental, psychosocial) that may affect a patient's food intake resulting in nutritional inadequacies
2. Screening for caries risk
   a) Determine the frequency of meals and snacks
   b) Identify habits, such as frequent use of gum, breath mints, cough drops, or antacids, that may contribute to caries risk
   c) Identify sources of simple and retentive carbohydrates in the diet

VII. ASSESSMENT OF NUTRITIONAL STATUS

A. Standards for dietary intake

1. Dietary Reference Intake (DRI) will replace the periodic revisions of the Recommended Dietary Allowances (RDA)
   a) Purpose—will encompass not only prevention of deficiency disease, but also
      (1) Role of nutrients in decreasing the risk of chronic and other diseases and conditions
      (2) Upper limits beyond which toxicity may occur
   b) Components
      (1) Estimated Average Requirement (EAR)—meets estimated needs of 50% of individuals in a given age and gender group
      (2) Adequate Intake (AI)—experimentally observed estimates of nutrient intake that appear to reduce the risk of chronic and other diseases and conditions; uncertainty in data prevents specific RDA
      (3) Recommended Dietary Allowance (RDA)—meets nutrient needs of 97% of healthy people
      (4) Tolerable Upper Intake Level (UL)—maximum intake that is unlikely to pose risk of adverse health effects in 97% of the population
2. Dietary guidelines
   a) Goals
      (1) Provide an adequate and balanced diet that meets the nutritional needs of an individual for maintenance, repair,

growth or development, and to maintain the living processes
   (2) Help reduce the risks of developing chronic degenerative diseases
b) Federal Dietary Guidelines
   (1) USDA Food Guide Pyramid
      (a) Visual representation of what foods should be eaten in greater quantities; eat mostly foods from the bottom of the pyramid that are high in fiber and antioxidant nutrients (e.g., vegetables and fruits) and fewer from the top (e.g., fats)
      (b) Foods in each group provide similar nutrient levels while providing variety
      (c) Recommendations
         i) 6 to 11 servings of breads, cereals, rice, and pasta
         ii) 3 to 5 servings of vegetables
         iii) 2 to 4 servings of fruit
         iv) 2 to 3 servings of dairy products
         v) 2 to 3 servings of meat, eggs, beans, and nuts
         vi) Spare use of fats, oils, and sweets
   (2) Dietary Guidelines for Americans
      (a) Eat a variety of foods
      (b) Maintain a healthy weight
      (c) Choose a diet low in fat, saturated fat, and cholesterol—less than 30% of calories should come from fat and less than 10% of calories from saturated fat

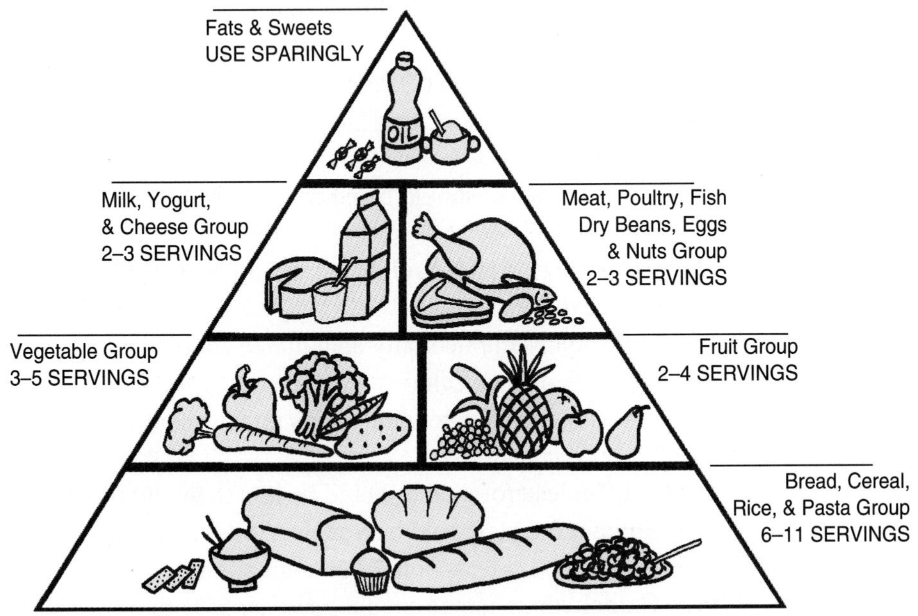

FIGURE 5-1. The Food Guide Pyramid

2000 Dietary Guidelines for Americans

ABCs for your health—Aim, Build, Choose

- Aim for fitness
  - Aim for a healthy weight
  - Be physically active each day
- Build for a healthy base
  - Let the Pyramid guide your food choices
  - Choose a variety of grains daily, especially whole grains
  - Choose a variety of fruits and vegetables daily
  - Keep food safe to eat
- Choose sensibly
  - Choose a diet that is low in saturated fat and cholesterol and moderate in total fat
  - Choose beverages and foods that limit your intake of sugar
  - Choose and prepare foods with less salt
  - If you drink alcoholic beverages, do so in moderation

(d) Choose a diet with plenty of vegetables, fruits, and grain products every day

(e) Use salt, sodium, sugars only in moderation

(f) Avoid alcoholic beverages; if one drinks, do so in moderation (1 drink/day for women, 2 drinks/day for men)

c) National groups

(1) American Cancer Society's Guidelines for Diet, Nutrition, and Cancer Prevention

(a) Choose most of the foods consumed from plant sources

(b) Limit intake of high-fat foods, particularly from animal sources

(c) Be physically active; achieve and maintain a healthy weight

(d) Limit consumption of alcoholic beverages, if one drinks

(2) American Heart Association Dietary Recommendations for Healthy People

(a) Total fat intake should be no more than 30% of total calories

i) Saturated fatty acid intake should be 8 to 10% of total calories

ii) Polyunsaturated fatty acid intake should be up to 10% of total calories

iii) Monounsaturated fatty acids intake should be 15% of total calories

iv) Cholesterol intake should be less than 300 mg/day

(b) Sodium intake should be less than 2400 mg/day, which is about 1 1/4 teaspoons of sodium chloride (salt)

(c) Carbohydrate intake should make up 55% to 60% or more of calories, with emphasis on increasing sources of complex carbohydrates

(d) Total calories should be adjusted to achieve and maintain a healthy body weight

(3) American Heart Association/National Cholesterol Education Program (AHA/NCEP)

(a) Step I Diet is the same as the recommendations for healthy people

(b) Step II Diet reduces saturated fat to 7% or less of total calories and cholesterol intake to less than 200 mg/day

B. Methods of evaluating dietary data

1. Use of dietary guidelines to determine overall dietary adequacy is most efficient in the dental office due to limited time and nutritional knowledge
2. Determine cariogenicity of dietary habits—evaluate frequency and type of retentive starches and sugars consumed
3. Computer analysis—enter all foods into a database

a) Evaluate overall nutrient intakes compared to RDAs—an intake below the RDA does not necessarily mean the patient is deficient

(1) Advantage—accurate and detailed information on nutrient intake

(2) Disadvantage—difficult to translate individual nutrients into the types of foods the patient needs to include in the diet to obtain the desired nutrients

b) Percentage of simple sugars—complex carbohydrates can be obtained

(1) Advantage—helpful in identifying sources of sugars

(2) Disadvantage—does not identify retentive starches and it is difficult to assess frequency of sugar exposure

VIII. NUTRITION ASSESSMENT AND COUNSELING

A. Methods of data gathering for nutrient assessment

1. Food Frequency Questionnaire (FFQ)

a) Consists of a multiple page survey listing a variety of foods and asking the patient how often the foods are consumed over a period of time—usually from 6 months to a year

b) Advantages

(1) Requires little "in office" time

(2) Allows analysis of food group/general nutrient intakes over time

c). Disadvantages

(1) Provides general dietary information

(2) Cannot evaluate daily frequency of sugar and snacking

(3) Relies on patient memory for frequency of intake over a long period

2. 24 hour dietary recall

a) Patient is asked to remember everything consumed during the past 24 hours; interviewer writes everything down and asks probing questions in order to gather more detail

b) Advantages

(1) Allows analysis of food group and nutrient consumption

(2) Can be done quickly
(3) Gathers data to evaluate sugar/fat intake
c) Disadvantages
(1) Patient may not accurately remember the kinds and amounts of food and beverage intake
(2) Interviewer needs experience asking open-ended questions
(3) Represents only 1 day of food intake, which may not be typical of the patient's usual diet
(4) There is a tendency to overreport low intakes and to underreport high intakes
3. 3-to-7-day food record
a) Requires patient to record the type and amount of food and beverages consumed
b) Advantages
(1) Allows evaluation of an average intake over a number of days
(2) Saves "in office" time
(3) Allows analysis of food group/nutrient consumption and eating patterns
c) Disadvantages
(1) Time-consuming for the patient and compliance is low
(2) Requires a highly trained person to evaluate the results obtained and develop individual recommendations

B. Nutrition Counseling

1. Components of nutrition counseling
a) Interviewing—obtaining information from the patient
b) Teaching—nonpersonal, transfer of information
c) Counseling—personalized working relationship with the patient to help him/her solve a problem or issue
d) Follow-up and monitor progress
2. Requirements for successful counseling
a) Provide conducive environment
(1) Physical environment—provide a private place with no interruptions or threatening surroundings (e.g., dental drill) and work with patient at eye level
(2) Patient readiness—work with patient who is not too tired or scared, in a hurry, or has past negative experiences, and is interested in self-help
(3) Counselor readiness—shares good attitude; not overstressed or in a hurry; provides an unbiased acceptance of all patients in word and body language

C. Interviewing Skills

1. Encourage patient to talk about his/her lifestyle and daily habits
2. Use open-ended questions to determine values, concepts, and attitudes
3. Use closed-ended questions to establish facts
4. Provide active listening—listen to what is being said and probe further; ask for clarification and acknowledge listening to patient
5. Be nonjudgmental—provide neither negative nor positive verbal or nonverbal judgments on patient's statements or habits

6. Provide attending skills—maintain eye contact, nod head, or use other means of confirmation to indicate listening without judgment

D. Teaching Skills

1. Determine patient's knowledge first
2. Clarify confusion; fill in knowledge gaps
3. Educate patient on the link between nutrition and oral and general health
4. Elicit continuous feedback to ensure patient comprehension
5. Provide appropriate amount of information to meet patient's needs; avoid being too simple or complex
6. Use appropriate visuals, including patient's own mouth and radiographs

E. Counseling Skills

1. Help patient assess his/her own diet
2. Have patient summarize results and findings
3. Have patient determine suggestions for changes
   a) Basic dietary adequacy
   b) Cariogenic dietary habits
4. Suggest basic diet adequacy
5. Suggest cariogenic risk factors
6. Have patient set goals for improvement
7. Provide suggestions and strategies when needed
8. Summarize with "reality check" and obtain verbal commitment for course of action
9. Monitor patient's progress from visit to visit

IX. NUTRITION CONSIDERATIONS IN THE LIFE CYCLE

A. Infancy

1. Early childhood caries—a pattern of severe caries beginning prior to 36 months of age affecting the primary maxillary anterior teeth
   a) 20% of children are at high risk, including Native Americans, Hispanics, and Native Alaskans
   b) Etiology—due to prolonged and frequent exposure to a bottle or breast-feeding, particularly at night and nap time
   c) Prevention—educate pregnant women about appropriate infant feeding practices and oral care before delivery
      (1) NEVER put an infant or child to bed with a bottle containing anything other than water
      (2) Avoid having infants sleep with mother and nurse at-will all night
      (3) Avoid using sweetened pacifiers
      (4) Begin weaning infants to a cup at 6 months; children should be completely weaned to a cup by age one

B. Childhood

1. Should eat foods high in nutrient and energy density to meet needs for growth and development; portion sizes are adjusted based on child's size and physiological needs

2. Children over age 2 years should eat a reduced-fat diet to decrease the risk of diet-related chronic diseases later in life
3. Excessive juice consumption (> 12 oz/day) may lead to
   a) Obesity due to excessive calories
   b) Short stature (results from juice replacing more nutrient-dense foods)
   c) Caries due to frequent exposure to fermentable carbohydrates

C. Adolescents—80% of an individual's average caries incidence occurs during adolescence

1. Dietary habits—adolescents exert new found independence in food choices
   a) Generally choose foods low in vitamin A, thiamin, iron, and calcium
   b) Eat fast foods and ready-to-eat snacks high in fat, sugar, protein, and sodium
2. Eating disorders—affect 5–11% of adolescents
   a) Anorexia nervosa—50% also practice bulimia
      (1) Diagnostic criteria
         (a) Fail to maintain minimal weight and height for age group
         (b) Fear of being overweight
         (c) Distorted body image
         (d) Amenorrhea in females
      (2) Oral manifestations may include
         (a) Angular cheilitis due to multiple nutrient deficiencies
         (b) Xerostomia resulting from parotid gland dysfunction
         (c) Dental erosion due to self-induced vomiting
   (b) Bulimia
      (1) Diagnostic criteria
         (a) Practice a minimum of two binges per week for 3 months; consume large quantities of high-calorie, carbohydrate-rich foods (average intake of food during a binge is 3400 calorie over an hour, with some patients ingesting as much as 50,000 calories in 24 hours)
         (b) Feel a lack of control
         (c) Compensatory actions to negate the binge's effects
            i) Use laxatives
            ii) Practice self-induced vomiting
            iii) Perform excessive exercise
            iv) Practice strict dieting or fasting
         (d) Overly concerned about body weight and shape
      (2) Oral manifestations
         (a) Perimolysis—enamel erosion on the lingual surfaces of the maxillary anterior teeth
         (b) Evidence of calluses or scars on the first knuckle of the index finger from induced vomiting
         (c) Traumatic palatal injuries or bruising from object used to induce vomiting
         (d) Possible xerostomia, due to dehydration from vomiting and laxatives

(e) Caries—an increase of 20% due to
i) Large amounts of fermentable and retentive carbohydrates eaten during a binge
ii) Exposure to acid during vomiting episodes
iii) Increase in xerostomia, which reduces the oral clearance of carbohydrates

c) Binge-eating disorder (BED)
(1) Diagnostic criteria—same binge-eating behaviors as the bulimic patient, but with no purging
(2) Oral manifestation includes increased caries rate due to the frequency of exposure to fermentable carbohydrates

D. Aging

1. Chronic disease—incidence and prevalence increases as the population ages
a) Cardiovascular disease (CVD) results from atherosclerosis that narrows the arteries and restricts blood flow, which can result in ischemia of the heart, brain, or extremities
(1) Risk factors include increasing age, gender, heredity, tobacco use, *hyperlipidemia,* hypertension, physical inactivity, high fat/saturated diets, diabetes mellitus, and obesity
(2) Prevention includes lowering blood pressure, normalizing lipid levels, maintaining glycemic control, reducing excess body fat, ceasing tobacco use, increasing physical activity, and consuming a healthy, low-fat diet
(a) Dietary therapy consists of an AHA/NCEP Step I diet
i) Increase use of soy products to replace animal fat
ii) Increase intake of soluble fibers to reduce serum lipid levels
iii) Increase intake of antioxidants to reduce oxidative damage
iv) Moderate salt intake to assist in lowering blood pressure
v) Maintain adequate levels of folate and vitamins B_6 and B_{12} to reduce homocysteine levels

2. Polypharmacy—use of multiple drugs at any one time
a) Xerostomia (dry mouth)—side effect of more than 400 medications including antihistamines, antihypertensives, antidepressants, and antipsychotics
(1) Signs and symptoms associated with xerostomia include
(a) Dysgeusia (changes in taste) due to low levels of saliva that aid in the dissolution of foods and allow the sensation of sweet, sour, salty, and bitter tastes
(b) Difficulty in speaking, swallowing (dysphagia), and chewing due to the lack of saliva to provide lubrication to the oral tissues
(c) Burning or soreness of the oral mucosa
(d) Increased susceptibility to oral *candidiasis;* saliva is needed to

i) Maintain the integrity of the mucous membranes, the first line of defense in innate immunity
ii) Limit growth of bacteria and prevent oral infections via antimicrobial agents, such as immunoglobulins and lysozymes

(e) Difficulty in wearing dentures
(f) Increase in the incidence of severe caries due to loss of saliva needed to
i) Provide substantial buffering capacity to maintain the oral pH near neutrality
ii) Provide some physical cleansing and diluting of toxic bacterial products
iii) Maintain mineral content of the teeth by aiding in ongoing remineralization

(2) Dietary recommendations to prevent caries should focus on
(a) Minimizing the frequency of meals and snacks
(b) Limiting sugary and retentive between-meal snacks such as candy, raisins, crackers, potato chips, pretzels, cookies, and dry cereal
(c) Encouraging consumption of fresh fruits, vegetables, and dairy products as snacks
(d) Encouraging frequent sips of water for hydration and lubrication of the oral mucosa
(e) Using sialogogues, such as xylitol in sugarless gum, to stimulate saliva
(f) Ending a meal or snack with cheese (anticariogenic) or rinsing with water when the patient cannot perform an oral hygiene regimen

(3) Tooth loss
(a) Denture wearers have 75% to 85% reduced masticatory efficiency
(b) Effects on dietary intake—patient alters food intake to reduce chewing or because of fear of choking, therefore patient
i) Consumes fewer meats, fresh fruits, and vegetables
ii) Relies on soft foods, which tend to be more retentive, increasing the risk of root caries for those with remaining teeth
iii) Consumes more refined carbohydrates and sucrose
iv) Loses teeth because of decrease in nutrient intakes of vitamin A, crude fiber, and calcium

X. ORAL CONDITIONS AFFECTING NUTRIENT INTAKE

A. Oral cancer

1. Accounts for about 3% of all cancers; long-term prognosis is generally poor
2. Effects on nutrient intake depend on the
   a) Patient's nutritional status before diagnosis

   b) Stage and site of the cancer
   c) Aggressiveness of therapy required in treating the cancer
3. Complications associated with oral cancer include
   a) Chronic pain
   b) Impaired swallowing and chewing, resulting in weight loss
   c) Speech difficulties
   d) Mucositis
   e) Xerostomia
   f) Physical disfigurement
   g) Oral infections, such as candidiasis
4. Nutrition recommendations
   a) Consume small, frequent high calorie/protein meals and snacks primarily consisting of liquid or soft, moist foods
      (1) Add whole milk or cream to puddings, cream soups, and milkshakes
      (2) Add extra cheese to foods
      (3) Add butter or margarine to mashed potatoes and scrambled eggs
      (4) Use pasteurized egg nog in milkshakes
      (5) Use commercial supplements or instant breakfast in whole milk for snacks
   b) Attempt to eat all solid foods before consuming liquids at meals to prevent early satiety

B. Oral and periodontal surgery

1. Effects on nutrient intake—usually minimal due to the short duration of inadequate nutrient intakes
   a) High-risk groups include those with a poor nutritional status before surgery (e.g., alcoholics, medically compromised patients, and those unable to consume adequate nutrition within 3 to 5 days postoperatively—this is of particular concern for diabetics)
2. Dietary recommendations for soft/liquid diet
   a) For the medically compromised patient, consult with physician and registered dietitian before surgery for recommendations to replete any nutrient deficiencies
      (1) Recommend a multivitamin supplement at 100% of RDA levels
      (2) Provide a list of nutrient-dense foods and beverages to have during postoperative recovery
   b) Postoperative care—nutrient requirements increase because of blood loss, increased catabolism, tissue regeneration, and host defense activities
      (1) A liquid diet may be required for the first 1 to 3 days
         (a) Milkshakes, ice cream, pudding, custards, instant breakfast drinks, and commercial liquid supplements provide calories, protein, and many of the essential nutrients needed for wound healing
         (b) Diabetic patients need to spread their carbohydrate intake evenly throughout the day to keep blood glucose

under control and may want to choose sugar-free or no-sugar-added products

(c) Continue the multivitamin supplement until eating returns to normal

(2) From days 3 to 7 postoperatively, the diet may progress from liquid to soft to normal as the patient tolerates

(a) Add fruit nectars and soft fruits such as applesauce and bananas to the liquid diet

(b) Additional soft foods include cottage cheese, yogurt, mashed potatoes, macaroni and cheese, scrambled eggs, and oatmeal

C. Oral lesions

1. May complicate nutrient intakes for anywhere from a few days to months
2. Apthous ulcers, mucositis, stomatitis, and esophagitis are inflammations of the mucous membranes lining the GI tract starting in the mouth
   a) Causes
      (1) Chemotherapy drugs including methotrexate, hydroxyurea, and 5-fluorouracil
      (2) Radiation to the head and neck
      (3) Immune suppression, as in AIDS
   b) Concerns
      (1) Ability to ingest enough food to provide adequate nutrition and prevent weight loss
      (2) Ability to perform home care procedures, which may prevent or reduce the severity of stomatitis
   c) Nutrition recommendations include a liquid or soft diet as discussed under oral cancer
   d) Poorly tolerated foods
      (1) Citrus fruit or juices, such as orange and grapefruit
      (2) Rough, coarse, or dry foods such as raw vegetables, granola, toast, and crackers
      (3) Spicy or salty foods
      (4) Textured or granular foods
      (5) Extremely hot or cold foods

review questions

DIRECTIONS Each of the questions or incomplete statements below is followed by suggested answers or completions. Select the **one** answer that is best in each case.

1. An adequate amount of nutrient intakes is needed by the oral tissues for all of the following EXCEPT one. Which one is the EXCEPTION?
   A. growth
   B. development
   C. catabolism
   D. maintenance

2. Essential amino acids must be obtained from the diet. They cannot be synthesized from other amino acids.
   A. The first statement is TRUE, the second is FALSE.
   B. Both statements are TRUE.
   C. The first statement is FALSE, the second is TRUE.
   D. Both statements are FALSE.

3. Which of the following is an example of an essential fatty acid?
   A. linoleic
   B. tropical oils
   C. lecithin
   D. oleic

4. Which of the following vitamins is NOT fat-soluble?
   A. A
   B. D
   C. C
   D. E

5. Modifiable risk factors for oral disease include all of the following EXCEPT one. Which one is the EXCEPTION?
   A. dietary factors
   B. oral hygiene habits
   C. health status of the hard and soft tissues
   D. genetics
   E. immunological response

6. The critical pH at which demineralization of the enamel occurs is
   A. 0.
   B. 2.0.
   C. 5.5.
   D. 7.0.
   E. 8.0.

7. Functions of saliva include all of the following EXCEPT one. Which one is the EXCEPTION?
   A. provides buffering capacity
   B. provides antimicrobial capacity
   C. speeds oral clearance of bacterial substrates
   D. provides growth medium for bacteria
   E. aids in remineralization of the tooth

8. Examples of retentive carbohydrates include all of the following EXCEPT one. Which one is the EXCEPTION?
   A. crackers
   B. cheese
   C. potato chips
   D. cookies
   E. pretzels

9. All of the following are common characteristics of water-soluble vitamins EXCEPT one. Which one is the EXCEPTION?
   A. required from the diet on a daily basis
   B. absorbed in the small intestine
   C. stored in the body for long periods
   D. easily destroyed

10. Good sources of calcium include all the following EXCEPT one. Which one is the EXCEPTION?
    A. fortified orange juice
    B. bread
    C. legumes
    D. milk
    E. yogurt

11. A high intake of dietary components that exert negative effects on bone mass include
    A. fat.
    B. sugar.
    C. calcium.
    D. alcohol.

12. A deficiency in which of the following nutrients has been associated with neural tube defects?
    A. thiamin
    B. folate
    C. calcium
    D. protein
    E. fat

13. Severe decay in early childhood is usually evident in
    A. primary first molars.
    B. mandibular central and lateral incisors.
    C. maxillary canines.
    D. maxillary central and lateral incisors.

14. A deficiency in vitamin A may result in
    A. rickets.
    B. abnormal bleeding.
    C. peripheral neuropathy.
    D. night blindness.

15. A bulimic patient may use all of the following methods to purge after binge eating EXCEPT one. Which one is the EXCEPTION?
    A. laxatives
    B. diuretics
    C. antidepressants
    D. excessive exercise
    E. vomiting

16. One of the MOST common drug-nutrient interactions that can increase the risk of dental caries is
    A. dysgeusia.
    B. dysphagia.
    C. xerostomia.
    D. dysphasia.

17. The calcium RDA standard for elderly individuals is below the standard set for the general population. This is because elderly people have decreased calcium absorption.
    A. The first statement is TRUE, the second is FALSE.
    B. Both statements are TRUE.
    C. The first statement is FALSE, the second statement is TRUE.
    D. Both statements are FALSE.

18. Diabetic patients may experience all of the following symptoms EXCEPT one. Which one is the EXCEPTION?
    A. frequent urination
    B. blurred vision
    C. decreased hunger
    D. increased infections

19. A normal fasting blood glucose level, in mg/dl, is
    A. 40 to 60.
    B. 80 to 120.
    C. 150 to 200.
    D. > 200.

20. One of the risk factors for osteoporosis is
    A. increased physical activity.
    B. tobacco use.
    C. estrogen therapy.
    D. toxic levels of vitamin D.

21. The MOST common nutritional deficiency among children and women of child-bearing age in the United States is
A. zinc.
B. vitamin C.
C. iron.
D. sodium.

22. Dairy products are good sources of all of the following nutrients, vitamins, and minerals EXCEPT one. Which one is the EXCEPTION?
A. calcium
B. zinc
C. vitamin D
D. protein
E. riboflavin

23. Which of the following factors decreases absorption of dietary iron?
A. vitamin C
B. lactose
C. hydrochloric acid
D. phytates
E. animal proteins

24. According to the Food Guide Pyramid, how many servings of bread and cereal are recommended daily?
A. 2 to 3
B. 2 to 4
C. 3 to 5
D. 6 to 11

25. The form of carbohydrate BEST used by tissues is
A. lactose.
B. maltose.
C. sucrose.
D. glucose.
E. fructose.

26. Carbohydrates provide 4 kcal/g and fats provide 7 kcal/g.
A. The first statement is FALSE, the second statement is TRUE.
B. The first statement is TRUE, and the second statement is FALSE.
C. Both statements are FALSE.
D. Both statements are TRUE.

27. Glucose is the sole source of energy for the
A. brain.
B. pancreas.
C. heart.
D. liver.
E. kidney.

28. Food sources of vitamin B_{12} include all of the following EXCEPT one. Which one is the EXCEPTION?
A. chicken
B. milk
C. pork
D. legumes
E. beef

29. Groups at high risk for many nutritional deficiencies include all of the following EXCEPT one. Which one is the EXCEPTION?
A. alcoholics
B. children
C. young adult males
D. elderly

30. The elderly have an increased need for vitamin D because of
A. decreased synthesis by the skin.
B. increased intake of dairy products.
C. increased absorption in the small intestine.
D. decreased intake of vitamin C.

31. Green leafy vegetables are sources of all of the following nutrients, vitamins, and minerals EXCEPT one. Which one is the EXCEPTION?
A. folate
B. vitamin B_{12}
C. carbohydrates
D. magnesium
E. iron

32. All of the following nutrients, vitamins, and minerals are involved in collagen synthesis EXCEPT one. Which one is the EXCEPTION?
A. vitamin C
B. copper
C. protein
D. iodine
E. zinc

33. Individuals with dentures have reduced masticatory efficacy, which results in increased intakes of
    A. fiber.
    B. protein.
    C. sucrose.
    D. calcium.
    E. vitamin A.

34. Sucrose is made up of the monosaccharides
    A. fructose and galactose.
    B. glucose and galactose.
    C. glucose and glucose.
    D. glucose and fructose.

35. The intrinsic factor is necessary for the absorption of
    A. amino acids.
    B. essential fatty acids.
    C. sucrose.
    D. vitamin B_{12}.

answers & rationales

1.

C. Catabolism is the destructive phase of metabolism in which complex substances are broken down to release nutrients and energy when the body has insufficient nutrients. The oral tissues, like the body, need nutrients for growth, maintenance, repair, and development.

2.

B. Essential amino acids must be obtained from the diet, because the body cannot synthesize them.

3.

A. Linoleic (omega-6) and linolenic (omega-3) are essential fatty acids that must be obtained from the diet. Tropical oils are saturated fats. Lecithin is a phospholipid that acts as an emulsifier for mixing water with oil, as in salad dressings. Oleic acid is a monounsaturated fatty acid found in olive and canola oils.

4.

C. Vitamin C is water-soluble. Vitamins A, D, E, and K are fat-soluble.

5.

D. Genetics is a risk factor that is not modifiable at this time. However, dietary factors, oral hygiene habits, immunological responses, and health status of oral tissues are modifiable factors.

6.

C. The pH at which the oral environment becomes acidic enough to cause minerals to be leached from the tooth surface is 5.5. This is the initial process in caries development. A pH of 7.0 and 8.0 is basic.

7.

D. Because saliva does not contain sucrose and functions as a pH buffer, it does not provide a growth medium for bacteria. Saliva also aids in the remineralization of teeth and the oral clearance of food, as well as provides antimicrobial properties.

8.

B. Cheese is composed of protein and fat. Its anticariogenic effect, due to its high calcium and phosphorus content, assists in raising the pH of saliva and buffers the acids produced by bacteria. Crackers, potato chips, pretzels, and cookies are all capable of producing energy for cariogenic bacteria.

9.

C. Water-soluble vitamins are not stored in the body for long periods, so they must be consumed daily. They are absorbed primarily in the small intestine and easily destroyed, most generally by heat.

10.

B. Bread has little calcium content, but is enriched with B vitamins. Legumes, milk, fortified juice, and yogurt are good sources of calcium.

11.

D. Excessive alcohol consumption has a negative effect on bone mass, a risk factor for osteoporosis, possibly because of its toxic effects on osteoblasts. Ninety-nine percent of calcium is found in the bones and teeth. Fat and sugar do not affect bone mass.

12.

B. The RDA for folate has been increased as a result of studies suggesting an association between low intakes and neural tube defects, such as spinal bifida. A deficiency in thiamin causes beriberi, which can damage the nervous and cardiovascular systems. A calcium deficiency is associated with rickets, osteoporosis, osteomalacia, and tetany. In the United States, there is rarely a deficiency associated with fat and protein.

13.

D. Maxillary central and lateral incisors are the first teeth affected in early childhood caries. The position of the tongue against the nipple causes pooling of the liquid around these teeth when there is extended contact with fermentable carbohydrates. The remaining teeth are protected by the position of the tongue.

14.

D. A deficiency in vitamin A causes night blindness. Rickets is caused by a deficiency in vitamin D and calcium. Vitamin K aids in the formation of prothrombin, a blood-clotting factor. Although a deficiency in vitamin E is rare, peripheral neuropathy is a symptom.

15.

C. The use of antidepressants does not assist in purging of excess calories consumed during a binging episode. However, the use of laxatives and diuretics, vomiting, and excessive exercise are all examples of purging.

16.

C. Xerostomia or dry mouth is a side effect of more than 400 different medications. Decreased saliva flow results in a loss of its buffering effects, thereby causing an increase in the incidence of caries. Dysgeusia is a change of taste a patient may experience. Dysphagia involves difficulty in swallowing and dysplasia describes abnormal growth or development.

17.

C. Because elderly people experience decreased calcium absorption, their need for calcium is higher than the RDA standards.

18.

C. Diabetics usually experience an increase in appetite. They may experience symptoms of frequent urination, blurred vision, and increased infections.

19.

B. The normal range for fasting blood glucose is between 80 and 120 mg/dl. Numbers below the normal range indicate hypoglycemia and numbers above this range indicate hyperglycemia.

20.

B. Individuals who smoke are at a higher risk for developing osteoporosis. Increased physical activity and estrogen therapy are advised as preventive and treatment measures, respectively. Toxic levels of vitamin D lead to calcium being deposited in soft tissues and irreversible cardiovascular and kidney damage.

21.

C. The most common nutritional deficiency of children and women of child-bearing age in the United States is iron deficiency. Vitamin C (sources include citrus fruits, broccoli, potatoes, and tomatoes) and zinc (found in protein-rich foods) are easily attained from the diet. A deficiency in sodium is rare because sodium is so readily available.

22.

B. Dairy products are good sources of protein, phosphorus, riboflavin, and vitamins A and D. Zinc is found primarily in protein-rich foods such as oysters, beef, eggs, and peanuts.

23.

D. Phytates (a salt of a phosphoric acid ester) bind calcium and reduce its absorption. Vitamin C and hydrochloric acid favor iron absorption. Animal proteins are good sources of iron. Lactose is the sugar found in milk.

24.

D. The recommended amount of servings per day for grains is 6 to 11. This provides a sufficient amount of carbohydrates, B vitamins, and fiber for a healthy diet. The recommended servings for dairy products and meat group per day is 2 to 3. It is recommended to have 2 to 4 servings of fruit and 3 to 5 servings of vegetables per day.

25.

D. Glucose is the form of carbohydrate used best by body tissues for energy. Maltose, lactose, and sucrose are disaccharides, which must be broken down into monosaccharides before entering the bloodstream. Fructose (levulose) is the sweetest of all the monosaccharides and is a product of the breakdown of sucrose.

26.

B. Carbohydrates provide 4 kcal/g and fats provide 9 kcal/g.

27.

A. Glucose is the sole source of energy for brain and red blood cells. Glucose is used by the pancreas, heart, liver, or kidney—but not as the sole source of energy as with the brain and red blood cells.

28.

D. Vitamin B_{12} is found only in animal sources, not in plant foods. Legumes are pods, such as peas and lentils. They are a plant source.

29.

C. Young adult males tend to have high intakes of nutrients and are not among the groups at risk for deficiencies. Elderly people, alcoholics, and children are all at risk for nutritional deficiencies. The elderly suffer from absorption problems. Children usually consume less calories per day than recommended by the RDA standards. Alcohol interferes with the storage of nearly all nutrients.

30.

A. There is a fourfold decrease in the synthesis of vitamin D by the skin in the elderly people. Dairy products assist in the absorption of vitamin D; however, elderly people may experience absorption problems. Vitamin C does not affect the absorption of vitamin D, but diets high in fiber can affect vitamin D absorption.

31.

B. Vitamin B_{12} is obtained from animal sources only. However, folate, carbohydrates, magnesium, and iron can be found in green leafy vegetables.

32.

D. Iodine helps regulate the basal metabolic rate. Protein, copper, zinc, and vitamin C are all involved in collagen synthesis and maintenance.

33.

C. Because denture wearers have reduced masticatory efficacy—75% to 85% less than natural teeth—an increase in the intake of sucrose and refined carbohydrates, foods easier to chew, is common. Foods rich in fiber, protein, calcium, and vitamin A require more biting and chewing.

34.

D. The disaccharide sucrose is made up of two monosaccharides—glucose and fructose. Glucose and galactose make up the disaccharide lactose. Two molecules of glucose make up maltose. The combination of fructose and galactose do not make up a disaccharide.

35.

D. The intrinsic factor is a protein made in the stomach. If this factor is absent, absorption of vitamin B_{12} is affected. Amino acids travel to the liver through the portal vein. The primary site for fat absorption is the small intestine. Sucrose is broken down into monosaccharides and then transported to the liver through the portal vein.

CHAPTER

6 Microbiology, Infectious Diseases, and Infection Control

Barbara L. Bennett, RDH, MS

contents

The study of microbiology is important for dental professionals to prevent the transmission of disease to themselves and their patients. Infection control is the mechanism by which the health professional controls disease transmission.

➤ MICROORGANISMS

I. BASIC CONCEPTS

A. Most numerous species on earth—part of normal environment

B. Same characteristics as more complex cells: metabolism, growth, reproduction

C. Microorganisms capable of producing disease—pathogens

D. Nomenclature—binomial system

1. Two-word name
2. Genus (capitalized) and species (lower case), with both italicized e.g., *Mutans streptococcus*

II. CLASSIFICATIONS

A. *Prokaryotes*—lack nucleus, unicellular, may be anaerobic or aerobic, smallest living organism with ability to survive independently of other organisms

1. Bacteria—*bacterium* means rod or staff
   a) Most play positive roles—necessary for many life processes
   b) Extremely adaptable to variable living condition
   c) All have cell walls
   d) Cause many diseases (pathogenic)
2. *Rickettsiae*—tiny bacteria transmitted by arthropods (ticks and lice)
3. *Chlamydiae*—half the size of rickettsiae, cannot be seen with light microscope
4. *Mycoplasms*—smaller than chlamydiae, only prokaryote without cell wall
5. *Cynobacteria*
   a) Formerly called blue-green algae
   b) Use photosynthesis
   c) Many "fix" nitrogen

B. *Eukaryotes*—possess a well-defined nucleus, organelles; more advanced life form

1. Algae (contain chlorophyll)—may have one or many cells
2. Protozoa—unicellular, nonphotosynthetic
3. Fungi (yeasts and molds)—nonphotosynthetic, classified by type of spores, mechanism of sexual and asexual spore formation, presence of mycelia
4. Slime molds—plasmodium

C. *Viruses*—classified according to type of nucleic acid, morphology, presence of envelope

D. *Helminths*—multicellular, usually parasites of human gastrointestinal (GI) tract or circulatory system

E. *Prions*—new classification, proteinacious infectious particles, defy many forms of sterilization

III. MEASUREMENT AND OBSERVATION OF MICROORGANISMS

A. Measurement units

1. Micrometer ($\mu m = 10^{-6}$ m)
2. Nanometer ($nm = 10^{-9}$ m)
3. Angstrom unit ($Å = 10^{-10}$ m)
4. Millimeter ($mm = 10^{-3}$ m)
5. Centimeter ($cm = 10^{-2}$ m)

B. Specimen preparation

1. Living specimens—hanging drop and temporary wet mount are preparations used
2. Staining
   a) Improves visualization of dead cells
   b) Some species differentiation
   c) Types
      (1) Acid/base—shows different cell components
      (2) Single dye (crystal violet, methylene blue, saffranin)
      (3) Differential staining—more than one dye used to group bacteria
         (a) Gram stain—cell wall thickness, shows penicillin sensitivity
            i) Gram positive—thick cell wall, stains purple or blue, penicillin sensitive
            ii) Gram negative—thin cell wall, stains red, resistant to penicillin
            iii) Acid fast—differentiates mycobacteria (*Mycobacterium tuberculosis*) by indicating presence of special cell wall lipids that resist depolarization
            iv) Dark field microscopy—necessary to visualize spirochetes

IV. BACTERIAL CELL STRUCTURE AND FUNCTION

A. Morphology

1. Cocci (single—coccus)
   a) Round or ovoid shape
   b) Occur in pairs (diplococci), chains (streptococci), four-square (tetrad), eight-cube (sarcinae), and clusters (staphylococci)
   c) Predominates in oral health
2. Bacilli (single—bacillus)
   a) Rodlike or cylindric
   b) Occurs in pairs (diplobacilli), chains (streptobacilli), rounded rods (coccobacilli), and with tapered ends (fusiform bacilli)
3. Spirilla (single—spirillum)
   a) Spiral or curved
   b) Vibrios—may be portion of a spiral

B. External cell structures

1. Surface coating (glycocalyx)
   a) Capsules—thick, organized polysaccharide and/or polypeptides attached to cell wall, protection from pathogens, drugs, phagocytosis, increases virulence (e. g., *Mutans streptococcus*)

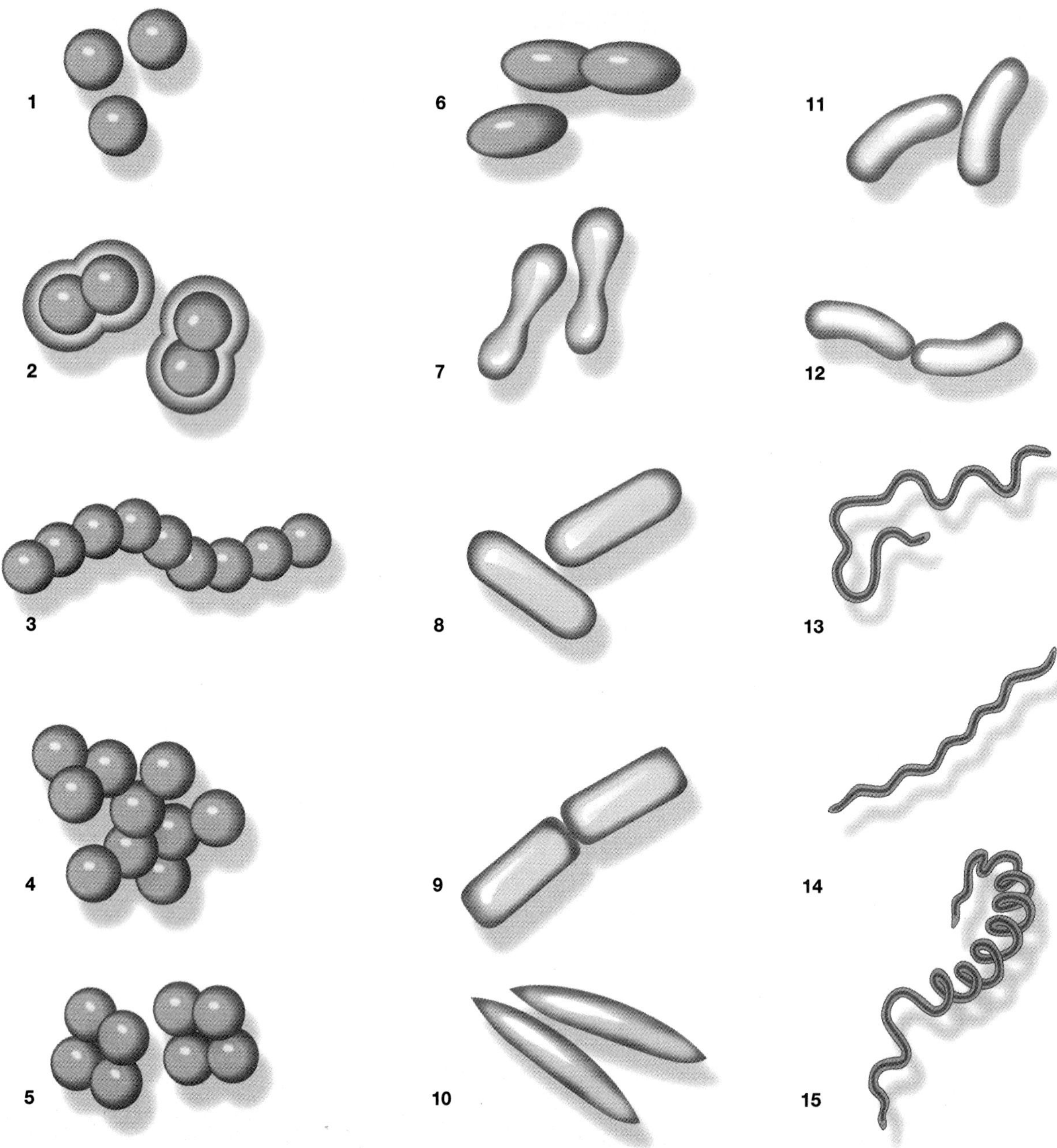

FIGURE 6-1. Variations in basic bacterial morphology. (*Adapted from Joklik WK, Willet HP, Amos DB, eds. Zinsser* Microbiology, *19th ed. E. Norwalk, CT: Appleton Lange 1984:25.*)

1. Single cocci. 2. Pairs of cocci. 3. Chains of cocci. 4. Clusters of cocci. 5. Cocci in tetrads. 6. Coccobacilli. 7. Club-shaped bacilli. 8. Bacilli with rounded ends. 9. Bacilli with square ends. 10. Bacilli with tapered ends (fusiforms). 11. Vibrios. 12. Spirillum. 13. Borrelia. 14. Treponema. 15. Leptospira.

b) Slime layer—a soluble mass of polysaccharides and/or polypeptides that are unorganized and loosely attached to the cell wall, protects and aids adherence

2. Appendages
   a) *Flagella*
      (1) Long, rigid protein strands
      (2) Aid in mobility
   b) Axial filaments
      (1) Form of locomotion used by spirochetes

(2) Aid in mobility

c) *Pili*

(1) Join bacteria in preparation for DNA transfer (also allows drug resistance if plasmids)

(2) Most common in gram-negative bacteria

(3) Provide attachment

d) *Fimbriae*

(1) Shorter, more numerous than pili

(2) Enables attachment of cell to surfaces (increases virulence)

C. Cell wall—peptidoglycan macromolecule that maintains shape, prevents cell rupture, supports flagella

1. Gram-positive
   a) Multilayers of peptidoglycan and teichoic acids
   b) Disrupted by penicillins and lysozymes
2. Gram-negative
   a) Lipoprotein-lipopolysaccharide-phospholipid outer membrane surrounding thin peptidoglycan layer
   b) Protects cell from phagocytosis, penicillin, lysozyme
   c) Disrupted by antibody lysis, mechanical forces (e.g., scaling), and complement

D. Plasma membrane

1. Phosopholipid bilayer with fluid mosaic protein layer interspersed
2. Functions in active transport, as cell barrier
3. Contains enzymes and protein receptors

E. Cell envelope

1. All external structures and appendages
2. Helps cell adhesion and maintenance
3. Responsible for staining characteristics

F. Internal cell structure

1. Cytoplasm—fluid space inside plasma membrane, site of biochemical activities, contains ribosomes, granules, chromatin body
2. Genome (nucleoid)—single chromosome of one molecule of DNA, closed loop without nuclear membrane in nucleoplasm of cell
   a) Plasmids—extrachromosomal DNA molecules that carry drug resistance information
   b) Transposons—DNA segments that can move without the benefit of homology
3. Ribosomes—composed of ribosomal ribonucleic acid (RNA) and ribosomal protein, function in protein synthesis
4. Mesosomes—folds in cytoplasmic membrane caused by drying (artifact)
5. Endospores—gram-positive cells form these dormant structures
   a) May remain in spore state for years, extremely resistant to heat, drying, chemical disinfection, and radiation
   b) "Live spore test" considered benchmark for sterilization
      (1) Steam and chemical vapor uses spores of *Bacillus stearothermophilus*

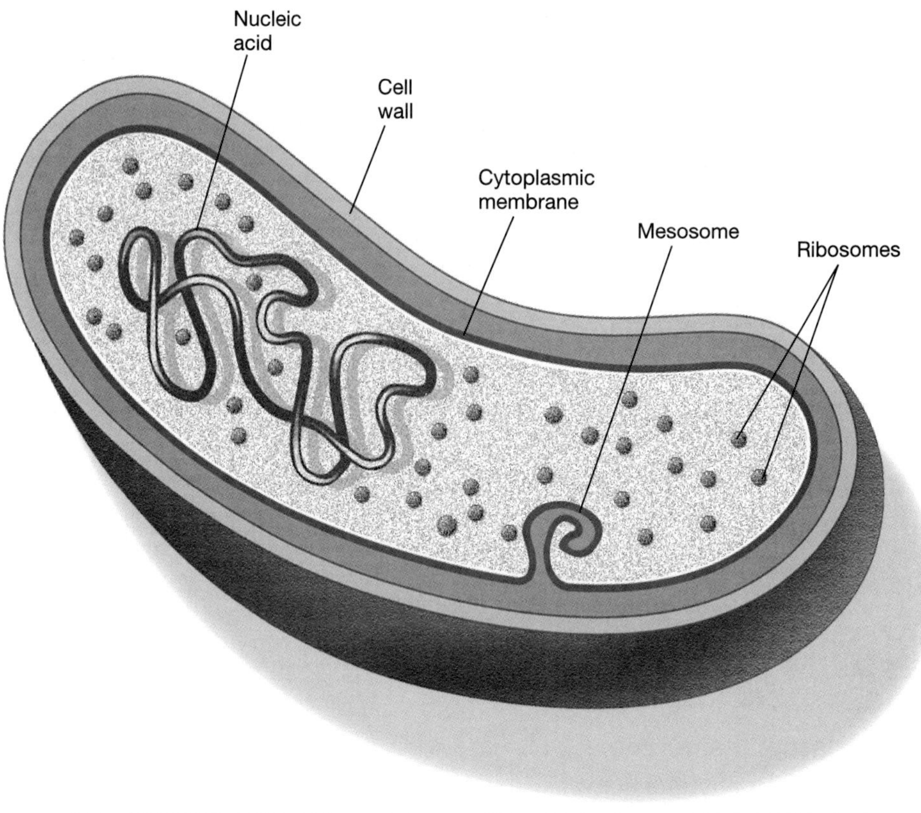

FIGURE 6-2. Composite procaryotic cell

(2) Dry heat and ethylene oxide sterilizers use spores of *Bacillus subtilis*

c) Produced by genera *Bacillus* and *Clostridium*

6. Inclusions—storage material, may include polysaccharide granules, granular sulfur, lipids, and vacuoles
7. Photosynthetic apparatus

V. EUKARYOTIC CELL STRUCTURE AND FUNCTION

A. Distinct nucleus bound by nuclear membrane; cell has nucleolus and membrane-bound organelles

B. Animal cells

1. Cell membrane surrounds cell and connects with internal membrane system
   a) Functions through active and passive transport in regulation of cell substances
   b) Important in drug sensitivity, phagocytosis, tumor formation, and immune response
2. Nucleus
   a) Controls physiology and reproduction of cell
   b) Composed of nuclear membrane, nucleoli (RNA synthesis), chromosomes (DNA), and nucleoprotein (chromatin)
3. Internal structures

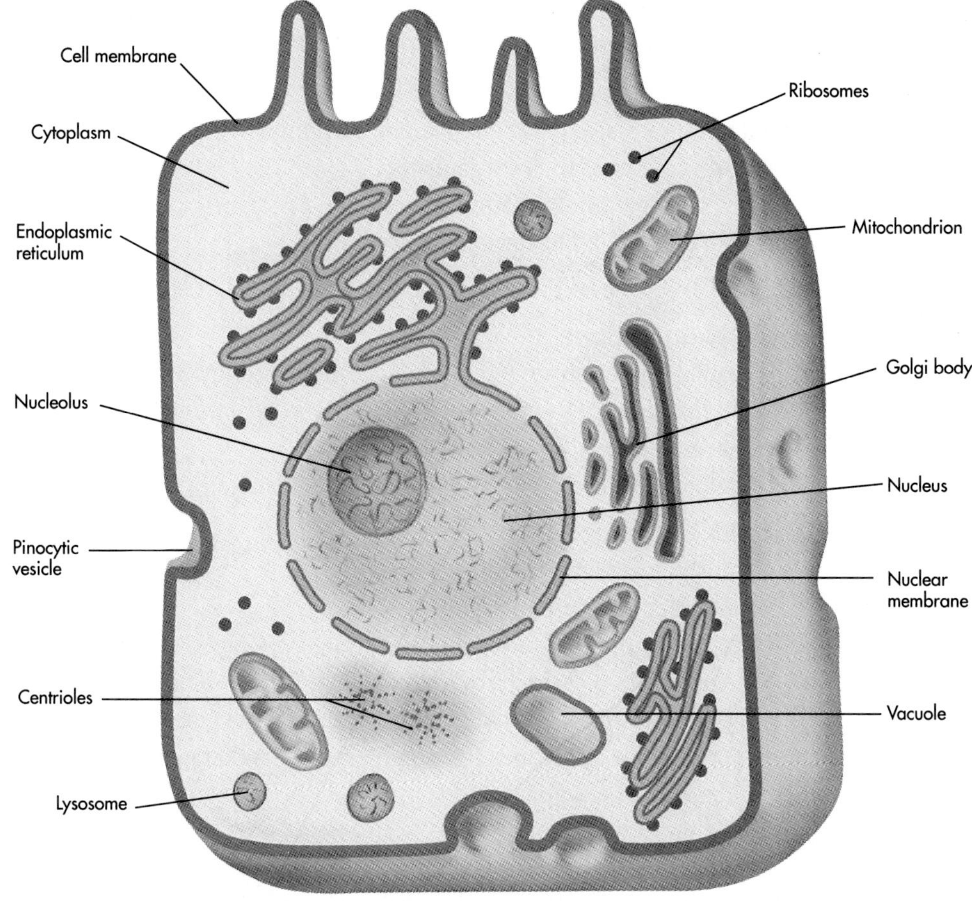

FIGURE 6-3. Diagram of the main structural components of a eucaryotic cell.

a) Mitochondria—energy production through adenosine triphosphate (ATP)
b) Golgi complex—protein packaging
c) Endoplasmic reticulum (ER)—protein synthesis, rough (has ribosomes attached) and smooth
d) Lysosomes—digestive enzymes
e) Cytoplasm—intracellular fluid, ions, nutrients, particles for cell function

➤ GROWTH AND CULTIVATION OF MICROORGANISMS

I. BACTERIAL GROWTH

A. Binary fission—one parent cell produces two new cells

B. Bacterial growth curve—phases

1. Lag phase—no increase in number, adjustment to environment
2. Log phase—cell numbers increase in exponential manner (logarithmic) most susceptible to antimicrobials at this phase
3. Stationary phase—viable cell numbers remain constant
4. Decline (death) phase—number of viable cells decrease

C. Generation time—time needed for cell to divide varies widely between species, usually around 20 minutes

D. Growth measurements

1. Increase in mass, numbers, weight, turbidity
2. Viable counts of microorganisms
    a) Bacteria—colony-forming units (CFU)
    b) Viruses—plaque-forming units (PFU)

II. CONDITIONS THAT AFFECT BACTERIAL GROWTH

A. Physical conditions

1. Thermal—may grow within a range, many around 30°C
2. Acid/alkaline (pH)—most organisms grow best around neutral pH, between 6 and 8
3. Osmotic pressure

B. Chemical conditions

1. Atmospheric requirements
    a) Aerobes—require oxygen
    b) Microaerophilic—low concentrations of oxygen
    c) Anaerobes—do not require oxygen
    d) Obligate anaerobes—cannot tolerate free oxygen
    e) Facultative anaerobes—aerobic organisms that can grow in the absence of oxygen
2. Nutrition requirements
    a) Heterotrophic—organic compounds needed for growth
    b) Autotrophic—use inorganic compounds
    c) Hypotrophic—obligate intracellular parasite

III. ANTIMICROBIAL AGENTS

A. Mechanisms of antimicrobial agents

1. Inhibition of cell wall synthesis (e.g., penicillins)
2. Disruption of cell membrane (e.g., polymycin)
3. Inhibition of cell wall synthesis (e.g., tetracyclines)
4. Inhibition of DNA synthesis (e.g., rifampin)
5. Competitive inhibition (e.g., sulfa drugs)

B. Antibody Assays—tests to determine exposure to antigen of a specific pathogen; also known as serological reactions

1. Titer—most dilute concentration of serum antibody that reacts with antigen
2. Enzyme-linked immunosuppressant assay (ELISA)—inexpensive enzyme test for HIV, other pathogens
3. Neutralization, precipitation, agglutination, flocculation; all common tests
4. Others: complement fixation, fluorescent antibody technique, radioimmunoassay, monoclonal antibodies, Western blot test

C. Antibiotic resistance and abuse

1. Many organisms resistant to common antibiotics
2. Multidrug resistant tuberculosis, *Escherichia coli, Psuedomonoas aeruginosa,* Methicillin resistant *Staphylococcus aureus*
3. Exchange of plasmids through pili, transfer of genetic material

IV. MICROBIAL DESTRUCTION

A. Definitions of procedures

1. *Sterilization*—destruction of all life forms, including spores
2. *Disinfectant*—chemical used to kill pathogenic microorganisms on a inanimate object, such as a table top
3. *Antiseptic*—chemical used to kill pathogenic microorganisms on a living organism, such as the surface of the human body
4. *Aseptic*—free of microorganisms
5. *Sanitize*—to reduce microbial populations to a safe level as determined by public health standards

B. Sterilization monitoring—critical for infection control effectiveness

1. Most reliable test of sterilization—killing of live bacterial endospores
   a) Steam and chemical vapor—*Bacillus stearothermophilus* spores
   b) Dry heat and ethylene oxide—*Bacillus subtilis* var. niger spores
   c) Should be monitored weekly
   d) Accurate documentation must be kept
   e) Control (unexposed, unsterilized) incubated at same time
2. Internal chemical indicators—"slow change indicators"
   a) Dyes change color when heat, steam, or gas reaches *inside* of load
   b) Gives warning of gross sterilizer malfunction, *not* proof of sterility
3. Chemical process indicators
   a) Dyes change color on short exposure to sterilizing conditions

TABLE 6-1 COMPARISON OF STERILIZATION METHODS

Method	Methodology	Advantages	Disadvantages
Steam under pressure	15–20 minutes 250–270°F 15–20 lb. pressure Coagulation of protein	Short cycle Good penetration Wide range of materials Packs may be used	Corrosion of instruments Dulls cutting edges Improper loading/poor penetration
Dry heat	1 hr, 320–350°F No pressure Oxidation of cell parts	Safe for metal instruments Does not dull cutting edge No rust, corrosion	Long cycle Poor penetration May destroy some materials
Unsaturated chemical vapor	20–30 minutes 270°F Automatic pressure Gas is toxic	Short cycle No rust, corrosion Does not dull edges Useful for orthodontic wire	Dry instruments before processing Destroys some plastics Ventilation needed
Ethylene oxide (ETO)	Room temp/8–10 hr 120°F 2–3 hours Gas is toxic	Safe for many materials Low temperature Reliable	Long cycle Expensive equipment Ventilation needed Aeration/24 hr.
Glutaraldehyde chloride dioxide	Immersion for 6–10 hours	Used for heat-sensitive items	Irritating to skin, lungs Unable to monitor

b) Not proof of sterilization, simply proof of instrument processing

4. Item classification for sterilization, disinfection, and cleaning
   a) *Critical*—items that penetrate oral soft tissue or bone; must be sterilized (e.g., surgical bur)
   b) *Semicritical* items—items that come in contact with mucous membranes; must be sterilized (e.g., dental mirror)
   c) *Noncritical* items—items that normally do not penetrate or contact mucous membranes, but that may be contaminated; require intermediate-level disinfection (e.g., dental chair)
5. Sterilization failures
   a) Overloading—steam, chemical, vapor cannot penetrate
   b) Improper packaging or timing
   c) Unit malfunction
   d) Improper unit operation or maintenance

C. Categories of chemical disinfectants

1. *High level*—inactivates all forms of bacteria and spores, fungi, and viruses. High level chemicals may also be classified as a sterilant, depending on length of contact with item
2. *Intermediate level*—inactivates many forms of microorganism spores
3. *Low level*—inactivates vegetative bacteria and some lipid-type viruses, does not destroy spores, tubercle bacilli, or nonlipid viruses such as polio

TABLE 6-2 COMPARISON OF DISINFECTANTS*

Disinfectant	Example	Scope	Advantages	Limitations
Halogens or chlorines	Sodium hypochlorite (bleach 1:10) EPA registered surface	Broad spectrum: Bacteriocidal Viricidal Tuberculocidal	Inexpensive Rapid action Broad spectrum	Unstable, mix daily Must preclean Corrosive to metals Irritating to skin
	Chlorine dioxide Not EPA registered	Same as above	Same as above	Same as above Unable to monitor biologically
Synthetic phenols	Omni II EPA registered surface	Broad spectrum: Tuberculocidal	Broad spectrum Compatible with most materials Residual action	Not sporicidal Mix daily May degrade some plastics Irritating to skin
	Chlorhexidine			Film accumulation Hard to rinse
Iodophors	Biocide EPA registered, Intermediate surface	Broad spectrum: Tuberculocidal Bactericidal Virucidal	Residual action Rapid actions Few reactions Broad spectrum	Stains surfaces Mix daily Inactivated by hard water Reacts with starch wipes
Glutaraldehyde	Cidex EPA registered immersion only—not surface	Chemical sterilant After 6–10 hours Most potent	Effective when immersed for long periods Active with organic matter	Prolonged time Rinse items Not for surfaces Severe tissue and lung irritation

*Disinfectants cannot be biologically monitored.

4. Criteria that products should have
   a) EPA approval
   b) Tuberculocidal, bacteriocidal, virucidal, and fungicidal effects
   c) Acceptable shelf life, use life, reuse life, and adequate instructions for use

D. Other disinfectants

1. Heavy metals—mercury, copper, silver
2. Alcohols—skin antiseptics
   a) Ethyl alcohol—reacts with organic matter, preclean
   b) Isoprophyl alcohol—"rubbing alcohol," skin cleaner
3. Hydrogen peroxide—rinse to debride wounds, effective against anaerobic organisms
4. Soaps and detergents—wetting agents, ionic (e.g., quaternary ammonium compounds), NOT acceptable as surface disinfectants

V. INFECTION CONTROL DURING DENTAL TREATMENT

A. Equipment should be selected according to the ease of disinfection and degree of contamination

1. Minimal surfaces requiring contact with contaminated hands
   a) Foot controls
   b) Recessed waste containers with opening in countertop
2. Smooth construction—minimal seams, buttons, exposed controls
3. Plastics, vinyls, laminates preferred
4. Carpet not recommended in treatment or laboratory areas

B. Surfaces should be compatible with disinfectants

C. Dental unit water lines (DUWL)—reduce colony-forming units (CFU) or "biofilms" of microorganisms

1. Water may be contaminated with pathogenic bacteria
   a) Gram-negative bacteria such as *Legionella pneumophila* (implicated in outbreaks of Legionnaire's disease)
   b) *Psuedomonas* dangerous to immunocompromised client
2. Check antiretraction valves for effectiveness
3. Self-contained water reservoir with sterile water
4. Bacterial filtration unit in water line
5. Flush lines at beginning of day for 3 to 5 minutes, 20 to 30 seconds between clients, and with disinfecting agent followed by rinse at end of day

D. General housekeeping—clean surfaces not associated with client treatment routinely with soap and water, minimize surface clutter

E. Preparation for client care

1. Surface disinfect noncritical items (those that do not penetrate or contact mucous membranes) exposed to treatment contamination
   a) Use disposable covers whenever possible (e.g., light handles)
   b) Use sterile forceps, overgloves, or paper towels as bridge between contaminated area and noncontaminated area
2. Effectiveness of surface disinfectant influenced by
   a) Number and type of microorganisms present

b) "Bioburden"—amount of organic matter (blood, saliva, or debris) on item being disinfected
c) Disinfectant used: intermediate-level, Environmental Protection Agency (EPA) registered, tuberculocidal,
d) Appropriate viricidal and fungicidal activity
e) Concentration and length of exposure—follow manufacturer's direction
f) Proper surface disinfection technique—spray/wipe/spray
   (1) Use heavy-duty gloves
   (2) Preclean (first spray) with aqueous-based disinfectant containing detergent
   (3) Wipe with dry paper towel using mechanical wiping action
   (4) Spray—reapply EPA-registered tuberculocidal hospital-grade disinfectant; leave moist for specified time

3. Use prearranged tray setups/cassettes, unit dose materials
4. Use disposables wherever appropriate
6. Surface barriers (single use covers) when appropriate

F. Infection control during client care

1. Reduce splatter, aerosol, and droplets
   a) Preprocedural rinse with antimicrobial mouthrinse
   b) Reduce aerosols during procedures
      (1) Use ventilation system with HEPA filtration
      (2) Use high-volume evacuation
      (3) Position client correctly
2. Minimize cross-contamination
   a) Designate noncontaminated and contaminated zone
      (1) Use overgloves to go into noncontaminated zones
      (2) Avoid touching unprotected surfaces once gloves have become contaminated
      (3) Protect charts, radiographs from contamination
      (4) Use barriers such as paper towels
      (5) Only equipment and supplies necessary for treatment should be in the noncontaminated area
   b) Waste disposal
      (1) Immediately dispose of contaminated waste on tray in small biohazard bag
      (2) Wipe instruments to minimize bioburden
3. Major source of Health Care Worker (HCW) infection—needlesticks
   a) Use special precautions when handing syringe and sharps
      (1) Angle sharp end away from HCW
      (2) Do not leave uncapped needles on tray
      (3) Never recap with a two-handed technique
         (a) Use "scoop" one-handed technique
         (b) Use commercially available needle capper
         (c) Hold cap with cotton pliers while recapping
         (d) Use the newer automatic recapping needles
   b) Never bend, break, or manipulate needles by hand
   c) Dispose in approved "sharps" container

d) Exposure incident protocol
   (1) Treat any percutaneous incident as potentially infectious
   (2) Immediately cleanse wound
      (a) Squeeze wound to promote bleeding
      (b) Cleanse under running water using antibacterial soap
      (c) Disinfect with bleach or iodophor
   (3) Source individual should be tested (same day) for anti-HIV and surface antigens to hepatitis B, hepatitis C—confidentially should be maintained (only employee informed of results)
   (4) Inform employer immediately: responsible for providing follow-up
   (5) Exposed HCW tested for HIV, HBV, HCV on day of exposure and counseled regarding postexposure evaluation, vaccinations
   (6) Although employer receives written report that employee was counseled, tested, informed of results, and needs further evaluation, findings are confidential

G. Post-treatment procedures

1. Treatment area decontamination
   a) All personal protective equipment (PPE) worn, including puncture-resistant nitrile gloves
   b) Removal of sharps and glass cartridges to approved container
   c) Flush water lines for 20 to 30 seconds
   d) Seal small biohazard bag, transport immediately to workplace-biohazard waste container
   e) Remove all disposable barriers, avoid contaminating clean surfaces
   f) Close instrument cassette, cover tray to avoid transporting airborne microorganisms
   g) If sterilization is delayed, place in holding solution to prevent bioburden from drying on instruments, sterilize ASAP
   h) Dispose of single-use items
   i) Clean suction tubing by flushing with commercial disinfecting solution
2. Infectious waste
   a) EPA regulates disposal and management of waste sharps, extracted teeth and tissue, blood and blood-soaked or blood-caked items. *Note: liquid or dried blood, saliva, and other body fluids are classified as other potentially infectious material (OPIM)*
   b) State and local regulations may vary from EPA
   c) ADA Council on Government Affairs and Federal Dental Services categorize waste as
      (1) Regulated waste (biohazardous)
         (a) Sharps: needles, disposable syringes, broken instruments, suture needles, scalpel blades, burs, local anesthetic cartridges, soft tissues, teeth, and other body tissues
         (b) Blood and blood-soaked items, liquid or semiliquid (OPIM)

(c) Articles caked with dried blood or OPIM

(2) Biomedical waste—solid medical waste, disposable items other than items listed above

(a) Masks, gloves

(b) Saliva ejectors, surface barriers

(c) Disinfection wipes, paper towels

(d) Rubber cups, rubber dams

(e) Client cups, bibs

(f) May be disposed of with trash unless there are local or state restrictions to the contrary

d) Waste management

(1) Biohazardous waste must be labeled and separated from other waste

(2) Disposal dependent on regulatory agencies: incineration, burial, sterilization

3. Instrument care

a) Recirculation area should be centrally located for efficiency

b) Handle contaminated instruments with heavy-duty gloves only

c) Processing should flow from contaminated area to noncontaminated

(1) Receiving area (containment), presoaking, waste disposal

(a) Precleaning removes organic debris (bioburden) that interferes with sterilization

(2) Decontamination—rinsing, ultrasonic cleaning, rinsing, drying

(a) Wet instruments interfere with sterilization from ethylene oxide and dry heat

(3) Packaging for sterilization

(4) Sterilization (may have more than one method)

(5) Storage

(6) Dispensing: trays prepared

d) Use separate area from treatment to avoid contamination from splatter

e) Ultrasonic cleaning safest, most efficient

(1) Follow manufacturer's directions

(2) Do not overload

(3) Cover unit to avoid aerosolization

(4) Manual scrub only when ultrasonic would damage equipment

VI. PROTECTING THE DENTAL HEALTH CARE WORKER (DHCW)

A. Immunizations

1. HBV—OSHA-required by employer to all workers with occupational exposure

a) Recombinant DNA HB vaccine given in deltoid muscle at 0, 1, 6 months

b) Postvaccination testing after last injection for presence of anti-HBV

2. Measles, mumps, rubella, tetanus, polio, chicken pox
3. Optional: influenza, pneumococcal vaccine
4. Boosters and reimmunization schedules should be maintained

B. Handwashing

1. Reduces transient and resident microorganisms on skin
2. Prevents person-to-person transmission
3. Prevents autogenous infection if skin becomes broken
4. Resident microorganisms: *Staphylococcus epidermis*, diphtheroids, micrococci
5. Gloves are NOT a substitute for routine handwashing
6. Wash before gloving, after carefully removing gloves, and after any break in glove
7. Use effective liquid antiseptic soap (should be gentle and nonirritating)
   a) Remove any jewelry
   b) Short handwash
      (1) Begin day with two consecutive 15-second handwashes with soap and water
      (2) Wash hands for 15 seconds between clients, before and after eating, using lavatory, or any contamination
   c) Surgical hand scrub—before surgical procedures with protocol posted
      (1) Five-minute scrub of hands, arms to elbow with repeated scrub and rinse using antimicrobial soap and soft sterile brush
      (2) Dry with sterile towel
8. Intact skin is a natural defense, use brush prudently
9. Use foot control for sink, or use paper towels to turn on and off
10. Keep nails short and cuticles groomed to avoid breaks in skin
11. Personnel with weeping dermatitis or lesions with exudate should avoid contact with saliva and blood
12. Recommended antimicrobial soaps
    a) Chlorhexidene gluconate 2% or 4%, with isopropyl (Bactoshield, Hibiclens)—has substantivity
    b) Parachlorometaxylenol 3% (Banique 3, Derm-septic)
    c) Povidone iodine 7.5% to 10.00% (Betadine)
    d) Triclosan

C. Gloves

1. Provide protection for client and oral health care worker
2. Prevent direct contact with potentially infectious materials
3. Cover abrasions and cuts that could be portals of entry for pathogenic microorganisms
4. Documented cases of transmission of HIV, HBV, herpes viruses transmitted from DHCW who did not wear gloves
5. Protocol for glove use
   a) Wear whenever anticipated contact with potentially infectious materials
   b) Wash hands before and after glove use

c) Do NOT wash gloves with antiseptics, causes "wicking"
d) Double gloving is NOT recommended

6. Types of gloves
   a) Single-use nonsterile gloves (examination gloves) adequate for most procedures, fits both hands, sized extra-small to extra-large
      (1) Latex: powdered or unpowdered
      (2) Vinyl
      (3) Nonvinyl (hypoallergenic)
   b) Single-use plastic overgloves ("food-handler gloves")
      (1) Nontreatment
      (2) Worn over treatment gloves to prevent contamination
      (3) Plastic
   c) Heat resistant gloves for handling hot items
7. Latex hypersensitivity
   a) Providers should be aware of symptoms, associated risks
      (1) *Immediate hypersensitivity*—eye itching, watering, coughing, wheezing, drop in blood pressure, anaphylaxis may occur within minutes of exposure
      (2) *Delayed hypersensitivity* (Type IV)—most common; occurs 48 hours later; dry, cracked, irritated or "weeping" skin
   b) Document in medical/dental records
   c) Provide latex-free gloves and armamentarium

D. Protective barriers for mucous membranes

1. Prevent exposure to droplets, aerosols, and splatter of potentially infectious particles (PIP)
2. Masks—prevents inhalation and direct contact with PIP and aerosols
   a) Effective masks filter 95% of particles 3.0 to 3.2 μm with minimal leakage
   b) Types
      (1) Glass fiber
      (2) Synthetic fiber
      (3) Dome
      (4) Tie-on
      (5) Ear loop
   c) Disposable particulate respirator (PRM) for use in treating infectious tuberculosis
      (1) Tight face seal to protect against inhalation of droplet nuclei
      (2) Greater filtration—99% for particles larger than 1 micron
   d) Minimizing contamination
      (1) Use new mask for each client or if mask becomes wet (wicking)
      (2) Put mask on before handwash
      (3) Adjust mask to fit tightly against face

(4) Avoid touching mask, protect from exposure to chemicals
(5) Keep mask on after procedure to avoid inhaling aerosols
(6) Remove mask overhead, touching only elastic or ties

3. Protective eyewear is worn during treatment, disinfection, sterilization, and laboratory procedures
   a) Risk of exposure of eyes to harmful chemicals, debris, potentially infectious materials
   b) Eyewear must cover entire orbit (top and side shields)
   c) Face shields provide most protection, used as an adjunct to glasses and masks for aerosol producing procedures
   d) Protective eyewear should be routinely provided to clients during treatment, be able to withstand immersion disinfection
   e) During treatment using ultraviolet radiation, special eyewear is needed

E. Protective clothing

1. Provides coverage to skin and street clothes from potentially infectious materials such as blood and saliva
2. May be disposable or reusable
3. Isolation gown is prototype
   a) Covers street clothing completely
   b) Long-sleeved, high collar, fits closely at neck, wrists
   c) Should be fluid resistant
4. Do not wear outside practice setting
5. Work shoes should be kept in practice area
6. Additional coverage such as plastic aprons, head covers, shoe covers, may be utilized during invasive procedures generating splash and splatter
7. Laundry
   a) Handle sparingly, outside client treatment area
   b) Transport for laundry or disposal in sealed, leakproof bag
   c) Launder separately at temperatures of 60 to 70°C or more, normal bleach
   d) Dry at high temperature (100°C)

➤ DISEASE TRANSMISSION

I. THE INFECTIOUS DISEASE PROCESS

A. Reservoir of infection

1. Potential sources of disease agents
2. Active disease cases, animals (zoonosis), water, food, soil

B. Portal of exit—mechanism for infectious agent to escape host (e.g., feces)

C. Routes of transmission

1. Direct contact
2. Indirect contact (fomites, contamination)
3. Accidental innoculation with instrument or needle
4. Arthropods—vectors such as ticks, fleas, spiders

Review of Blood Components

Formed Elements (cellular components)

1. Erthryocytes (RBCs)—function in oxygen transport through hemoglobin; disposal of CO_2, mature RBC has no nucleus.
2. Leukocytes (WBCs)—function in immune and inflammatory response; antigen-antibody response; phagocytosis—ingestion and disposal of invader by certain leukocytes
   a. Granular leukocytes
      - Polymorphonuclear neutrophils (PMNs)*
        No color when stained
        Most numerous inflammatory cell in any stage of infection
        55% to 65% of WBCs in blood, few in tissue
        First line of defense, first to respond, phagocytic
        Short-lived scavenger cell with powerful bacteriocidal enzymes: collagenase, lysozyme
      - Basophils (1% of WBCs in circulation)
        Stain blue
        Rich in granules of histamine, heparin, serotonin-released in allergic reaction
        React with IgE on sensitized surface of mast cells (in connective tissue of respiratory and GI tract)
      - Eosinophils*
        Stain red
        Mediate allergic response
        Reject parasitic worms
   b. Nongranular leukocytes
      - Monocytes
        3% to 8% of WBCs in normal circulating blood
        Lifespan of a few hours
        Migrate into tissue and become macrophages
        Take on characteristics of specific tissues, may live for months or years
        Macrophages attack pathogens, participate in immune response
      - Lymphocytes—small cells, slightly larger than RBC, large nucleus with small amounts of cytoplasm
        Originate from blood-forming stem cells in bone marrow
        Each type of lymphocyte has cluster designation marker (epitopes) or CD markers expressed on their cell membrane (e.g., CD4+ helper cell)
        B lymphocytes or B cells—bursa-derived cell, precursors of plasma cells that produce antibodies, concentrated in lymphoid tissue, participates in humoral immunity
        T lymphocytes or T cells—thymus-derived cell that participates in cellular immunity
        Helper T cells—help other immune cells to increase efficiency; presents macrophage with antigen to B cell, release lymphokines (chemicals that signal immune system)
        Cytotoxic T cells—kills cells infected with viruses, intracellular bacterial pathogens, some tumors
        Suppressor T Cells—regulates immune response

Natural killer cells—lymphocytes without membrane surface markings on B or T cells

Kill certain types of tumor and virus-infected cells

3. Thrombocytes (platelets)—involved in blood coagulation

Fluid Portion of Blood

Plasma—90% water, 10% proteins (albumin, globulins, fibrinogen, non-protein nitrogenous material, carbohydrates and fats, inorganic salts, and bicarbonate buffers)

*Indicates cell with phagocytic abilities

II. THE IMMUNE SYSTEM

A. Nonspecific resistance

1. Normal and indigenous flora (e.g., *S. epidermis*)
2. Natural barriers: intact skin, mucous membranes, nasal hairs, stomach acid, cough reflex, secretions such as tears, mucus, vaginal fluids
3. Blood components such as leukocytes
4. Lymphatic system—transports WBCs and removes foreign cells and debris via lymphatic vessels, lymph fluid, lymphocytes, and reticuloendothelial system
5. Inflammation
   a) The sum of the body's reaction to injury or invasion of pathogenic organisms
   b) The process by which repair and regeneration of damaged tissue takes place
   c) Some damage to host cell is directly related to inflammatory by-products
      (1) For example, collagenase released by PMNs to destroy invading bacteria also destroys collagen of principal gingival fibers as secondary result.
   d) Cardinal signs of inflammation—usually related to effects of vasodilation
      (1) Heat
      (2) Redness or erythema
      (3) Edema
      (4) Pain
      (5) Loss of function
   e) Sequence of events during inflammatory process
      (1) Injury or introduction of invader
      (2) Immediate constriction of microcirculation
      (3) Dilatation of small blood vessels
      (4) Increased permeability of small blood vessels
      (5) Exudate leaves small blood vessels
      (6) Blood viscosity increases, causing microcirculation to decrease

(7) Margination and pavementing of WBCs on edge of blood vessels
(8) WBCs go into tissue and phagocytose foreign material
(9) Cellular and tissue debris is removed

6. Antimicrobial substances produced by the body
   a) Lysozyme—nonspecific enzyme found in tears, saliva that digests peptidoglycan of gram-positive bacteria
   b) Interferon—antiviral protein produced on exposure to viruses, inhibits viral replication
   c) Complement—group of proteins that function in a cascading series of immunological reactions, stimulated by antigen-antibody activity
   d) Interleukins—lymphokyine produced by white blood cells that act on other white blood cells—important in cellular immunity

B. Specific resistance: immunity—a condition under which an individual is protected from disease—specific to individual disease causing organism

1. Active immunity—developed after antigens enter the body and the antibody is produced in response
   a) *Naturally acquired*—result of exposure to disease or developing illness (e.g., "catching chickenpox")
   b) *Artificially acquired*—development of antibodies after intentional exposure to antigens (e.g., HBV immunization)
2. Passive immunity—antibodies enter body from an outside source
   a) *Naturally acquired* (congenital immunity)—antibodies pass into fetal circulation from mother's bloodstream via the placenta; lasts 3 to 6 months
   b) *Artificially acquired*—intentional injection of antibody-rich serum into circulation (e.g., gamma globulin)
3. Cell-mediated immunity (CMI): protects against viral infections, fungi, some tumor cells, causes transplant rejection
   a) T lymphocytes produce cytokines (such as macrophage-activating factor) in response to altered cell surface
   b) T lymphocyte works with macrophages, B lymphocytes
   c) Responsible for delayed hypersensitivity response (Type IV)
4. Humoral—antibody-mediated immunity (AMI)
   a) Good against bacterial infections
   b) Upon stimulation, activated B lymphocytes transform into plasma cells
   c) Plasma cells produce antibodies
   d) Antibodies react with specific antigen
   e) Antigen-antibody complex activates complement, which destroys in the following ways
      (1) Bacteria are lysed
      (2) Bacteria are more susceptible to phagocytosis
      (3) Chemotaxis attracts PMNs and macrophages
      (4) Histamine is released, amplifying inflammatory response
   f) Five classes of immunoglobins (Ig) used interchangeably with "antibody"

(1) IgM—largest, first to appear in circulation, starts agglutination and bacteriolysis
(2) IgA—primary defense on exposed mucosal surfaces, secretory IgA in saliva, body cavities
(3) IgE—major role in allergic reactions, sensitizes mast cells and basophils to release histamine, heparin starting Type I reactions
(4) IgG—classic gamma globulin, 75% of circulating antibodies, "maternal antibody"—crosses placenta
(5) IgD—trace antibody, probably regulator

C. Errors in the immune response

1. Hypersensitivity reactions—exaggerated or inappropriate response that causes tissue damage, initiating antigen termed *allergen*
   a) Type I—classic, immediate, anaphylactic, IgE antibody mediated
      (1) Mast cells, basophils, release of histamines, prostaglandins, heparin
      (2) Genetic, affects 10% of population
      (3) Asthma, urticaria, angioedema, "hay fever," anaphylaxis
      (4) Allergens—pollen, dust, pets, foods, medications
   b) Type II—cytotoxic, antibody reacts with cell surface antigen causing cell death
      (1) Complement activates
      (2) Rh incompatibility: hemolytic disease of the newborn
      (3) Blood transfusion reactions
   c) Type III—immune complex reactions, antibody reacts with soluble antigen, fixes complement, activating an "immune complex"
      (1) Usually complexes adhere to macrophages and are destroyed
      (2) If remain in circulation, cause blood vessel permeability, damage to blood vessels, tissue destruction results (Arthus reaction)
      (3) May be cause of autoimmune diseases such as systemic lupus erythematosus
      (4) Examples—serum sickness, farmer's lung, bacterial endocarditis
   d) Type IV—Cell-mediated, delayed hypersensitivity
      (1) Sensitized T lymphocyte interacts with antigen
      (2) Lymphokines released, adversely affecting body cells
      (3) Usually 48 hours after exposure to antigen
      (4) Examples: Contact dermatitis, TB skin test, poison ivy
      (5) NO antibody involved
2. Autoimmune diseases (autoallergic)—body usually recognizes itself and does not attack its own tissues
   a) Autoimmune disorders—body attacks tissue as "nonself"
   b) Examples: rheumatoid arthritis, lupus erythematosus, Graves' disease
3. Immunosuppression—increased susceptibility to infection due to defective functioning of immune system

a) Examples
   (1) Drug induced: corticosteroids, cyclosporine; infections common
   (2) Acquired immunodeficiency syndrome (AIDS)—irreversible disease caused by a defect in cell-mediated immunity that allows development of opportunistic infections and cancers, with a high mortality rate
      (a) Etiology—lentivirus of human retrovirus family
      (b) Infects lymphocytes (especially CD4+ helper T cells), macrophages, and other immune defense cells
      (c) CDC definition—T-lymphocyte count < 200 cells or CD4+ < 14%, and any of the following conditions: candidiasis of bronchi, trachea, lungs, and esophagus; invasive cervical cancer, coccidiomycosis, cryptococcosis, cytomegalovirus, HIV-related encephalopathy, chronic herpes simplex, disseminated or extrapulmonary histoplasmosis, isoporiasis, Kaposi sarcoma, Burkitt's or immunoblastic lymphoma, lymphoma of the brain, *Mycobacterium tuberculosis, avium, Pneumocystis carinii* pneumonia, recurrent pneumonia, progressive multifocal leukoencephalopathy, recurrent *Salmonella* septicemia, toxoplasmosis of the brain, and HIV wasting syndrome
      (d) Transmission: exposure to infected blood, sexual contact, perinatal, with cofactors such as genital herpes increasing transmission rate
      (e) Oral manifestations
         i) Kaposi sarcoma: neoplastic vascular, pigmented lesion of mucous membrane or skin (blue, purple, brown)
         ii) Oral and esophageal candidiasis
         iii) Herpetic lesions
         iv) Hairy leukoplakia
         v) Linear gingival erythema, necrotizing ulcerative periodontitis
         vi) Human papillomavirus
         vii) Lymphoma
         viii) Recurrent aphthous ulcers
      (f) No known cure, treated with antiviral agents (synthetic nucleotide analogs such as azidothymidine (AZT), dedeoxyinosine (ddI), dedeoxycytidine (ddC), and protease inhibitors

D. Factors that affect immune response (host state)

1. Abnormal physical conditions
   a) Congenital defects of heart, kidney
   b) Trauma, burns, surgery, infection or inflammatory condition
      (1) Entrance for pathogenic microorganism
      (2) Altered physiological defense

2. Systemic diseases
   a) Alcoholism
   b) Diabetes mellitus
   c) Neoplasms such as leukemia
   d) Immunosuppressive disorders such as HIV
   e) Malnutrition
   f) Genetic disorders such as chemotactic leukocyte defect
3. Prostheses and transplants
   a) Nidus for infection
   b) Therapy may include suppression of normal immune response to avoid transplant rejection
4. Drug therapy
   a) Steroids suppress immune response
   b) Chemotherapeutic agents suppress immune response
5. Extreme youth or age
   a) Infant dependent on maternal antibodies for first 3 to 6 months
   b) Decreased immune response in elderly

➤ INFECTIOUS DISEASES SPECIFIC TO THE DENTAL HEALTH PROVIDER

Infections of Epithelial Tissues

I. VIRAL INFECTIONS

A. Herpes simplex

1. Etiological agent—herpes simplex viruses HVS 1(oral) and HVS 2 (genital), even in health it is present in saliva
2. Transmitted through oral or ocular secretions and also through fomites
3. Retrovirus establishes latent infection in nerve ganglion; reactivates on stress, sunlight, illness
4. Acute herpetic gingivostomatitis in children
   a) Fever, malaise, localized lymphadenopathy, anorexia, numerous yellow vesicles that rupture and ulcerate, leaving erythemic margins
   b) Painful, duration 7 days, palliative treatment, usually self-limiting
5. Herpetic whitlow—infection of fingers
6. Herpes labialis—"cold sores, fever blisters," erythematous base with vesicles; prodromal burning and tingling
7. Ocular herpes—may cause blindness, attacks conjunctiva and cornea
8. Treatment—antiviral agents such as acyclovir

B. Varicella zoster virus—etiological agent for chickenpox, herpes zoster (shingles)

1. Chickenpox—mode of transmission: mucosa of upper respiratory tract via droplets
   a) Highly infectious childhood disease
   b) Clinical symptoms—fever, malaise, rash with vesicle formation
   c) Oral lesions may occur
   d) Vaccine available

2. Shingles—reactivation of latent virus in dorsal root ganglion of sensory nerves
   a) Follows nerve pathway—thoracic area most commonly affected, ophthalmic division of trigeminal nerve second most common
   b) Same etiology as chickenpox, different manifestation of infection
   c) Primarily affects adults: malaise, fever, severe pain with rash and vesicles
   d) Occurs along nerve trunk

C. Measles

1. Etiology—rubeola virus
2. Mode of transmission—respiratory droplets spreading to lymphoid tissue
3. Virus is spread throughout epithelial body surfaces
   a) Koplik's spots—first clinical sign; small spots on buccal mucosa
   b) Skin rash follows, fever, may have secondary bacterial infections
4. Vaccine available

D. Rubella virus (German measles)

1. Mode of transmission—respiratory droplets
2. Clinical findings—malaise, low-grade fever, rash, lymphadenopathy
3. Vaccine available

E. Mumps (infective parotiditis)

1. Etiology—paramyxovirus
2. Mode of transmission—respiratory droplets
3. Inflammation of parotid gland, meninges, testicles
4. Vaccine available

F. Infectious mononucleosis

1. Etiology—Epstein-Barr virus (also causes hairy leukoplakia (HIV+), chronic fatigue syndrome, Burkitt's lymphoma (HIV+), and some nasopharyngeal tumors
2. Mode of transmission—direct contact with saliva

VII. BACTERIAL INFECTIONS

A. Lyme disease

1. Etiological agent—spirochete *Borrelia burgdorferi*
2. Mode of transmission—deer tick bites
3. Neurological and arthritic problems caused by antigen-antibody complex (type III hypersensitivity reaction)
4. Clinical findings—bulls-eye lesion, headaches, fever, myalgia, lymphadenopathy, cardiac disease, neurological problems, arthritis
5. Vaccine available

B. Tetnus

1. Etiology—*Clostridium tetani*
2. Mode of transmission—spores enter anaerobic wound site, produce tetanus toxin (usually "puncture wound")

3. Clinical findings: trismus or "lock-jaw," facial muscle spasms, dysphagia, breathing difficulty
4. Vaccine available

C. Streptococcal infections

1. Etiology—*Streptococcus pyogenes* (group A beta-hemolytic)
2. Mode of transmission—rapidly spreads from portal of entry
3. Clinical findings
   a) Scarlet fever—acute upper respiratory tract inflammation, bright red oral mucosa, sequelae include rheumatic fever and hemorrhagic glomerulonephritis
   b) Erysipelas—"invasive strep," angry skin eruptions

D. Staphylococcal infections

1. Etiology—*Staphylococcus aureus*
2. Mode of transmission—entry into wound
3. Clinical findings—furuncles (boils), carbuncles, impetigo, "scalded baby syndrome"
4. Carried in anterior nares, fomites such as stethoscopes
5. Most strains resistant to penicillin—methicillin-resistant *Staphlylococcus aureus* (MRSA) serious problem in hospitals
6. Common nosocomial infection

E. *Pseudomonas aeruginosa* infections

1. Common in water supplies and dental unit water lines
2. Pathogenic in immunocompromised client, burn victims, common nosocomial infection
3. Clinical findings—external ear infections, rash associated with hot tubs, swimming pools

VIII. FUNGAL INFECTIONS

A. Candidiasis

1. Etiology—*Candida albicans,* normal part of flora of skin, mucosa
2. Opportunistic infection manifested in immunocompromised patients
3. Predisposing factors—use of broad-spectrum antibiotics, immunological defects (HIV), diabetes mellitus, pregnancy, and malnutrition
4. Clinical findings
   a) Intraoral lesions
   b) Angular chelitis (perleche)—infection at corner of mouth may be secondarily infected with *S. aureus*

Respiratory Tract Infections

I. UPPER RESPIRATORY TRACT INFECTIONS

A. "Common cold"

1. Etiology—rhinovirus, adenovirus, coronavirus, respiratory syncyntial virus
2. Clinical findings—nasal obstruction, "runny nose," sore throat, cough, dyspnea
3. Self-limiting, palliative treatment only

B. Diphtheria

1. Etiology—*Corynebacterium diphtheriae*
2. Pathogenesis—droplets carry bacteria into mucous membrane, damage caused by systemic toxin
   a) Edema, lymphadenopathy of neck
   b) Pseudomembrane on tonsils, blocks airway
3. Vaccine available
4. Detected with Schick test

C. Streptococcal pharyngitis ("strep throat")

1. Etiology—*Streptococcus pyogenes*
2. Mode of transmission—respiratory droplets, ingestion of contaminated substance
3. Clinical findings—severe inflammation of throat and tonsils, pain, fever

II. LOWER RESPIRATORY TRACT INFECTIONS

A. Tuberculosis (TB)

1. Etiology—*Mycobacterium tuberculosis*
2. Mode of transmission—inhalation of droplet nuclei, direct inoculation, ingestion of contaminated food or water. Long incubation period: 28 to 47 days
3. Risk factors—immunocompromised patient, chronic alcoholism, diabetes mellitus, HIV, poor nutrition, prolonged contact with those with disease
4. Clinical symptoms—early: low-grade fever, weight loss, fatigue, slight cough; later: elevated temperature in afternoon, night sweats, weakness, persistent cough (may be bloody)
5. Diagnosis—positive purified derivative (PPD) of TB injected subcutaneously as Mantoux skin test. Reaction to test indicates need for chest x-ray.
   a) Positive skin test indicates antibodies exist, not necessarily active TB
   b) HIV patients with TB may test negatively due to anergy
6. Multidrug resistant TB occurs when medication is not taken properly
7. T-cell mediated, HIV patients at high risk due to lack of T-cell response
8. Granulomas called tubercles; tissue destruction: caseous necrosis

B. Pertussis or "whooping cough"

1. Etiology—*Bordetella pertussis*
2. Clinical findings—paroxysmal cough
3. Vaccine available

C. Pneumonia—inflammation of lungs, caused by many species of microorganisms

1. Bacterial
   a) Pneumococcal pneumonia
      (1) Etiology—*Streptococcus pneumoniae*
      (2) Spread by droplets, carrier state exists

(3) Risk factors—extremes of age, lowered resistance, bacteremia
(4) Clinical findings—sudden onset of high fever, chills, chest pain, dry cough
(5) Vaccine available

b) *Klebsiella pneumoniae*—more serious, common in alcoholics, immunocompromised

2. Mycoplasmal pneumonia "walking pneumonia," mild presentation
3. Fungal—*Pneumocystis pneumonia*
   a) Spores inhaled
   b) Disease occurs in immunocompromised (e.g., HIV)
4. *Chlamydia pneumoniae*—intracellular organisms
5. Viral pneumonia—many viruses implicated

D. Legionnaire's disease

1. Etiology—*Legionella pneumonphilia*
2. Mode of transmission—inhalation of contaminated aerosols
3. Clinical findings—influenza-like disease with pneumonia, GI hemorrhage, respiratory failure
4. Multiplies in municipal water supplies, cultured from dental unit water lines

E. Influenza

1. Etiology—rapidly mutating virus
2. Mode of transmission—airborne droplets, contact with contaminated object
3. Clinical findings—body aches, fever, headaches, dry cough, malaise
4. Secondary bacterial infections may lead to more serious illness
5. Vaccine available, recommended for DHCW

F. Histoplasmosis

1. Etiology—fungus: *Histoplasma capsulatum*
2. Mode of transmission—inhalation of spores carried in feces of birds and bats
3. Clinical findings—Skin lesions, meningitis
4. Indigenous to Mississippi River Valley, common infection among farmers

G. *Hantavirus* pulmonary virus

1. Etiology—*Hantavirus*
2. Mode of transmission—inhalation of deer mice excretions
3. Clinical findings—severe respiratory distress, rapid onset, hemorrhage of lungs

H. Cytomegalovirus (CMV)

1. Etiology—Cytomegalovirus (herpes virus)
2. Mode of transmission—congenital, contact with body fluids, inhalation of respiratory droplets, especially in children in day-care settings
3. Clinical findings—infectious mononucleosis, pneumonitis, severe disease manifestations in the fetus; including fetal death, prematurity, retardation, blindness, chronic liver disease
4. Serious complications in the immunodeficient patient

➤ INFECTIONS OF THE GASTROINTESTINAL TRACT

I. VIRAL INFECTIONS

A. Hepatitis A (HAV)

1. Mode of transmission—oral-fecal route due to contaminated food or water, personal contact in unsanitary conditions, blood transfusions in early stage of active disease (rare)
2. Clinical findings—disease occurs much more frequently in children, who present with few if any signs and symptoms
   a) Preicteric phase—abrupt onset of influenza-like illness, fever, headaches, vomiting, nausea, abdominal pain, tender, palpable liver
   b) Icteric phase—rare in children, continuation of symptoms for days to a month, anicteric form (without jaundice) two to three times more prevalent, 90% of patients recover completely
   c) Immunity—Anti-HAV detectable in blood within 2 weeks of onset
      (1) Immunity follows infection
      (2) No carrier state
      (3) Vaccine (Havrix) available, early immunization recommended
         (a) Food handlers, travelers to foreign countries, children
         (b) Administered 2 weeks before expected exposure, booster for adults

B. Hepatitis B

1. Mode of transmission—blood-borne pathogen, percutaneous and permucosal exposure, infected blood transfusions (screened since 1985), exposure to infected body fluids or contaminated needles, and perinatal transmission
2. Terms to know
   a) Hepatitis B surface antigen (HBsAg) (Australian antigen)—surface marker in acute, chronic, and carrier states of HBV
   b) Antibody to hepatitis B surface antigen (anti-HBsAg)—represents immunity
   c) Hepatitis B e antigen (HBeAg)—high titer indicates high infectivity or development of chronic liver disease and carrier state
   d) Antibody to hepatitis B e antigen (anti-HBeAg)—indicates low infectivity
   e) Hepatitis B core antigen (HBcAg)—indicates acute, chronic, or resolved state
   f) Antibody to HBcAg (anti-HBcAg)—indicates prior HBV infection
   g) IgM class antibody to hepatitis B core antigen (IgM anti-HBc)—indicates recent HBc infection
3. Clinical Findings
   a) HBV infection (does not occur in response to vaccine)
   b) Similar to HAV, although slower onset and longer duration

c) Most patients asymptomatic, but jaundice and acute disease do occur
  (1) Symptoms described above with some skin rashes, itching, joint pain
  (2) End of icteric phase corresponds with recovery
  (3) 5% to 10% will develop carrier state
    (a) HbsAg detectable after 6 months
    (b) Carriers usually asymptomatic and undetected
    (c) High incidence of cirrhosis or hepatocellular carcinoma (cancer of liver)

4. Immunity
  a) Serologic presence of anti-HBsAg indicates immunity
  b) Vaccines available
    (1) Early vaccine derived using inactivated HBsAg from plasma ofchronic HBV carriers (Heptavax)
    (2) Recombinant DNA HB vaccine: uses recombinant DNA technology to synthesize HbsAg in yeast culture (Recombivax HB)
      (a) 99% immunity in children, drops to 95% in adults
      (b) Three doses: 0, 1, 6 months; postvaccination testing within 1 month for high-risk groups, including DHCW
      (c) Better response when injection is given in deltoid muscle rather than buttock
    (3) Passive immunization for postexposure prophylaxis—hepatitis B immune globulin given within 24 to 48 hours of exposure

C. Hepatitis C (Formerly known as transfusion associated non-A, non-B hepatitis)

1. Mode of transmission—percutaneous exposure to contaminated blood and plasma products (blood now tested in the United States), IV drug use, sexual transmission, perinatal exposure
2. Clinical findings—insidious onset, few or no clinical symptoms, some patients develop abdominal discomfort, nausea and vomiting, few develop icteric phase; chronic liver disease develops in 50% to 85%, progresses to liver cancer or cirrhosis
3. Prevention—universal precautions, testing of donated blood

D. Hepatitis D (formerly delta hepatitis)

1. Mode of transmission—HDV cannot cause infection without presence of HBV
  a) Occurs after multiple exposures to HBV such as IV drug users or patients with hemophilia
  b) Similar transmission to HBV: contaminated blood, body fluids, contaminated needles, sexual contacts, perinatal transfer
2. Clinical findings—severe infection (coinfection or superinfection of HBV), abrupt onset, may cause fulminant hepatitis.

E. Hepatitis E (formerly known as enterically transmitted non-A, non-B hepatitis)

TABLE 6-3 COMPARISONS OF HEPATITIS VIRUSES

Etiological Agent	Incubation (I) and Communicable Period (C)	Vaccine
Hepatitis A (HAV)	I—15–50 days C—2–3 weeks before jaundice	Havrix Given to children Foreign travelers Military Food handlers Day care workers
Hepatitis B (HBV)	I—45–160 days C—presence of HbsAg Carrier state: 5–10%	Genetically engineered vaccine Recombivax Children HCWs Military
Hepatitis C (HCV)	I—2–26 weeks C—chronic in 50–85%/carrier	None exists
Hepatitis D (HDV)	I—uncertain C—uncertain	Vaccine for HBV confers immunity
Hepatitis E (HEV)	I—15–60 days C—duration of illness	None
Hepatitis G	Unknown	None

1. Mode of transmission—oral-fecal, enteric, outbreaks associated with contaminated water sources, inadequate sewage disposal
2. Clinical findings—nausea, vomiting, high mortality in pregnant women
3. Prevention—proper sanitation, handwashing before food handling

F. Hepatitis G

1. Mode of transmission—bloodborne, coinfection with HCV
2. Disease modality still unknown

II. BACTERIAL INFECTIONS

A. Food poisoning agents (often toxin producing)

1. Botulism
   a) Etiology—*Clostridium botulinum*
   b) Mode of transmission—contaminant of food products (improperly cooked or preserved)
   c) Clinical findings—toxin produced; nerve damage causes speaking difficulties, inability to swallow, heart failure, respiratory paralysis
   d) Sudden infant death syndrome may be linked to infant botulism
2. Staphylococcal food poisoning
   a) Etiology—staphylococci (usually *S. aureus*) produced toxin from unrefrigerated foods
   b) Clinical findings—violent vomiting, diarrhea 1 to 8 hours after ingestion of enterotoxin

➤ OTHER IMPORTANT DISEASES

I. SEXUALLY TRANSMITTED DISEASES

A. Syphilis

1. Etiology—*Treponema pallidum* (anaerobic spirochete)
2. Mode of transmission—primarily by sexual contact with skin or mucous membranes
3. Spirochete crosses the placenta—congenital syphilis occurs
4. Spirochete can pass through break in skin, intact mucous membranes
5. Organisms spread rapidly through lymphatic system and bloodstream, affecting all organs
6. Clinical findings
   a) Primary stage: single granulomatous lesion at point of contact ("chancre")
      (1) Asymptomatic
      (2) Highly contagious
      (3) Lasts 3 to 5 weeks, heals spontaneously with no scar
   b) Secondary stage—patient may be asymptomatic for 2 to 6 months before symptoms occur
      (1) Flulike symptoms
      (2) Shallow painless ulcers—"mucous patches" on lips, soft palate, and tongue that are highly contagious
      (3) Swollen lymph nodes
      (4) Maculopapular rashes on face, hands, feet
   c) Tertiary stage—may take years to develop
      (1) "Gumma"—inflammatory granulomatous lesions on tongue, perforating palate, facial bones
      (2) Gumma is not contagious, usually asymptomatic
      (3) Central nervous system (CNS) involvement leads to loss of fine motor coordination, personality changes
      (4) Major cause of death—cardiovascular system involvement
   d) Congenital syphilis: Hutchinson's triad
      (1) Tooth development affected:
         (a) Hutchinson's incisors—notched, "screwdriver" appearance
         (b) "Mulberry molars"—irregular first molars
      (2) Cranial nerve damage
         (a) Deafness
         (b) Impaired vision
         (c) Meningitis
      (3) Poor formation of long bones
      (4) High infant mortality rate

B. Gonorrhea

1. Etiology: *Neisseria gonorrhoeae,* a gram-negative, aerobic diplococcus
2. Mode of transmission—Sexual contact spreads microorganism throughout genitourinary tract, into reproductive system causing pelvic inflammatory disease (PID)

3. Clinical findings
    a) Women at higher risk than are men
        (1) Usually asymptomatic
        (2) May have vaginal discharge, backache, abdominal pain
    b) Men may experience frequent, painful urination
    c) Gonoccoccal glossitis, pharyngitis
        (1) Oral infection including pharyngitis, glossitis, stomatitis
        (2) May include areas of ulceration, tissue sloughing
    d) Gonococcal ophthalmia—newborn's eyes may become infected during birth, treating eyes with 1% silver nitrate prevents blindness
    e) Complications include sterility, meningitis, disseminated infections

C. Chlamydia (Chlamydial urethritis or nongonococcal urethritis (NGU)

1. Etiology—*Chlamydia trachomatis*
2. Mode of transmission—sexual contact (grows only in living tissue)
3. Clinical findings—gonorrhea-like symptoms, although milder
    a) Leading cause of PID, sterility in women
    b) Called "silent epidemic," affecting 3 to 5 million women annually in United States
4. Chlamydial ophthalmia—disease affecting eyes of infant born to an infected mother; requires erythromycin therapy to prevent blindness
5. Chlamydial pneumonia—develops in exposed infants, implicated in myocardial infarctions in adults

II. DISEASES OF THE CIRCULATORY SYSTEM

A. Rheumatic fever

1. Etiology: Beta-hemolytic group A streptococcus
2. Mode of transmission—hypersensitivity reaction developing after streptococcal infection; inflammation of heart valves, abnormal growth of connective tissue, valve scarring occurs
3. Clinical findings—fever, polyarthritis, malaise, inflammation of heart (carditis)
4. Sequelae of carditis
    a) Defective heart valves
        (1) Narrowing of valve opening—stenosis
        (2) Failure of valve to close completely—valvular insufficiency
    b) Antibiotic premedication needed before dental treatment to prevent bacterial endocarditis

B. Infective endocarditis (bacterial endocarditis, subacute bacterial endocarditis)

1. Etiology—microbial invasion of heart valves or endocardium, usually associated with normal flora of respiratory or intestinal tract
    a) Usually streptococci (α-hemolytic) and staphylococci
    b) Yeasts, fungi, and viruses have also been implicated

2. Mode of transmission—dental procedures may introduce microorganisms into bloodstream (bacteremia), and they lodge on defective heart valves
3. Risk factors
   a) Cardiac abnormalities such as heart valves damaged by rheumatic fever, congenital heart defects, prosthetic heart valves, and arteriosclerosis
   b) Intravenous drug users
   c) Infections at portals of entry; poor oral hygiene, trauma to oral tissues (dental procedures)
   d) Individuals with compromised immune response
4. Clinical findings
   a) Symptoms appear within 2 weeks
   b) Fever, malaise, anemia, weakness, arthralgia, muscle weakness, and heart murmur
   c) Vegetative clusters of microorganisms lead to emboli, diminished heart function
   d) High mortality rate, susceptibility to reinfection
5. Consult with physician, prophylactic antibiotic premedication required
6. Stress importance of oral health to prevent nidus of infection

III. INFECTIONS OF THE NERVOUS SYSTEM AND SENSORY ORGANS

A. Meningitis—inflammation of the covering of the brain

1. Etiology—variety of causes, high mortality rate
   a) Aseptic meningitis—caused by viruses, bacteria, chemicals, mycoplasms, and chlamydias
      (1) Acute onset, stiff neck, severe headache, fever
   b) Meningococcal meningitis—*Neisseria meningitidis*
      (1) Mode of transmission—inhalation of respiratory droplets
      (2) Headache, stiff neck, vomiting, coma within hours
   c) Haemophilus meningitis—*Haemophilus influenzae b*
      (1) Mode of transmission—inhalation of respiratory droplets
      (2) Respiratory disease, stiff, arched neck, headache
      (3) Primarily affects children, HIB vaccine available

B. Rabies

1. Etiology—rabies virus
2. Mode of transmission—bite of rabid animal
3. Incubation period of 4 to 6 weeks
4. Clinical findings—painful throat spasms, inability to swallow, convulsions, respiratory paralysis, and death

C. Poliomyelitis

1. Etiology—poliomyelitis virus
2. Mode of transmission—oral route into intestines
3. Clinical findings—destruction of motor neurons in spinal cord, leading to flaccid paralysis (may be mild to severe)
4. Vaccine available

D. Toxoplasmosis

1. Etiology—*Toxoplasma gondii*
2. Mode of transmission—contact or inhalation of contaminated cat feces, raw meat, soil, rodents, or through placenta to fetus
3. Clinical findings—age dependent
   a) Adults—resembles infectious mononucleosis
   b) Congenital infection—stillbirth, severe psychomotor defects, blindness, deafness

E. Cryptococcoses

1. Etiology—*Cryptococcus neoformans*
2. Mode of transmission—inhalation of dehydrated fungus from bird droppings (especially pigeons)
3. Clinical findings—Meningitis common in immunocompromised patients; disseminated disease affects skin, lungs, and other organs

F. Conjunctivitis—inflammation of eye, various causes

1. Etiology
   a) Bacterial: *Haemophilus aegyptius*—common in warm climates, purulent discharge from eyes
   b) Viral
      (1) Chlamydia *trachomatis* (trachoma)
         (a) Associated with poor sanitation and personal hygiene
         (b) Inflammation of conjunctiva: scarring, secondary infection, partial or complete blindness
      (2) Coxsackievirus A 24—hemorrhagic conjunctivitis
      (3) Ocular herpes
         (a) Herpetic keratoconjunctivitis; corneal ulcers
         (b) May recur
         (c) May cause blindness
         (d) Use of safety glasses has greatly reduced incidence in health care workers

➤ MICROORGANISMS OF THE ORAL CAVITY

I. NORMAL ORAL ENVIRONMENT

A. Composition of oral flora influenced by many factors

1. Nutrients available
   a) Nutrients—fermentable carbohydrates and amino acids required
      (1) Exogenous sources—dietary sugars from host's diet provide acid and extracellular, insoluble carbohydrates (dextrans, glucans) that provides adhesion mechanism to tooth surface
      (2) Endogenous sources such as gingival exudate, saliva, epithelial cells and leukocytes, and metabolic by-products from other bacteria
2. pH requirements—dietary sugars provide an acidic medium
   a) Bacteria that are *aciduric* (tolerant of low pH values) and *acidogenic* (acid producing) become predominant
      (1) *Mutans streptococcus*, and related strains of streptococci
      (2) Lactobacilli

b) Lactic acid produced by breakdown of fermentable carbohydrates (primarily sucrose), starches implicated to a lesser extent
c) If acidogenic plaque is exposed to sugar, immediate acid production may cause pH to drop low enough to decalcify tooth surface in minutes
   (1) Below 4.5 for enamel, 6.0 to 6.7 for root surfaces
   (2) Depending on salivary flow and amount of plaque, pH remains low for 20 to 120 minutes after each sugar exposure

3. Concentration of oxygen—plaque is predominantly a gram-positive, facultative mass, even on exposed surfaces
4. Saliva flow
   a) Adequate flow rate is necessary to decrease susceptibility to caries
      (1) Needed to buffer salivary acids
      (2) Flow helps remove bacteria from oral structures
   b) Provides components for bacterial attachment to teeth; components may also inhibit bacterial growth or attachment to teeth
      (1) Glycoprotein's high molecular weight inhibits adherence
      (2) Secretory IgA inhibits microbial attachment
      (3) Antibacterial components (lysosyme, lactoperoxidase)

B. Composition of oral microbiota

1. Mucous membranes—type of surface affects type and number of microorganisms present
   a) Cheek—predominantly *S. sanguis, S. salivarius*
   b) Gingival crevice—predominantly *B. melaninogenicus*
   c) Tongue—*S. salivarius*
   d) Streptococci most common species in healthy mouth, make up over 50% of mass
2. Saliva—organisms derived from plaque and tongue (e.g., *S. salivarius*)
3. Tongue, large surface area provided by papilla
4. Gingival sulcus—as cleaning ability decreases, bacteria proliferate, gingival crevicular fluid increases, pathogenicity increases
   a) As the periodontal pocket deepens, flora changes from gram-positive, motile aerobes to predominately gram-negative, nonmotile anaerobes
   b) Periodontal pocket primary source of periodontal pathogens
5. Tooth surface plaque (* indicates ability to cause caries)
   a) Smooth surfaces—*S. sanguis* first colonizer, will be replaced by *Mutans streptococcus*
   b) most strongly cariogenic bacteria in animals, *S. milleri**, *S. mitior* and *S. sobrinus** as plaque remains undisturbed on tooth surface
      (1) *Mutans streptococcus* requires hard surface, will disappear with extractions, reappears with denture placement
         (a) Homofermentive lactic acid former
         (b) Produces insoluble glucans as attachment mechanism to tooth
         (c) High sucrose diet associated with increase in *Mutans streptococcus*

(2) *Mutans streptococcus* most closely associated with caries in epidemiological studies

c) Occlusal pits and fissures—morphology allows plaque to remain undisturbed—common caries site; causative organisms include

(1) *Mutans streptococcus**

(2) Acidogenic lactobacilli* (increase as sugar intake increases)

(a) Causative role in caries not as strong as other species

(b) Carious lesions act as retention sites

(c) Found mainly in fissurcs

d) Interproximal surfaces—difficulty in access in cleansing allows plaque to proliferate—*Mutans streptococcus** most common species

e) Root surfaces—apical migration of the gingival margin exposes cementum

(1) Extremely susceptible to caries

(2) *Mutans streptococcus* (also causative organism in root surface caries)

(3) *Actinomyces viscosus, A. naeslundii* ferment glucose to lactic acid, primary species implicated in root caries

f) Prerequisites for caries formation

(1) Cariogenic bacteria

(2) Nutrient source (fermentable carbohydrates) of substrate for acid production; increase in dietary sucrose will increase cariogenic bacteria

(3) Ability to produce extracellular, insoluble glucans for adhesion to tooth structure

(4) Susceptible host

C. Supragingival plaque

1. Thin layer of 1 to 20 cells
2. Mostly gram-positive facultative anerobic organisms

a) *S. sanguis, A. viscosus, A. naeslundii* predominate

b) Other species include *A. israelii, Mutans streptococcus, Veillonella, Fusobacterium,* and *Treponema capnocytophaga*

D. Subgingival plaque results from apical migration of supragingival plaque

1. Early in the disease, supragingival plaque influences the subgingival population
2. As periodontal disease progresses, the flora changes to more anerobic, gram negative, nonmotile forms

II. MICROBIOLOGY OF PERIODONTAL, PERIAPICAL, AND ORAL-FACIAL DISEASES

A. *Gingivitis*—gingival inflammation in response to bacterial plaque and its metabolic by-products; reversible as compared with:

1. Early stages

a) Plaque up to 100 times thicker than in health, and is more complex

   b) Predominated by *Actinomyces* species and gram-positive organisms
2. Chronic—increase in gram negative, anerobic organisms
   a) Rods predominate
   b) *Actinomyces, Fusobacterium, Bacteroides,* and spirochetes present

B. *Chronic periodontitis*—inflammatory changes extend into deeper periodontal structures, resulting in loss of alveolar bone

1. Deepening periodontal pocket provides favorable environment for bacteria
2. May be multiple diseases with similar characteristics, having different bacterial populations
3. Progression is usually episodic, dependent on effectiveness of host response
4. Microorganisms include
   a) *Prevotella intermedia*
   b) *Porphyromonas gingivalis*
   c) *Fusobacterium* species
   d) Spirochetes
   e) *Eubacterium* species
   f) *Bacteroides forsythus*
   g) *Campylobacter rectus*

C. Aggressive periodontitis (formerly prepubertal and juvenile periodontitis)—associated with immune defects; neutrophils or monocytes have defective chemotaxis or impaired function

1. Genetic or familial tendency
2. Prepubertal disease may affect primary teeth
3. Disease may be localized or generalized
   a) Localized lesions affecting permanent first molars and/or incisors
   b) Generalized disease results in rapid overall pattern of bone loss
4. Atypical—sparse amounts of thin plaque
5. Microbiota present
   a) *Capnocytophaga* species (invades tissue, rare in children)
   b) *Actinobacillus actinomycetemcomitans*
   c) *Prevotella intermedius, Eikenella corrodens*
   d) *Porphyromonas gingivalis*
6. Gram-negative, anerobic bacteria predominate
7. Host defense defective, usually impaired neutrophil function
8. Associated with rapid loss of alveolar bone

D. Necrotizing periodontal diseases—acute anaerobic infection causing ulceration of gingival margins; may progress to destruction of gingiva and underlying bone

1. Interproximal areas affected first, may result in loss of cratering of interdental papilla

2. Predisposing factors include smoking, stress, poor nutrition, and poor oral hygiene
3. Symptoms include foul odor, extreme pain, sloughing of gingiva
4. Predominant microorganisms
   a) *P. intermedia*
   b) Intermediate-sized spirochetes (*Treponema* species)
   c) *Fusobacterium* species
5. Such rapid destruction of periodontal attachment and bone occurs that pocketing is not present, alveolar bone may be exposed with sequestration
6. Localized or generalized
7. Occurs in HIV-infected person—does not respond well to therapy

F. Pregnancy and hormonally related gingivitis

1. *P. intermedia*
2. Bacteria are black pigmented

G. Linear gingival erythema (formerly HIV gingivitis)

1. May have similar presentation to ANUG, but does not respond well to local therapy
2. Fiery, discontinuous, red outline of free gingival margin, extensive, spontaneous bleeding
3. Painful, with progression to periodontitis without treatment
4. Occurs in patients infected with HIV

H. Factors influencing progression of disease

1. Invasion of tissue by bacteria (e.g., spirochetes, *Capnocytophaga* species)
2. Bacterial products may cause destruction of tissue
   a) Endotoxins (lipopolysaccharides) activate complement, produce fever and shock, and interfere with normal function of blood homeostasis; associated with gram-negative bacterial cell walls
   b) Exotoxins are soluble substances secreted by gram-positive cells that are very toxic to other organisms (e.g., botulism)
   c) Enzymes (lysozyme, collagenase, hyaluraonidase) cause destruction of oral tissue and interfere with normal immune function
3. Plaque bacteria present an antigenic challenge, some local destruction results from inflammatory process (e.g., immune complex, cell-mediated)
4. Humoral immunity
   a) Lymphocytes, plasma cells present in area of plaque
   b) Plasma cells produce antibodies
   c) Complement is activated by bacterial endotoxin, or bacterial antigen-antibody complexes
5. Cellular immunity
   a) Cell-mediated immunity causes release of lymphokines or osteoclast-activating factor
   b) The progression of periodontal disease may be due to these components of cellular immunity

I. Infections of the periapical and oral-facial tissues

1. Infections may include
   a) Periodontal and periapical abscesses
   b) Endodontically involved infections
   c) Postsurgical and extraction wound infections, including alveolar osteitis (dry socket)
   d) Sinus tract (draining fistulas) infections
   e) Cellulitis (Ludwig's angina)
   f) Injuries as a result of trauma
   g) Osteomyelitis
   h) Pericoronitis
   i) Infections of periodontal origin
2. Bacteria cultured from these infections are predominantly gram-negative bacilli such as *Prevotella* and *Porphyromonas*
3. Acute endodontic infections harbor obligate anerobic bacteria (e.g., *P. intermedia*)
4. Ludwig's angina
   a) May be caused by normal oral flora gaining access through abscessed tooth
   b) Aerobic or facultative organisms along with anaerobic microorganisms
   c) Rapidly spreading, diffuse swelling of the floor of the mouth and neck
   d) Blockage of airway becomes life-threatening
   e) Infected mandibular molars, thin lingual cortical plate of mandible are predisposing factors.
5. Actinomycosis—opportunistic infection after injury that introduces contaminated debris into tissue
   a) Etiology—*A. israellii, A. naeslundii* (gram-positive member of normal oral microbiota)
   b) Facial swelling below angle of jaw, chronic superficial mass, abscess with sinus, and chronic discharge

review glossary

Aerosol artificially generated collections of particles (often pathogenic and capable of producing infection) suspended in air.

Anergy a diminished reactivity to a specific antigen because of immunosuppression. (e.g., negative skin test in TB-infected individual due to immunosuppression caused by HIV).

Antibody a soluble protein molecule produced and secreted by body cells in response to an antigen, capable of binding and inactivating that specific antigen

Antigen a substance capable of producing a specific immune response and reacting with an antibody, usually a large molecular weight protein.

Asepsis no living pathogens present; a sterile state.

Antigenic determinant the specific molecular binding area on the surface of the cell that activates an immunological response.

Bacteremia presence of microbes in a normally sterile bloodstream.

Carrier a person harboring a specific infectious agent with no clinical manifestations and who serves as a source of potential infection; may be chronic or temporary.

Cell-mediated (cellular) immunity T-lymphocytes and macrophages are the predominant cells participating; Type IV (delayed hypersensitivity) is termed cell-mediated immunity.

Chemotaxis the process by which phagocytic cells are attracted to the area of invasion by pathogenic organisms.

Communicable stage of a disease the time during which the infectious agent may be transferred from an infected person to another; the communicable period may include or overlap the incubation period.

Complement a step-by-step process (the complement cascade) by which more than 20 serum proteins mediate the antigen-antibody process.

Contamination when an infectious agent is on a body surface.

Cytokine a substance (e.g., lymphokines, interleukins, and interferons) produced by cells that affects other cells (e.g., lymphocytes and macrophages) and that mediate the immune response.

Cytoloysis the breaking apart (lysis) of bacteria or cells such as tumor or red blood cells, from the activation of complement.

DHCW dental health care worker.

Disinfection pathogenic microorganisms are destroyed by direct contact with chemical or physical agents.

Droplet a very small drop, such as a particle of moisture expelled during sneezing, coughing, or talking that may carry potentially infectious agents.

Endemic the constant presence of an infectious agent or disease within a geographic area.

Endogenous infection acquired as a result of self microflora.

Epidemic widespread cases of disease in a region, greater than the expected number of cases for that population.

Fomite or fomes an inanimate material or object on which pathogen agents may be carried.

Hapten a molecule that is not intrinsically immunological, but that may produce a response if combined with a specific antibody.

HCW health care worker.

Histocompatible transplant antigens are shared; unlikely to cause rejection response.

Humoral immunity a population of activated B lymphocytes become plasma cells, which produce specific antibodies in response to stimulus by a specific antigen; mediated by complement.

Hypersensitivity reactions exaggerated or inappropriate response to an antigen; classified as Type I, Type II, Type III, or Type IV.

Immunity the resistance a person has against a disease.

Immune response the development of immunity or resistance to a foreign substance, which can be antibody mediated (humoral), cell-mediated (cellular), or both.

Immunoglobin a glycoprotein composed of L and H chains that functions as an antibody. The five subclasses based on the antigenic determinants are: IgA, IgD, IgG, IgM, IgE.

Incubation period the interval of time between the first contact with the infectious agent and the appearance of clinical symptoms and signs of the disease.

Infection the state caused by the invasion, development, or multiplication of the infectious agent in the body; may be *primary* (original), *latent* (no clinical symptoms), *recurrent* (reactivation of primary infection), *acute* (rapid onset, abrupt resolution), *chronic* (slow onset, long duration), *localized* (confined to a particular area), or *generalized* or *systemic* (invades bloodstream and lymphatic system).

Interferon a low-molecular weight protein produced by infected cells that protects noninfected cells from viral infections. Also mediates immune response.

Interleukin a cytokine that stimulates or affects the functions of lymphocytes and other cells.

Jaundice (icterus) yellowish coloring of skin, mucous membranes, sclerae, and bodily excretions due to hyperbilirubinemia and deposition of bile pigments.

Major histocompatibility complex (MHC) a cluster of genes that determines the histocompatibility of the species, determining what substances will be considered foreign or antigenic.

Microbiota the living microscopic organisms of an area.

Nosocomial infection acquired as a result of a hospital stay.

Opportunist bacteria that are normally benign that invade the host under favorable conditions.

Opsonization the coating of an antigen or infectious agent by antibodies or complement that facilitates uptake of the foreign particle into the phagocytic cell.

Pandemic a widespread epidemic affecting the populations of extensive areas, perhaps the whole world.

Parenteral infection by route other than alimentary tract, such as intramuscular, intravenous, or subcutaneous.

Parotiditis inflammation of the parotid gland.

Pathogen a microorganism, or other substance that causes disease. An opportunistic pathogen causes disease when the immune system is compromised

Percutaneous through, or by way of, the skin.

Permucosal through, or by way of, a mucous membrane.

Personal protective equipment (PPE) those items mandated by OSHA, such as barrier gowns, masks, safety glasses, and face shields that protect the HCW from transmission of disease.

Phagocytosis the process by which certain immunological cells ingest and destroy other cells.

Prodromal early signs or warnings of impending disease.

Retrovirus RNA is the core genetic material of this virus; the enzyme reverse transcriptase is required to convert RNA to proviral DNA.

Sequelae long-term or permanent damage to organs or tissue as a result of disease.

Seroconversion the presence of antibodies is changed from negative (seronegative) to positive (seropositive) after exposure to the etiological agents of the disease.

Serological marker or diagnosis specific laboratory finding of an antibody or an antigen that identifies a disease.

Sign objective, observable and measurable changes in the client's condition (e.g., fever).

Symptom subjective changes reported by the client (e.g., pain).

STD sexually transmitted disease.

Surveillance observation of occurrence and spread of a disease to effect disease control; a public health objective.

Susceptible host a person or organism not possessing resistance against an infectious agent.

Toxemia presence of toxin in bloodstream.

Transmission (horizontal) one individual passes an infectious agent to another.

Transmission (vertical) an infectious agent is passed from one generation to another, across the placenta, or through breast milk.

Universal precautions (universal standards) the philosophy of infection control in which all human blood and some human bodily fluids are treated as if known to be infected with blood-borne pathogens (BBP).

Vector the carrier that transfers an infectious microorganism from one host to another. Biological vectors may be arthropods, insects, or other living carriers in whose body the microorganism multiplies.

Vehicle the object or substance serving as an intermediary in which the infectious organism is transported and introduced into a new susceptible host.

Virion the complete virus particle consisting of the nucleoid (genetic information) and the capsid (protective protein shell).

Virulence the degree of pathogenicity; ability to invade host, toxin production, number of microorganisms present

Virus a subcellular entity that gains entrance to living cells and is capable of replication only within those cells; may contain DNA or RNA.

Window period the time between exposure resulting in infection and the serological antibody marker; the infectious agent is transmissible, but the antibody test is negative.

DIRECTIONS Each of the questions or incomplete statements below is followed by suggested answers or completions. Select the **one** answer that is best in each case.

1. All of the following are nonspecific host defenses against disease EXCEPT one. Which one is the EXCEPTION?
   A. intact skin or mucous membranes
   B. saliva, tears, and vaginal fluids
   C. antibody-antigen complex
   D. antagonism by resident microbiota
   E. pH of the stomach
2. Immunoglobins are classified as
   A. carbohydrates.
   B. complex proteins.
   C. lipids.
   D. simple amino acid chains.
3. The immunoglobin found in saliva and in other body secretions is
   A. IgE.
   B. IgD.
   C. IgA.
   D. IgM.
   E. IgG.
4. The predominate cell found in acute inflammatory reactions is
   A. macrophage.
   B. neutrophil.
   C. lymphocytes.
   D. basophils.
5. Chemotaxis is a function of which of the following cell types?
   A. lymphocytes
   B. erythrocytes
   C. neutrophils
   D. plasma cells
6. Passive immunity is BEST defined as
   A. species immunity.
   B. a state of temporary insusceptibility to an infectious agent.
   C. individual immunity.
   D. an immunity mediated by hormones.
7. Which of the following markers indicates immunity to HBV?
   A. Hepatitis B surface antigen
   B. antibody to Hepatitis B surface antigen
   C. presence of Delta agent
   D. Hepatitis B "e" antigen
8. The presence of antibodies to HBeAg represents
   A. infectivity.
   B. acute infection.
   C. immunity.
   D. a carrier state.
   E. low infectivity.
9. Contact dermatitis exemplifies which of the following types of hypersensitivity?
   A. Type I
   B. Type II
   C. Type III
   D. Type IV

10. Which of the following parts of an antibody combine with the antigen?
    A. Fc
    B. Fab
    C. hinge region
    D. polypetide

11. Which of the following cells synthesize antibodies?
    A. mast
    B. stem
    C. plasma
    D. fibroblast

12. Which of the following genera are gram-negative, comma-shaped rods?
    A. *Treponema*
    B. *Actinomyces*
    C. *Vibrio*
    D. *Staphylococcus*

13. Which of the following bacteria are carried on the skin, in the anterior nares, and are responsible for the transmission of many nosocomial infections?
    A. *Mutans streptococcus*
    B. *Staphylococcus aureus*
    C. *Treponema pallidum*
    D. *Actinomyces naeslundii*

14. Hepatitis B represents which type of immunity?
    A. acquired-active
    B. acquired-passive
    C. natural-active
    D. natural-passive

15. What is the immunoglobin that predominates in a Type I hypersensitivity reaction?
    A. IgA
    B. IgE
    C. IgG
    D. IgD
    E. IgM

16. Which of the following indicates the effectiveness of sterilization?
    A. change of color on autoclave tape or bag
    B. live spore test
    C. following time and temperature requirements exactly
    D. monitoring patients for disease

17. Introduction of a pathogen from a species other than human is termed
    A. heterozygous.
    B. homozygous.
    C. zoonosis
    D. autogenous

18. RNA and DNA are found in which cell organelle?
    A. mitochondria
    B. endoplasmic reticulum
    C. nucleus
    D. ribosomes

19. In which type of plaque is *Actinobacillus actinomycetemcomitans* found?
    A. thin gram-negative
    B. thin gram-positive
    C. thick gram-negative
    D. thick gram-positive

20. The varicella zoster virus is responsible for which ONE of the following diseases?
    A. herpes simplex I
    B. shingles
    C. measles
    D. infectious mononucleosis

21. All of the following increase the virulence of a pathogen EXCEPT one. Which one is the EXCEPTION?
    A. endotoxins
    B. pili
    C. capsules
    D. microtubules
    E. enzyme production

22. Tissue grafted from one species to another is termed
    A. autocraft
    B. homograft
    C. heterograft
    D. homoplastic

23. The microorganisms MOST likely to be found in a microscopic plaque sample of a patient with ANUG would be

A. spirochetes and *Prevotella intermedia.*
B. *Fusobacterium.*
C. *Actinobacillus actinomycetemomitans.*
D. *Porphyromonas gingivalis* and *Prevotella intermedia.*

24. The FIRST cells that travel to the site of injury are
A. B lymphocytes.
B. T lymphocytes.
C. polymorphonuclear neutrophils.
D. thrombocytes.

25. The bacteria type MOST likely to be seen in mature plaque is
A. gram-positive cocci and a few rods.
B. gram-negative cocci and rods.
C. vibrios and spirochetes.
D. filamentous forms and fusobacterium.

26. Which of the following bacteria are predominate in pregnancy gingivitis?
A. *S. salivarius*
B. *Prevotella intermedia*
C. *Porphymonas gingivalis*
D. *Mutans streptococcus*

27. Affinity for the hard tooth surface is characteristic of
A. *S. mitior* and *S. pyogenes.*
B. *Mutans streptococcus* and *S. salivarius.*
C. *Mutans streptococcus* and *S. sanguis.*
D. *Lactobacillus* and *S. mutans*

28. Bacteria that have the ability to initiate caries on smooth surface enamel must be able to
A. produce mucin.
B. produce proteolytic enzymes.
C. produce extracellular insoluble glucans.
D. survive in a high pH environment.

29. Which of the following acids is formed in large quantities after degradation of sucrose by *Mutans streptococcus?*
A. lactic
B. acetic
C. linoleic
D. lipoteichoic

30. The principal site for the growth of spirochetes, fusobacteria, and other anaerobes is
A. supragingival dental plaque.
B. the gingival margin.
C. the gingival sulcus.
D. saliva.

31. The most likely species of microorganism to predominate in a necrotic root canal is
A. *S. salivarius.*
B. *Mutans streptococcus*
C. *P. intermedia.*
D. *S. sanguis.*

answers & rationales

1.

C. Antibodies are a host defense made in response to specific antigens. Each antibody is specifically designed to fit the surface markers on a specific antigen. Intact skin and mucous membranes are nonspecific host defenses that act as a barrier to harmful substances or organisms. Saliva, tears, and vaginal fluids are nonspecific host defenses that contain IgA to inactivate pathogens. They also serve as a mechanism to flush the invaders away. Resident microflora are nonspecific host defenses that compete for nutrients and surface area. *S. epidermis* is a harmless microorganism that may inhibit the growth of pathogenic *S. aureus* on the skin's surface. The pH of the stomach is extremely low, due to the presence of hydrochloric acid. This nonspecific host defense kills most microorganisms on contact.

2.

B. Immunoglobins are a class of structurally related proteins, with an important role in specific host defense. Immunoglobins are not carbohydrates, lipids, or simple amino acid chains.

3.

C. Saliva and other body secretions contain the immunoglobin IgA. It is considered the secretory antibody. IgE is the immunoglobulin that is responsible for Type I hypersensitivity reactions. IgE combines with the surface of the antigen, activating basophils, and mast cells to release histamine and other inflammatory products. IgD is a trace antibody responsible for regulating the antibody-antigen process. IgM appears only in the bloodstream. It is the first antibody to appear and starts agglutination and bacteriolysis. IgG is the main immunoglobin the blood, composing up to 75% of the total defense. It is able to cross the placental barrier to protect the fetus.

4.

B. Neutrophils or polymorphonuclear neutrophils (PMNs) are the first line of defense in the inflammatory response and are the most numerous inflammatory cell in any stage of infection. Macrophages are larger phagocytic cells than neutrophils and are present in chronic and acute infections, but not in the same numbers. Lymphocytes may be either T or B lymphocytes and are activated by the presence of PMNs, monocytes, and macrophages. Basophils are a granulocytic WBC that increase in number in myeloproliferative diseases.

5.

B. Neutrophils are attracted to the site of invasion by chemotaxis (chemical attraction). Failure of the chemotactic factor plays a role in diseases of host response such as juvenile periodontitis. Lymphocytes are presented to the antigen by macrophages. Erythrocytes are red blood cells, and are not involved in chemotaxis. Plasma cells are produced by B lymphocytes are the precursors to antibodies. They are not involved in chemotaxis.

6.

B. Passive immunity is a state of temporary insusceptibility to an infectious agent, due to the introduction of antibodies from another source. These antibodies may be passed from mother to fetus, or may be given in the form of immunoglobin injection of preformed antibodies. Species immunity is that immunity a whole species has toward a certain pathogen and is not considered passive. Individual immunity is protection from a specific pathogen, due to the formation of antibodies. Hormones have no specific relation to immunity.

7.

B. Formation of antibodies to the hepatitis B surface antigen indicates immunity. The presence of both hepatitis B surface and "e" antigens indicate infectivity. The presence of the delta agent indicates coinfection with hepatitis D.

8.

E. The presence of antibodies to HBeAg indicates low infectivity, but not necessarily complete elimination of the disease. The presence of HBeAg indicates infectivity. The presence of HBsAg indicates acute infection, whereas the presence of antibodies to HBsAg indicates immunity. The presence of HBsAg may indicate a carrier state, if it persists longer than 6 months.

9.

D. Contact dermatitis is a type of delayed hypersensitivity or Type IV reaction. This type of reaction usually occurs 2 to 3 days after exposure to the allergen and is mediated by the T lymphocyte. Type I indicates immediate hypersensitivity, mediated by the antibodies produced by IgE. Examples are anaphylactic reactions, asthma, and hay fever. Type II hypersensitivity reactions are cytotoxic reactions such as blood transfusion reactions and hemolytic disease of the newborn. Type III hypersensitivity reactions are immune complex reactions that may be responsible for autoimmune diseases such as systemic lupus erythematosus. Both Type II and III are antibody mediated.

10.

B. The Fab or fragment antigen-binding portion of the antibody combines with the antigen. These consist of variable regions with two chains that are responsible for the specificity of the antibody. The Fc (fragment crystallizable) fragment of the antibody contains sites where immune cells of the host will bind. The hinge region is the area where the Fab and the Fc fragments combine. The antibody is a "y" shaped molecule with a light polypeptide chain and a heavy polypeptide chain, however, these chains are not the antigen attachment site.

11.

C. Plasma cells, found in the bone marrow and connective tissue, synthesize antibodies. Mast cells release histamine, serotonin, and heparin when activated by IgE. Stem cells manufacture T or B lymphocytes, and fibroblasts manufacture collagen.

12.

C. *Vibrio* is a genus of gram-negative, comma-shaped bacterial rods. *Treponema* are spiral-shaped bacteria or spirochetes. *Actinomyces* are rod-shaped bacteria, whereas Staphylococci are grape-shaped clusters of round bacteria.

13.

B. *Staphylococcus aureus* is a common microscopic resident of skin, and resides in the anterior nares. It is easily spread from hospital workers to patients through careless infection control practices. In addition, once established, it is resistant to many common antibiotics. It is one of the most common causes of nosocomial or hospital-transmitted infections. *Streptococcus mutans* is the primary bacterium implicated in the transmission of human caries. *Treponema pallidum* is the causative organism of syphilis in humans. *Actinomyces naeslundii* is the primary bacterium implicated in human root caries.

14.

A. Vaccination represents active-acquired immunity since it is artificial stimulation of the body's production of antibodies to the hepatitis B virus. Acquired passive immunity is the artificial introduction of antibodies in response to a disease threat. Natural active immunity is achieved when the body is exposed to a disease and produces antibodies in response to the immunological challenge. Natural passive immunity is a short-lived immunity that is transferred from one organism to another, such as fetal antibodies crossing the placenta.

15.

B. IgE is the antibody that predominates in a Type I hypersensitivity (classic allergic) reaction. IgA is the antibody that is present in body secretions and on mucous membranes. IgG is the primary antibody in the blood. IgD is a trace antibody, responsible for regulating antibody-producing cells. IgM is the first antibody to appear in the bloodstream and starts the process of agglutination and bacteriolysis.

16.

B. The live spore test is the only definitive test to measure effective sterilization. The change in color of tape or markings on the bag indicates only that the proper temperature was reached, not that all microorganisms were killed. Even when time and temperature requirements are followed, there still can be ineffective pressure or temperature achieved to kill all microorganisms. Monitoring patients would be extremely difficult and therefore not conclusive proof that sterilization had been achieved, especially when patients do not report illnesses.

17.

C. A zoonosis is the introduction of a pathogen from another species, especially the animal family. Heterozygous is defined as having different allelic genes at one locus, which may result in the manifestation of a recessive genetic condition. Homozygous is defined as having the same allelic genes at one locus, resulting in dominance of a manifestation of a gene's expression. An autogenous infection is the introduction of the patient's own microflora into injured tissue, causing a local or systemic post-treatment infection.

18.

C. The nucleus is the site of genetic determination and metabolic functioning for the cell and contains chromosomes, DNA, and the nucleolus, which holds RNA. The mitochondria are responsible for the production of the cell's energy, via adenosine triphosphate (ATP). The endoplasmic reticulum is responsible for protein and lipid synthesis and packaging. Rough endoplasmic reticulum contains the tiny granules of RNA in the form of ribosomes, which manufacture proteins. Smooth endoplasmic reticulum contain enzymes that synthesize lipids, especially those used to make membranes. Ribosomes are a granule of ribonucleoprotein, which is the site of protein synthesis as directed by mRNA.

19.

A. *Actinobacillus actinomycetemcomitans* is a small gram-negative coccoid facultative organism. It is uncommon in that it thrives in thin plaque layers, and may cause diseases such as juvenile periodontitis in relatively clean mouths.

20.

A. Herpes simplex I is a virus that presents as vesicles typically found above the waist and around and in the mouth. It is caused by a different virus in the Herpesviridae family. The varicella zoster virus, a member of the herpes virus family, is responsible for two different manifestations of the same etiological agent. In children, the virus presents itself as a common childhood illness called chickenpox, usually a mild vesicular disease. In adults, the latent virus in dorsal root ganglions is reactivated, closely following areas of innervation, and producing an extremely painful rash and vesicles along the nerve trunk. Measles is caused by the rubeola virus. Infectious mononucleosis is caused by the Epstein-Barr virus.

21.

D. Microtubules are protein structures within flagella and responsible for movement, as well as functioning in the spindle apparatus of the cellular division process of mitosis. They do not increase the virulence of pathogens. Endotoxins, or lipopolysaccharides, are part of the gram-negative cell wall and increase the virulence of those microorganisms. They have the ability to activate, complement, or disrupt cellular homeostasis, and lead to the destruction of the periodontal attachment apparatus. Pili and fimbrae are attachment mechanisms for microorganisms that allow them to adhere to body structures, usually mucous membranes. Pili also function as a means of exchange of genetic material (important in the transference of drug resistance between species) and as a receptor site for viruses. Bacteria with pili are more pathogenic than those of the same genera without pili. Capsules, or slime layers, are protective mechanisms for bacteria and aid in their virulence. Bacteria that are able to synthesize polymers with a well-defined outer limit that attaches to the cell wall are said to have capsules. If the outer limit is not as well defined, it is called a slime layer or glycocalyx. Bacteria able to synthesize these structures are more virulent and more pathogenic. *Mutana streptococcus* are able to produce a capsule that allows for adherence to tooth structure. Enzyme production by bacteria allows for greater virulence and tissue destruction.

22.

C. Heterograft (xenograft) is the correct term for tissue grafted from another species. Autograft is the term to define tissue grafted from one's own body. Homograft (allograft) refers to tissue grafted from the same species. Hemoplastic is another term for homograft and allograft.

23.

A. Spirochetes and *P. intermedia* are the predominate bacteria found in ANUG. Fusobacterium are also found in ANUG, but not as commonly as spirochetes and *P. intermedia. A. actinomycetemomitans* is not usually found in ANUG. *Porphyromonas gingivalis* and *Prevotella intermedia* are commonly found in adult periodontitis.

24.

C. Polymorphonuclear neutrophils (PMNs) are the first cells to respond to immunological challenge or injury. B lymphocytes must be activated by complement and macrophages. T lymphocytes must be activated by complement and macrophages. Thromocytes or platelets are involved in blood clotting.

25.

C. Vibrios and spirochetes are the bacterial markers for the maturation of plaque, appearing as early as 4 to 7 days in the rapid plaque formers. Gram-positive cocci and a few rods occur in early plaque. Few gram-negative cocci exist in plaque. Filamentous forms and *Fusobacterium* occur in the early to middle stages of plaque development.

26.

B. *Prevotella intermedia* predominates in all types of hormonal gingivitis. *S. salivarius* are not linked to the development of gingivitis. It is a common inhabitant of saliva. *Porphymonas gingivalis* are common in all types of periodontal disease, but are not considered the primary etiological agent in pregnancy gingivitis. *Mutans streptococcus* are implicated as the primary etiologic agent in human caries.

27.

C. *Mutans streptococcus* and *S. sanguis* are considered colonizers of tooth structure. Both of these bacteria need to adhere to a hard surface. *S. mitior* and *S. pyogenes* are found on both soft and hard tissues of the oral cavity. *Mutans streptococcus* do require hard tooth surfaces, but *S. salivarius* are commonly found in saliva and soft oral tissues. *Lactobacillus* causes caries but has no ability to adhere to hard tooth surfaces. It must inhabit a pit, fissure, or existing lesion.

28.

C. "Colonizers" such as *Mutans streptococcus* and *S. sanguis* are able to adhere to tooth structure due to their ability to produce extracellular insoluble glucans. This allows them to remain in contact with the surface long enough to initiate caries. Mucin is produced by salivary glands and used for lubrication. Proteolytic enzymes may break down the fibrous structure of the periodontal attachment, but do not initiate caries. Bacteria capable of initiating caries do so by producing acid and thereby lowering the pH of the oral environment.

29.

A. Lactic acid is produced by the degradation of sucrose by *Mutans streptococcus* and the *Lactobacillus* sp. Acetic acid, or vinegar, is not produced by *Mutans streptococcus.* Linoleic acid is an essential fatty acid, and not produced by *Mutans streptococcus*. Lipoteichoic acid is a component of gram-positive cell walls and is not produced by *Mutans streptococcus*.

30.

C. Spirochetes, *Fusobacterium*, and other anaerobes thrive in the low oxygen environment of the gingival sulcus. Supragingival plaque is heavily populated with gram-positive facultative anaerobes. The gingival margin is heavily populated with gram-positive facultative anaerobes. Saliva is primarily populated with gram-positive facultative anaerobes.

31.

C. *P. intermedia* is consistently found in necrotic root canals. *S. salivarius* is found primarily in saliva and in those soft tissue surfaces coated with saliva. *Mutans streptococcus* are facultative anaerobes that usually do not dominate the microbiota in a necrotic root canal. S. *sanguis* is an early colonizer of hard tooth structure and is not found in necrotic root canals.

CHAPTER

7 Oral Pathology

Joseph E. Baughman, DDS

contents

The study of oral pathology focuses not only on diseases that affect the oral cavity, but also on systemic diseases that may exhibit oral manifestations.

I. TERMINOLOGY AND DEFINITIONS

A. Terminology Based on Appearance and Consistency

1. Color
   a) Pink or coral pink—color of normal mucosa
   b) *Erythematous*—implies red or inflamed
   c) *Leukoplakia*—implies white lesion; does not rub off
   d) Blue-black or reddish-purple—implies amalgam, melanin, or a vascular lesion
2. *Nodule*—small, firm, palpable lesion above or below surrounding surface level
   a) *Pedunculated*—narrow base that grows on a stalk
   b) *Sessile*—wide base without stalk
   c) *Hypertrophy*—increase of tissue size due to an increase in cell size
   d) *Hyperplasia*—increase of tissue size due to an increase in cell numbers
3. *Papule*—small, elevated growth usually < 5 mm in diameter
4. *Macule*—small, nonelevated lesion usually of a different color
5. *Vesicle*—fluid-filled blister < 5 mm in diameter
6. *Bulla* (plural = bullae)—fluid-filled blister > 5 mm in diameter
7. *Pustule*—vesicle or bulla filled with pus
8. *Corrugated*—wavy elevations and depressions, also wrinkled
9. *Fissured*—deep grooves with no cracks or ulcerations
10. *Papillary*—rough surface with small projections (cauliflower-like)

B. Radiographic Terminology

1. *Unilocular*—only one radiolucent compartment
2. *Multilocular*—several radiolucent compartments with the same or varied sizes
3. Honeycombed—several radiolucent compartments of the same size
4. *Well-circumscribed*—well-defined border with clearly defined margins
5. Diffuse—poorly identifiable margins that blend into normal tissue
6. *Sclerotic*—appears more radiopaque than normal

II. ANOMALIES OF THE ORAL CAVITY

A. Mucosal Anomalies

1. Abnormalities of the tongue
   a) Ankyloglossia—tongue-tie; lingual frenum is too short or attached too anteriorly
   b) Lingual varices—enlarged tortuous veins on ventral surface of tongue
   c) Fissured—deep dorsal surface grooves; usually developmental on adults
   d) Hairy—proliferation of filiform papillae; color varies due to chromogenic bacteria

   e) Central papillary atrophy (median rhomboid glossitis)—erythematous area located in midline of tongue, anterior to circumvallate papillae and devoid of filiform papillae
   f) Geographic (migratory glossitis)—erythematous areas devoid of filiform papillae usually with a yellowish-white border; areas appear to migrate, but in reality one area heals and another appears
2. Abnormalities of other mucosal tissue
   a) Fordyce granules—yellowish clusters of submucosal sebaceous glands
   b) Leukoedema—opalescent (milky) hue of the buccal mucosa resulting from increased intracellular edema
   c) Lip pits—blind sacs found in the vermillion zone or commissures, cause is usually congenital
   d) Melanin pigmentations—focal brownish areas that may be racial in origin or indicative of a systemic disease (e.g., Addison's disease or Peutz-Jeghers syndrome)
   e) Retrocuspid papilla—fibrous elevation lingual to mandibular canines
   f) *Leukoplakia*—not a diagnosis, but a clinical description of a white lesion that does not rub off
      (1) Etiology—usually resulting from chronic irritation with hyperkeratosis
      (2) Clinical manifestations—may be premalignant with use of high-risk factors (e.g., tobacco or alcohol)
   g) Lichen planus—skin disease
      (1) Etiology—unknown
      (2) Oral manifestations
         (a) White or gray thread-like papules in a linear or reticular arrangement (Wickham's striae)
         (b) Plaque-like form (more common on the dorsum of the tongue)
         (c) Bulbous and/or erosive form (see vesiculoerosive diseases)
      (3) Clinical manifestations—more commonly seen in nervous, high-strung individuals
      (4) Treatment—none unless symptomatic (e.g., erosive), then corticosteroids are prescribed

B. Dental Anomalies

1. Abnormalities in size and shape of teeth
   a) Concresence—joining of adjacent teeth by cementum only
   b) Dens in dente (Dens invaginatus)—tooth within a tooth; enamel is deposited within the pulp chamber due to the invagination of enamel organ
   c) Dilaceration—abnormal root curvature caused by trauma during tooth formation
   d) Enamel pearl—development of excess enamel on root due to misplaced ameloblasts
   e) Macrodont—denotes large tooth

(1) Relative—large tooth compared with the rest of dentition
(2) Absolute—truly enlarged tooth

f) Microdont— denotes a small tooth
(1) Relative—small tooth compared with the rest of dentition
(2) Absolute—truly small tooth; peg lateral is most common

g) Regional odontodysplasia (ghost teeth on x-ray)—evidence of thin enamel and dentin with large pulp chambers

h) Talon cusp—accessory cusp found on the maxillary and mandibular anteriors

i) Taurodontism—elongated pulp chamber with short roots

2. Abnormalities in number of teeth
   a) Anodontia—missing teeth; examples include
      (1) Total
      (2) Partial
      (3) Congenital—failure to develop and may be due to a syndrome (e.g., ectodermal dysplasia)
      (4) Acquired—through extraction(s)
   b) Fusion—two teeth are fused into one, resulting in a macrodont; therefore, fewer than normal complement of teeth are present
   c) Supernumerary—extra teeth; mesiodens is most common; usually microdont in size, and may be a result of a syndrome (e.g., cleidocranial dysplasia or dysostosis)
   d) Gemination (twinning)—two clinical crowns are evident with usually one root; results in greater than normal number of teeth; usually macrodont in size; result of tooth bud attempting to split
3. Abnormalities in tooth structure
   (a) Enamel hypoplasia—defect in enamel organic matrix formation
      (1) Etiology—possible factors include
         (a) Genetic (e.g., Amelogenesis imperfecta)
         (b) Environmental (e.g., drug ingestion, fever)
         (c) Metabolic (e.g., vitamin deficiency)
         (d) Disease (e.g., congenital syphilis)
   b) Enamel hypocalcification—defect in enamel mineralization
      (1) Etiology—genetic, environmental, metabolic, or disease
      (2) Oral manifestations—results in defects in tooth color
      (3) Treatment—none if mild; cosmetic if moderate to severe
   c) Amelogenesis imperfecta—abnormal enamel
      (1) Etiology—genetic or environmental
      (2) Oral manifestations
         (a) Enamel frequently fractures leaving restorations elevated above the surrounding dentin
         (b) May be an isolated defect or affect several or all teeth
      (3) Clinical manifestations
         (a) Classified according to mode of transmission, appearance, or etiology

(b) Radiographically, teeth exhibit thin, absent, or defective enamel

(4) Treatment—full coverage restorations

d) Dentinogenesis imperfecta—abnormal dentin

(1) Etiology—usually genetic

(2) Oral manifestations—enamel may fracture due to defective dentinoenamel junction (DEJ)

(3) Clinical manifestations—no pulp chamber or canals are visible on radiographs

(4) Treatment—full coverage restorations

e) Dentinal dysplasia—abnormal dentin

(1) Etiology—usually genetic

(2) Oral manifestations—roots are short and conical

(3) Clinical manifestations—periapical pathology is frequently seen on x-ray

(4) Treatment—usually extraction because of periapical pathology

III. CYSTS

A. Odontogenic Cysts

1. Radicular cyst (periapical cyst)—most common intraoral cyst

a) Etiology—pulpal pathology, which usually results in a nonvital tooth; epithelial lining probably results from rests of Malassez

b) Clinical manifestations—radiographically, cyst may resemble a periapical abscess or dental granuloma (inflamed granulation tissue with no epithelium)

c) Treatment—endodontics, apicoectomy, or extraction with bony curettage

2. Residual cyst—radicular cyst that remains after tooth extraction

3. Dentigerous cyst (follicular cyst)—surrounds crown of unerupted tooth

a) Etiology—epithelial lining develops from reduced enamel epithelium

b) Clinical manifestations

(1) Cyst attaches at cementoenamel junction (CEJ)

(2) Unilocular radiolucency is evident with well-defined margins

(3) Increased risk of neoplasm forming if left untreated

c) Treatment—enucleation of cyst, assisted eruption of tooth, or extraction

4. Primordial cyst—develops in place of missing tooth

a) Etiology—epithelial lining develops from remnants of enamel organ

b) Clinical manifestation—usually a unilocular radiolucency is evident

c) Treatment—surgical removal; enucleation

5. Eruption cyst—soft tissue cyst

a) Etiology—hematoma in the path of eruption

b) Clinical manifestations—usually little or no epithelial lining is evident; fluid buildup is found in path of eruption between crown and soft tissue
c) Treatment—none or lance overlying gingiva to assist in eruption of tooth

6. Lateral periodontal cyst—unilocular or multilocular lucency usually located in mandibular premolar area on lateral aspect of root
   a) Etiology—epithelial rests in periodontal ligament
   b) Treatment—surgical removal
7. Gingival cyst—soft tissue cyst
   a) Etiology—result of epithelium from rests of Serres (remnants of dental lamina)
   b) Oral manifestations—swelling usually located on attached gingiva
   c) Treatment—enucleation, if any
8. Odontogenic keratocyst—multilocular, rarely unilocular, radiolucency with poorly defined margins
   a) Etiology—epithelial remnants of odontogenic apparatus
   b) Clinical manifestations—produces keratin; locally aggressive with a high recurrence rate; and may be indicative of basal cell nevus syndrome
   c) Treatment—aggressive; complete surgical removal

D. Nonodontogenic Cysts

1. Median palatal cyst—unilocular radiolucency in midline of palate
   a) Etiology—epithelium from rests; remnants are from fusion of palatal shelves
   b) Clinical manifestations—radiolucency in midline of palate with or without soft tissue swelling
   c) Treatment—surgical removal
2. Nasopalatine duct cyst (cyst of the incisive canal)—located more anteriorly than median palatal cyst
   a) Etiology—epithelium from rests of nasopalatine duct
   b) Clinical manifestations—unilocular radiolucency in midline of palate, apical to maxillary centrals (frequently heart-shaped due to superimposed anterior nasal spine)
   c) Treatment—surgical removal
3. Median mandibular cyst—unilocular radiolucency in mandibular midline
   a) Etiology—epithelium from fusion of rests of mandibular process
   b) Clinical manifestations—radiolucency in midline of mandible
   c) Treatment—surgical removal
4. Globulomaxillary cyst—inverted pear-shaped unilocular radiolucency between maxillary canine and lateral incisor
   a) Etiology—epithelium from fusion rests or odontogenic rests
   b) Oral manifestations—divergence of roots and convergence of crowns; may exhibit fluctuant soft tissue swelling of gingiva

c) Treatment—surgical removal

5. Simple bone cyst—pseudocyst of bone with no epithelial lining
   a) Etiology—considered to be from trauma
   b) Oral manifestations—unilocular or multilocular lucency that scallops between and around the roots
   c) Treatment—surgery; reveals an empty bony cavity
6. Aneurysmal bone cyst—pseudocyst of bone with no epithelial lining
   a) Etiology—considered to be from trauma; histology of blood-filled cavities with peripheral multinucleated giant cells
   b) Clinical manifestations—multilocular/honeycombed lucency
   c) Treatment—curettage of bony defect
7. Stafne cyst (defect)—pseudocyst
   a) Clinical manifestations
      (1) No bony cavity evident, only thinning of mandible
      (2) Unilocular, well-defined lucency inferior to mandibular canal
   b) Treatment—none; only an anatomic variation
8. Branchial cleft cyst (lymphoepithelial cyst)—soft tissue cyst in lateral neck area, anterior to sternocleidomastoid muscle
   a) Etiology—epithelium is from trapped rests of branchial clefts
   b) Oral manifestations—yellowish nodule frequently found on ventral side of tongue and floor of mouth
   c) Treatment—surgical removal
9. Thyroglossal duct cyst—soft tissue cyst in midline of neck or posterior portion of tongue
   a) Etiology—epithelium is from remnants of thyroglossal duct (tract)
   b) Treatment—surgical removal
10. Nasolabial cyst—soft tissue cyst in nasolabial fold or maxillary canine area
    a) Etiology—epithelium trapped in fusion line of maxillary labial processes
    b) Clinical manifestations—fluctuant soft tissue swelling inferior and lateral to alae
    c) Treatment—surgical removal
11. Epidermoid cyst—soft tissue cyst; contains only tissue derived from ectoderm
    a) Etiology—trapped epithelium or pleuripotential cells
    b) Clinical manifestation—fluctuant swelling usually found in floor of mouth
    c) Treatment—surgical removal
12. Dermoid cyst—soft tissue cyst
    a) Etiology—pleuripotential cells; contains tissue derived from ectoderm, mesoderm, and/or endoderm
    b) Clinical manifestation—fluctuant swelling usually found in floor of mouth
    c) Treatment—surgical removal

IV. BENIGN NEOPLASMA

A. Nomenclature

1. *Neoplasia* ("new growth")—implies an uncontrolled growth
2. *Tumor*—implies swelling; frequently used interchangeably with neoplasm
3. *Benign*—implies a growth; cannot metastasize (spread to other locations from point of origin); hence, it is not cancer
4. *Malignant*—has ability to metastasize; therefore, it is cancer
5. *Hyperplasia*—increase in size resulting from an increase in cell numbers; similar to neoplasia, but is usually a response to stimuli or an irritant
6. *Hypertrophy*—increase in size resulting from an increase in size of individual cells; mimics neoplasia clinically and is usually a response to stimuli
7. -oma—suffix added to end of tissue type to imply a benign neoplasm of that tissue (e.g., fibroma, neoplasm of fibrous connective tissue; adenoma, neoplasm of glandular tissue); not all tumors with "oma" suffix are benign (e.g., melanoma is skin cancer)

B. Odontogenic Tumors (Neoplasms)

1. Ameloblastoma—slow-growing, benign, but locally invasive tumor of ameloblasts
   a) Etiology—ectodermal origin; histologically several types are classified
   b) Oral manifestations—usually swelling or bony expansion; may be evident only on radiograph
   c) Clinical manifestations
      (1) Multilocular (small unilocular lesions) radiolucency with poorly defined margins
      (2) Peak incidence is in adults, rarely in children
   d) Treatment—wide surgical excision; recurrence is common
2. Ameloblastic fibroma—slow-growing benign tumor made up of ameloblasts and fibroblasts
   a) Etiology—odontogenic origin (ectodermal and mesodermal components)
   b) Clinical manifestations
      (1) More frequently seen in children and adolescents
      (2) Usually unilocular in form (occasionally multilocular)
      (3) Most have well-defined margins
   c. Treatment—surgical enucleation; recurrence is unusual
3. Odontogenic adenomatoid tumor (OAT)—slow-growing benign tumor
   a) Etiology—ectodermal origin
   b) Oral manifestations—most frequently found in anterior part of maxilla and may or may not involve impacted teeth
   c) Clinical manifestations
      (1) Early lesions are present as unilocular radiolucencies; older lesions show multiple radiopaque foci

(2) If an impacted tooth is involved, it is frequently mistaken for a dentigerous cyst (except radiolucency encompasses more than just crown of tooth)
(3) Usually found in young patients

d) Treatment—conservative surgical enucleation; recurrence is rare

4. Calcifying epithelial odontogenic tumor (CEOT)—also known as Pindborg tumor (slow-growing benign tumor)
   a) Etiology—ectodermal origin
   b) Clinical manifestations
      (1) May or may not involve unerupted teeth
      (2) Slight tendency for tumor to invade locally
      (3) Radiographs show unilocular or multilocular radiolucency with poorly defined margins and scattered radiopaque foci
      (4) Tumor may produce amyloid
      (5) Usually seen in adults
   c) Treatment—wide surgical excision; recurrence is common
5. Odontogenic myxoma—slow-growing benign tumor
   a) Etiology—mesodermal origin; cell of origin thought to be stellate reticulum
   b) Oral manifestations—may cause scalloped tooth resorption
   c) Clinical manifestations
      (1) Presents itself as a multilocular (small lesion may be unilocular) radiolucency with poorly defined margins
      (2) May be locally invasive
      (3) Usually seen in young adults
   d) Treatment—wide surgical excision; recurrence is common
6. Odontoma—benign tumor that forms enamel, dentin, and cementum
   a) Types
      (1) Compound odontoma—formation of well-organized microdonts
         (a) Oral manifestations—most commonly found in anterior teeth
         (b) Treatment—surgical removal with no recurrence
      (2) Complex odontoma—disorganized haphazard formation of enamel, dentin, and cementum
         (a) Oral manifestations—involve no developed teeth; most commonly found in posterior portion of mandible
         (b) Treatment—surgical removal with no recurrence
7. Cementoma (periapical cemental dysplasia)—hyperplasia of the cementum
   a) Etiology—cells probably arise from pluripotential cells in periodontal ligament (PDL)
   b) Oral manifestations—most commonly found in anterior portion of mandible at apices
   c) Clinical manifestations
      (1) Early stages are entirely radiolucent and resemble periapical pathology, but teeth remain vital

      (2) Older lesions become progressively more radiopaque
   d) Treatment—none
8. Cementoblastoma—true neoplasm of cementum
   a) Etiology—derived from PDL cells
   b) Clinical manifestations
      (1) Usually tumor is all radiopaque with apex of root obliterated on x-ray film
      (2) Usually located in mandibular premolar and molar areas
      (3) Pain may be patient's chief complaint
   c) Treatment—root amputation (or extraction) and enucleation of tumor

C. Benign Mucosal Neoplasms

1. Fibroma—most common intraoral soft tissue neoplasm
   a) Clinical manifestations
      (1) Forms may be sessile, pedunculated, or only hyperplasia in response to stimuli (e.g., irritation = irritation fibroma)
      (2) Color is of normal mucosa unless neoplasm is secondarily ulcerated
      (3) Can occur anywhere intraorally
   b) Treatment—surgical excision with no recurrence
2. Ossifying fibroma—fibroosseous lesion that may occur in soft tissue (peripheral ossifying fibroma) or in bone (central ossifying fibroma) (see Neoplasms of the bone)
   a) Etiology
      (1) Odontogenic origin
      (2) Cells of origin are probably from pluripotential cells in PDL
      (3) Histology consists of essentially dense fibrous connective tissue with spicules of vital bone forming with neoplasm
   b) Oral manifestations—development usually occurs on gingiva
   c) Clinical manifestations
      (1) Peripheral ossifying fibroma mimics fibroma, but texture may be more firm
      (2) Form may be sessile or pedunculated
   d) Treatment—surgical excision with no recurrence
3. Cementifying fibroma—same as ossifying fibroma except it forms cementum within neoplasm instead of bone
   a) Etiology—cells are probably from pluripotential cells in PDL
   b) Clinical manifestations—include a peripheral and central variety (see Neoplasms of the bone)
   c) Treatment—none or surgical removal
4. Ossifying-cementifying fibroma—same as above except it forms bone and cementum within neoplasm
   a) Etiology—cells are probably from pluripotential cells in PDL
   b) Clinical manifestations—also include a peripheral and central variety (see Neoplasms of the bone)
   c) Treatment—none or surgical removal
5. Lipoma—neoplasm of adipose (fat) tissue

a) Clinical manifestations—may occur anywhere in oral cavity; form is sessile or pedunculated and of soft texture
b) Treatment—surgical excision with no recurrence

6. Pyogenic granuloma—reactive hyperplasia resulting from a local irritant (usually calculus)
   a) Etiology—histology consists of inflamed granulation-type tissue with numerous capillaries
   b) Clinical manifestations
      (1) Called granuloma gravidarum (pregnancy tumor) if it occurs in pregnant patient; result of an exaggerated response to hormonal stimuli
      (2) Usually a pedunculated hemorrhagic-colored mass arising from crevicular sulcus
      (3) Bleeds readily on manipulation
      (4) May become quite large or may undergo spontaneous remission
      (5) Older lesions may become sclerotic (fibrous tissue replacement) and eventually resemble a fibroma
   c) Treatment—surgical excision with removal of irritant; lesion may recur
7. Giant cell tumor (giant cell granuloma)—neoplasm of multinucleated giant cells
   a) Etiology—unknown
      (1) Histology consists of granulation-type tissue with numerous multinucleated giant cells
      (2) Multiple giant cell tumors of bone may be seen in patients with hyperparathyroidism
   b) Clinical manifestations
      (1) Varieties—peripheral (soft tissue) and central (intraosseous) (see Neoplasms of the bone)
      (2) Similar presentation as a pyogenic granuloma
      (3) Soft tissue lesions tend to be "liver" colored
      (4) Form is pedunculated and tends to grow from crevicular sulcus
   c) Treatment—surgical excision with recurrence rare
8. Granular cell tumor (granular cell myoblastoma)—neoplasm of cells exhibiting a granular cytoplasm (myoblastoma—previous terminology used when cell of origin was thought to be a myoblast)
   a) Etiology—considered to be of primitive neural cell origin
      (1) Histologically, epithelium may proliferate (pseudoepitheliomatous hyperplasia) into underlying lamina propria in 50% of cases, mimicking squamous cell carcinoma, except lesion is benign
   b) Oral manifestations—most commonly occurs on dorsal portion of tongue, but occasionally occurs elsewhere in oral cavity
   c) Clinical manifestations
      (1) Sessile elevation (nodule), frequently exhibiting a central depression
      (2) Almost exclusively found in adults

d) Treatment—surgical excision with no recurrence

9. Congenital epulis (of the newborn)—tumor of gingiva that is present at birth
   a) Etiology—unknown
      (1) Histologically resembles granular cell tumor in adults, but cells are thought to be of a different origin
   b) Clinical manifestations—soft tissue mass; usually occurs on maxillary anterior gingiva, but may arise in mandible
   c) Treatment—surgical excision with no recurrence
10. Papilloma—epithelial neoplasm induced by papilloma virus
   a) Oral manifestations—occurs anywhere intraorally as a pedunculated (occasionally sessile) mass with small papillary projections or cauliflower-like surface
   b) Treatment—surgical excision with recurrence unusual
11. Epulis fissuratum (denture hyperplasia)—not a true neoplasm
   a) Clinical manifestations—reactive hyperplasia caused by an overextended, poor fitting denture; denture flange sits in groove or crevice created by lesion
   b) Treatment—surgical excision and remake denture

D. Benign nerve tumors

1. Neuroma—neoplasm of neural tissue
   a) Clinical manifestations
      (1) True neoplasm of nerve tissue referred to as plexiform neuroma
      (2) Form may be sessile or pedunculated
      (3) Intraosseous or soft tissue; soft tissue neoplasm exhibits color of normal mucosa; intraosseous form is usually a unilocular radiolucency
      (4) Hyperplasia of neural processes due to trauma is referred to as traumatic neuroma
         (a) Occurs when nerve process is amputated and degenerates while myelin tube (conduit) remains
         (b) If scar tissue obstructs myelin conduit as nerve process regenerates, it continues to proliferate creating a neoplasm of nerve tissue
   b) Treatment—surgical excision with no recurrence

2) Neurofibroma—neoplasm of neural elements and fibrous connective tissue
   a) Clinical manifestations
      (1) May occur anywhere intraorally
      (2) Multiple neurofibromas may be indicative of von Recklinghausen's syndrome (potential of neurofibromas to undergo malignant transformation)
   b) Treatment—surgical excision with no recurrence (except von Recklinghausen's syndrome)

3. Neurilemoma (schwannoma)—neoplasm of Schwann cells (produce myelin sheath)
   a) Forms

(1) Intraosseous or soft tissue—usually a unilocular lucency; color is of normal mucosa
(2) Sessile or pedunculated

b) Treatment—surgical excision with no recurrence

E. Vascular neoplasms

1. Hemangioma—neoplasm of blood vessels
   a) Etiology—usually congenital; three types based on histology
      (1) Cellular hemangioma—composed only of endothelial cells; no vascular channels formed
      (2) Capillary hemangioma—composed of small vascular channels
      (3) Cavernous hemangioma—composed of large dilated channels
   b) Oral manifestation—most commonly found on tongue
   c) Clinical manifestations
      (1) Enlarges slowly
      (2) Superficial lesions are sessile-red or bluish-red; deeper lesions are of normal color and only palpable or slightly elevated on surface; vascular color not readily detectable in deeper lesions
      (3) May develop in bone as poorly defined multilocular/honeycombed lucencies
   d) Treatment—use sclerosing agents or surgical excision for small lesions; no recurrence
2. Lymphangioma—neoplasm of lymphatic vessels
   a) Etiology—usually congenital
   b) Oral manifestations—most commonly found on tongue
   c) Clinical manifestations
      (1) Cystic hygroma—congenital lymphangioma in neck
      (2) Sessile in form and color is of normal mucosa
      (3) May only be palpable or cause slight elevation of surface mucosa
   d) Treatment—use of sclerosing agents or surgical excision with no recurrence

F. Neoplasms of muscle

1. Rhabdomyoma—neoplasm of striated (voluntary) muscle
   a) Oral manifestation—sometimes found on tongue
   b) Clinical manifestations—lesions are usually sessile in form, deep, and only palpable or cause slight elevation of surface mucosa
   c) Treatment—surgical excision with no recurrence
2. Leiomyoma—neoplasm of smooth (involuntary) muscle
   a) Etiology—origin is in smooth muscle wall of blood vessels
   b) Oral manifestations—rarely found intraorally
   c) Clinical manifestations
      (1) Occurs in association with blood vessels
      (2) Sessile in form, palpable, or may cause slight elevation of surface mucosa
   d) Treatment—surgical excision with no recurrence

G. Salivary gland neoplasms

1. Pleomorphic adenoma (mixed tumor)—slow-growing, encapsulated, sessile neoplasm of glandular tissue
   a) Etiology—consists of ectodermal and mesodermal derivatives (mixed)
   b) Clinical manifestations—most commonly found in parotid gland extraorally and in minor salivary glands of palate intraorally
   c) Treatment—surgical excision with chance of recurrence owing to incomplete removal
2. Monomorphic adenoma—glandular neoplasm
   a) Oral manifestations—most commonly found in upper lip
   b) Clinical manifestations
      (1) Consists of one cellular element (monomorphic)
      (2) Sessile form may only be palpable or cause elevation of surface mucosa
   c) Treatment—surgical excision with no recurrence
3. Warthin's Tumor (papillary cystadenoma lymphomatosum)—glandular neoplasm
   a) Etiology—ductal epithelial proliferation within lymphoid aggregates
   b) Clinical manifestations—seen predominantly in parotid gland of males, rarely intraorally and occasionally bilaterally; palpable or elevation of the surface
   c) Treatment—surgical excision with no recurrence

H. Neoplasms of the bone

1. Exostosis—hyperplasia of the bone
   a) Oral manifestations
      (1) Frequently seen on alveolar process
      (2) Specific areas, such as palate (midline) and lingual of mandible (premolar areas) are referred to as palatal torus or mandibular tori, respectfully
   b) Clinical manifestations
      (1) Not a true neoplasm of bone (osteoma)
      (2) Consists of a hard texture with color of normal mucosa unless secondarily ulcerated
      (3) Large lesions frequently exhibit a lobular shape
      (4) On radiographs, there is evidence of more radiopaque bone with poorly defined margins
      (5) No malignant potential
   c) Treatment—none, unless there is interference with speech and mastication, then surgical excision; occasional slow recurrence
2. Osteoma—slow-growing neoplasm of bone
   a) Etiology—arises from periosteum or endosteum
   b) Clinical manifestations
      (1) Almost exclusively found in membranous bones of skull and face in older adults; most commonly found in sinus and on medial surface of ascending ramus or inferior border of mandible
      (2) Detected by palpation or visual asymmetry of area

    (3) Usually sessile in form and occasionally pedunculated
    (4) Radiographically, appears as a solitary mass of dense bone with well-defined margins
    (5) Multiple osteomas may be indicative of Gardner's syndrome (osteomas and intestinal polyps; polyps may undergo malignant transformation)
  c) Treatment—surgical excision with no recurrence
3. Chondroma—neoplasm of cartilage
  a) Oral manifestation—rarely found intraorally, but may be seen in maxillary anterior or mandibular premolar area and at symphysis; locally invasive
  b) Treatment—surgical excision with rare recurrence
4. Central ossifying fibroma (fibroosseous lesion of bone)—same as soft tissue neoplasm, but located within bone
  a) Clinical manifestation—seen on radiographs as an unilocular radiolucency with varying degrees of radiopacities; usually asymptomatic
  b) Treatment—surgical removal if symptomatic
5. Central cementifying fibroma—same as soft tissue neoplasm and central ossifying fibroma stated above, but with spicules of cementum
  a) Treatment—surgical removal if symptomatic
6. Central cementifying-ossifying fibroma—same as above, but produces cementum and bone
7. Fibrous dysplasia (monostotic fibroosseous lesion of the jaws)—unilateral asymptomatic enlargement of maxilla or mandible
  a) Etiology—unknown, but trauma and infection are suspected
  b) Oral manifestations—may cause malalignment of teeth
  c) Clinical manifestations
    (1) Considered a neoplasm because of the enlargement
    (2) Radiographs vary from unilocular to multilocular, well-defined radiolucencies to fine trabeculations
    (3) Described as a "gound glass" appearance that blends into surrounding normal bone
  d) Treatment—removal of lesion and/or recontouring of bone
8. Central giant cell tumor of bone—similar to soft tissue neoplasm
  a) Clinical manifestations
    (1) Consists of neoplastic, large, multinucleated cells
    (2) Radiographically, a unilocular or multilocular radiolucency is seen with poorly defined margins
    (3) Multiple neoplasms are seen in patients with hyperparathyroidism
  b) Treatment—surgical removal; treat endocrine disorder if hyperparathyroidism exists

V. SALIVARY GLAND PATHOLOGY

A. Inflammation and stone formation

1. *Sialadenitis*—inflammation of salivary gland tissue
  a) Etiology—may be trauma, mucus retention, or inspissation

b) Clinical manifestations—may result in enlargement of gland and be acute or chronic
c) Treatment—removal or correction of etiology

2. *Sialodochitis*—inflammation of salivary gland duct
   a) Etiology—possible mucus retention or stone formation, but usually trauma
   b) Clinical manifestation—erythematous oriface of duct; may result in mucus retention if inflammation occludes duct
   c) Treatment—removal of etiology
3. *Sialolithiasis*—stone formation
   a) Etiology—unknown; may be due to mineralization of mucus plug within the duct
   b) Clinical manifestation—calcified obstruction may cause mucus retention with swelling; may be palpable and/or visible on radiographs
   c) Treatment—removal
4. Xerostomia—dryness of mouth owing to reduced salivary flow
   a) Etiology—result of inflammation, atrophy, autoimmune disease, or drugs/medications
   b) Clinical manifestation—oral dryness; may cause mucosal changes
   c) Treatment—salivary stimulants or saliva substitutes
5. Sjögren's syndrome—lymphocytic infiltration of salivary glands resulting in loss of function
   a) Etiology—autoimmune
   b) Oral manifestations
      (1) Dry mouth (xerostomia)—may lead to erythema of mucosal surfaces
      (2) Tongue may exhibit atrophy of papillae
   c) Clinical manifestations
      (1) Dry eyes (xerophthalmia)—resulting from destruction of lacrimal glands; results in damage referred to as keratoconjunctivitis sicca
      (2) Frequently other autoimmune processes are characteristic of syndrome
   d) Treatment—steroids, pilocarpine (stimulates salivary flow), and saliva and tear substitutes
6. Necrotizing sialometaplasia—necrosis of salivary gland tissue with metaplasia of ducts
   a) Etiology—caused by infarction of blood supply to the area; amount of destruction is dependent on degree of infarction
   b) Oral manifestation—necrosis of tissue in palate
   c) Treatment—palliative, self-limiting

B. Mucous extravasation and retention

1. Mucocele
   a) Etiology—result of trauma to salivary gland duct and extravasation of mucin into surrounding connective tissue; granulation tissue with inflammation surrounds inspissated mucin histologically
   b) Oral manifestations
      (1) Most commonly found in lower lip

(2) Superficial lesions may present as sessile in form with bluish or translucent swelling; deep lesions may only be palpable or cause elevation of normal-appearing vermillion zone or mucosa

(3) Swellings may fluctuate in size depending on salivary flow

c) Treatment—surgical excision of involved gland and duct

2. Mucus retention phenomenon—same as above without rupture of salivary gland duct

a) Etiology—resulting from obstruction of duct by mucus plug or sialolith, resulting in mucin retention without extravasation into surrounding connective tissue

b) Clinical manifestations

(1) Extravasation or retention result in similar clinical presentation as stated with mucocele

(2) Distinction may be evident only histologically

(3) May occur anywhere minor salivary glands are located

c) Treatment—surgical excision

3. Ranula—not a diagnosis, but a clinical description of swelling in floor of mouth

a) Etiology—frequently resulting from mucus retention as a result of obstruction of submandibular (Wharton's) duct

b) Treatment—removal of etiology

VI. INFECTIOUS DISEASES

A. Bacterial diseases

1. Tuberculosis—contagious lung disease

a) Etiology

(1) Caused by *Mycobacterium tuberculosis,* a Gram-negative, acid-fast bacillus

(2) Histologically, classified as granulomatous inflammation with caseous (cheeselike) necrosis and Langerhans giant cells (multinucleated giant cell with nuclei arranged in horseshoe-shaped pattern around periphery of cytoplasm)

b) Oral manifestations

(1) Lesions present as progressively enlarging painful ulcerations probably caused by infected sputum

(2) Oral ulcerations heal as respiratory disease becomes quiescent

c) Clinical manifestations

(1) Portal of entry is through respiratory tract

(2) Lung lesions heal with calcification of necrotic areas visible on chest radiographs

(3) Chronic cough significant in medical history

(4) Involvement of nodes in head and neck area are referred to as scrofula

(5) Involvement of internal viscera referred to as miliary TB

(6) May involve bone as tuberculous osteomyelitis

(7) Purified protein derivative (PPD)—positive test exhibited by erythematous inflammation and induration at injection site within 48 hours

d) Treatment—long-term isoniazid, rifampin, or other antituberculous drugs

2. Syphilis—bacterial disease
   a) Etiology—caused by *Treponema pallidum,* a spirochete contracted by intimate contact or transplacentally
   b) Three stages with characteristic lesions
      (1) Primary stage—chancre lesion; usually occurs at site of inoculation as a deeply cratered ulceration frequently exhibiting a "piled-up" periphery
         (a) Oral manifestations—chancres exhibit whitish membrane that may not be diagnostic of syphilis
         (b) Treatment—antibiotic therapy
      (2) Secondary stage—evidence of pruritic rash on skin and or mucous patches on the mucosal surfaces
         (a) Oral manifestations
            (i) Lesions are widespread and not associated with site of inoculation
            (ii) Skin lesions exude clear fluid when scratched and contains the spirochete
            (iii) Mucous patches may also exhibit a whitish membrane teeming with spirochete
         (b) Treatment—secondary stage may recur frequently and requires antibiotic therapy
      (3) Tertiary stage—gumma (gummatous necrosis)
         (a) Oral manifestations
            (i) Occurs years after primary stage
            (ii) Lesions fatal if they occur in vital structures
         (b) Treatment—none

2. Gonorrhea—sexually transmitted disease
   a) Etiology—caused by *Neisseria gonorrhoeae,* a diplococcus
   b) Oral manifestations—oral lesions are rare, but, if present, resemble nonspecific ulcerations containing microorganism
   c) Treatment—antibiotics

4. Actinomycosis—bacterial infection
   a) Etiology
      (1) Resulting from *Actinomyces israelii,* a normal inhabitant of the oral cavity
      (2) Organism causes disease when implanted in the deep wounds or extraction sites protected from free oxygen (anaerobe)
   b) Clinical manifestations—forms fistulae that tend to drain through the skin, exuding colonies of the microorganism as yellowish grit referred to as sulfur granules
   c) Treatment—long-term antibiotics

B. Viral diseases

1. Herpes simplex—two forms: primary and secondary
   a) Primary herpes simplex—first exposure to virus

(1) Oral manifestations
   (a) Begins as pinpoint vesicles anywhere intraorally and periorally
   (b) Vesicles quickly rupture, leaving small ulcerations
(2) Clinical manifestations
   (a) Most common in young children; may become endemic in child-care facilities from one infected individual
   (b) Patient may exhibit fever, malaise, or lymphadenopathy; or symptoms may be mild to subclinical
(3) Treatment—bed rest, fluids, and no aspirin
(4) Remission in 10 to 14 days

b) Secondary herpes simplex (recurrent herpes)
(1) Oral manifestations
   (a) Most intraoral lesions occur on attached mucosa as small pinpoint vesicles that quickly rupture leaving small pinpoint ulcerations; several ulcerations may coalesce to form larger ulcerations
   (b) Most common site is on hard palate lingual to first molars
   (c) Lip lesions (herpes labialis) occur frequently
(2) Clinical manifestations
   (a) Transmission is by direct contact
   (b) Virus resides in trigeminal ganglia, then migrates down nerve process when immunity is compromised or stressed (usually occurs in same location with each outbreak)
   (c) Prodromal tingling may precede eruption of vesicles
   (d) Herpetic eczema (skin) is uncommon
   (e) Herpetic whitlow (finger) was common in dentistry before wearing gloves
(3) Treatment—palliative only; antiviral drugs demonstrate efficacy and heal without scarring in 10 to 14 days

2. Herpes zoster (shingles)
   a) Etiology—caused by varicella-zoster virus, the same virus that causes chickenpox
   b) Oral manifestations—lesions present as small vesicles that quickly rupture intraorally and on skin
   c) Clinical manifestations
      (1) Usually occurs in adults (regardless of prior history of chickenpox)
      (2) Lesions are usually unilateral (follow dermatomes) and rarely cross midline
      (3) May persist for weeks, while neuralgia may persist for months
      (4) Prodromal burning sensation is common
   d) Treatment—antiviral drugs; only viral disease treatable with steroids
3. Hand-foot-and-mouth disease—coxsackievirus disease
   a) Oral manifestation—causes vesicles with ulcerations intraorally

b) Clinical manifestations
(1) Vesicular papules are found on palms of hands and soles of feet
(2) Usually found in young children
(3) Lesions are distributed, which aids in distinguishing hand-foot-and-mouth disease from other viral diseases
c) Treatment—palliative
d) Remission—spontaneous in 10 to 14 days
4. Herpangina—coxsackievirus disease
a) Oral manifestation—vesicular-ulcerative lesions occur in soft palate and pharyngitis
b) Treatment—palliative
c) Remission—5 to 10 days
5. Mononucleosis—infectious disease
a) Etiology—caused by Epstein-Barr virus
b) Oral manifestations—palatal petechiae common in prodromal stages
c) Clinical manifestations—fever, malaise, pharyngitis, lymphadenopathy, and splenomegaly
d) Treatment—palliative
6. Mumps—viral parotitis, but may affect any major salivary gland
a) Clinical manifestations—parotids are most commonly affected; frequently causes bilateral, tender enlargement
b) Treatment—palliative
7. Measles (rubeola)—paramyxovirus skin eruption
a) Oral manifestations—evidence of occasional oral ulcerations; Koplik's spots (erythematous macules) with necrotic centers are common on buccal mucosa opposite molars; typically precedes skin lesions
b) Treatment—palliative
8. German measles (rubella)
a) Etiology—viral-induced disease
b) Oral manifestations—enamel hypoplasia has been associated with rubella; similar in appearance to rubeola, but without Koplick's spots
c) Clinical manifestations—birth defects occur if contracted during first trimester (include blindness, deafness, and cardiovascular abnormalities)
9. AIDS (acquired immunodeficiency syndrome)—HIV (RNA virus with reverse transcriptase) disease causes depletion of CD4 lymphocytes (T-cell) and compromises immune system; results in death as a result of opportunistic infections or malignancies
a) Routes of transmission
(1) Intimate contact with fluid exchange
(2) Contact with contaminated blood or blood products
(3) Transplacental
b) Oral manifestations
(1) Includes unexplained candidiasis (see Fungal diseases)

(2) Hairy leukoplakia (Epstein-Barr virus induced)—hyperkeratotic proliferation of papillae on lateral borders of tongue that are usually found bilaterally
(3) Opportunistic malignancies
(a) Kaposi's sarcoma (purplish-red macules or papules most commonly found on palate)
(b) Linear gingival erythema (LGE)—distinct erythematous line involving marginal gingiva
(4) Necrotizing ulcerative periodontitis (NUP)—rapidly progressive periodontal disease without concomitant local factors
c) Clinical manifestations
(1) Symptoms—flu-like within weeks of infection, but may be subclinical
(2) Incubation period—highly variable
(3) Opportunistic infections are evident
d) Treatment—multiple drug regiments without cure at this time

C. Fungal diseases

1. Candidiasis (thrush, moniliasis)
a) Etiology—caused by *Candida albicans,* which is frequently part of the normal oral flora
b) Forms
(1) White curds—rub off (pseudomembranous)
(2) Localized erythematous—found especially under removable prostheses (denture sore mouth)
(3) Leukoplakic areas—do not rub off (hypertrophic candidiasis), but heal with antifungal medications
c) Oral manifestation—angular cheilitis frequently occurs due to *Candida*
d) Clinical manifestations
(1) Opportunistic organism evident especially with antibiotic, steroid, chemotherapy use and diabetes mellitus
(2) Any unexplained candidiasis causes suspicion for compromised immunity (e.g., HIV)
e) Treatment—antifungal medications with possible recurrence
2. Histoplasmosis—infectious disease
a) Etiology—caused by *Histoplasma capsulatum;* histology shows histiocytes and macrophages with organisms in cytoplasm exhibiting a clear halo (mucopolysaccharide capsule)
b) Oral manifestations
(1) May cause ulcerations and/or granulomatous inflammation
(2) Lesions occur as a result of infected sputum
c) Clinical manifestation
(1) Portal of entry is through respiratory tract and inhalation of dust (especially bird droppings) containing spores
(2) Endemic in Ohio and Mississippi River valleys
d) Treatment—long-term therapy with amphotericin B and other antifungals with possible recurrence

3. Coccidioidomycosis
   a) Etiology—caused by *Coccidioides immitis*
   b) Oral manifestations
      (1) Lesions are not common, but when present consist of ulcerations and granulomatous
      (2) Inflammation is present resulting from infected sputum
   c) Clinical manifestation
      (1) Portal of entry is through respiratory tract by inhalation of spores
      (2) Endemic in southwestern United States
   d) Treatment—use of amphotericin B or ketoconazole with possible recurrence

VII. VESICULOEROSIVE DISEASES

A. Viral-induced (see Infectious Diseases, viral)

1. Herpes simplex—also classified as a vesiculoerosive disease because of clinical presentations of small vesicles
   a) Clinical manifestations—vesicles rupture to leave small areas of ulceration
   b) Treatment—bed rest, fluids, and no aspirin
2. Herpes zoster—classified also as a vesiculoerosive disease
   a) Clinical manifestation—vesicles rupture, leaving small areas of ulceration
   b) Treatment—antiviral drugs, the only viral disease treatable with steroids
3. Hand-foot-and-mouth disease—coxsackievirus
   a) Clinical manifestations
      (1) Predilection to cause vesicles in soft palate, pharynx, and cutaneous areas of hands and feet in young children
      (2) Short duration
   b) Treatment—palliative
4. Herpangina—coxsackievirus
   a) Clinical manifestations
      (1) Predilection for vesicular eruptions of soft palate and pharynx
      (2) May be confused with primary herpetic stomatitis
      (3) Short duration
   b) Treatment—palliative
5. Measles
   a) Clinical manifestations
      (1) Intraoral vesicles possible
      (2) Koplik's spots may occur on buccal mucosa
   b) Treatment—palliative

B. Autoimmune

1. Recurrent aphthous ulcers (RAU)—minor aphthae
   a) Etiology—unknown, but immune dysfunction is suspected
   b) Oral manifestations
      (1) Painful lesions are evident that are usually < 5 mm in dimension

(2) have a shallow yellow fibrinous center with an erythematous nonelevated margin
(3) Lesions are usually single, but may occur in crops
(4) Adjacent lesions may coalesce to form larger areas of ulceration
(5) Usually heal in 7 to 10 days without scarring
(6) Multiple and multisystem lesions may be suggestive of Beçhet's syndrome
(7) Most frequently found on freely moveable portion of mucosa

c) Treatment—palliative
(1) Multiple and frequent recurrence may respond to supervised steroid therapy
(2) Topical tetracycline reduces likelihood of secondary bacterial infection
(3) Recurrence is likely

2. Beçhet's syndrome—multisystem disease usually presenting with ocular, oral, and genital lesions
a) Etiology—suspected to be autoimmune
b) Clinical manifestations
(1) Oral lesions—resemble RAU and tend to occur in multiple crops
(2) Ocular lesions—include uveitis and/or conjunctivitis
(3) Genital lesions—also exhibit painful ulcerations
c) Treatment—supervised steroid therapy, but may undergo spontaneous remission

3. Reiter's syndrome—multisystem disease
a) Etiology—unknown, but autoimmune dysfunction is suspected
b) Clinical manifestations—frequently manifesting ocular, oral, and genital lesions
(1) Oral lesions—resemble multiple RAU
(2) Ocular lesions—include uveitis or conjunctivitis
(3) Genital lesions—include balanitis, nongonococcal urethritis
(4) Patients frequently exhibit arthritis
c) Treatment—anti-inflammatory drugs

4. Major aphthae—periadenitis mucosa necrotica recurrens (PMNR); Sutton's disease
a) Etiology—considered to be an immune dysfunction
b) Oral manifestations
(1) Large, cratered ulcerations of mucosal surfaces with "piled-up" erythematous margins of long duration
(2) Ulcers heal in weeks to months, usually with scarring
c) Treatment—supervised steroid therapy

5. Erythema Multiforme—disease affecting skin and mucous membranes
a) Etiology—unknown, although an immune dysfunction is suspected and infections or drugs may precipitate onset
b) Oral manifestations
(1) Lesions may exhibit multiple RAU-type or larger ulcerations

(2) Vesicles may occur early or exist at margins of ulcers

c) Clinical manifestations—classic skin lesion presents as multiple concentric circles of erythema and normal color skin

d) Treatment—supervised steroid therapy with possible recurrence

6. Stevens-Johnson syndrome—multisystem disease of erythema multiforme; usually involves ocular, oral and genital regions
   a) Clinical manifestations
      (1) Oral and genital lesions exhibit erythema multiforme
      (2) Ocular lesions consist of conjunctivitis or uveitis
   b) Treatment—supervised steroid therapy with possible recurrence
7. Lupus erythematosus—chronic skin or systemic disease
   a) Etiology—considered to be autoimmune
   b) Types
      (1) Chronic discoid—affects the skin and mucous membranes
      (2) Systemic—multisystem disease that is occasionally fatal
   c) Oral manifestations
      (1) Lesions present as erythematous plaques or erosions affecting buccal mucosa, gingiva, palate, and vermillion zone
      (2) Ulcerations are seen frequently
   d) Clinical manifestations
      (1) Antibodies are formed against cell nucleus or other cytoplasmic antigens
      (2) "Butterfly" rash is frequently seen affecting the malar processes; bilaterally connects across bridge of nose
      (3) Females are affected more frequently than males
      (4) Patients complain of malaise, weakness, and an occasional low-grade fever
      (5) Increased sensitivity to ultraviolet radiation is not uncommon
   e) Treatment—long-term steroids and antimalarial drugs
8. Erosive (bullous) lichen planus (see Anomalies of the oral cavity, Anomalies of other mucosal tissue)—skin disease affecting basal layer of epithelium
   a) Etiology—suspected to be autoimmune
   b) Forms
      (1) Erosive and bullous—least common; exhibits erythematous erosions and ulcerations most common on posterior buccal mucosa and attached gingiva
      (2) Bullous lichen planus—variant of erosive in which vesicles or bullae precede ulcerations
      (3) Wickham's striae—may be visible at periphery of lesion; may or may not accompany skin lesions
   c) Treatment—steroid therapy; may undergo spontaneous remission with possible recurrence
9. Pemphigus (pemphigus vulgaris, pemphigus vegetans)—skin disease
   a) Etiology—autoimmune; histologically an intraepithelial separation (above the basal cell layer) with Tzanck cells (free-floating epithelial cells)

b) Oral manifestations
  (1) Lesions present as aphthae-like ulcerations or large irregular ulcerations with erythematous margins
  (2) Vesicles or bullae may precede ulcerations
c) Clinical manifestations
  (1) Antibodies are directed against desmosomes resulting in acantholysis (loss of cell-to-cell adhesion)
  (2) Individuals may exhibit a positive Nikolsky's sign (sloughing of epithelium after minor trauma)
  (3) May have ethnic or genetic predisposition
d) Treatment—steroids

10. Pemphigoid (benign mucous membrane pemphigoid, cicatricial [scar-forming] pemphigoid)—autoimmune disease that affects basal layer membrane area; antibodies are directed against hemidesmosomes resulting in subepithelial separation
  a) Oral manifestations
    (1) Lesions exhibit painful ulcerations with erythematous margins on any mucosal surface
    (2) Desquamative gingivitis—clinical description of possible pemphigoid; positive Nikolsky's sign is frequently noted
  b) Clinical manifestations—bullous pemphigoid is considered a variant of cicatricial pemphigoid, but autoimmune findings are not consistent
  c) Treatment—steroids; may undergo periods of remission and exacerbation

VIII. BLOOD DYSCRASIAS

A. Vocabulary

1. *Purpura*—general term for submucosal, subcutaneous bleeding
2. *Petechiae*—small, pinpoint, nonelevated red spot of submucosal bleeding
3. *Ecchymosis*—purple or purplish-red, nonelevated area of submucosal bleeding, larger than a petechiae
4. *Hematoma*—purple or purplish-red, elevated area of submucosal bleeding
5. *Epistaxis*—spontaneous nose bleed
6. *Hematuria*—blood in urine
7. *Hemoptysis*—coughing up blood
8. *Hemolysis*—rupture of erythrocytes with loss of hemoglobin
9. *Erythropenia*—decrease in circulating red blood cells (RBCs)
10. *Leukopenia*—decrease in circulating white blood cells (WBCs)
11. *Thrombocytopenia*—decrease in circulating platelets

B. Clotting disorders

1. Thrombocytopenia (idiopathic thrombocytopenic purpura)—disease of platelets resulting in a decrease in numbers
  a) Etiology
    (1) Idiopathic—unknown
    (2) Secondary thrombocytopenic purpura—drugs, chemicals, or radiation

(3) Immune thrombocytopenic purpura—autoimmune

b) Oral manifestations

(1) Include spontaneous gingival bleeding, ecchymoses, petechiae, or purpura

(2) Invasive procedures, including a prophylaxis, are contraindicated while platelet count is depressed

c) Clinical manifestations—correlate with decreased platelets (e.g., bruise easily, hematuria, and epistaxis)

d) Treatment

(1) Primary—may undergo spontaneous remission or transfusion, steroids, and splenectomy

(2) Secondary—elimination of etiology, if possible, and again patient may undergo spontaneous remission, transfusion, steroids, or splenectomy

2. Nonthrombocytopenic purpura—spontaneous bleeding

a) Etiology

(1) Capillary fragility or defect in platelet function (e.g., aspirin ingestion, nonsteroid anti-inflammatory drugs, and autoimmune disease)

(2) Von Willebrand's disease—genetic form of nonthrombocytopenic purpura

b) Treatment—same as for thrombocytopenia

3. Hemophilia—genetic disease resulting in a deficiency of a clotting factor

a) Types

(1) Hemophilia A—factor VIII deficiency (X-linked transmission)

(2) Hemophilia B—factor IX deficiency (X-linked transmission)

(3) Hemophilia C—factor XI deficiency (questionable transmission)

b) Oral manifestations

(1) Include spontaneous gingival bleeding, purpura, petechiae, ecchymoses, and epistaxis

(2) Invasive procedures including prophylaxis is contraindicated until missing factor is replaced

c) Treatment—replace missing factor

C. Disorders of red blood cells

1. Anemia—disorder of oxygen-carrying capability either in RBCs or defect in hemoglobin molecule

a) Etiology—may be a result of dietary deficiencies, genetic or autoimmune

b) Oral manifestations—angular cheilitis, atrophy of oral mucosa, erythema of tongue (with or without burning), and loss of filiform and fungiform papillae in severe or chronic cases

c) Clinical manifestations—pallor and fatigue

d) Treatment—replace deficiency; with pernicious anemia, B_{12} injections are given to bypass gastrointestinal tract where intrinsic factor is missing

e) Types
   (1) Dietary
      (a) Iron deficiency anemia
      (b) Pernicious anemia—deficiency in vitamin B_{12} (cobalamin) caused by a loss of intrinsic factor; may have an autoimmune component
      (c) Folate deficiency—also referred to as megaloblastic anemia
   (2) Genetic
      (a) Thalassemia autosomal dominant—results in an amino acid change in hemoglobin molecule
         i) Thalassemia major—severe form that results from homozygous inheritance
         ii) Thalassemia minor—milder form that results from heterozygous inheritance
      (b) Sickle cell anemia
         i) Autosomal dominant disease that affects predominantly blacks and individuals of Mediterranean descent
         ii) Defect is also an amino acid substitution in hemoglobin molecule, causing RBCs to assume a sickle shape and leading to congestion within capillaries and ischemia of the tissue
         iii) Sickle cell disease is most severe form resulting from homozygous inheritance
         iv) Sickle cell trait is a milder form resulting from heterozygous inheritance

2. Aplastic anemia—results in a severe decrease of all circulating blood cells including RBCs, WBCs (leukopenia), and platelets (thrombocytopenia)
   a) Etiology
      (1) Primary aplastic anemia—unknown
      (2) Secondary aplastic anemia—chemical or radiation
   b) Clinical manifestations—primarily suggestive of leukopenia and thrombocytopenia, which include infections and spontaneous hemorrhage
   c) Treatment
      (1) Primary aplastic anemia—supportive, but usually fatal
      (2) Secondary aplastic anemia—remove etiology
3. Polycythemia—abnormal increase in RBC count; either absolute or relative
   a) Etiology
      (1) Neoplastic (primary polycythemia)
      (2) Decrease in oxygen (secondary polycythemia)
      (3) Decreased plasma volume (relative polycythemia)
   b) Oral manifestations—evidence of red to purple mucosa, submucosal ecchymoses, petechiae or hematoma, and spontaneous bleeding
   c) Treatment—chemotherapy and/or removal of etiology

D. Disorders of white blood cells

1. Agranulocytosis—severe reduction in circulating granulocytes, especially neutrophils, resulting from either a defect in production or accelerated destruction
   a) Etiology
      (1) Primary form—unknown
      (2) Secondary form—drugs, chemicals, or radiation
   b) Clinical manifestations—severe infections with fever, malaise, and necrotizing ulcerations
   c) Treatment—antibiotics and transfusions
2. Cyclic neutropenia—periodic cycles of neutrophils decrease with cycles of normal count, usually over 3 to 4 weeks
   a) Etiology—genetic and autosomal dominant
   b) Oral manifestations—severe infections, ulcerations, gingival, and periodontal infections
   c) Treatment—antibiotics and transfusions

IX. ENDOCRINE DISORDERS

A. Diabetes mellitus—disease involving utilization of glucose primarily because of insulin deficiency or resistance

1. Etiology—genetic, autoimmune, viral, and environmental factors
2. Types
   a) Type 1 (IDDM)—insulin-dependent, caused by insulin insufficiency; juvenile onset
      (1) Characteristics—islets of Langerhans cells are destroyed (possibly autoimmune) or cease to produce adequate insulin
      (2) Oral manifestations—increased susceptibility to infection, xerostomia, gingival and periodontal complications, with severe bone loss in uncontrolled cases
      (3) Clinical manifestations—polydipsea (increased thirst), polyuria (increased urination), and polyphagia (increased appetite), but with loss of weight
      (4) Treatment—insulin replacement
   b) Type 2 (NDDM)—non-insulin-dependent; most common form of diabetes; adult-onset; insulin secreted, but ineffective in controlling glucose metabolism
      (1) Characteristics—healing time prolonged
      (2) Oral manifestations—can be same as with type 1
      (3) Clinical manifestations—can be same as with type 1
      (4) Treatment—diet modifications, exercise, and oral hypoglycemics

B. Hyperthyroidism—excessive thyroid hormone secretion

1. Etiology—hyperplasia or tumor of the pituitary gland
2. Oral manifestations—bone loss, premature eruption of teeth, and early development of periodontal disease
3. Clinical manifestations—exophthalmus (protruding eyes), weakness, and unusual reddish hue to skin

4. Treatment—surgery, medication, radiation of thyroid, or radioactive iodine

C. Hypothyroidism—decreased thyroid hormone secretion

1. Etiology—autoimmune, lack of dietary iodine, drugs, and pituitary dysfunction
2. Types
   a) In children—referred to as cretinism
   b) In adults—referred to as myxedema
3. Oral manifestations—thickened lips, delayed tooth eruption; in children macroglossia; in adults primarily macroglossia
4. Treatment—supplemental thyroid hormone

D. Hyperparathyroidism—multisystem disease; increased secretion of parathyroid hormone

1. Etiology—usually owing to parathyroid adenoma
2. Oral manifestations
   a) Increased radiolucency of bone
   b) Cystic-like spaces in maxilla and mandible
   c) Tendency to develop multiple central giant cell tumors
3. Clinical manifestations—weakness, anorexia, polyuria, polydipsea, fatigue, constipation, hypercalcemia, calcifications in internal organs (especially kidneys and pancreas), gastric ulcers and bone demineralization
4. Treatment—removal of adenoma and possible removal of one or more parathyroids

E. Addison's disease—inadequate production of adrenal steroids

1. Etiology—autoimmune, malignancy, or necrosis of adrenal tissue
2. Oral manifestations—paraoral and intraoral pigmentation
3. Clinical manifestation—bronzing of skin; facial pigmentation
4. Treatment—steroid replacement therapy

X. ORAL CANCER

A. Soft tissue

1. Squamous cell carcinoma—most common primary intraoral malignancy
   a) Etiology (risk factors)—sun exposure (lips, paraoral), tobacco and alcohol use
   b) Oral manifestations
      (1) Especially with high-risk factors, leukoplakic plaques (those with premalignant potential), and erythroplakia (red lesions)
      (2) Speckled leukoplakia (red and white combination)
      (3) *Exophytic* ulcerative mass
      (4) Most commonly found in floor of mouth, ventral and lateral borders of tongue, soft palate, paraphyrangeal area, and retromolar pad
   c) Clinical manifestations—locally invasive with metastasis to regional nodes, liver, and lungs
   d) Treatment—surgery, radiation, and chemotherapy

2. Verrucous carcinoma—variant of squamous cell carcinoma
   a) Etiology (risk factors)—primarily tobacco use
   b) Oral manifestations—slow-growing exophytic red and white mass exhibiting a pebbly surface; locally invasive, but low potential for metastasis
   c) Treatment—surgical excision
3. Basal cell carcinoma—epithelial malignancy rarely seen intraorally
   a) Etiology (risk factors)—considered to be sun exposure; cells of origin are basal layer of epithelium
   b) Clinical manifestations
      (1) Slightly elevated nodule, frequently evidenced with a central depressed area or ulceration that refuses to heal
      (2) Low metastatic potential
      (3) Basal cell nevus syndrome—autosomal dominant syndrome manifested by multiple odontogenic keratocysts, multiple basal cell carcinomas, and other skeletal anomalies
      (4) Most commonly found on face
   c) Treatment—surgical removal
4. Fibrosarcoma—malignancy of fibroblasts
   a) Oral manifestations—rapidly growing soft tissue mass with induration; rarely seen intraorally
   b) Treatment—surgery and radiation therapy
5. Rhabdomyosarcoma—malignancy of skeletal muscle; rapidly growing submucosal mass with induration
   a) Oral manifestations—rarely occurs intraorally, but may occur on tongue and floor of mouth
   b) Treatment—primarily surgical removal

B. Salivary gland

1. Mucoepidermoid carcinoma—malignancy composed of epidermoid cells and mucin-secreting cells
   a) Oral manifestations—slow-growing, enlarged submucosal or intraglandular mass with indistinct margins
   b) Clinical manifestations
      (1) Most commonly found in parotid gland
      (2) Also seen, but less frequently, in submandibular, sublingual, and minor salivary glands
      (3) Low metastatic potential
   c) Treatment—surgical excision
2. Adenoid cystic carcinoma—slow-growing malignancy most commonly found in minor salivary glands
   a) Oral manifestations
      (1) Firm, unilobular mass within a major salivary gland with some tenderness on palpation
      (2) Slow-growing mass intraorally with indistinct borders, induration, and a propensity for mucosal ulceration
   b) Clinical manifestations
      (1) May be locally invasive with predilection for neural and bony invasion and metastasis to lungs
      (2) Usually found to be well advanced at time of diagnosis

c) Treatment—surgical excision

3. Malignant pleomorphic adenoma—malignancy arising from a preexisting, long-standing, benign pleomorphic adenoma
   a) Oral manifestations—firm, unilobular mass within a major salivary gland, with accelerated growth, tenderness, pain, and indistinct borders
   b) Clinical manifestations—epithelial, mesenchymal (or both) elements may undergo malignant transformation with tendency for metastasis
   c) Treatment—surgical removal

C. Bone

1. Osteosarcoma—malignant tumor of bone
   a) Oral manifestations—more commonly found in mandible than maxilla
   b) Clinical manifestations
      (1) Most common in the 25 to 40 age group; however, when present in younger age group, it is most commonly found in long bones
      (2) Poorly defined radiolucent and/or radiopaque lesions are evident
      (3) May present as a "starburst" appearance on occlusal films
      (4) Pain may be present if peripheral nerves are involved
   c) Treatment—chemotherapy and/or surgery
2. Ewing's sarcoma—bone malignancy
   a) Etiology—disputed origin
   b) Clinical manifestations
      (1) Most commonly found in younger age group
      (2) Irregular diffuse radiolucency of the jaws is evident
      (3) May show "onion-skin" appearance (multiple layers) on occlusal films
   c) Treatment—radiation and/or surgery; prognosis is poor
3. Multiple myeloma—malignancy of plasma cells affecting bone
   a) Clinical manifestations
      (1) Radiographs exhibit several sharply punched-out radiolucent areas
      (2) Lateral skull films are frequently involved
   b) Treatment—chemotherapy
4. Chondrosarcoma—malignancy of cartilage resulting in bone lesions
   a) Oral manifestations—mandible and maxilla are affected with poorly defined radiolucencies
   b) Clinical manifestations
      (1) Occasional scattered calcifications may be seen
      (2) Occurs in any age group
   c) Treatment—wide surgical excision; prognosis is poor

D. Blood

1. Leukemias—group of disorders characterized by proliferation of atypical white blood cells; classified according to the type of cell (e.g., monocytes, lymphocytes, granulocytes) or onset of disease (e.g., acute or chronic)

a) Types
   (1) Acute—more common in young age group
   (2) Chronic—more common in young adults and older
b) Oral manifestations—range from gingival engorgement, spontaneous hemorrhage, ulcerations, to opportunistic infections
c) Treatment—radiation and chemotherapy

2. Lymphomas (non-Hodgkin's lymphoma)— malignancy of lymphocytes more common in lymphatic system, but may spill over into general circulation; classified according to microscopic appearance
   a) Clinical manifestations—usually presents as a lymphadenopathy; occasionally involves soft tissues and bone
   b) Treatment—radiation, surgery, chemotherapy

E. Metastic disease

1. Metastic tumors
   a) Etiology—histologically, metastasis resembles primary tumor
   b) Clinical manifestations
      (1) Lesions exhibit poorly defined radiolucencies and ragged resorption of roots
      (2) Most common lesions are found in lungs, prostate, breast, thyroid, and kidneys (prostate, breast, and lung lesions may exhibit foci of calcifications within radiolucency)
      (3) Occasionally metastatic site may be first manifestation (occult metastasis)
      (4) Tumors may metastasize to jaw
   c) Treatment—dependent on primary tumor and extent of spread

XI. SYNDROMES

A. Basal cell nevus syndrome—autosomal transmission

1. Clinical manifestations
   a) Include multiple odontogenic keratocysts (OKC), multifocal basal cell carcinoma, hypertelorism, palmer pitting, palmer and plantar keratosis, and bifid ribs
   b) Not all manifestations are seen in all patients
   c) Multiple OKC and basal cell carcinomas are most consistent

B. Beçhet's syndrome (see Vesiculoerosive diseases)—chronic, autoimmune disease producing ocular, oral, and genital lesions

C. Cleidocranial dysplasis (dysostosis)—autoimmune dominant transmission

1. Oral manifestations—underdeveloped premaxilla and multiple supernumerary teeth, frequently impacted owing to crowding
2. Clinical manifestations—results in enlarged skull, long neck, sloping shoulders, and ability to approximate shoulders because of nondevelopment or partial absence of one or both clavicles

D. Cyclic neutropenia—autosomal dominant condition exhibiting recurring cycle of neutrophil depletion and regeneration

1. Oral manifestations
   a) Severe gingivitis that may progress to periodontitis with recurring attacks
   b) Bone loss does not repair between episodes
2. Clinical manifestations—symptoms are related to neutropenia and include fever, malaise, and pharyngitis
3. Treatment—management of neutropenia and antibiotic coverage

E. Down Syndrome—chromosomal abnormality (extra or partial excess of chromosome 21)

1. Oral manifestations
   a) Macroglossia with protrusion of tongue
   b) Fissured tongue
   c) High arched palate
   d) Enamel hypoplasia
   e) Microdontia
   f) Early periodontal disease
2. Clinical manifestations
   a) Broad flat face
   b) Open cranial sutures
   c) Epicanthal folds
   d) Open mouth
   e) Prognathism
   f) Cardiac abnormalities
   g) Mental retardation

F. Ectodermal dysplasia—X-linked recessive transmission

1. Etiology—abnormalities of tissues derived from ectoderm, especially the hair, skin, nails, teeth, and adnexal glandular structures
2. Oral manifestations—partial or complete congenital anodontia with teeth conical in shape when present

G. Fibromatosis gingivae (idiopathic gingival fibromatosis)—suspected autosomal dominant trait

1. Oral manifestations—dense, diffuse, smooth, or nodular fibrous enlargement of gingiva with or without inflammation
2. Treatment—gingival resection; recurrence is common

H. Gardner's syndrome—autosomal dominant transmission

1. Oral manifestations—multiple impacted and/or supernumerary teeth
2. Clinical manifestations
   a) Polyps of the colon, osteomas of the bones, and sebaceous cysts of the scalp and back
   b) Polyps may undergo malignant transformation

I. Papillon-Lefèvre Syndrome—autosomal recessive transmission

1. Oral manifestations—premature destruction of periodontium
2. Clinical manifestations—exhibits reddish-white scaly hyperkeratosis of palmer and plantar surfaces
3. Treatment—aggressive periodontal therapy; prognosis is poor

J. Peutz-Jeghers syndrome—autosomal dominant transmission

1. Oral manifestations—oral pigmentations; pigmented macules involve buccal mucosa, gingiva, and hard palate
2. Clinical manifestations—intestinal polyposis; polyps have a moderate risk of malignant transformation

K. Reiter's syndrome (see Vesiculoerosive diseases)

1. Etiology—unknown
2. Oral manifestations—ulcerations resembling recurrent apthous ulcers
3. Clinical manifestations—arthritis, urethritis, balanitis, and conjunctivitis

L. Stevens-Johnson syndrome (see Vesiculoerosive diseases)—chronic disease exhibiting ocular, oral, and genital lesions of erythema multiforme

M. Von Recklinghausen's disease—autosomal dominant transmission

1. Oral manifestations—tumors are most common on lateral borders of tongue, but can occur anywhere
2. Clinical manifestations
   a) Multiple nerve tissue tumors on skin, brain, and internal viscera
   b) Café au lait ("coffee with cream") pigmentation is common on skin

N. White sponge nevus (Canon's disease)—autosomal dominant transmission

1. Oral manifestations—thick, corrugated, white appearance on buccal mucosa bilaterally
2. Clinical manifestations—may be present at birth or develop around puberty

DIRECTIONS Each of the questions or incomplete statements below is followed by suggested answers or completions. Select the **one** answer that is best in each case.

1. Which of the following terms defines a fluid-filled lesion usually less than 5 mm in its greatest dimensions?
   A. bulla
   B. pustule
   C. vesicle
   D. papule
   E. macule
2. All the following are mucosal anomalies of the oral cavity EXCEPT one. Which one is the EXCEPTION?
   A. fissured tongue
   B. concresence
   C. ankyloglossia
   D. hairy tongue
   E. central papillary atrophy
3. White threadlike papules in a linear or reticular pattern—frequently found on the buccal mucosa—are MOST likely
   A. leukoedema.
   B. lichen planus.
   C. fordyce granules.
   D. pemphigus.
   E. hyperkeratosis.
4. A tooth root exhibiting an unusual curvature is referred to as a(n)
   A. concresence.
   B. dilaceration.
   C. taurodontism.
   D. anodontia.
   E. macrodont.
5. A tooth exhibiting two clinical crowns with usually one root is probably the result of
   A. fusion.
   B. concresence.
   C. dens in dente.
   D. gemination.
   E. amelogenesis imperfecta.
6. Dentinogenesis imperfecta is a condition with abnormal dentin. On radiographs, it frequently appears with the absence of pulp chambers and canals.
   A. The first statement is TRUE, the second statement is FALSE.
   B. Both statements are TRUE.
   C. The first statement is FALSE, the second statement is TRUE.
   D. Both statements are FALSE.
7. All of the following are odontogenic cysts EXCEPT one. Which one is the EXCEPTION?
   A. primordial
   B. residual
   C. dentigerous
   D. nasopalatine duct
   E. radicular

8. Which of the following cysts is frequently the oral manifestation of basal cell nevus syndrome?
   A. globulomaxillary
   B. primordial
   C. odontogenic keratocyst
   D. periapical
   E. incisive canal

9. Which of the following terms implies an increase in cell size, but not cell numbers?
   A. hyperplasia
   B. neoplasia
   C. hamartoma
   D. hypertrophy
   E. choristoma

10. An odontogenic tumor, in which cells arise from the inner enamel epithelium and demonstrate locally invasive potential, is a(n)
    A. odontogenic adenomatoid tumor.
    B. compound odontoma.
    C. odontogenic myxoma.
    D. ameloblastoma.

11. All of the following odontogenic neoplasms are derivatives of ectoderm EXCEPT one. Which one is the EXCEPTION?
    A. ameloblastoma
    B. odontogenic myxoma
    C. odontogenic adenomatoid tumor
    D. calcifying epithelial odontogenic tumor

12. Which of the following odontogenic tumors, MOST commonly present at the apices of mandibular anteriors, consists of varying radiolucencies and radiopacities?
    A. ameloblastoma
    B. odontogenic myxoma
    C. cementoma
    D. odontogenic keratocyst
    E. calcifying epithelial odontogenic tumor

13. The MOST common intraoral soft tissue neoplasm is a(n)
    A. cementoma.
    B. lipoma.
    C. papilloma.
    D. epulis fissuratum.
    E. fibroma.

14. Which of the following neoplasms manifests as a hemorrhagic, pedunculated mass and is usually an exaggerated response to a local irritant?
    A. pyogenic granuloma
    B. fibroma
    C. lipoma
    D. epulis fissuratum
    E. peripheral giant cell tumor

15. Which of the following neoplasms is viral induced?
    A. pyogenic granuloma
    B. lipoma
    C. papilloma
    D. epulis fissuratum
    E. peripheral giant cell granuloma

16. A neoplasm of cells that produces myelin is defined as
    A. neuroma.
    B. neurilemoma.
    C. neurofibroma.
    D. hemangioma.

17. A purplish-red neoplasm, found on the dorsum of the tongue, MOST likely is a
    A. lymphangioma.
    B. fibroma.
    C. rhabdomyoma.
    D. pyogenic granuloma.
    E. hemangioma.

18. The MOST likely origin of a leiomyoma neoplasm is in the
    A. intrinsic muscles of the tongue.
    B. extrinsic muscles of the tongue.
    C. mylohyoid muscle.
    D. striated muscles of the pharynx.
    E. smooth muscles surrounding blood vessels.

19. All of the following are common salivary gland tumors found in the parotid EXCEPT one. Which one is the EXCEPTION?
    A. Warthin's
    B. pleomorphic adenoma
    C. mixed
    D. monomorphic adenoma

20. Which bone lesion is occasionally seen in patients with hyperparathyroidism?
    A. chondroma
    B. osteoma
    C. exostosis
    D. fibrous dysplasia
    E. central giant cell tumor

21. Inflammation of a salivary gland duct is known as
    A. sialadenitis.
    B. sialodochitis.
    C. sialolithiasis.
    D. sialometaplasia.

22. The etiology of necrotizing sialometaplasia is due to a(n)
    A. infarction of blood supply to that portion of the gland.
    B. stone formation in the duct of the involved gland.
    C. inflammation in the gland proper.
    D. obstruction in the glandular duct.

23. Which of the following is a clinical description, not a diagnosis, of swelling in the floor of the mouth?
    A. mucocele
    B. mucus duct cyst
    C. ranula
    D. mucus retention phenomenon
    E. mucus extravasation phenomenon

24. Tuberculosis may manifest oral ulcerations. These ulcerations heal as the disease becomes quiescent.
    A. The first statement is TRUE, the second statement is FALSE.
    B. The first statement is FALSE, the second statement is TRUE.
    C. Both statements are TRUE.
    D. Both statements are FALSE.

25. The cutaneous manifestation of secondary syphilis is a
    A. mucus patch.
    B. mucosal ulceration.
    C. gummatous necrosis.
    D. pruritic rash.

26. "Sulfur granules" may be a manifestation of
    A. tuberculosis.
    B. gonorrhea.
    C. syphilis.
    D. shingles.
    E. actinomycosis.

27. The MOST frequent oral site of recurrent herpes is the
    A. floor of the mouth.
    B. dorsum of the tongue.
    C. buccal mucosa.
    D. labial mucosa.
    E. hard palate.

28. Shingles is also known as
    A. herpes simplex.
    B. herpes zoster.
    C. herpangina.
    D. rubeola.
    E. hand-foot-and-mouth disease.

29. Which of the following diseases may exhibit prodromal Koplik's spots?
    A. shingles
    B. rubeola
    C. herpangina
    D. herpes simplex
    E. rubella

30. Epstein-Barr virus is implicated as the etiology in which of the following conditions?
    A. thrombocytopenia
    B. mononucleosis
    C. herpangina
    D. pernicious anemia

31. Periadenitis mucosa necrotica recurrens is known as
    A. major aphthae.
    B. minor aphthae.
    C. Beçhet's syndrome.
    D. Reiter's syndrome.
    E. Stevens-Johnson syndrome.

32. Which of the following diseases demonstrates antibodies against desmosomes?
    A. pemphigoid
    B. erythema multiforme
    C. lupus erythematosus
    D. pemphigus
    E. erosive lichen planus

33. All of the following are multisystem diseases EXCEPT one. Which one is the EXCEPTION?
    A. Beçhet's syndrome
    B. Reiter's syndrome
    C. Stevens-Johnson syndrome
    D. amelogensis imperfecta

34. Which of the following bleeding disorders is a result of a deficiency of factor IX?
    A. hemophilia A
    B. hemophilia B
    C. hemophilia C
    D. thrombocytopenia
    E. erythroblastosis fetalis

35. A term that specifically implies a spontaneous nose bleed is
    A. hematoma.
    B. hemoptysis.
    C. purpura.
    D. petechiae.
    E. epistaxis.

36. Aplastic anemia is a disease exhibiting deficiencies in which of the following circulating blood counts?
    A. red blood cells
    B. granulocytes
    C. agranulocytes
    D. hemoglobulin
    E. all blood cells

37. Which of the following diseases manifests episodes of infections and normality?
    A. cyclic neutropenia
    B. agranulocytosis
    C. aplastic anemia
    D. polycythemia
    E. thrombocytopenia

38. Which of the following diseases may manifest bronzing of the skin?
    A. Basal cell nevus syndrome
    B. Peutz-Jeghers syndrome
    C. Addison's disease
    D. hyperparathyroidism
    E. diabetes mellitus

39. Cancer of the glandular tissue is appropriately defined as
    A. liposarcoma.
    B. lymphangiosarcoma.
    C. glandular sarcoma.
    D. adenocarcinoma.

40. A cyst located in the midline apical to the maxillary central incisors would MOST likely be a
    A. nasopalatine duct.
    B. thyroglossal duct.
    C. globulomaxillary.
    D. branchial cleft.
    E. median mandibular.

answers & rationales

1.

C. A vesicle is a small fluid-filled lesion usually less than 5 mm in diameter. A bulla, by definition, is a large fluid-filled lesion usually greater than 5 mm in diameter. A pustule is a lesion filled with pus—a more specific fluid content. Papules and macules are lesions that are not filled with fluid.

2.

B. Concresence is a dental anomaly characterized by the joining of adjacent teeth by cementum only. Fissured and hairy tongue, ankyloglossia, and central papillary atrophy are mucosal anomalies of the oral cavity.

3.

B. Lichen planus is an autoimmune disease which frequently exhibits white threadlike papules in a linear pattern (Wickham's striae). Leukoedema is a term which refers to a milky opalescent hue to the buccal mucosa due to increased intracellular edema. Fordyce granules are a yellow submucosal aggregate of sebaceous glands. Pemphigus is an autoimmune skin disease exhibiting oral ulcerations. Hyperkeratosis is a general term implying increased keratin production with no linear pattern.

4.

B. Dilaceration refers to a root that exhibits unusual curvature. Concresence implies adjacent teeth joined together only by the cementum. Taurodontism describes abnormally elongated pulp chambers. Anodontia refers to the absence of one or more teeth—congenital or acquired. A macrodont is a large tooth.

5.

D. Gemination implies twinning of a tooth. Fusion is the joining of two teeth to form one tooth—usually one less than the normal number. Concresence does not affect the crowns since joining is accomplished by cementum only. Dens in dente implies a tooth within a tooth—enamel is within a pulp chamber. Amelogenesis imperfecta is abnormal enamel formation and does not affect tooth numbers.

6.

B. The etiology of dentinogenesis imperfecta is usually genetic, clinically manifesting no pulp chambers or canals.

7.

D. A nasopalatine duct cyst is nonodontogenic. It is a unilocular radiolucency found in the midline of the palate, apical to the maxillary central incisors. Primordial, residual, dentigerous, and radicular cysts are all odontogenic.

8.

C. Multiple odontogenic keratocysts are frequently seen in basal cell nevus syndrome. These multilocular cysts are radiolucent with poorly defined margins. A globulomaxillary cyst is found between the maxillary lateral incisor and canine. The primordial cyst is intraosseous and found in place of a missing tooth. Periapical cyst is another term for radicular cyst involving a nonvital tooth. An incisive canal cyst is developmental and located in the incisive canal.

9.

D. Hypertrophy implies a cellular enlargement only. Hyperplasia implies an increase in cells numbers. Neoplasia implies a tumorous growth owing to an increase in cell numbers. Hamartoma is a neoplasia of cells native to a given area and choristoma is a neoplasia of cells foreign to a given area.

10.

D. Ameloblastoma is a slow-growing benign neoplasm of ameloblasts that arises from the inner enamel epithelium. Odontogenic adenomatoid tumor is noninvasive of odontogenic origin. Compound odontoma is a noninvasive tumor-forming tooth structure. Odontogenic myxoma is a tumor arising from cells of the stellate reticulum.

11.

B. Odontogenic myoxoma is a slow-growing benign tumor of mesodermal origin. Ameloblastoma, odontogenic adenomatoid, and calcifying epithelial odontogenic tumors are entirely from ectodermal derivation.

12.

C. Cementomas are commonly found at the apices of mandibular incisors. The lesion can be entirely radiolucent, then mixed radiolucent/radiopaque to entirely radiopaque in older lesions. Ameloblastoma is not commonly found at the apices of the mandibular incisors and shows no variation in radiolucencies or radiopacities. Odontogenic myxoma is not commonly found at the apices of mandibular incisors and is entirely radiolucent. An odontogenic keratocyst is not an odontogenic tumor, but a cyst. A calcifying epithelial odontogenic tumor is not dependent on existing teeth and not commonly found at the apices of mandibular incisors.

13.

E. Fibroma is the most common intraoral soft tissue neoplasm. A cementoma is not a soft tissue neoplasm, but composed of intraosseous cementum. A lipoma is a neoplasm of adipose tissue not commonly found intraorally. A papilloma is an epithelial neoplasm, but not as common as the fibroma. Epulis fissuratum is a fibrous hyperplasia due to a poor fitting denture and is not as common as the fibroma.

14.

A. Pyogenic granuloma is a reactive hyperplasia of granulation-type tissue. It is usually hemorrhagic and pedunculated in response to a local irritant. Fibroma is usually not hemorrhagic in appearance. Lipoma is a neoplasm of adipose tissue and not hemorrhagic in appearance. Epulis fissuratum is a reactive neoplasm that develops in response to a poor fitting denture and is not hemorrhagic in appearance. Peripheral giant cell tumor is usually liver color in appearance when it is present in the soft tissue.

15.

C. The etiology of papilloma is the human papilloma virus. Pyogenic granuloma is a reactive neoplasm in response to a local irritant. Lipoma is a neoplasm of adipose tissue and not viral-induced. Epulis fissuratum is a reactive neoplasm in response to a poor fitting denture. Peripheral giant cell granuloma has an unknown etiology; however, it is not suspected as being viral-induced.

16.

B. Neurilemoma is a neoplasm of Schwann cells, which produces myelin sheath. Neuroma is a neoplasm of neural tissue. Neurofibroma is a neoplasm of neural elements and fibrous connective tissue. Hemangioma is a neoplasm of blood cells.

17.

E. A hemangioma is most commonly found on the tongue, frequently hemorrhagic in nature. Lymphangioma is a common neoplasm found on the tongue, but not discolored. Fibroma is usually the color of normal mucosa, unless secondarily inflamed. Rhabdomyoma is a neoplasm of striated muscle usually the color of normal mucosa as well. Pyogenic granuloma is not normally found on the tongue and usually arises from the crevicular gingiva.

18.

E. Leiomyoma is sessile in form, palpable, and may cause slight elevation of the surface mucosa. Its origin intraorally is in the smooth muscle walls of blood vessels. The remaining striated muscles may involve rhabdomyoma, a neoplasm of voluntary muscles.

19.

D. Monomorphic adenoma is a glandular neoplasm most commonly found in the upper lip. Warthin's tumor is almost exclusively found in the parotid gland. Pleomorphic adenoma (another name for mixed tumor) is most commonly found in the parotid gland.

20.

E. It is not unusual to find a central giant cell tumor in patients with hyperparathyroidism. Chondroma (cartilaginous neoplasm), osteoma (bony neoplasm), and exostosis (bony neoplasm) are not associated with hyperparathyroidism. Fibrous dysplasia is a fibrous and bony proliferation and not associated with hyperparathyroidism.

21.

B. Sialodochitis implies inflammation of a gland duct. Sialadenitis implies inflammation of a gland proper. Sialolithiasis implies salivary gland stone formation. Sialometaplasia implies histological glandular epithelium changes.

22.

A. The etiology of necrotizing sialometaplasia is from interruption of the blood supply. Stone formation, inflammation in the glandular proper, and obstruction and inflammation of the glandular duct do not cause necrosis in the salivary gland.

23.

C. Ranula is only a clinical description and does not imply etiology. Mucocele is a generic diagnosis of either mucous extravasation or retention. Mucous duct cyst implies an obstruction with the duct epithelium forming, a cyst-like lesion. Mucous retention phenomenon implies obstruction of a duct with mucus retention. Mucous extravasation phenomenon implies rupture of a duct with mucus spillage into surrounding connective tissue.

24.

C. Tuberculosis is a disease involving the respiratory system. Symptoms include chronic coughs and occasionally oral ulcerations resulting from coughing up infected sputum.

25.

D. Cutaneous implies skin and pruritic implies itching. Mucous patch and mucosal ulceration are mucous manifestations, not cutaneous manifestations. Gummatous necrosis is a manifestation of tertiary syphilis.

26.

E. Actinomycosis is a bacterial disease that produces pus with granules. The granules appear yellow, similar to a grain of sulfur, but actually are colonies of the microorganism. Tuberculosis, gonorrhea, syphilis, and shingles do not produce pus-containing "sulfur granules."

27.

E. The most common intraoral site of recurrent herpes is usually adjacent to the maxillary first molars. The floor of the mouth, dorsum of the tongue, and buccal and labial mucosa are rarely sites for recurrent herpes.

28.

B. Herpes zoster is frequently referred to as shingles. Herpes simplex is also referred to as "fever blisters." Herpangina is seasonal pharyngitis. Rubeola is measles, and hand-foot-and-mouth disease are seasonal vesicles in the appropriate sites, respectively.

29.

B. With rubeola, there's evidence of erythematous macules located near the parotid papillae before the measles rash. Shingles, herpangina, herpes simplex, and rubella show no evidence of Koplik's spots.

30.

B. Epstein-Barr is implicated in mononucleosis as well as hairy leukoplakia of AIDS. Thrombocytopenia is a bleeding disorder caused by inadequate or missing platelets. Herpangina is a coxsackievirus disease. Pernicious anemia results from a lack of intrinsic or extrinsic factors associated with vitamin B_{12} deficiency.

31.

A. Periadenitis mucosa necrotica recurrens are large ulcers also known as major aphthae. Minor aphthae are small ulcers. Beçhet's syndrome involves ocular, oral, and genital minor aphthae. Reiter's syndrome also involve the ocular, oral, and genital with lesions, but not aphthae. Stevens-Johnson syndrome involves ocular, oral, and genital erythema multiforme.

32.

D. Pemphigus is an autoimmune disease that destroys desmosomes. Pemphigoid is an autoimmune disease that destroys hemidesmosomes. Erythema multiforme is an autoimmune disease causing "target lesions" on the skin. Lupus erythematosus is an autoimmune disease with antinuclear antibodies. Erosive lichen planus is a disease affecting the basement membrane.

33.

D. Amelogenesis imperfecta is a dental defect resulting in severe hypoplasia or hypocalcification of the enamel. Beçhet's, Reiter's, and Stevens-Johnson syndromes are multisystem diseases.

34.

B. Hemophilia B is a bleeding disorder as a result of a deficiency of factor IX. Hemophilia A is a deficiency of factor VIII. Hemophilia C is a deficiency of factor XI. Thrombocytopenia is a deficiency in platelets and erythroblastosis fetalis notes Rh incompatibility.

35.

E. Epistaxis is a spontaneous nose bleed. Hematoma is an elevated area of submucosal bleeding. Hemoptysis refers to coughing up blood. Purpura is a general term for submucosal bleeding. Petechiae is a small, pinpoint, nonelevated area of submucosal bleeding.

36.

E. Aplastic anemia results in a severe decrease in red blood cells, white blood cells, and platelets—not just circulating red blood cells, granulocytes, agranulocytes, and hemoglobin.

37.

A. Cyclic neutropenia is a disorder of the white blood cells that exhibits cycles between normal blood counts and deficiencies of neutrophils. Agranulocytosis has a severe reduction in circulating granulocytes, especially neutrophils. Aplastic anemia results in a severe decrease of all circulating blood cells. With polycythemia, there is an abnormal increase in red blood cells. With thrombocytopenia, there is an abnormal decrease in circulating platelets.

38.

C. With Addison's disease, there is frequently evidence of a bronze discoloration of the skin. Basal cell nevus syndrome manifests skin cancers, skeletal abnormalities, and multiple OKCs. Peutz-Jeghers syndrome manifests oral and pcrioral pigmentations with intestinal polyps. Hyperparathyroidism is a multisystem disease that manifests bone demineralization. With diabetes mellitus, skin discoloration is not commonly encountered.

39.

D. "Adeno" implies glandular. Carcinoma implies a malignancy of ectodermal origin from which glandular tissue originates. Liposarcoma is a malignancy of adipose tissue, a mesodermal derivative. Lymphangiosarcoma is a malignancy of lymphatic tissue, also a mesodermal derivative. Glandular sarcoma is a malignancy of ectodermal origin, therefore designated as a carcinoma.

40.

A. A nasopalatine duct cyst is unilocular and develops in the incisive canal. A thyroglossal duct cyst develops in the neck and a branchial cleft cyst develops in the lateral part of the neck. A globulomaxillary cyst develops between the maxillary lateral incisor and canine. A median mandibular cyst develops in the midline of the mandible.

CHAPTER

8 Pharmacology

Ruth Tornwall RDH, MS
Frieda Pickett, RDH, MS

contents

Pharmacology is the study of drugs and their effects on living organisms. A *drug* is a chemical substance used for the diagnosis, prevention, or treatment of a disease or condition.

I. DRUG ACTION AND TERMINATION

A. *Receptors*—macromolecules located on or within cell membranes that the drug must bind with to be effective; lock and key fit (specific drug binding with specific receptor; Figure 8-1)

1. *Agonist*—drug has affinity for receptor, which produces an effect
2. *Antagonist*—drug has affinity for the receptor; produces no effect
   a) Competitive antagonist—interacts with same receptor site as agonist and competes with the agonist
   b) Noncompetitive antagonist—binds to a receptor site different from the binding site for the agonist but reduces the maximal response of the agonist

B. Drug-binding forces—the chemical binding of a drug to a receptor site

1. *Covalent bonds*—sharing of an electron by a pair of atoms; strong bond often irreversible (tetracycline to dentin)
2. *Ionic bonds*—an electrostatic attraction between ions of opposite charge (most common mechanism for drug binding), reversible, easily made and easily broken
3. *Hydrogen bonds*—special type of interaction between polar molecules, weaker than ionic bonds
4. *Van der Waals Forces*—weak interactions that develop when two atoms are placed in close proximity

C. *Log-dose effect curve*—log of the dose (*x*-axis) versus the intensity of response (*y*-axis) (Figure 8-2)

1. *Potency*—amount of a drug needed to produce desired therapeutic effect
2. *Affinity*—tendency for a drug to bind to a receptor site
3. *Efficacy*—the desired therapeutic response obtained from a drug when a sufficient amount of drug is administered; not related to potency
4. Ceiling effect (*plateau*)—therapeutic effect cannot be increased with a higher dose of the drug

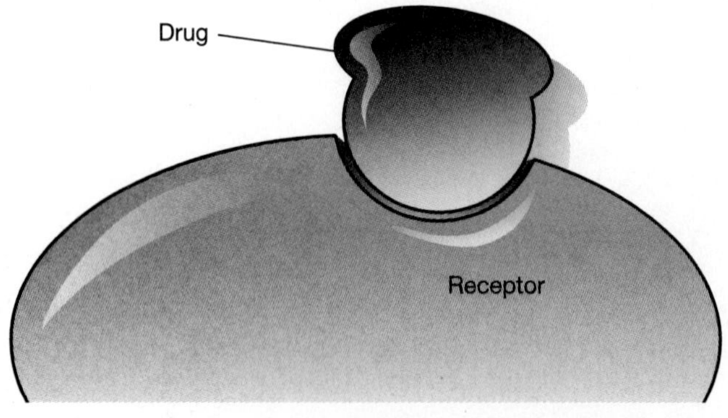

FIGURE 8-1. Drug–receptor interaction

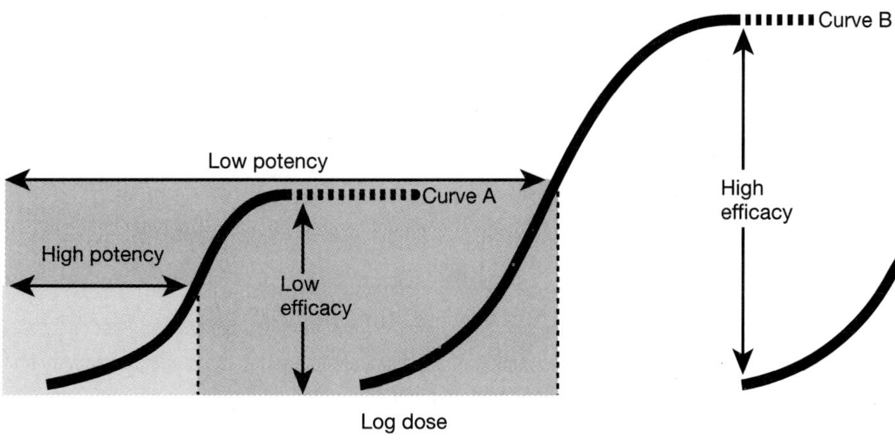

FIGURE 8-2. Log-dose effect curve

5. Effect dose (ED50)—dose that produces a therapeutic response in 50% of the subjects given the drug
6. Lethal dose (LD50)—dose of the drug that produces death in 50% of the subjects given the drug
7. *Therapeutic Index* (TI)—ratio of the median lethal dose (LD50) to the median effective dose (ED50); express the safety of the drug; the greater the TI, the safer the drug.

D. Factors altering drug's effect

1. *Placebo effect*—a perceived effect that occurs after taking an inactive substance
2. Patient noncompliance—patients takes medication incorrectly or not at all
3. Drug interaction—effect may be modified by previous or concomitant administration of another agent

E. Routes of administration—affects drug onset and duration of response

1. *Enteral*—placed directly into the gastrointestinal (GI) tract by oral or rectal administration
   a) Oral (PO)—by mouth, slower onset of action, may be affected by presence of food in the GI tract
   b) Rectal—given as suppositories, creams, enemas for local (hemorrhoids) or systemic (antiemetic) effects; slower onset of action
2. *Parenteral*—bypasses the GI tract and includes various injection routes
   a) *Intravenous* (IV)—placed directly into the blood, rapid predictable response; route of choice for emergencies
   b) *Intramuscular* (IM)—placed directly into the muscle
   c) *Subcutaneous* (SC, SQ)—under the skin (e.g., insulin)
   d) *Intradermal*—into the dermis, small amounts of drugs (e.g., local anesthetic and tuberculin skin test)
   e) *Intrathecal*—injected into the spinal subarachnoid space; used for treatment of certain forms of meningitis

f) *Intraperitoneal*—into the peritoneal cavity
g) *Inhalation* (INH)—inhaled into the lungs (gaseous, microcrystalline, volatile drugs, and bronchodilators)
h) *Topical*—includes local application to oral mucous membranes, skin, and other epithelial surfaces for local or systemic effects (e.g., anesthetic)
i) *Transdermal*—provides continuous controlled release of medication through semipermeable membrane after application to intact skin (e.g., estrogen/nicotine patches)

F. *Pharmacokinetics*—study of what happens to a drug once it enters, circulates, and leaves the body; what factors influence absorption, distribution, metabolism, and excretion (ADME)

1. Absorption—process by which drug molecules are transferred from the site of administration to circulating fluids
   a) Transport mechanism
      (1) *Simple diffusion*—substance moves from high concentration to low concentration
      (2) *Active transport*—substance is transported against gradient across a biological membrane by "carriers" that furnish energy for transportation of drug
      (3) *Facilitated diffusion*—drug is transported down the concentration gradient at a greater rate than passive diffusion; bound to specific carrier proteins
   b) Effects of ionization
      (1) More ionized (water-soluble), increases and facilitates absorption over the surface area
      (2) pH of the tissues at site of administration and dissociation characteristics of the drug determine ease with which the drug will travel through the tissues
   c) Lipid solubility—the more lipid-soluble (nonionized), the more readily the drug crosses the biological membranes
2. Distribution—drug is distributed throughout the body by plasma proteins in blood
   a) Protein binding—drug is bound reversibly to plasma proteins, a storage site; a bound drug is not free to exert its action
   b) Unbound drug—can cross membranes to site of action, bind to cell receptor, causes an action
   c) Constant equilibrium—drugs remain in constant equilibrium between the unbound and bound form
   d) Redistribution—drugs move from the site of action to other nonspecific sites
3. Metabolism (*biotransformation*)—most common site is liver; body changes the drug to be excreted by the kidneys; microsomal enzyme-dependent
4. Excretion—drugs and their metabolites eliminated via urine, bile, sweat, saliva, lungs, tears, and milk; kidney is the major organ of drug excretion

II. ADVERSE REACTIONS—undesirable reactions of drug effects

A. Toxic effect—exceeds the amount of desired effect; dose-related, predictable

B. Side effect—a dose-related reaction not part of the desired therapeutic outcome; occurs when the drug acts on a nontarget organ

C. *Idiosyncratic reaction*—unexpected reaction to drug, not predictable; most likely to affect the very young and old

D. *Drug allergy*—varies from a mild rash to anaphylaxis; antigen–antibody reaction; not dose-related and not predictable; can be divided into four types of reactions depending on the type of antibody or cell-mediated reaction

E. Interference with natural defense mechanism—certain drugs may reduce the body's ability to fight infection

F. *Teratogenic*—adverse effect of a drug on the fetus, producing deformities

III. DRUG INTERACTIONS—the action of a drug on the effectiveness or toxicity of another drug administered earlier, simultaneously, or later; results in undesired drug effect

A. Definitions

1. *Potentiation*—interaction of two or more drugs resulting in a greater-than-expected effect
2. *Antagonism*—clinical response is reduced by administration of second agent
3. *Summation*—combined activities of two or more drugs that elicit identical or related pharmacological effects; effect is not greater
4. *Synergism*—combination of two or more agonists producing an effect greater than can be achieved by the maximum does of one of those drugs

B. Mechanisms of interaction

1. Pharmacokinetic
   a) Absorption alterations
      (1) Absorbed on large surface area—altered pH may affect disintegration or dissolution
      (2) Bound or chelated drugs may decrease effect
      (3) Altered GI tract motility absorption may increase or decrease effect
   b) Distribution alterations
      (1) *Plasma–protein binding*—affected by other drugs with greater affinity causing second drug to have greater unbound concentration
      (2) *Blood–brain barrier*—some drugs cannot cross the central nervous system (CNS) tissue membranes
   c) Metabolism alterations

(1) A drug may induce hepatic microsomal enzyme production and result in a lessened effect of another drug
(2) A drug may decrease microsomal enzymes resulting in accumulation of another drug, increasing pharmacological effect

d) Excretion alterations
(1) Bound drugs cannot be filtered in glomerulus, remain in circulation
(2) Tubular reabsorption may be affected by altered pH

2. Pharmacodynamic—sympathetic and parasympathetic nervous system posses sites for drug interactions to occur; have opposite effects

IV. DRUGS USED IN DENTISTRY

A. *Autonomic drugs*—drugs that exert stimulating or inhibiting effects on the two divisions of the autonomic nervous system (ANS), both parasympathetic (PANS) and sympathetic (SANS)

1. *Cholinergic* or parasympathetic drugs stimulate the PANS; neurotransmitter is acetylcholine and the termination is by acetylcholinesterase

a) Receptors
(1) Muscarinic—postsynaptic tissue that responds to muscarine
(a) Eye—miosis, contraction for near vision
(b) Heart—bradycardia, decreased blood pressure
(c) Lungs—bronchoconstriction
(d) Uterus—contraction
(e) Urinary bladder—contraction
(f) Nasopharyngeal—increased secretions
(g) GI tract—increased motility
(2) Nicotinic—ganglia stimulated by nicotine
(a) All autonomic ganglia—stimulation of post-ganglionian neuron
(b) Skeletal muscle—contraction

b) Mechanism
(1) Direct action—drug acts like acetylcholine at the receptor site
(a) Choline esters—bethanechol (Urecholine)
(b) Other—pilocarpine (Salagen)
(2) Indirect action—drug inhibits the enzyme cholinesterase, causing acetylcholine buildup at receptor site

c) Pharmacological effects
(1) Cardiovascular system
(a) Direct effect—decreased force and rate of contraction, decreased cardiac output, smooth muscle relaxation of blood vessels
(b) Indirect effect—increased heart rate and cardiac output
(2) GI system
(a) Direct effect—excitation of smooth muscle leading to salivation

(b) Indirect effect—lacrimation, urination, increased stomach acid production, and diarrhea

(3) Eye—accommodation for near vision, miosis, and decrease in intraocular pressure

d) Adverse reactions—extensions of pharmacological effects

e) Treatment of overdose

(1) Pralidoxime (2-PAM, Protopam) regenerates acetylcholinesterase

(2) Atropine—antimuscarinic, does not block nicotinic effects

f) Dental use of pilocarpine—treatment of xerostomia when functional salivary gland tissue is present

2. *Anticholinergic* (parasympatholytic)—inhibits the effects of the PANS; blocks muscarinic receptors throughout the body and nicotinic receptors at high doses

a) Pharmacological effects

(1) CNS—low doses, sedation; high doses, stimulation

(2) Cardiovascular system—low doses, bradycardia; high doses, tachycardia

(3) Eye—increases in intraocular pressure, cycloplegia, mydriasis

(4) Smooth muscle—relaxation of the respiratory and GI smooth muscle

(5) Exocrine glands—reduction of secretions in the respiratory, GI, and genitourinary tracts

b) Adverse reaction—extension of the drug's pharmacological effects

c) Contraindications—patients with glaucoma, prostatic hypertrophy, constipation, urinary retention, and cardiovascular disease

d) Clinical uses

(1) Preoperative medication

(a) Dries up secretions

(b) Blocks the vagal slowing of the heart resulting from general anesthesia

(2) GI disorders—reduces increased motility and acid secretions

(3) Ophthalmologic examination—full visualization of the retina and relaxation of the lens

(4) CNS—treatment of motion sickness, sleep aid, treatment of Parkinson-like symptoms for antipsychotic drugs

e) Examples of drugs

(1) Atropine (Sal-Tropine)—prototype agent to decrease salivary flow and respiratory secretions, increase heart rate, and dilate pupils

(2) Scopolamine (Transderm Scōp)—antimotion sickness

(3) Propantheline (Pro-Banthine)—reduce GI motility as it creates a dry mouth for orthodontic and other dental procedures

4. *Adrenergic* (sympathomimetic)—stimulates the effects of the SANS

a) Neurotransmitter—norepinephrine (NOR)
   (1) Synthesis and inactivation—NOR released from nerve endings, inactivation occurs through dissipation, reuptake by presynaptic nerve terminals or enzymatic breakdown
b) Receptors—effects on organs and tissues
   (1) alpha α
      (a) Eye (iris)—mydriasis
      (b) Arteries—vasoconstriction
   (2) beta β
      (a) β_1 (heart)—increased force and rate of contraction
      (b) β_2 (eye)—relaxation of distant vision
      (c) Lungs—bronchodilation
      (d) Skeletal smooth muscle—contraction
      (e) Uterus—relaxation
c) Mechanism
   (1) Direct action—NOR, epinephrine, and isoproterenol produce effects directly on a receptor site by stimulating the receptor
   (2) Indirect action—agents (amphetamine) release endogenous NOR, which then produces a response
   (3) Mixed action—agents (ephedrine) can stimulate the receptor directly or release endogenous NOR to cause a response
d) Pharmacological Effects
   (1) CNS—stimulate excitation, alertness, anxiety, apprehension, restlessness, and tremors (at higher doses)
   (2) Cardiovascular system
      (a) Heart—increases the force and rate of contraction; increase blood pressure
      (b) Vessels
         i) *vasoconstriction* of smooth muscle (α), which increases total peripheral resistance
         ii) *vasodilation* of skeletal muscle arteries (β_2), which decreases total peripheral resistance
      (c) Blood pressure—increases
      (d) Eye—decreases in intraocular pressure
      (e) Respiratory system—bronchial relaxation
      (f) Metabolic effects—hyperglycemia (glycogenolysis), decreased insulin release
      (g) Salivary glands—decreases salivary flow
e) Toxic reactions—extensions of pharmacological effects of anxiety, tremors, palpitation and arrhythmias
f) Uses
   (1) Vasoconstriction
      (a) Prolonged action—added to local anesthetic solutions
      (b) Homeostasis—topically or infiltrated locally to stop bleeding
      (c) Decongestion—incorporated into nose drops or sprays
   2) Cardiac effects—treatment of shock is controversial; treatment of cardiac arrest

(3) Bronchodilation—treatment of asthma or anaphylaxis
(4) CNS stimulation—treatment of attention deficit hyperactivity disorder (ADHD) and narcolepsy

g) Examples of adrenergic agents
(1) Epinephrine (adrenaline)
(a) Receptor stimulated: $\alpha\beta$
(b) Use: acute asthma attack, anaphylaxis, vasoconstrictor in local anesthesia
(2) Levonordefrin
(a) Receptor stimulated: α
(b) Use: vasoconstrictor added to local anesthesia
(3) Phenylephrine (NeoSynephrine)
(a) Receptor stimulated: α
(b) Use: OTC nose drops or sprays
(4) Isoproterenol (Isuprel)
(a) Receptor stimulated: β
(b) Use: treatment of asthma
(5) Pseudoephedrine (Sudafed)
(a) Receptor stimulated: β
(b) Use: OTC products for common cold
(6) Dopamine (Inotropin)
(a) Receptor stimulated: $\alpha\beta$
(b) Use: treatment of shock
(7) Amphetamine
(a) Receptor stimulated: $\alpha\beta$
(b) Use: treatment of obesity

h) Dental concerns—patients who use OTC medications may not inform health care provider; drugs interact with vasoconstrictor added to local anesthetic; these drugs interact with many other drugs.

4. *Adrenergic blocking agents* (sympatholytic)—inhibits the effects of the SANS, blocks all adrenergic receptors (a combination of receptors, or may block only α, β_1, or β_2 receptors)
a) Clinical uses—hypertension, angina, cardiac arrhythmias, myocardial infarction, glaucoma, prophylactic treatment of migraine headaches, Raynaud's disease
b) Examples
(1) α blocking agents—tolazoline (Priscoline), prazosin (Minipress), phentolamine (Regitine)
(2) β blocking agents (note *-olol* in generic names)
(a) Nonselective—affects the heart and lungs; propranolol (Inderal) and nadolol (Corgard)
(b) Selective—affects the heart; metoprolol (Lopressor) and atenolol (Tenormin)
(3) α and β blocking agents end in *-alol*
(a) labetalol—used for hypertension

B. Nonopioid analgesics—general considerations of pain; *perception*, the physical component, involves a message carried through nerves to the cerebral cortex; and *reaction,* the

psychological component, involves the patient's emotional response

1. Salicylates (aspirin)
   a) Site of action—primarily at peripheral nerve endings
   b) Mechanism—ability to inhibit the enzyme cyclooxygenase and thereby, prostaglandin synthesis
   c) Pharmacological effects
      (1) Analgesia—mild to moderate pain
      (2) Antipyretic—reduces elevated body temperature owing to ability to block prostaglandin synthesis in hypothalamus
      (3) Anti-inflammatory—reduces inflammation levels to treat mild to moderate pain
      (4) Uricosuric—decreases excretion of uric acid
      (5) Antiplatelet—prevents platelets from sticking to each other
   d) Adverse reactions
      (1) GI—simple dyspepsia, vomiting, or gastric bleeding
      (2) Bleeding altered
         (a) *Platelet adhesivesness*—irreversibly interferes with clotting mechanism
         (b) *Hypoprothrombinemia*—inhibits prothrombin synthesis
      (3) *Reye's syndrome*—may cause hepatoxicity and encephalopathy in children with chickenpox or influenza
      (4) *Hypersensitivity*—a true allergy is uncommon, cross-hypersensitivity exists between aspirin and nonsteroidal anti-inflammatory agents
      (5) Aspirin overdose (*salicylism*)—tinnitus, headache, nausea, vomiting, dizziness, dimness of vision
   e) Drug interactions—many interactions caused by aspirin binding to plasma proteins
      (1) Warfarin—an increased risk for bleeding and hemorrhaging
      (2) Probenecid—interferes with uricosuric effect
      (3) Methotrexate—can cause increased serum concentration, resulting in toxicity
      (4) Sulfonylureas—can cause a hypoglycemia effect
      (5) Antihypertensives—reduces the effect of angiotensin-converting enzyme (ACE) inhibitors, β blockers, and loop diuretics (requires several doses over a few days)
2. Nonsteroidal anti-inflammatory agents/drugs (NSAIAs/NSAIDs)
   a) Site of action—same as aspirin
   b) Mechanism—same as aspirin
   c) Pharmacological effects: analgesia, antipyretic, anti-inflammatory
   d) Adverse reactions
      (1) Gastrointestinal—GI irritation, pain, bleeding problems
      (2) CNS—sedation, dizziness, confusion, mental depression, headache
      (3) Blood clotting—reversibly inhibits platelet aggregation
      (4) Oral—ulcerative stomatitis, gingival ulcerations, xerostomia

e) Therapeutic uses
   (1) Pain control—greater than aspirin, equal to or greater than some opioids (propoxyphene); useful for dental pain
   (2) Anti-inflammatory—rheumatoid arthritis and osteoarthritis, useful in dental pain
   (3) *Dysmenorrhea*—reduces excess of prostaglandin in uterine wall that produces painful contractions

f) Examples
   (1) OTC NSAIDs
      (a) Ibuprofen (Motrin, Advil)—most common, oldest OTC and can be prescription
      (b) Naproxen sodium (Aleve)—different in duration of action
      (c) Ketoprofen (Orudis KT)—similar to ibuprofen
   (2) Prescription NSAIDs
      (a) Ketorolac (Toradol)—oral and injectable dose form, useful for short-term management of moderate to severe pain
      (b) Naproxen (Naprosyn)

3. Acetaminophen (N-acetyl para-aminophenol [NAPAP])—Tylenol
   a) Pharmocological effects—analgesic (mild, integumental pain), antipyretic
   b) Adverse reactions
      (1) *Hepatic necrosis*—massive doses or usual doses over a long period have been reported to cause liver damage
      (2) *Nephrotoxicity*—associated with long-term consumption, risk is further increased if also taking aspirin or NSAID
   c) Drug interactions—major drug interaction is with alcohol

C. Opioid analgesics and antagonists

1. Classification—narcotic from poppy plant
   a) Mechanism of action at receptor site—agonist, mixed agonist/antagonist
   b) Chemical structure—useful when allergies present
   c) Potency—based on amount of pain relief needed, type pain (visceral, mod-severe)
2. Mechanism—bind to receptors located in CNS, producing altered perception of and response to pain
   a) *Mu* (μ)—respiratory depression, euphoria, analgesia
   b) *Kappa* (κ)—miosis, sedation, analgesia
   c) *Sigma* (σ)—dysphoria, hallucinations, anxiety, respiratory and vasomotor situation
3. Pharmacological effects
   a) Analgesia—depends on strength of agent; morphine, strongest; codeine, weakest
   b) Sedation and euphoria—not main effect, produce sedation by κ-receptor stimulation, potentiates analgesia and relieves anxiety
   c) Cough suppression—depresses cough center in medulla, producing antitussive effect (codeine)
   d) GI effects—constipation, nausea and vomiting, used to treat diarrhea symptomatically (paregoric)

4. Adverse reactions
   a) Respiratory depression—reduce rate and depth of respiration, produces vasodilation increasing intracranial pressure, should not be used in patients with head injuries
   b) Nausea and emesis—stimulates chemoreceptor trigger zone (CTZ) in brain
   c) Constipation—tonic contraction of the GI tract, slows GI motility, tolerance to this effect does not develop
   d) Miosis—pinpoint pupils, tolerance to this effect does not develop
   e) Urinary retention—increase smooth muscle time
   f) CNS effects—anxiety, restlessness, nervousness
   g) Abuse—can occur with all opioids
5. Examples
   a) Agonists
      (1) Morphine—prototype
      (2) Meperidine (Demerol)
      (3) Hydromorphone (Dilaudid)—orally effective for severe pain
      (4) Methadone—treatment of opioid addicts and for analgesia
      (5) Oxycodone (Percodan)—combined with aspirin or acetaminophen (Percocet) for synergistic effect on moderate to severe pain
      (6) Codeine (Empirin #3, Tylenol #3)—weak compared with morphine, combined with nonopioid agent for synergistic effect
   b) Agonist/antagonist
      (1) Pentazocine (Talwin)—produces analgesic sedation and respiratory sedation
   c) Antagonists
      (1) Naloxone (Narcan)—pure narcotic antagonist, drug of choice for treating agonist or mixed opioid overdose, reverses opioid-induced respiratory depression
      (2) Naltrexone (ReVia)—maintenance of opioid-free state; dental pain must be treated with nonopioid analgesics in patients taking this drug

D. Anti-infective agents

1. General Principles
   a) Therapeutic indications—acute dental pain with fever; treatment of abscesses and certain periodontal diseases; prophylaxis
   b) Patient—best defense against a pathogen is host response
   c) Infection—virulence, number of organisms present, and invasiveness of the microorganism are important in deciding acuteness, severity, and spreading tendency of infection
   d) Anti-infective administration carries risks; benefits versus risks must be weighed
   e) Definitions
      (1) *Anti-infective*—acts against or destroys infections

(2) *Anti-bacterial*—acts against bacteria
   (a) *bactericidal*—kills bacteria
   (b) *bacteriostatic*—inhibits or retards growth of bacteria
(3) *Antibiotic agents*—produced by another microorganism to kill or inhibit the growth or multiplication of bacteria
(4) *Antimicrobial*—acts against microorganism
(5) *Antiviral*—acts against viruses
(6) *Blood level*—concentration of anti-infective agent present in blood serum
(7) *Minimum inhibiting concentrations* (*MIC*)—lowest concentration needed to inhibit visible growth of an organism on media after incubation for 18 to 24 hours
(8) *Resistance*—occurs when microorganisms are unaffected by an antimicrobial agent, may be natural (always has been resistant) or acquired (develops resistance)
(9) *Spectrum*—range of action of a drug
(10) *Superinfection,* suprainfection—infection caused by the overgrowth of microbes different from the causative microorganism (e.g., *Candida* infection after antibiotic therapy)
(11) Culture and sensitivity—all infections not responding to antimicrobial therapy should be cultured and sensitivity tests performed (application of antimicrobial agent to culture to determine effective antibiotic); also cases of serious infections and infection in compromised patients
(12) General adverse reactions
   (a) Superinfection
   (b) Allergic reactions—ranges from mild to fatal anaphylaxis
   (c) Drug interactions
      i) Oral antibiotics—reduced effectiveness of oral contraceptives
      ii) Oral anticoagulants—increase the effect of the anticoagulant
      iii) Other anti-infective agents—antibodies may compete for same receptor and should not be given together (erythromycin and clindamycin); a bacteriostatic agent may stop the organism from growing so that the bactericidal does not work effectively (erythromycin and penicillin)
   (d) GI—nausea, vomiting
   (e) Pregnancy—risk to the fetus must be considered
   (f) Rule—use agent with a narrow spectrum that is susceptible to microorganism causing infection or for prophylaxis

2. Antibiotics
   a) Penicillins
      (1) Mechanism—inhibits cell wall synthesis; bactericidal

(2) Groups
 (a) Penicillin G/penicillin V—narrow spectrum
 (b) Penicillinase—resistant penicillin
 (c) Ampicillin/amoxicillin
 (d) Extended-spectrum penicillin
(3) Pharmocokinetics
 (a) Administered orally or parenterally but not topically due to allergy sensitization potential
 (b) Peak blood levels—immediately when used intravenously, 30 minutes to 1 hour if given orally or intramuscularly
 (c) Half-life—30 minutes to 1 hour
 (d) Metabolized—kidney, excreted in urine
 (e) Acid stability—penicillin G is unstable in acid environment of the stomach and is administered parenterally; penicillin V is acid-stable and given orally
(4) Adverse reactions
 (a) Gastrointestinal upset
 (b) Allergic reactions—mild to anaphylactic
(5) Penicillin G/penicillin V
 (a) Spectrum—includes gram-positive cocci and certain gram-negative cocci; not resistant to penicillinase, 90% of oral infections are gram-positive
 (b) Penicillin G—prototype, parenteral; potassium salt given IV produces most rapid and highest blood level; given IM, produces intermediate blood levels
 (c) Penicillin V—well absorbed with oral administration, used in the treatment of dental infections because it kills microorganisms in 90% of dental infections
 (d) Examples
  i) Penicillin G
  ii) Penicillin G procaine (Crysticillin)
  iii) Penicillin G benzathine (Bicillin L-A)
  iv) Penicillin V (Pen-Vee K, V-Cillin K)
(6) Penicillinase—resistant penicillins
 (a) Reserved for use only against penicillinase-producing staphylococci
 (b) Prototype—dicloxacillin (Dynapen, Dycill)
(7) Ampicillin/amoxicillin
 (a) Spectrum—gram-positive cocci, some enterococci; not penicillinase resistant
 (b) Amoxicillin—a relative of ampicillin, preferred for higher blood levels (better absorbed), less frequent dosage, absorption not impaired by food
  i) Drug of choice in American Heart Association (AHA) antibiotic prophylaxis regimen, to prevent infective endocarditis and in antibiotic prophylaxis for selected total joint replacement (2 grams 1 hour before procedure).

(c) Augmentin—amoxicillin plus clavulanic acid (inhibits B-lactamases produced by bacteria), has been used in treatment of mixed periodontal infection
(d) Examples
i) Ampicillin (Polycillin, Omnipen)
ii) Amoxicillin (Amoxil, Trimox)
(8) Extended spectrum penicillin
(a) Spectrum—broader than penicillin G, both gram-positive and gram-negative, special activity against *Pseudomonas aeruginosa,* not penicillinase-resistant
(b) Used parenterally to treat systemic infections
(c) Examples
i) Carbenicillin
ii) Piperacillin
iii) Ticarcillin
b) Macrolides
(1) Mechanism—inhibits bacterial protein synthesis at the 50 S subunit, bacteriostatic
(2) Adverse reactions
(a) GI—abdominal cramps, nausea, vomiting and diarrhea
(b) *Cholestatic jaundice*—primarily seen with estolate but also with ethyl succinate
(3) Therapeutic uses—drug of choice in penicillin-allergic patient, other specific infections, not effective against the anaerobic species in dental infections
(4) Spectrum
(a) Erythromycin—works primarily against gram-positive organisms, similar to penicillin V
(b) Azithromycin (Zithromax)
i) Mild to moderate infections of upper/lower respiratory tract
ii) May have activity against some anaerobes
iii) Adverse reactions—stomatitis, candidiasis, dizziness, vertigo, nausea, vomiting, hepatoxicity
iv) Recommended for use in antibiotic prophylaxis in people who are allergic to penicillin
(c) Clarithromycin (Biaxin)
i) Similar effects, uses, and adverse reaction as azithromycin
ii) Used to kill *Helicobacter pylori* in gastric ulcers
(5) Pharmacokinetics
(a) Broken down in gastric fluid, therefore has enteric coating (erythromycin)
(b) Administer 2 hours before or 2 hours after meals, blood levels peak in 1 to 4 hours after ingestion
(6) Examples
(a) Erythromycin base (E-Mycin)
(b) Erythromycin stearate (Erythrocin)
(c) Erythromycin ethylsuccinate (E.E.S., Pediamycin)

(d) Erythromycin estolate (Ilosone)

c) Tetracyclines
- (1) Mechanisms of action—inhibits bacterial protein synthesis at 30 S subunit, bacteriostatic
- (2) Pharmacokinetics—given orally, rapid absorption, kidney excretion mainly; doxycycline excreted in feces
- (3) Spectrum—considered broad-spectrum antibiotics, effective against wide variety of gram-positive and gram-negative bacteria, both aerobes and anaerobes, cross-resistance can occur
- (4) Adverse reactions
  - (a) GI—anorexia, nausea, vomiting; related to local irritation from altered flora
  - (b) Effects on teeth and bones—should not be used during pregnancy or in children up to 9 years of age, forms covalent bond with enamel causing intrinsic staining
  - (c) *Hepatoxicity*—increases with IV use
  - (d) Superinfection—over growth of *C. albicans* (thrush, vaginitis)
  - (e) Photosensitivity—exaggerated sunburn with exposure to sun
- (5) Drug Interactions
  - (a) Cations—decreased intestinal absorption, include dairy products, antacids, and mineral supplements
    - i) Doxycycline (Vibramycin)—can take with food
  - (b) Enhanced effect of drugs—oral sulfonylureas
  - (c) Reduced tetracycline effect—barbiturates and phenytoin
  - (d) Reduce effectiveness of oral contraceptives, bactericidal antibiotics
- (6) Uses
  - (a) Medical—acne, pulmonary infections in patients with chronic obstructive pulmonary disease (COPD)
  - (b) Dental—periodontal infections
- (7) Examples
  - (a) Tetracycline (Achromycin V, Sumycin)
  - (b) Doxycycline (Vibramycin)
  - (c) Minocycline (Minocin)

d) Clindamycin (Cleocin)
- (1) Mechanism—inhibits bacterial protein symphysis at 50 S subunit, bacteriostatic
- (2) Pharmacokinetics—orally well absorbed; topically, IM or IV more then 90% bound to plasma proteins, drug excreted as inactive metabolite in urine and feces
- (3) Spectrum—effective against gram-positive organisms and some anaerobe species, cross-resistance between clindamycin and erythromycin
- (4) Adverse reactions
  - (a) GI effects—diarrhea, *pseudomembranous colitis (PMC)*, potentially fatal

(b) Other effects—superinfections, allergy, *neutropenia, thrombocytopenia, agranulocytosis*

(5) Uses

(a) Oral infections caused by bacteroides species, some staphylococcus infections, acne

(b) An alternative regimen for antibiotic prophylaxis

(c) Good for bone infections

e) Metronidazole (Flagyl)

(1) Mechanism—trichomonacidal, bactericidal

(2) Pharmacokinetics—well absorbed orally with peak blood levels 1 to 2 hours after ingestion, 60% to 80% excreted in urine

(3) Spectrum—effective against trichomonacidal, ambicidal and obligate anaerobes such as bacteroides species

(4) Adverse reactions

(a) GI effects—disulfiram-like reaction if taken with alcohol, precaution if chlorhexidine rinse is prescribed

(b) Oral effects—metallic taste

(c) CNS effects—headache, dizziness

(5) Uses

(a) Sexually transmitted diseases and serious anaerobic infections of abdomen, skeleton, and female genital tract

(b) Dental—anaerobic periodontal infections

f) Cephalosporins

(1) Mechanism—chemically related to the penicillins, inhibits bacterial cell wall synthesis

(2) Pharmacokinetics—administered orally, IM, or IV; well absorbed, excreted in urine

(3) Spectrum—effective against most gram-positive cocci, penicillinase-producing staphylococci, some gram-negative bacteria; three generations of agents, extent of antimicrobial action depends on generation

(4) Adverse reactions

(a) GI effects—diarrhea, nausea, vomiting, and abdominal pain; minimized if taken with food or milk

(b) Other—nephrotoxicity, superinfection

(c) Allergy—cross-sensitivity with penicillin

(5) Uses

(a) Respiratory infection, sexually transmitted diseases, or various mixed infection used parenterally in hospitals

(b) Dental use limited to treatment of infection resistance to penicillin, ineffective against more narrow-spectrum antibiotics

(c) Alternative antibiotic in antibiotic prophylaxis

(6) Examples

(a) 1st generation

i) Cephalexin (Keflex)

ii) Cefadroxil (Duricef)

iii) Cefazolin (Ancef)

(b) 2nd generation—Cefaclor (Ceclor)
(c) 3rd generation—Cefixime (Suprax)

g) Aminoglycosides
(1) Mechanism—inhibits bacterial protein synthesis at 30 S subunit, bactericidal, broad antibacterial spectrum
(2) Pharmacokinetics—only administered IV or IM, plasma blood levels must be monitored
(3) Spectrum—effective against most gram-negative bacilli, resistance to agents can be rapid
(4) Adverse reactions
(a) Ototoxicity—toxic to 8th cranial nerve
(b) Nephrotoxicity—concentrates in the renal cortex
(c) Neuromuscular blockade—if given in combination with general anesthetic or skeletal muscle relaxant, it can produce apnea
(5) Uses
(a) Treatment of aerobic gram-negative infections when other agents are ineffective
(b) Treatment of hospitalized patients with serious gram-negative infections
(6) Examples
(a) Gentamicin
(b) Neomycin

h) Sulfonamides
(1) Mechanism—competitive antagonist of para-aminobenzoic acid (PABA); antimetabolite, bacteriostatic
(2) Pharmacokinetics—given orally with varying absorption depending on agent given; metabolites or free drug excreted in urine
(3) Spectrum—many gram-positive and some gram-negative bacteria; *Chlamydia*
(4) Adverse reactions—photosensitivity, allergic reactions, renal crystallization (crystalluria); patient should increase fluid intake
(5) Uses—Urinary tract infection, otitis media, not used frequently in dental infections as other agents are more effective
(6) Examples
(a) Sulfamethoxazole
(b) Trimethoprim (Septra, Bactrim)
(c) Sulfamethizole (Thiosulfil)

i) Quinolones (Fluoroquinolone)
(1) Mechanism of action—inhibits to nucleic acid (i.e., DNA) and synthesis, bactericidal
(2) Pharmacokinetics—well absorbed, half-life of 4 hours; antacids interfere with its absorption
(3) Spectrum—wide range of gram-negative and gram-positive organisms
(4) Adverse reactions—GI effects, hypersensitivity

(5) Uses
(a) Indicated for lower respiratory tract, skin, bone and joint, urinary tract infections
(b) Not used in dentistry because the spectrum does not match that of the oral flora
(6) Examples—generic name "floxacin"
(a) Ciprofloxacin (Cipro), Ofloxacin (Floxin)
(b) Lomefloxacin (Maxaquin)
(c) Norfloxacin (Noroxin)

3. Antifungal agents—seen more frequently in the immunocompromised patient; fungal infections managed in the dental office are mucocutaneous (affecting skin or mucosa)
a) Nystatin (Mycostatin, Nilstat)
(1) Mechanism—binds to sterols in the fungal cell membrane, changes membrane permeability
(2) Spectrum—fungicidal and fungistatic against a variety of yeasts and fungi
(3) Dosage forms—aqueous suspension (contains 50% sucrose), *pastille* (also contains sugar); dental hygienist should recommend fluoride rinse after therapy
(4) Uses—treatment and prevention or oral candidiasis
b) Clotrimazole (Mycelex)
(1) Mechanism—alteration of cell membrane permeability; cellular constituents lost
(2) Spectrum—tinea species and *Candida* species
(3) Dosage forms—*troches* (dissolves in mount 5x/day for 2 weeks)
(4) Uses—local treatment of oropharyngeal candidiasis
c) Ketoconazole (Nizoral)
(1) Mechanism—alters cellular membrane and interferes with intracellular enzymes
(2) Spectrum—wide variety of fungal infections including many systemic fungal infections
(3) Pharmacokinetics—absorbed systemically, requires an acid environment
(4) Dosage forms—oral tablets
(5) Adverse reactions
(a) GI—nausea and vomiting
(b) Hepatoxicity
(c) Pregnancy and nursing—teratogenic potential, risk to benefit must be considered
(d) Drug interactions—H_2 blockers, anticholinergic agents, antacids, warfarin, and cyclosporine
d) Fluconazole (Diflucan)
(1) Mechanism—prevents synthesis of ergosterol in the fungal cell by inhibiting fungal cytochrome P450 enzymes
(2) Dosage forms—oral tablets or IV
(3) Uses

(a) Treatment of cryptococcal meningitis or pharyngeal and esophageal candidiasis
(b) Serious systemic *Candida* infections
(c) Prophylactic agent against candidiasis in immunocompromised patients
(d) Treatment of *Candida* that does not respond to other agents

4. Antiviral agents—obligate intracellular organisms that use DNA/RNA from host's cells, killing virus often requires harming host cell; the herpes virus of most interest to dentist; immunocompromised patients may have oral symptoms
   a) Acylovir (Zovirax)
      (1) Mechanism—interferes with DNA polymerase and inhibits DNA replication
      (2) Spectrum—herpes simplex viruses, papilloma viruses
      (3) Dosage forms—oral, topical, IV
      (4) Adverse reactions—burning, nausea, CNS effects
      (5) Uses
         (a) Topical—initial herpes genitalis, limited non-life-threatening initial and recurrent mucocutaneous herpes simplex
         (b) Oral—initial and management of viral lesions in immunocompromised and nonimmunocompromised patients
         (c) Parenteral—severe initial herpetic infections in immunocompromised patient
         (d) New agents
            i) Famciclovir (Famvir)
            ii) Valacyclovir (Valtrex)
   b) Penciclovir (Denavir)
      (1) Available topically for primary and recurrent herpes simplex
      (2) Shown to reduce pain and duration of lesions
      (3) Advantage—higher concentration so it stays in the cells longer
5. Antituberculosis agents
   a) Patients with tuberculosis are difficult to treat because of their inadequate defense mechanisms
   b) Tubercle bacilli develop resistant strains easily, have long periods of inactivity
   c) Most drugs not bactericidal, high dose cannot be used owing to toxicity
   d) Multiple drug combinations frequently required
      (1) Isoniazid (INH)
         (a) Mechanism—bactericidal only against growing tubercle bacilli
         (b) Adverse reactions—CNS effects, hepatoxicity, hepatitis
         (c) Uses—alone as prophylaxis, in combination with rifampin and pyrazinamide (PZA) or other agents

(2) Rifampin (Rifadin)
  (a) Mechanism—inhibition of DNA-dependent RNA polymerase
  (b) Adverse reactions—GI irritation
  (c) Uses—in combination with other antitubercular agents
(3) Ethambutol (Myambutol)
  (a) Uses—synthetic tuberculostatic agent effective against *Mycobacterium tuberculosis,* resistance develops very rapidly when used alone; used in combination therapy
  (b) Adverse reactions—optic neuritis

E. Local anesthetics (LA)—drugs derived from PABA that produce a loss of sensation in a localized area of the body

1. General principles
  a) Two groups—esters and amides
  b) Structure
    (1) Aromatic nucleus (lipophilic)
    (2) Linkage (ester or amide followed by an aliphatic chain)
    (3) Amino groups (hydrophilic)
  c) Site of action—nerve membrane
  d) Mechanism of action
    (1) Reduces transient increase in sodium flow into nerve membrane
    (2) Binds water-soluble ionized form of LA to calcium ion receptor site
    (3) Receptor channel is blocked and sodium conduction decreases
    (4) Results in a decrease in rate of depolarization
    (5) Prevents nerve conduction in blocking pain threshold
  e) Ionization factors
    (1) LAs are weak bases
    (2) LAs occur in equilibrium between two forms
      (a) Lipophilic free base
      (b) Hydrophilic hydrochloride salt
      (c) Characteristics of two forms
        i) Free base—uncharged, unionized, unstable, basic, and fat-soluable (lipophilic)
        ii) Hydrochloride salt—charged, ionized, stable, acidic, and water-soluable (hydrophilic)
      (d) Proportion of base and salt determined by pK_a of LA and pH of surrounding tissue environment
      (e) Dental carpule pH less than 7.4—allows for ionized form and increases water solubility, also increases stability of LA in carpule
      (f) Injection into tissue with pH of 7.4—allows LA to be available in free base form, providing for greater tissue penetration
      (g) Inflammation of tissue may lower pH, resulting in less LA absorbed—slower onset action, reduction of potency

2. Pharmacology
   a) Reversibly blocks peripheral nerve condition of small unmyelinated fibers
   b) Loss of nerve function occurs in following order
      (1) autonomic
      (2) cold
      (3) warmth
      (4) pain
      (5) touch
      (6) pressure
      (7) vibration
      (8) proprioception
      (9) motor response
   c) Nerve function returns in reverse order
3. Pharmacokinetics
   a) Absorption—rate dependent on tissue vasculartiy and route of administration
      (1) Warmth and massage increase vasodilatory activity, cold temperature decreases vasodilatory ability
      (2) Spread over area affected by degree of ionization
   b) Distribution
      (1) Distributed throughout body
      (2) Higher vascular organs higher concentrations of anesthetics
      (3) Lipid solubility of a particular local anesthetic affects potency of agent
   c) Metabolism
      (1) Esters
         (a) Hydrolyzed by plasma pseudocholinesterase and liver esterases
         (b) Procaine—hydrolyzed to PABA
      (2) Amides
         (a) Metabolized by liver
         (b) Prilocaine metabolized to orthotolidine, which can produce methemoglobinemia if given in large doses
   d) Excretion—metabolites and some unchanged drug esters and amides excreted by the kidneys
4. Adverse reactions
   a) Factors influencing toxicity
      (1) Drug
      (2) Concentration
      (3) Route of administration
      (4) Rate of injection
      (5) Vascularity
      (6) Patient's weight
      (7) Rate of metabolism and excretion
   b) CNS effects—restlessness, tremors, convulsions
   c) Cardiovascular effects—myocardial depression and cardiac arrest

d) Local effects—hematoma, injection technique or excessive volume administered
e) Malignant hyperthermia
f) Pregnancy and nursing—use elective dental treatment, usual doses of LA given to nursing mothers will not affect health or normal nursing infant
g) Allergy—rash to anaphylactic shock
(1) Esters—more allergic potential than amides
(2) Alternative drug—diphenhydramine (Benadryl)
(3) Other ingredients may produce allergic reactions—sulfite agents

5. Composition of LA solutions
a) Vasoconstrictor—epinephrine, norepinephrine (Levophed), levonordefrin (Neo-Cobefrin)—retards absorption reduces systemic toxicity
b) Antioxidant—sodium metabisulfite, sodium bisulfite, acetone sodium bisulfite; retards oxidation
c) Alkalinizing agent—sodium hydroxide; adjust pH of solution to between 6 and 7
d) Sodium chloride—makes solution isotonic

6. Topical anesthetics
a) Lidocaine—amide, topically effective
b) Benzocaine—ester, used topically, lacks significant systemic toxicity
c) Cocaine—ester of benzoic acid, naturally occurring vasoconstrictor effect, no dental application

F. Antianxiety agents—referred to as either sedative-hypnotic or antianxiety drugs; some patients may require agents before dental appointment

1. Definitions
a) *Sedative*—a small dose will produce mild CNS depression causing reduction of activity and anxiety
b) *Hypnotic*—a large dose will produce greater CNS depression resulting in sleep
c) *Minor tranquilizers*—action similar to sedative, hypnotics
d) *Major tranquilizers*—antipsychotic activity

2. Benzodiazepines
a) Mechanism—exerts effects in CNS
b) Pharmacokinetics
(1) well absorbed orally
(2) available in many forms
(3) highly protein bound, non-ionized, lipid soluble, crosses blood-brain barrier easily
(4) metabolized by oxidation, duration of action varies with agent
c) Effects
(1) Behavioral—anxiety reduction at low doses, drowsiness and sleep at higher doses

(2) Anticonvulsant—prevention of seizures associated with local anesthetic toxicity; drug of choice for treatment of status epilepticus

d) Adverse reaction
   (1) CNS effect—fatigue, drowsiness, muscle weakness, ataxia
   (2) Amnesia—episodes can last several hours (usually at time of dosing)
   (3) Visual effects—contraindicated in angle-closure glaucoma
   (4) Dental—xerostomia
   (5) *Phlebitis*—when given parenterally
   (6) Pregnancy and lactation—increased risk of congenital formation when taking agent in first trimester; Food and Drug Administration (FDA) pregnancy categories D and X
   (7) Abuse—less than other sedative-hypnotic agents
   (8) Overdose—flumazenil (Romazicon) benzodiazepine antagonist

e) Drug interactions—additive with other CNS depressants

f) Uses
   (1) Anxiety control
   (2) Insomnia management
   (3) Treatment of epilepsy—diazepam drug of choice for status epilepticus, convulsions from local anesthetic overdose
   (4) Treatment of alcoholism
   (5) Control of muscle spasms
   (6) Medication before surgery

g) Examples—diazepam (Valium), lorazepam (Ativan)

3. Buspirone (BuSpar)
   a) Mechanism—binds to serotonin and dopamine receptors
   b) Pharmacological effect—anxioselective; produces less CNS depression
   c) Two to four weeks to be effective—not for dental anxiety

4. Barbiturates
   a) Mechanism—interacts with γ-aminobutyric acid (GABA) receptor
   b) Pharmacokinetics—well absorbed orally and rectally; short and intermediate-acting, metabolized by liver; long-acting, renal excretions as free drug
   c) Pharmacological effects
      (1) CNS depression
         (a) small dose, sedation
         (b) large doses, disinhibition and euphoria
         (c) at high doses, anesthesia with respiratory and cardiovascular depression, finally cardiac arrest
      (2) Anticonvulsant—long-acting used in treatment of epilepsy
   d) Adverse reactions
      (1) Sedation or hypnotic doses—exaggerated CNS effect in elderly and debilitated patients with liver or kidney impairment

(2) Anesthetic doses—high concentration used for intubation or very short procedure; no significant analgesic effects (does not block reflex response to pain)

e) Acute poisoning—cause of death for overdose is respiratory depression

f) Contraindications—absolutely contraindicated in patients with intermittent or positive family history of *porphyria*

g) Drug interactions—potent stimulators of liver microsomal enzyme production, involved in many drug interactions

h) Uses—determined by duration of action

(1) Ultrashort—IV for induction of general anesthesia; thiopental (Pentothal)

(2) Short and intermediate—little use; abused; replaced by benzodiazepines; Secobarbital (Seconal)

(3) Long-acting—used for treatment of epilepsy; phenobarbital (Luminal)

3. Nonbarbituarate sedative hypnotic—offers no advantage over barbiturates

a) Examples

(1) Chloral hydrate (Noctec)

(a) Rapid onset, short duration of action

(b) Used for preoperative sedation for children in dentistry

(c) Produces gastric irritation

(2) Meprobamate (Equanil, Miltown)

(a) Minor tranquilizer for daytime sedation; has anticonvulsant action

(b) Some muscle relaxant properties

4. Centrally acting muscle relaxants

a) Action effects the CNS causing skeletal muscle relaxation

b) Two common examples, methocarbamol (Robaxin) and cyclobenzaprine (Flexeril), exert effects indirectly on the CNS

c) Indicated or adjunct to rest and physical therapy for relief of muscle spasm associated with acute painful musculoskeletal conditions

G. General anesthetics

1. General considerations

a) Anesthesia produced by group of chemical substances that are potent CNS depressants

b) Produce reversible loss of consciousness and insensitivity to painful stimuli

c) Administered in hospital operating rooms; used also by oral and maxillofacial surgeons in hospital or in office; nitrous oxide used in dental office to allay patient anxiety

2. Stages and planes of anesthesia

a) Stage I—analgesia

b) Stage II—delirium or excitement; move through smoothly and quickly

c) Stage III—surgical anesthesia; four planes, most treatment in this phase

d) Stage IV—respiratory or medullary paralysis; reverse stage immediately or patient will die; stage not used

3. Classification of anesthetic agents
   a) Inhalation anesthetics
      (1) Gases—nitrous oxide; used in Stage I or to produce conscious analgesia
      (2) Volatile liquids—halogenated hydrocarbons, ethers
   b) Intravenous agents
      (1) Barbiturates
      (2) Opioids
      (3) Neuroleptics
      (4) Benzodiazepines
4. Examples
   a) Nitrous oxide–oxygen (N_2O–O_2)
      (1) Colorless gas with little or no odor; least soluble in blood of all inhalation anesthetics—used for conscious anesthesia during dental treatment
      (2) Cannot be used alone to give surgical anesthesia because of low potency
      (3) Normal concentration of N_2O—10% to 50% (average 35%)
      (4) Advantages
         (a) Rapid onset
         (b) Easy to administer
         (c) Rapid recovery
         (d) Acceptable for children
      (5) Pharmacological effects
         (a) CNS effects—analgesia and amnesia
         (b) Circulatory effects—minimal; peripheral vasodilation
         (c) GI—patient should be warned to avoid a large meal within 3 hours of appointment time to prevent vomiting
      (6) Adverse reactions/contraindications
         (a) Faulty equipment—could pose a hazard for dental team members (spontaneous abortion, genetic effect)
         (b) Respiratory obstruction—upper respiratory obstruction (stuffy nose)
         (c) *Chronic obstructive pulmonary disease* (COPD)—respiration driven by lack of oxygen, could cease to breathe with high oxygen levels
         (d) Emotional instability—patients taking psychotherapeutic medication should be evaluated before use
         (e) Pregnancy—use at all is questionable; first trimester critical; incidence of spontaneous abortion increased in female operating personnel
         (f) Abuse—chronic abuse may result in neuropathy
   b) Halogenated hydrocarbons
      (1) Halothane (Fluothane) is nonirritating to bronchial mucous membranes
      (2) Possible occurrence of postanesthetic hepatitis, popularity diminished

c) Halogenated ether
   (1) Enflurane (Ethrane) induction and recovery rapid; depresses respiration; alteration in encephalographic activity; reduced blood pressures, muscle relaxation
   (2) Isoflurane (Forane)—same as other halogenated ethers; useful and popular

d) Ultra short-acting barbituates
   (1) Examples—methohexital sodium (Brevital), thiopental sodium (Pentothal)
   (2) Rapid onset, short duration—does not provide analgesia
   (3) Used for rapid induction to stage III anesthesia
   (4) Adverse reaction—laryngospasm and bronchospasm
   (5) Contraindication—status asthmaticus, porphyria, and known hypersensitivity

e) Ketamine (Ketalar)
   (1) Produces dissociative anesthesia—disrupts association pathways in brain
   (2) Given IV or IM with rapid onset of action
   (3) May produce delirium and hallucinations during recovery

f) Opiates
   (1) Used as adjunctive drugs to general anesthesia in preanesthetic medication and also to provide analgesia
   (2) Examples
      (a) Morphine
      (b) Fentanyl (Sublimaze)

g) Benzodiazepine
   (1) Midazolam (Versed)—useful for induction of anesthesia

H. Emergency drugs

1. General considerations
   a) Choice of drugs for dental office emergency; kit depends on individual circumstance, experience, and personal preference
   b) Some drugs may only be used by those with advanced cardiac life support (ACLS) training
2. Drugs
   a) Epinephrine
      (1) Actions—cardiac stimulation, vasoconstriction, bronchial dilation, elevation of blood glucose
      (2) Dosage—0.3 to 0.5 ml of 1:1000 dilution every 5 to 20 minutes as needed, up to three doses, IM or SQ
   b) Diphenhydramine (Benadryl)
      (1) Actions—antihistamine used in the treatment of some allergic reactions
      (2) Dosage—50 mg IM, IV of 10 mg/ml
   c) Diazepam (Valium)
      (1) Action—drug of choice for most convulsions if drug is needed, toxic reaction to local anesthetic
      (2) Dosage—5 to 10 mg IV
   d) Naloxone (Narcan)
      (1) Action—drug of choice for opioid-induced apnea

(2) Dosage—0.4 mg (1 ml) IV, may be given SQ or IM, onset of action 2 minutes by IV

e) Oxygen

(1) Action—restoration of oxygen saturation of hemoglobin

(2) Dosage—100% via nasal inhalation if spontaneous breathing, must use with positive-pressure ventilation if respiration arrested

f) Aromatic ammonia spirits

(1) Action—irritation of respiratory mucosa, stimulation of respiratory muscle movement, mobilization of venous return

(2) Dosage—0.3 ml

g) Glucose

(1) Action—restoration of blood glucose level for maintenance of brain function

(2) Dosage—operator judgment, requires 10 minute onset time, use oral form of sucrose (soft drink, juice) in conscious patient, supplied as viscous solution in tubes

h) Morphine

(1) Action—given patient who has suffered an acute infarction to relieve pain and allay apprehension

(2) Dosage—10 mg/ml

i) Methoxamine

(1) Action—adrenergic agonist with a-adrenergic properties, produces mild increase in blood pressure

(2) Dosage—10 mg/mL

j) Nitroglycerin (Nitrostat)

(1) Action—relaxation of vascular smooth muscle, reduced cardiac work

(2) Dosage—0.3 to 0.4 mg every 5 minutes, up to 3 doses

(3) Caution—orthostatic hypotension may occur; onset of dose occurs with 2 to 4 minutes, if chest pain returns or worsens, assume myocardial infarction

k) Hydrocortisone (Solu-Cortef)

(1) Action—corticosteroid used for allergic reactions, anaphylaxis, and adrenal crisis

(2) Dosage—50 mg/mL

l) Dextrose

(1) Action—used IV to manage hypoglycemic episodes when diabetic is unconscious and cannot swallow

m) Metaproterenol

(1) β_2-adrenergic agonist useful in management of bronchoconstriction

(2) Dosage—two puffs

V. DRUGS THAT MAY AFFECT PATIENT TREATMENT

A. Cardiovascular drugs

1. Cardiovascular disease—disease of heart and blood vessels

a) Hypertension, angina, stroke, atherosclerosis, congestive heart failure

   b) Leading cause of death in the United States
   c) Hypertension most common CV disease, African Americans at high risk
   d) Stress during dental treatment major factor in causing emergency
2. Dental implications
   a) Contraindications to treatment—MI within 6 months; unstable angina, uncontrolled congestive heart failure (CHF), arrhythmia; severe hypertension
   b) Vasoconstrictor limitation in local anesthesia (1:100,000, aspirating technique)
   c) Risk factors for infective endocarditis (valvular disease, previous infective endocarditis [IE], congenital heart disease); require antibiotic premeditation
   d) Precautions with pacemaker patient (vitalometer, electrosurgical unit, electromagnetic ultrasonic scaler)
3. Cardiac glycosides
   a) Causes failing heart muscle to contract more efficiently, increases cardiac output, oxygenation of tissues
   b) Right sided CHF, edema in extremities; left sided CHF, edema in lungs
   c) Digoxin—digitalis-type drug (foxglove plant)
      (1) Increases force and efficiency of cardiac muscle contraction
      (2) Reduces edema by increasing glomerular filtration rate
      (3) Reduces heart rate
      (4) Indicated for treatment of CHF, arrhythmia
      (5) Adverse reactions of digitalis-type drugs
         (a) GI—nausea, vomiting, salivation, gagging (overdose); anorexia
         (b) CV—arrhythmia (overdose)
         (c) CNS—headache, sedation, visual disturbances, weakness, confusion
      (6) Drug interactions—diuretics, sympathomimetic drugs (arrhythmia); tetracycline, erythromycin (digoxin toxicity)
      (7) Dental management
         (a) Observe for signs of toxicity; if present, refer to physician
         (b) Use epinephrine with caution, low doses, aspirating syringe
         (c) Monitor pulse for bradycardia, arrhythmia
         (d) Semisupine or upright chair position—pulmonary congestion, GI side effects
4. Antiarrhythmic agents
   a) Heart rhythm—sinoatrial (SA) node (right atrium), arteriovenous (AV) node (Purkinje fibers, ventricles)
   b) Major drugs used for arrhythmia (abnormal rhythm pattern)
      (1) Quinidine—myocardial depressant, both direct and indirect actions
      (2) Lidocaine—emergency use primarily, ventricular tachycardia
      (3) Side effects—nausea, vomiting, hypotension; allergy—*thrombocytopenia*
      (4) Management—monitor vital signs

5. Antianginal drugs
   a) *Angina*—pain, heavy feeling, discomfort in chest area, referred pain to jaw or arms due to lack of oxygenation of heart muscle, precipitated by stress
   b) Major drugs—nitrites, nitrates, beta blockers, calcium channel blockers
      (1) Nitroglycerin—acute episodes, sublingual administration, use patient's medications
      (2) Amyl nitrite—emergency use, inhalation (banana oil smell); abused drug
      (3) Beta blockers (propranolol, nadolol, metoprolol, atenolol)—block adrenergic stimulation to heart, slows heart rate; prophylactic use
      (4) Calcium channel blockers (verapamil, diltiazem, nifedipine, amlodipine)—inhibits calcium binding during contraction, reduces workload on heart muscle; prophylactic use
   c) Action—reduces oxygen requirement of cardiac muscle, vasodilation
   d) Dental implications of treating a patient with angina
      (1) Medical history follow-up questions on control, vital signs
      (2) Check expiration date on patient nitroglycerin prescription
      (3) Manage side effects of agents—hypotension, xerostomia; gingival hyperplasia (calcium channel blockers, except amlodipine, isradipine)
6. Antihypertensive agents
   a) Types of hypertension—essential, secondary, malignant; etiology—usually unknown, 140/90 mild hypertension
   b) Stepped-care regimen—reduced alcohol, reduced salt, no smoking; exercise program, weight reduction, combination drug therapy
   c) Major drugs used—diuretics, blocking agents, inhibitors
      (1) Action of thiazide, loop and potassium-sparing diuretics—diuresis
      (2) Action of adrenergic blocking drugs—vasodilation, decrease peripheral resistance, decrease heart rate
      (3) Action of calcium channel blockers—coronary vasodilation
      (4) Action of angiotensin-converting enzyme inhibitors—prevents formation of angiotensin II that causes vasoconstriction
      (5) Agents for severe hypertension—clonidine, guanethidine, reserpine, hydralazine
   d) Side effects of antihypertensives—postural hypotension, xerostomia, blood dyscrasia, dizziness; gingival hyperplasia (calcium blockers)
   e) Dental implications of treating a hypertensive patient
      (1) Measure vital signs each appointment, stress reduction protocol
      (2) Manage side effects as needed

(3) Avoid opioids (caution: increased sedation); with healthy person, maximum .2 mg; cardiac patient, maximum .04 mg with epinephrine (1:100,000)

7. Anticoagulants
   a) Use of anticoagulants—prevent blood clots, thin blood consistency
      (1) Indication—*stroke,* thromboembolitic disease, *myocardial infarction*
   b) Drugs used by injection—heparin, enoxaparin
      (1) Action of heparin—dissolves blood clots, whereas warfarin prevents formation of clots
   c) Drug used by oral administration—warfarin (Coumadin)
      (1) Action of warfarin—vitamin K antimetabolite, interferes with synthesis of clotting factors
   d) Dental management
      (1) Caution in dental procedures causing bleeding; direct pressure, apply oxidized cellulose
      (2) Use acetaminophen for analgesia, not aspirin or NSAIDs
      (3) Physician consult for International Normalized Ratio (INR) or prothrobin time
      (4) Antibiotics can potentiate effects of warfarin
   e) Other blood-altering agents—ticlopidine, streptokinase, dipyridamole, pentoxifyline
8. Antihyperlipidemics
   a) Drugs indicated to lower cholesterol—cholestyramine, gemfibrozil, niacin, lovastatin, simvastatin, probucol
   b) Dental implications for patient taking antihyperlipidemics
      (1) Monitor vital signs; at risk for cardiovascular disease
      (2) Monitor liver function if prescribing drugs
      (3) Postural hypotension possible with niacin
9. Dental implications of cardiovascular disease
   a) Consider contraindications to dental treatment
   b) Observe situations indicating physician consultation
   c) Stress reduction protocol
   d) Vasoconstrictor limitation, postural hypotension

B. Anticonvulsant agents—used for prevention or control of two types of seizures

1. Types of generalized seizures (loss of consciousness in both)
   a) Absence (*petit mal*)
      (1) Drug therapy—ethosuximide or valproic acid
      (2) Absence—does not fall to floor
   b) Tonic-clonic (*grand mal*)
      (1) Drug therapy—valproic acid, phenytoin, phenobarbital, carbamazepine
      (2) Associated with "aura"
      (3) Jerking movements
      (4) Status epilepticus—continuous seizures, emergency treatment is diazepam injection

2. Partial seizures—simple or complex (psychomotor)
   a) Seizures last minutes versus seconds in absence type
   b) Aura can occur in complex partial seizures
   c) Drug therapy—carbamazepine, phenytoin, phenobarbital, primidone
3. Drugs used to treat seizures—CNS depressants
   a) Action—prevent spread of abnormal electric discharges in brain; drugs used depend on seizure type
   b) Adverse reactions relevant to dental treatment
      (1) CNS depression results in impaired learning
      (3) Opioid drugs—reduce dose if prescribed by dentist
      (3) Nausea, vomiting, anorexia—consider semisupine chair position
      (4) Blood dyscrasis—reduced healing, low host resistance
   c) Numerous drug interactions—consult with physician before prescribing
   d) Types of CNS depressants
      (1) Barbiturates—phenobarbital most common type, used in tonic-clonic and partial seizures
         (a) Used alone or in combination with other anticonvulsants
         (b) Sedation, excitement, confusion common
         (c) Stomatitis—refer to physician, drug therapy needs changing
      (2) Hydantoins—phenytoin (Dilantin) most common type, used in tonic-clonic and partial seizures
         (a) 50% patients develop gingival hyperplasia
            i) Anterior interproximal, facial—initial enlargement
            ii) Fibrotic, does not bleed easily, surgical removal
            iii) Strict plaque control necessary to minimize overgrowth
         (b) Has narrow therapeutic index—adverse reactions, drug interactions common
            i) Nausea, vomiting, confusion, dizziness, skin reactions possible
            ii) Vitamin D and folate deficiency—oral mucosal ulceration, glossitis
      (3) Valproic acid (Depakene) and divalproex sodium (Depakote)—all seizure types
         (a) Indigestion, nausea, vomiting frequent
         (b) Prolonged bleeding, anticoagulation possible—blood tests needed before dental procedures causing bleeding, avoid prescribing aspirin, NSAIDs
         (c) Excessive CNS depression with other CNS depressant drugs
      (4) Carbamazepine (Tegretol)—structurally related to tricyclic antidepressants, anticonvulsant activity
         (a) Used to treat trigeminal neuralgia (tic douloureux)
         (b) Serious blood dyscrasias—aplastic anemia, agranulocytosis; report petechia, infection, poor healing to physician

(c) Adverse reactions—nausea, dizziness, confusion, xerostomia, skin reactions, blood pressure changes; chewable tablet contains sugar—suggest home fluoride for caries control

(d) Drug interactions frequent—antibiotics, analgesics

(5) Ethosuximide (Zarontin)

(a) Drug of choice for absence seizures

(b) Side effects include GI upset, drowsiness, blood dyscrasias, gingival enlargement, glossitis

(6) Benzodiazepines—oral forms and parenteral forms

(a) Cloazepam (Klonopin), chlorazepate (Tranzene)—oral route

(b) Diazepam (Valium), lorazepam (Ativan)—parenteral for status epilepticus

(c) GI, CNS side effects possible—oral side effects of xerostomia, coated tongue, thirst, painful gingivae

4. Management of dental patients with seizures

a) Detailed medical history review—seizure history; drug effects, interactions

b) Management of systemic and oral side effects of drugs

c) Stress management plan, observe for tonic-clonic signs—move patient to floor if possible, tilt head to side, remove objects from mouth, do not insert gauze-wrapped tongue blade

C. Psychotherapeutic drugs

1. Types of psychiatric disorders—organic or functional

a) Organic—congenital or caused by injury or disease

b) Functional—psychotic disorders, no biochemical abnormality

(1) Schizophrenia—loss of perception of reality

(2) Depression—loss of self worth

(3) Bipolar disorder—alternating periods of elation and depression

2. Types of Psychotherapeutic Drugs

a) Antipsychotic drugs indicated for schizophrenia

(1) Phenothiazines are most frequently used

(a) Chlorpromazine (Thorazine)—sedation, xerostomia side effects

(b) Thioridazine (Mellaril), trifluoperazine (Stelazine), prochlorperazine (Compazine), other phenothiazines used

(2) Action—calm emotions, *antiemetic* effect

(3) Adverse reactions—sedation, orthostatic hypotension, *extrapyramidal effects* (parkinsonism, akathisia, *tardive dyskinesia*), anticholinergic effects (xerostomia, blurred vision, constipation), blood dyscrasias

(4) Drug interactions—potentiate CNS depressants (decrease dose of opioids), epinephrine safe for dental use, anticholinergic agents (increased effects)

(5) Temporomandibular joint (TMJ) pain can result from extrapyramidal effects, tardive dyskinesia can make oral procedures difficult

(6) Dental management relates to drug side effects, medication compliance

b) Antidepression—drugs used may be prescribed for other conditions; question patient about why being used

(1) First generation agents (tricyclic agents, others)

(a) Examples—amitriptyline (Elavil), doxepin (Sinequan), imipramine (Tofranil), amoxapine, desipramine, nortriptyline (Pamelor); monoamine oxidase inhibitors (MAOIs)

(b) Adverse effects of tricyclics—CNS (sedation, tremors), xerostomia, orthostatic hypotension, myocardial toxicity (MI, CHF, tachycardia) with overdose

i) Dental implications—use epinephrine with caution (hypertension), xerostomia (home fluoride, saliva substitutes), tremors (electric toothbrushes)

ii) MAOIs are infrequently used—numerous drug interactions, food interactions (aged cheese, wine, fish) precipitating hypertensive crisis

(2) Second generation agents

(a) Examples—selective serotonin reuptake inhibitors (SSRIs): fluoxetine (Prozac), sertraline (Zoloft), paroxetine (Paxil), fluvoxamine (Luvox)

(b) Other second-generation agents—trazadone (Desyrel), bupropion (Wellbutrin), nefazodone (Serzone)

(c) Adverse effects of SSRIs—tremors (fluoxetine), nausea, xerostomia, taste changes

(d) Adverse effects of bupropion—GI distress, constipation, dry mouth, headache, tremors, agitation, dizziness, risk of seizures (rare)

(3) Lithium (Eskalith, Lithobid)

(a) Disorders treated

i) Anxiety

ii) Phobia

iii) Bipolar disorder

iv) Obsessive-compulsive disorder

(b) Adverse effects—tremors, thirst, nausea, vomiting; use NSAIDs with caution (decreased clearance of lithium)

(c) Management consideration during treatment

i) Communication problems—patient behavior problems

ii) Ensure patient has taken medication, check dosage

iii) Depression can affect motivation for self-care practices

iv) Narcotics for dental pain—give short course, no refills

3. Dental management implication for adverse effects, drug incompatibilities

a) Home fluoride (xerostomia), electric toothbrush (tremors)

b) Sit upright for 1 to 2 minutes at end of appointment before dismissal (orthostatic hypotension)

D. Autacoid and antihistamine drugs

1. Pathophysiology of histamine response
   a) Autacoid is a naturally occurring substance involved in host response
      (1) Host response
         (a) Histamine released from mast cells during allergic reaction, inflammation
         (b) Pharmacological effects—vasodilation, capillary permeability, bronchoconstriction, itching (H_1) increased gastric acid secretion (H_2)
         (c) Adverse effects of histamine—anaphylaxis most serious
2. Antihistamine drugs
   a) Antihistamines block histamine receptors (H_1, H_2), numerous agents
      (1) Older H_1 blockers—used for allergic rhinitis, antimotion sickness
         (a) Adverse effects—sedative effects, dry mouth, nervousness, convulsions (high doses)
      (2) Newer nonsedating H_1 blocking agents—loratadine (Claritin), fexofenadine (Allegra)
      (3) H_2 receptor blockers—cimetidine (Tagamet), famotidine (Pepcid), ranitidine (Zantac), nizatidine (Axid)—used to treat GI disorders
3. Pharmacological effects of prostaglandin (PG), thromboxanes, leukotrienes, kinins
   a) Produced in response to inflammation, injury
   b) Smooth muscle contraction or relaxation—depends on type of PG; used to induce midtrimester abortions
   c) Platelet adhesiveness affected
   d) Increase body temperature, heat rate, capillary permeability
   e) Liberated as part of the periodontal inflammation process—role in erythema, edema, alveolar bone resorption
      (1) Leukotrienes are derived from arachidonic acid, play role in asthma and periodontal inflammation
      (2) Kinins formed by proteolytic enzymes—role in periodontal inflammation, shock, chronic allergy, anaphylaxis
      (3) Substance P—peptide acts as neurotransmitter in brain, hormone in intestines; causes vasodilation, hypotension

E. Adrenocorticosteroid drugs—hormones sereted by adrenal cortex (corticosteroids), which include both glucocorticoids and mineralocorticoids

1. Major glucocorticoid—cortisol (hydrocortisone), most frequently used
   a) Indication—Addison's disease, asthma, systemic inflammatory disease, emergency uses (shock)
   b) Dose forms—topical, oral, parenteral, inhalational
      (1) Systemic effects—oral, parenteral mainly
         (a) Prednisone most common oral form

(b) Topical forms used in dentistry—triamcinolone (Kenalog), fluocinonide (Lidex)

(2) Inhalational forms—oral candidiasis may result (rinse mouth after use)

2. Physiology of adrenal cortex function—fight or flight mechanism
   a) Hydrocortisone released by adrenal cortex in response to stress
   b) Steroids (hydrocortisone) inhibit release of adrenocorticotropic hormone (ACTH)
      (1) Therapeutic use—anti-inflammatory effect, suppression of allergic reactions
      (2) Long-term exogenous steroid therapy—suppresses adrenal function
         (a) Adrenal crisis occurs in stress—increase dose of steroid preparation before stressful dental treatment
      (3) Adverse reactions proportional to dosage, prolonged therapy
         (a) Abnormal fat distribution—moon face, buffalo hump, hyperglycemia, weight gain, muscle wasting
         (b) Increased infection, masked infection
         (c) Personality, behavior changes; peptic ulcer
         (d) Impaired wound healing, osteoporosis, glaucoma, cataracts
         (e) Fluid retention, hypertension, adrenal crisis
3. Medical and dental uses of glucocorticoids
   a) Topical—oral ulcerations, desquamative gingival lesions
   b) Injectable—TMJ arthritis
   c) Chronic systemic diseases—asthma, autoimmune diseases
4. Synthetic corticosteroid products
   a) Equivalent doses of products compared with hydrocortisone
   b) Topical products classified by potency—hydrocortisone weakest, betamethasone most potent
5. Dental implication and management
   a) Avoid aspirin—GI effects, peptic ulcer possibility
   b) Monitor blood pressure
   c) Examine oral tissues for masked infection, osteoporosis, delayed wound healing
   d) Possibility of adrenal crisis in stressful dental procedures—increase dose of corticosteroid
      (1) Doses > 20 mg to 60 mg/day hydrocortisone or 5 mg to 15 mg prednisone/day—increase dose to two to three times the daily dose before stressful dental procedure
      (2) Rule of twos—if > 20 mg cortisone for 2 weeks within 2 years, increase dose

F. Hormones

1. Pituitary hormone—desmopressin—treats diabetes insipidus, clotting disorders (hemophilia A, von Willebrand's disease)
2. Thyroid hormone—thyroxine, levothyroxine (Synthroid)—treats hypothyroidism (myxedema, cretinism)

- a) Effects on physiological function—needed for growth and development, regulates basal metabolic rate; goal of treatment, bring to euthyroid state
  - (1) Oral—edema in tongue, face, delayed eruption, exfoliation
  - (2) Thyroid hormone requires iodine for synthesis
  - (3) Goiter is hypertrophy of hypofunctioning thyroid gland—no dental treatment until physician consultation completed
- b) Drug interaction—use CNS depressants (opioids) with caution
- c) Hyperthyroidism (Graves' disease)—oversecretion of thyroid hormone
  - (1) Epinephrine contraindicated, stress can precipitate thyroid storm
  - (2) Excessive sweating, protruding eyes, anxiety—signs of hyperthyroidism, need physician consult before stressful dental procedure
  - (3) Thyroidectomy or antithyroid drugs (radioactive iodine)

3. Pancreatic hormones—glucagon and insulin are produced and secreted by the beta cells in the islets of Langerhans
   - a) Diabetes mellitus—hyperglycemia, glycosuria, severe periodontal disease
     - (1) Type 1 (formerly IDDM)—ultimate insulin deficiency, insulin injections
       - (a) Etiology—heredity, virus induced autoimmune response; onset in youth
       - (b) Types of insulin—rapid, intermediate, long (zinc for extended effect)
         - i) Injected before breakfast—if meal not consumed risk of insulin shock
         - ii) Treatment—give sugar, juice if conscious
     - (2) Type 2 (formerly NIDDM)—hypofunction of beta cells
       - (a) Etiology—heredity, obesity; onset in adult usually
       - (b) Drug treatment can include insulin or oral antidiabetic drugs
         - i) Sulfonylureas—tolbutamide, glyburide, glipizide (second-generation agents) increase insulin secretion by beta cells
         - ii) Alpha-glucosidase inhibitors (acarbose, miglitol)—slows breakdown of carbohydrates in intestines, can antagonize treatment for insulin shock
         - iii) Biguanide-metformin (Glucophage)—increases insulin secretion and treats insulin resistance
         - iv) Meglitinides (repaglinide, nateglinide)—stimulates insulin secretion
         - v) Thiazolidinediones (pioglitazone, rosiglitazone)—increases insulin sensitivity
       - (c) Drug interactions—aspirin, sulfonamides, barbiturates
4. Female sex hormones—estrogens, progesterone, used in hormone replacement therapy

a) Secreted primarily by ovaries—oral contraception, menstrual disturbances, osteoporosis, hysterectomy or menopause indications for treatment
b) Types of estrogen—conjugated estrogens (Premarin), estradiol, ethinyl estradiol, esterified estrogens
(1) Side effects—gingival bleeding, exaggerated inflammation, nausea, hypertension, dry socket
(2) Management—good plaque control, semisupine position, monitor vital signs
c) Progestins—progesterone (parenteral), medroxyprogesterone (oral), levonorgestrel (oral)
(1) When uterus is intact, added to estrogen hormone replacement therapy to prevent uterine cancer
d) Oral contraceptives can contain combinations of estrogens and progestins
(1) Drug interactions with oral contraceptives—antibiotics, high doses of acetaminophen, benzodiazepines
(2) Instruct to use additional form of birth control if antibiotics prescribed
e) Estrogen receptor inhibitor—tamoxifen (treatment of breast cancer)

5. Male sex hormones—testosterone, anabolic steroids
a) Medical use—treatment of breast cancer, hormone replacement therapy
b) Anabolic steroids are Schedule III controlled drugs—illicit use to build muscle mass

G. Respiratory drugs—used to treat asthma, COPD, bronchoconstriction

1. Pathophysiology of asthma—allergic response characterized by reduced expiratory airflow, mucus collection, airway restriction
a) Drugs for asthma—adrenergic agonists, corticosteroids, theophylline, ipratropium bromide, cromolyn, leukotriene inhibitors (newest)
b) Action—produce bronchodilation or reduce symptoms of asthma
(1) Adrenergic drugs—epinephrine, albuterol, metaproterenol, pirbuterol
(2) Corticosteroids—triamcinolone, flunisolide, beclomethasone; inhalation agents, candidiasis possible, rinse after use
(3) Cromolyn (Intal)—used for prophylaxis, not for acute asthma symptoms
(4) Theophylline—bronchodilator (asthma, COPD); drug interacts with erythromycin (theophylline toxicity)
(5) Ipratropium bromide (Atrovent), inhalation route, bronchodilator (asthma, COPD)
2. COPD—irreversible airway obstruction from chronic bronchitis or emphysema
3. Other drugs to treat respiratory diseases

a) Nasal decongestants—constrict blood vessels of nasal membranes
   (1) Chronic use—rebound swelling and congestion
   (2) Side effects—increased adrenergic effects (tachycardia, hypertension)
b) Expectorants and mucolytics—promote removal of mucus from respiratory tract; agents—guaifenesin (Robitussin), acetylcysteine (Mucomyst)
c) Antitussives—cough suppressant action; agents—codeine, dextromethorphan

4. Side effects of drugs to treat respiratory diseases
   a) Dry mouth, adrenergic stimulation, candidiasis, reduced host resistance
   b) Basis for contraindication of nitrous oxide with COPD—hypoxia needed for breathing stimulus
5. Management of dental patient with respiratory diseases
   a) Stress reduction to prevent acute symptoms
   b) Physician consultation for steroid supplementation
   c) Nitrous oxide contraindicated in COPD, aspirin and sulfite preservative in local anesthetic/vasoconstrictor may cause asthma attack
   d) Monitor vital signs—semisupine chair position if airway obstructed
6. Metered dose inhalers
   a) Advantages—medications go directly to site of action, good bronchodilator effect, accurate dose, rapid onset of action, convenient to carry
   b) Disadvantages—difficult for child to use, decreased action if overused

H. Gastrointestinal drugs—actions of drugs used to treat or alleviate symptoms of GI disease

1. Neutralize gastric HCI (antacids)—acute gastritis, ulcers
   a) Sodium bicarbonate, calcium carbonate, aluminum and magnesium salts, magnesium-aluminum hydroxide gel, sucralfate
   b) Interactions—alters absorption of tetracyclines
2. Prevent release of acids (H_2-blockers, proton pump inhibitors, prostaglandin)—ulcers, GERD (gastroesophageal reflux disease)
   a) Cimetidine (Tagamet), ranitidine (Zantac), famotidine (Pepcid)—H_2-receptor antagonists
      (1) Interactions—antacids, smoking
      (2) Side effects affecting dental treatment—confusion, dry mouth, taste alteration, blood dyscrasias; delayed drug metabolism of drugs metabolized by P450 pathway (cimetidine, ranitidine)
   b) Omeprazole (Prilosec)—a proton pump inhibitor
   c) Misoprostol (Cytotec)—prostaglandin
3. Promote intestinal movement (laxatives, GI stimulants)—constipation, GERD, gastric stasis
   a) Laxatives—bulk (cellulose), lubricants (mineral oil), stimulants (bisacodyl), stool softeners, saline laxative (magnesium sulfate)

   b) GI stimulates—metoclopramide, affects upper GI tract
4. Minimize fluid and electrolyte imbalance (antidiarrheals)
   a) Kaolin and pectin (Kaopectate)—adsorbent action
   b) Opioids—diphenoxylate (Lomotil) and loperamide (Imodium), decrease GI peristalsis
5. Prevent vomiting (antiemetics)
   a) Anticholinergecs/antihistamines—dimenhydrinate (Dramamine), diphenhydramine (Benadryl), hydroxyzine (Atarax)
   b) Trimethobenzamide (Tigan)—acts on chemoreceptor trigger zone in brain
   c) Prochlorperazine (Compazine), promethazine (Phenergan)—phenothiazine antipsychotic drugs
   d) Cannabinoid drugs—dronabinol (Marinol), marijuana substance
6. Management of dental patient with GI disease
   a) Sodium agents—contraindicated in patient on sodium-restricted diet
   b) Be aware of potential drug interactions
   c) GI disease symptoms may require semisupine chair position
   d) Manage side effects (dry mouth, sedation, dizziness) as needed

I. Antineoplastic drugs—cancer chemotherapy agents that interfere with the cell cycle to destroy malignant cells

1. Agents—a group that depends on mechanism and site of action
   a) Alkylating agents—nitrogen mustard, nitrosoureas, miscellaneous agents
   b) Antimetabolites—methotrexate, fluorouracil, mercaptopurine, effective in rapidly growing neoplasms
   c) Others—plant alkaloids, antibiotics, hormones
      (1) Tamoxifen (Nolvadex)—blocks estrogen receptors in breast
      (2) Paclitaxel (Taxol)—used for ovarian cancer, Kaposi's sarcoma
2. Oral complications of antieoplastic agents—poor healing, bleeding, xerostomia, *mucositis* (oral ulceration), taste disturbances
   a) Before initiation of chemotherapy—eliminate dental disease
   b) Management—alcohol-free fluoride products, palliataive rinse for oral ulceration, strict plaque control, warning to prevent injury in self-care methods, chlorhexidine
   c) Physician consult, WBC, platelet count before dental procedures
   d) Dental appointment during week before chemotherapy
3. Adverse drug effects
   a) Bone marrow depression—*leukopenia,* agranulocytosis, thrombocytopenia, anemia
   b) GI sloughing—bloody diarrhea, stomatitis (mucositis), vomiting
   c) Immunosuppression—poor healing, inability to fight infection

review questions

DIRECTIONS Each of the questions or incomplete statements below is followed by suggested answers or completions. Select the **one** answer that is best in each case.

1. When the drug molecule approaches close enough to the receptor so that the attractive forces between them causes binding, it has
   A. intrinsic activity.
   B. affinity.
   C. an antigen/antibody reaction.
   D. acceptor binding.

2. When a drug binds to a receptor and interferes with an agonist binding, it is called a
   A. placebo.
   B. displacing ion.
   C. competitive antagonist.
   D. full agonist.

3. Oral administration of a drug would be contraindicated when
   A. respiratory inflammation is present.
   B. immediate onset of action is necessary.
   C. the stomach is full.
   D. sterile technique is required.

4. Biotransformation of drugs occurs primarily in the
   A. bloodstream.
   B. kidney.
   C. liver.
   D. stomach.

5. A dental patient becomes sleepy after administration of an antihistamine. This *effect* would be termed a(n)
   A. toxic effect.
   B. hyperreaction.
   C. contraindication.
   D. idiosyncracy.
   E. side effect

6. A drug is available to bind to a receptor when it is in a(n)
   A. plasma protein-bound form.
   B. unbound form.
   C. nonionized form.
   D. ionized form.

7. Action of norepinephrine is terminated by being
   A. broken down by acetocholinesterase.
   B. reabsorbed by the adrenergic nerve termina.
   C. metabolized.
   D. none of the above.

8. Under the effects of the sympathetic nervous system, a person will experience
   A. increased energy.
   B. increased respiration.
   C. increased blood pressure.
   D. increased heart rate.
   E. all of the above.

9. The route of administration used MOST often in emergencies is
   A. oral.
   B. rectal.
   C. sublingual.
   D. intravenous.
   E. intramuscular.

10. In dentistry, a cholinergic drug is used to
    A. produce a dry field for taking impressions.
    B. calm an anxious patient before a dental procedure.
    C. increase salivary flow to treat xerostomia.
    D. reduce the chance of getting an infection.
    E. potentiate a local anesthetic agent.

11. Aspirin is contraindicated in the dental patient with a medical history of
    A. heart failure.
    B. ear surgery.
    C. adult-onset diabetes.
    D. mental psychoses.

12. Overdose of narcotic analgesics usually produces death from
    A. convulsions.
    B. respiratory depression.
    C. brain abscess.
    D. liver failure.
    E. kidney failure.

13. A superinfection is defined as
    A. a massive or virulent infection.
    B. overgrowth of a nonsusceptible bacterium capable of producing its own infection.
    C. an overgrowth of body flora bacteria as a result of immunological response to disease.
    D. none of the above.

14. Which of the following antibiotics is MOST often required for orodental infections?
    A. penicillin.
    B. erythromycin.
    C. tetracycline.
    D. nystatin.

15. If the patient is allergic to penicillin G and has an oral infection, the indicated antibiotic is
    A. penicillin V.
    B. ampicillin.
    C. tetracycline.
    D. erythromycin.

16. Which of the following is the MOST common side effect of erythromycin?
    A. gastrointestinal
    B. dermatological
    C. hematological
    D. allergenic

17. The patient needs a broad-spectrum antibiotic such as tetracycline. The patient should be cautioned not to use Fem-iron tablets.
    A. The first statement is TRUE. The second statement is FALSE.
    B. The first statement is FALSE. The second statement is TRUE.
    C. Both statements are TRUE.
    D. Both statements are FALSE.

18. Sulfonamides are not considered to be antibiotics because they
    A. are semisynthetic chemicals.
    B. only inhibit bacterial growth.
    C. are not produced by microorganisms.
    D. are organic chemicals.

19. Which of the following drugs is important in treating candidiasis?
    A. Nystatin
    B. Amphotericin B
    C. Candicidin
    D. Griseofulvin
    E. Flucytosine

20. The major organ for elimination of drugs is the
    A. intestines.
    B. bowels.
    C. kidney.
    D. lungs.
    E. skin.

21. The mechanism of action of local anesthetics is to
    A. block nerve synapses.
    B. coagulate nerve protein reversibly.
    C. depolarize persistently the nerve membrane.
    D. block nerve conduction by preventing nerve depolarization.

22. Drug allergy is an adverse reaction resulting from a
    A. previous sensitization to some drug.
    B. failure to apply topical anesthetic before injection.
    C. contact with a nonspecific protein.

D. drug interaction from a competitive blocking agent.
E. drug interaction on a plasma ion.

23. A local anesthetic with epinephrine is an example of a favorable drug reaction called
A. potentiation.
B. competitive antagonist.
C. intrinsic activity.
D. affinity.

24. A patient taking diazepam regularly to treat generalized anxiety disorder is most likely to complain of
A. ptyalism.
B. xerostomia.
C. palatal petechia.
D. gingival hyperplasia.
E. buccal mucosal keratinization

25. All of the following drugs are used for sedation EXCEPT one. Which one is the EXCEPTION?
A. Equanil
B. Miltown
C. Librium
D. Valium
E. Coumadin

26. Nitrous oxide is contraindicated for use in which of the following conditions?
A. diabetes
B. emphysema
C. hypertension
D. heart disease

27. When considering Guedel's classification of general anesthetics, stage II includes
A. regular respiration.
B. bradycardia.
C. loss of vomiting reflex.
D. hypotension.
E. unconsciousness.

28. The drug of choice for emergency treatment of status epilepticus is
A. phenobarbital.
B. phenytoin.
C. trimentadione.
D. hydantoin.
E. diazepam.

29. The single most useful agent in resuscitative procedures is
A. aromatic ammonia spirits.
B. antihistamine tablets.
C. epinephrine by injection.
D. oxygen.

30. Contraindications to dental treatment for the cardiovascular patient include all of the following EXCEPT one. Which one is the EXCEPTION?
A. within 6 months after myocardial infarction
B. within 6 months after cardiac transplant
C. presence of unstable angina pectoris
D. presence of uncontrolled arrhythmias
E. presence of uncontrolled, severe hypertension

31. Which one of the following statements describes the major effect of digoxin on the failing heart?
A. increases the force and efficiency of myocardial contraction
B. suppresses parasympathetic effects that slow heart rate
C. blocks formation of messenger chemicals that promote vasoconstriction and cardiac edema
D. acts synergistically with sympathetic nervous system to reset sympathetic tone of SA node

32. Physician consultation to determine the International Normalized Ratio (INR) is required before treating the patient taking which of the following drugs?
A. nifedipine (Procardia XL)
B. ibuprofen (Motrin)
C. warfarin (Coumadin)
D. menadiol (Synkayvite)

33. Of the following barbiturates, which is indicated for tonic-clonic seizures?
A. ethosuximide (Zarontin)
B. phenobarbital (Solfoton)
C. phenytoin (Dilantin)
D. clonazepam (Klonopin)

34. Which of the following drugs might be included in the drug history of a patient being treated for schizophrenia?
    A. chlorpromazine (Thorazine)
    B. trifluoperazine (Stelazine)
    C. thioridazine (Mellaril)
    D. prochlorperazine (Compazine)
    E. all of the above

35. Which of the following second-generation drugs is most commonly used to treat major depression?
    A. lithium (Eskalith)
    B. fluoxetine (Prozac)
    C. amtriptyline (Elavil)
    D. bupropion (Wellbutrin)

36. Of the following adverse reactions, which is associated with prolonged hydrocortisone therapy?
    A. osteoporosis
    B. desquamative gingival lesions
    C. abnormal weight loss
    D. toxic goiter

37. During stressful procedures, adrenal crisis should be anticipated in which of the following situations?
    A. 10 mg hydrocortisone/day within 2 years of appointment
    B. 5 mg prednisone/day for 2 weeks within 2 years of appointment
    C. 5 mg cortisone for 2 days within 2 years of appointment
    D. twice daily topical application of triamcinolone for 2 years before appointment

38. Which of the following drugs is a proton pump inhibitor used in combination with antibiotics for treating peptic ulcer?
    A. cimetidine (Tagamet)
    B. bismuth subsalicylate (Pepto-Bismol)
    C. kaolin and pectin (kaopectate)
    D. omeprazole (Prilosec)

answers & rationales

1.

B. The degree of attraction between a drug and receptor is called affinity. Intrinsic activity refers to the ability of a drug molecule to stimulate the receptor and produce an effect. Receptors that cannot initiate a response are known as acceptors. An antigen/antibody response is a host immune response.

2.

C. The antagonist produces its effect by preventing an agonist from occupying its receptor site. The result is no intrinsic activity. An agonist is a drug capable of binding to a receptor, simulating it, and producing a response. A placebo is an inert substance given in place of a drug.

3.

B. Drugs given orally must be absorbed through the stomach or intestines and also into the hepatic portal circulation, resulting in a much slower onset of action. Food in the stomach is sometimes required for the absorption of the drug. Many drugs that are used to treat respiratory disease are administered by use of a metered-dose inhaler.

4.

C. The liver is the most important organ for drug biotransformation. Other organs play a special role in metabolism, but the liver is the most important organ.

5.

E. A side effect is a dose-related reaction that is not part of the desired therapeutic outcome. A toxic reaction is an extension of the pharmacologic effect on the target organ resulting in an excessive effect. An idiosyncratic reaction is a genetically related abnormal drug response. A contraindication refers to a reason for not prescribing a drug.

6.

B. A drug that is bound is unavailable to go to the site of action; therefore, a drug must be in its unbound form to get to the site of action and bind to the receptor to produce an effect. Nonionized and ionized forms will affect a drug's absorption.

7.

B. Norepinephrine is terminated principally by its reuptake into the nerve ending, removing it from the site of action. The enzymes monoamine oxidase and catechol-O-methyltransferase play a minor role in the metabolism of norepinephrine and epinephrine. Acetylcholine is metabolized by acetylcholinesterase to yield inactive substances.

8.

E. The SANS effects will increase energy, respiration, blood pressure, and heart rate.

9.

D. IV administration produces the most rapid drug response because the injection is made directly into the blood. Oral administration of drugs must be absorbed through the small intestine, delaying its onset of action. Drugs given rectally are poorly and irregularly absorbed. Sublingual administration of drugs is a topical route and generally used for localized effects. The intramuscular route may be used for drugs that are irritating or for suspensions.

10.

C. Cholinergic drugs stimulate gland cell secretion, resulting in increased salivary flow. Anticholinergic can be used to produce a dry field before some dental procedures. Cholinergic drugs are not used to treat anxiety. Cholinergic drugs are not used to prevent infection or to increase the effect of local anesthetics.

11.

C. A combination of aspirin and sulfonyloreas can cause a hypoglycemic effect. Aspirin may be used to prevent unwanted clotting in heart failure. Aspirin does not affect those patients with a history of ear surgery or mental psychoses.

12.

B. The usual cause of death from an overdose is respiratory depression. This is related to a decrease in the sensitivity of the brainstem to carbon dioxide, which reduces the rate and depth of respiration. A narcotic may adversely affect the kidney and liver, but failure is not usually the cause of death. Convulsions or brain abscesses are not the usual cause of death from an overdose of narcotics.

13.

B. A superinfection is an infection caused by the proliferation of microorganisms different from those causing the original infection. An immunological response of the host does not result in an overgrowth of bacteria. A virulent infection is not the definition of superinfection.

14.

A. Penicillin is often used for the treatment of dental infections because of its bactericidal potency, lack of toxicity, and spectrum action, which includes many oral flora. Erythromycin is active against the same aerobic microorganism as penicillin. It is the drug of first choice against these microorganisms in penicillin-allergic patients, but it is not effective against the anaerobic *Bacteroides* species and would not be effective for infections caused by those microorganisms. In aerobic gram-positive infections, penicillins offer a clear advantage over tetracyclines, but they are rarely the drug of choice for a specific infection. Nystantin is an antifungal agent.

15.

D. The drug of choice against infections in penicillin-allergic patients is erythromycin. Penicillin V and ampicillin are from the same family as penicillin G. Tetracycline is a broad-spectrum antibiotic and is rarely the drug of choice for a specific infection.

16.

A. Side effects most often associated with erythromycin administration are gastrointestinal. Dermatological and hematological effects are not problems. Allergic reactions to erythromycin are uncommon.

17

C. Fem-iron tablets have cations in them. Divalent and trivalent cations decrease the intestinal absorption of tetracycline by chelating with it. These products should not be taken within 2 hours of ingesting tetracycline.

18.

C. Sulfonamides cannot be classified as antibiotics because they are not produced by living organisms. Penicillin G is the only naturally occurring penicillin. All others are semisynthetic. The sulfonamides are bacteriostatic against many gram-positive and some gram-negative bacteria.

19.

A. Nystantin is used for both the treatment and prevention of oral candidiasis in susceptible cases. Amphotericin B, griseofulvin, and flucytosine are used in other types of fungal infections.

20.

C. The most important organ of excretion is the kidney. However, drugs may be removed from the body by any organ that makes contact with the outside environment.

21.

D. After combining with the receptor, local anesthetics block the conduction of nerve impulses by decreasing the permeability of the nerve cell membrane to sodium ions preventing nerve depolarization.

22.

A. For a drug to produce an allergic reaction, it must act as an antigen and react with an antibody in a previously sensitized patient. The reaction is not dependent on the dose nor is it predictable.

23.

A. Potentiation is the interaction of two or more drugs resulting in an effect that is greater than expected. A competitive antagonist is a drug that has affinity for or combines with the receptor and produces no effect. Intrinsic activity refers to the ability of a drug molecule to stimulate the receptor and produce an effect. Affinity refers to the degree of attraction between a drug and the receptor.

24.

B. Benzodiazepines have been reported to cause xerostomia. Benzodiazepines do not cause excessive salivation, palatal petechia, gingival hyperplasia, or lichen planus.

25.

E. Coumadin is an anticoagulant. Equanil, Miltown, Librium, and Valium may all be used for sedation.

26.

B. Nitrous oxide is contraindicated for patients with respiratory obstruction, COPD, emotional instability, and pregnancy. Diabetes hypertension and heart disease are not contraindications.

27.

E. Stage II begins with unconsciousness and is associated with involuntary movement and excitement. Sympathetic stimulation produces tachycardia and hypertension. Respiration becomes irregular and emesis and incontinence can occur. Stage II can be uncomfortable for the patient and so should be passed through quickly.

28.

E. Diazepam (Valium) is the drug of choice for the treatment of status epilepticus. Phenobarbital, phenytoin, trimethadione, and hydantoin are used to treat seizures but are not the drug of choice for this situation.

29.

D. Oxygen is the most important drug in the emergency kit. It is indicated in most emergencies, especially if respiratory difficulty is a problem.

30.

B. There is no specific time frame for cardiac transplant recipients to receive dental treatment after transplantation. The time depends on the progress of the individual patient and requires a physician consult.

31.

A. The major effect of digoxin on the failing heart is to increase the force and efficiency of the myocardial contraction. As digoxin increases the cardiac output, the sympathetic tone is decreased, with a decrease in the heart rate as the end result.

32.

C. Warfarin's action is to decrease synthesis of clotting factors and requires the INR to determine the patient's clotting ability; the other agents do not work by the same mechanism.

33.

B. Phenobarbital (Solfoton) is the only barbiturate listed as a choice. Clonazepam (Klonopin) is a benzodiazepine derivative. Phenytoin (Dilatin) is the prototype for the hydantoin group. Ethosuximide (Zarotin) is an anticonvulsant of a miscellaneous group used to treat absence (petit mal) seizures.

34.

E. All of these drugs could be used to treat schizophrenia.

35.

B. Prozac is the only drug listed that is among the top 20 most prescribed drugs.

36.

A. A major risk factor for osteoporosis is long-term prednisone therapy. Hydrocortisone does not cause desquamative gingival lesions but may be used to treat them. It is not used in the treatment of toxic goiters. Long-term use causes weight gain, not weight loss.

37.

B. This distractor follows the "rule of twos" in adrenal drug therapy, the other distractors do not.

38.

D. Omeprazole is the only proton pump inhibitor listed. Cimetidine is an antihistamine. Bismuth subsalicylate is an antidiarrheal. Kaolin is an antidiarrheal combination product.

CHAPTER

9 Patient Assessment and Preventive Dentistry

Lauri Wiechmann, RDH, MPA

contents

➤ PATIENT ASSESSMENT

Patient assessment is defined as the critical analysis and evaluation or judgment of a particular condition, situation, or other subject of appraisal.

I. COMPONENTS

A. Social history—gathering personal information about the patient such as the essential data for an appointment and legal implications (e.g. care of a minor)

B. Health history—incorporates subjective and objective information to obtain comprehensive medical data; may include the following information

1. Conditions that may complicate dental hygiene treatment
2. Diseases that require special precautions or premedications
3. Physical conditions presently being treated by a physician
4. Allergic conditions
5. Current medications
6. Current diseases/conditions

C. *Vital signs*—monitoring and recording blood pressure, pulse, temperature, and respiration; contributes to a proper systemic evaluation of patient in conjunction with a complete medical history

1. Blood pressure—force at which blood is pumped against the walls of the arteries
   a) *Diastole*
      (1) Minimum amount of pressure exerted against the walls of the vessels
      (2) Phase of the cardiac cycle in which the heart relaxes between contractions
   b) *Systole*
      (1) Maximum amount of pressure exerted against the walls of the vessels
      (2) Involves contraction or period of contraction during which left ventricle of heart contracts and blood is forced into aorta and pulmonary artery
   c) Armamentarium—sphygmomanometer, manometer, and stethoscope
      (1) *Sphygmomanometer*—consists of an inflatable cuff, pressure bulb for inflating the cuff, and a manometer, a device to read the pressure
         (a) Inflatable cuff—made of a nonelastic material and fastened with Velcro
         (b) Size of cuff is determined by size of patient's arm
         (c) Proper size width is 20% greater than the diameter of the arm (Figure 9-1)
      (2) Types of *manometers*
         (a) Mercury—contains a column of mercury that rises with an increase in pressure as cuff is inflated; includes tabletop and wall-mounted units or free-standing on wheels; most reliable recorder of blood pressure

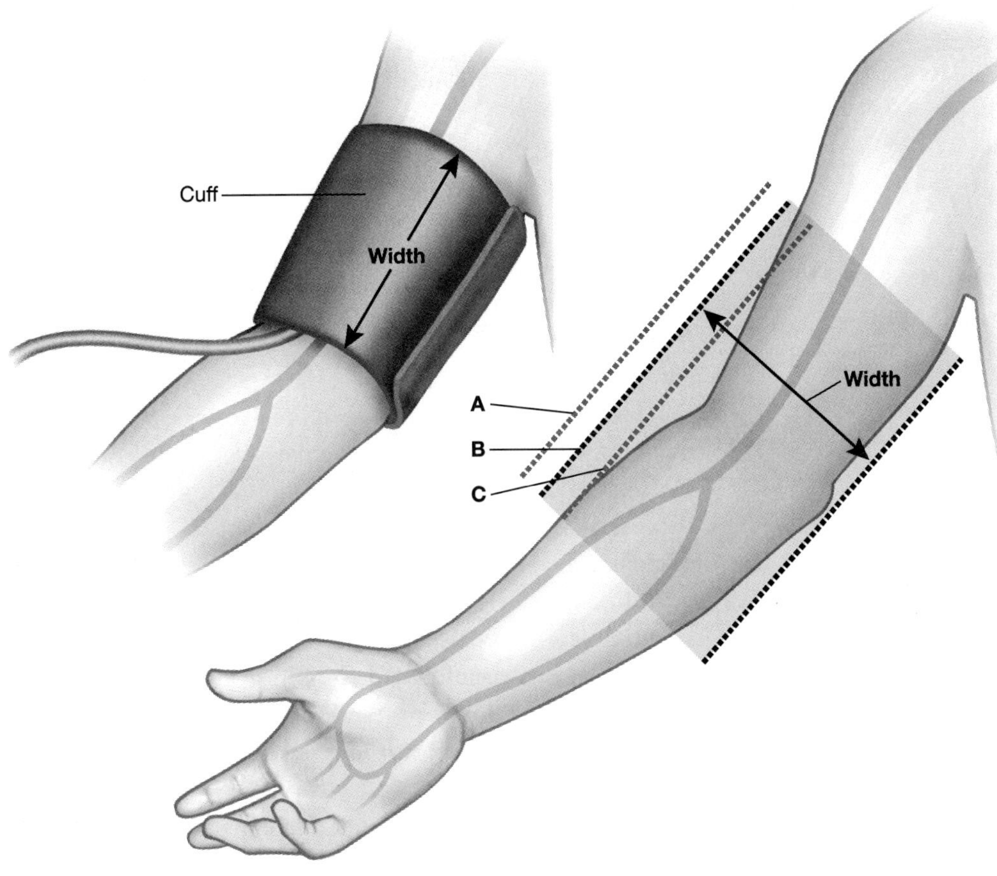

FIGURE 9-1. Selection of cuff size. A) too wide; B) proper width—20% greater than diameter of the arm; C) too narrow

(b) Aneroid—contains a circular gauge for registering pressure; needle rotates as pressure rises; accurate and less awkward to use than a mercury manometer because gauge is attached to blood pressure cuff

(c) Electronic—provides a digital readout on a lit display; does not require a stethoscope like the other two; costly and least likely to give an accurate reading

(3) Stethoscope—listening aid that amplifies body sounds; components include

(a) Earpieces

(b) Binaurals—connects the earpieces to the tubing

(c) Tubing—connects the binaurals to the chestpiece

(d) Chestpiece—amplifies sound; consists of the bell on one side and diaphragm on the other

i) Diaphragm—flat side covered by a thin plastic disk; best for amplifying high-pitched sounds (i.e., lungs)

ii) Bell—cone-shaped side; best for amplifying low-pitched sounds (i.e., heart and vascular)

d) Normal range for adults—systolic, 90–140; diastolic, 60–90

e) Screening for hypertension

(1) < 140/90—proceed with routine dental procedures
(2) 140/90 to 160/95—recheck blood pressure before dental procedure; if still elevated, refer to physician for evaluation in 3 months
(3) 160/95 to 180/105—recheck blood pressure before dental procedure; if still elevated, advise patient to see physician in 1 month; call physician before starting treatment
(4) > 180/105—recheck blood pressure before dental procedure; if still elevated, refer to physician immediately; DO NOT treat patient

f) Factors that affect blood pressure
(1) Increase of blood pressure—result of exercise, eating, use of stimulants, and oral contraceptives
(2) Decrease of blood pressure—result of fasting, rest, use of depressants, fainting, loss of blood, or shock

2. Body temperature

a) Types of thermometers
(1) Disposable—single use (effective for preventing cross-contamination); usually made of thin strips of plastic with a specially treated dot or strip indicator that changes color according to temperature; readings are not as accurate as other thermometers
(2) Mercury—consists of a thin glass tube with a mercury-filled bulb at the end; mercury is heated by body temperature, causing an expansion in the hollow center of the glass
(3) Electronic—provides a digital readout of the temperature; time efficient and decreases cross-contamination
(4) Tympanic—placed in ear; measures infrared energy emitted from eardrum (tympanic membrane)

b) Normal range (Table 9-1)
(1) Adult—98.6°F to 100.6°F
(2) Child—96°F to 100.6°F; higher in infancy and decreases as the child ages

c) Factors that affect body temperature
(1) Time of day—highest in afternoon and early evening; lowest during sleep and early morning
(2) Increase of temperature—response to exercise, hot beverages, smoking, infection, dehydration, hyperthyroidism, myocardial infarction, and tissue injury
(3) Decrease of temperature—response to starvation, hemorrhage, and physiological shock

3. Pulse—intermittent throbbing sensation felt when fingers are pressed against an artery; indirect measurement of cardiac output

a) Palpation sites
(1) Brachial artery—located in bend of elbow (antecubital space)
(2) Carotid artery (carotid pulse)—located at side of neck
(3) Facial artery—located at side of face at border of mandible
(4) Radial artery (radial pulse)—located at wrist

TABLE 9-1 VITAL SIGNS						
	Age					
Vital Signs	**0–1 year**	**1–6 years**	**6–11 yrs**	**11–16 years**	**Adult**	**Elderly**
Temperature (°F)	96–99.5	98.5–99.5	98.5–99.6	98.6–100.6	98.6–100.6	97.2–99.6
Pulse (beats per minute)	80–160	75–130	70–115	55–110	60–100	60–100
Respirations (per minute)	26–40	20–30	18–24	16–24	12–20	12–24
Blood pressure (mm Hg)						
Systolic	74–100	80–112	84–120	94–120	90–140	100–150
Diastolic	50–70	50–80	54–80	62–88	60–90	60–90

b) Normal range
   (1) Adult —60–100 beats/minute
   (2) Child—70–105 beats/minute
4. Respirations—involves inhalation and exhalation; indicates how well the body is providing oxygen to the tissues
   a) Normal range
      (1) Adult—12–20 breaths/minute
      (2) Child—16–40 breaths/minute; slows down as the child gets older

D. Dental history—gathering past and present dental information; may include following information

1. Chief complaint, discomfort, and/or pain
2. Previous dental/dental hygiene care, including care from specialists
3. Personal habits, including oral hygiene and grinding
4. Patient's attitude toward dental care and importance of a healthy mouth
5. Intraoral examination—observation and palpation of structures within oral cavity
6. Extraoral examination—observation and palpation of structures of the head and neck outside of oral cavity
7. Observation methods of intraoral/extraoral examinations
   a) *Palpation* (Figure 9-2)
      (1) *Bilateral*—use both hands at same time to examine corresponding structures on opposite sides of body
      (2) *Bimanual*—use finger(s) and/or thumb from each hand; apply simultaneously
      (3) *Digital*—use single finger
      (4) *Bidigital*—use finger and thumb of same hand
   b) *Auscultation*—process of listening to body sounds
   c) *Inspection*—performing a visual examination of body and overall appearance

E. Dental examination

1. Caries—lesion of hard tissues of teeth that ranges from changes at molecular level to gross tissue destruction and cavity formation

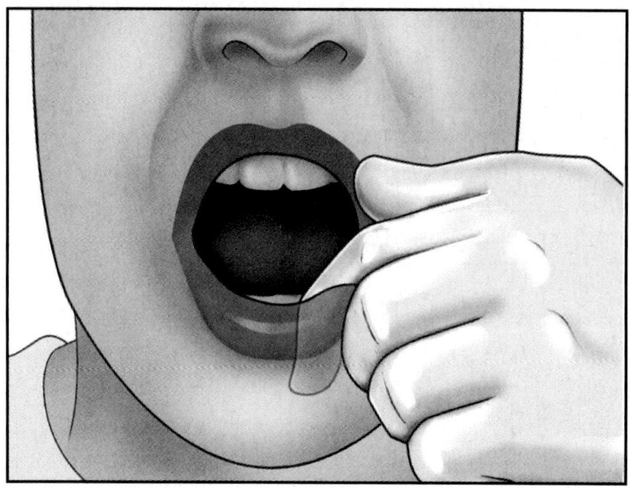

Digital palpation—Use index finger. Example—detect the presence of exostosis on the border of the mandible.

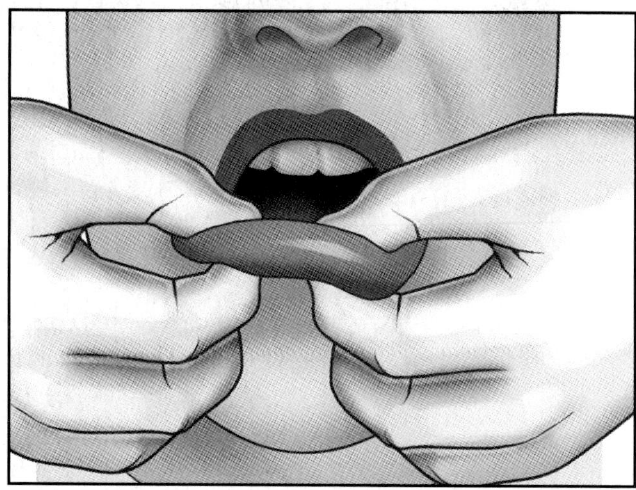

Bidigital palpation - Use finger and thumb of same hand. Example—Palpate the lips.

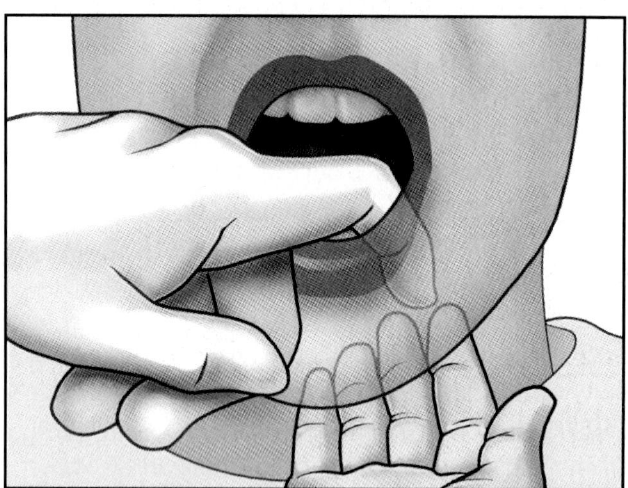

Bimanual palpation—Use finger(s) and/or thumb from each hand. Example—palpate floor of mouth.

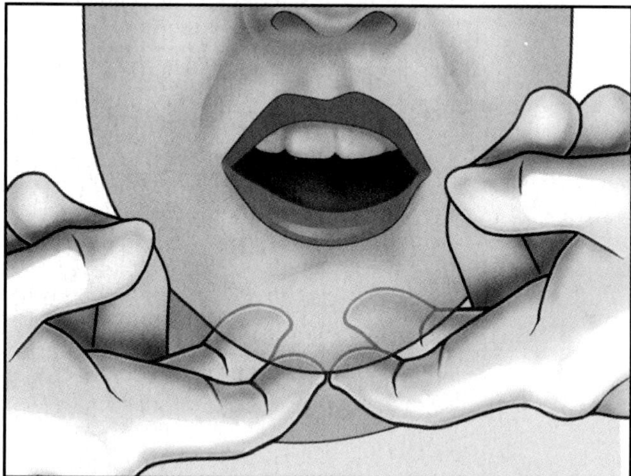

Bilateral palpation - Use both hands at same time to examine corresponding structures on opposite sides of body. Example—examine submental nodes.

FIGURE 9-2. Palpation methods of the oral cavity

a) Process of caries formation—pathological process of demineralization and remineralization
   (1) *Demineralization*—loss of mineral apatite from tooth structure
   (2) *Remineralization*—repair of tooth structure after acidogenic episodes
   (3) Bacterial involvement
      (a) *Streptococcus mutans*—associated with coronal caries; appear in large numbers during initial phase of developing carious lesions; have ability to ferment mannitol and sorbitol; mainly produce lactic acid
      (b) *Lactobacillus* species—found in greater numbers in more advanced, smooth-surface lesions

(c) *L. casei*—shown to colonize white spot lesions before cavitation

(d) *Actinomyces odontolyticus*—also associated with progression of a lesion

b) Detection of caries

(1) Direct visual—includes facial, lingual and occlusal lesions; may need to utilize mirror for transillumination

(2) Radiographs—require proper angulation with no horizontal overlapping; best for viewing interproximal caries

(3) Explorer—use for pit and fissure examination; and to follow margin of restorations

(4) Characteristic changes in the color and translucency of enamel may be seen

(a) Chalky white areas of demineralization

(b) Grayish-white discoloration of marginal ridges with dental caries of underlying proximal surface

(c) Grayish-white color spreading from margins of restorations caused by recurrent decay

(d) Yellowish-brown to dark brown color of tooth structure with an open carious lesion

c) Classification of caries—Dr. G.V. Black's classification (Figure 9-3)

(1) Class I—involves pit and fissure surfaces (occlusals of premolars and molars, facials and linguals of molars, and linguals of maxillary incisors)

(2) Class II—involves proximal surfaces of premolars and molars

(3) Class III—involves proximal surfaces of incisors and canines, but NOT incisal angle

(4) Class IV—involves proximal surfaces of incisors and canines, INCLUDING incisal angle

(5) Class V—involves cervical one third of facial or lingual surfaces (not pits and fissures)

(6) Class VI—involves incisal edges of anterior teeth and cusps of posterior teeth

d) Types of dental caries

(1) Pit and fissure—involves occlusal surfaces of posterior teeth as well as lingual pits of maxillary incisors

(2) Smooth surface—involves intact enamel surfaces other than pit and fissure locations

(3) Root surface—involves any area on the root

(4) Recurrent (secondary)—involves tooth surface adjacent to an existing restoration

(5) Rampant—involves rapid and extensive development of cavitation from time of initial incipient lesion

(6) Nursing bottle—develops from a prolonged exposure to a sugar substance in a bottle; form of rampant decay

2. Abrasion—loss of tooth structure from a mechanical cause
3. Attrition—loss of tooth structure from tooth-to-tooth contact
4. Erosion—loss of tooth structure through a chemical process

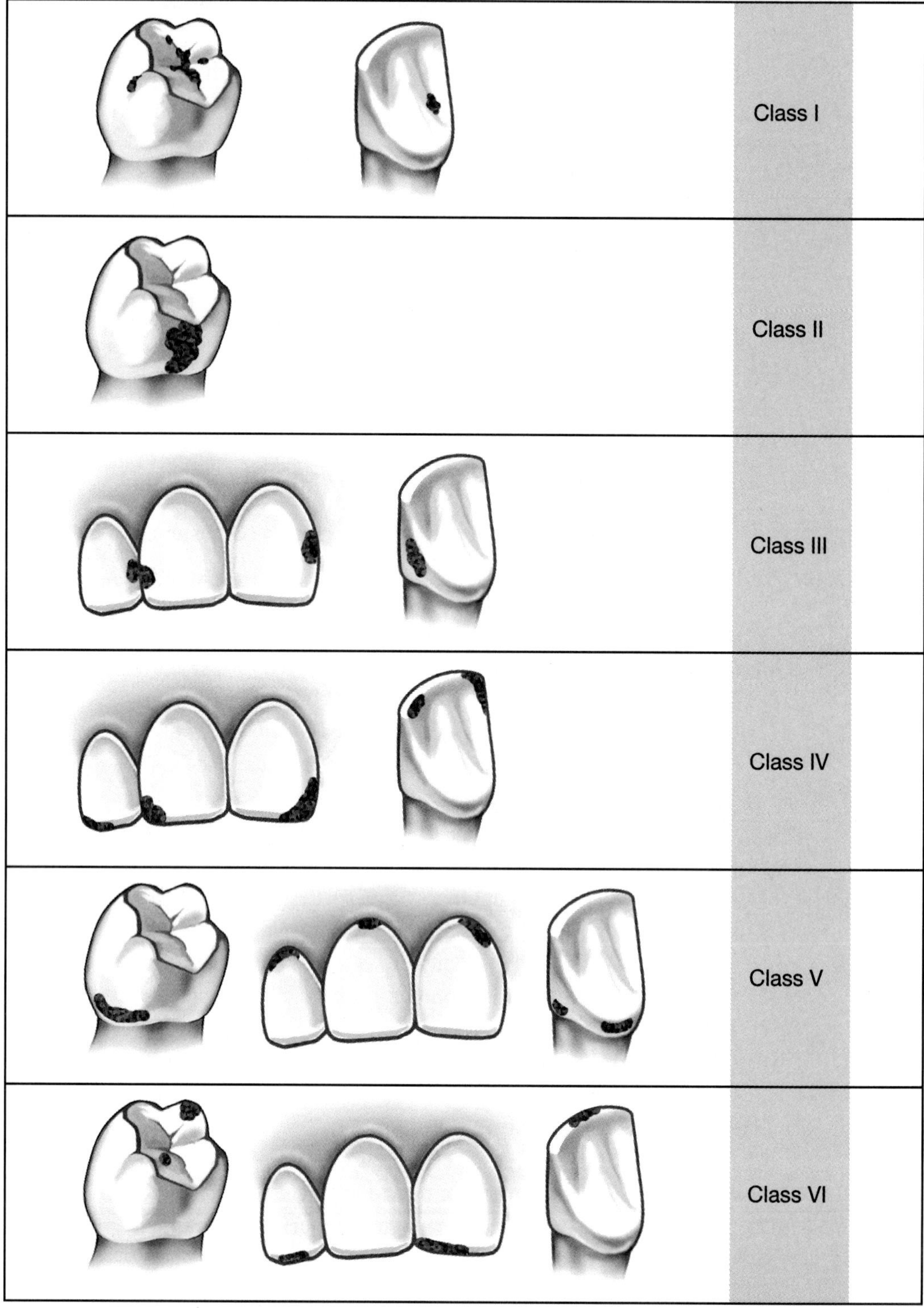

FIGURE 9-3. Black's classification of dental caries and restorations

F. Occlusal examination

1. Angle's classification of occlusion (Figure 9-4)
   a) Class I—Neutrocclusion
      (1) Molar relation—mesiobuccal cusp of permanent maxillary first molar is in alignment with buccal groove of permanent mandibular first molar

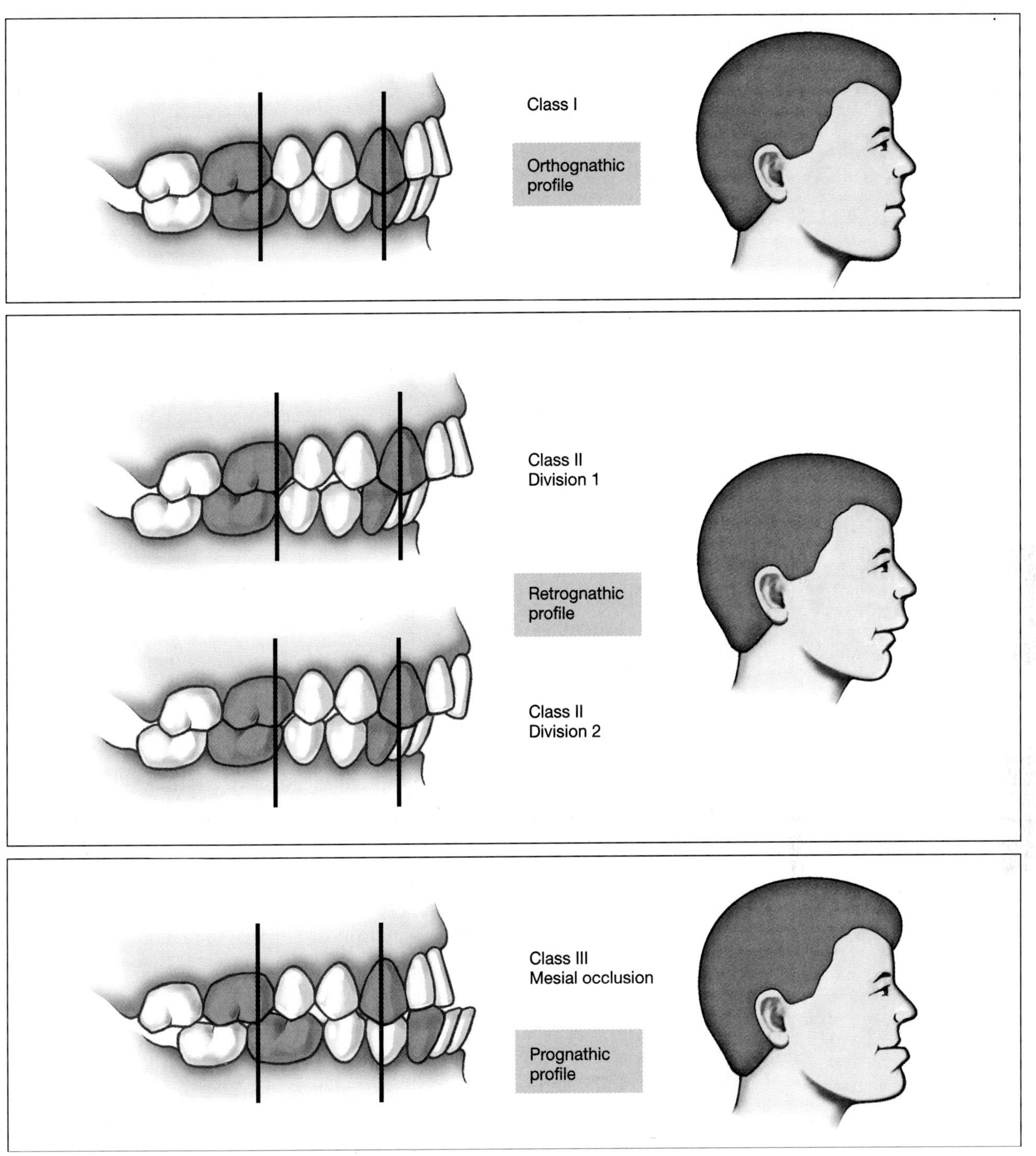

FIGURE 9-4. Occlusal relationships: Class I (*top*); Class II, division 1 (*middle top*), Class II, division 2 (*middle bottom*); Class III (*bottom*)

(2) Canine relation—maxillary permanent canine occludes with distal half of mandibular canine and mesial half of permanent mandibular first premolar

b) Class II—Distocclusion

(1) Molar relation—mesiobuccal cusp of permanent maxillary first molar is mesial to buccal groove of permanent mandibular first molar

(2) Canine relation—distal surface of permanent maxillary canine is mesial to mesial surface of permanent mandibular canine by a minimum width of half a premolar
(a) Division I—molar and/or canine relationship is same, but with permanent maxillary incisors protruded (toward facial)
(b) Division II—molar and/or canine relationship is the same but with one or more of permanent maxillary incisors retruded (toward lingual)

c) Class III—Mesiocclusion
(1) Molar relation—mesiobuccal cusp of permanent maxillary first molar is distal to buccal groove of permanent mandibular first molar
(2) Canine relation—mesial surface of permanent maxillary canine is distal to distal surface of permanent mandibular canine by a minimum width of half a premolar

2. *Overjet*—horizontal distance between labioincisal surface of mandibular incisors and linguoincisal surfaces of maxillary incisors
3. *Overbite*—vertical distance by which maxillary incisors overlap mandibular incisors
   a) Normal overbite—incisal edges of maxillary incisors are within incisal third of mandibular incisors
   b) Moderate overbite—incisal edges of maxillary incisors are within middle third of mandibular incisors
   c) Severe (deep) overbite—incisal edges of maxillary incisors are within cervical third of mandibular incisors
4. *Crossbite*—may occur unilaterally or bilaterally
   a) Posterior—maxillary or mandibular teeth are either facial or lingual to their normal position
   b) Anterior—maxillary incisors are lingual to mandibular incisors
5. *End-to-End*—cusp-to-cusp occlusion of maxillary and mandibular molars and premolars
6. *Edge-to-Edge*—incisal edge-to-incisal edge occlusion of maxillary and mandibular incisors and canines
7. *Openbite*—lack of occlusal or incisal contact between one or more of maxillary and mandibular teeth
8. Defective restorations—to determine, utilize an explorer to trace around margins of restoration; evidence of a grayish-white color spreading from margins of restorations caused by recurrent decay
9. Demineralized areas—noted visually as "white spot" lesions
10. Root anatomy—utilize explorer to detect location of anatomic depressions, root anomalies, calculus, and decay

G. Periodontal assessment—gathering data involving supporting and surrounding tissues of teeth

1. Sulcus/pocket measurements—using a periodontal probe, measure from gingival margin to base of sulcus

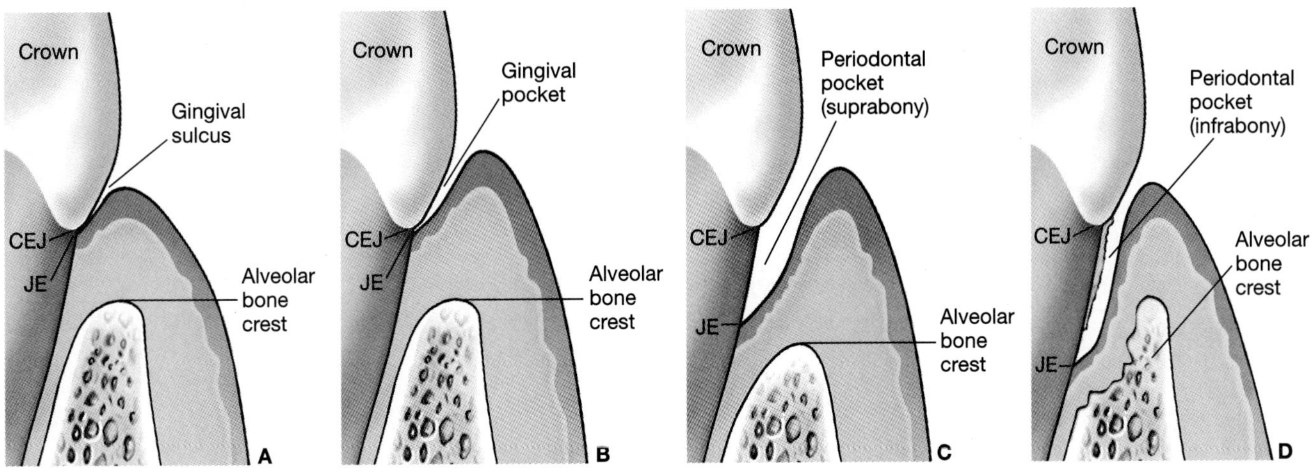

FIGURE 9-5. Types of pockets: A) healthy; B) gingivitis; C) suprabony; D) infrabony

a) Definition—crevice or groove between free gingiva and tooth
b) Types of Pockets (Figure 9-5)
   (1) *Gingival*—gingival margin is coronal to cementoenamel junction (CEJ) because of inflammation of gingival tissues; there is no loss of periodontal attachment
   (2) *Suprabony*—base of pocket is coronal to crest of alveolar bone
   (3) *Infrabony (intrabony)*—base of pocket is below or apical to crest of alveolar bone

2. Mobility—movement of tooth
   a) Classification—includes N, 1, 2, 3 or I, II, III
      (1) N = normal, physiological
      (2) 1 or I = involves slight horizontal mobility, greater than normal
      (3) 2 or II = involves moderate horizontal mobility, greater than a 1 mm displacement
      (4) 3 or III = involves severe mobility and may move in all directions (vertical as well as horizontal)
   b) Techniques for determining mobility
      (1) Use two single-ended blunt instruments
      (2) Rock the tooth facial-lingually to test for horizontal mobility
      (3) Test vertical mobility by placing blunt end of one instrument on occlusal or incisal surface while depressing tooth
3. Clinical attachment level (Figure 9-6)
   a) Definition—measure probing depth from CEJ (or other fixed point) to location of probe tip at coronal level of attached periodontal tissues
   b) Measurement technique—select a fixed point on tooth (CEJ is usually used) and measure from that point to base of sulcus/pocket
   c) Determine amount of attached gingiva

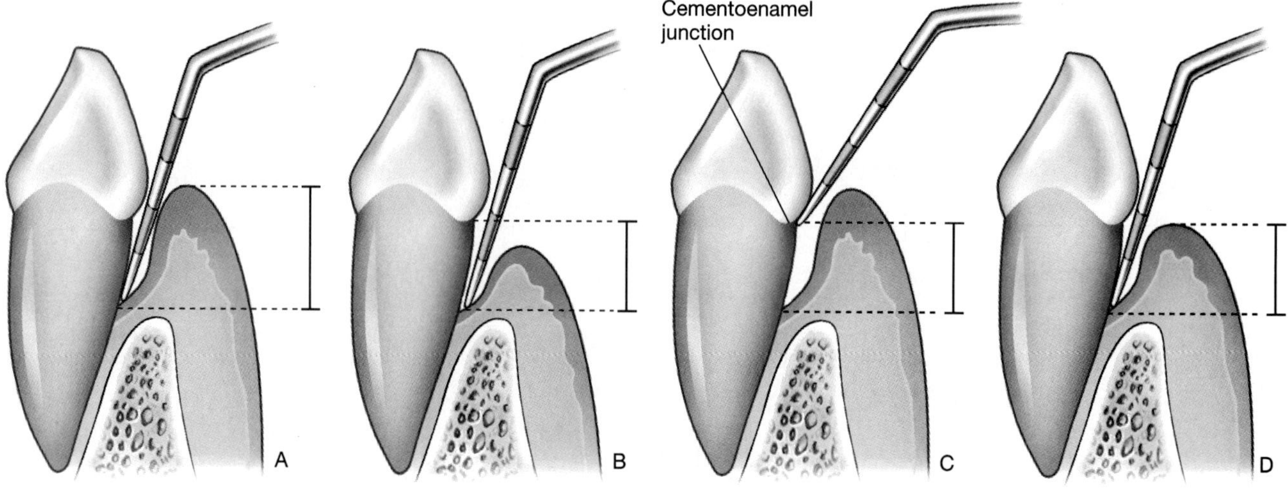

FIGURE 9-6. Clinical attachment level: A) probing depth—measure pocket from attached gingiva to gingival margin; B) recession present—measure from CEJ to attached gingiva; C) gingival margin covers CEJ—locate CEJ, measure distance to CEJ, then subtract from probing depth; D) gingival margin is at CEJ—measure from CEJ to attached gingiva

(1) On external surface of gingiva, measure from mucogingival junction to gingival margin (determines total gingiva)
(2) Measure probing depth
(3) Subtract probing depth from total gingival measurement (amount of attached gingiva)

4. Loss of attachment—junctional epithelium migrates toward apex of tooth
   a) *Furcation*—involves anatomic area of a multirooted tooth where roots either bifurcate or trifurcate
      (1) Classification (Figure 9-7)
         (a) Class I—evidence of early bone loss in furca area; probe can enter furca on either side; can be determined by moving probe from side to side

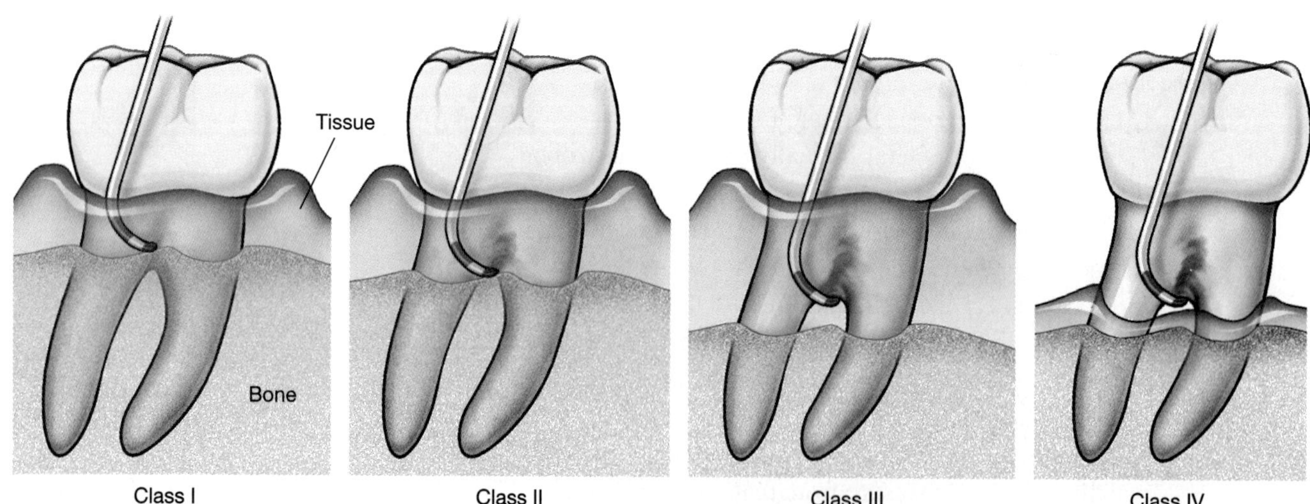

FIGURE 9-7. Classification of furcation involvement

(b) Class II—evidence of moderate bone loss in furcation area; probe can enter furca, but cannot pass between roots
(c) Class III—evidence of severe bone loss in furcation area; probe can pass between roots through entire furcation area
(d) Class IV—same as Class III with exposure resulting from gingival recession

(2) Anatomic features
(a) *Bifurcation*—divergence of root trunk into two roots
(b) *Trifurcation*—divergence of root trunk into three roots

(3) Technique for determining furcation—furcation probe is instrument of choice used to examine topography of furcation area; accessing furcated areas includes
(a) Maxillary first premolars—involves mesial and distal aspects under contact area
(b) Maxillary molars—includes mesial, buccal, and distal surfaces
(c) Mandibular molars—involves facial and lingual surfaces

b) *Recession*—exposure of root surface that results from apical migration of junctional epithelium; (Figure 9-8)
(1) Visible recession—measured from CEJ to gingival margin
(2) Total (actual) recession—measured from CEJ to base of pocket

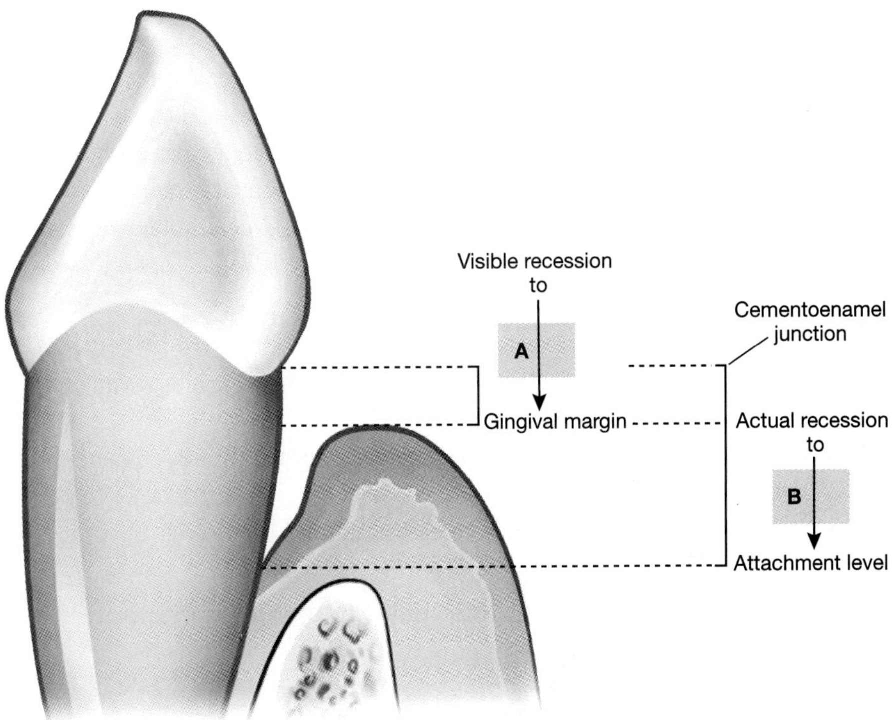

FIGURE 9-8. Gingival recession: A) visible—measured from CEJ to gingival margin; B) actual—measured from CEJ to base of pocket

(3) Apparent recession—exposed root surface that is visible on clinical examination

5. Gingival description—differentiating among normal, healthy tissues and diseased tissues
   a) Healthy
      (1) Color—uniformly pink or coral pink
      (2) Contour—not enlarged, fits tightly around tooth
      (3) Consistency—firm; attached gingiva firmly bound
      (4) Texture—free gingiva is smooth; attached gingiva is stippled
   b) Diseased
      (1) Color—for acute disease, bright red; for chronic disease, a bluish hue (bluish pink or bluish red)
      (2) Contour—enlarged, swollen
      (3) Consistency—for acute disease, soft, spongy, and loss of stippling; for chronic disease, firm, hard, stippled, and fibrotic
      (4) Texture—for acute disease, smooth and shiny; for chronic disease, hard, firm, stippled (sometimes more than normal)
      (5) Bleeding on probing—indicates diseased gingival tissues; ulcerated pocket wall bleeds on gentle probing
6. Bacterial composition—made up of pathogenic microorganisms that produce gingivitis and periodontal disease
   a) Healthy—consists of predominantly Gram-positive, aerobic cocci and rods
   b) Diseased—consists of predominantly Gram-negative, anaerobic spirochetes, vibrios, and rods
7. Occlusal trauma—may result from excessive forces and/or lack of bony support
   a) Occlusal forces are transmitted to the periodontal attachment apparatus
      (1) Force can cause changes in bone and connective tissue
      (2) Changes affect tooth mobility and clinical probing depth
   b) Mode of treatment—establish periodontal health, then apply occlusal therapy to help reduce mobility and regain bone loss due to traumatic occlusal forces

H. Caries/nutritional counseling

1. Designed to help patient study individual oral problems and understand need for changing habits
2. Explain specific changes in diet necessary for improved general and oral health
3. Encourage elimination of sugar-containing foods and substitute low/no sugar foods

I. Pulp vitality testing—method used to test a suspected nonvital tooth

1. Device—pulp tester (*vitalometer*)
   a) Types
      (1) Battery-operated—hand-held, battery-operated device
         (a) Advantages—portable, easy to use

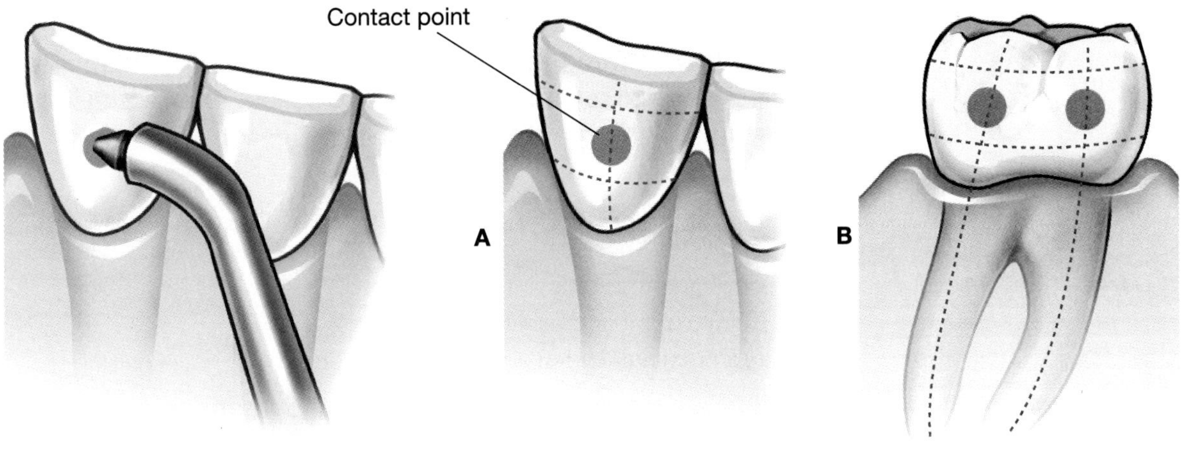

FIGURE 9-9. Position of pulp tester: A) place pulp tester in middle third of tooth; B) placement of pulp tester on multirooted tooth

(b) Disadvantages—battery can run out

(2) Plug-in—requires electrical energy from outlet

(a) Advantages—more dependable than battery operated

(b) Disadvantages—not self-contained

b) Contraindications—do not use on patient with a cardiac pacemaker or any electronic life-support device

c) Technique for use

(1) Dry teeth to be tested—isolate teeth with cotton rolls (prevents current from passing to gingiva)

(2) Moisten tip of tester with a small amount of toothpaste or other electrolyte

(3) Apply tester tip

(a) Test at least one tooth other than the one in question (preferably an adjacent tooth) and then same tooth on contralateral side (this determines normal response)

(b) Place tester (without applying pressure) to middle or gingival third of tooth surface (Figure 9-9)

(4) Start with rheostat at zero; advance slowly, but steadily, until patient signals that a sensation is felt

(5) Test each tooth at least twice and average readings

(6) Record averaged number of all teeth tested in patient's chart

(7) Considerations to take when applying tester tip—avoid contact with gingiva or other soft tissues and metallic restorations

➤ PREVENTIVE DENTISTRY

Preventive dentistry includes the management of behaviors to prevent oral disease, the coordination and delivery of primary preventive oral hygiene services, the provision of secondary preventive intervention to prevent further disease, and the facilitation of the patient's access to care and implementation of oral care goals.

I. PREVENTION

A. *Primary prevention*—involves techniques and agents to forestall onset and reverse progress of disease, or arrest disease process before treatment becomes necessary

1. Examples
   a) Mechanical and chemical plaque removal
   b) Use of fluorides
   c) Sugar discipline
   d) Use of pit and fissure sealants
   e) Patient education and health promotion

B. *Secondary prevention*—involves routine treatment methods to terminate a disease and restore tissues to as normal as possible

1. Examples
   a) Deep scaling
   b) Restorations
   c) Periodontal debridement
   d) Endodontics

C. *Tertiary prevention*—involves using measures necessary to replace lost tissues and rehabilitate patients so physical capabilities and/or mental attitudes are as near to normal as possible after secondary prevention has failed

1. Examples
   a) Prosthodontics
   b) Implants

II. PLANNING

A. Patient needs—involves inner forces that drive a person to action

1. *Maslow's hierarchy of needs*—developed by Abraham Maslow, humanistic psychologist; includes five levels of basic human needs: physiological, safety (security), love (social), self-esteem (ego), and self-actualization (self-fulfillment) (Figure 9-10)

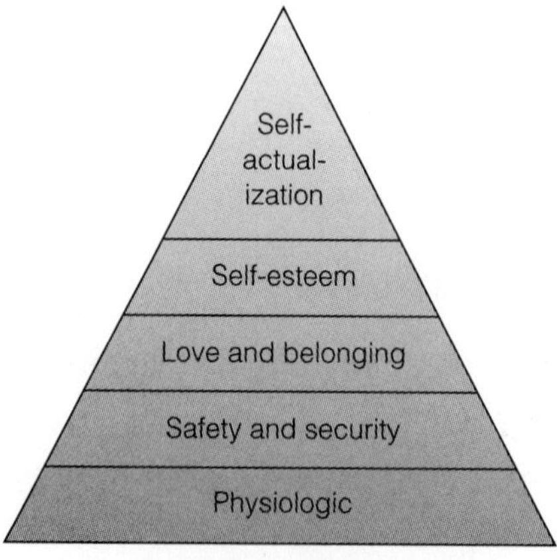

FIGURE 9-10. Maslow's hierarchy of needs

a) Physiological needs—includes those needs necessary to maintain body homeostasis (food, water, oxygen, sleep)
b) Safety (security)—controls number of hazards that can cause physical and mental damage as well as guaranteeing a stable and predictable environment
c) Love (social)—focuses on group acceptance, opportunity to give and receive friendship
d) Self-esteem (ego)—involves feelings of self-worth including achievement, confidence, competence, and status
e) Self-actualization (self-fulfillment)—focuses on a positive tendency for development, growth, and self-enhancement

2. *Health belief model*—based on views that an individual's decision to engage in healthy behavior depends on three components
   a) Patient's chance of susceptibility to disease
   b) If occurrence of disease will have some impact on patient's life
   c) If the benefits of taking action outweigh barriers to that action

B. Priorities—involves judgments made concerning relative importance of one diagnosis/decision over another

C. Goals of the appointment(s)—include broad-based statements that identify specific indicators to measure patient performance

1. Related specifically to dental hygiene diagnosis
2. Reflects patient's expected outcomes
3. Guides the dental hygiene and patient interventions required to achieve desired outcome

III. PRINCIPLES OF LEARNING

A. Concepts

1. Learning is more effective when an individual is physiologically and psychologically ready to learn
2. Motivation is essential for learning
3. Learner has to recognize and understand what is being taught and will learn only what is useful
4. Learning takes place more rapidly when what is being taught has meaning

B. Learning ladder—designed to demonstrate how individuals learn in a sequential series of steps (Figure 9-11)

1. Unawareness—possessing limited or inaccurate information
2. Awareness—obtaining correct information, but does not possess any personal meaning
3. Self-interest—recognizing prospective objective with slight inclination to act
4. Involvement—attitude is influenced and action is forthcoming
5. Action—new concepts and practices are tested
6. Habit—commitment is reached in performing behavior

IV. PRINCIPLES OF TEACHING

A. Show, Tell, Do—effective in helping children overcome a fearful situation

1. Show and tell patient what service will be provided
2. Provide service

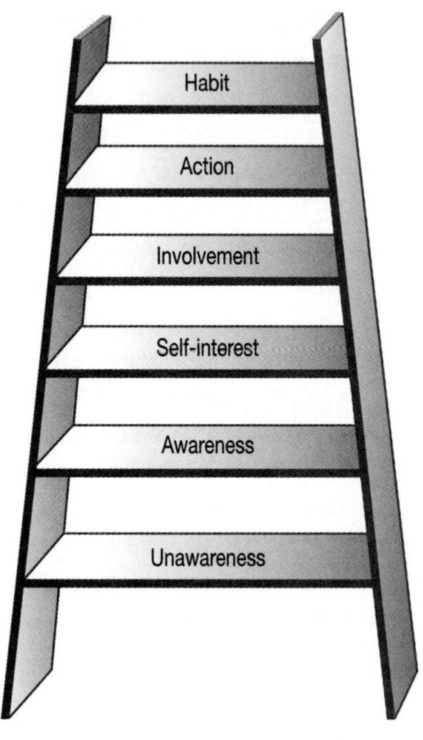

FIGURE 9-11. Learning ladder

V. PLAQUE DEVELOPMENT

A. Plaque is a dense, organized bacterial system embedded in an intermicrobial matrix that adheres closely to teeth, calculus, and other structures in oral cavity

B. Life Cycle

1. Acquired pellicle
    a) Organic layer that forms within a couple of hours on a cleaned tooth surface
    b) Includes four stages of formation
        (1) Bathing of tooth by salivary fluids containing protein constituents
        (2) Selective absorption of certain negatively and positively charged glycoproteins
        (3) Loss of solubility of absorbed proteins
        (4) Alteration of glycoproteins by enzymes from bacteria and oral secretions
2. Bacterial colonization—accumulation of bacterial flora
    a) Types of bacteria
        (1) Supragingival—consists of a newly formed deposit (contains various Gram-positive species) and mature plaque (contains facultative anaerobic microorganisms)
        (2) Subgingival—contains motile, Gram-negative rods and spirochetes
    b) Timeline of colonization
        (1) Days 1 to 2—made up primarily of Gram-positive cocci: *Streptococcus mutans* and *Streptococcus sanguis*

(2) Days 2 to 4—includes predominantly cocci, increasing numbers of Gram-positive filamentous forms and slender rods
(3) Days 4 to 7—increase in filaments and more mixed flora with rods, filamentous forms, and fusobacteria; plaque located near gingival margin begins to develop a more mature flora (Gram-negative spirochetes and vibrios)
(4) Days 7 to 14—contains predominately spirochetes and vibrios, with an increase in white blood cells; more Gram-negative and anaerobic organisms are found
(5) Days 14 to 21—continual increase of spirochetes and vibrios, white blood cells, Gram-negative and anaerobic organisms

c) Supragingival plaque
(1) Origin—salivary microorganisms are selectively attracted to glycoproteins from acquired pellicle
(2) Location—extends from coronal to margin of free gingiva
(3) Distribution—begins on proximal surfaces and other protected areas
(4) Adhesion
(a) Attached bacterial plaque—firmly attach to acquired pellicle, other bacteria, and tooth surfaces
(b) Unattached (surface) bacterial plaque—loose; washed away by saliva or during swallowing
(5) Retention—found on rough surfaces of teeth or restorations, malpositioned teeth, and carious lesions
(6) Source—saliva

d) Subgingival plaque
(1) Origin—downward growth of bacteria from supragingival plaque
(2) Location—extends apically to base of sulcus
(3) Distribution—shallow pocket; undisturbed area in mouth
(4) Adhesion
(a) Attached bacterial plaque—includes tooth surface, subgingival pellicle, and calculus
(b) Unattached (loose) bacterial plaque—floats between adherent plaque on tooth and pocket epithelium
(5) Retention—pocket holds plaque against tooth; overhanging margins that extend into sulcus can also hold plaque
(6) Nutritional sources—include gingival crevicular fluid, inflammatory exudate, and leukocytes

3. Bacterial Mineralization—addition of mineral elements, such as calcium and phosphorus, to bacterial plaque; results in a hardened deposit

a) Supragingival calculus
(1) Nutrient source—saliva
(2) Color—white, creamy yellow, or gray; may be stained with food and/or beverages, tobacco, and other pigmenting agents

(3) Distribution—most commonly found near opening of salivary gland ducts; facial surfaces of maxillary molars and lingual surfaces of mandibular anterior teeth

b) Subgingival calculus

(1) Nutrient source—gingival crevicular fluid and inflammatory exudate

(2) Color—light to dark brown, dark green, or black

(3) Distributions—heaviest amount on proximal surfaces, lightest on facial surfaces; occurs with or without associated supragingival calculus deposits

C. Identification Methods

1. Plaque

a) Disclosing agents—selective dye in a solution, tablet, or lozenge form used to identify bacterial plaque on surfaces of teeth

b) Direct vision—plaque may be stained with beverages, food, or other pigmented agents making it easier to view; thick plaque may appear dull, with a furlike appearance

c) Tactile—plaque may feel slimy or slippery

2. Calculus

a) Visual examination

(1) If calculus is not stained, it may be necessary to utilize compressed air to “dehydrate” it to view supragingivally; deflect gingival margin for observation subgingivally

(2) Diseased gingival margin does not adapt closely to tooth surface where calculus is present

(3) Transillumination of anterior teeth depicts supragingival calculus as a dark, opaque, shadow-like area on proximal surface

b) Gingival tissue color change—dark calculus may reflect through gingival tissue

c) Tactile—utilization of probe or explorer can be used to detect supragingival and/or subgingival calculus deposits

VI. REMOVAL OF BACTERIAL PLAQUE—an essential component of the therapeutic approach in preventing and controlling many dental diseases

A. Manual toothbrushes

1. Components

a) Head—working end; consists of tufts of bristles that are made of nylon filaments or natural bristles from boar’s hair; all filaments should be soft and end-rounded

b) Handle—portion of toothbrush that is grasped

c) Shank—section that connects head to handle

2. Characteristics of an effective toothbrush—includes size, shape, and texture to conform to patient comfort

a) Size—should be selected based on size of patient’s mouth; large enough to remove plaque effectively, yet small enough to access all areas of the mouth

b) Shape

(1) Handle—modification may include angled, offset, angled and offset, small and narrow, large and wide, rounded, and squared; handle should allow patient to comfortably grasp toothbrush

(2) Head—may be designed in a diamond style or square; brushing plane may be flat, rippled, dome-shaped, or bilevel

c) Texture/firmness—involves bristle resistance to pressure; composition involves tufted or multitufted and diameter of bristle

(1) Tufted—five or six tufts long and three tufts across

(2) Multitufted—10 or 12 tufts in three or four rows; positioned in close proximity allowing for greater force during use

(3) Diameter—usual range for adult toothbrush bristles is between 0.007 and 0.015 inches (filament size)

3. Types of toothbrushes

a) Adult toothbrushes

(1) Soft toothbrush—bristles 0.007 to 0.009 inches in diameter

(2) Medium toothbrush—bristles 0.010 to 0.012 inches in diameter

(3) Hard toothbrush—bristles 0.013 to 0.014 inches in diameter

(4) Extra hard toothbrush—bristles 0.015 inches in diameter

b) Child toothbrush—bristles are shorter and diameter is reduced to 0.005 inches

4. Toothbrushing

a) General objectives

(1) Remove plaque and disturb reformation

(2) Clean teeth of food, debris, and stain contained in plaque

(3) Stimulate gingival tissues

(4) Used to apply dentifrice or therapeutic agents

b) Methods

(1) Horizontal—position bristles perpendicular to crown of tooth; brush in a back-and-forth horizontal pattern

(2) Fones—position bristles perpendicular to crown of tooth; brush in a circular (rotary) motion

(3) Leonard—up-and-down brushing motion over facial surfaces of closed posterior teeth

(4) Stillman—position bristles at a 45-degree angle to apex of tooth, with part of brush resting on gingiva and other part on teeth; move brush using a vibratory motion while applying slight pressure; lift brush and repeat in next area

(5) Charter—place brush at a 90-degree angle to long axis of tooth so bristles are gently forced between teeth, but do not rest on gingiva; move brush in several small rotary motions keeping bristles in contact with gingival margin

(6) Bass—place brush at a 45-degree angle to tooth apex; apply gentle pressure so bristles enter sulcus; use a vibratory motion (horizontal jiggle) to activate bristles

(7) Roll—position bristles parallel to and against attached gingiva; turn wrist to flex bristles first against gingiva and then facial surface; roll bristles coronally

c) Modified techniques
   (1) Modified Stillman and Charters—position bristles in same position as original method, then gently begin a vibratory motion; slowly press-roll bristles coronally continuing vibratory motion during roll
   (2) Bass—sulcular brushing is done either before or after use of rolling method
d) General considerations when recommending a specific technique
   (1) Consider patient's oral health status: number of teeth, alignment, mouth size, removable prostheses, orthodontic appliances, periodontal status, and gingival condition
   (2) Review patient's systemic health status, muscular and joint diseases, and mental capabilities
   (3) Patient's age
   (4) Patient's interest and motivation
   (5) Patient's manual dexterity
   (6) Ease and effectiveness in explaining and demonstrating toothbrushing technique

B. Automatic (powered) toothbrushes—battery or electrical

1. Components
   a) Head—usually smaller than manual toothbrushes; removable to allow for replacement; three basic patterns
      (1) Reciprocating—back-and-forth motion
      (2) Arcuate—up-and-down motion
      (3) Elliptical—combination of reciprocating and arcuate motions
   b) Shank—connects into handle
   c) Handle—contains power device (battery or electric current); portion of toothbrush that is held
2. Indications for use
   a) Parental brushing of children
   b) Physically and mentally compromised
   c) Elderly
   d) Arthritic/poor dexterity
   e) Poorly motivated
   f) Patients who require a large handle
3. Methods of use—follow manufacturer's directions

C. Dental floss

1. Types
   a) Waxed—contains wax coating
      (1) Indications for use—normal contact areas, irregular tooth surfaces, defective or overhanging restorations
      (2) Contraindications—tight contact areas
   b) Unwaxed
      (1) Indications for use—tight contact areas
      (2) Contraindications—crowded teeth, heavy calculus deposits, defective or overhanging restorations

c) Tape—broad and flat waxed floss
(1) Indications for use—interdental space without tight contact areas
(2) Contraindications—none
d) Polytetrafluoroethylene—made of synthetic material
(1) Indications for use—tight contact areas and rough proximal tooth surfaces
(2) Contraindications—none
e) Tufted floss (Super Floss)—contains a portion of waxed floss, followed by thicker tufted floss, and then a portion of flexible plastic at the end
(1) Indications for use—bridges and diastemas
(2) Contraindications—presence of interdental papilla

2. Method of use
a) Use approximately 18 inches of floss
b) Wind bulk of floss around middle finger of one hand and remaining floss lightly around same finger of other hand
c) Secure floss with thumb and index finger of each hand leaving 3/4 to 1 inch of floss between hands
d) Use thumb and index finger to guide floss between teeth using a see-saw motion
e) Once past contact point, adapt floss to each interproximal surface by creating a C-shape
f) Move floss in an apical-coronal motion several times
g) Repeat procedure on adjacent interproximal tooth with care to prevent damage to interproximal papilla
h) Gently guide floss out of contact area using see-saw motion
i) Obtain clean area of floss for next tooth

3. Accomplishments achieved by using floss
a) Removes plaque and debris that adhere to teeth, restorations, orthodontic appliances, fixed prostheses, interproximal gingiva, and implants
b) Aids in identifying presence of subgingival calculus, overhanging restorations, and interproximal carious lesions
c) Reduces gingival bleeding
d) May be used as a vehicle for applying polishing or chemotherapeutic agents to proximal or subgingival areas

D. Interdental brush—small, spiral bristle brush; core of brush that holds bristles may be made of plastic, wire, or a nylon-coated wire

1. Indications for use
a) Provides plaque removal at interproximal areas, in and around furcations, orthodontic bands, and fixed prostheses with large spaces present
b) Provides gingival stimulation
c) Applies chemotherapeutic agents

2. Contraindications—avoid using when healthy interproximal papilla is present

3. Method of use
   a) Moisten brush
   b) Insert at an angle approximating normal gingival contour
   c) Activate by using an in-and-out motion

E. Single tufted brush—single-tufted or group of small tufts (e.g., end-tuft and unituft)

1. Indications for use—use on regions not easily reached with other devices
   a) Irregular gingival margins around migrated or malposed teeth
   b) Lingual and palatal tissues that elicit a gag reflex with a full-size toothbrush
   c) Distal areas of most posterior teeth
   d) Orthodontic appliances
   e) Pontics
   f) Precision attachments associated with crown and bridge or implant abutments
2. Contraindications—avoid using when a normal contact area presents itself with interproximal papilla
3. Method of use
   a) Direct end of tuft into proximal area and along gingival margin
   b) Combine rotating motion with intermittent pressure
   c) Use sulcular brushing stroke

F. Toothpicks—utilized with a holder, the toothpick can be more effectively applied at proper angle and access hard-to-reach areas (Figure 9-12)

1. Indications for use
   a) Plaque removal at and just beneath gingival margin
   b) Interdental cleaning of concave proximal tooth surfaces

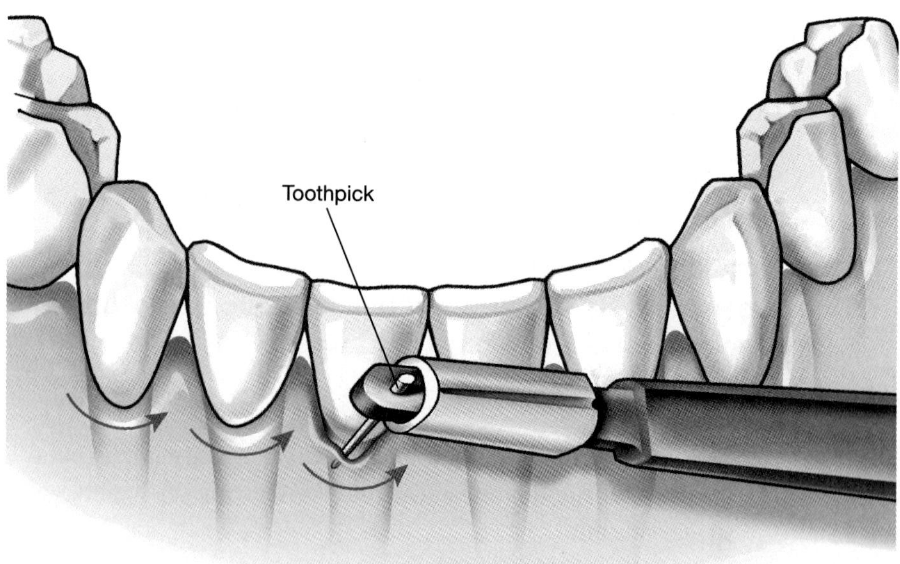

FIGURE 9-12. Use of toothpick in holder. Apply toothpick perpendicular to gingival margin and trace gently around the margin.

   c) Exposed furcation areas
   d) Orthodontic appliances
   e) Application of chemotherapeutics
   f) Fixed prostheses
2. Contraindications—avoid subgingival insertion or vigorous proximal use to prevent gingival damage
3. Method of use
   a) Moisten toothpick
   b) Apply toothpick perpendicular to gingival margin
   c) Use moderate pressure, trace around gingival margin of each tooth

G. Wedge stimulators—plastic or wooden triangular aids used for removing plaque (Figure 9-13)

1. Indications for use—interdental areas with tooth surfaces and no interdental gingiva
2. Contraindications—avoid using in presence of interdental gingiva
3. Method of use
   a) Soften wood
   b) Insert wedge from facial aspect with flat surface of triangular base resting on gingiva and tip of wedge angled coronally
   c) Move wedge in and out while applying moderate pressure and using a burnishing stroke

H. Gauze strips—6-inch piece of gauze bandage

1. Indications for use—proximal surfaces of teeth adjacent to edentulous areas, teeth that are widely spaced, or implant abutments

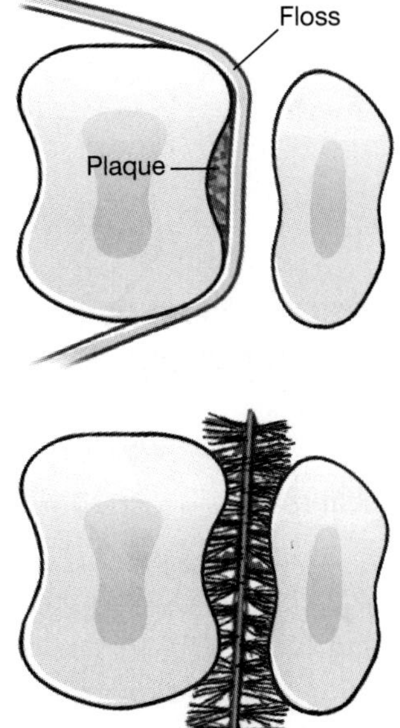

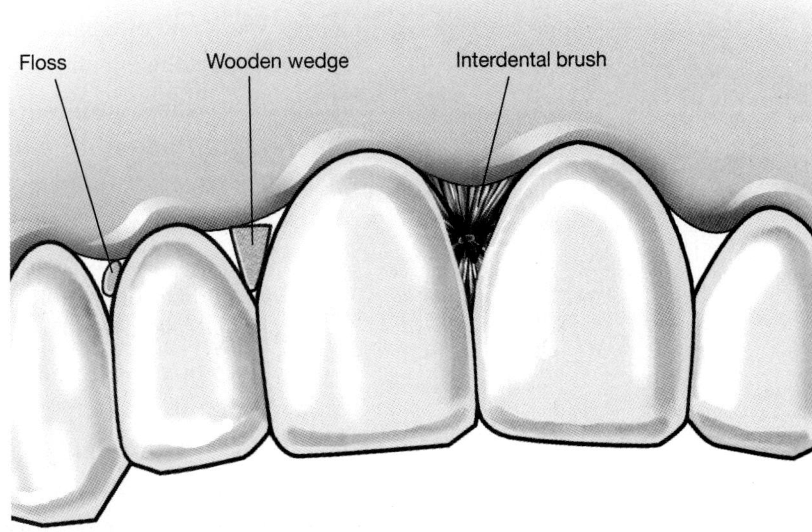

FIGURE 9-13. Use of wooden wedge, interdental brush, and floss

2. Contraindications—interproximal spaces with presence of interdental gingiva
3. Method of use
   a) Fold in half a 1-inch wide, 6-inch long gauze bandage
   b) Place fold toward gingiva
   c) Adapt gauze by wrapping it around the exposed proximal surface to facial and lingual line angles
   d) Activate by using a "shoeshine" stroke from facial to lingual

I. Knitting yarn

1. Indications for use
   a) Proximal cleaning in areas where interdental papillae have receded
   b) Abutments of fixed prostheses
   c) Isolated teeth
   d) Teeth separated by diastemas
   e) Distal surface of most posterior teeth
2. Contraindications—avoid using wool yarn where interdental gingiva is present
3. Method of use
   a) Fold yarn in half using approximately 8 inches
   b) Thread and tie approximately 8 inches of dental floss
   c) Insert floss through contact area and draw yarn into embrasure
   d) Clean tooth surface with a facial-lingual stroke

J. Pipe cleaner

1. Indications for use
   a) Proximal surfaces where interdental gingiva is missing
   b) Open furcation areas
2. Contraindications—avoid using on implants and where interdental gingiva is present and furcation areas are not exposed
3. Method of use
   a) Use one third of a regular pipe cleaner
   b) Work end of cleaner through space
   c) Activate using an in-and-out motion

K. Rubber tip stimulator—conical or pyramidal flexible rubber or plastic tip attached to a handle or to end of toothbrush

1. Indications for use
   a) Cleans debris from interdental area
   b) Removes plaque at and just below gingival margin
2. Contraindications—none
3. Method of use
   a) Place tip at 90-degree angle to long axis of tooth
   b) Utilize moderate pressure while tracing along gingival margin or use an in-and-out motion in open embrasure area

L. Floss holder—Y-shaped or C-shaped yokes with handle allowing patient to manipulate floss by holding handle

1. Indications for use for patients who
   a) Have large hands

   b) Are physically challenged
   c) Lack normal dexterity
   d) Have caregivers providing oral care
   e) Prefer not to put hands in mouth
2. Contraindications—none
3. Method of use
   a) Tightly secure floss between two prongs of yoke
   b) Use same technique as described for flossing

M. Bridge (floss) threader—blunt-ended, needle-like device made of a stiff, yet flexible, plastic or a plastic loop where floss is inserted

1. Indications for use; carries floss
   a) Through embrasure areas under contact points too tight for floss insertion
   b) Between proximal surface and gingiva of abutment teeth of fixed prostheses
   c) Under pontics
   d) Around orthodontic appliances
   e) Under splinting
2. Contraindications—avoid using in areas where regular flossing can be utilized
3. Method of use
   a) Insert floss into threader
   b) Direct end of threader into target area
   c) Disengage floss from threader to adapt to tooth surface
   d) Utilize flossing technique previously described

N. Oral irrigator—targeted application of a pulsated or steady stream of water or other irrigant used for cleansing and/or therapeutic purposes

1. Indications for use—flush away loosely adherent microflora located coronal to gingival margin
2. Contraindications—avoid using on patients with a possible risk to subacute bacterial endocarditis
3. Method of use
   a) Direct jet tip toward interdental area holding tip at right angle to long axis of tooth
   b) Start on lowest pressure setting, increase slightly over time depending on condition of gingiva and tissue comfort
   c) Lean over sink
   d) Trace around each tooth spending extra time at interproximal areas

VII. DENTIFRICES—substance used with a toothbrush or other applicator to remove bacterial plaque, materia alba, and debris from gingiva and teeth for cosmetic purposes, and for applying specific agents to tooth surfaces for therapeutic purposes

A. Types

1. *Cosmetic*—improves appearance of teeth (i.e., to remove stain)

2. *Therapeutic*—reduces some disease in mouth
   a) Fluoride-containing dentifrice—contains up to 260 mg of fluoride; safe and effective fluoride content for over-the-counter dentifrice is 0.22% for NaF, 0.76% for MFP, and for 0.4% SnF_2
   b) Baking soda-peroxide-fluoride dentifrice (e.g., Mentadent)—combination of 0.75% stable peroxide gel, baking soda, and 1100 ppm sodium fluoride
   c) Antimicrobial dentifrices
      (1) Chemical compounds used to supplement usual brushing and flossing in mechanical plaque control
      (2) Stannous salts have reported activity against caries, plaque and gingivitis
         (a) Marketed in United States as Crest Gum Care
         (b) Has shown superior efficacy in antimicrobial, plaque acidogenicity, gingivitis or gingival bleeding, and tartar control
      (3) Triclosan—broad-spectrum antibacterial agent effective against wide variety of bacteria
         (a) Marketed in United States as Colgate Total
         (b) Approved by FDA in July 1997 as the first dentifrice to help prevent gingivitis, plaque, and caries
         (c) Received ADA's Seal of Acceptance for its benefit in reducing gingivitis, plaque, caries, and tartar

B. Components

1. Humectants—retain moisture and prevent drying once exposed to air; help stabilize preparation
2. Preservatives—prevent bacterial growth; help prolong shelf life
3. Sweetening agents—impart pleasant flavor for patient acceptance
4. Flavoring agents—make dentifrice desirable; mask other ingredients that may have a less pleasant flavor
5. Coloring agents—enhance attractiveness

C. Other dentifrices

1. Antitartar
   a) Tetrasodium phosphate and disodium dihydrogen pyrophosphate (e.g., Crest Tartar Control)
   b) Zinc citrate trihydrate—tartar control versions for Aim and Close-Up
   c) ADA seal has not been awarded to anticalculus products because ADA considers calculus inhibition a cosmetic effect; seal is awarded due to anticaries effect of these products
2. Antihypersensitivity—active agents include potassium nitrate, strontium chloride, and sodium citrate

VIII. FLUORIDE—salt of hydrofluoric acid; stored primarily in bones and teeth

A. Actions of fluoride

1. Enters dental plaque and affects bacteria by depressing their production of acid, thereby reducing possibility of demineralization of teeth

2. Reacts with mineral elements on surface of tooth to make enamel less soluble to acid end-products of bacterial metabolism
3. Facilitates remineralization of teeth that have been demineralized

B. Systemic—pertaining to or affecting whole body

1. Sources
    a) Community water fluoridation
    b) Dietary fluoride supplements including fluoride drops, tablets, and lozenges, and vitamins with fluoride
    c) Occurs naturally in food
2. Community water fluoridation
    a) Fluoride is added to community drinking water supply
    b) Most economical method of caries prevention
    c) Cost varies depending on size of community and cost of installation and running of a water fluoridation plant; ranges from \$0.12 to \$5.41/person/year or an average of \$0.51/person/year
    d) Benefits—inhibits dental caries in primary and permanent teeth; inhibits coronal and root caries
    e) Range—0.7 to 1.2 ppm; hotter climate = lower end of range, colder climate = higher end of range
3. Dietary supplements—include liquid drops, tablets, lozenges, and oral rinses; ingested and absorbed into blood system (Table 9-2)
    a) People benefitting from fluoride supplements are those who
        (1) Use a private water supply that does not have natural fluoride and is not practical to fluoridate
        (2) Have access to less than optimum fluoride in the water
        (3) Live in community where water supply has not yet been fluoridated
    b) Method of use
        (1) May be prescribed on an individual basis for use at home or administered to school classroom groups
        (2) If in tablet form, chew first (added topical effect)
        (3) Swish mixture (either liquid or chewed tablet mixed with saliva) for 1 minute
        (4) Do not eat or drink for 30 minutes

C. Topical—localized; on the surface; pertaining to a particular spot

1. Professionally applied—decreases caries by 30% to 40%
    a) Indications for use
        (1) Primary teeth

TABLE 9-2 SUPPLEMENTAL FLUORIDE DOSAGES

	Concentration of Fluoride in Water (ppm)		
Age	**≤ 0.3**	**0.3 to 0.6**	**≥ 0.6**
6 mo to 3 yr	0.25	0	0
3 to 6 yr	0.5	0.25	0
6 to 16 yr	1	0.5	0

(2) Posteruptive (postmaturation) period—2-year period of maturation after tooth has erupted
(3) Active caries—new carious lesions at regular maintenance appointment
(4) Secondary/recurrent caries—adjacent to previous restorations
(5) Wearing orthodontic appliances
(6) Compromised salivary flow
(7) Teeth supporting an overdenture
(8) Exposed root surfaces
(9) Lack of compliance and conscientious efforts for daily bacterial plaque removal
(10) Low or no fluoride in drinking water
(11) Early carious lesions

b) Types
- (1) Stannous fluoride
  - (a) Recommended and approved concentration is 8%
  - (b) pH is between 2.4 to 2.8
  - (c) Aqueous solutions are not stable due to formation of stannous hydroxide and stannic oxide; solutions must be prepared immediately before use
  - (d) Taste is bitter and metallic
  - (e) May cause extrinsic brown staining of teeth and gingival irritation
  - (f) Consists of 19,360 ppm of fluoride
- (2) Sodium fluoride
  - (a) Recommended for use in 2% concentration
  - (b) Recommended 4 applications be given 1 week apart for children ages 3, 7, 10, and 13
  - (c) Has an acceptable taste
  - (d) Does not discolor teeth or cause gingival irritation
  - (e) pH is 9.2 (basic)
  - (f) Consists of 9040 ppm of fluoride
- (3) Acidulated phosphate fluoride
  - (a) Recommended for use in 1.23% concentration; generally obtained by use of 2.0% NaF and 0.34% hydrofluoric acid
  - (b) Available as an aqueous solution or gel in *thixotropic* base—gel that is able to liquefy when agitated and revert to a gelatinous state on standing
  - (c) pH is between 3.0 to 3.5
  - (d) Consists of 12,300 ppm of fluoride
  - (e) Causes surface roughening, pitting or etching of porcelain and composite restorations
- (4) Varnishes
  - (a) Recommended especially for children
  - (b) Contains 5% sodium fluoride; treatment usually requires only 0.3 to 0.5 ml of varnish, which contains 3 to 6 mg of fluoride
  - (c) Retained for 24 to 48 hours

c) Application methods
   (1) Paint-on technique (solution or gel)
      (a) Isolate teeth utilizing cotton rolls and cotton roll holders—maxillary and mandibular of one side for adults, maxillary and mandibular separately for children
      (b) Place dry-angle over Stensen's duct opening
      (c) Activate saliva ejector
      (d) Dry teeth
      (e) Moisten all teeth with fluoride, starting with mandibular arch first
      (f) Start timer for appropriate length of time
      (g) Keep surfaces moistened throughout the timing; press solution or gel into interproximal areas
      (h) At end of timing, wipe teeth briefly to remove excess gel or solution
      (i) Instruct patient to expectorate and not swallow
      (j) Proceed to other half of mouth
      (k) Instruct patient not to eat or drink for at least 30 minutes after application
   (2) Tray technique (gel or foam)
      (a) Choose appropriate tray size—deep enough to cover entire exposed enamel
      (b) Seat patient in upright position
      (c) Load fluoride into tray—2 ml maximum for children and 2.5 ml maximum for adults (avoid overfilling)
      (d) Dry teeth thoroughly with air syringe
      (e) Insert mandibular tray and press against teeth
      (f) Insert maxillary tray and press against teeth
      (g) Insert saliva ejector between trays
      (h) Place cotton roll between trays on opposite side to prevent dislodging of trays
      (i) Leave in place for appropriate amount of time
      (j) Remove trays and request patient to expectorate, making sure patient does not swallow fluoride
      (k) Remove remaining fluoride with suction device
      (l) Instruct patient not to eat or drink for at least 30 minutes

2. Self-applied—includes prescription and over-the-counter products
   a) Application methods
      (1) Custom tray—fill tray with appropriate amount and type of fluoride (APF 0.5%, NaF 1.1%, and SnF_2 0.4%) and leave in mouth for designated amount of time
      (2) Rinse—patient swishes for 1 minute with appropriate amount of fluoride and then expectorates
      (3) Toothbrushing—fluoride gel or paste is used two or three times daily
   b) Types
      (1) Stannous fluoride—daily rinse (0.63%) and brush-on gel (0.4%) forms

(2) Sodium fluoride—daily (0.05%) and weekly (0.2%) rinses, and 1.19% gel applied in tray
(3) Acidulated phosphate—0.5% brush-on or gel applied in tray

c) Indications for use
  (1) Stannous fluoride
    (a) 0.63% daily rinse—use for high susceptibility to root surface caries and dentinal hypersensitivity
    (b) 0.4% brush on gel—use for high caries rate and hypersensitivity
  (2) Sodium fluoride
    (a) 0.05% daily rinse—use on children over 6 years of age and adults with caries susceptibility
    (b) 0.2% weekly rinse—use for school-based programs
    (c) 1.19% gel in a tray—use for rampant caries and when patient is undergoing radiation therapy
  (3) Acidulated phosphate fluoride—0.5% brush-on gel or applied in tray for rampant caries

3. Toxicity—state or quality of being poisonous
  a) Acute fluoride toxicity—rapid intake of an excess dose over a short time; average lethal dose is 4 to 5 grams. *Note:* Generally death from acute fluoride toxicity occurs within 4 hours of ingestion
    (1) Signs
      (a) Nausea (caused by formation of hydrofluoric acid in the stomach)
      (b) Vomiting
      (c) Hypersalivation
      (d) Abdominal pain
      (e) Diarrhea
      (f) Cramping of arms and legs due to drop in blood calcium
      (g) Bronchospasm
      (h) Cardiac arrest
      (i) Ventricular fibrillation
      (j) Fixed and dilated pupils
      (k) Hyperkalemia and hypocalcemia
    (2) Treatment—urgency of treatment is based on number of multiples of 5mg/kg of fluoride ingested. *Note:* The blood reaches its maximum level 1/2 to 1 hour after ingestion of fluoride (Table 9-3)
      (a) Induce vomiting (e.g., ipecac syrup or digital stimulation)
      (b) Ingest fluoride-binding agents (e.g., milk, lime water, liquid or gel antacids that contain aluminum or magnesium hydroxide)
      (c) Seek medical attention, if needed (maintain blood calcium levels with intravenous calcium, gastric lavage, and/or blood dialysis)

TABLE 9-3 EMERGENCY TREATMENT FOR ACUTE FLUORIDE TOXICITY

Milligram Fluoride Ion per Kilogram of Body Weight	Treatment
Less than 5mg/kg	1. Ingest fluoride-binding agent. 2. Observe for a few hours. 3. Induced vomiting is NOT necessary.
More than 5mg/kg (toxic dose)	1. Induce vomiting. 2. Ingest fluoride binding. 3. Seek medical attention.
More than 15mg/kg (lethal dose)	1. Seek medical attention. 2. Induce vomiting. 3. Begin cardiac monitoring.

b) Chronic—long-term ingestion of fluoride in amounts that exceed approved therapeutic levels
  (1) Factors that increase severity of chronic fluoride toxicity
    (a) Increase in consumption of naturally fluoridated water
    (b) Elevated intake of fluoride in food
    (c) Nutritional diseases
    (d) Low calcium diets

c) Dental fluorosis—developmental defect of enamel that occurs when an excessive amount of fluoride is ingested during period of enamel formation
  (1) Hypomineralized fluorotic region appears as matte white or opaque
  (2) Usually symmetrical in mouth
  (3) Different clinical degrees of fluorosis include
    (a) Normal—no fluorosis
    (b) Questionable—few white flecks or white spots (snow-capping); usually involve incisal edges of anterior teeth or cusps of posterior teeth
    (c) Very mild—small opaque areas involving < 25% of surface
    (d) Mild—white opacities are more extensive, but involve < 50% of surface
    (e) Moderate—all enamel surfaces are affected with frequent brown staining
    (f) Severe—discrete pitting, brown stains are widespread, with all enamel surface affected; teeth are not discolored at time of eruption—discoloration is due to posteruptive uptake of exogenous stains from diet

IX. MOUTH RINSES

A. Types

1. Cosmetic—improve appearance of oral cavity (e.g., reduce oral malodor)

2. Therapeutic—reduce some disease in mouth (e.g., dental caries, bacterial plaque, gingivitis); *does not* kill all bacteria in mouth; it reduces the number

B. Ingredients

1. Oxygenating agents
   a) Purpose—cleanse by effervescent action; short-lasting antimicrobial effect; -only as long as oxygen is being released
   b) Adverse effects—long-term use results in overgrowth of bacteria resulting in black hairy tongue
   c) Other information —common ingredients include hydrogen peroxide, sodium perborate, and urea peroxide
2. Chlorhexidine gluconate—0.12% prescription plaque control rinse
   a) Purpose
      (1) Absorbed into teeth and pellicle
      (2) Time-released over 12 to 24 hours (substantivity), prolonging bacteriocidal effect
      (3) Lysis cell wall consisting of Gram-positive and -negative microorganisms and fungi
   b) Adverse effects
      (1) Brown staining of teeth
      (2) Temporary loss of taste
      (3) Bitter taste
      (4) Dryness, soreness, and burning sensation of mucosa
      (5) Epithelial desquamation
      (6) Discoloration of teeth, tongue, and restorations
      (7) Slight increase in supragingival calculus formation
   c) Additional information
      (1) Available in other parts of world as 0.2% solution
      (2) Used as a preprocedural rinse to lower oral bacterial count
      (3) Decreases supragingival bacterial plaque formation and inhibits development of gingivitis
      (4) Used for short-term adjunctive therapy after surgical treatment that limits mechanical plaque control
      (5) Used on selective patients to control inflammation in necrotizing ulcerative gingivitis
      (6) Used on selective patients to encourage and motivate when oral hygiene has been neglected for a period of time
      (7) Suppresses growth of *Streptococcus mutans*
      (8) Should not be used immediately before or after regular toothbrushing as it is inactivated by most dentifrice surfactants
      (9) Used as a 30-second rinse, twice daily, with 1 oz of solution
      (10) Common names include Peridex and Perioguard
3. Essential oils/phenolic compounds
   a) Purpose—antiplaque and antigingivitis compounds
   b) Adverse effects—has a bitter taste
   c) Other information
      (1) Active ingredients include thymol, menthol, eucalyptol, and methyl salicylate

(2) Original formula contains 26.9% alcohol; other variety contains 21.6% alcohol
(3) Reduces both plaque accumulation and severity of gingivitis by up to 34%
(4) Common name is Listerine

d) Quaternary ammonia compounds
(1) Purpose
(a) Decreases bacterial cell wall permeability and metabolism
(b) Possesses no substantivity
(c) Recommended to control halitosis, not gingivitis

e) Sanguinarine—alters bacterial cell wall structure and may inhibit bacterial adhesion

f) Stannous fluoride
(1) Purpose
(a) May possess antiplaque properties
(b) May alter bacterial cell metabolism or cell adhesion properties
(c) May reduce plaque for a short-time; long-term benefits are unknown

X. PIT AND FISSURE SEALANTS

A. Composed of an organic polymer (resin) that flows into the pits or fissures and bonds to enamel surface mainly by mechanical retention

B. Thin plastic coating placed in pits and fissures of teeth to act as a physical barrier to decay

C. Types

1. Light cured (*photopolymerization*)—material hardens when exposed to an ultraviolet or visible blue light
   a) Operator initiates polymerization at any suitable time
   b) Requires a special curing light
   c) No mixing or measuring of materials is necessary
   d) Has a short polymerization time (20 to 30 seconds)
   e) Has less porocities than self-cured, after hardening process is complete
2. Self-cured (*autopolymerization*)—material hardens because of reaction between monomer and catalyst
   a) Mixing of monomer and catalyst creates a strong chemical bond
   b) Setting time cannot be controlled once catalyst is added
   c) Has a long polymerization time (1 to 3 minutes)

D. Criteria for placement

1. Indications for use—deep occlusal fissures, fossas, or lingual pits
2. Contraindications
   a) Patient behavior does not permit a dry field throughout the procedure
   b) Open occlusal carious lesion exists
   c) Caries exist on other surfaces of same tooth
   d) Large occlusal restoration is already present

3. Probable indications
   a) Fossa is well isolated from another fossa with a restoration
   b) Area is confined to a fully erupted fossa even though the distal fossa is impossible to seal due to inadequate eruption
   c) Intact occlusal surface is present where contralateral tooth surface is carious or restored
   d) Incipient lesion exists in pit and fissure

E. Clinical procedure

1. Remove deposits and debris
   a) All heavy stains, deposits, and debris should be off crown surface before applying sealant
   b) Use a polishing cup and brush with pumice (containing no fluoride) or an air polisher
2. Isolate tooth
   a) Keep tooth clean and dry eliminating possible contamination by saliva
   b) Keep material from contacting oral tissues and patient from swallowing material
   c) Use a rubber dam, cotton rolls, and bibulous pads over opening of parotid (Stensen's) duct
3. Dry tooth
   a) Prepare for acid etch
   b) Eliminate moisture and contamination
   c) Use air syringe and high volume evacuation to help keep area dry and free from saliva
4. Acid etch
   a) Purpose
      (1) Creates micropores to increase surface area, which provides retention for sealant
      (2) Removes contamination from enamel
      (3) Provides antibacterial action
   b) Procedure using phosphoric acid (15%–50%)
      (1) Liquid—apply continuously with brush, sponge, or cotton pellet using a dabbing motion; low viscosity allows for easy flow into pit or fissure, but may be difficult to control
      (2) Gel etch—apply gel and leave undisturbed; tinted gel with thick consistency allows for increased visibility and control, but may be difficult to rinse off tooth surface
      (3) Etch for 15 to 60 seconds—follow manufacturer's directions
5. Rinse thoroughly 10 to 15 seconds with water syringe; apply suction to prevent saliva from reaching etched surface and dry. *Note:* Repeat etching process if surface does not appear white and chalky
6. Replace cotton rolls, if needed
7. Apply sealant material—follow manufacturer's directions; allow liquid sealant to flow freely onto etched enamel surface, avoiding marginal ridges and cusp tips; avoid overfilling to a high, flat surface

8. Curing process
   a) Photopolymerization
      (1) Wear eye protection
      (2) Cover entire tooth surface, keeping tip distance approximately 2 mm from tooth
      (3) Cure for 20 to 30 seconds, in accordance with manufacturer's instructions
   b) Autopolymerization—takes approximately 2 to 3 minutes; check with explorer for hardness
9. Postapplication inspection
   a) Explorer—feel for a hard, smooth surface; if incomplete coverage or air bubbles are detected, a reapplication of the sealant material is necessary
   b) Articulating paper—locate high spots; adjust as required
10. Follow-up evaluation should be performed every 6 months

DIRECTIONS Each of the questions or incomplete statements below is followed by suggested answers or completions. Select the **one** answer that is best in each case.

1. The maximum amount of pressure exerted against the walls of blood vessel is called
   A. pulse.
   B. diastolic pressure.
   C. systolic pressure.
   D. cardiac output.

2. To determine the proper size of a blood pressure cuff, the width needs to be 20%
   A. less than the diameter of the upper arm.
   B. greater than the diameter of the upper arm.
   C. less than the diameter of the lower arm.
   D. greater than the diameter of the lower arm.

3. All of the following are types of manometers EXCEPT one. Which one is the EXCEPTION?
   A. mercury
   B. aneroid
   C. titanium
   D. electronic

4. All of the following factors can INCREASE blood pressure EXCEPT one. Which one is the EXCEPTION?
   A. fainting
   B. stimulants
   C. use of oral contraceptives
   D. eating

5. All of the following factors can DECREASE body temperature EXCEPT one. Which one is the EXCEPTION?
   A. starvation
   B. hyperthyroidism
   C. hemorrhage
   D. physiological shock

6. Which of the following arteries is found in the antecubital space?
   A. radial
   B. facial
   C. carotid
   D. brachial

7. Which of the following palpation methods involves using both hands at the same time to examine corresponding structures on opposite sides of the body?
   A. bilateral
   B. bimanual
   C. digital
   D. bidigital

8. Using G.V. Black's classification system, which of the following is the correct description of a Class V carious lesion?
   A. radiographic decay on the mesial of #30
   B. explorer detectable decay on the occlusal of #30
   C. explorer detectable decay on the mesial-lingual cusp tip of #30

D. explorer detectable decay on the lingual cervical third of #30

9. A patient presents with the following occlusal classification: The mesial surface of the permanent maxillary canine is distal to the distal surface of the permanent mandibular canine by at least the width of a premolar. Which of the following is the patient's occlusal classification?
   A. Class I
   B. Class II, Division I
   C. Class II, Division II
   D. Class III

10. An anterior crossbite involves the maxillary incisors being facial to the mandibular incisors. A posterior crossbite involves the facial cusps of the maxillary posterior teeth being positioned facial to the facial cusps of the mandibular posterior teeth.
   A. The first statement is TRUE, the second statement is FALSE.
   B. Both statements are TRUE.
   C. The first statement is FALSE, the second statement is TRUE.
   D. Both statements are FALSE.

11. A periodontal assessment of #19 reveals 3 mm from the cementoenamel junction (CEJ) to the gingival margin and 4 mm from gingival margin to the base of the pocket. In millimeters, what is the total (actual) amount of recession?
   A. 1
   B. 3
   C. 4
   D. 7

12. In the principles of learning, from the lowest to highest stages of the learning ladder, which of the following is the correct order?
   A. awareness, unawareness, involvement, self-interest, action, habit
   B. unawareness, awareness, involvement, action, self-interest, habit
   C. unawareness, awareness, self-interest, involvement, habit, action
   D. unawareness, awareness, self-interest, involvement, action, habit

13. All of the following describe supragingival calculus EXCEPT one. Which one is the EXCEPTION?
   A. Its nutrient sources are gingival crevicular fluid and inflammatory exudate.
   B. Its color can vary depending on agents that pigment it.
   C. It is commonly located on the facial of maxillary molars.
   D. It is commonly located on the lingual of mandibular incisors.

14. All of following are objectives of toothbrushing EXCEPT one. Which one is the EXCEPTION?
   A. remove calculus and disturb reformation
   B. remove food debris
   C. stimulate gingival tissues
   D. apply therapeutic agents

15. Placing the toothbrush at a 45-degree angle to the apex of the tooth, with part of the brush resting on the gingiva and the other part on the tooth, represents which of the following toothbrushing methods?
   A. Bass
   B. Charters
   C. Fones
   D. Stillman

16. Which of the following factors do NOT need to be considered when recommending a specific toothbrushing technique?
   A. patient's oral health
   B. size of toothbrush
   C. patient's systemic health status
   D. patient's manual dexterity

17. All of the following patients should be considered when recommending an automatic toothbrush EXCEPT one. Which one is the EXCEPTION?
   A. elderly
   B. those who require a large handle
   C. those with arthritis or poor manual dexterity
   D. those with orthodontia

18. Which type of dental floss would be MOST appropriate for normal contact areas?
    A. polytetrafluoroethylene
    B. tape
    C. unwaxed
    D. waxed

19. All of the following indicate use of a single-tufted brush (end-tuft, uni-tuft) EXCEPT one. Which one is the EXCEPTION?
    A. distal area of the most posterior tooth
    B. pontics
    C. irregular gingival margins around migrated or malposed teeth
    D. interdental cleaning of concave proximal tooth surfaces

20. The action of an oral irrigating device flushes away
    A. loosely adherent microflora located apical to the gingival margin.
    B. loosely adherent microflora located coronal to the gingival margin.
    C. attached microflora located apical to the gingival margin.
    D. attached microflora located coronal to the gingival margin.

21. All of the following are types of therapeutic dentifrices EXCEPT one. Which one is the EXCEPTION?
    A. fluoride-containing dentifrice
    B. baking soda-peroxide-fluoride dentifrice
    C. antimicrobial dentifrice
    D. antitartar dentifrice

22. Which of the following components of a dentifrice prevents bacterial growth and prolongs shelf life?
    A. humectant
    B. preservative
    C. sweetening agent
    D. flavoring agent

23. Which of the following active ingredients is found in antitartar dentifrice?
    A. potassium nitrate
    B. strontium chloride
    C. zinc citrate trihydrate
    D. sodium citrate

24. Where is fluoride primarily stored in the body?
    A. small intestine
    B. kidneys
    C. bloodstream
    D. bones and teeth

25. Which method of systemic fluoride is MOST economical for caries prevention?
    A. community water fluoridation
    B. dietary fluoride supplements
    C. naturally occurring in food
    D. professional fluoride treatment

26. What is the appropriate dietary fluoride supplement, in milligrams, for a 3-year-old patient who lives in an area with 0.4 ppm of fluoride in the water?
    A. none
    B. 0.25
    C. 0.5
    D. 1

27. All of the following indicate use of a professional topical fluoride EXCEPT one. Which one is the EXCEPTION?
    A. wearing orthodontic appliances
    B. compromised salivary flow
    C. low community water fluoridation level
    D. primary teeth

28. For an adult patient, the maximum amount of fluoride recommended for a professionally applied topical treatment (tray technique), in milliliters, is:
    A. 0.2.
    B. 0.25.
    C. 2.
    D. 2.5.

29. Which of the following professional topical fluorides has a recommended concentration of 1.23%?
    A. acidulated phosphate fluoride
    B. monofluorophosphate
    C. sodium fluoride
    D. stannous fluoride

30. What is the first sign of acute fluoride toxicity?
    A. abdominal pain
    B. diarrhea
    C. nausea
    D. vomiting

31. All of the following factors increase the severity of chronic fluoride toxicity EXCEPT one. Which one is the EXCEPTION?
    A. increase in consumption of naturally fluoridated water
    B. swallowing an excess amount of fluoride during a professional fluoride treatment
    C. elevated intake of fluoride in food
    D. low-calcium diet

32. In mouth rinses, which of the following ingredients provides cleansing by an effervescent action?
    A. chlorhexidine gluconate
    B. essential oils
    C. oxygenating agents
    D. stannous fluoride

33. All of the following are adverse effects of chlorhexidine gluconate EXCEPT one. Which one is the EXCEPTION?
    A. bitter taste
    B. brown staining of teeth
    C. epithelial desquamation
    D. white pitting of teeth

34. Which of the following relates to autopolymerization of dental sealants?
    A. setting time cannot be controlled once catalyst is added
    B. shorter polymerization time
    C. no mixing of materials
    D. requires a special curing light

35. While examining the TMJ, the hygienist notes a popping sound. What type of assessment skill is used to hear the sound?
    A. observation
    B. palpation
    C. auscultation
    D. olfaction

36. While assessing the dentition, the hygienist notices a suspicious area around the margin of an occlusal restoration and radiographically, a radiolucent area is evident. What type of decay is MOST likely?
    A. incipient
    B. arrested
    C. recurrent
    D. root

37. Upon examining a patient's profile, the hygienist notices that the upper lip is protruded 6 mm to the lower lip. What is the MOST likely occlusal relationship?
    A. prognathic
    B. retrognathic
    C. orthognathic
    D. normal

38. What is the malrelationship of teeth when vertical space is between the mandibular and maxillary arches?
    A. openbite
    B. edge-to-edge
    C. end-to-end
    D. crossbite

39. A patient demonstrates flossing between teeth #s 24 and 25. As the floss is moved from #24 to #25, it is kept in a horizontal position resulting in tissue trauma. Which gingival tissue is involved?
    A. attached
    B. gingival margin
    C. free gingival margin
    D. interdental papilla

40. When the gingival margin migrates coronally, it is described as
    A. recession.
    B. a periodontal pocket.
    C. pseudopocket.
    D. bulbous papilla.

answers & rationales

1.

C. Systolic pressure is the period during which blood is forced into the aorta and pulmonary artery, resulting in the maximum amount of pressure exerted against the walls of the blood vessel. Pulse is the intermittent throbbing sensation felt when the fingers are pressed against an artery. It is an indirect measurement of the patient's cardiac output. The diastolic pressure is the minimum amount of pressure exerted against the walls of the vessels. It is the phase of the cardiac cycle in which the heart relaxes between contractions.

2.

B. The proper size of a blood pressure cuff is 20% greater than the diameter of the arm. If the cuff is too large, the reading will be lower than the actual one. If the cuff is too small, the reading will be higher than the actual one.

3.

C. Titanium is NOT a type of manometer. Mercury, aneroid, and electric are types of manometers.

4.

A. Fainting does NOT cause an increase, but rather a decrease in blood pressure. Use of stimulants and contraceptives and eating cause an increase in blood pressure.

5.

B. Hyperthyroidism is NOT a factor in decreasing temperature. Starvation, hemorrhage, and physiological shock can decrease body temperature.

6.

D. The brachial artery is found in the antecubital space of the elbow. The radial artery is found on the radial portion (thumb-side) of the wrist. The carotid artery is lateral to the larynx. The facial artery is found crossing the border of the mandible.

7.

A. The bilateral palpation technique uses both hands at the same time to examine corresponding structures on opposite sides of the body. The bimanual technique utilizes finger(s) and thumb from each hand simultaneously. Bidigital technique involves the use of a finger and thumb of the same hand. Digital technique involves the use of a single finger.

8.

D. The Class V category involves the cervical third of either the facial or lingual surface—not the pits and fissures. Class II decay is on the proximal surface of any posterior tooth. Decay on the occlusal surface of a tooth is a Class I. Class VI caries is evident on the cusp tip of a tooth.

9.

D. Class III occlusal relationship involves the mesial surface of the permanent maxillary canine located distally to the distal surface of the permanent mandibular canine by at least the width of a premolar. When the maxillary canine occludes with the distal half of the mandibular canine and the mesial half of the mandibular first premolar, it is a Class I occlusion. When the distal surface of the maxillary canine is mesial to the mesial surface of the mandibular canine, by a minimum width of half of a premolar, it is a Class II occlusion.

10.

D. Both statements are false. In an anterior crossbite, the maxillary incisors are located lingually to the mandibular incisors. In a posterior crossbite, the maxillary posterior teeth are located lingual to the respective mandibular posterior teeth.

11.

D. The total amount of recession is 7 mm as a result of the distance measured from the CEJ to the base of the pocket; 3 mm is the amount of recession and 4 mm is the depth of the gingival sulcus.

12.

D. The correct order for the stages of the learning ladder, from lowest to highest, is unawareness, awareness, self-interest, involvement, action, habit (Hint: Unusual Apes Sit In A Hut).

13.

A. The nutrient source for supragingival calculus is saliva, NOT gingival crevicular fluid and inflammatory exudate, which are the nutrient sources for subgingival calculus. The color of supragingival calculus can vary depending on agents, which can pigment it. Common coloring agents include food and bacteria. Calculus is commonly located on the facial of maxillary molars and lingual of the mandibular incisors, adjacent to where salivary glands are located.

14.

A. Calculus cannot be removed with a toothbrush since it is a mineralized deposit. It must be removed with hand or ultrasonic/sonic instrumentation. Objectives of toothbrushing include removing food debris, stimulating gingival tissues, and applying therapeutic agents such as fluoride.

15.

D. The Stillman brushing technique involves placing the brush at a 45-degree angle to the tooth, with part of the bristles on the soft tissue and part on the tooth. The Bass method of toothbrushing involves placing the brush at a 45-degree angle to the apex of the tooth, applying a gentle pressure so the bristles enter the sulcus. With the Charters method, the toothbrush is placed at 90 degrees to the long axis of the tooth. The bristles are gently placed between the teeth, but do not rest on the gingiva. The Fones method includes brushing both arches at the same time. The bristles are placed perpendicular to the crown of the tooth and the brush is activated using a large circular motion.

16.

B. The size of the toothbrush does NOT need to be considered when recommending a specific toothbrushing technique, but should be considered when determining which toothbrush to recommend to the patient. The patient's oral health and systemic health status and manual dexterity should be considered when recommending a specific toothbrushing technique.

17.

D. An automatic toothbrush is NOT indicated for orthodontic patients; it is recommended for the elderly, those with arthritis/poor manual dexterity, and those who may require a large handle.

18.

D. Waxed dental floss is most appropriate for normal contact areas. Polytetrafluoroethylene dental floss is made of a synthetic material and is indicated for use in tight contact areas and/or rough tooth surfaces, because it is less likely to shred. Dental tape is broad and flat waxed floss indicated for spaces without tight contact areas. Unwaxed floss is indicated in tight contact areas.

19.

D. A single tufted brush is not used for interdental cleaning of concave proximal tooth surfaces because of its size. The distal of most posterior teeth, pontics, and irregular gingival margins around migrated or malposed teeth are areas indicated for a single-tufted brush.

20.

B. An oral irrigating device flushes away loosely adherent microflora located coronally to the gingival margin. It is efficient in disrupting microflora that is NOT attached to the tooth structure or gingival tissue on the coronal portion of the tooth only.

21.

D. Antitartar dentifrice is NOT a type of therapeutic dentifrice. The ADA considers calculus inhibition a cosmetic benefit. Therapeutic dentifrices containing fluoride, baking soda-peroxide-fluoride, and antimicrobial agents reduce disease in the mouth.

22.

B. The preservative in dentifrice prevents bacterial growth, which prolongs the shelf life of the product. Humectants retain moisture in a dentifrice and sweetening agents impart a pleasant flavor for patient acceptance. Flavoring agents make the toothpaste desirable and mask other unpleasant flavors.

23.

C. Zinc citrate trihydrate is an active ingredient in antitartar dentifrices. Potassium nitrate, strontium chloride, and sodium citrate are found in antihypersensitivity dentifrices.

24.

D. Fluoride is primarily stored in bones and teeth in the human body. Fluoride is rapidly absorbed by the small intestine, excreted via the kidneys, and can be found in the bloodstream.

25.

A. Community fluoridation is the most economical systemic method for caries prevention. Dietary fluoride supplements and foods that naturally contain fluoride are sources of systemic fluoride, but are not as economical as community fluoridation. Professional fluoride treatment is a topical form of fluoridation.

26.

B. A 3-year-old child would require a supplemental fluoride of 0.25 if the community water supply is < 0.4 ppm of fluoride. However, a 3-year-old may be prescribed 0.5 mg of fluoride if the concentration of community fluoride is less than 0.3 ppm. A supplement of 1 mg would never be prescribed to a 3-year-old.

27.

C. Low community water fluoridation level is NOT an indication for applying professional topical fluoride. However, wearing orthodontic appliances, having a compromised salivary flow, and primary teeth are indications for use of a professional topical fluoride treatment.

28.

D. An adult patient would receive 2.5 ml of fluoride during a professional fluoride treatment.A child fluoride treatment would contain 2.0 ml of fluoride. It is important to administer the correct amount to receive the full benefit of fluoride. Administering too much fluoride could cause acute fluoride toxicity if swallowed.

29.

A. Acidulated phosphate fluoride has a recommended concentration of 1.23%. This is obtained by combining 2.0% sodium fluoride and 0.34% hydrofluoric acid. Monofluorophosphate is found in dentifrices only. Professionally, sodium and stannous fluorides are available at 2.0% and 8.0%, respectively.

30.

C. The first sign of acute fluoride toxicity is nausea. Following nausea, the patient may also experience vomiting, abdominal pain, and diarrhea.

31.

B. Swallowing an excess amount of fluoride during a professional fluoride treatment is an example of acute, not chronic fluoride toxicity. Factors that increase the severity of chronic fluoride toxicity include an increase in the consumption of fluoridated water, elevated intake of fluoride in food, and a low-calcium diet.

32.

C. Oxygenating agents cleanse the mouth by an effervescent action. Chlorhexidine gluconate is an antimicrobial that has bactericidal effects. Essential oils are the active ingredients in Listerine and have both antigingivitis and antiplaque effects. Stannous fluoride is a therapeutic agent.

33.

D. Chlorhexidine gluconate does NOT produce white pitting of teeth. Bitter taste, brown staining of teeth, and epithelial desquamation are adverse effects of chlorhexidine gluconate.

34.

A. Autopolymerization or self-cured sealants require the mixing of a monomer and a catalyst. Once the catalyst is added, the setting time cannot be controlled. Light cured or photopolymerization involves a shorter polymerization time, no mixing of materials, and a special curing light.

35.

C. The examination skill of auscultation involves listening to the sounds made by various structures and functions. Observation involves the visual deviation of the structures. While palpating the TMJ, the dental hygienist would feel the popping sensation. Olfaction is an examination skill of smell.

36.

C. Recurrent decay is a lesion that occurs at the margin(s) of an existing restoration. An incipient lesion can be arrested before permanent damage to the tooth has occurred. With arrested decay, remineralization has occurred. Root caries are found on the root surfaces, not on the occlusal surfaces.

37.

C. The patient presents with a retrognathic profile, which is associated with a Class II occlusal relationship. Normal occlusion and Class I malocclusion present with an orthognathic profile. Class I malocclusion is differentiated from a normal occlusion because of malposed teeth. Class III malocclusion involves a prognathic facial profile.

38.

A. An openbite is the lack of occlusal or incisal contact between one or more maxillary and mandibular teeth. Edge-to-edge malrelationship involves the anterior teeth only. The teeth meet on the incisal edges. End-to-end malrelationship is similar to edge-to-edge, except it involves the posterior teeth. Crossbite malrelationship is present when the maxillary teeth are positioned lingually to the mandibular teeth.

39.

D. The interdental gingiva is traumatized when the floss is not lifted toward the incisal edge while moving from one tooth to the next. The attached gingiva is not affected by flossing because it is located apical to the interdental gingiva. The gingival and free gingival margins are interchangeable terms describing the tissue closest to the crown of the tooth.

40.

C. Pseudopocket is a term used when the marginal gingiva has moved coronally and produced an artificially deepened sulcus. Recession is the apical migration of the gingival margin. A periodontal pocket results from loss of attachment of gingival tissues. Bulbous papilla is a clinical characteristic of diseased gingiva involving the interdental papilla.

CHAPTER

10 Periodontal Instrumentation

Barbara Stubbs, RDH, MS

contents

I. BASIC INSTRUMENT DESIGN

A. Parts

1. Handle—designed for holding instrument; identify instrument by design name and number stamped on handle; available in various weights, diameters, and surface textures
   a) Weight—hollow metal handle is lighter in weight than solid metal handle; increases tactile sensitivity, reduces hand fatigue, and helps prevent *repetitive strain injury* (RSI)
   b) Diameter—easier to control handle with a larger diameter; reduces muscle cramping and helps prevent RSI
   c) Surface texture—easier to control in a wet environment if handle is knurled (serrated); helps prevent RSI
2. Working end—performs function (work) of instrument; consists of face, back, lateral surfaces, and cutting edges; has three sections—heel, middle, and tip (or toe)
3. Shank—metal rod between handle and working end that extends instrument length
   a) Types
      (1) Simple—designed for instrumentation of anterior teeth; shank is bent in one plane only
      (2) Complex—designed for subgingival instrumentation of posterior teeth; shank is bent in two planes
      (3) Functional—encompasses entire shank from working end to handle
         (a) Short—accesses coronal surfaces of teeth
         (b) Long—accesses coronal and root surfaces of teeth
      (4) Terminal (lower)—section of shank nearest to working end; begins below working end and extends to first shank bend
   b) Flexibility—determined by function of instrument
      (1) Flexible—provides most tactile information; needed for detection of subgingival calculus and removal of light calculus and endotoxins (e.g., explorers and area-specific curets such as “finishing” Graceys)
      (2) Moderately flexible—provides some tactile information; needed for removal of small or medium-sized calculus deposits (e.g., universal curets)
      (3) Rigid—provides little tactile information; needed for removal of large calculus deposits (e.g., sickle scalers and rigid curets)

B. Types

1. Mouth mirror—assessment instrument
   a) Functions
      (1) Retracts patient’s cheek or tongue for improved visibility and patient protection
      (2) Provides indirect vision of surfaces that cannot be viewed directly
      (3) Reflects light onto a dark area in mouth

(4) Provides *transillumination* to reflect light (e.g., through an anterior tooth)

b) Description

(1) Working end is round

(2) Used in all phases of dental hygiene procedures

(3) Fogging is minimized by gently rubbing mirror against buccal mucosa or dipping in commercial mouth rinse

2. Explorer—assessment instrument

a) Function—provides superior tactile information in locating supragingival and subgingival calculus deposits, tooth surface irregularities and defects, overhanging margins and other defects in restorations, and decalcification and caries; available in a variety of designs

b) Description

(1) Fine, wirelike working end that terminates to a sharp point

(2) Types include Shepherd hook, straight, pigtail, cowhorn, Orban-type, and 11/12

3. Periodontal probe—assessment instrument

a) Functions

(1) Assesses periodontal health

(2) Measures lesions and overjets

b) Description—blunt, rod-shaped working end marked in millimeter units

(1) Calibrated—straight probe is available in plastic or metal in several different designs and calibration patterns, color-coded styles, as well as computerized pressure-sensitive

(a) Used to measure sulcus and pocket depths, recession, *clinical attachment levels,* and width of attached gingiva

(b) Assesses consistency of gingival tissue

(c) Evaluates presence of bleeding and *suppuration* (purulent exudate)

(d) Measures other oral structures

(2) Furcation—curved probe is used to detect extent of attachment loss in furcated areas; extent of furcation is denoted as a classification, not a millimeter measurement

(3) Examples—Novatech series (right-angle tip) and Nordent PCL JB 2-4 (color coded)

4. Periodontal file

a) Functions

(1) Crushes large supragingival or subgingival calculus deposits

(2) Roughens burnished calculus to facilitate deposit removal with another instrument

(3) Also used to smooth margins of amalgam restorations

b) Description

(1) Rigid shanked instrument with a working end that is thin in width and either rounded, oblong, or rectangular in shape

(2) Has multiple straight cutting edges which are at 90- to 105-degree angles to the shank

(3) Used with a pull stroke

c) Designs
   (1) Paired working ends—consists of four working ends that are needed to instrument all surfaces of a tooth—mesial, distal, facial, and lingual
   (2) Double-ended—designed for use on facial/lingual surfaces or mesial/distal surfaces; each working end offers a single-surface application
d) Examples—Hirschfield 3/7, 5/11, 9/10 and Orban 10/11 and 12/13

5. Hoe
   a) Functions
      (1) Used to remove large, heavy supragingival calculus
      (2) Subgingival use is limited by design (in current practice, sonic and ultrasonic scalers are generally used for this purpose)
   b) Description
      (1) Single cutting edge angled at 90 to 100 degrees to the shank
      (2) Designed like the periodontal file in that four working ends are needed to instrument each surface of a tooth (see Periodontal file)
      (3) Used with a pull stroke
6. Chisel
   a) Functions—used to dislodge heavy calculus particularly from exposed proximal surfaces on mandibular anteriors; use is limited
   b) Description
      (1) Double-ended push instrument with either a straight or curved shank
      (2) Blade is continuous with shank
      (3) Cutting edge is formed with tip beveled at a 45-degree angle
      (4) Used only in a horizontal direction with a push stroke
7. Sickle scaler
   a) Functions
      (1) Used to remove heavy supragingival calculus deposits from all aspects of tooth crown (facial, lingual, mesial, distal)
      (2) Design not recommended for subgingival use because of possible soft tissue trauma and excessive removal of cementum
   b) Description
      (1) Working end has pointed back and is triangular in cross section
      (2) Two cutting edges on each working end meet at a point called the tip
      (3) Cutting edges are at same level and may be straight or curved
      (4) Face is perpendicular (90-degree angle) to terminal shank
      (5) Straight-shank sickle (anterior instrument) is often single-ended because same end may be used on mesials and distals

(6) Bent-shank sickle may be used on anteriors and/or posteriors and is usually double-ended, with one end designed for mesials and other end for distals

c) Examples

(1) Anterior sickle scalers—OD1, Jacquette-30, Jacquette-33, Towner-U15, Goldman-H6, Goldman-H7, H 6/7, Whiteside-2

(2) Posterior sickle scalers—Jacquette 14/15, Jacquette 31/32, Jacquette 34/35, Mecca 11/12, Ball 2/3, Catatonia 107/108, 204 SD, IPFW 204

8. Curet

a) Function—used to remove deposits supragingivally and subgingivally on crown and root surfaces

b) Description

(1) Designed with a long or short, rigid or flexible, simple or complex, functional shank

(2) Designed with paired mirror-image working ends (available as one double-ended curet or a pair of single-ended curets)

(3) Working ends have rounded backs and are semicircular in cross section; curves upward toward a rounded toe

c) Types (universal, area-specific, and finishing curets)

(1) Universal curet—implies that one double-ended working end can be used on all anterior and posterior tooth surfaces

(a) Function—designed to remove light or moderate supragingival and subgingival calculus

(b) Description—lateral surfaces form two parallel cutting edges that curve upward toward rounded toe and are at the same level (cutting edge is not self-angulated)

i) Each working end has two cutting edges—both cutting edges are used

ii) Face is perpendicular to terminal shank

iii) Terminal shank is not parallel with handle

iv) Functional shank designs vary in length and rigidity

(c) Examples—Columbia 2R/2L, 4R/4L, 13/14; Barnhart 1/2, 5/6; Younger-Good 7/8; Langer 1/2, 3/4, 5/6; Rule 3/4; Indiana University 13/14; HU 1/2; Bunting 5/6; Mallery 1/2

(d) Suggested applications

i) Columbia 13/14—works well in anterior areas or areas with slight to moderate probing depths

ii) Columbia 4R/4L—has longer terminal shank than Columbia 13/14; works well in deeper pockets in posterior areas

iii) Columbia 2R/2L—has longer terminal shank than Columbia 4R/4L and is ideal for use in deep facial or lingual pockets

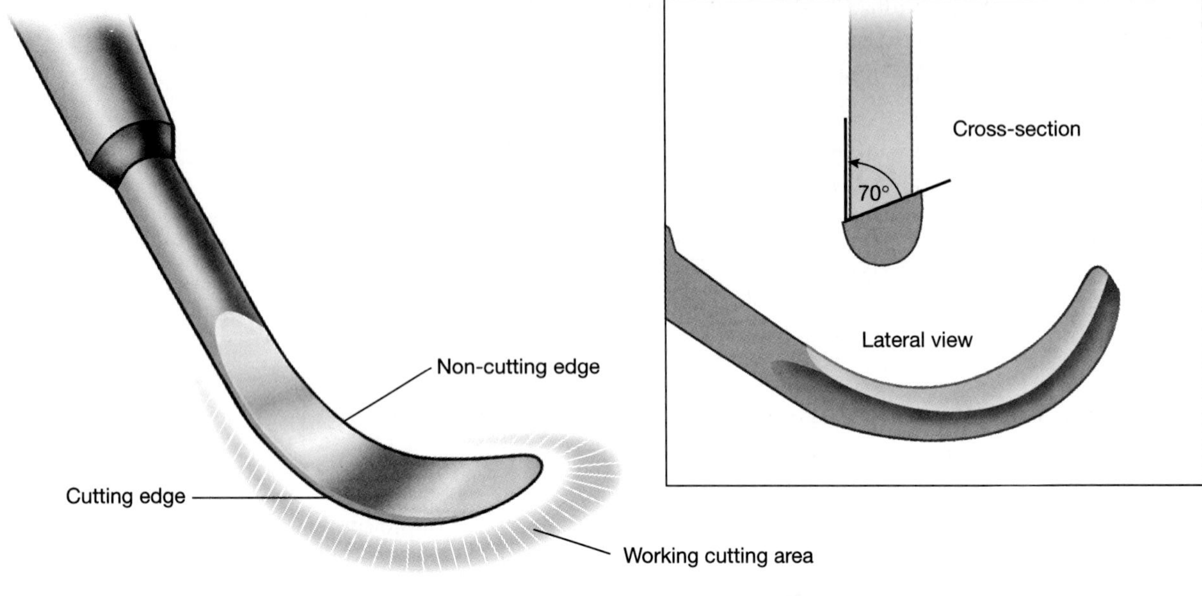

FIGURE 10-1. Area-specific curet.

(2) Area-specific curet—implies that a single area-specific curet can be applied only to certain tooth surfaces and areas of mouth
   (a) Function
      i) Depending on the rigidity of shank, it is designed to remove light to moderate supragingival and subgingival calculus and endotoxins
      ii) Ideal for adapting to root morphology
   (b) Description—lateral surfaces form two cutting edges that curve upward toward rounded toe
      i) Face is offset or tilted at a 60- to 70-degree angle to terminal shank and cutting edges are at different levels (cutting edge is self-angulated)
      ii) Only one cutting edge (lower, longer cutting edge) per working end is used
      iii) Designed with longer terminal shanks for access to middle- and apical-third of root

TABLE 10-1	AREAS OF USE FOR STANDARD GRACEY SERIES
Gracey 1/2	Anterior teeth
Gracey 3/4	Anterior teeth
Gracey 5/6	Anterior and premolar teeth
Gracey 7/8	Posterior teeth (facial and lingual)
Gracey 9/10	Posterior teeth (facial and lingual)
Gracey 11/12	Posterior teeth (mesial)
Gracey 13/14	Posterior teeth (distal)

TABLE 10-2 OTHER GRACEY CURETS	
Gracey 15/16 Curet	Modification of Gracey 11/12 for superior access to mesial surfaces of posterior teeth
Gracey 17/18 Curet	Modification of Gracey 13/14 with accentuated angles for superior access to distal surfaces of posterior teeth
Gracey Mesial-Distal Curet	Modification of combination of Graceys 11, 12, 13, and 14 on double-ended instruments; G11/14 and G12/13 allows clinician to complete all surfaces on either the facial or lingual aspect of a sextant without changing instruments
Gracey Prophy Series	Shorter and more rigid shank than the Standard series
Rigid Gracey Series	Standard length, but with a more rigid shank and working end
Hu-Freidy After-Five Series	Thinner working end; terminal shank is 3 mm longer than standard Gracey series
Hu-Freidy Mini-Five Series	Thinner working end shortened to half the length of standard Gracey series; terminal shank is also 3 mm longer than standard Gracey series

iv) Functional shank is more complex and varies in length and rigidity

(c) Examples of area-specific curets—Standard Gracey series, Hu-Freidy After-Five Series, Hu-Freidy Mini-Five series, Hu-Freidy Vision Curvette series, Kramer-Nevins series, Turgeon series, and Nordent SC GR 1-2 MDC

(3) Finishing curet (Gracey)—has flexible shank and is intended for light scaling

II. BASIC PRINCIPLES OF INSTRUMENTATION

A. Grasp—recommend modified pen grasp

B. Fulcrum (finger rest)—acts as a support beam for hand and wrist to pivot on during instrumentation; common error in instrumentation technique is a weak fulcrum resulting in poor stroke control and tissue trauma

1. Intraoral
   a) Hold ring finger straight with tip resting on incisal, occlusal, or occlusolingual/occlusofacial line angles of tooth
   b) Ideal fulcrum is established on a stable tooth in the same arch and as close as possible to tooth being instrumented (1 to 4 teeth away)
2. Advanced
   a) Use if basic intraoral fulcrum is not effective or possible
   b) Useful in achieving parallelism for deep pocket access or when edentulous areas preclude use of basic fulcrum
   c) Includes extraoral fulcrum on chin or cheek, cross-arch fulcrum, opposite arch fulcrum, modified intraoral fulcrum,

finger-on-finger fulcrum, piggy-back fulcrum, and stabilized fulcrum

C. Adaptation—place lead third (toe) of cutting edge in contact with tooth surface in preparation for stroke

D. Angulation

1. Establish correct angle between instrument face and tooth surface (< 90-degree angle and > 45-degree angle)
2. Ideal angulation for scaling is 60 to 80 degrees
3. Incorrect angulation > 90 degrees may result in trauma to epithelial lining of pocket
4. Incorrect angulation of < 45 degrees may result in burnished calculus deposits

E. Insertion

1. Insert face at a 0-degree angulation to tooth surface until working end is positioned at base of pocket
2. Establish a 60- to 80-degree face-to-tooth angulation before initiating a stroke

F. Lateral pressure—use index finger or thumb to press inward against handle to engage cutting edge and apply pressure to tooth before and during activation of stroke

G. Motion activation

1. Move instrument to produce an oblique, circumferential (horizontal), or vertical stroke
2. Hand, wrist, and arm should move as a single unit and rotate to produce each stroke
3. Avoid fatiguing finger-powered strokes

H. Handle roll

1. Roll instrument handle between and during strokes, as strokes progress around tooth to reestablish correct adaptation of leading third of cutting edge to tooth
2. This is particularly important at line angles, depressions, furcations, and root concavities

I. *Assessment stroke* (exploratory or placement stroke)

1. Use relaxed grasp and feather-light pressure
2. Apply many overlapping, long, flowing, sweeping strokes
3. Apply multidirectional strokes and cover entire root surface to detect calculus, overhanging restorations, and other tooth surface irregularities
4. Use with explorers, curets, thin sonic and ultrasonic tips
5. Perform with curets, sonic and ultrasonic instruments during periodontal debridement to determine if working strokes have been successful in deposit removal
6. Use explorer to evaluate for complete removal of deposits

J. Working stroke—use appropriate pressure and stroke to debride tooth surfaces

1. Calculus removal work stroke—use with sickle scalers, curets, sonic and ultrasonic tips to remove calculus deposits

a) Hand-activated instruments—use firm pressure and limited short, controlled, scraping, pull strokes beginning beneath deposit and proceeding coronally
b) Sonic and ultrasonic instruments—use light pressure and sweeping, brushlike push-pull strokes in an erasing motion

2. Root surface debridement work stroke (formerly called root planing)—use with area-specific curets and slim sonic and ultrasonic tips to remove residual calculus granules and endotoxins from root surfaces
   a) Apply long multidirectional, controlled overlapping strokes (by using vertical stroke series followed by oblique and circumferential series) with very light even pressure
   b) Work in long, narrow sections or tracts beginning each stroke at base of pocket and ending at cementoenamel junction (CEJ)
   c) Avoid firm pressure and too many strokes that may result in unnecessary removal of cementum
   d) Know pocket topography and root anatomy (locations of furcations and root concavities) to help facilitate thorough root surface debridement
   e) Refer to comprehensive periodontal charting and radiographs often during instrumentation

III. USE OF PERIODONTAL PROBE

A. Sulcus and pocket depth measurement—measure distance, in millimeters, from base of pocket to gingival margin

1. Use basic probing technique with a calibrated probe
2. Position probe parallel to long axis of tooth
3. Gently insert probe to base of pocket
4. Work around entire circumference of tooth in strokes 1 to 2 mm apart
5. Chart six measurements per tooth (3 depths on facial aspect and 3 on lingual aspect), recording deepest measurement in each area
6. Slant probe slightly under contact to assess interdental col area

B. Extent of inflammation—evaluate presence of bleeding and/or purulent exudate (suppuration) on probing

C. Calculus detection—use probe to detect location of calculus deposits

D. Recession—use calibrated probe to measure distance from gingival margin to exposed CEJ

E. Clinical attachment level (attachment level; probed level of attachment)

1. Use calibrated probe to measure distance from CEJ to junctional epithelium
2. Best clinical indicator of bone support because bone level is approximately 2 mm apical to junctional epithelium
3. Methods used to determine attachment level
   a) Gingival margin is at CEJ—measure distance from base of pocket to CEJ

b) Gingival margin is receded apically to CEJ—measure distance from base of pocket to CEJ
c) Gingival margin is 1 mm or greater coronal to CEJ—measure distance from base of pocket to gingival margin (overall measurement), then measure distance from CEJ to gingival margin and subtract from overall measurement

F. Width of attached gingiva—determine by measuring with a calibrated probe

1. On external surface of gingiva, measure distance from gingival margin to mucogingival junction to obtain total width of gingiva
2. Insert probe into sulcus and measure probing depth
3. Subtract probing depth from total width of gingiva

G. Gingival consistency—determine by placing length of calibrated probe against the free gingiva and applying gentle pressure

1. Slight indentation and blanching of tissue will quickly disappear if it is healthy
2. Tissue will remain blanched and indented for a few seconds if edematous
3. Tissue will not exhibit blanching and indentation if fibrotic

H. Size of lesions or deviations—use calibrated probe to measure and document width, length, height, or depth of lesion, or other deviation from normal

I. Classification of furcation involvement

1. Use furcation probe to detect and classify extent of furcation involvement
2. Attempt insertion of probe into buccal, lingual, mesial, and distal furcations to determine extent of bone loss and classify
3. Classifications
   a) Class I: Slight bone loss in furcation area; furcation concavity can be detected but probe cannot be inserted into furcation
   b) Class II: Partial bone loss in furcation area; furcation probe can be inserted into furcation but does not pass through it
   c) Class III: Complete bone loss in furcation area; furcation probe passes between roots completely through furcation
   d) Class IV: Same as Class III but furcation is exposed clinically due to gingival recession

J. Assessing mobility

1. Horizontal mobility
   a) Place blunt handle ends of two single-ended instruments (e.g., mirror and probe) to opposite sides of each tooth
   b) Apply alternating pressure from the facial and lingual aspects and assess facial-lingual mobility
2. Vertical mobility—apply vertical pressure with end of blunt handle to occlusal or incisal
3. Classifications
   a) N = normal physiological mobility (all teeth exhibit slight normal mobility)

b) Grade I = slight mobility; up to 1 mm horizontal displacement in facial-lingual direction

c) Grade II = moderate mobility; > 1 mm horizontal displacement in facial-lingual direction

d) Grade III = severe mobility; > 1 mm displacement in both vertical and horizontal directions

IV. USE OF EXPLORER

A. Shepherd hook and straight explorers—each is an unpaired explorer with strong rigid shank ideally suited for caries detection in the following areas

1. Pit and fissures—explore posterior occlusal surfaces and anterior lingual cingulum areas
2. Smooth surfaces—explore facial, lingual, and proximal aspects of crowns
3. Root surfaces caries—explore exposed roots commonly found in geriatric patients owing to gingival recession
4. Recurrent decay—explore along restorative margins

B. Orban-type explorer—unpaired explorer best suited for use in deep, narrow pockets of anterior teeth or facial and lingual surfaces of posterior teeth

C. 11/12 Explorer—paired explorer with mirror-image working ends

1. Description—universal instrument
   a) Adapts to all anterior and posterior surfaces
   b) Well suited to adapt in deep pockets, especially on proximal surfaces of posterior teeth and in other limited access areas owing to its long, complex functional shank
2. Determine correct working end as follows
   a) Use on anterior teeth
      (1) Position terminal (lower) shank parallel to long axis of anterior tooth surface and adapt working end to tooth
      (2) Tip of correct working end will curve toward tooth
      (3) Use one working end on all surfaces toward operator from a given aspect (facial or lingual); opposite end is used on all surfaces away from operator from the same aspect (facial or lingual)
   b) Use on posterior teeth
      (1) Correct working end is established when terminal (lower) shank is parallel to proximal surface
      (2) Use one working end on distobuccal, buccal, and mesiobuccal surfaces of each tooth in a sextant; opposite working end is used on distolingual, lingual, and mesiolingual surfaces of teeth in same sextant

D. Pigtail and cowhorn explorers

1. Each is paired with mirror-image working ends and is a universal instrument, adapting to all anterior and posterior surfaces
2. Best suited for use in normal sulci or shallow pockets
3. Operated same as 11/12 explorer

V. USE OF SICKLE SCALER

A. Use of anterior sickle (single-ended)

1. Design—two cutting edges on a single working end; one cutting edge is used on all surfaces toward operator, opposite cutting edge on same working end is used on all surfaces away from operator
2. Strokes (application)
   a) Begin at midline on facial or lingual surface of tooth
   b) Adapt leading third of cutting edge
   c) Establish 60- to 80-degree face-to-tooth surface angulation
   d) Activate pull strokes working toward proximal surface

B. Use of posterior sickle (double-ended)

1. Design—two cutting edges per working end
   a) Use one cutting edge from distofacial line angle to just past center of distal surface; use opposite cutting edge of same working end from distofacial line angle to just past center of mesial surface
   b) Use both cutting edges of one working end on entire facial aspect of the posterior sextant; use the two cutting edges of opposite working end on the entire lingual aspect of the same sextant
2. Strokes (application)
   a) Position terminal shank parallel to the long axis of tooth and adapt working end to proximal surface
   b) Adapt correct cutting edge
   c) Begin strokes at distofacial line angle with tip pointed distally
   d) Adapt leading third of cutting edge
   e) Establish 60- to 80-degree face-to-tooth surface angulation
   f) Activate pull strokes to just past center of distal surface
   g) Lift and turn instrument so leading third of opposite cutting edge of same working end is adapted at distofacial line angle with tip pointed mesially
   h) Establish 60- to 80-degree face-to-tooth surface angulation
   i) Activate oblique strokes to just past center of mesial surface

VI. USE OF UNIVERSAL CURETS—one double-ended universal curet can be applied to all anterior and posterior tooth surfaces; each working end has two cutting edges

A. Use of universal curet on anterior surfaces

1. Strokes (application)
   a) Position terminal (lower) shank parallel to long axis of tooth and adapt working end
   b) Establish correct cutting edge, accomplished when instrument face tilts toward tooth
   c) Use one working end on all surfaces toward operator and opposite working end on all surfaces away from operator
   d) Adapt leading third of cutting edge
   e) Insert at midline on facial or lingual surface of tooth

f) Establish 60- to 80-degree face-to-tooth surface angulation
g) Activate pull strokes working toward proximal surface

B. Use of universal curet on posterior surfaces—technique is same as posterior sickle scaler

VII. USE OF AREA-SPECIFIC CURETS—use only one cutting edge (lower, longer cutting edge) on each working end

A. Use of an area-specific curet on anterior surfaces

1. Strokes (application)
   a) Select one double-ended, area-specific curet appropriate for anterior teeth
   b) Position terminal shank parallel to anterior tooth and adapt a working end
   c) Establish correct working end (face of blade will tilt toward tooth)
   d) Use one working end on all surfaces toward operator; use opposite working end on all surfaces away from operator
   e) Adapt leading third of lower cutting edge
   f) Insert at midline on facial or lingual surface of tooth
   g) Establish 60- to 80-degree face-to-tooth surface angulation
   h) Activate pull strokes working toward proximal surface

B. Use of area-specific curet on posterior surfaces

1. Strokes (application)
   a) Select curet appropriate for surface (e.g., Gracey 13 or 14 for distal surface, Gracey 11 or 12 for mesial surface)
   b) Adapt lower cutting edge to a proximal surface—correct curet and cutting edge are adapted when terminal shank is parallel to proximal surface
   c) Insert by adapting leading third of lower cutting edge to tooth surface at angles to ensure overlapping strokes
   d) Establish 60- to 80-degree face-to-tooth surface angulation and activate pull strokes across surface—mesial curets can be used from distofacial or distolingual angle to midline of mesial surface
   e) Use at least four area-specific curets (e.g., Gracey 11, 12, 13, and 14) or two double-ended Gracey curets (e.g., Gracey 11/12 and 13/14) to complete facial and lingual aspects of a posterior sextant
   f) Debride each root as if it were a single-rooted tooth, if furcation involvement is present

VIII. PARADIGM SHIFT IN NONSURGICAL PERIODONTAL THERAPY

A. Old paradigm includes scaling and root planing

1. Treatment objectives
   a) Complete mechanical removal of plaque, calculus, and cementum
   b) Achieve hard, glassy, smooth root surfaces
   c) Promote effective daily plaque control by patient

2. Instrumentation
   a) Scaling—use firm pressure with hand-activated instruments for calculus removal
   b) Root planing—use moderate to firm pressure with hand-activated instruments to remove residual calculus and necrotic, altered cementum
   c) Ultrasonic and sonic instrumentation—use of hand-activated instrumentation preferred over ultrasonic and sonic instrumentation; concept that ultrasonic or sonic instrumentation must be followed by root planing with hand instruments for complete removal of deposits and altered cementum
3. Misconceptions
   a) Belief that endotoxins are firmly bound and absorbed into cementum; therefore this "altered" cementum and all residual calculus must be eliminated with extensive root planing before healing can occur
   b) Removal of cementum is an essential component of nonsurgical periodontal therapy
   c) Evaluate success of therapy immediately following instrumentation; based on calculus removal and attainment of smooth root surfaces

B. New paradigm involves periodontal debridement

1. Treatment objectives
   a) Establish an environment favorable to periodontal health and maintenance
   b) Mechanically remove all detectable plaque and plaque retentive factors such as calculus deposits
   c) Mechanically remove endotoxins from root surfaces (specifically complex lipopolysaccharides [LPS] found in cell walls of Gram-negative bacteria)
   d) Facilitate shift in oral flora from disease-related to health-related organisms
   e) Stimulate patient's immune response
   f) Promote effective daily plaque control
   g) Reevaluate healing response after initial therapy to identify areas of persistent inflammation that may need additional nonsurgical treatment; determine whether surgical treatment is necessary
   h) Stop progress of disease and allow for tissue healing
   i) Institute maintenance program to maintain periodontal health
2. Instrumentation
   a) Supragingival and subgingival debridement—use appropriate pressure with hand-activated instruments to remove the type of calculus present
   b) Root surface debridement
      (1) Use light, overlapping strokes with hand-activated or power-driven instruments for removal of all plaque and endotoxins (LPS) from entire root surface

(2) Root surface debridement does NOT include purposeful and aggressive cementum removal

(3) Cementum is intentionally conserved

c) Ultrasonic and sonic instrumentation

(1) As a result of advances in ultrasonic tip design and a new approach to periodontal therapy, ultrasonic instrumentation is no longer restricted to supplemental role of gross calculus removal

(2) Primary role in periodontal instrumentation since the late 1980s

(3) Modern units with modified tips have proven equally effective as hand scaling in periodontal debridement

(4) Some clinical research suggests ultrasonics may be more effective than hand-activated instruments in deep pockets and furcations (majority of practitioners, however, continue to rely on hand instrumentation)

3. Antimicrobial adjuncts—use antimicrobial agents and antibiotics as needed to control disease (e.g., use of antimicrobial irrigation devices and/or rinses, antimicrobial solution vs. water in ultrasonic unit, systemic antibiotics, and tetracycline fibers)

4. Assessment of host response—assess factors influencing immune response (e.g., neutrophil deficiencies, smoking, pregnancy, medications, diabetes and other systemic illnesses)

5. New concepts

a) Complete calculus removal is extremely challenging, especially in deeper pockets

b) Healing can occur in spite of residual calculus

c) Endotoxins are not incorporated into cementum and do not "alter" cementum; they loosely adhere to cementum and are easily removed

d) Excessive removal of cementum is not necessary and may be detrimental to the periodontium; therefore, debridement techniques should not include intentional removal of cementum

e) Key to successful treatment involves restoration of delicate balance between oral flora and host immune response

f) Success of treatment is NOT evaluated by root smoothness, but is determined by absence of inflammation and infection, healing and repair of damaged periodontal tissues, and cessation of progress of periodontal disease

IX. POWER-DRIVEN SCALERS

A. Involve a rapidly vibrating water-cooled tip that fractures and dislodges calculus deposits and flushes debris from pockets

B. Types—units are classified as ultrasonic or sonic

1. Ultrasonic instruments

a) Magnetostrictive

(1) Description of unit

(a) Houses electric generator in a portable unit with power and water adjustment controls

        (b) Includes handpiece with a variety of insert (tip) designs
        (c) Connects to electrical and water outlets
        (d) Activates power by using foot control
    (2) Mechanism of action
        (a) Converts electrical energy into mechanical energy in the form of vibrations
        (b) Electrical current creates a magnetic field and expansion and contraction of metal stacks in handpiece insert; causes vibration of tip
        (c) Generates heat; therefore water flow through tip serves as coolant and water lavage
    (3) Vibrations—range from 25,000 to 35,000 cycles/second
    (4) Tip (insert)—moves in elliptical pattern; all four surfaces of tip are active, which permits debridement with the most easily adapted tip surface (back, sides, or front)
  b) Piezoelectric (piezoceramic)
    (1) Description of unit
        (a) Houses electric generator in a portable unit with power and water adjustment controls
        (b) Includes handpiece with a variety of insert (tip) designs
        (c) Connects to electrical and water outlets
        (d) Activates power by using foot control
    (2) Mechanism of action
        (a) Converts electrical energy into mechanical energy in the form of vibrations via quartz or metal alloy crystal transducer
        (b) Produces no magnetic field
        (c) Generates less heat than magnetostrictive types
        (d) Water flow through tip serves as coolant and lavage
    (3) Vibrations—range from 25,000 to 50,000 cycles/second
    (4) Tip (insert)—moves in a linear pattern (back and forth); only two surfaces of tip (both sides) are active
        (a) Reduces hammering through linear movement, but limits number of active surfaces; thus adaptation of tip-to-tooth morphology is restricted
        (b) Use of tip-tightening and loosening tool is necessary
2. Sonic instruments
  a) Description—small air-driven scaler handpiece that attaches directly to dental unit
    (1) Screw working tips onto handpiece
    (2) Turn water switch of dental unit to ON
    (3) Activate power by using dental unit rheostat
  b) Mechanism of action
    (1) Driven by compressed air rather than electrical current
    (2) Produces vibrations by air pressure passing over metal rod contained within handpiece
    (3) Generates no heat
    (4) Reduces frictional heat at tip-to-tooth interface and provides water lavage with water coolant

c) Vibrations—ranges from 2000 to 6300 cycles/second; slower rate of vibration results in lowered capacity for heavy calculus removal; light to moderate calculus can be effectively removed

d) Tip

(1) Movement of tip is elliptical or orbital

(2) All four surfaces of tip are active

(3) Requires use of tip-loosening tool

D. Advantages of ultrasonic and sonic instrumentation

1. Modified tip designs—as effective as hand-activated instrumentation for periodontal debridement

a) Resemble periodontal probe, thinner in diameter than standard ultrasonic and sonic tips, and are significantly smaller than hand-activated curets

b) Provide greater tactile sensitivity and maximum access to deep, narrow pockets and superior adaptation to root anatomy including furcations and root concavities (standard Gracey curets are too large to enter 50% of all molar furcations)

c) Inserts easily beneath tight gingival margins

d) Removes less cementum than standard ultrasonic tips or hand-activated instruments and provides more conservative approach to periodontal therapy

2. Less soft tissue trauma—due to tips having no cutting edge; results in faster healing rates

3. Flushing action (water lavage)

a) Penetrates to base of pockets and flushes out blood and loosened debris (plaque, calculus, endotoxins)

b) Improves visibility during instrumentation

c) Provides antibacterial effect through acoustic streaming and cavitation

(1) *Acoustic streaming*—continuous stream of water creates pressure within confines of pocket and removes bacteria from pockets; Gram-negative motile rods are particularly sensitive to acoustic streaming

(2) *Cavitation*—spray of tiny bubbles is released at instrument tip; bubbles collapse and produce shock waves referred to as cavitation, which tears apart bacterial cell walls at treatment site; promotes flushing of pocket debris

4. Reduces instrumentation time—removes heavy calculus and stain in less time than with hand-instrumentation

5. Increases patient comfort—reduces instrumentation pressure and time, which is less fatiguing for patient

6. Reduces operator fatigue—decreases effort in removing heavy calculus and stain; offers a lighter grasp and pressure than with hand instrumentation

7. May reduce chance of injury to clinician because tips do NOT have cutting edges

8. Overhang removal—special tips are available for safe, effective removal of amalgam overhangs

9. Cement removal—accomplishes removal of excess crown, bridge, or orthodontic cement

E. Disadvantages of ultrasonic and sonic instrumentation

1. Aerosol production
   a) Releases oral microorganisms, blood, saliva, and debris into air in form of an aerosol
   b) Can be minimized through
      (1) Using antimicrobial pretreatment mouth rinse
      (2) Positioning patient properly (supine with head turned to side)
      (3) Using high-volume evacuation
      (4) Cupping cheeks or lips for water containment
      (5) Reducing water flow slightly
      (6) Using focused-spray ultrasonic inserts
2. Impeded visibility from water spray
   a) Problem can be minimized by
      (1) Keeping mirror face thoroughly wet
      (2) Using high-volume evacuation
      (3) Reducing water flow slightly
3. Contraindications for some patients—use is NOT recommended on patients with any of the following conditions
   a) Communicable diseases that can be transmitted via aerosols (e.g., tuberculosis, hepatitis, strep throat, flu, respiratory infections)
   b) Unshielded cardiac pacemaker—magnetostrictive ultrasonic instruments should NOT be used on or near these patients
   c) High susceptibility to infection—includes patients who are debilitated, have organ transplants, uncontrolled diabetes, or immunosuppression from disease or chemotherapy
   d) Respiratory or pulmonary disease or difficulty in breathing (e.g., asthma, emphysema, cystic fibrosis, mouth breathing)—because of high infection risk and danger of aspiration of bacterial plaque
   e) Difficulty in swallowing or compromised gag reflex (e.g., muscular dystrophy, paralysis, multiple sclerosis)
   f) Young age—primary and newly erupted teeth have large pulp chambers that are more susceptible to injury from vibrations and heat from ultrasonic instruments
   g) Certain dental conditions
      (1) Avoid use on demineralized tooth surfaces, dentinal hypersensitivity, porcelain crowns, laminate veneers, composite resin restorations, and titanium implant abutments
      (2) Amalgam and gold restorations may also be potentially damaged
      (3) Avoid close and prolonged contact with restorations

F. Treatment modifications for contraindications from dental conditions

1. Use plastic ultrasonic and sonic tips on titanium implant abutments

2. Reduce volume of water on magnetostrictive systems on patients sensitive to cold water—warmer water increases patient comfort
3. Use dentin desensitizing treatments or local anesthetic for sensitive patients who need ultrasonic instrumentation

G. Armamentarium

1. Types of tips (inserts)
   a) Sonic tips are available in sickle, universal, and probe-shaped designs
   b) Ultrasonic tips are available in a wide variety of designs resembling periodontal probes, chisel scalers, sickle scalers, and curets, as well as a ball-ended furcation and concavity design
2. Tip Selection
   a) Select larger, stronger standard tips for heavy or tenacious calculus removal
   b) Select modified thin tips for deplaquing and removing light to moderate calculus and endotoxins—thin tips are available in "straight" or "right and left" curved designs resembling a furcation probe
      (1) Modified (thin) straight tip designs—used primarily for preventive care and deplaquing; thin straight tips can be used on any surface in any quadrant and are well suited for patients with case type I gingivitis, exhibiting 3 to 4 mm gingival pockets with bleeding and inflammation, and minimal to no bone loss
      (2) Modified (thin) curved right and left tip designs—well suited for negotiating periodontal pockets > 4 mm deep; use for instrumenting periodontal case types II, III, and IV
         (a) Right tip is designed for use on all surfaces on mandibular right facial, mandibular left lingual, maxillary right lingual, and maxillary left facial
         (b) Left tip is designed for use on all surfaces on mandibular right lingual, mandibular left facial, maxillary right facial, and maxillary left lingual
         (c) Both right and left tips are needed to completely instrument a quadrant
2. Work area—use of barriers, surface disinfection, and laminar airflow systems are particularly important because of aerosol production
3. Operator protection
   a) Wear gown with high neck and long sleeves
   b) Cover hair
   c) Wear high bacterial filtration efficiency (HBFE) face mask, protective eyewear, face shield, and gloves; change face mask every 20 minutes in an aerosol-producing environment to prevent moisture penetration
4. Patient protection
   a) Drape patient with plastic drape, towel or bib, and tissues
   b) Place protective eyewear and cover hair
   c) Request patient to turn off hearing aid(s)

H. Ultrasonic procedures

1. Flush water lines—connect sterilized ultrasonic handpiece to connector tubing; flush over sink for 5 minutes at beginning of day and for 3 minutes between patients
2. Select tip(s)—base selection of tip shape on patient's health or disease status, root anatomy (including furcations and concavities) and type and location of deposits to be removed
3. Insert tip into ultrasonic handpiece—hold handpiece upright and fill with water; release foot pedal and insert sterilized tip until it snaps into place (process must be repeated each time tip is changed)
4. Adjust frequency, water, and power settings—make adjustments while holding tip over sink; correct settings ensure maximum instrument efficiency and comfort for operator and patient
   a) Frequency—involves number of cycles per second (cps)
      (1) Controls speed of movement of tip—higher the frequency, faster the vibration and increased ability to remove tenacious deposits (more heat is also generated at higher frequencies)
      (2) Units may have either manual or automatic frequency control (manual tuning or autotuning)
         (a) Manual tuning units—require frequency adjustments for each tip
         (b) Tuning frequency also controls pattern of water spray from tip
         (c) Unit is correctly tuned when a fine mist with a rapid drip is produced at tip—obtained by adjusting power setting
   b) Water setting
      (1) Adjust water volume so a maximum mist or "halo" surrounds the tip with no excessive dripping of water; once set, water control needs little adjustment
      (2) Deliver water coolant to tip through internal or external water supply
      (3) Maintain water stream directly over tip; insufficient water can result in instrument overheating and damage to dental pulp
      (4) Use antimicrobial solution in place of water irrigation, when indicated and if unit permits
   c) Power (length of stroke [amplitude])—controls distance tip travels in a single vibration; higher the power, longer the stroke, and greater the "chipping" action of tip
      (1) Higher power settings—increase deposit removal ability and are best suited for initial debridement of moderate to heavy calculus or tenacious deposits using general purpose rigid tips; greater damage to tooth surfaces is associated with higher power settings
      (2) Low to medium power settings—appropriate for sulcular and pocket debridement and light instrumentation using

modified thin tips; use of low power with smaller, shorter strokes are needed for root surface debridement

(3) Basic power setting principle—avoid high settings; with thinner tip, lower the power setting needed; use lowest power setting possible at which a particular tip functions properly

(4) Power boost feature—some units have a manual or automatic feature that can override manual power settings to temporarily boost power as needed

5. Position patient in supine position—turn patient's head to right while instrumenting treatment areas on patient's right side and left while instrumenting treatment areas on left side
6. Position high speed suction—place on lowest side where water pools; operator working alone may link saliva ejector to high speed suction and request patient's assistance with suctioning
7. Establish grasp and fulcrum—use light, relaxed pen or modified pen grasp with light intraoral or extraoral fulcrum
8. Activate tip—position tip near tooth surface and activate tip before adaptation and insertion
9. Select active tip surface—use active tip surface that best conforms to tooth surface being instrumented; back and sides of tip are primarily used
10. Adapt tip to tooth—adapt last several millimeters of an active tip surface
    a) Direct tip apically with length parallel to long axis of tooth or at no more than a 15-degree angle with tooth surface (similar to placement of a periodontal probe)
    b) Utilize convex curvature of back of tip in furcation anatomy
    c) Direct point of tip away from tooth and toward tissue (opposite of hand instrumentation principles); NEVER use point of tip on tooth surfaces—dull point may still damage tooth structure
    d) Slant tip or assume a perpendicular relationship to long axis of tooth when instrumenting proximal surface to ensure adequate coverage under contact
11. Plan sequence—review location of calculus with an explorer; plan systematic sequence to minimize number of times tips must be changed
12. Activate strokes—use light overlapping strokes in sweeping or erasing-type motion
    a) Keep tip in constant motion in continuous looping pattern (avoid using heavy pressure that can damage or remove tooth structure)
    b) Apply multidirectional strokes to cover entire root surface
    c) Release foot pedal to aid in water control or to allow patient a brief rest
13. Evaluate
    a) Periodically explore/evaluate debrided areas with inactive tip
    b) Evaluate a completed quadrant or sextant with explorer

I. Sonic procedures

1. Flush water lines—switch dental unit water to ON position; hold dental handpiece line over sink and activate a steady stream of water for 5 minutes at beginning of day and for 1 minute between patients to flush system
2. Connect sterilized sonic handpiece to dental unit line and turn dental unit water OFF
3. Insert sterilized sonic tip—hand tighten tip (be careful of sharp point)
   a) Do not tighten tip with sonic handpiece wrench
   b) Lock tip onto handpiece by stepping on dental unit rheostat
   c) Turn dental unit water back ON
4. Adjust water
   a) Hold handpiece tip over sink in a vertical position
   b) Activate power with dental unit rheostat
   c) Adjust dental unit water control until fine mist appears at tip
5. Establish patient position, clinician's grasp and fulcrum, adaptation and instrumentation technique—similar to those for an ultrasonic instrument (see steps 5–13 on p. 371)
6. Change tips—position handpiece horizontally over sink
   a) Remove tip with sonic handpiece wrench while activating rheostat
   b) Select new tip, hand tighten, and activate rheostat to lock into place

X. GINGIVAL CURETTAGE—involves debriding soft tissue wall of periodontal pocket

A. Inadvertent (incidental) curettage—unintentional (accidental) removal of soft tissue lining of periodontal pocket with hand or ultrasonic instruments during normal subgingival instrumentation; different from intentional curettage

B. Intentional curettage

1. Description
   a) Deliberate removal of diseased soft tissue lining of periodontal pocket
   b) Includes removal of junctional and pocket epithelium and immediate subadjacent connective tissue
   c) Accomplished with sharp hand-activated curet, ultrasonic instrument, or with use of chemicals
2. Rationale
   a) May be included after periodontal instrumentation in attempt to promote pocket reduction through tissue shrinkage and new connective tissue attachment
   b) Necessity for and additional benefits of curettage are currently highly questioned
3. Procedure with hand-activated curet
   a) Anesthetize soft tissues
   b) Activate a sharp curet with face of blade at a 70-degree angle to soft tissue pocket wall

c) Apply digital pressure to outer surface of facial or lingual gingiva to provide support against instrument; move along pocket wall to remove epithelial lining

4. Post-treatment procedures
   a) Irrigate site with normal saline solution
   b) Apply pressure with sterile gauze moistened in normal saline to facilitate readaptation of tissue, stop bleeding, minimize clot thickness, and promote healing
   c) Apply periodontal dressing as needed

XI. DENTAL IMPLANTS

A. Osseointegrated dental implant—stable functional replacement for a single tooth, several, or all teeth; consists of an anchor, abutment, and prosthetic crown; bridge, fixed, or removable denture; restores natural tooth function

1. Parts
   a) Anchor—metal fixture inserted into bone
   b) Abutment—metal attachment connected to anchor by center screw; acts as a connection between implant anchor and prosthetic appliance
   c) Implant—anchor and abutment; titanium is preferred material owing to its biocompatibility with bone; others include vanadium, vitallium, ceramic, cobalt alloys, or aluminum

B. Candidate selection criteria

1. Need for tooth replacement
2. Good physical, mental, and oral (periodontal) health
3. Consistent and effective daily plaque control
4. Adequate manual dexterity to ensure daily plaque control procedures
5. Sufficient quantity and quality of alveolar bone to retain dental implant
6. Cooperation and communication with dental team
7. Signed informed consent

C. Benefits

1. Improve function (mastication and speaking), appearance, self-confidence and self-esteem
2. Enhance patient comfort
3. Decrease alveolar bone resorption, tissue ulceration, and pressure
4. Eliminate direct forces on gingiva and alveolar crest
5. Preserve remaining alveolar bone
6. Increase retention of prosthetic appliance

D. Risks

1. Improper patient selection
2. Development of dehiscence (a hole in the buccal or labial plate of alveolar process) as a result of placing implant in area of insufficient bone
3. Improper control of immediate stress or load resulting from pressure placed on implant too soon after initial surgery
4. Rejection of implant—inability of body to accept metal implant

5. Inadequate time allowed for healing and interface development
6. Failure to osseointegrate—inadequate fusion of bone to implant anchor
7. Development of *periimplantitis*—involves inflammation and infection in periimplant tissues (gingiva around implant abutment) resulting from inadequate personal or professional oral hygiene care
8. Inadequate manufactured quality of dental implant or prosthetic design

E. Types of dental implants

1. *Endosseous implant*
   a) Most widely used
   b) Implant is placed within bone

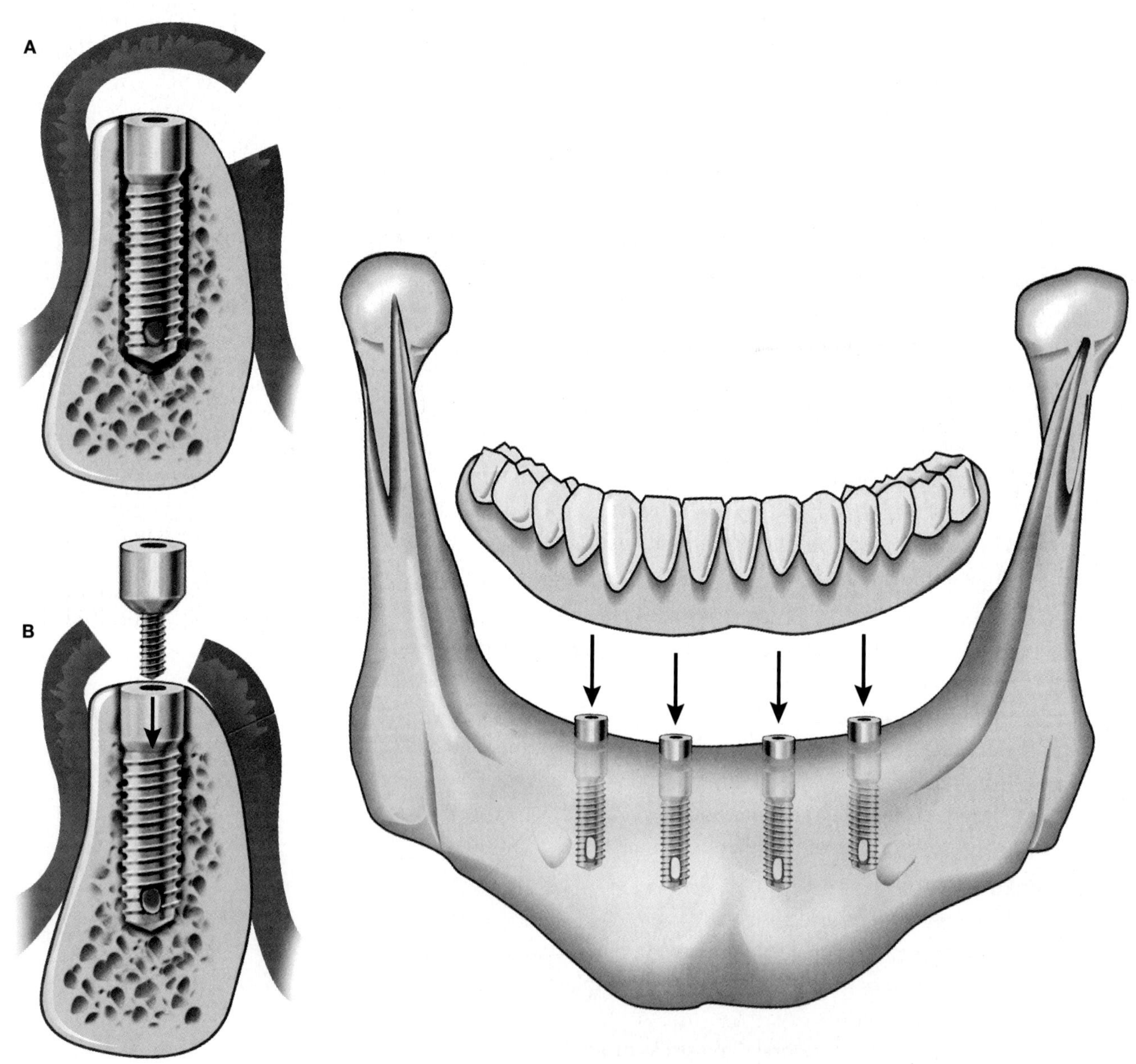

FIGURE 10-2. Endosseous implant. A) first surgery; B) second surgery

c) Abutment posts protrude through oral tissues to support removable prosthetic overdenture (attached to abutment by magnets, O-rings, or clips), dentist-retrievable denture (attached to abutment with tiny screws), or fixed prosthetic crown or bridge

d) Procedure involves two surgeries
   (1) First surgery
      (a) Implant anchor (blade, screw, or cylinder) is inserted through an intraoral incision into a hole drilled in bone
      (b) Periosteum is sutured closed over anchor
      (c) Tissues are allowed to heal and osseointegrate for 4 to 6 months in maxilla and 3 to 6 months in mandible
      (d) In *osseointegration,* bone cells grow around and directly fuse to metal anchor—success of implant is dependent on osseointegration
   (2) Second surgery
      (a) Top of anchor is surgically reexposed and abutment is attached onto anchor by a center screw
      (b) Periosteum is sutured so abutments protrude through periosteum
      (c) Healing caps are temporarily placed on abutments
      (d) Gingival tissues heal in 3 weeks in maxilla and 1 week in mandible

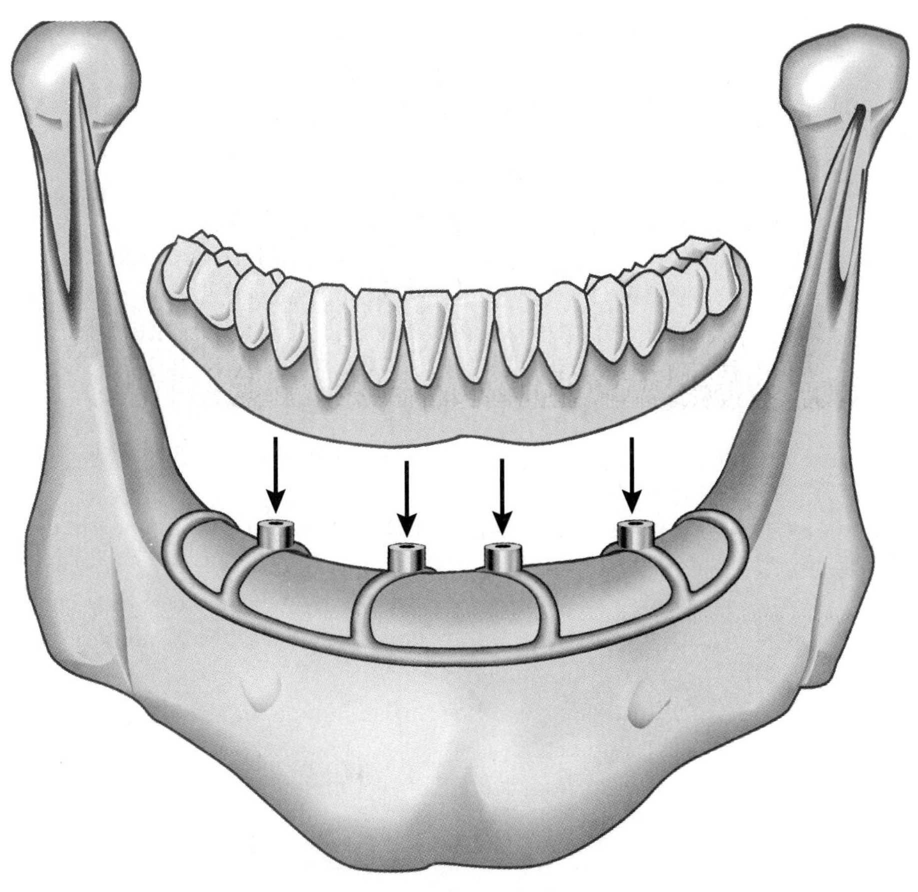

FIGURE 10-3. Subperiosteal implant

(e) Biological seal forms and attaches healthy periimplant soft tissues to implant abutment

e) Prosthetic phase—fixed or removable dental appliance is fabricated and attached to implant abutments

2. *Subperiosteal implant*
   a) Metal framework is placed over bone and under periosteum
   b) Metal posts on framework protrude through oral tissues to support prosthesis
   c) System used when width or depth of bone is insufficient for endosseous implants
   d) Procedure involves two surgeries
      (1) First surgery
         (a) Intraoral incision is made to expose alveolar bone
         (b) Impression is taken of alveolar bone
         (c) Surgical site is closed
         (d) Dental laboratory fabricates metal framework from impression and model
      (2) Second surgery
         (a) After surgical reexposure, metal framework is placed over alveolar bone and under periosteum
         (b) Surgical site is closed
         (c) Metal posts on framework protrude through gingiva to attach a fixed or removable prosthetic appliance
         (d) No osseointegration occurs with this type of implant
3. *Transosteal implant*—metal framework is placed through mandible
   a) Rarely used and, when so, strictly on mandible (cannot be placed in maxilla)
   b) Used when patient has an atrophic edentulous mandible or a congenital or traumatic deformity of mandible
   c) Procedure involves drilling holes in chin through an extraoral incision and inserting an implant consisting of five to seven parallel pins into mandible—two terminal pins protrude through gingiva and act as abutments to attach dental appliance

F. Professional implant maintenance procedures—involves working with dentist and patient to maintain gingival health and bone support for implant

1. Assessment—collect, analyze, and document following patient data
   a) Changes in medical history
   b) Location of implants—prudent to ask new patients if they have any dental implants; it may not be evident without radiographs
   c) Conditions of oral mucosa
   d) Discomfort, pain, swelling, inflammation, or infection associated with implants
   e) Color, texture, consistency of periimplant tissues
   f) Periodontal probing depths
      (1) Routine probing of implants is controversial because of possibility of disturbing the biological seal, leading to local infection and implant failure

(2) Current consensus—probing should NOT be performed routinely on implants; probe only when problem is suspected, using a plastic probe

g) Bleeding on probing (if performed)

h) Presence of exudate in sulci around implant abutments

i) Amount of plaque and calculus accumulation

j) Salivary percolation at periimplant sulcus—breakdown of biological seal is indicated if bubbles form at sulcus on application of vertical pressure to implant

k) Mobility of implant or implant prosthesis—check screw retention, horizontal and vertical mobility of implant; loose screw can cause mobility of dental prosthesis and implant

l) Results of microbiological monitoring tests

m) Marginal bone height surrounding implant anchor—determined by radiographs taken at appropriate intervals, and as needed

n) Oral hygiene knowledge, beliefs, and habits

2. Periodontal debridement of implants

a) Periimplant irrigation

(1) Precede and follow scaling with antimicrobial solution such as 0.12% chlorhexidine gluconate, particularly when periimplantitis is present

(2) Deliver solution to periimplant sulcus with either a plastic disposable syringe or powered oral irrigation unit

b) Materials contraindicated for use on implant abutments—avoid the following materials that may scratch or alter abutment surface

(1) Metal sonic and ultrasonic tips, scalers, probes, explorers and other metal instruments—metal easily scratches abutments

(2) Prophylaxis cup or brush polishing with abrasive paste or flour of pumice

(3) Air polishing device—use is controversial

(4) Acidulated phosphate fluoride—corrodes titanium implant abutments

c) Materials indicated for use on implant abutments

(1) Plastic probe

(2) Plastic, plastic-tipped, Teflon-coated, and wood-tipped scalers—used safely for calculus removal (use of graphite and gold-tipped scalers is controversial)

(3) Plastic ultrasonic or sonic scaler tips

(4) Rubber cup, rubber point, or porte polisher with gel dentifrice or tin oxide

(5) Low concentration of neutral sodium fluoride

d) Plaque and calculus removal—supragingival calculus formation is more common than subgingival calculus on implant abutments

(1) Lateral pressure—apply little pressure to remove calculus from implants; attachment of calculus to implant is weak; occasional tenacious deposits can be removed with plastic ultrasonic or sonic tips

(2) Apply basic skills—use basic operator and patient positioning, grasp, and fulcrum; AVOID fulcruming on implant
(3) Activation of strokes—apply light pressure with hand-activated and ultrasonic scaling strokes
(4) Direction of scaling strokes—apply strokes in vertical, oblique, or horizontal direction away from periimplant tissues
(5) Variety of implant scalers—includes standard sickle, universal, and Gracey curet designs, as well as the following
(a) Universal—used on apical portion of prosthetic framework; activate strokes in facial-to-lingual direction
(b) Lingual—used on lingual aspect of abutment; activate vertical strokes
(c) Facial—used on facial aspect of abutment; activate vertical strokes
(d) Wrench-type—wraps around mesial and distal aspects of abutment; activate vertical strokes
(6) Stain removal—not routinely performed on dental implants; porte polisher is instrument of choice for polishing implants; polish gently with nonabrasive agent when selective stain removal is indicated
(7) Plaque removal—remove plaque on implant abutments and underneath prosthetic appliance by buffing with G-Floss, Postcare Implant Flossing Cord, Super Floss, dental floss and/or tape used with a floss threader, moistened ribbon, yarn, or gauze
(8) *Caution:* care must be taken not to scratch implant or disrupt biological seal while scaling or polishing

3. Planning patient's disease-control program
a) Designing a home care plan
(1) Tailor to patient's preference, motivation, compliance, and dexterity
(2) Consider implant abutment length and position, and prosthetic design
(3) Access for plaque removal between appliance and gingival tissue and health of periimplant tissues
b) Providing home care instructions
(1) Provide oral/written instructions and educational pamphlets to patient
(2) Demonstrate self-care procedures and observe patient practice
(3) Instructions must be reinforced and modified as appropriate at recall visits

4. Continuing care schedule
a) Oral hygiene instruction—give immediately after implant abutment insertion and at each recall visit
b) Recall maintenance visits—schedule every 3 months for first year, then every 3 to 4 months thereafter

c) Radiographic evaluation—x-ray study of implant, bone, and periodontal structures every 3 months for first year, then annually thereafter unless otherwise indicated
d) Removal of fixed prosthetic appliances (e.g., dentist-retrievable denture)—dentist removes fixed prosthesis to check implant stability, assess gingival health, and clean appliance annually at recall maintenance appointment
e) Visits to dentist or oral surgeon—schedule annual follow-up visits with practitioner who placed implant
f) Follow-up for signs of infection—return to general dentist in 10 to 14 days or refer to specialist

G. Patient oral physiotherapy aids and procedures

1. Patient warnings
   a) Caution patient never to use safety pin, paper clip, or other metal objects to self-clean implants or abutments
   b) Warn against using hard bristle brushes that can damage implant abutment surface and lead to gingival and periimplant recession
   c) Avoid conventional metal-wired interdental brushes
2. Disclosing agent—use disclosing agent with magnifying intraoral mirror, face mirror, and pen light to evaluate plaque control on implant abutment, dental appliances, restorations, and natural teeth twice weekly
3. Brushes—use combination of soft-bristle toothbrushes as needed to remove plaque from implant abutment, dental appliances, restorations, and natural teeth
   a) Small, compact head toothbrush—for general use and on appliances; direct bristles at a 45-degree angle toward soft tissues; use two to three times daily
   b) Uni-tuft interspace brush—tapered or flat; especially useful for reaching facial and lingual surfaces of implants; use two to three times daily
   c) Plastic nylon-coated interdental brush—tapered or flat; especially useful for reaching interproximal surfaces of implants; use at least once daily
   d) Motor-powered rotary brushes—recommend to patients with limited manual dexterity; use on LOW power, one to two times daily
4. Implant abutment floss aids
   a) Types
      (1) G-Floss
      (2) Postcare Implant Flossing Cord (red = thick; green = thin)
      (3) Super Floss
      (4) Dental floss and/or tape used with a floss threader
      (5) Moistened ribbon, yarn, or gauze
   b) Instruction for use
      (1) Loop aid around implant abutment
      (2) Crisscross and pull back and forth in a shoeshining motion

(3) Wrap in a C-shape and use in back-and-forth polishing motion to clean around accessible natural teeth and under fixed bridges, connecting bars, or implant overdenture
(4) Use at least once daily

5. Rubber tip stimulator
   a) Tapered
   b) Use to remove debris from all tooth surfaces and gingival sulcus
   c) May also use to stimulate and massage periimplant tissue once daily
6. Wooden wedge stimulator, wooden pick, or porte polisher—use for plaque removal as needed
7. Dentifrice
   a) Recommend use of fine abrasive or gel anticalculus dentifrice twice daily
   b) Use of abrasive dentifrice can alter implant abutment surface
8. Antimicrobial agent
   a) Recommend a 30-second rinse with 0.12% chlorhexidine gluconate twice daily for 5 to 7 days immediately after abutment connection surgery
   b) Thereafter, apply as needed to specific sites with cotton swabs, brushes, or other oral hygiene aids
9. Oral irrigator—use as indicated when periimplant inflammation is present
   a) Use with caution and never at implant junction
   b) Use only with horizontal tip and flow placed on LOW setting
   c) Use solutions such as phenolic, plant alkaloid, or 0.12% chlorhexidine gluconate mouth rinse
   d) Use only as needed

XII. POLISHING

A. Purpose

1. Removes extrinsic stains from surfaces of teeth
2. Superficial polishing of crowns considered a cosmetic procedure with minimal therapeutic benefits (stains are not etiological factors for any disease or destructive process)
3. Selective procedure not needed by every patient especially on a routine basis

B. *Selective polishing*

1. Perform after scaling and other periodontal treatment is completed
2. Assess for presence of unsightly stains and determine need to polish teeth, restorations, and removable prostheses
3. Polish only selected surfaces where objectionable stain is noted

C. Effects of polishing

1. Beilby (polish) layer—removes and redeposits surface material; fine scratches and surface irregularities are filled in by fine particulate being removed
2. Bacteremia—antibiotic premedication indicated for risk patients
3. Aerosol production

a) Accompanies polishing with handpiece and prophylaxis angle as well as air polishing
b) Porte polisher produces very little aerosol
c) Aerosols contraindicate polishing for patients with, and who are highly susceptible to, infection via contaminated aerosols (e.g., asthma, emphysema, other respiratory diseases, breathing or swallowing difficulties, and immunosuppression)

4. Spatter of polishing agent and contaminants—patient and operator need protective eyewear
5. Removal of tooth structure—removes fluoride-rich surface layer of enamel
   a) Loss of enamel from repeated polishing over time can be significant
   b) Rapid removal of cementum and dentin occurs owing to softness and porosity
   c) Avoid polishing newly erupted teeth (they are more porous and less mineralized), areas of thin enamel (e.g., amelogenesis imperfecta, areas of abrasion) demineralization, and exposed cementum and dentin
6. Increased roughness of tooth surfaces—can create grooves and scratches
7. Heat production
   a) May cause pain or discomfort and damage to dental pulp from frictional heat of rubber cup
   b) Primary teeth, which have large pulp chambers, are particularly susceptible to heat damage
8. Trauma to gingival tissues—gingival epithelium can be abraded by rubber cup polishing at too high a speed, extended application of rubber cup with abrasive agent, or incorrect air-polishing technique
9. Reaction to abrasive particles—polishing agent and microorganisms can be forced into tissues by rotation of rubber cup, which can result in inflammation and/or delayed healing; polishing is contraindicated immediately after subgingival instrumentation in patients with deep periodontal pockets and for patients with soft, spongy gingiva
10. Increased tooth sensitivity—abrasive agent uncovers dentinal tubules ends and thus increases sensitivity; avoid areas of existing dentinal hypersensitivity
11. Surface damage to restorative materials—application of abrasive polishing agents can roughen surfaces of gold, amalgam, composite, and porcelain restorations, as well as titanium implants, and is therefore contraindicated for restored root surfaces

D. Indications for polishing (by any method)

1. Removal of unsightly stains—remove stains not otherwise removed during toothbrushing or periodontal instrumentation
2. Prepares teeth for sealants, restorative procedures, or orthodontic bonding
3. Patient motivation—encourages patient to maintain improved appearance

E. Procedures common to all polishing methods

1. Clinician preparation—wear gown with high neck and long sleeves, cover hair; wear mask, protective eyewear, faceshield, and gloves
2. Patient preparation
   a) Administer antibiotic premedication for all patients at risk
   b) Use antimicrobial pretreatment mouthrinse
   c) Use plastic drape, towel or bib, protective eyewear, and hair covering
   d) Coat lips with nonpetroleum lip lubricant
   e) Give patient extra tissues
3. Patient position—place in normal supine with head turned to right or left
4. Moisture containment—cup patient's cheeks and lips to contain water, saliva, and abrasive agent
5. Modified pen grasp—rest handpiece in 'V' between thumb and index finger
6. Fulcrum—use extraoral or intraoral fulcrum (same or opposite arch)
7. Initial stain removal
   a) Remove stains incorporated in plaque and calculus along with deposits during scaling
   b) Remove thick, heavy stains with ultrasonic and/or hand-activated instruments to avoid excessive polishing
      (1) Select ultrasonic tip that is more rounded and broad (vs. thin and pointed) for greater coverage and less tooth surface damage
      (2) Use hand-activated hoe, sickle, and curet—curet adapts well to stained curvatures of teeth
8. Use of coarser polishing agents
   a) When coarser polishing agent is needed for moderate stain removal, follow up with a fine polishing agent
   b) Use fresh rubber cup or wooden point with fine polish
9. Interproximal stains
   a) Use dental tape with abrasive agent to remove interproximal stains remaining after polishing (avoid use of abrasive in contact area)
   b) Use finishing strips for interproximal stain removal only when all other methods fail
10. Floss—rinse and floss to remove debris and abrasive particles retained between teeth

F. Power-driven polishing with rubber cup and bristle brush

1. Selection of polishing agent
   a) Use least abrasive agent first, moving to more abrasive agent if first fails to remove stain
   b) Use of over-the-counter toothpaste may be ample for professional use when stain is minimal— may also be used when stain is absent and patient requests polishing in spite of selective polishing education
2. Abrasive agents available for polishing structures

   a) Enamel—Super-fine silex (silicon dioxide), zirconium silicate, calcium carbonate (chalk or whiting), pumice flour or superfine pumice, and tin oxide
   b) Metallic restorations—pumice flour or superfine pumice, calcium carbonate, tin oxide, and levigated alumina
   c) Composite restorations—aluminum oxide (alumina)
   d) Porcelain restorations—diamond polishing paste
   e) Laboratory use only—use rouge on gold and precious metal alloys; use coarse (lab) pumice on mouthguards
3. Commercial polishing preparations—contain an abrasive (e.g., pumice), water, humectant (e.g., glycerin), binder (e.g., agar), artificial sweetener, and flavoring agent
4. Application principles for abrasives
   a) Rate of tooth surface abrasion and generation of frictional heat are increased by greater quantities of abrasive in polishing agent, speed of application, and pressure
   b) Therefore, use wet agents, low speeds, and light, intermittent pressure
5. Polishing equipment
   a) Handpiece—autoclavable, belt-driven, or motor-driven slow (low) speed handpiece; 6000 to 10,000 rpm; three basic designs: straight, contra-angle, and right angle
   b) Prophylaxis angle—disposable or autoclavable, contra- or right-angle attachment
   c) Rubber cup, rubber tip, and bristle brush attachments—disposable; three basic types: threaded stem for threaded right angle, snap-on for button-end right angle, and mandrel stem for latch-type contra-angle
6. Procedures for using prophylaxis angle
   a) Switch dental unit water to OFF position
   b) Use high-volume suction
   c) Fill cup with abrasive agent and almost bring into contact with tooth surface (but not touching) before activating handpiece
   d) Apply steady pressure with toe to rheostat to produce even, low speed
   e) Apply light pressure with rubber cup so edges flare slightly
   f) Use intermittent, light pressure (1 to 2 seconds contact) in small dabbing, circular strokes
   g) Turn entire handpiece to adapt cup to distal, facial/lingual, and mesial aspects
   h) Work from gingiva toward incisal or occlusal of each tooth
   i) Adapt cup rim to tooth concavities (e.g., lingual fossa of anterior teeth)
   j) Keep rubber cup filled with polishing agent to prevent frictional heat buildup in the tooth
   k) Keep working end moving at all times
   l) Restrict use of bristle brush to occlusal surfaces—soften bristles in hot water before use
   m) Use rubber tip on occlusal surfaces or under orthodontic wires

G. Air-powered polishing

1. Description—also called airpolishing, air-powder polishing, air-abrasive polishing, and airbrasive polishing
   a) Air-powered device delivers slurry of warm water, sodium bicarbonate powder, and air through a handpiece
   b) System includes air, water, power lines, foot control, autoclavable handpiece sheath, nozzle, and wire nozzle-cleaning tool
   c) Available in combination ultrasonic scale/airbrasive units
2. Advantages of air polishing
   a) Removes plaque and stain as effectively as rubber cup polishing and requires less time
   b) Effective on chlorhexidine, tobacco, and coffee stains
   c) Effective on stain in difficult access areas (e.g., occlusal pits and fissures)
   d) Less abrasive than rubber cup polishing with traditional prophylaxis pastes
   e) Efficiently removes plaque, stain, and debris from teeth with orthodontic appliances
   f) Effective for root detoxification on periodontally diseased roots
3. Disadvantages of air polishing
   a) Aerosol production—once a significant problem; can be nearly eliminated by use of disposable aerosol-reduction device fitted on nozzle of air polisher and connected to suction
   b) Use of mirror for indirect vision—not usually possible unless aerosol-reduction device is used
   c) Spray may be uncomfortable for patient and inconvenient for clinician unless aerosol-reduction device is used
   d) Contraindications for use includes
      (1) All contraindications for polishing in general as with any method
         (a) High susceptibility to infection transmissable via aerosols
         (b) Difficulty swallowing or breathing
         (c) Communicable diseases transmissable via aerosols
         (d) Patients at risk for bacteremia require premedication
         (e) Exposed cementum or dentin
         (f) Areas of hypersensitivity and demineralization
         (g) Thin enamel
         (h) Soft, spongy gingiva
         (i) Immediately after instrumentation in deep pockets
         (j) Primary or newly erupted teeth
         (k) Restored tooth surfaces
         (l) Titanium implants
      (2) Patients on restricted sodium diet—including patients with controlled hypertension
      (3) Patients with end-stage renal disease
      (4) Use on acrylic denture materials

(5) Use on most restorative materials may
(a) Cause pitting and wear of composite resins, porcelain, and dental cements
(b) Erode cement and damage margins of dental castings
(c) Wear dental sealants
(d) Result in matte finish with prolonged or excessive use on polished metal surfaces
(e) Remove and alter surface titanium on dental implants (use is controversial on implants)

4. Procedures for air polishing
   a) Connect water and air lines—use caution not to switch air and water lines; unit will malfunction
   b) Flush water line—flush line for 2 to 5 minutes before first use each day
   c) Use three foot control positions
      (1) OFF offers a continuous air spray
      (2) First position releases water spray only for rinsing teeth and tongue
      (3) Second position releases cleaning slurry
   d) Powder and water delivery
      (1) Adjust amount of powder delivered by turning indicator on top of chamber (12:00 maximum; 6:00 minimum)
      (2) Adjust water volume with water control
   e) Direct nozzle tip SLIGHTLY apically at the following angles:
      (1) Anterior facial and lingual surfaces—60 degrees to surface
      (2) Posterior facial and lingual surfaces—80 degrees to surface
      (3) Posterior occlusal—90 degrees to surface
   f) Direct center of spray onto middle third of tooth surfaces; AVOID directing into sulcus
   g) Use constant circular motion keeping nozzle 3 to 4 mm from tooth surface
   h) Limit application time to 1 to 2 seconds per surface
   i) Clean 4 to 6 tooth surfaces, then rinse with water-only foot control position
   j) Use both hands to cup and shield spray unless using aerosol-reduction device
   k) Place gauze over lip and cheek to protect from spray unless using aerosol-reduction device

H. Cleaning removable dentures—basic methods

1. Ultrasonic cleaning—procedure of choice
   a) Use solution designated for stain and calculus removal and follow manufacturer's directions
   b) Rinse with warm (never hot) water
   c) Use moderately stiff brush to scrub free solution and loosened debris
2. Combination manual and power-driven
   a) Remove calculus by scaling, being careful not to scratch denture

b) Polish only external surfaces (polishing internal surface of denture may alter fit)
c) Soften bristle brush in hot water and use to polish nonmetal parts with very wet superfine pumice
d) Polish metal parts with rubber cup and tin oxide
e) Rinse thoroughly with warm (never hot) water

3. Dental lathe in laboratory
   a) Polish nonmetal parts with wet rag wheel and fine pumice
   b) Polish metal parts, other than clasps, with separate wet rag wheel and tin oxide
   c) Use porte polisher and tin oxide on clasps
   d) Rinse thoroughly with warm (never hot) water

XIII. INSTRUMENT SHARPENING

A. Advantages

1. Reduces number of strokes required for deposit removal and therefore saves time
2. Reduces operator fatigue in fingers, hand, and wrist
3. Provides greater instrument control owing to less pressure required for deposit removal
4. Reduces possibility of burnishing deposits and scratching or grooving roots
5. Increases tactile sensitivity

B. Stationary instrument–moving stone technique

1. Determine design characteristics of the instrument-working end
   a) Face and lateral surface of the sickle scaler, universal curet, and area-specific curet meet in internal angle of 70 to 80 degrees
   b) Sharp cutting edge is a line—has length, but no width
   c) Dull cutting edge is rounded—has length and width
2. Lubricate stone (optional)
   a) Reduces frictional heat
   b) Use sterile oil for natural and synthetic sharpening stones
3. Grasp instrument handle in palm of hand, rest hand on countertop, and position working end
   a) Point toe (tip) directly toward operator
   b) Position face parallel to counter top
      (1) Universal curet—lower shank is perpendicular to countertop
      (2) Area-specific curet—lower shank is NOT perpendicular to countertop
4. Grasp lower portion of stone and initially position stone perpendicular to instrument face
5. Tip lower portion of stone toward instrument's lateral surface and establish 70- to 80-degree angle between stone and instrument face
6. Move stone in short up-and-down strokes and finish in downward stroke
7. Sharpen cutting edge in sections (heel, middle, and toe thirds)
8. Sharpen one cutting edge (lower) per working end on area-specific curet

9. Sharpen two cutting edges per working stroke end on universal curet and sickle scaler
10. Continue sharpening strokes to round back of working end of curet
11. Use semicircular strokes to round back of working end of curet
12. Evaluate sharpness of cutting edge(s) with plastic sharpening test stick

review questions

DIRECTIONS Each of the questions or incomplete statements below is followed by suggested answers or completions. Select the **one** answer that is best in each case.

1. Which of the following instrument designs is LEAST likely to provide tactile sensitivity?
   A. flexible shank
   B. moderately flexible shank
   C. rigid shank
   D. hollow metal handle

2. All of the following represent functions of a straight, calibrated probe EXCEPT one. Which one is the EXCEPTION?
   A. assess attachment loss
   B. evaluate the presence of bleeding
   C. measure recession
   D. detect fractures in teeth
   E. measure lesions

3. Which one of the following instruments is used with a push stroke?
   A. periodontal file
   B. chisel
   C. hoe
   D. sickle
   E. curet

4. Which of the following instruments is recommended to remove light subgingival calculus deposits?
   A. hoe
   B. chisel
   C. sickle scaler
   D. curet

5. Which of the following instruments has a "self-angulated" cutting edge?
   A. Columbia 13/14
   B. Barnhart 1/2
   C. Jacquette-33
   D. Gracey 11/12
   E. Columbia 4R/4L

6. Tooth #30 has a Class III furcation involvement. Which of the following Gracey curets is BEST suited for scaling the distobuccal aspect of the mesial root?
   A. 1/2
   B. 5/6
   C. 7/8
   D. 11/12
   E. 13/14

7. When scaling with a sickle or curet, the IDEAL angulation, in degrees, between the instrument face and tooth surfaces should be
   A. 15.
   B. 45.
   C. 70.
   D. 90.

8. On a Gracey curet, which part of the cutting edge should be adapted to the tooth surface in preparation for a working stroke?
   A. leading third
   B. middle third
   C. heel third
   D. toe

9. Which one of the following work strokes should be performed with firm pressure?
   A. calculus removal with an ultrasonic instrument
   B. calculus removal with a sonic instrument
   C. calculus removal with an hand-activated instrument
   D. root surface debridement with an hand-activated instrument
   E. root surface debridement with an ultrasonic instrument
10. When a furcation probe can completely pass between the roots, with no tissue recession present, the furcation is classified as Class
    A. I.
    B. II.
    C. III.
    D. IV.
    E. V.
11. Tooth #23 can be displaced 2 mm in a facial-lingual direction, but no vertical mobility can be detected. The degree of mobility should be classified as
    A. N.
    B. Grade I.
    C. Grade II.
    D. Grade III.
    E. Grade IV.
12. Which one of the following is a characteristic of the NEW paradigm in nonsurgical periodontal therapy?
    A. root planing with firm pressure
    B. intentional and aggressive cementum removal
    C. hard, glassy, smooth root surfaces
    D. use of antimicrobial adjuncts
13. Which of the following materials is NOT acceptable to use on a dental implant?
    A. graphite
    B. plastic
    C. wood
    D. stainless steel
14. Which of the following descriptions does NOT reflect correct positioning of the air-polishing nozzle tip?
    A. nozzle is directed at 60-degree angle to anterior facials and linguals
    B. nozzle is directed at 90-degree angle to posterior facials and linguals
    C. spray is centered onto the middle third of tooth surface
    D. nozzle is kept 3 to 4 mm away from tooth surface
15. Of the following power-driven scalers, which one utilizes a tip that is activated on two surfaces (sides)?
    A. magnetostrictive
    B. piezoelectric
    C. sonic
    D. Titan
16. Which of the following instruments is LEAST likely to adequately access and debride a Class III furcation?
    A. modified (thin) ultrasonic tip
    B. standard Gracey curet
    C. Hu-Friedy After-Five curet
    D. Hu-Friedy Mini-Five curet
17. Which of the following is the BEST method for polishing dental implants?
    A. porte polisher with tin oxide
    B. prophylaxis cup with flour of pumice
    C. prophylaxis brush with medium abrasive paste
    D. air polishing
18. In the OLD paradigm of nonsurgical periodontal therapy, the success of treatment was evaluated in terms of the
    A. absence of inflammation and infection.
    B. healing and repair of damaged periodontal tissues.
    C. cessation of progress of periodontal disease.
    D. complete removal of calculus and root smoothness.
19. Air polishing can be safely and efficiently performed on patients with
    A. extensive composite and porcelain restorations.
    B. orthodontic appliances.
    C. controlled hypertension.
    D. Addison's disease.

20. Which of the following power-driven scalers has the LEAST capacity for heavy calculus removal?
    A. magnetostrictive
    B. piezoelectric
    C. sonic
    D. there is no difference
21. Contraindications for use of ultrasonic scalers are for all of the following conditions EXCEPT one. Which one is the EXCEPTION?
    A. respiratory infection
    B. acute necrotizing ulcerative gingivitis
    C. emphysema
    D. demineralized tooth structure
    E. composite resin restorations
22. All of the following procedures are routinely performed at dental implant maintenance appointments EXCEPT one. Which one is the EXCEPTION?
    A. applying periimplant antimicrobial irrigation prior to scaling
    B. assessing horizontal and vertical mobility to implant
    C. probing entire dentition including implant
    D. checking for salivary percolation in peri-implant sulcus
    E. taking radiographs at appropriate intervals
23. A linear movement pattern working tip is characteristic of which of the following power-driven scalers?
    A. magnetostrictive
    B. piezoelectric
    C. sonic
    D. Titan
24. Which of the following ultrasonic tips is MOST appropriate to use to debride a 6 mm pocket on the lingual surface of tooth #18?
    A. standard universal
    B. modified (thin) straight
    C. modified (thin) curved right
    D. modified (thin) curved left
25. Which of the following dental implants is placed within the bone and MOST widely used?
    A. supraperiosteal
    B. subperiosteal
    C. transosteal
    D. endosseous
26. The BEST method to use for removal of heavy tobacco stain is
    A. ultrasonic scaling.
    B. rubber cup polishing with a coarse abrasive.
    C. bristle-brush polishing with a coarse abrasive.
    D. hand scaling.
27. All of the following oral hygiene aids can be safely used to clean dental implant abutments EXCEPT one. Which one is the EXCEPTION?
    A. Super Floss
    B. dental tape
    C. yarn
    D. pipe cleaner
    E. shoelace
28. All of the following are disadvantages of ultrasonic instrumentation EXCEPT one. Which one is the EXCEPTION?
    A. periodontal debridement
    B. aerosol production
    C. impeded visibility
    D. inconvenience of water spray
    E. operator hearing shifts
29. All of the following applications should be used during ultrasonic debridement EXCEPT one. Which one is the EXCEPTION?
    A. overlapping strokes
    B. multidirectional strokes
    C. use of light pressure
    D. high power setting
    E. use of modified (thin) tip
30. All of the following principles are involved with correct rubber cup polishing technique EXCEPT one. Which one is the EXCEPTION?
    A. Position rubber cup on tooth before activating handpiece.
    B. Apply light pressure to slightly flare rubber cup edges.
    C. Use intermittent, dabbing, circular strokes.
    D. Keep rubber cup filled with polishing agent.

answers & rationales

1.
C. Shank flexibility is necessary to detect tooth irregularities and subgingival deposits. Rigid shanks provide little tactile information for the clinician. A flexible shank provides the greatest tactile information, whereas the moderately flexible shank provides some tactile sensitivity.

2.
D. The periodontal probe is not the appropriate instrument to use to detect fractures in teeth. However, it is an excellent instrument to use to assess attachment loss, evaluate the presence of bleeding, and measure recession and lesions.

3.
B. The chisel is used only in a horizontal direction with a push stroke to dislodge heavy calculus from the facial, lingual, and interproximal surfaces. The periodontal file, hoe, sickle, and curet are used with a pull stroke.

4.
D. Curets are designed to remove light to moderate supragingival and subgingival calculus. The hoe offers limited use subgingivally, but can be used to remove heavy supragingival calculus. The sickle scaler removes calculus supragingivally.

5.
D. Area-specific curets, such as the Gracey 11/12, have a longer (self-angulated) cutting edge that is used during instrumentation. The Columbia 13/14, Barnhart 1/2, Jacquette-33, and Columbia 4R/4L have cutting edges on both sides.

6.
E. The Gracey 13/14 is designed to be used on distal surfaces of posterior teeth. When furcation involvement is present, each root is debrided as if it were a single-rooted tooth. The Gracey 1/2 is designed to use on anterior teeth. The Gracey 5/6 is used on anterior and premolar teeth. The Gracey 7/8 is designed for application on facial and linguals of posterior teeth. The Gracey 11/12 is designed for mesial surfaces of posterior teeth.

7.
C. The correct angulation between the instrument face and tooth surface is less than 90 degrees and greater than 45 degrees. A 70-degree angle is considered ideal.

8.
A. The curet is correctly adapted for a working stroke when the leading third of the cutting edge is in contact with the tooth surface and conforms to the contour of the tooth. Using the toe, middle, or heel third in preparation for a working stroke would increase the possibility of soft tissue trauma.

9.
C. Only a calculus removal work stroke, with hand-activated instruments, is executed with moderate to heavy (firm) pressure. Calculus removal with ultrasonic or sonic instruments should be used with light pressure. Root surface debridement with hand-activated or ultrasonic instruments should be used with a light pressure.

10.

C. Class III furcations, with complete bone loss, are located below the gingival margin and allow for a furcation probe to pass completely between the roots. Because there is slight bone loss with Class I furcations, the probe cannot be inserted into the furcation. With Class II furcations, there is partial bone loss, and the probe can be inserted into the furcation only. With a Class IV furcation, the probe can pass between the furcation with clinical evidence of the furca due to the presence of gingival recession. There is no Class V classification for furcation involvement.

11.

C. Grade II represents moderate mobility in which the tooth can be displaced greater than 1 mm in a facial-lingual direction, but cannot be displaced vertically. N denotes normal physiological mobility—all teeth exhibit slight normal mobility. Grade I represents slight mobility—up to 1 mm facial-lingual displacement. Class III denotes severe mobility with displacement greater than 1 mm horizontally as well as vertically. There is no Grade IV classification for mobility.

12.

D. The new paradigm in nonsurgical periodontal therapy includes the use of various antimicrobial agents and antibiotics. The old paradigm includes using mechanical removal of deposits through scaling and root planing, intentionally removing cementum from root surfaces to obtain a hard, glossy result.

13.

D. Stainless steel instruments should be avoided because metal easily scratches and damages the surfaces of implant abutments. The use of plastic and wood-tipped scalers are safe to use on dental implants. The use of graphite is controversial at this time.

14.

B. The air-polishing nozzle tip should be directed slightly apical at an 80-degree angle to posterior facial and lingual surfaces. The air-polishing nozzle tip should be used in a constant circular motion 3 to 4 mm from the tooth surface. It can be applied at 60 degrees to the posterior occlusal surfaces. Also, the spray should be directed in the middle third of the tooth, avoiding spray into the sulcus.

15.

B. The piezoelectric ultrasonic tip vibrates in a linear movement pattern, which limits the number of active tip surfaces to its two sides. A magnetostrictive scaler moves in an elliptical pattern using all four surfaces of the tip. A sonic scaler tip moves in an elliptical or orbital motion using all four sides. Titan is an example of a sonic scaler.

16.

B. The standard Gracey curet has the largest diameter working end of all the instruments listed. Smaller diameter working ends, such as the modified (thin) ultrasonic tip, and Hu-Friedy After-Five/Mini-Five curets, provide better access into furcation areas.

17.

A. The porte polisher is the instrument of choice for polishing dental implants. A nonabrasive agent, such as tin oxide, is recommended to use on dental implants because of its susceptibility to surface scratching. Use of a rubber cup with pumice and prophylaxis brush with medium abrasive paste may scratch or alter the abutment surface(s). The use of air-polishing is controversial.

18.

D. The success of treatment in the old paradigm (nonsurgical periodontal treatment) was determined by root smoothness and complete removal of calculus, not by the patient's response to therapy.

19.

B. Air-polishing can be used to safely and efficiently remove plaque, stain, and debris on patients with orthodontic appliances. Air polishing can cause pitting and wear on composite and porcelain restorations. It is not recommended for patients on a restricted sodium diet, including patients with controlled hypertension. Patients with a risk of an acid-base imbalance, such as in Addison's disease, should not have an air polisher used on them.

20.

C. Sonic instrument tip vibrations range from 2000 to 6300 cycles/second (cps) compared with 25,000 to 50,000 cps in magnetostrictive and piezoelectric ultrasonic instruments. The slower rate of vibration in sonic instruments results in a lower capacity for heavy calculus removal.

21.

B. Ultrasonic instrumentation provides an effective means of debridement in cases of acute necrotizing ulcerative gingivitis. Before ultrasonic instrumentation, an antimicrobial pretreatment rinse and removal of soft debris with a toothbrush are recommended to minimize aerosolized bacteria. It is not advised to use ultrasonic scaling on patients with respiratory or pulmonary diseases or who may have difficulty breathing, such as those with a respiratory infection or emphysema, because of a high infection risk and danger of aspiration of bacterial plaque. Damage of composite resin restorations and demineralized tooth structure could also result from use.

22.

C. The current consensus includes that probing should NOT be routinely performed on dental implants. Probing implants should be done only when a problem is suspected because of the possibility of disturbing the biological seal, leading to local infection and implant failure. It is protocol to provide the following procedures at the dental implant maintenance appointments: apply periimplant antimicrobial irrigation before scaling, assess mobility, check for salivary perculation in periimplant sulcus, and take radiographs at appropriate intervals.

23.

B. The piezoelectric is the only power-driven scaler with a linear movement pattern. A magnetorestrictive tip moves in an elliptical pattern and a sonic (Titan) tip moves in an elliptical or orbital motion.

24.

C. Modified (thin) curved right and left tips are designed for light deposit removal and negotiating periodontal pockets greater than 4 mm. The right tip is designed for use on the mandibular right facial and left lingual, as well as the maxillary right lingual and left facial surfaces. The modified (thin) curved left tip is designed for use on the mandibular left buccal and right lingual surfaces and maxillary right and left lingual surfaces. Modified (thin) straight tip designs are used primarily for preventive care and deplaquing on any surface, especially cases exhibiting 3- to 4-mm pockets with bleeding and inflammation. Standard universal tips are used for heavy or tenacious calculus removal.

25.

D. Endosseous implants are surgically placed within the alveolar bone and represent the most widely used type of dental implant. A subperiosteal implant is placed over the bone and under the periosteum and most commonly used when the width or depth of the bone is insufficient for an endosseous implant. A transosteal implant is placed through the mandible and rarely used. There is no supraperiosteal implant.

26.

A. Removal of heavy stains should begin with ultrasonic instruments before polishing. It reduces instrumentation time and operator fatigue. The use of coarse abrasives can do damage to the enamel.

27.

D. Use of metal-wired pipe cleaners should be avoided because metal objects damage implant abutment surfaces. Super Floss, dental tape, yarn, and shoelaces can be used to safely clean implant abutments.

28.

A. Because of advances in ultrasonic tip design and a new approach to periodontal therapy, ultrasonic instrumentation is no longer restricted to gross calculus removal. Ultrasonic instrumentation, with modified tip designs, has been proven equally effective as hand-activated instrumentation for periodontal debridement. Ultrasonic scalers produce aerosol from the water spray, impede visibility, and can cause operator hearing shifts.

29.

D. Removal of light deposits and root surface debridement should be accomplished with modified (thin) ultrasonic tips and LOW power settings. High power settings are used with standard (general purpose) rigid tips for removal of moderate-heavy or tenacious calculus.

30.

A. The rubber cup should be activated just before making contact with the tooth surface. This allows the clinician the opportunity to adjust the speed of the rotating rubber cup to the desired setting before making contact with the tooth.

CHAPTER

11 Oral and Maxillofacial Radiology

Gail Williamson, RDH, MS

contents

Thanks to Mr. Mark Dirlam, graphic artist, and Mr. Mike Halloran and Mr. Thomas Meador, photographers, at the Illustrations Department at Indiana University School of Dentistry, for their skilled assistance and preparation of the radiographic illustrations. Thanks to Edwin T. Parks, DMD, MS, and Sally Phillips, RDH, BS, for their review of chapter materials.

I. RADIATION PHYSICS

A. *Radiation*—transmission of energy through space and matter in the form of waves or particles

B. Types of radiation

1. *Electromagnetic radiation*—transmission of wave energy through space and matter as a combination of electric and magnetic fields
   a) Characteristics
      (1) Have no mass
      (2) No electrical charge
      (3) Travel at the speed of light in a straight but oscillating path
      (4) Exists in a wide range of magnitudes or energy continuum (Fig. 11-1)
      (5) Dualistic nature—some characteristics best explained by wave theory, some by quantum theory
   b) Wave theory—radiation propagated in form of waves
      (1) Wave motion—wavelength; one wavelength is the distance from crest to crest or valley to valley
      (2) Frequency—number of crests or valleys per unit time
      (3) Wavelength and frequency determine energy level; short wavelength and high frequency = high energy level
   c) Quantum theory
      (1) Describes electromagnetic radiation as small bundles of energy called quanta or photons
      (2) Transfer of energy occurs as a flux of quanta or photons; each photon travels at the speed of light and contains specific amount of energy
      (3) Quantum theory useful for describing interaction of radiation with atoms and the production of x-rays
   d) Examples
      (1) Long wavelengths—radar, television, radio
      (2) Short wavelengths—visible light, ultraviolet light, x-rays

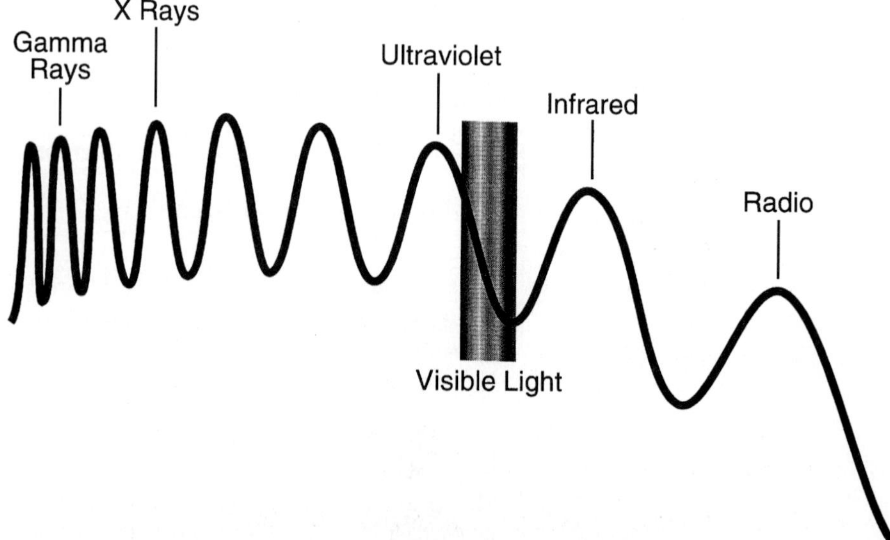

FIGURE 11-1. The electromagnetic spectrum

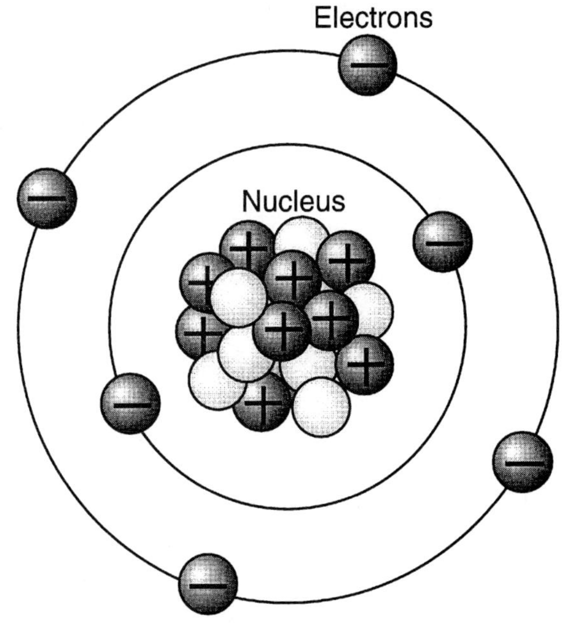

FIGURE 11-2. The subatomic particles: protons, neutrons, and electrons

2. *Particulate radiation*—atomic nuclei or subatomic particles that travel at high velocity
   a) Characteristics
      (1) Have mass and energy
      (2) All particles have an electrical charge except neutrons
      (3) Travel in straight lines at high speeds
   b) Examples
      (1) Alpha particles, beta particles, and cathode rays (electrons)
      (2) Nucleons—protons (+) and neutrons (Fig. 11-2)

C. Some specific properties of x-rays useful in imaging

1. Able to penetrate matter
2. Differentially absorbed by matter
3. Capable of producing a latent image that can be transformed into a visible image
4. Causes certain substances to fluoresce such as intensifying screens

D. Ionization—process by which a neutral atom acquires a positive or negative charge

1. Electromagnetic radiation and particulate radiation of sufficient energy can interact with atoms and create ion pairs
2. Ion pair: + ion = atom with lost electron, – ion = the ejected electron
3. Mechanism by which biological systems are altered or damaged
4. Examples of ionizing radiation
   a) Electromagnetic—ultraviolet light, x-rays, gamma rays
   b) Particulate—alpha particles, beta particles, protons

II. PRODUCTION OF RADIATION

A. X-ray generating equipment and components

1. Control panel components
   a) Main on/off switch

b) *Milliamperage (mA) selector*—adjusts amount or flow of electrical current
   (1) 1 mA =1/1000 ampere
   (2) Typically fixed at a specific mA such as 10 mA
c) *Kilovoltage (kVp) selector*—adjusts potential difference or rate of electrical current
   (1) 1 kVp = 1000 volts
   (2) Usually fixed at 70 kVp
   (3) Variable kVp machines range from 50 to 100 kVp
d) *Timer*—regulates the length of x-ray exposure, calibrated as fraction of a second
   (1) Formats
      (a) Standard fractions of a second (1/2 second)
      (b) Decimal fractions of a second (.50 second)
      (c) Impulses (30 impulses/second)
   (2) Conversion
      (a) To convert exposure time in seconds to impulses, multiply by 60 ($1/2 \times 60 = 30$ impulses)
      (b) To convert impulses to exposure time in seconds, divide by 60 ($30 \div 60 = 30/60$ or 1/2 or .50)
e) Exposure switch/button—engages system to produce x-rays
f) X-ray emission light/audible signal—indicates when x-rays are being produced

2. *X-ray tubehead*—metal encasement housing the x-ray production components (Fig. 11-3):
   a) X-ray tube—air-evacuated leaded glass tube with unleaded glass window to allow x-rays to leave x-ray tube
   b) *Cathode* (–) *electrode*
      (1) Molybdenum metal focusing cup
      (2) Tungsten filament—thin wire
      (3) Controlled by low voltage (8 to 12 volts) electrical circuit
   c) *Anode* (+) *electrode*
      (1) Copper metal sheath or rod
      (2) Tungsten metal "target" (focal spot) embedded on the surface of copper rod
      (3) Controlled by high-voltage (50,000 to 100,000 volts) circuit
   d) Transformers—devices used to alter electrical current
      (1) *Step-down transformer* or low voltage (mA) circuit; decreases electrical current from 110 or 220 volts to 8–12 volts to heat tungsten filament
      (2) *Step-up transformer* or high voltage (kVp) circuit; increases electrical current from 110 or 220 to 50 to 100 kVp to produce x-rays
      (3) *Autotransformer*—allows selection of variable kVp settings on x-ray units with a kVp range
   e) Oil—surrounds x-ray tube and serves to dissipate heat
   f) X-ray *filter*—millimeter layers of aluminum metal used to filter x-ray beam

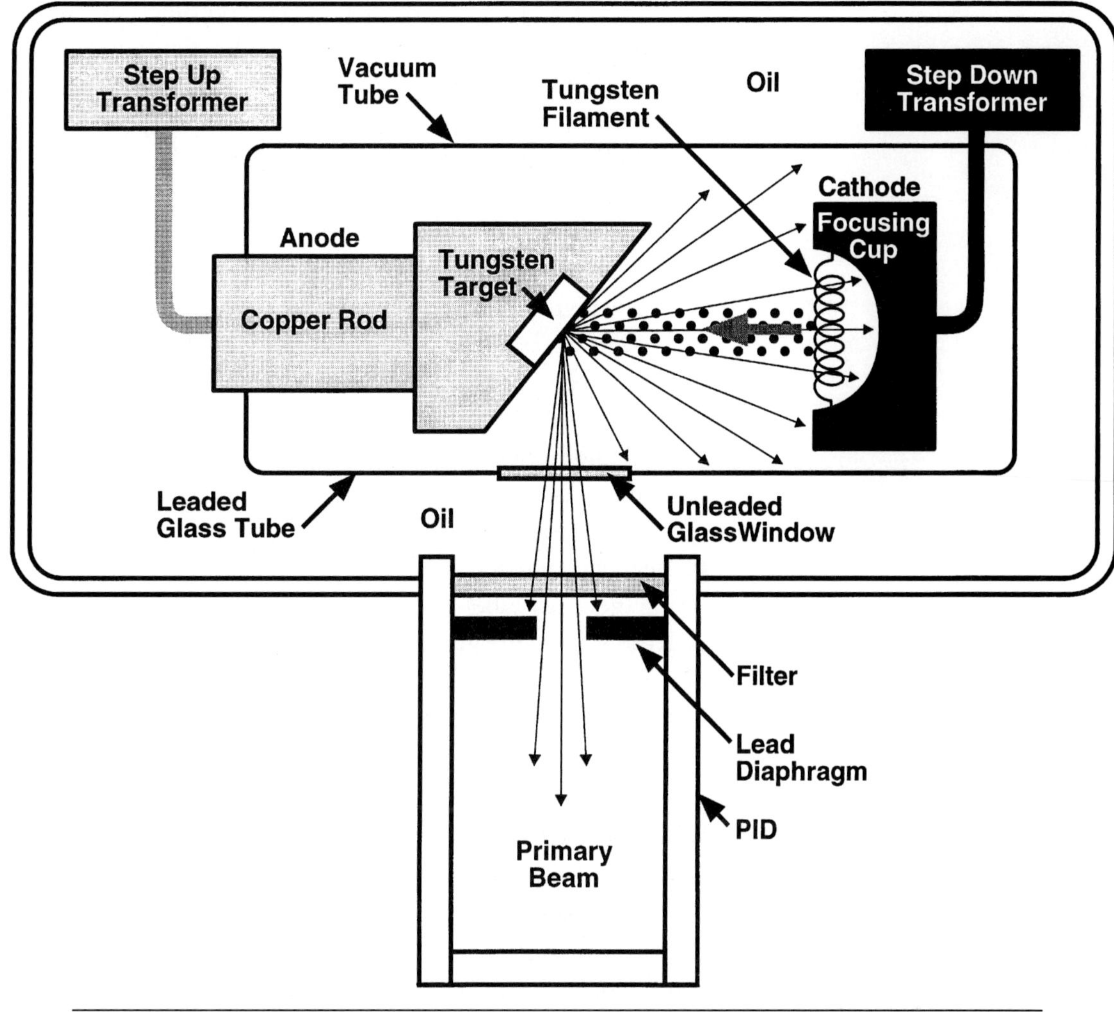

FIGURE 11-3. Components of an x-ray tubehead

g) *Lead diaphragm* or collimator—device that restricts size of x-ray beam
h) *PID* (position indicating device) or x-ray cone—device that guides the x-ray beam toward patient and receptor

B. Production of x-rays

1. Turn on the machine and set the exposure factors—mA, kVp, time
2. Depress the exposure button to activate the system to produce x-rays
3. Heat the tungsten filament
   a) Controlled by the mA setting via the step-down transformer
   b) Filament is heated to incandescence, creating an electron cloud; referred to as thermionic emission
   c) Provides a source of particles to use for producing x-rays
   d) Once the filament is heated, a time delay switch applies power to the high-voltage circuit
4. Electrons set in motion
   a) + charged anode attracts the electrons from the – charged cathode

b) Speed of the traveling electrons is controlled by the kVp setting via the step-up transformer; the higher the kilovoltage, the greater the speed

5. Anode target bombardment
   a) Cathode electron particles interact with the tungsten target atoms; < 1% (≈.2%) of the interactions produce x-rays
      (1) *Bremsstrahlung (general or braking) radiation*—interactions at or near the nucleus that suddenly stop or brake high-speed electrons; major source of x-ray photons
      (2) *Characteristic radiation*—K, L shell interactions that dislodge an electron, attracting an electron from the next shell to fill the vacancy; minor source of x-ray photons
   b) Cathode electron particles interact with outer electron shells of tungsten target atoms; > 99% (≈99.8%) of the interactions produce heat
6. Heat is conducted via the copper sheath/rod into the oil surrounding the x-ray tube
7. X-rays leave the glass tube via the unleaded glass window
8. Primary x-ray beam
   a) Filtered with aluminum to remove long wavelength x-rays
   b) Collimated to reduce the size of the x-ray beam
   c) Guided through the PID (x-ray cone) for patient radiography

III. IMAGE RECEPTORS

A. Intraoral radiographic film—used for direct imaging (x-ray interaction with film emulsion)

1. Film composition
   a) Film wrappings
      (1) Outer plastic or paper cover—protects film from light and moisture
         (a) Plain white side directed toward x-ray source
         (b) Colored side indicates film speed and single or double film packet; side placed away from x-ray source
      (2) Inner black paper—protects film from light and moisture
      (3) Lead foil—located between black paper and outer cover
         (a) Reduces film fog by absorbing secondary radiation scattering back from patient's tissues
         (b) Helps reduce patient exposure by attenuating the primary beam after penetrating the film base
   b) Film identification dot—convex on source side of the film, concave on the other
      (1) Used to determine patient's right and left sides
      (2) Placed coronally on periapicals and toward x-ray source
      (3) Corresponds to white side or exposure side of film
   c) Film base and emulsion
      (1) Film base—polyester plastic material with a blue tint
         (a) Provides stiffness with some flexibility
         (b) Tint reduces eye fatigue
      (2) *Film emulsion*—gelatin matrix with a suspension of silver halide crystals

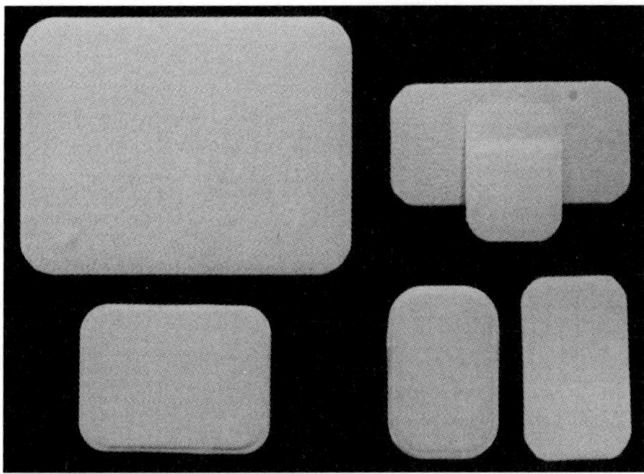

FIGURE 11-4. Intraoral film. Size 4 occlusal (*top left*); Size 3 bitewing (*top right*); Size 2, 0, and 1 periapicals (*bottom, from L to R*)

(a) Silver halide crystals or grains
   i) 95% silver bromide
   ii) Small amount of silver iodide
   iii) Sulfur-containing crystal lattice contaminant (sensitivity speck) increases sensitivity of silver bromide crystals

(3) Adhesive—aids in adherence of emulsion to film base

(4) Supercoating—gelatin layer over emulsion that helps prevent scratching

2. Film size and purpose (Fig. 11-4)
   a) *Periapical* (sizes 0, 1, 2)—records entire tooth or group of teeth and surrounding structures
   b) *Bitewing* (sizes 0, 1, 2, 3)—records interproximals of posterior teeth crowns and supporting alveolar bone
   c) *Occlusal* (size 4)—records large portion of either maxilla or mandible; used to view broader area or to localize objects
   d) Surveys—combination of several periapical and/or bitewing films
3. *Film speed*—refers to sensitivity of silver halide emulsion to radiation; the more sensitive the film emulsion, the less x-ray exposure required
   a) American National Standards Institute (ANSI) speeds
      (1) A (slowest), F (fastest)
      (2) Current available speeds—D (Ultraspeed), E (Ektaspeed) and F (Insight); E speed is twice as fast as D and requires half the exposure, F speed requires 20% exposure of E speed film

B. Extraoral radiographic film—used for indirect imaging (x-ray interaction with intensifying screens)

1. Sizes and types of extraoral projections
   a) Lateral jaw (5 in. × 7 in.)—records right or left side of the jaws
   b) Panoramic (5 in. or 6 in. × 12 in.)—records entire maxilla, mandible, and immediately adjacent structures

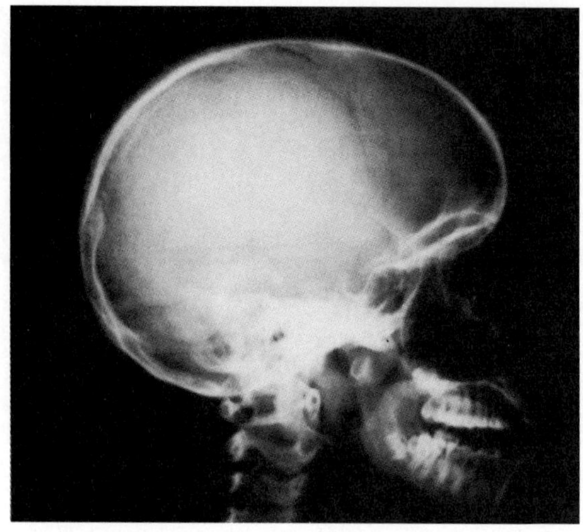

FIGURE 11-5. Lateral head plate

c) Skull projections (8 in. × 10 in.)—record entire skull in various ways to view specific anatomy, symmetry, and disease processes
   (1) Lateral head plate—common projection used for orthodontics to assess facial growth (Fig. 11-5)
   (2) Waters projection—view useful for examining maxillary sinuses as well as frontal and ethmoid sinuses

2. *Cassettes*—film holder for extraoral radiographs that contains two intensifying screens
3. *Intensifying screens*—screens fluorescence upon exposure to x-rays
   a) Reduces patient radiation dose
   b) Sum of x-rays and fluorescent light emitted by the screen phosphors exposes the film
   c) Basic components
      (1) Base—plastic support material
      (2) Reflecting layer—reflect light emitted from phosphor layer back to the film
      (3) Phosphor layer—light-sensitive phosphorescent crystals suspended in plastic material
         (a) Calcium tungstate screens—emit blue and blue-violet light
            i) Must be matched with blue light-sensitive film
            ii) Slower crystals that require more x-ray exposure
         (b) Rare earth screens—emit green light
            i) Must be matched with green light-sensitive film
            ii) Faster crystals that require at least one-half the x-ray exposure of calcium tungstate screens

IV. EXPOSURE FACTORS

A. Visual characteristics

1. *Density*—overall degree of blackness or darkness on the radiograph

a) Factors affecting density—exposure factors (mA, time, kVp), source-film distance, subject (patient) thickness

2. *Contrast*—difference in densities among various regions on a radiograph
   a) Factors affecting contrast—kVp, subject contrast (thickness, density, atomic number), film contrast (ability to display differences in subject contrast), film processing
3. *Sharpness*—ability of a radiograph to define an edge
   a) Factors affecting sharpness—focal spot size, movement, film emulsion grain size, intensifying screen fluorescence
4. *Resolution*—ability of a radiograph to record and demonstrate separate structures that are close together
   a) Factors affecting resolution—focal spot size, movement, film emulsion grain size, intensifying screen fluorescence

B. Exposure factors

1. *mA*—controls quantity or number of x-rays
   a) Function of tube current, usually fixed at specific mA
   b) Affects film density or degree of film darkening
      (1) Dependent on quantity or number of x-rays reaching the film; more x-rays → dark image, few x-rays → light image
      (2) Low density—light image from low mA setting; to darken the image, increase the mA setting
      (3) High density—dark image from high mA setting; to lighten the image, decrease the mA setting
   c) A change in mA changes the quantity or number of x-rays produced; rule of thumb
      (1) An increase of 5 mA will increase the number of x-rays
         (a) To maintain original film density, divide time by 2
         (b) 5 mA @ .30 sec. = 10 mA @ .15 sec.
      (2) A decrease of 5 mA will decrease the number of x-rays
         (a) To maintain original film density, multiply time by 2
         (b) 10 mA @ .20 sec. = 5 mA @ .40 sec.
2. *Exposure time*—controls length of time that x-rays are produced
   a) Most frequently altered exposure factor
   b) A change in time alters quantity or number of x-rays
   c) Affects film density or degree of film darkening
      (1) Dependent on quantity or number of x-rays reaching film; more x-rays → dark image, few x-rays → light image
      (2) Low density—light image from decreased exposure time setting or premature release of exposure button; to darken image, increase time setting and complete exposure cycle
      (3) High density—dark image from increased exposure time setting; to lighten image, decrease exposure time setting
3. *Milliampere-seconds* (*mAs*)—combined density factor; product of milliamperage and time
   a) 10 mA × .30 seconds = 3 mA
   b) 15 mA × .20 seconds = 3 mA
   c) Most significant density factor

4. *kVp*—controls quality or penetrating power of x-rays; minor factor in controlling quantity of x-rays
   a) Chiefly affects contrast or range of densities on radiograph
   b) Scale of contrast is affected because of altered penetrating power
      (1) Long scale contrast (> 70 kVp)—many shades of grays, blacks, whites; described as low contrast
      (2) Short scale contrast (≤ 70 kVp)—few shades, mostly blacks or whites; described as high contrast
   c) A change in kVp will alter the quantity or number of x-rays affecting film density; rule of thumb
      (1) Each 15 kVp increase will increase the number of x-rays
         (a) To maintain original film density, divide time by 2
         (b) 60 kVp @ .50 sec. = 75 kVp @ .25 sec.
      (2) Each 15 kVp decrease will decrease the number of x-rays
         (a) To maintain original film density, multiply time by 2
         (b) 85 kVp @ .15 sec. = 70 kVp @ .30 sec.
   d) Altering kVp without adjusting time
      (1) Increasing kVp will increase film density and decrease contrast
      (2) Decreasing kVp will decrease film density and increase contrast
5. *Source-film distance*—distance from the source of x-rays to the film affects beam intensity (number and energy of x-rays) and, consequently, film density; a long distance decreases beam intensity and film density, a short distance increases beam intensity and film density
   a) *Inverse square law*—intensity of x-ray beam varies inversely with square of the source-film distance
      (1) Formula

$$\frac{I1}{I2} = \frac{D2^2}{D1^2}$$

      (2) Sample problem:
         (a) I1 = .10 sec, D1 = 8″, D2 = 16″
         (b) $x = \frac{.10 \times 16^2}{8^2} = .40$ sec.
      (3) Applications
         (a) PID length changes (Fig. 11-6)
         (b) Distance from open end of PID to skin surface
         (c) Radiation safety principle
      (4) Strategies for inverse square law problems
         (a) Determine if problem refers to PID change or operator safety
         (b) PID change
            i) Determine distance factor—has the distance doubled, tripled, or quadrupled?
            ii) Square the factor ($2^2 = 4$, $3^2 = 9$, $4^2 = 16$)
            iii) Multiply squared factor × the original time for new exposure time

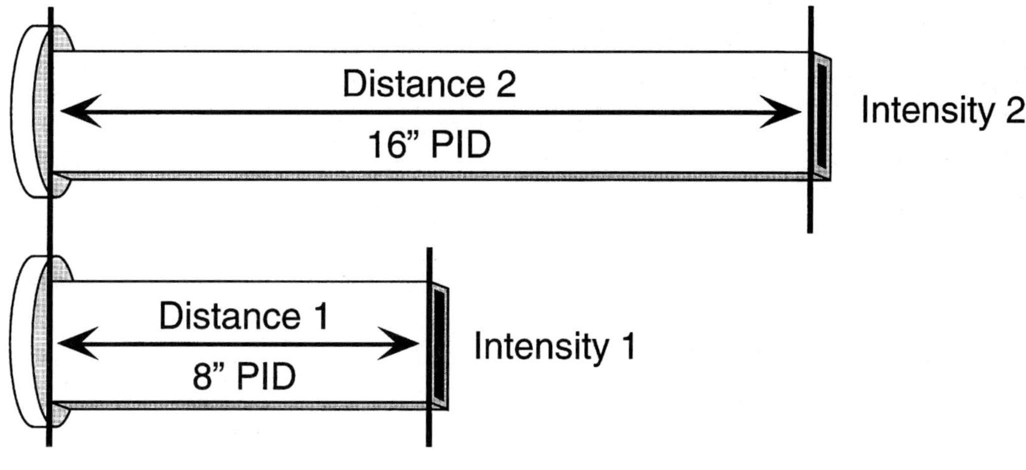

FIGURE 11-6. The Inverse Square Law is applied to a change in the length of the PID

- (c) Operator distance and beam intensity
  - i) Establish distance from source (6)
  - ii) Square the distance (36)
  - iii) Invert the distance = x-ray beam intensity at 6 foot distance is 1/36 of the original intensity
- (5) *Filtration*—removes less penetrating x-rays, improves beam quality
  - (a) *Inherent filtration*—unleaded glass window and oil bath that x-ray beam passes through
  - (b) *Added filtration*—metal filter, usually aluminum, installed by manufacturer
  - (c) *Total filtration*—sum of inherent and added filtration
    - i) 1.5 mm Al @ < 70 kVp
    - ii) 2.5 mm Al @ ≥ 70 kVp
- (6) *Collimation*—restricts size of x-ray beam
  - (a) Collimators
    - i) Lead collimator with diaphragm
    - ii) Lead-lined PIDs—preferably long, open-ended, rectangular PIDs; further collimate or restrict the size of x-ray beam
    - iii) Reduces volume of tissue exposed at skin surface
    - iv) Area of exposure at skin surface should not exceed 2.75 inches or 7 cm in diameter

V. INTRAORAL RADIOGRAPHIC TECHNIQUES

A. Rules of accurate image formation

1. Use as small focal spot as possible (determined by manufacturer); affects image unsharpness and magnification
2. Place film as close to structure as possible (short object-film distance); minimizes image unsharpness and magnification
3. Use longest source-object distance possible (PID); minimizes image unsharpness and magnification

4. Place film parallel (both vertically and horizontally) to structures to be imaged; minimizes shape distortion, improves anatomic accuracy
5. Direct central ray perpendicular (at a right angle) to the object and film; minimizes shape distortion, improves anatomic accuracy

B. Intraoral technique theories

1. *Paralleling technique*
   a) Applies most of the rules of accurate image projection to periapical radiography
   b) Film packet placed parallel to long axes of teeth
   c) Central ray directed perpendicular to teeth and film packet center
   d) Most accurate periapical technique
2. *Bitewing technique*
   a) Used to record interproximal surfaces of tooth crowns in occlusion and alveolar bone height
   b) Typically used to record posterior tooth crowns; sometimes used to record anterior tooth crowns
   c) Most accurate view of interproximal surfaces and alveolar bone height
3. *Bisecting angle technique*
   a) Applies one of the rules of accurate image projection to periapical radiography
   b) Film packet placed against the lingual surfaces of teeth and bone
   c) Based on geometry of equilateral triangles; central ray directed perpendicular to an imaginary line that "bisects" or divides angle formed by long axes of teeth and film packet
   d) Images have shape distortion; not as anatomically accurate in imaging structures as paralleling or bitewing techniques

VI. RADIATION BIOLOGY AND SAFETY

A. *Radiation biology*

1. Definition—study of effects of ionizing radiation on biological or living systems
2. *Attenuation*
   a) Absorption or transfer of x-ray energy to the material or matter through which it passes
   b) X-radiation entering a biological system begins to lose its energy and can produce various effects
   c) Photon interactions with matter
      (1) *Compton scattering*
         (a) Occurs when an x-ray photon interacts with outer orbital electron in absorber atom
            i) Photon gives up some of its energy by ejecting an outer electron from shell (recoil e– or Compton e–)
            ii) Results in ionization of absorber atom (+ ion), ejected electron (– ion)
            iii) Colliding photon is scattered in a different direction and continues to give up its energy through further interactions

(b) 62% of the photons from the dental x-ray beam undergo Compton scattering
i) 30% of the scatter escapes the patient tissues
ii) Remainder contributes to film fog
(2) *Photoelectric effect*
(a) Occurs when an x-ray photon of sufficient energy collides with a K shell electron in absorber atom
i) Photon gives up its energy by ejecting electron from the K shell (recoil e– or photoelectron)
ii) Results in ionization of absorber atom (+ ion), ejected electron (– ion)
iii) Vacancy in the K is filled by L shell electron, which releases characteristic radiation; 80% of photoelectron interactions occur at K shell level
(b) 30% of photons absorbed from the dental x-ray beam are absorbed by the photoelectric effect
i) Energy is absorbed by patient
ii) Does not result in film fog
(3) No interaction—9% of x-rays pass through without any interaction
(4) *Coherent scattering* (Thompson effect, classical scattering or unmodified scattering)
(a) Low-energy photon passes near outer electron in absorber atom
i) Causes electron to vibrate at same frequency as the photon; excitation
ii) No x-ray energy is transferred to the atom, no damage done
iii) Only effect is change in direction of x-ray photon
(b) Accounts for $< 8\%$ of interactions in dental examinations
(c) Has little effect on film fog

B. Effects of ionizing radiation on living systems

1. *Direct effect*
a) Direct alteration of biological molecules such as proteins, carbohydrates, and nucleic acids
(1) Energy is absorbed by molecule
(2) Energy transferred between unstable intermediate molecules
(3) Stable damaged molecules formed
(a) Rearrangements from dissociation of molecules into free radicals (atoms or molecules with unpaired electrons in valence shell)
(b) Differ in structure and function from original molecules
b) Accounts for $\approx 33\%$ of radiation-induced biological damage
2. *Indirect effect*
a) Ionization or radiolysis of the H_2O molecule
(1) Water is predominant molecule in biological system, approximately 80% by weight
(2) Breakdown of H_2O molecule

(a) Production of free radicals; hydroxyl free radical believed to be most destructive
(b) Leads to production of H_2O_2, a major toxin due to its reactivity in achieving ground state
(c) Reactions result in formation of new molecules with different chemical and biological properties than the original

(3) Accounts for ≈ 66% of radiation-induced biological damage

3. *Linear energy transfer* (*LET*)—measure of rate at which energy is transferred from incident radiation to tissue along path radiation is traveling
   a) The higher the LET, the greater the tissue damage; protons and alpha particles have high LET and are more damaging than x-rays
   b) X-rays have a relatively low LET and are sparsely ionizing; ionize relatively few atoms and/or biomolecules and less likely to cause a direct biological effect
4. Cell sensitivity
   a) *Somatic*—all tissues of the body except reproductive
      (1) Somatic effects of radiation are not passed along to future generations
      (2) Include cancer and other disorders that do not involve the reproductive or genetic tissues
      (3) Follow a linear, threshold dose-response; a certain dose is necessary before demonstrable damage occurs
   b) *Genetic*—reproductive cells
      (1) Genetic effects of radiation occur only in reproductive cells and can be passed to future generations
      (2) Include alterations of chromosomes that may result in mutations in future generations
      (3) Believed to occur in a linear, nonthreshold, dose-response model; no dose is considered safe
   c) *Law of Bergonie-Tribondeau*—describes cells most sensitive to effects of radiation
      (1) Mitotic activity—high mitotic rate and history
      (2) Growth and development—primitive or immature
      (3) Degree of differentiation—undifferentiated without specialized function
      (4) Cells with a large nucleus/cytoplasm ratio
   d) Categories of cell/tissue sensitivity—radiosensitive to radioresistant
      (1) High sensitivity—small lymphocyte, bone marrow, reproductive cells, intestinal mucosa
      (2) Intermediate sensitivity—connective tissue, small blood vessels, growing bone and cartilage, salivary glands, lungs, kidneys, liver
      (3) Low sensitivity—optic lens, mature erythrocytes, muscle, nerve

e) *Target or critical organ concept*
(1) Various somatic tissues are designated as critical organs for radiological health purposes
(2) Concept based on radiosentivity and potential effects
(3) Critical organs include female breast, skin, thyroid, lens of the eye, hematopoietic tissues, genetic tissues

5. Other factors
a) Area of exposure
(1) Whole-body—radiation exposure to entire body
(2) Localized—radiation exposure restricted to specific area of the body
b) *Latent period*—time interval between irradiation and development of an observed biological effect
(1) Short-term, early, or acute effects
(a) May occur minutes, hours, or weeks after exposure
(b) Usually result of high dose to whole body
(c) Ultimate early effect is death
(2) Long-term, late, or chronic effects
(a) May occur months, years, or decades after exposure
(b) Result of low dose received over a long time
(c) May have no observable effect or result in cancers later in life
c) *Cumulative effect*—residual injury without repair from repeated radiation exposure

C. Units of radiation measurement

1. Systems
a) Standard or traditional units (Roentgen, rad, rem)
b) International units (C/kg, gray sievert)
2. *Exposure dose*—measure of radiation quantity or exposure and refers to the ability of x-rays to ionize air; measure is taken at the skin surface before radiation has penetrated patient's tissues
a) *Roentgen (R)*—amount of radiation capable of ionizing 1.6×10^{12} ion pairs per gram of air; $1.0\ R = 2.58 \times 10^{-4}$ C/kg of air
b) Coulombs per kilogram (C/kg); 1 C/kg $= 3.88 \times 10^3$ R (3876 R)
3. *Absorbed dose*—used to measure quantity of any type of ionizing radiation received by a mass of any type of matter including patient's tissues
a) *rad*—1.0 rad = .01 gray (divide rad by 100 to equal gray)
b) *gray (Gy)*—1 Gy = 100 rads (multiply gray by 100 to equal rad)
c) Units may be expressed in smaller units such as mR (millirad, .001 R = 1 mR) or cGy (centigray, .01 gray = 1 cGy)
4. *Dose equivalent*—measure used to compare biological effects or damage an exposed individual might expect to occur from (RBE, relative biological effectiveness) different types of radiation
a) DE = AD (absorbed dose) × QF (quality factor); quality factor for x-rays is 1
b) *rem (Roentgen equivalent man)*—1.0 rem = .01 sievert (divide rem by 100 to equal sievert)

c) *sievert (Sv)*—1 Sv = 100 rems (multiply sievert by 100 to equal rem)
d) Units may be expressed in smaller units such as mRem (millirem; .001 Rem = 1 mRem) or cSv (centisievert; .01 sievert = 1 cSv)

D. Radiation safety and protection for dental patients

1. Guiding principles
   a) *ALARA*—As Low As Reasonably Achievable
   b) Risk vs. benefit decision—determination that the benefit of radiographic examination outweighs risk
   c) Minimize exposure, maximize diagnostic result
2. Somatic reduction measures
   a) *Selection criteria*—guidelines for prescribing dental radiographs; used to determine need, type, and frequency of radiographic examinations
      (1) Based on positive historical findings, positive clinical signs and symptoms, patient risk factors, type of visit (new or recall patient), patient age, and type of dentition
      (2) Produces high-yield, individualized radiographic examinations that influence diagnosis and treatment
      (3) Ensures maximum patient benefit with minimum of patient exposure
   b) Film speed—using E speed film instead of D speed film produces a 40% to 50% exposure reduction; F speed film further reduces E speed exposures by 20%
   c) Rare earth intensifying screens for extraoral radiography result in 50% reduction compared with calcium tungstate screens
   d) Correct processing and quality assurance procedures reduce patient exposure by avoiding retakes
   e) Primary beam collimation—rectangular collimation reduces skin surface dose 60% to 70%
   f) Aluminum filtration—estimated 57% reduction in exposure by removing low energy, longer wavelength x-rays
   g) Kilovoltage range
      (1) Lower kilovoltage settings result in higher skin doses than higher kilovoltage settings
      (2) An 80 kVp setting results in a 45% reduction in exposure compared with using 60 kVp
   h) Paralleling technique with film holding devices and beam alignment guides standardize technique and reduce retakes
   i) Lead shields—.25 mm lead minimum
      (1) Thyroid collar—50% exposure reduction to thyroid
      (2) Apron—aids in shielding bone marrow sites in the chest and abdomen
      (3) Apron—primary gonadal shield

E. Radiation safety and protection for dental personnel

1. *Maximum permissible dose (MPD)*
   a) Radiation exposure not expected to cause appreciable bodily injury to a person at any time during life

   b) Whole body dose limit for occupational exposure = 5 rems/year (0.05 Sv or 50 mSv); 1.25 rem/calendar quarter (0.0125 Sv or 12.5 mSv)
   c) Whole body dose limit for pregnant radiation users and non-occupationally exposed individuals = 0.5 rems (0.005 Sv or 5 mSv); 1/10 occupational MPD
   d) Goal—achieve an occupational exposure dose as close to 0 as possible by adhering to radiation safety and protection rules
2. *Maximum accumulated dose* (*MAD*)—accumulated lifetime dose limit for occupationally exposed workers
   a) Formula—*MAD* = N (age) − 18 (legal age for radiation worker) × 5 rems/year
   b) Example—MAD for a 35-year-old radiation worker: MAD = (35 − 18) × 5 = 85 rems or 850 mSv
3. Radiation sources
   a) *Background radiation*—ionizing radiation ubiquitous in the environment and encountered in daily life
      (1) Natural—radiation exposure from radon (55%), cosmic radiation (8%), terrestrial radiation (8%), and internal source radiation (11%); greatest contributor ≈ 82%
      (2) Artificial or manufactured—medical x-rays (11%), dental x-rays (.30%), nuclear medicine (4%), consumer products (3%); totals ≈ 18%
      (3) Other sources—occupational (< .03%), nuclear fuel (< .03%), nuclear fallout (< .03%); totals < .10%
      (4) Average annual effective dose from all sources = 3.60 mSv
   b) Dental sources
      (1) *Primary*—radiation generated at target and collimated by PID; used for patient radiography
      (2) *Secondary*—scatter radiation produced by interaction of primary radiation with the patient's facial tissues
      (3) *Leakage*—radiation emitted from tubehead encasement during exposure
4. Safety rules and protection measures
   a) Avoid primary beam
      (1) Do not stand in or near primary beam or its path
      (2) Do not hold x-ray head, PID, or patient in place
      (3) Do not hold films in patient's mouth
   b) *Distance and position rule* (Fig. 11-7)
      (1) Stand 6 feet from source of x-rays
      (2) Preferred operator position—between 90° to 135° to the primary beam
   c) Barriers
      (1) *Primary barrier*—designed to attenuate primary beam; common primary barriers are operatory walls
      (2) *Secondary barrier*—intended to absorb secondary and leakage radiation; secondary barriers are ceiling and floor

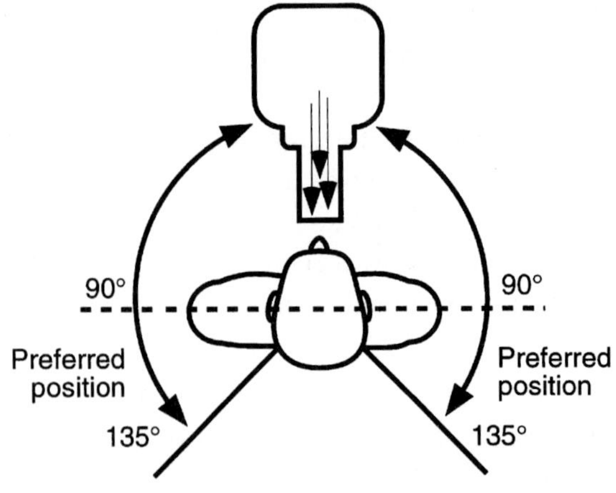

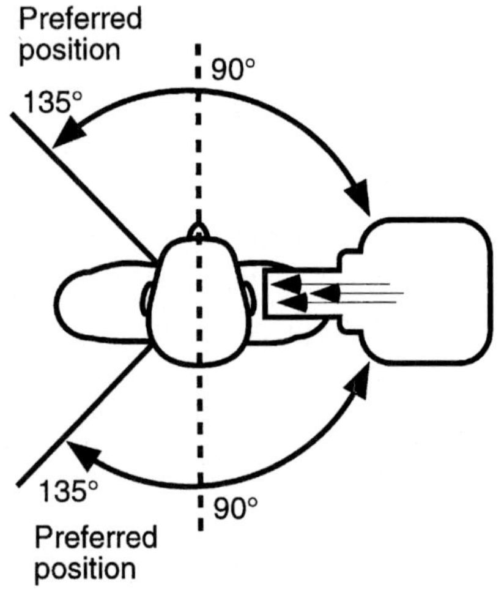

FIGURE 11-7. For optimum operator safety, the clinician should stand 6 feet from the x-ray source, at a 90–135° angle to the primary beam

d) Radiation monitoring
   (1) Pocket/badge dosimeter worn at chest/waist level
   (2) Monitors MPD for one individual; only for occupational exposure
   (3) Analyzed quarterly—dentist responsible for evaluation and monitoring of reports

VII. RADIOGRAPHIC INFECTION CONTROL

A. Operator protection

1. Universal precautions recommended—gloves, masks, eyewear, work attire

B. Operatory preparation and clean-up

1. Intraoral x-ray unit
   a) Precleaning and disinfection procedures
      (1) Spray-wipe-spray technique with ADA-accepted water-based surface disinfectant-detergent
      (2) Surface disinfectant-detergent must remain in contact with surface for 10 minutes to achieve disinfection

   b) Prepare x-ray head, PID, control panel, exposure switch, work surface; cover with plastic barriers
   c) Postprocedure clean up—use gloves to carefully remove covers, properly dispose of instruments, place clean barriers with fresh gloves
   d) If barrier techniques are not used, precleaning and disinfection procedures must be completed between patients
2. Panoramic x-ray machines
   a) Preclean, disinfect, and cover control panel, exposure button, chin rest, head, temple support, and handgrips
   b) After film exposure, remove gloves and wash hands to handle cassette
   c) Postprocedure clean up—use gloves to remove covers, properly dispose of bitepiece, place clean barriers with fresh gloves
   d) If barrier techniques are not used, precleaning and disinfection procedures must be completed between patients

C. Film handling

1. Organize film and sterile instruments on covered surface away from x-ray source
   a) Keep exposed and unexposed film separated
   b) Lay out films in survey order; place exposed films in plastic cup
2. Film barriers—use film barrier bag or commercially covered film packets for daylight loading automatic processors

D. Conventional darkroom processing procedures

1. After completing intraoral procedures, replace soiled gloves with fresh gloves, use paper towel or overgloves to open darkroom door
2. Shell films in safelight conditions—drop films out on clean paper towel without touching the film
3. Properly dispose of contaminated film wrappings, container, and gloves
4. Wash and dry hands
5. Handle films on edges and insert into processor

E. Daylight loader automatic processors

1. Use film barrier-covered film packets
2. With gloves, drop film packets out of barrier into a cup or onto a towel
3. Remove and dispose of contaminated gloves; wash and dry hands
4. Open daylight loader window and cover bottom surface of unit with paper towels or plastic wrap
5. Place film receptacle and powderless gloves into unit, close window
6. Insert hands through sleeves, put on gloves, shell films and insert films into processor
7. Remove gloves, withdraw hands through the sleeves
8. Open window, fold covering materials over waste materials, remove and correctly dispose waste materials

VIII. DARKROOM PROCESSING AND QUALITY ASSURANCE

A. Darkroom requirements

1. Design—adequate size for processing activities, convenient arrangement of equipment, proper ventilation
2. White light tight environment
   a) Typical light leaks occur around doorframe, ceiling tiles, vents, wall seams
   b) Seal leaks with black masking tape or weather stripping
3. Environmental conditions
   a) Temperature—70°F/21°C
   b) Humidity—50% to 70%
   c) Cleanliness—essential for quality processing and avoidance of artifacts
4. *Safelight conditions*—adequate darkroom illumination without compromising image quality
   a) Safelight lamps, filters, and bulbs
      (1) Filters white light (green and blue spectrum) to which film is most sensitive
      (2) Filters
         (a) Red filter (GBX-2)—safe for both intraoral and extraoral film; requires a 15-watt incandescent bulb
         (b) Orange filter (ML-2)—safe for intraoral film only; requires a 10-watt incandescent bulb
      (3) Working distance and time
         (a) Safelight lamps mounted 4 feet from counter surface
         (b) Five-minute working time under safelight lamps

B. Processing chemicals

1. General principles
   a) Wetting—softens emulsion so developer chemicals can act on emulsion
   b) Development—transforms latent image into visible image via reduction of exposed silver halide crystals
   c) Rinsing—stops development and removes excess chemicals from emulsion
   d) Fixation—removes unexposed silver halide crystals from the emulsion
   e) Washing—removes all excess chemicals from the emulsion
   f) Drying—removes the water from the emulsion
2. Developer solution components
   a) Metol (Elon) (reducing agent)—brings up the gray tones
   b) Hydroquinone (reducing agent)—brings up the black tones and contrast
   c) Sodium carbonate (activator)—softens and swells emulsion
   d) Potassium bromide (restrainer)—prevents reducing agents from developing the unexposed silver halide crystals
   e) Sodium sulfite (preservative)—prevents rapid oxidation
   f) Water (solvent)—medium for dissolving chemicals

3. Fixer solution components
   a) Ammonium or sodium thiosulfate (fixing agent)—clears away the unexposed, undeveloped silver halide crystals
   b) Acetic or sulfuric acid (neutralizer/acidifier)—stops development by neutralizing developer chemicals
   c) Aluminum chloride (chrome alum) or sulfide (hardener)—shrinks and hardens the emulsion
   d) Sodium sulfite (preservative)—prevents chemical deterioration
   e) Water (solvent)—medium for dissolving chemicals
4. Automatic processing solutions—formulated for mechanical transport systems and higher temperature processing
   a) Chemical differences
      (1) Phenidone replaces metol for gray tone production
      (2) Hardening agent (gluteraldehyde) and antiswelling agent (sulfide compounds) added to developer to prevent emulsion from sticking to the rollers
      (3) Additional hardening agent added to fixer to prevent emulsion from sticking to the rollers
5. *Replenishment*—restores the ability of the processing chemicals to perform their function without changing the entire volume
   a) Ready-to-use developer or fixer solution added daily to solution reservoirs
   b) Replenished solutions should be replaced with fresh chemicals every 2 to 4 weeks under normal conditions, more frequently when indicated
   c) Solution lifespan is dependent on use factor—exposure to air, temperature

C. Automatic processing systems

1. Automatic processing system components
2. Processing solutions—formulated for mechanical transport systems higher temperature processing
3. Sequence: developer, fixer, rinse, dry
4. Temperature—ranges from 83°F (28°C) to 105°F (40°C)
   a) Heating element controls the temperature of developer solution
   b) Rollers designed to rotate at a speed compatible with the developer temperature
5. Time—average processing cycle is 4.5 to 5.5 minutes
6. Film feed—insert films slowly, allowing space among films
7. Drying chamber—blows films dry before exit
8. External film receptacle—receives finished radiographs
9. Maintenance
   a) Daily
      (1) Replenish each solution with 4 to 7 ounces of chemicals after the equivalent of 4 to 6 full mouth or panoramic surveys
      (2) Clean rollers daily by running cleaning sheets through the processor; cleaning sheets should not be reused due to solution contamination potential

b) Weekly—rollers should be removed and cleaned
  (1) Rinse under warm water
  (2) Spray with special cleaner and allowed to sit for 10 minutes
  (3) Wipe clean with separate sponges
  (4) Rinse with water and excess water removed before re-installation
c) Every 2 to 4 weeks
  (1) Thorough cleaning of entire machine and roller system
  (2) Replace with fresh chemicals, fill the fixer reservoir first
d) Monthly
  (1) Inspect moving parts for wear
  (2) Lubricate moving parts as needed
  (3) Check dryer, remove accumulated dust
e) Every 3 months use a system cleaner to clean entire processing unit
f) Cleaning procedures should be completed with a protective gown, utility gloves, mask, eyewear, and adequate ventilation

D. Manual processing

1. Equipment
  a) Stainless steel solution tanks, film racks, solution stirrers
  b) Temperature regulator—mix hot and cold running water
  c) Overflow pipe—maintains a clean, circulating water bath
  d) Floating thermometer—determine temperature and development time
  e) Darkroom timer—used to time the development, fixation and wash cycles
2. Solution sequence and time (follow manufacturer's directions)
  a) Development—5 minutes @ 68°F (20°C)
  b) Rinse—(30 seconds) stops development
  c) Fixation—10 minutes @ 68°F (20°C)
    (1) Films can be viewed after 3 minutes following a brief 30-second rinse
    (2) Films must be returned to the fixer solution for 7 more minutes to equal a total of 10 minutes
  d) Wash—running water for 20 minutes @ 68°F (20°C)
  e) Drying cycle—films can be air dried or placed in a commercial film dryer
3. Temperature and time
  a) Time of development is inversely proportional to temperature of water bath
  b) As temperature increases, time of development decreases
4. Solution maintenance and change
  a) Replenishment
    (1) Replenish each solution with 8 ounces of chemicals (depending on size of tanks); may require some solution to be removed to replenish
    (2) Level of solution should be adequate to cover all films
  b) Change solutions every 3 to 4 weeks

(1) Solution reservoirs and master tank should be cleaned with commercial cleaner
(2) Thoroughly rinse before reassembly
(3) Fill fixer tank first, then developer
(4) Fill water bath, stir solutions

c) Cleaning procedures should be completed with a protective gown, utility gloves, mask, eyewear, and adequate ventilation

E. Quality assurance

1. Action plan used to ensure production of high quality, diagnostic images while minimizing costs and exposure to personnel and patients
2. X-ray machine
   a) Periodically tested by qualified service representative or radiation physicist per state law requirements
      (1) X-ray output
      (2) Kilovoltage calibration
      (3) Half value layer—aluminum filtration
      (4) Timer accuracy
      (5) Milliamperage reproducibility
      (6) Collimation
   b) Office maintenance
      (1) Check arm for drifting—tighten as needed
      (2) Check x-ray head and PID for drifting—tighten as needed
3. Safelight and darkroom conditions
   a) Check for proper safelight filter and distance
   b) Inspect for light leaks in total darkness
      (1) Mark leaks with chalk
      (2) Eliminate with black masking tape or weather stripping
   c) Coin test
      (1) Place coin on unwrapped film in total darkness, let it remain 5 minutes, process film
      (2) If coin image is present, light leak exists and needs to be eliminated
      (3) After white leaks eliminated, repeat coin test to evaluate safelight conditions
4. Film processing quality control (Fig. 11-8)
   a) Stepwedge—test device with graduated layers of metal, configured similar to a staircase
      (1) Used to produce test images such as reference and/or check films for solution monitoring
      (2) Commercial—graduated layers of aluminum or copper
      (3) Homemade—graduated layers of lead foil taped together
   b) With a fresh film, produce a control film or reference radiograph at bitewing exposure time and process in fresh solutions
   c) Expose a check film each day and process as usual
   d) Compare check film to control or reference film—if visible difference between two films, there is a processing problem
   e) Resolve processing problem such as temperature adjustment, replenishment, or solution change before patient films are processed

FIGURE 11-8. Film processing quality control procedures involve the production of reference (*top left*) and check (*top right*) films using an alumunum stepwedge (*bottom*)

5. Image receptor quality assurance
   a) Film storage—cool, dry place away from x-ray source, chemical fumes @ 50°F to 70°F and 30% to 50% relative humidity
   b) Cassettes examined monthly for damage and function; replace as needed
      (1) Rigid—defective hinges, latches
      (2) Flexible—open seams, defective latch mechanisms
      (3) Screens inspected for cracks or defects, clean periodically
         (a) Clean with cotton ball or gauze and special screen cleaner
         (b) Wipe dry with fresh cotton ball or gauze
         (c) Air dry before closing cassette; wet screens will stick together and tear the screens upon opening
6. Viewbox care
   a) Inspect monthly, replace light bulbs when needed
   b) Operatory viewbox—preclean, disinfect and cover; place mounted radiographs under clear plastic cover
   c) Change cover between patients

IX. INTRAORAL TECHNICAL AND PROCESSING ERROR IDENTIFICATION AND CORRECTION

A. Technical errors and artifacts

1. Vertical angulation errors—deviation from true long axis dimension
   a) *Foreshortening*—too much vertical angulation used (Fig. 11-9)
      (1) Shape distortion resulting in an image shorter than actual structure
      (2) Correction—decrease the vertical angulation, place film parallel to the teeth long axes
   b) *Elongation*—not enough vertical angulation used (Fig. 11-10)
      (1) Shape distortion resulting in an image longer than actual structure

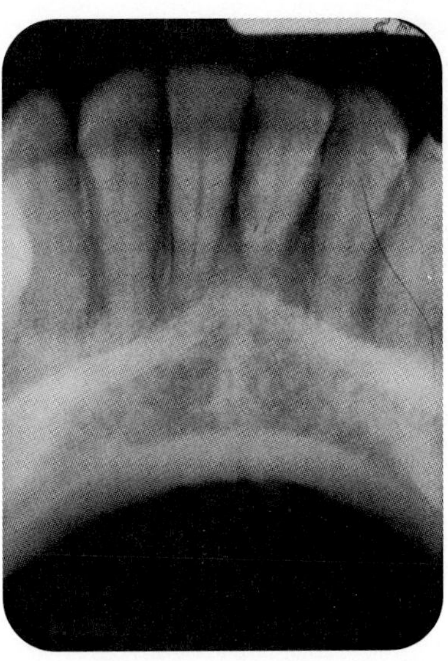

FIGURE 11-9. Foreshortened image of the lower anterior teeth

(2) Correction—increases vertical angulation, make sure film is not distorted

2. *Horizontal angulation* errors—diagonal entry to proximal contacts (Fig. 11-11)
   a) Results in overlapping of interproximal contacts and widening of the image horizontally
   b) Correction—direct central ray perpendicular to the labial/buccal surfaces of the teeth crowns
3. *Cone cut* errors—lack of centering x-ray beam over the film (Fig. 11-12)
   a) Results in partial exposure of film; clear zone with no image
   b) Correction—direct central ray to film center and central ray entry point

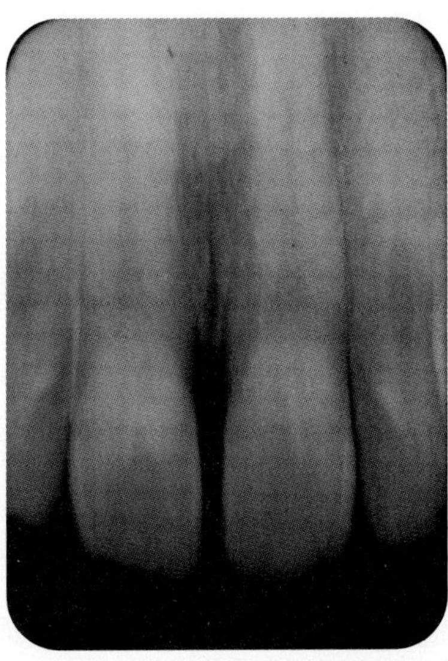

FIGURE 11-10. Elongated image of the maxillary incisor teeth

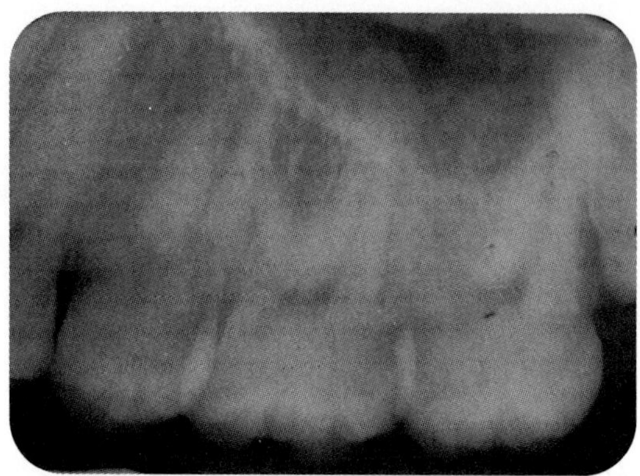

FIGURE 11-11. Horizontal angulation error

4. Film placement errors—improper film location or orientation relative to anatomic area
   a) Inadequate coverage of area (periapicals/bitewings)
   b) Inadequate apical coverage (periapicals)
   c) Backward placement of the film packet—lead foil pattern and opposite orientation of the mounted film
   d) Correction—follow film descriptions for correct film location, position dot or white side of film toward the x-ray source
5. Film bending errors—improper film folding, creasing, or crimping, which interferes with image quality
   a) Creasing film before exposure results in white artifacts; creasing or crimping film before and after exposure results in black artifacts
   b) Correction—limit film bending
      (1) Use appropriate film size
      (2) Use film packet edge cushions to minimize patient discomfort
      (3) Handle films carefully during film holder insertion or removal

B. Exposure errors

1. Overexposure
   a) Results in high-density or dark film
   b) Correction—reduce exposure time, check for small patient size

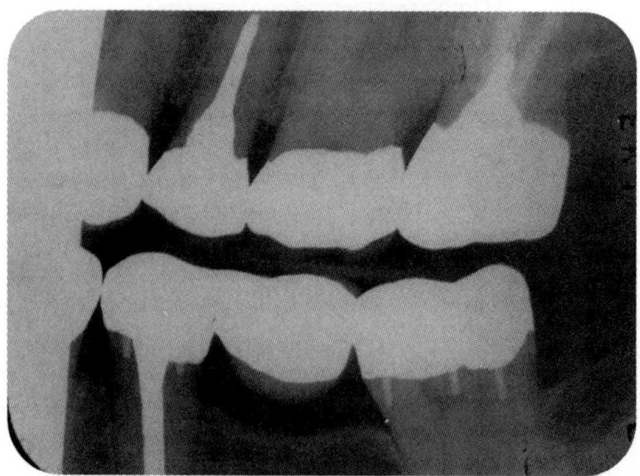

FIGURE 11-12. Cone cut error

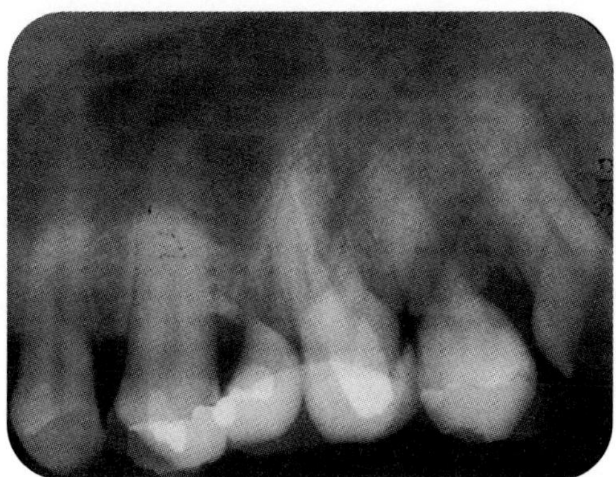

FIGURE 11-13. Double-exposed film

2. Underexposure
   a) Results in low-density or light film
   b) Correction—increase exposure time, check for large patient size, make sure exposure button was not released too soon
3. Double exposure (Fig. 11-13)
   a) Bizarre pattern of superimposed images
   b) High-density appearance
   c) Accompanied by blank, transparent unexposed film
   d) Correction—separate unexposed film from exposed film
4. Unexposed film
   a) Results in blank, transparent appearance of film base
   b) Correction—separate unexposed film from exposed film

C. Patient management and patient preparation errors

1. Movement—motion unsharpness
   a) Results in blurred image of recorded structures
   b) Correction—stabilize film placement and instruct patient to remain still during entire exposure
2. Eyewear and removable prostheses errors (Fig. 11-14)
   a) Results in radiopaque images of these items superimposed over dental structures
   b) Correction—instruct patient to remove glasses and removable prostheses before radiographic procedures
3. Thyroid collar and lead apron placement errors
   a) Results in lead shield image superimposed over dental structures
   b) Correction—place shields so that they do not interfere with the path of the x-ray beam and film

D. Processing errors and artifacts

1. Film handling errors
   a) Emulsion scratches—white areas where emulsion has been removed from film base
   b) Black static electricity artifacts—tree or branchlike in shape owing to friction or rough film handling
   c) Partial or complete white light exposure of film—black zone or completely black image

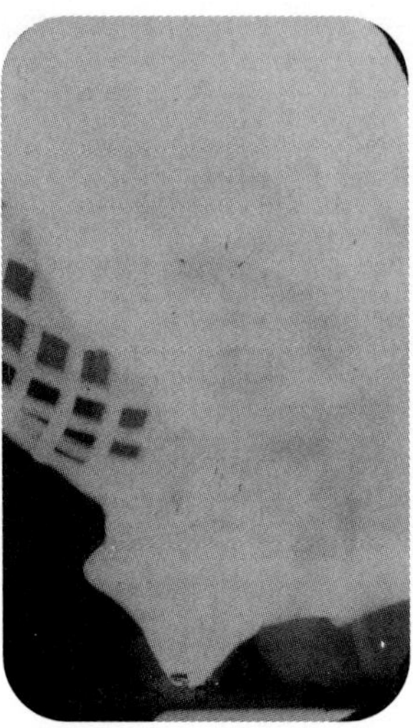

FIGURE 11-14. Radiopaque image of removable prosthesis superimposed over dental structures

   d) Correction—handle the films carefully, separate films gently, and handle on edges in safelight conditions
2. Solution contamination errors
   a) Black or gray droplet artifacts or fingerprints from precontamination with developer or fluoride solution
   b) White droplet artifacts or fingerprints from precontamination with fixer solution
   c) Brown-yellow artifacts from inadequate film washing
   d) Corrections—use clean, dry hands to handle films on clean, covered darkroom working surfaces; allow proper film washing with clean, circulating water
3. Automatic processing errors
   a) Dark image (also applies to manual processing)
      (1) Overdevelopment owing to high processing temperature without time adjustment
      (2) Over-replenishment
      (3) White light leaks or improper safelight conditions
   b) Light image (also applies to manual processing)
      (1) Underdevelopment owing to low processing temperature without time adjustment
      (2) Under-replenishment
   c) Brown image from exhausted developer solution
   d) Green image from inadequate fixation or exhausted fixer
   e) Streaked image owing to dirty rollers; dirty image from dirty water bath
   f) Film feed artifacts—film overlapping and gear marks
   g) Corrections—use time-temperature processing methods with fresh or properly replenished solutions and clean wash water; insert films slowly to allow space between films
4. Solution sequence errors
   a) Fixer placed in developer reservoir results in a blank, transparent image; fixer removes entire film emulsion leaving the plastic base

b) Drain, thoroughly clean and rinse solution reservoirs; replace with fresh chemicals

X. PANORAMIC RADIOGRAPHY AND ERROR CORRECTION

A. Criteria for a diagnostic panoramic radiograph

1. Entire maxilla and mandible recorded including the temporomandibular joints
2. As anatomy allows, symmetrical display of structures right to left
3. Slight smile or slight downward curve of the occlusal plane
4. Good representations of the teeth with minimal over or undermagnification
5. Overlapping of posterior interproximal surfaces is expected
6. Tongue positioned against palate to eliminate palatoglossal air space
7. Minimal or no cervical spine shadow
8. Acceptable film density and contrast
9. Free of technical, film handling, and processing errors

B. Panoramic imaging concepts

1. Tomography—body sectioning method of revealing a depth of tissue or image layer called the focal trough
2. Focal trough is a predetermined layer or thickness of structures that will be imaged in focus on the film; correct patient positioning is essential for optimal results
3. X-ray source has a vertical slit aperture and directs the x-ray beam in a lingual to labial direction through structures: fixed at -10°
4. Accomplished by simultaneous movement of the x-ray head and film cassette in opposite directions during exposure
5. Side of the patient's dental arches closest to the film is recorded in focus while the side closest to the x-ray source is blurred out of focus
6. Resulting image is uniformly magnified owing to the long object-film distance with some posterior contact overlapping
7. Ghost images or remnant images from the opposite side may superimpose over the desired structures
   a) Structures that ghost tend to be thicker and will not be completely blurred out of focus
   b) Ghost images appear on the opposite side, higher on the film than the original structure, and are magnified and blurred more in the vertical than the horizontal plane
   c) Examples of structures that ghost include the rami, lower border of the mandible, chin rest, some right/left side markers and earrings
8. Panoramic machines vary in style but operate based on the preceding principles and allow operator to select appropriate mA and kVp; time is fixed
9. Cassettes—5 or 6 × 12 inch rigid or flexible cassette (type compatible with machine) with intensifying screens

C. Panoramic radiographic technique

1. Preexposure preparation
   a) Use proper infection control procedures to preclean and disinfect unit and place sterile bitepiece
   b) Load cassette in safelight conditions

c) Place into cassette holder on machine
d) Instruct patient to remove all metallic objects from the head and neck region including earrings, necklaces, barrettes, hairpins, intraoral prostheses, hearing aids, eyeglasses
e) Place panoramic lead apron (long front and back panel), fully clearing the back of the neck region; do not use a thyroid collar (Fig. 11-16–Lead apron artifact)
f) Explain procedure to the patient and instruct the patient to remain still during entire exposure
g) Exposure factor considerations—obesity, large bone structure, racial differences, frail or small bone structure, edentulous; adjust mA and kVp as needed

2. Patient positioning requirements
   a) Stands or sits with straight spine
   b) Anterior teeth bite end-to-end in bitepiece groove
   c) Head planes
      (1) Midsagittal (horizontal) plane is positioned perpendicular to the floor
      (2) Occlusal (vertical) plane is positioned parallel to the floor; Frankfort and ala-tragus plane also used
      (3) Anteroposterior (forward-backward) plane is aligned with a specific landmark per manufacturer
   d) Tongue pressed against palate
   e) Lips and eyes closed

D. Identification and correction of common errors

1. Patient positioning errors
   a) Cervical spine error
      (1) Spinal column is slumped
      (2) Creates a pyramid to column-shaped radiopacity superimposed over the anterior teeth
      (3) Correction—instruct patient to sit or stand tall with spine erect, make sure chin rest is high enough to maintain straight spine position
   b) Midsagittal plane errors
      (1) Patient's head tilted to one side
         (a) Side tilted toward film is imaged smaller in width, and side toward x-ray source is imaged larger in width, one side is higher than the other
         (b) Correction—center midsagittal plane and align it perpendicular to floor
      (2) Patient's head rotated to one side (Fig. 11-15):
         (a) Side rotated toward film is imaged smaller in width and side toward x-ray source is imaged larger in width
         (b) Correction—center the midsagittal plane and align it perpendicular to floor
   c) Vertical head plane errors
      (1) Patient's head is tilted upward

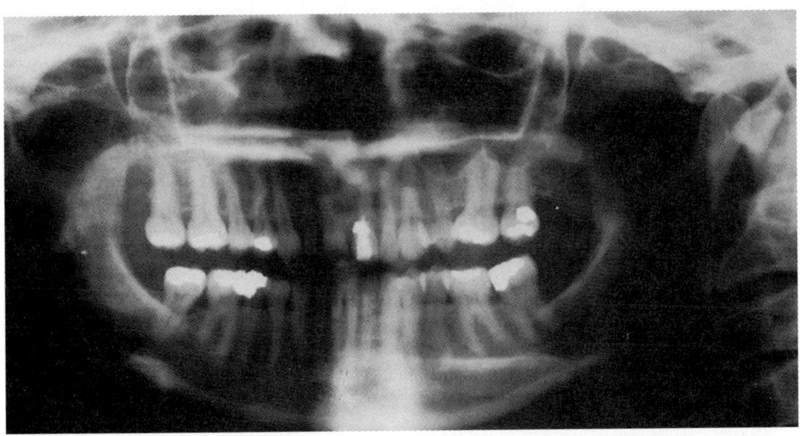

FIGURE 11-15. Panoramic midsagittal image error

(a) Upper teeth are blurred and larger in width, hard palate is superimposed over maxillary teeth apices, condyles may be cut off, occlusal plane flat or frowned

(b) Correction—move head down and align occlusal plane parallel to floor

(2) Patient's head is tilted downward (Fig. 11-16)

(a) Lower teeth are blurred and larger in width with foreshortened apices, condyles may be cut off, severe grin to the occlusal plane

(b) Correction—move head up and align occlusal plane parallel to floor

d) Anteroposterior plane errors

(1) Patient is positioned too far forward (Fig. 11-17)

(a) Teeth are blurred and smaller in width, severe overlapping of teeth (especially premolars), spine may be superimposed over the ramus areas

(b) Correction—move the head back toward x-ray source and align with landmark, make sure teeth are end-to-end in bitepiece groove

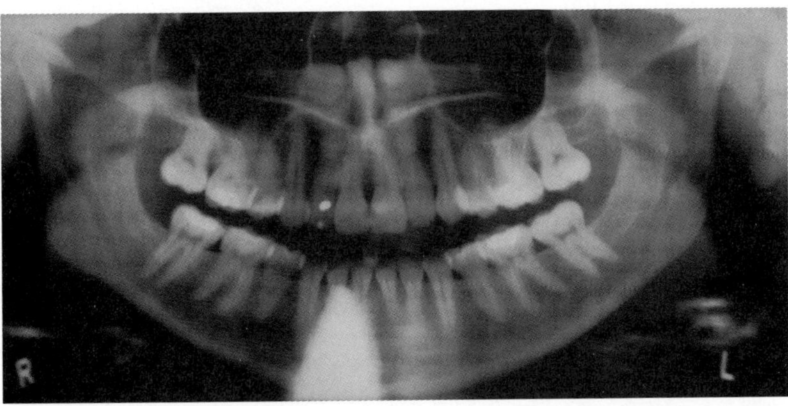

FIGURE 11-16. Panoramic vertical head plane error

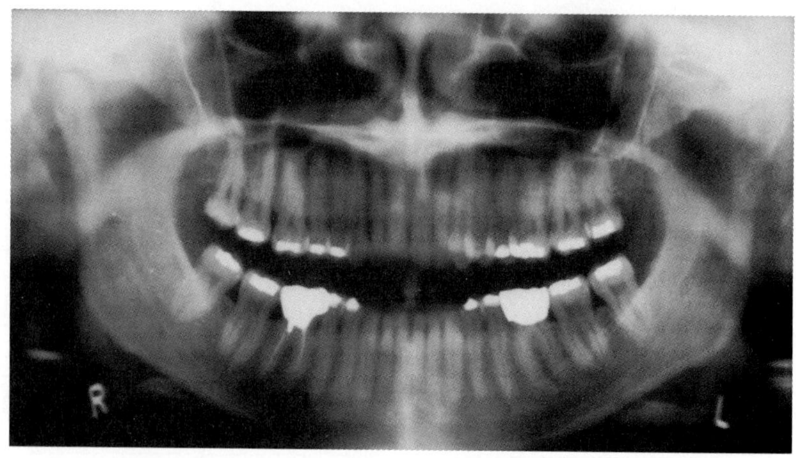

FIGURE 11-17. Panoramic anteroposterior plane error

(2) Patient is positioned too far backward
(a) Teeth are blurred and larger in width, excessive ghosting of each ramus and spine, image too large for film
(b) Correction—move head forward toward the film and align with landmark, make sure teeth are end-to-end in bitepiece groove

e) Patient preparation errors—metallic objects left in place, producing radiopaque artifacts
(1) Objects include earrings, necklaces, napkin chain, eyeglasses, intraoral prostheses, barrettes
(2) Correction—instruct patient to move head and neck metallic objects

f) Patient moves during exposure causing motion unsharpness
(1) Make sure patient is capable of cooperating with procedure
(2) Correction—instruct patient to close eyes and remain still during entire exposure cycle

g) Patient does not press tongue against palate
(1) Radiolucent air space artifact is created in maxillary apical region
(2) Correction—instruct patient to swallow and press tongue against roof of mouth; close lips around bitepiece

h) Exposure errors
(1) Double exposure
(a) Bizarre pattern of superimposed images with high-density appearance
(b) Correction—process film immediately after exposure, be sure to keep unexposed and exposed cassettes separated from each other
(2) Overexposure
(a) Results in high-density or dark film
(b) Correction—reduce kVp/mA, check for small patient size

(3) Underexposure
(a) Results in low-density or light film
(b) Correction—increase kVp/mA, check for large patient size

i) Operational errors
(1) Cassette resistance
(a) Produces alternating white and black vertical bands or lines from cassette contact with patient's shoulder
(b) Correction—make sure patient's spine is straight, head is erect, and shoulders down; avoid placing inferior aspect of cassette against patient's shoulder

(2) Incomplete exposure
(a) Results in partially exposed image
(b) Correction—maintain constant pressure on exposure button until cycle of machine rotation is complete

XI. LOCALIZATION TECHNIQUES

A. *Tube shift technique*—compares change in position of object between two images taken at different horizontal or vertical angulations (Fig. 11-18)

1. Two film comparison is required such as two periapicals, a periapical and bitewing, periapical and topographical occlusal
2. Object movement is compared with movement of x-ray head, not PID or x-ray cone
3. Alternate terms for this technique—buccal object rule, Clark's rule and the SLOB rule
4. SLOB Acronym
   a) S = same; L = lingual; O = opposite; B = buccal
   b) If object moves in same direction as x-ray head, object is lingual in location
   c) If object moves in opposite direction to x-ray head, object is buccal in location

B. *Right angle technique*—compares position of objects between two images taken at right angles to one another (Fig. 11-19)

1. Two-film comparison—central ray (CR) directed perpendicular to film
   a) Paralleling technique periapical—CR perpendicular to long axes of teeth
   b) Cross-sectional occlusal—CR perpendicular to occlusal plane of teeth
2. Comparison of two films determines location of object(s) in question

XII. RADIOGRAPHIC ANATOMY

A. Radiopaque vs. radiolucent

1. *Radiopacities*
   a) Structures that are dense structurally and absorb x-rays either fully or partially
   b) Results in little or no change in emulsion
   c) Appear white or shades of white/gray after film processing

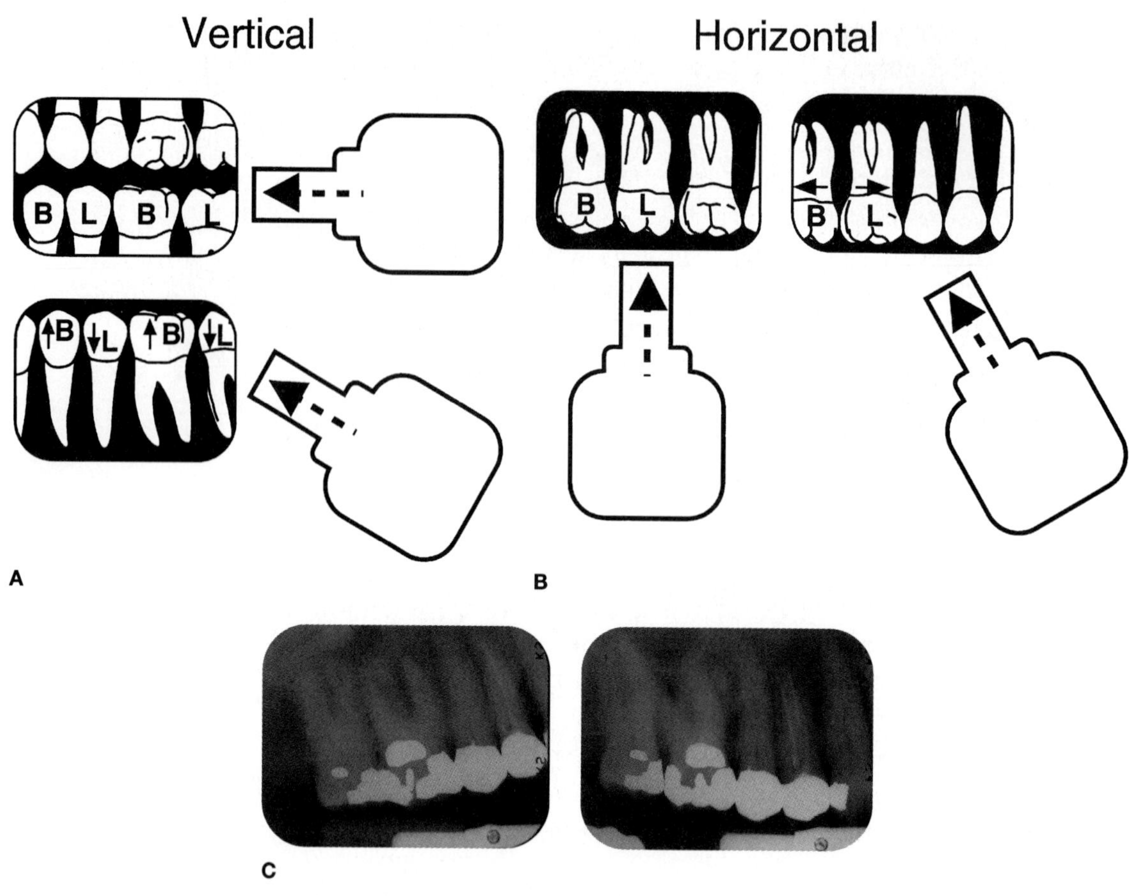

FIGURE 11-18. In the SLOB rule, objects move in a particular direction relative to the movement of the x-ray head. A) illustrates how lingual objects move the same direction as the x-ray head and how buccal objects move opposite the direction of the x-ray head in the vertical plane. B) demonstrates the same pattern of object movement in the horizontal plane. C) Application of the SLOB rule requires a two-film comparison. Compare the molar and premolar periapical radiographs and observe that the CV amalgam restorations move the same direction as the horizontal movement of the x-ray head. In addition, notice that the filled pulp canals on tooth #5 have become separated. The lingual canal moves forward, the same as the movement of the x-ray head, while the buccal canal moves opposite the x-ray head.

2. *Radiolucencies*
    a) Structures that are not dense structurally and allow x-rays to pass through
    b) X-rays interact with film emulsion
    c) Appear black or shades of black after film processing

B. Maxillary anatomic landmarks (Fig. 11-20 a–g)

1. Maxillary tuberosity (*a*)
    a) Molar region—distal to third molar
    b) Heel or rounded end of alveolar ridge
    c) Radiopaque
2. Coronoid process of mandible
    a) Molar region—inferoposterior corner of film
    b) Triangular or thumb-shaped bone
    c) Radiopaque
3. Pterygoid plates
    a) Molar region—distal to tuberosity

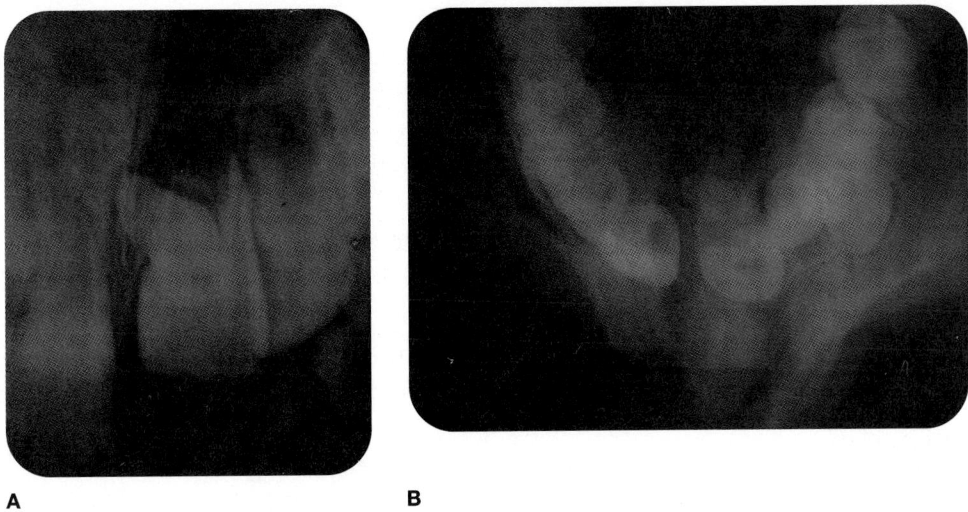

FIGURE 11-19. The right angle technique of localization compares the position of an object on two films taken at right angles to one another. A) This anterior periapical was taken with the central ray at a right angle to the teeth long axes. B) This cross-sectional maxillary occlusal was taken with the central ray directed at a right angle to the incisal/occlusal plane. The comparison of these two films confirms that the mesiodens is impacted lingual to #9.

   b) Medial pterygoid plate or pterygoid hamulus—small finger-like bone
   c) Lateral pterygoid plate—thin wing of bone
   d) Both radiopaque
4. Zygomatic process and bone (*b*)
   a) Molar and premolar region—superior to molar teeth
   b) Zygomatic process—U-shaped radiopacity above first molar
   c) Zygomatic bone—broad radiopacity extending away from zygomatic process in posterior direction
   d) Alternate name—malar process/malar bone

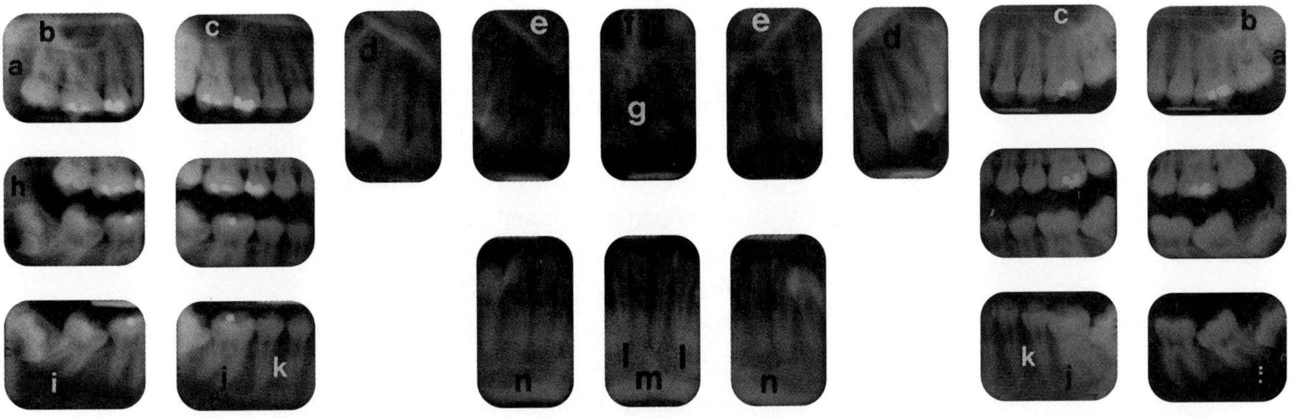

FIGURE 11-20. Anatomic landmarks that appear on this full mouth survey include: a) maxillary tuberosity; b) zygomatic process; c) maxillary sinus; d) inverted Y; e) nasal fossa; f) nasal septum; g) incisive foramen; h) external oblique ridge; i) mandibular canal; j) internal oblique ridge; k) mental foramen; l) mental ridge; m) genial tubercles surrounding the lingual foramen; n) inferior border of the mandible

5. Maxillary sinus (*c*)
   a) Molar, premolar, and canine region—oblong cavity superior to posterior teeth
   b) Alternate name—maxillary antrum
   c) Radiolucent body with fine radiopaque borders
6. Inverted Y (*d*)
   a) Canine and lateral incisor region—superior to teeth roots
   b) Bony septum between maxillary sinus and nasal fossa
   c) Radiopacity dividing two radiolucent cavities
7. Nasal fossae (*e*), nasal septum (*f*), and anterior nasal spine
   a) Lateral and central incisor region—superior to incisor teeth roots
   b) Fossae—radiolucent oblong cavities
   c) Septum—radiopaque vertical band dividing the fossae
   d) Spine—radiopaque triangular point of bone at base of nasal septum
8. Incisive foramen (*g*)
   a) Central incisor region—between roots of central incisors
   b) Oval, diamond, or heart-shaped radiolucency
   c) Alternate name—nasopalatine foramen
9. Midpalatine suture
   a) Central incisor region—midline, between central incisor teeth
   b) Thin, vertical linear radiolucency
   c) Alternate names—median palatal, maxillary suture, or intermaxillary suture

C. Mandibular anatomic landmarks (Fig. 11-20 h–n)

1. External oblique ridge or line (*h*)
   a) Molar region—crosses third molar crown
   b) Diagonal outer ridge of anterior ramus
   c) Radiopaque diagonal stripe
2. Mandibular canal space (*i*)
   a) Molar and premolar region—inferior to molar roots
   b) Diagonal radiolucent tube or ribbon with fine radiopaque borders
   c) Alternate name—inferior alveolar canal space
3. Internal oblique ridge or line (*j*)
   a) Molar and premolar region—crosses molar roots
   b) Diagonal inner ridge of anterior ramus
   c) Radiopaque diagonal stripe
   d) Alternate name—mylohyoid ridge or line
4. Mental foramen (*k*)
   a) Premolar and canine region—adjacent to premolar roots
   b) Circular radiolucency
   c) Sometimes misinterpreted as periapical pathology
5. Submandibular fossae
   a) Molar and premolar region—between internal oblique ridge and lower border of the mandible

b) Cavity on lingual surface of the mandible for submandibular gland
c) Poorly defined radiolucency with sparse trabecular pattern

6. Mental ridge (*l*)
   a) Canine and incisor region—inferior to teeth roots
   b) Radiopaque inverted V-shaped or triangular ridge
7. Genial tubercles (*m*)
   a) Incisor region—inferior third of anterior mandible
   b) Radiopaque ring of bone
   c) Alternate name—mental spines
8. Lingual foramen
   a) Incisor region—inferior third of anterior mandible
   b) Pinpoint radiolucency often surrounded by genial tubercles
9. Inferior or lower border of mandible (*n*)
   a) Possible to be seen on any mandibular periapical
   b) Radiopaque horizontal band

D. Anatomic landmarks on panoramic radiographs (in addition to previously described anatomic landmarks) (Fig. 11-21a–ee)

1. Maxillary
   a) Nasal conchae (*x*)—radiopaque ovoid bones located on lateral aspects of nasal cavity (turbinates)
   b) Hard palate (*u*)—radiopaque, horizontal band superior to maxillary teeth that forms roof of oral cavity

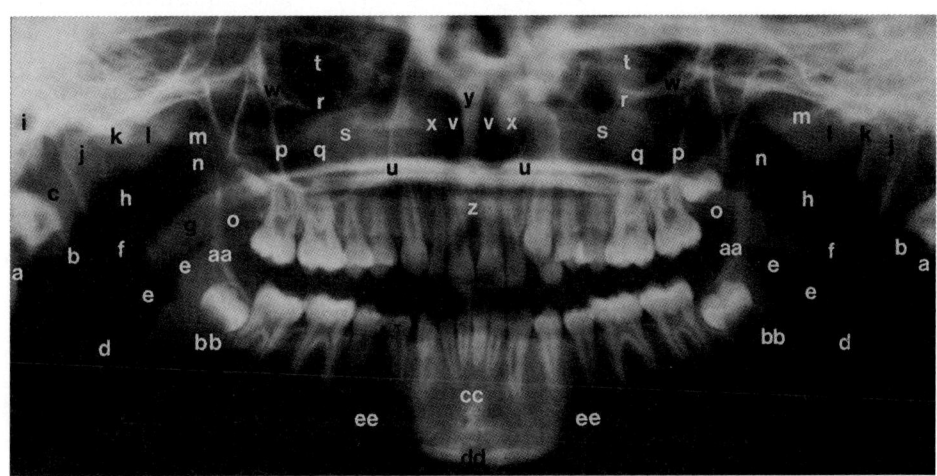

FIGURE 11-21. Anatomic landmarks that are demonstrated on this panoramic radiograph include: a) cervical spine; b) styloid process; c) ear soft tissue; d) angle of the mandible; e) oropharyngeal air space; f) mandibular foramen; g) soft palate; h) nasopharyngeal air space; i) external auditory meatus; j) mandibular condyle; k) articular eminence; l) zygomatic arch; m) zygomaticotemporal suture; n) coronoid process; o) maxillary tuberosity; p) zygomatic process; q) maxillary sinus; r) infraorbital canal; s) infraorbial foramen; t) orbit; u) hard palate; v) nasal fossa; w) rim of the orbit; x) nasal conchae; y) nasal septum; z) incisive foramen; aa) external oblique ridge; bb) ghost of the opposite ramus and inferior border of the mandible; cc) genial tubercles and lingual foramen; dd) inferior border of the mandible; ee) mental foramen

2. Mandible
   a) Mandibular condyle (*j*)—radiopaque, rounded articular process of the mandible
   b) Angle of mandible (*d*)—radiopaque intersection of ramus and body of mandible
   c) Mandibular foramen (*f*)—radiolucent opening into mandibular canal on medial surface of ramus
3. Adjacent structures
   a) Rim of orbit (*w*)—radiopaque bone cavity surrounding orbit (eye socket); orbit (*t*) is radiolucent
   b) Infraorbital canal (*r*)—radiolucent tubular structure with parallel radiopaque borders extending from floor of orbit to infraorbital foramen
   c) Infraorbital foramen (*s*)—radiolucent circular external opening of infraorbital canal located on anterior surface of maxilla
   d) Pterygomaxillary fissure (*loop between m and w*)—radiolucent inverted teardrop-shaped space between posterior maxilla and pterygoid plates
   e) External auditory meatus (*i*)—radiolucent ovoid opening of ear canal
   f) Zygomaticotemporal suture (*m*)—radiolucent diagonal junction between zygomatic process (*p*) of temporal bone and temporal process of zygomatic bone; processes form zygoma
   g) Zygomatic arch (*l*)—radiopaque horizontal bony process that attaches to temporal bone
   h) Glenoid fossae (*above j*)—radiolucent cavity in temporal bone where mandibular condyle rests
   i) Articular eminence (*k*)—radiopaque bony prominence on inferior surface of zygomatic arch anterior to glenoid fossae
   j) Cervical spine (*a*)—radiopaque vertebrae in neck region
   k) Styloid process (*b*)—radiopaque slender, pointed projection extending downward from temporal bone
   l) Hyoid bone—radiopaque, U-shaped bone in neck
4. Soft tissues
   a) Nasal soft tissue—faint radiopacity of tip and ala of nose
   b) Soft palate (*g*)—faint radiopacity extending downward from posterior aspect of hard palate
   c) Ear lobes (*c*)—faint radiopacity of fleshy part of ear inferior to external auditory meatus
   d) Tongue—faint radiopacity representing lateral and dorsal surfaces of tongue (*above z*)
   e) Lips—faint radiopacity of upper and lower lip
5. Air-space images
   a) Nasopharyngeal (*h*)—radiolucent airway of pharynx and nasal cavity located above soft and hard palate
   b) Oropharyngeal (*e*)—radiolucent airway of pharynx and oral cavity located below soft palate
   c) Palatoglossal (*below u*)—radiolucent space between dorsum of tongue and hard palate

XIII. FILM MOUNTING AND DUPLICATION

A. Film mounting procedures

1. Labial mounting—film dot convexities toward operator, patient's right and left; ADA-accepted standard for film mounting
2. Lingual mounting—film dot concavities toward operator, operator's right and left
3. Film mount selection
   a) Plastic or cardboard frame material opaque to light
   b) Number of film windows matches orientation and number of radiographs
   c) Organizes film survey to reflect patient's oral cavity
   d) Proper labeling and identification—include patient's full name, date of survey, dentist's office, and operator
4. Mounting procedure
   a) Orient film dot convexity uniformly
   b) Identify film types
      (1) Bitewings—crowns in occlusion, horizontal placements (usually), smile appearance of occlusal plane
      (2) Anterior periapicals—vertical placements of the crowns and apices of canine and incisor teeth
      (3) Posterior periapicals—horizontal placements of crowns and apices of premolar and molar teeth
      (4) Arrange films in order, then mount with respect to
         (a) Tooth morphology
         (b) Anatomic landmarks
         (c) Natural order and progression of dentition
         (d) Match restorations and missing teeth from film to film
         (e) Check for smile appearance or curve of occlusal plane

B. Film duplication procedures

1. *Film duplication*—process of copying radiographs by passing ultraviolet light through an original survey and exposing film designed for duplication
2. Duplication film has a single emulsion
   a) Emulsion side has a light, dull appearance
   b) Nonemulsion side has a dark, shiny appearance
   c) Sheet duplication film does not have a film identification dot
   d) Direct reversal film; whiteness is deposited rather than blackness
3. Light exposure of duplication film is opposite to principles of x-ray film exposure
   a) Low-density or light original radiographs require less light exposure on duplication
   b) High-density or dark original radiographs require more light exposure on duplication
4. Good contact between duplication film and mounted radiographs necessary to prevent blurring and fuzziness of duplicated image

5. Duplication procedure
   a) Place correctly organized radiographs into flat pocket mount
   b) Take survey into darkroom and continue procedures under safelight conditions
   c) Place mounted film survey with front of mount placed toward the duplicator light box surface for labially mounted radiographs
   d) Place emulsion side of duplication film on lingual side of mounted radiographs
   e) Close lid of duplicator, pressing duplication film firmly against the survey, and latch it
   f) Set timer on light box for appropriate amount of light exposure; press timer button and observe exposure
   g) Process exposed duplication film and evaluate results; repeat if necessary
   h) Trim, label, identify right and left sides of finished film using original survey as reference

XIV. INTERPRETATION

A. Viewing conditions

1. Subdued background lighting
2. Viewbox used for even light distribution and transillumination
3. Eliminate excess light around films/mount
4. Use systematic approach when making observations
5. Magnification is useful for examining small details

B. Caries (Fig. 11-22)

1. Cavity preparation and restoration classification
   a) Class I—All pit and fissure cavities
      (1) Occlusals of molars and premolars
      (2) Occlusal two thirds of facial and lingual surfaces of molars
      (3) Lingual pits of maxillary incisors
   b) Class II—cavities on proximal surfaces of molars and premolars
   c) Class III—cavities on proximal surfaces of incisors and canines not involving incisal angle
   d) Class IV—cavities on proximal surfaces of incisors and canines involving incisal angle
   e) Class V—cavities on gingival one third of facial or lingual surfaces of all teeth
   f) Class VI—Cavities on the incisal edge of anterior teeth or the cusp tips on posterior teeth
2. Interproximal caries
   a) Carious lesions that occur just below the contacts of the teeth
   b) Best found radiographically on bitewings
   c) Typical shape—horizontal V-shaped or triangular radiolucency
   d) Degree classification
      (1) Incipient (Class/Type I)—lesion has penetrated less than halfway through the enamel layer

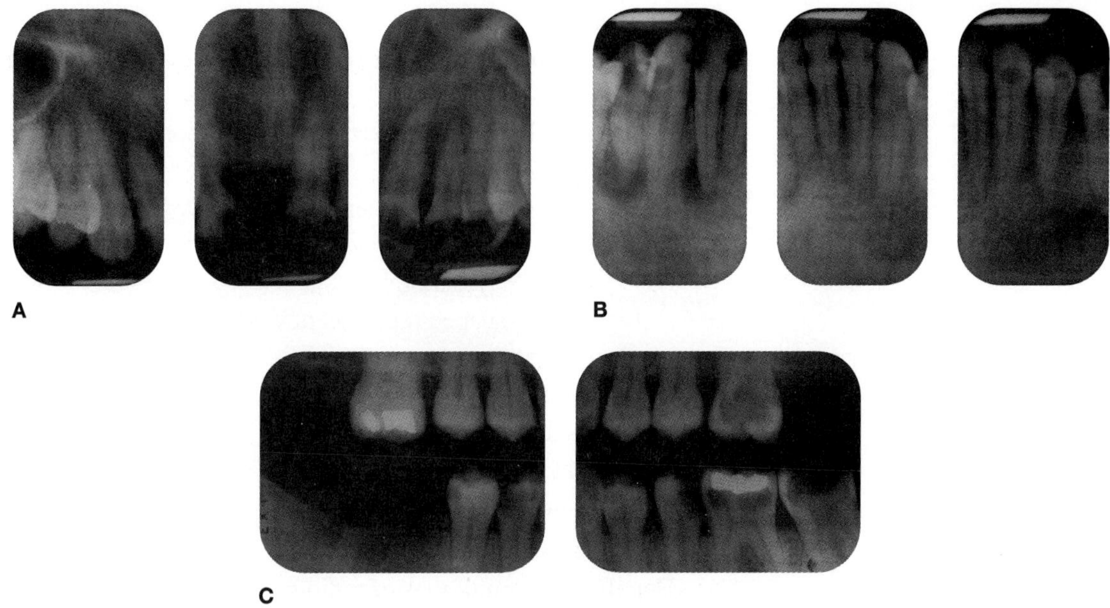

FIGURE 11-22. A) The maxillary anterior periapicals display the following carious lesions: CIII lesions—#6 mesial, #7 mesial and distal, #9 distal, #10 distal; CIV lesions—#9 mesial, #10, mesial and #11 mesial; CV lesion—#6 facial, #9 facial, #10 facial, #11 facial, B) The mandibular anterior periapicals display the following carious lesions: CII lesions—#20 distal and occlusal, #21 distal, #28 mesial, occlusal and distal, #29 mesial and distal; CIII—#22 mesial and distal, #23 mesial and distal, #24 mesial and distal, #25 mesial, #26 mesial and distal, #27 mesial; CIV lesions—#25 distal; CV lesions—#21 facial, #22 facial, #27 facial. C) The premolar bitewing views display the following carious lesions: CII lesions—#3 mesial and distal, #4 mesial and distal, #5 mesial and distal, #12 mesial and distal, #13 mesial and distal, #14 mesial, occlusal and distal, #18 mesial, occlusal, distal, buccal and lingual, #19 mesial and distal, #20 mesial, occlusal and distal, #21 mesial and distal, #28 mesial, occlusal and distal, #29 mesial and distal; CIII lesions—#6 distal, #11 distal, #27 distal; CV lesions—#12 buccal, #19 buccal, #20 buccal, #21 buccal

(2) Moderate (Class/Type II)—lesion has penetrated more than halfway through the enamel layer but does not involve the dentinoenamel junction (DEJ)

(3) Advanced (Class/Type III)—lesion has penetrated through the DEJ and spread less than halfway to the pulp

(4) Severe (Class/Type IV)—lesion has penetrated through the DEJ and spread more than halfway to the pulp or involves the pulp

3. Occlusal caries
   a) Caries involving the pits and fissures of posterior teeth
   b) Radiographically apparent once through the occlusal enamel layer
   c) Typical shape—triangular radiolucency with the base broadening as the dentin is invaded
4. Buccal and lingual caries
   a) Caries of the cervical third of the facial or lingual surfaces of the crown
   b) Typical shape—crescent or dot radiolucency in the cervical third of the crown
   c) May be confused with Class V radiolucent tooth-colored restorations

5. Root caries
   a) Carious involvement of cementum and dentin of exposed root surfaces
   b) Typical shape—diffuse rounded inner border without lateral tooth edge
   c) May be confused with cervical burnout
      (1) Phenomenon of x-ray penetration of cementoenamel junction (CEJ) anatomy
      (2) Wedge-shaped radiolucency adjacent to CEJ
      (3) Lateral root edge is seen
6. Recurrent caries
   a) Caries that occur around margins of existing restorations
   b) Typical shape—radiolucent halo below interproximal or occlusal margin

C. Periodontal disease

1. Benefits and limitations of radiographs
   a) Benefits
      (1) Depiction of bone height and density
      (2) Permits evaluation of root length and shape
      (3) View periodontal ligament (PDL) widening
      (4) View normal anatomy relative to bony defects
      (5) Periapical coverage of teeth
      (6) Observe moderate to advanced furcation involvement and local irritants
   b) Limitations
      (1) Inability to evaluate incipient bone loss
      (2) Unable to determine presence or absence of periodontal pockets or level of epithelial attachment
      (3) Unable to determine morphology of bone defects, buccal/lingual bone status, mobility, or early furcation involvement
2. Classification of periodontal disease progression
   a) Case Type I
      (1) Gingivitis
      (2) No radiographic changes
      (3) Alveolar bone 1.5 to 2.0 mm from CEJ
   b) Case Type II
      (1) Early or mild periodontitis
      (2) Radiographs may show crestal lamina dura changes, triangulation, 20 to 30% bone loss
      (3) Alveolar bone 3 to 4 mm from CEJ
   c) Case Type III
      (1) Moderate periodontitics
      (2) Radiographs show mild to moderate bone loss, 30% to 50%
      (3) Alveolar bone 5 to 7 mm from CEJ
      (4) Furcation involvement, bony defects
   c) Case Type IV
      (1) Advanced periodontitis
      (2) Radiographs show severe bone loss, > 50% bone loss

(3) Alveolar bone ≥ 8 mm from CEJ

(4) Severe destruction of periodontal structures, advanced furcation involvement and bony defects

d) Case Type V

(1) Refractory periodontitis

(2) Multiple disease sites despite therapy

(3) Continued, rapid bone loss

3. Early disease observations

a) Crestal bony changes—loss of sharp angle between crestal lamina dura and alveolar crest, decreased bone density (radiolucent)

b) PDL widening near bony crests (triangulation)

c) Widened vascular channels

4. Evaluation of bone loss—determined by comparing bony margins to plane of adjacent CEJs

a) Normal appearance

(1) Bone crests—anterior crests are pointed, posterior crests are flat and angular

(2) Normal height—1.5 to 2.0 mm from CEJ

(3) Bone crests are radiopaque, with lamina dura extending from lateral root surfaces across crestal bone with trabeculated underlying bone

(4) Periodontal ligament space—linear radiolucency (0.25 to 0.40 mm wide) located between tooth root and lamina dura

b) Types of bone loss

(1) Horizontal bone loss—bony margin is parallel to plane of adjacent CEJs (Fig. 11-23)

(2) Vertical bone loss—bony margin is diagonal to plane of adjacent CEJs (Fig. 11-24)

(3) Localized or generalized condition

(4) Degree classification—mild (slight), moderate, advanced (severe)

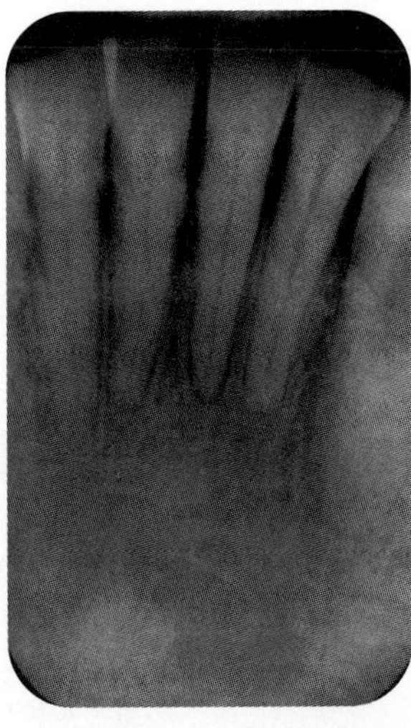

FIGURE 11-23. Horizontal bone loss

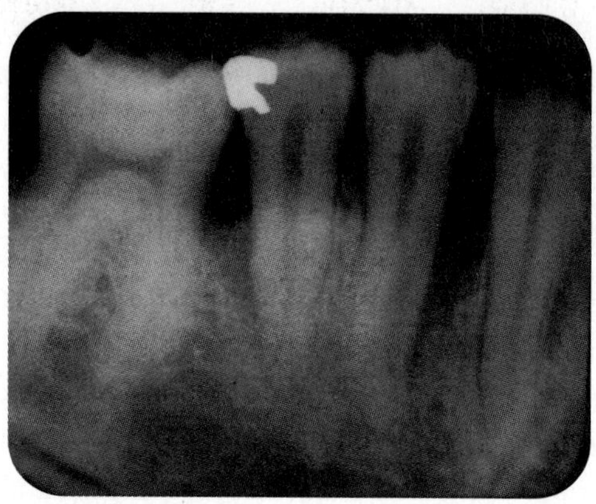

FIGURE 11-24. Vertical bone loss

c) Evaluation of bony defects—areas of decreased bone density that vary in size, shape, and location
d) Local factors and irritants
   (1) Calculus deposits—radiopaque spurs, rings, ledges
   (2) Faulty restorations—overhanging margins, poor proximal contours
   (3) Occlusal trauma—may widen PDL or thicken lamina dura or both
   (4) Areas of food impaction
   (5) Root morphology and crown-root ratio
e) Furcation involvement (Fig. 11-25)
   (1) Advanced bone loss that exposes furcation areas of multi-rooted teeth
   (2) Radiographic appearance—area of decreased bone density (radiolucency) within furcation
   (3) Class II and Class III furcation involvement visible radiographically

D. Periapical disease—most common types

1. Periapical granuloma
   a) Most common aftermath of pulpitis
   b) Round radiolucency with well-defined radiopaque border

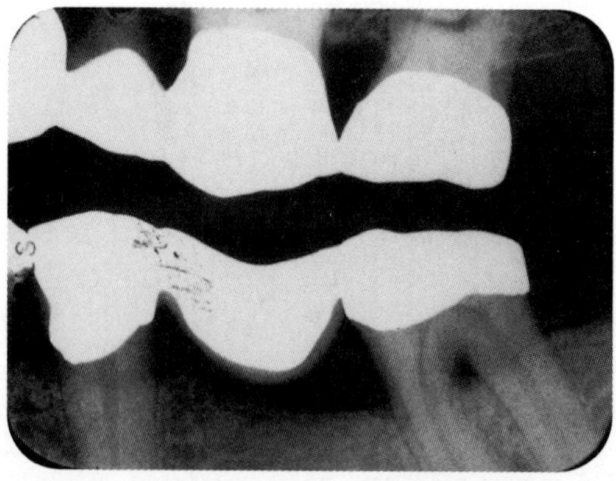

FIGURE 11-25. Class II and Class III furcation involvement

c) Vary in size, may show some trabeculations within lesion
d) Nonvital tooth, usually asymptomatic

2. Periapical cyst
   a) Often sequela of periapical granuloma
   b) Nonvital tooth, usually asymptomatic
   c) Radiographic presentation similar to periapical granuloma
   d) Often larger, more radiolucent with fewer central trabeculations than periapical granuloma
   e) May involve more than one tooth
3. Chronic periapical abscess
   a) May develop after an acute periapical abscess or in existing periapical granuloma
   b) Radiolucent lesion with diffuse, irregular borders that blend into the bony pattern
   c) Often extends beyond tooth apex and involves lateral aspects of root
   d) Involved tooth usually asymptomatic
   e) Fistulous tract may be found clinically
4. Condensing osteitis or chronic focal sclerosing osteomyelitis
   a) Reaction of bone to infection
   b) Typically involves mandibular first molars in young people
   c) Well-circumscribed radiopaque mass surrounding apex or apices of carious or heavily restored tooth
   d) Root outline visible
   e) Sclerotic bone may have distinct or diffuse border

review questions

DIRECTIONS Each of the questions or incomplete statements below is followed by suggested answers or completions. Select the **one** answer that is best in each case.

1. All of the following descriptions are characteristic of electromagnetic radiation EXCEPT one. Which one is the EXCEPTION?
   A. some types can ionize human tissue
   B. include visible and ultraviolet light
   C. travel in an oscillating motion
   D. include alpha and beta particles
   E. energies vary in wavelength

2. All of the following descriptions are characteristic of x-ray energy EXCEPT one. Which one is the EXCEPTION?
   A. form of particulate radiation
   B. cause certain substances to fluoresce
   C. produce a latent image on a receptor
   D. capable of penetrating matter
   E. differentially absorbed

3. Which of the following accurately describes the anode electrode?
   A. aluminum focal spot
   B. source of x-rays
   C. controlled by low-voltage circuit
   D. surrounded by molybdenum focusing cup

4. The step-down transformer is responsible for all of the following activities EXCEPT one. Which one is the EXCEPTION?
   A. supplies current to the cathode electrode
   B. is operated by the mA switch
   C. decreases electrical current
   D. creates a potential difference

5. What is bremsstrahlung radiation?
   A. Radiation produced by particle interaction at the P or Q shell level of target atoms.
   B. X-ray photons generated as a result of particle interaction at or near the nucleus of target atoms.
   C. Thermal energy produced by particle interaction at the outer shell levels of target atoms.
   D. A minor source of particle energy generated.

6. All of the following statements are correct regarding intraoral film EXCEPT one. Which one is the EXCEPTION?
   A. Intraoral film consists of a plastic film base coated with silver halide crystals.
   B. The purpose of the lead foil is to reduce film fog by absorbing scatter radiation.
   C. The color-coded side of the film packet is directed toward the x-ray source.
   D. The outer covering of the film packet is either plastic or paper.

7. Fluorescent light and x-rays produce the latent image on intraoral radiographs. The visible image on an extraoral film is the result of chemical processing of the exposed film.
   A. The first statement is TRUE. The second statement is FALSE.
   B. The first statement is FALSE. The second statement is TRUE.

C. Both statements are TRUE.
D. Both statements are FALSE.

8. Which of the following is the most common method of altering film density?
   A. changing the milliamperage setting
   B. adjusting the kilovoltage peak
   C. changing the length of the PID
   D. altering the exposure time

9. The x-ray machine is set at 10mA, 60 kVp, and .80 second. It is necessary to change the kilovoltage setting to 90 kVp.To maintain the same film density, what would be the new exposure time at 90 kVp?
   A. 1.60 seconds
   B. 1.20 seconds
   C. .40 second
   D. .20 second
   E. .10 second

10. Collimation of the x-ray beam produces all of the following outcomes EXCEPT one. Which one is the EXCEPTION?
    A. increases intensity of x-ray beam
    B. restricts size of x-ray beam
    C. reduces exposure to patient
    D. minimizes image magnification
    E. improves image sharpness

11. The x-ray machine is equipped with a short 4-inch PID and the exposure factors are set at 15 mA, 80 kVp, and .10 second. If the PID is changed to a 12-inch length, what should the exposure time be at the new distance?
    A. .20 second
    B. .40 second
    C. .90 second
    D. 1.00 second
    E. 1.60 seconds

12. Which of the following phrases is MOST representative of long scale contrast?
    A. produced by reduced x-ray penetration of the involved structures
    B. described as high contrast with a black or white appearance
    C. type of contrast preferred for carious lesion diagnosis
    D. described as low contrast with few shades between black and white
    E. demonstrates a broad range of densities on the processed radiograph

13. Which of the following phrases does NOT accurately describe x-ray beam filtration?
    A. amount of required filtration depends on the kilovoltage setting
    B. includes inherent filtration such as the window and oil
    C. platinum is the most common filter material
    D. total filtration includes inherent and added
    E. improves quality of x-ray beam

14. All of the following phrases are consistent with the paralleling technique EXCEPT one. Which one is the EXCEPTION?
    A. A short position indicating device is used.
    B. It is the preferred method for taking radiographs.
    C. The film is placed parallel to the long axes of the teeth.
    D. The central ray is directed at a right angle to the teeth and film.
    E. It produces images with the least unsharpness, magnification and shape distortion.

15. From the list below, select the factor that would BEST achieve the anatomic accuracy of an image.
    A. focal spot size
    B. object-film distance
    C. source-object distance
    D. object-film parallelism

16. All of the following phrases are descriptive of Compton scattering EXCEPT one. Which one is the EXCEPTION?
    A. Photon interaction occurs with electron in the K shell of absorber atom.
    B. It produces a scattered photon of lower energy called a recoil electron.
    C. 62% of x-ray beam photons undergo Compton scattering.
    D. It results in ionization of the involved absorber atom.
    E. It contributes to film fog.

17. All of the following accurately describe the indirect effects of x-radiation EXCEPT one. Which one is the EXCEPTION?
    A. ionization event
    B. production of free radicals
    C. direct alteration of biomolecules
    D. radiolysis of water
    E. 66% of induced biological damage

18. Which of the following cells or tissues are NOT highly sensitive to the effects of radiation?
    A. bone marrow
    B. small blood vessels
    C. small lymphocyte
    D. sperm and ova

19. Which of the following is consistent with the dose equivalent?
    A. compares biological effects of different types of radiation
    B. quantifies the radioactivity of x-rays
    C. measure of ability of x-rays to ionize air
    D. measure of radiation exposure

20. Using the following would result in patient exposure reduction EXCEPT one. Which one is the EXCEPTION?
    A. lead-lined thyroid collar
    B. 16-inch PID rather than an 8-inch PID
    C. rectangular collimation
    D. rare earth intensifying screens
    E. a low kilovoltage

21. In the developer, what is the function of the reducing agent hydroquinone?
    A. removes the unexposed, undeveloped silver bromide crystals
    B. stops development by neutralizing chemical carryover
    C. reaction provides the black tones and contrast of the image
    D. softens the film emulsion to speed development

22. Which one of the following quality assurance procedures is NOT accurately described?
    A. The coin test is used to evaluate x-ray machine function such as output, kilovoltage calibration, and milliamperage reproducibility.
    B. Solution monitoring involves the comparison of a control film taken at the time of solution change and a daily check film.
    C. On a monthly basis, inspect cassettes for damage and function and clean the intensifying screens.
    D. Preclean, disinfect and cover operatory viewboxes in preparation for patient care and replace light bulbs as needed.

23. To correct the technical error of overlapping, it is necessary to
    A. increase the vertical angulation to reduce the overlapping of the structures.
    B. place the film so that it is parallel to the long axes of the teeth to be recorded.
    C. direct the horizontal angle through the interproximal surfaces of the teeth of interest.
    D. decrease the positive vertical angle and move the x-ray beam in a more posterior direction.

24. All of the following descriptions indicate backward placement of an intraoral film packet EXCEPT one. Which one is the EXCEPTION?
    A. The colored side of the film packet was placed toward the x-ray source.
    B. The film identification dot convexity was directed toward x-ray source.
    C. The pattern of the lead foil appears on the processed radiograph.
    D. The processed film has a low-density appearance.

25. Which of the following does NOT cause a high-density radiograph?
    A. white light leaks or improper safelight conditions in the darkroom
    B. overdevelopment owing to a high processing temperature

C. under-replenishment of the processing solutions
D. double exposure of a film

26. Panoramic ghost images display certain radiographic features. Which of the following features is NOT characteristic of ghost images?
   A. Typical structures that produce ghosts include the ramus areas and metal earrings.
   B. Ghost images are reversed and appear on the same side as the original structure.
   C. Ghost images appear magnified and blurred in the horizontal and vertical plane.
   D. Ghost images appear higher on the film than the original structure.

27. Which guideline does NOT aid in the production of a diagnostic panoramic radiograph?
   A. place occlusal plane parallel to the floor
   B. lead apron clears back of the neck
   C. patient stands or sits with erect spine
   D. have patient place tongue in floor of mouth

28. Which of the following selections is NOT descriptive of the tube shift method of object localization?
   A. also referred to as Clark's rule or the buccal object rule
   B. object movement is compared to movement of the PID
   C. buccal objects move in the opposite direction
   D. lingual objects move in the same direction
   E. requires at least a two-film comparison

29. Select the landmark that is radiopaque and recorded on posterior periapicals.
   A. genial tubercles
   B. mandibular foramen
   C. zygomatic bone
   D. maxillary sinus

30. Compared with intraoral radiographs, all of the following landmarks are found ONLY on panoramic radiographs EXCEPT one. Which one is the EXCEPTION?
   A. external auditory meatus
   B. cervical spine
   C. hyoid bone
   D. coronoid process

31. Which one of the following selections is NOT an accurate description of carious lesions?
   A. Carious lesions that occur on the proximal surfaces of incisors and canines are classified as Class III lesions.
   B. The typical radiographic presentation of a Class V lesion is a crescent or dot radiolucency.
   C. Frequently, a recurrent carious lesion occurs under the proximal margin of a restoration.
   D. Class II lesions are best found radiographically and located just below the contacts of posterior teeth.
   E. An incipient carious lesion is one that is proximal and has penetrated to the DEJ.

32. All of the following selections describe the benefits of radiographs in periodontal disease assessment EXCEPT one. Which one is the EXCEPTION?
   A. can determine the level of epithelial attachment
   B. observe periodontal ligament widening
   C. observe the apical regions of the teeth
   D. evaluate root length and shape
   E. view bone height and density

33. Which of the following descriptions is NOT consistent with the normal radiographic presentation of periodontal structures?
   A. Anterior bone crests are narrow and pointed.
   B. Posterior bone crests are flat and angular in shape.
   C. Normal bone height is 1.0 to 3.0 mm from the CEJ.
   D. Bone crests are radiopaque with the lamina dura outlining the bony septa.
   E. The periodontal ligament space is a linear radiolucency surrounding the tooth root.

34. All of the following radiographic observations are consistent with early periodontal disease EXCEPT one. Which one is the EXCEPTION?
    A. triangulation
    B. decreased bone density
    C. widened vascular channels
    D. thickening of the lamina dura
    E. loss of a sharp angle between the crestal lamina dura and bone crest

35. How does the periapical cyst differ from the periapical granuloma?
    A. usually larger and may involve more than one tooth
    B. demonstrates central trabeculations within lesion
    C. round radiolucency with a well-defined border
    D. tooth usually asymptomatic
    E. involves a nonvital tooth

answers & rationales

1.

D. Alpha and beta particles are not electromagnetic radiations. They are considered particulate radiation. Electromagnetic radiation has the following characteristics. It travels in a wave motion and has energies with varied wavelengths. Some types of electromagnetic radiation can ionize human tissue. Visible and ultraviolet light are some familiar examples of this type of energy.

2.

A. X-ray energy is not a form of particulate radiation. X-rays are a form of electromagnetic radiation and are not particles. X-ray energy is classified as causing certain substances to fluoresce, produce a latent image, differentially absorbed, and capable of penetrating matter.

3.

B. X-rays are generated by electron bombardment of the anode target. The anode is housed inside the x-ray tube and is composed of a copper rod with a tungsten metal target, controlled by the high voltage circuit. X-rays are generated by electron bombardment of the anode target. The molybdenum focusing cup is located in the cathode, not the anode.

4.

D. The step-up transformer, rather than the step-down transformer, creates a potential difference between the anode and cathode in the x-ray production system. The step-down transformer is operated by the mA switch, supplies a low-voltage current to the cathode to heat the tungsten filament and produce free electrons (electron cloud) at the cathode.

5.

B. Bremsstrahlung radiation is breaking or general radiation produced by particle interaction at or near the nucleus (K or L) shells of target atoms, not outer shells (P or Q). These interactions are the major source of x-ray photons.

6.

C. This would produce an image error owing to improper placement of the film in relation to the x-ray source. In all instances, the white side of the film packet is directed toward the x-ray source. The intraoral film packet consists of the base, which is coated with halide crystals, the lead foil, which reduces film fog, and the plastic or paper outer covering.

7.

B. In extraoral radiography, it is the sum of the fluorescent light and x-rays that expose the film, rather than x-rays alone as with intraoral radiography. The visual image is the result of chemical processing.

8.

D. The most common method of altering film density is by changing the exposure time. Some intraoral x-ray machines have fixed milliamperage and kilovoltage settings, only allowing variations in exposure time. Changing the length of the PID isn't a common method of altering film density.

9.

D. The rule of thumb for altering kilovoltage is for every 15 kVp increase, divide the time by 2. In this problem, the kVp was increased from 60 to 90, requiring two reductions in the exposure time.

10.

A. Collimation restricts the primary beam of radiation, reducing the area of exposure at the skin surface. In addition, it keeps the x-rays more parallel to one another and improves image geometry. Intensity is altered when the source-object distance is changed from distance to another. Optimum collimation infers a 16-inch PID, which would decrease beam intensity and require an increase in exposure time if changed from a shorter PID.

11.

C. In this inverse square law problem, the PID was changed from 4-inch to 12-inch. The law states that intensity varies as the square of the source-film distance. Since the distance tripled, square 3 and multiply the original time by 9 to calculate the new exposure time to equalize the x-ray beam intensity at 12 inches.

12.

E. Long-scale contrast is produced at higher kilovoltage settings by greater beam penetration of structures. This produces many shades of gray on the processed film, lowers contrast, and is preferred for periodontal diagnosis—not carious lesions—because more subtle changes can be observed.

13.

C. The most common filter material used in dental x-ray machines is aluminum. The amount of added aluminum filtration is determined by the kilovoltage setting.

14.

A. The paralleling technique utilizes a long PID rather than a short PID. The longer cone is used to counteract the magnification that occurs from a slightly increased object-film distance as well as to minimize image unsharpness.

15.

D. Anatomic accuracy is best achieved when the film is placed parallel to the teeth of interest, and the central ray is directed perpendicular to the teeth and film. Focal spot size, object-film distance, and source-object distance affect geometric rather than anatomic accuracy of an image.

16.

A. Photon interaction occurs with electron in the K shell of absorber atom. Compton scattering is the result of photon interaction with outer electron shells of the absorber atom.

17.

C. The indirect effects of x-radiation occur through ionization or radiolysis of water molecules and produce free radicals that cause various reactions in the formation of new molecules. It is estimated that 66% of induced biological damage occurs via this process. The direct alteration of biomolecules results when radiation interacts with the DNA of the cells.

18.

B. Small blood vessels are categorized as having intermediate sensitivity rather than high sensitivity to the effects of radiation. Bone marrow, small lymphocytes, and sperm and ova are highly sensitive to the effects of radiation.

19.

A. The dose equivalent is used to compare the biological effects (relative biological effectiveness) of different types of radiation. It does not measure the radiation exposure or ability to ionize air, or quantify the radioactivity of x-rays.

20.

E. Lower kilovoltage produces a higher skin dose than higher kilovoltage. Use of lead-lined thyroid collar, rectangular 16-inch PID, and rare earth-intensifying screens reduce radiation exposure to the patient.

21.

C. Hydroquinone is the developer reducing agent that generates the black tones and contrast of the radiographic image. In the fixing solution, the sodium thiosulfate removes the unexposed, undeveloped silver bromide crystals. Water stops the developing process. Sodium carbonate softens the film emulsion to speed development.

22.

A. The coin test is a quality assurance procedure for evaluating white light leaks and safelight conditions in the darkroom. Solution monitoring, inspection of cassettes, and infection control for the viewboxes are quality assurance procedures.

23.

C. To correct overlapping, direct the horizontal angle through the interproximal surfaces of the teeth.

24.

B. If the film was placed backwards, the film dot concavity was placed toward the x-ray source.

25.

C. Under-replenishment of the processing solutions would produce a low-density image. Over-replenishment of the processing solutions would produce a high-density image. Double exposure, white light, and overdevelopment would produce high-density images.

26.

B. Ghost images are not reversed, but they appear on the opposite side of the original structure rather than the same side. Typical structures that ghost are the ramus areas and metal earrings. Ghost images also appear magnified and blurred in the horizontal and vertical plane and higher on the film than the original structure.

27.

D. In panoramic radiography, the tongue should be placed on the palate rather than the floor of the mouth and the lead apron should be placed so that it clears the back of the neck. The patient should sit or stand with an erect spine and be positioned with the occlusal plane parallel to the floor.

28.

B. In the tube shift method of object localization, the object movement is compared with the movement of the x-ray head rather than the PID. The tube-shift method of localization is also referred to as Clark's rule or buccal object rule. This means that buccal objects move in the opposite direction, and lingual objects move in the same direction, and at least two films are required for comparison.

29.

D. The radiopaque posterior landmark includes the zygomatic bone. The genial tubercles are radiopaque but appear on a mandibular anterior periapical. The mandibular foramen and maxillary sinus are radiolucent.

30.

D. The coronoid process appears in both intraoral and panoramic films. Of the landmarks listed, the external auditory meatus, cervical spine, and hyoid bone appear only on panoramic films.

31.

E. An incipient lesion is defined as one that has penetrated less than halfway through the enamel and does not involve the DEJ.

32.

A. The epithelial attachment is soft tissue in origin and, therefore, the level of attachment cannot be determined on dental radiographs; however, the remaining selections benefit periodontal disease assessment.

33.

C. The normal alveolar bone height, as measured on dental radiographs, is 1.5 to 2.0 mm from the CEJ and should not be confused with probing depths. The remaining descriptions are consistent with normal radiographic appearances of periodontal structures.

34.

D. Thickening of the lamina dura is more of a response to occlusal trauma than periodontal disease. Triangulation, decreased bone density, widened vascular channels, and loss of a sharp angle between the crestal lamina dura and bone crest are early radiographic signs of periodontal disease.

35.

A. The periapical cyst is the sequela of the periapical granuloma and is often larger and involves more than one tooth. Both the periapical cyst and periapical granuloma are round radiolucencies with well-defined borders and central trabeculations within the lesion that involve nonvital, asymptomatic teeth.

CHAPTER

12 Periodontology

Marilyn Stolberg, DDS

contents

Periodontology involves the diagnosis, treatment, and prevention of diseases associated with the periodontium.

I. TISSUES OF THE PERIODONTIUM

A. Gingiva

1. Components
   a) Free gingiva—located at crest of alveolus; not attached, outer boundary of sulcus
   b) Free gingival groove—located at inferior border of free gingiva, point opposite of alveolar crest, depression
   c) Attached gingiva—located below free gingival groove; lies over underlying bone
   d) Mucogingival junction—located where attached gingiva ends
   e) Alveolar mucosa—located below mucogingival junction
   f) Gingival sulcus—denotes space between gingiva and tooth
   g) Col—consists of nonkeratinized tissue located between lingual and facial papilla
   h) Interdental papilla—denotes tissue that occupies interdental space between two adjacent teeth
   i) Epithelial attachment—located at base of sulcus, where epithelium attaches to tooth
   j) Epithelium—contains both keratinized and nonkeratinized tissues
      (1) Keratinized—consists of oral epithelium
      (2) Nonkeratinized—consists of sulcular and junctional epithelium
   k) *Sulcular (crevicular) fluid*—serum-like fluid that passes from gingival connective tissue through tissues into the sulcus; an inflammatory exudate
      (1) Characteristics
         (a) Less fluid is present in healthy gingiva than in diseased gingiva
         (b) Amount of fluid may be proportionate to severity of inflammation
   l) Connective tissue
      (1) Known as *lamina propria*
      (2) Vascular and has nerve tissue
      (3) Components
         (a) *Fibroblasts*—produce *collagen* and *elastic fibers;* collagen gives connective tissue its strength
         (b) Composed of *mast cells, macrophages, histiocytes, plasma cells,* and *lymphocytes*
   m) Gingival fiber groups
      (1) Marginal gingiva—consists of dense fiber bundles made of collagen
      (2) Functions of fibers
         (a) Brace gingiva against tooth
         (b) Assist gingiva to withstand forces of mastication

(c) Connect free marginal gingiva to cementum and attached gingiva

(3) Types of fiber groups

(a) Gingivodental—located on facial, lingual, and interproximal surfaces

(b) Circular—encircles tooth

(c) Transseptal—located interproximally and forms horizontal bundles

B. Periodontal ligament (PDL)—consists of connective tissue fibers (collagen) that surround root and connect tooth to bone

1. Functions
   a) Transmit occlusal forces to bone
   b) Attach teeth to bone
   c) Maintain gingival tissues in their proper relationship to teeth
   d) Resist impact of occlusal forces
   e) Protect nerves and vessels from injury by surrounding root with soft tissue
   f) Supply nutrients to remaining periodontal structures—bone, cementum, and gingiva
   g) Transmit touch, pressure, and pain through sensory nerve fibers
2. Fiber bundles
   a) Made of collagen
   b) Attach to cementum and bone by *Sharpey's fibers*
   c) Not visible on radiograph, but space where they are located can be seen on radiograph as radiolucent line surrounding root of tooth
   d) Principal fibers—arranged in distinct groups
      (1) Transseptal—extend interproximally over alveolar crest; embedded in cementum of two adjacent teeth
      (2) Alveolar crest—located apically to junctional epithelium and extend obliquely from cementum to alveolar crest
      (3) Horizontal—extend at right angles to long axis of tooth
      (4) Oblique—extend from cementum in a coronal direction to the bone; largest and most significant fiber group
      (5) Apical—extend from cementum at root apex to base of tooth socket
      (6) Interradicular—found only in multirooted teeth; extend from cementum at furcation to bone in furcation area
3. Remodeling
   a) Cells found in PDL (e.g., fibroblasts, cementoblasts, osteoblasts) can remodel bone and cementum
   b) Fibers adapt to occlusal stimuli and increase in size when occlusal forces increase

C. Cementum—consists of calcified tissue covering tooth root

1. Types
   a) *Acellular cementum*—covers cervical one third to one half of root

(1) No cells are present
(2) Contains calcified Sharpey's fibers
(3) Plays a significant role in supporting tooth in socket

b) *Cellular cementum*—formed after tooth has erupted
(1) Located more apically than acellular cementum; compensates for lost tooth crown length that occurs with attrition
(2) Less calcified than acellular
(3) Fewer Sharpey's fibers present

2. Patterns of formation—continuous process with periods of greater and lesser activity
a) Arranged in layers or lamellae
b) Form more rapidly at apex

3. Cementoenamel junction (CEJ)—defines tooth's anatomic crown; useful in assessing attachment loss or bone loss
a) Types
(1) Cementum overlaps enamel—60% to 65%
(2) Cementum meets enamel, not overlapping—30%
(3) Cementum and enamel do not meet (dentin is exposed)—5% to 10%

4. Anomalies
a) *Hypercementosis*—localized or generalized, prominent thickening of cementum often accompanied with nodular overgrowth at apex; numerous etiologies, including Paget's disease
b) Cementicles—globular masses of cementum that lie free in PDL or adhere to root surface

D. Alveolar process—portion of mandible and maxilla that forms and supports tooth sockets; occurs with tooth eruption

1. Disappears after a tooth is lost
2. Bones that make up alveolar process
a) Dense outer plate (*cortical bone*)—includes facial and lingual compact bone
b) *Socket wall*—made up of compact bone (cortical bone); holds ends of PDL—Sharpey's fibers; lamina dura
c) *Cancellous bone*—located between outer cortical plates and socket wall; less dense and spongy; contains trabeculae

3. Parts
a) *Alveoli*—tooth sockets
b) *Interdental septum*—area of bone between teeth
(1) Composed of facial and lingual cortical plates, socket walls, and underlying cancellous bone
(2) Shape is determined by size and shapes of crowns of approximating teeth

c) Bone coverings—composed of vascular connective tissue containing osteogenic cells
(1) *Periosteum* covers outer bone surface
(2) *Endosteum* covers inner bone surface

4. Bone remodeling
    a) Continuous changing of bone
    b) Can be removed (resorbed) or added (formed)
    c) Function, age, and systemic factors determine changes in bone

II. RISK FACTORS

A. Definition—attributes or exposures that increase probability that a disease will occur

B. Causes—environmental conditions, habits, or other diseases that increase or decrease patient's susceptibility to periodontal infection

C. Identification—analyze information obtained from oral examination, clinical studies of periodontium, and medical/dental histories

D. Categories

1. Unchanging risk factors
    a) Include gender, genetic factors, congenital immunodeficiencies, past history of periodontal disease, and congenital systemic diseases
    b) Contribute to periodontal problems—factors include diabetes and conditions or diseases involving reduction of neutrophil numbers or function
    c) Risk factors do not change, even if periodontal health is restored
2. Changing risk factors
    a) Include poor oral hygiene, age, certain medications, tobacco and alcohol use, stress, acquired immune system deficiencies, acquired endocrine diseases, acquired inflammatory diseases, nutritional deficiencies, and tooth restorations, which enhance plaque accumulation or inhibit normal function
    b) Contribute to periodontal problems as well
    c) Risk factors that can be removed or changed
        (1) Poor oral hygiene—primary factor in gingival and periodontal disease
        (2) Tobacco use
            (a) One of the most significant risk factors in development and progression of periodontal disease
            (b) Users exhibit greater bone loss, increased pocket depths, and calculus formation
            (c) Users exhibit same or less gingival inflammation and same levels of plaque accumulation as nonsmokers
            (d) Nicotine and other toxic substances in tobacco alter host's ability to neutralize infection by reducing neutrophils' effectiveness
            (e) Alters periodontal tissue vasculature; reduces immunoglobulin levels and antibody responses to bacterial plaque

(3) Nutritional status
   (a) Secondary factor in etiology of periodontal disease
   (b) Deficiencies of nutrient elements associated with wound healing may contribute to gingival and periodontal disease progression
   (c) Nutrients important for wound healing include
      i) Protein—repairs tissue and increases resistance to infection
      ii) Vitamin C—promotes collagen formation, tissue synthesis, and wound healing
      iii) Folic acid—enhances red blood cell maturation, tissue synthesis, and cell proliferation
      iv) Vitamin B_{12}—enhances red blood cell maturation, tissue synthesis, and cell proliferation
      v) Vitamin A—increases resistance to infection and promotes tissue synthesis; deficiency affects integrity of epithelium
      vi) Vitamin K—affects prothrombin formation
      vii) Iron—promotes red blood cell formation
      viii) Zinc—enhances connective tissue formation, wound healing, and protein synthesis

(4) Side effects—certain medications may have impact on gingival/periodontal tissues and their response to periodontal treatment; severity of periodontal reaction to medications varies among patients
   (a) Gingival hyperplasia—medications associated with gingival hyperplasia include
      i) Phenytoin (Dilantin)
      ii) Calcium channel blockers
         - Diltiazem (Cardizem, Dilacor)
         - Nifedipine (Procardia)
         - Primidone
         - Valproic acid
         - Verapimil (Calan, Isoptin, Verelan)
      iii) Cyclosporine
   (b) Xerostomia—medication categories associated with xerostomia include:
      i) Anorectics (Dexadrine, amphetamine, dextroamphetamine, Adipex-P, and Pondimin)
      ii) Anticholinergics (Atrovent, Artane, Bentyl)
      iii) Anticonvulsants (Valium)
      iv) Antidepressants (Anafranil, Asendin)
      v) Antihistamines (Seldane, Benadryl)
      vi) Antihypertensives
         - Diuretics (Lasix)
         - Central adrenergic inhibitors (Catapres, Aldomet)
         - Peripheral adrenergic antagonists (Minipres)
         - Calcium-channel blockers (Calan)

- Angiotensin-converting enzyme (ACE) inhibitors (Capoten, Vasotec, Monopril)

vii) Antiparkinson (L-dopa, Dopar, Artane)
viii) Antipsychotics (Clozapine, Clozaril, Haldol)
ix) Muscle relaxants (Flexeril)
x) Acne treatment (Accutane)

(c) Altered host resistance—medications that may alter host resistance to infection include
i) Antibiotics
ii) Insulin
iii) Oral hypoglycemics
iv) Systemic corticosteroids

(d) Abnormal bleeding—medications that may cause abnormal bleeding include
i) Aspirin
ii) Dipyridamole
iii) Nonsteroidal anti-inflammatory drugs (NSAIDs)
iv) Phenytoin (Dilantin)
v) Quinidine
vi) Methyldopa

(5) Dental restorations, whose design or material contributes to plaque retention, can contribute to development of gingival inflammation and periodontal destruction

(e) Risk factors and periodontal disease—Risk factors that demand most attention in management of periodontal disease —smoking and diabetes

III. ORAL FACTORS OTHER THAN MICROORGANISMS THAT AFFECT PERIODONTAL HEALTH

A. Calculus (mineralized plaque)

1. Sources of minerals are precipitated salts that originate in saliva and sulcular (crevicular) fluid
2. Inorganic content is mainly calcium phosphate, with lesser amounts of calcium carbonate and other organic compounds
3. Deposits are classified by their location (supragingival or subgingival)

a) Supragingival calculus
(1) Attaches coronal to gingival margin
(2) Displays chalky, creamy white appearance
(3) Mineralization results from saliva
(4) Relatively easy to remove
(5) Deposits occur on, but are not limited to, buccal surfaces of maxillary molars, opposite Stensen's duct, and lingual surfaces of mandibular anterior teeth, opposite Wharton's duct

b) Subgingival calculus
(1) Attaches apical to gingival margin
(2) Displays dark brown-black appearance
(3) More difficult to remove than supragingival calculus
(4) Mineralization results from sulcular fluid
(5) Deposits occur on all root surfaces in sulcus or pocket

4. Significant in gingival and periodontal disease because it contributes to bacterial plaque accumulation owing to its porous surface; inhibits plaque removal and is a tissue irritant

B. Plaque control—primary factor in reduction or elimination of gingival and periodontal disease

1. Conditions that can temporarily or permanently affect plaque control or removal include
   a) Faulty restorations
   b) Partial dentures
   c) Orthodontic appliances
   d) Malocclusion

C. Other conditions that can affect periodontal health

1. Unreplaced missing teeth—increase risk of migration of teeth and loss of bone support
2. Mouth breathing—dehydrates exposed gingival tissue causing tissue to become enlarged and inflamed; affects maxillary incisal area
3. Excess occlusal forces—can result in compression and necrosis of periodontal ligament and root, as well as cementum and alveolar process resorption

IV. SYSTEMIC FACTORS INFLUENCING PERIODONTAL DISEASES

A. Periodontitis associated with systemic diseases

1. General Information
   a) Periodontal disease is directly related to presence of microorganisms in periodontal structures
   b) Involves large quantities of pathogenic bacteria
   c) Host response is modified by systemic disease
   d) Composition of microorganisms or host's ability to respond to microorganisms has impact on health of periodontal tissues
   e) Microorganisms affect periodontal tissues and, in some cases, general systemic health of individual
   f) Destruction of tissues results in ulcerated sulcular epithelium—portal of entry for microorganisms or their toxins to invade circulatory systems, distributing microorganisms systemically
   g) Studies support significant correlation between periodontal diseases and specific systemic diseases
2. Specific systemic diseases
   a) Diabetes
      (1) Uncontrolled diabetics have increased risk of developing periodontal disease, with severity of periodontal disease being greater
      (2) Patients with poorly controlled blood glucose levels have increased risk for developing acute periodontal abscesses and chronic inflammatory periodontal diseases
         (a) Hyperglycemia, associated with uncontrolled diabetes, exacerbates inflammatory destruction, and impaired wound healing

(b) Metabolic compounds accumulate in tissue and contribute to vascular inflammatory and neural complications

(3) Diabetics may have impaired polymorphonuclear (PMN) leukocyte function, which will alter the inflammatory response—exaggerated inflammatory response

(4) More difficult to control diabetes in presence of periodontal disease

b) Cardiovascular disease

(1) Periodontal disease puts individual at increased risk for heart disease including heart attacks and stroke

(2) Circulating periodontal pathogens may result in small blood clots that can block arteries

c) Human immunodeficiency virus (HIV) infection

(1) Periodontal disease associated with HIV infection is a rapid progression of chronic periodontitis

(2) HIV invades T-4 (T-helper) lymphocytes (with CD4 receptor cells)

(3) Virus binds to CD4 lymphocyte cell surface

(4) Number of CD4 lymphocytes decreases

(5) Ultimately, there is a depressed immune function, which is a significant factor in development of HIV-associated periodontal disease

(6) With HIV infection, there may be inadequate function of PMN leukocytes, which will alter the inflammatory response

d) Neutrophil disorders

(1) Significant in development and progression of periodontal diseases because neutrophil function is critical to well-functioning inflammatory response

(2) Primary neutrophil defects or disorders

(a) *Agranulocytosis*—acute disease; white blood cell count drops

(b) *Cyclic neutropenia*—involves periodic episodes of abnormally low number of neutrophils

(c) *Chediak-Higashi syndrome*—inherited metabolic disorder with neutrophils containing perioxidase-positive inclusion bodies

(d) Lazy leukocyte syndrome

(3) Neutrophil defects or impairment secondary to other systemic conditions

(a) Papillon-LeFèvre syndrome

(b) Down syndrome

(c) Inflammatory bowel disease

(d) *Addison's disease*—chronic adrenal insufficiency

e) Pregnancy

(1) Evidence suggests that pregnant women with periodontal disease are at increased risk of delivering low birth weight infants; circulating inflammatory products and toxins that occur as a result of the periodontal disease may effect fetal development

V. MICROBIOLOGY OF PERIODONTAL DISEASES

A. Microorganisms

1. Accumulation around gingival margins is associated with majority of periodontal diseases
2. Found in bacterial plaque (biofilm) in gingival sulcus or pocket
3. Only a small number (approximately 12) found in oral cavity are associated with gingival or periodontal diseases
4. Bacteria associated with gingival or periodontal diseases have properties that are especially damaging or destructive to structures of periodontium—maintain similar structural or toxic characteristics (e.g., Gram-negative anaerobic)
5. Bacteria cause tissue damage by substances they release or as a consequence of host's inflammatory and immune response (some have tissue-invasion properties; others have enzymes that break down connective tissue)

B. Bacterial characteristics—use following characteristics to identify or categorize bacteria

1. Morphotypes (shapes)
   a) Cocci—ball-shaped and spherical
   b) Rods—long and thin
      (1) Bacilli—rectangular in shape
      (2) Filaments—threadlike
      (3) Fusiforms—threadlike, with tapered ends
   c) Spirochetes—spiral, with fibrils (little fibers) in cell wall
2. Cell wall—identifying characteristic of bacteria
   a) Characteristics
      (1) Contains receptor proteins that contribute to bacteria's adherence
      (2) Lipopolysaccarides are destructive endotoxins that cause inflammatory or immune host response
      (3) May have fimbriae or pili (projections of cell wall) contributing to bacterial adhesion to tooth or other bacteria
      (4) Contains polysaccharides—long-chained, sticky carbohydrates
         (a) Glucans help bacteria stick together
         (b) Salivary enzymes destroy peptidoglycan found in bacterial wall
   b) Gram stain properties
      (1) Gram-positive bacteria will pick up Gram stain (a violet stain) in cell wall
      (2) Gram-negative bacteria will *not* pick up Gram stain in cell wall
3. Oxygen needs influence where bacteria can survive
   a) *Aerobic*—require oxygen to survive
   b) *Anaerobic*—do not survive in an oxygen-rich environment
   c) *Facultative anaerobe*—can use oxygen, but can survive if no oxygen is present

4. Bacterial metabolism
    a) *Fermentors*—Gram-positive bacteria metabolize carbohydrates, including saccharides, resulting in fermentation
    b) *Nonfermentors*—food source includes proteins (amino acids or peptides)

C. Classification of periodontal bacteria—bacteria associated with periodontal disease are generally Gram-negative, anaerobic

1. Supragingival plaque
    a) Formation begins shortly after plaque is removed
        (1) *Pellicle*—acellular, organic layer is deposited on tooth surface within minutes after tooth surface is cleaned
            (a) Aids in attachment of bacteria
            (b) Provides receptors for bacteria to adhere
            (c) Allows initial layer of bacteria to attach
        (2) Bacterial attachment
            (a) After first layer of bacteria attaches, many other bacterial species will accumulate in colonies
            (b) Composition varies among individuals and as plaque matures
            (c) Mature plaque is allowed to accumulate on tooth surface for extended period
    b) Types of bacteria
        (1) Gram-positive species—accumulate in new plaque; cocci are predominant
        (2) Facultative anaerobic microorganisms increase in number as plaque matures; these create environment that is suitable for anaerobic bacteria to colonize
2. Subgingival plaque
    a) Accumulates in layers on tooth surface and also as loosely adhered plaque close to sulcular tissue *after* supragingival plaque is established
    b) In these areas, motile, Gram-negative rods and spirochetes will increase
    c) Tissue-associated plaque (loosely adherent) is free-floating in sulcus or pocket
    d) More toxic than attached plaque—significant factor in periodontal destruction
    e) Types of bacteria frequently associated with periodontal disease
        (1) Most frequently implicated microorganisms
            (a) *Porphyromonas gingivalis* (*P.gingivalis*)
            (b) *Actinobacillus actinomycetemcomitans* (*Aa*)
            (c) *Prevotella intermedia* (*P. intermedia*)
        (2) Other microorganisms, with lesser significance
            (a) *Bacteroides forsythus*
            (b) *Fusobacterium* sp.
            (c) *Peptostreptococcus micros*
            (d) *Campylobacter rectus*

(e) *Treponema denticola*
(f) Enteric rods
(g) *Streptococcus* sp.
(h) *Actinomyces* sp.

D. Virulence of periodontal pathogens

1. Tissue destruction
   a) Depends on pathogenicity or virulence of microorganisms and host's ability to protect body from destructive nature of microorganisms
   b) May occur as result of direct invasion of bacteria into inflamed sulcus and because of substances that are components of bacteria or bacterial by-products
   c) Bacteria may also trigger inflammatory or immune response
   d) Methods of destruction may vary because microorganisms have different destructive characteristics
2. Bacterial infection with *Aa*, *P. gingivalis* and *P. intermedia* have greatest significance
3. Nature of bacterial plaque is significant; sulcular ulceration allows bacteria and/or by-products to invade gingival connective tissue
4. Host response is significant
5. Tobacco, alcohol, stress, or systemic conditions alter immune response
6. Pathogenic bacteria can produce
   a) *Proteolytic enzymes*
      (1) *Collagenase* degrades collagen
      (2) *Hyaluronidase* can increase tissue permeability and contribute to bone resorption
      (3) *Chondroitinase* can increase tissue permeability
      (4) *Proteases* break down noncollagenous proteins and increase capillary permeability
   b) Bacterial waste products—include hydrogen sulfide
   c) Toxins
      (1) Leukotoxin disturbs PMN leukocytes
      (2) Endotoxin is found in cell wall of Gram-negative bacteria
         (a) Include lipopolysaccharides, which can cause tissue necrosis and initiate inflammation and immune response
         (b) Some stimulate bone resorption

E. Microbial plaque

1. Emphasis is on control of plaque formation and retention
2. Periodontal microflora
   a) Gingival health—includes Gram-positive cocci and short rods
   b) Gingivitis—includes Gram-negative bacteria—*Fusobacterium nucleatum, Veillonella parvula, Actinomyces viscosus, P. intermedia*
   c) Adult periodontitis—includes *A. actinomycetemcomitans, P. gingivalis, P. intermedia, B. forsythus, Eikenella corrodens, F. nucleatum, C. rectus, Treponema* sp.

d) Refractory Adult periodontitis—includes variety of microorganisms, but not limited to *B. forsythus, F. nucleatum, C. rectus, P. gingivalis, P. micros*
e) Generalized and localized juvenile periodontitis—includes *A. actinomycetemcomitans, Prevotella* sp., *P. gingivalis, Capnocytophaga sputigena, E. corrodens, Eubacterium* sp.
f) Generalized prepubertal gingivitis—includes *P. intermedia, A. actinomycetemcomitans, E. corrodens, C. sputigena*
g) Localized prepubertal periodontitis—includes *F. nucleatum, Selenomonas* sp., *C. rectus, B. forsythus, Capnocytophaga* sp.
h) Acute necrotizing ulcerative gingivitis and necrotizing ulcerative periodontitis—includes *P. intermedia, F. nucleatum, Borrelia vincentii,* and spirochetes
i) HIV-associated gingivitis and periodontitis—includes *Candida albicans, P. gingivalis, P. intermedia, A. actinomycetemcomitans, F. nucleatum, C. rectus*
j) Rapid progressive periodontitis—includes *A. actinomycetemcomitans, P. gingivalis, P. intermedia, Bacteroides capillus, B. forsythus, E. corrodens, C. rectus*

F. Immune response

1. Inflammation—results from tissue response to irritation or injury
   a) Vessels become permeable to certain phagocytic cells (e.g., PMN leukocytes and macrophages)
   b) Phagocytic cells travel to area of injury
      (1) Bacterial invaders are engulfed by the phagocytic cells and destroyed by enzymatic activity
      (2) Bacterial breakdown products attract antibodies that facilitate immobilization and destruction of invader cells
   c) Mast cells release histamine-producing vasodilatation, which tends to cause swelling and increase bleeding when tissue surface is interrupted
   d) Certain lymphocytes produce elements capable of inducing bone resorption
   e) Plasma cells travel to area of injury and produce immunoglobulins, which have ability to neutralize enzymes and toxin produced by bacteria

VI. CLINICAL ASSESSMENT

A. Periodontal assessment

1. Appearance of gingival tissues can provide information about past or present gingival disease
2. Clinical attachment loss
   a) Identifies distance from CEJ to base of sulcus or pocket
   b) Best indicator of damage to periodontium
   c) Increase in attachment loss indicates progression of periodontal disease
3. Furcation—identification and measurement
   a) Loss of attachment on multirooted teeth results in exposure of root furca to oral environment

b) Use furcation probe or explorer to detect furcation involvement
c) Access to furcation varies depending on number of tooth roots
(1) Mandibular molars—2 roots; access from buccal and lingual
(2) Maxillary molars—3 roots; access from buccal, mesial, and distal
4. Tooth mobility—degree a tooth is able to move in horizontal or apical direction; some mobility is physiological and not due to periodontal disease
5. Tooth positioning—malposed teeth may increase plaque retention resulting in increase in periodontal destruction
6. Lost tooth—increases risk of pathological migration of teeth (teeth may drift or tip away from their physiological position, resulting in occlusal trauma and increased bone destruction)
7. Dentition assessment
a) Caries—harbor bacteria
b) Restoration status—restorations should be intact without defective margins; margins that promote plaque retention increase risk of tissue inflammation and recurrent caries
c) Proximal contact relationships—open contacts allow for food impaction and debris accumulation; tight contacts make flossing difficult
d) Unusual wear patterns on teeth may suggest occlusal trauma
e) Tooth anomalies, such as hypoplastic areas or extra cusps, can increase risk of plaque retention
8. Radiographic examination
a) Provides information about calcified structures, such as bone and tooth
b) Full mouth radiographs and periapical and vertical bitewings are valuable for periodontal assessment
c) Assists in recognizing both normal and abnormal structures
d) Used to detect caries, bone and periapical pathology, and calcified deposits
e) Aids in identifying integrity of margins of restorations
f) Used for periodontal assessment
(1) Normal bone patterns
(a) Height or crest of alveolar bone should be 1 to 2 mm apical to tooth's CEJ
(b) Contour of alveolar bone should follow contour of CEJ
(c) Lamina dura is intact with alveolar ridge—appears as a white (radiopaque) line that outlines tooth roots and alveolar crest
(d) Periodontal ligament space will be visible as a black (radiolucent) area between tooth root and lamina dura—width of periodontal ligament space should be uniform from tooth to tooth

(e) Cancellous bone will be radiopaque, but less dense than lamina dura; within cancellous bone are irregular patterns known as trabeculae that surround marrow spaces

(2) Indicators of bone destruction in periodontal disease

(a) Patterns of bone loss can be horizontal or vertical, both of which can be identified on radiographs

(b) Radiographs do not identify initial bone destruction; by the time bone destruction is radiographically identified, disease has progressed

(c) Horizontal bone loss is a reduction of bone height, with distance between bone and CEJ being > 2 mm

(d) Vertical bone loss is an angular loss of bone height that leaves a gap or trough between bone and tooth root surface

(3) Changes in furcation involvement—as a result of bone loss, furcation of multirooted teeth may be exposed and no longer encased in alveolar bone; may not always be visible on radiograph, and if so, it will appear as radiolucent area at furca

(4) Changes in periodontal disease

(a) Changes in radiodensity of lamina dura—crest of lamina dura will be less well defined; appearance at crest may have breaks or be fuzzy

(b) Radiolucent wedges are apparent at alveolar crest adjacent to tooth root surfaces

(c) Slight radiolucent projections will extend from alveolar crest in apical direction

VII. AMERICAN ACADEMY OF PERIODONTOLOGY (AAP) DISEASE CLASSIFICATION—categorizes periodontal diseases by appearance or amount of periodontal destruction

A. Case Type I—gingival disease

1. Involves inflammation of gingiva characterized clinically by changes in color, gingival form, position, surface appearance, and presence of bleeding and/or exudate

B. Case Type II—early periodontitis

1. Involves progression of gingival inflammation into deeper periodontal structures and alveolar bone crest, with slight bone loss
2. Evidenced by slight loss of connective tissue attachment and alveolar bone

C. Case Type III—moderate periodontitis

1. Involves more advanced stage of periodontitis, with increased destruction of periodontal structures and noticeable loss of bone support, possibly accompanied by increase in tooth mobility
2. Evidence of possible furcation involvement in multirooted teeth

D. Case Type IV—advanced periodontitis

1. Involves further progression of periodontitis with major loss of alveolar bone support usually accompanied by increased tooth mobility
2. Evidence of furcation involvement in multirooted teeth is likely

E. Case Type V—refractory periodontitis

1. Includes patients with multiple disease sites that continue to demonstrate attachment loss after appropriate therapy—also includes patients with recurrent disease at single or multiple sites
2. Sites presumably continue to be infected by periodontal pathogens no matter how thorough or frequent treatment is provided

VIII. GINGIVITIS—reversible inflammation of the gingiva

A. Accumulation of plaque is directly related to development of gingivitis

B. Chronic plaque-associated gingivitis—an inflammatory response to irritant bacterial plaque; majority of gingivitis falls in this category

C. Other conditions of gingiva may alter its appearance or be caused by microbial infection

1. Acute necrotizing ulcerative gingivitis (ANUG)—acute gingival disease that results in destruction and cratering of gingival tissues, especially interdental papilla
   a) Accompanied with severe pain, excess salivation, spontaneous gingival bleeding, and foul breath odor with metallic taste
   b) Associated with *P. intermedia, F. nucleatum, B. vincentii,* and spirochetes
   c) Risk factors include stress, malnutrition, smoking, and immunosuppression
2. Primary herpetic gingivostomatitis is an acute viral infection that presents with numerous intraoral ulcerations
   a) Etiology—herpes simplex virus
   b) Patient will be febrile and have oral pain
   c) More common in children than adults
   d) After acute infection subsides, virus remains dormant in a nerve ganglion and may subsequently cause episodes of recurrent or secondary herpes—most commonly seen as herpes labialis
3. Hormone-induced gingivitis is exaggerated tissue response to local irritant plaque; may occur when there are fluctuations in hormones, including pregnancy, puberty, oral birth control medication, and steroid therapy

IX. PERIODONTITIS—inflammation of periodontal tissues and loss of connective tissue

A. Presence or accumulation of plaque may initiate periodontal disease, but it is not the only factor involved in its development and progression

B. Etiology of periodontal diseases is more complex than etiology of gingival disease

C. Nature and severity of the diseases are related to virulence of bacteria and host's ability to resist bacterial invasion

1. Similar microorganisms do not cause all periodontal diseases, nor does every form of periodontal disease cause same pattern of tissue destruction
2. Some forms of periodontal disease are easier to treat than others

D. Pathogenesis of periodontitis

1. Bacterial infection with *Aa*, *P. gingivalis,* and *P. intermedia* has greatest significance
2. Nature of bacterial plaque is significant—sulcular ulceration allows bacteria and/or by-products to invade gingival connective tissue
3. Host response is significant
4. Tobacco, alcohol, stress, or systemic conditions alter immune response

E. Types—numerous periodontal diseases are identified with unique etiology, characteristics, and age of onset (1989 World Workshop in Clinical Periodontics)

1. Adult periodontitis
   a) Includes gingival inflammation, pocket formation, possible mobility, and bone loss
   b) Some contributing factors include ineffective oral hygiene, malposed teeth, and poorly contoured restorations
2. Prepubertal periodontitis
   a) Generalized—affects primary teeth, involves rapid alveolar bone destruction, associated with leukocyte abnormalities, and is accompanied by middle ear, skin, and upper respiratory infections
   b) Localized—affects few teeth, exhibits less gingival inflammation and bone destruction, and is not accompanied by other infections
3. Juvenile periodontitis
   a) Localized—rapid attachment and vertical bone loss at incisors and first molars; minimal plaque is present
   b) Generalized—generalized rapid attachment and bone loss; minimal plaque is present
4. Rapidly progressive periodontitis—rapid onset, with rapid and severe bone loss; episodic; amount of plaque varies
5. Acute necrotizing ulcerative periodontitis
   a) Sudden onset, pain, necrosis, and cratering of interdental papillae and spontaneous bleeding
   b) Usually localized in anterior regions
   c) Accompanied by foul breath, metallic taste, and excess salivation
6. Refractory periodontitis—resistant to repeated routine treatment methods

F. Updated nomenclature—November 1999 *Annuals of Periodontology* published a new classification system for periodontal diseases and conditions intended to recognize shortcomings in the existing classification system, which came from the 1989 World Workshop in Clinical Periodontics

1. This new system is being incorporated into both clinical practice and education
2. Because literature using the 1989 classification system is still widely used, reference to both 1989 and 1999 classification systems are included
3. In addition to renaming some diseases, and adding others, there is clarification of the designation of periodontitis as a manifestation of systemic diseases; refractory periodontitis has been eliminated
4. Gingival diseases—new category
   a) Dental plaque-induced gingival diseases
      (1) Associated with dental plaque only
      (2) Modified by systemic factors
      (3) Modified by medications
      (4) Modified by nutrition
   b) Non-plaque induced gingival lesions
      (1) Specific bacterial origin
      (2) Viral origin
      (3) Fungal origin
      (4) Genetic origin
      (5) Gingival manifestations of systemic conditions
      (6) Traumatic lesions (factitious, iatrogenic, accidental
      (7) Foreign body reactions
      (8) Not otherwise specified (NOS)
5. Chronic peritonitis—replaces term adult periodontitis
   a) Localized
   b) Generalized
6. Aggressive periodontitis—replaces term early-onset periodontitis
   a) Localized
   b) Generalized
7. Periodontitis as a manifestation of systemic diseases
   a) Associated with hematological disorders
      (1) Acquired neutropenia
      (2) Leukemia
   b) Associated with genetic disorders
      (1) Familial and cyclic neutropenia
      (2) Down syndrome
      (3) Leukocyte adhesion deficiency syndromes
      (4) Papillon-LeFevre syndrome
      (5) Chediak-Higashi syndrome
      (6) Histiocytosis syndromes
      (7) Glycogen storage disease
      (8) Infantile genetic agranulocytosis
      (9) Cohen syndrome

(10) Ehlers-Danlos syndrome
(11) Hypophosphatasia

8. Necrotizing periodontal diseases—replaces term necrotizing ulcerative periodontitis
   a) Necrotizing ulcerative gingivitis (NUG)
   b) Necrotizing ulcerative periodontisis (NUP)
9. Abscesses of the periodontium—new category
   a) Gingival abscess
   b) Periodontal abscess
   c) Pericoronal abscess
10. Periodontitis associated with endodontic lesions—new category
11. Developmental or acquired deformities and conditions—new category
   a) Localized tooth-related factors that modify or predispose to plaque-induced gingival diseases/periodontitis
   b) Mucogingival deformities and conditions around the teeth
      (1) Gingival/soft tissue recession
      (2) Lack of keratinized gingiva
      (3) Decreased vestibular depth
      (4) Aberrant frenum/muscle positions
      (5) Gingival excess
      (6) Abnormal color
   c) Mucogingival deformities and conditions on edentulous ridges
   d) Occlusal trauma

X. NONSURGICAL PERIODONTAL THERAPY (soft tissue management)—provided by dental professional

A. Objectives

1. Remove bacterial plaque to restore periodontal health
2. Slow or stop progression of periodontal disease
3. Prepare tissues for surgical therapy

B. Definitions of nonsurgical periodontal therapies

1. Scaling—removal of calculus and stain from surfaces of teeth with hand-activated instruments and/or sonic and ultrasonic scalers
2. Root planing—smoothing of root surfaces, including removal of rough cementum or dentin that is impregnated with calculus and endotoxins
3. SRP—combines scaling and root planing
4. Periodontal debridement—nonsurgical removal of tooth surface irritants
5. Prophylaxis—involves mechanical plaque control procedures that can be performed by dental hygienist or dentist to prevent and control periodontal diseases, such as scaling, polishing, and flossing
6. Coronal polishing—removal of stains and bacterial plaque (nonmineralized deposits) from surface of teeth with a hand or rotary instrument; frequently accomplished using a rubber cup with polishing agent on a slow speed handpiece
7. Selective polishing—polishing only surfaces of teeth that have extrinsic stain and visible plaque

8. Gingival curettage—removal of epithelial lining of periodontal pocket by scraping surface with an instrument, such as a curet

C. Goals of nonsurgical periodontal therapy—correct and preserve dentition in state of health, comfort, and function with appropriate esthetics throughout lifetime of individual

1. Treatment goals
   a) Eliminate and control etiological factors causing disease
   b) Maintain periodontal health
   c) Prevent recurrence of disease
2. Specific nonsurgical treatment objectives
   a) Establish conditions conducive to reattachment of connective tissue and healing of periodontal tissues
   b) Eliminate microorganisms, calculus, and other irritants on and within tooth surface to reduce inflammation
   c) Promote connective tissue regeneration
   d) Make root surface biologically acceptable to gingival tissues

D. Techniques—use of hand-activated instrumentation and sonic/ultrasonic scalers

E. Antibiotics in the treatment of periodontal disease—used because mechanical removal (scaling, debridement) may not always be effective

1. Certain periodontal situations benefit from use of antibiotics when used in conjunction with mechanical debridement
2. Treatment is intended to alter subgingival bacteria flora
3. Antibiotics may be provided systemically or locally
   a) Systemic antibiotics—selection must be determined based on nature of pathogen
      (1) Tetracycline (minocycline, doxycycline)—proved successful for treatment of certain periodontal diseases (a low dose of doxycycline hyclate [Periostat] is an effective enzyme suppressor, including collagenase)
         (a) Can accumulate in high concentrations in gingival sulcus
         (b) Blocks production of collagenase
         (c) *Aa* is highly susceptible to tetracycline
      (2) Metronidazole (Flagyl, MetroGel, Protostat)
         (a) Useful for oral soft tissue infections resulting from Gram-negative bacilli (*Bacteroides*) and Gram-positive spore-forming bacilli (*Clostridium*)
         (b) Targets anaerobes
         (c) Used in combination with other antibiotics (e.g., Helidac [metronidazole and tetracycline])
         (d) Useful for patients with ANUG or HIV
      (3) Penicillin—not considered effective in treatment of periodontal disease
         (a) Periodontal pathogens are resistant to penicillin
         (b) Enzymes produced by periodontal pathogens tend to break down the penicillin, making it ineffective

(c) Augmentin (amoxicillin and clavulanic acid) has been found helpful for treating *Bacteroides* infections

b) Local delivery—places antibiotic or antimicrobial at site of infection; occurs after mechanical care (scaling, root planing, debridement)

(1) Tetracycline embedded fiber (Actisite)—placed in periodontal pocket

(a) Delivers high level of antibiotic directly to diseased site

(b) Fiber is left in pocket for 10 days, then removed

(2) Chlorhexidine contained in gelatin strip (PerioChip)

(a) Biodegradable in 10 days

(b) Useful in treating adult periodontitis and maintenance patients

(c) Used in pockets > 5 mm

(d) Low risk of antibacterial resistance

(3) Doxycycline gel (Atridox)

(a) Injected into periodontal pocket

(b) Conforms to periodontal pocket and solidifies

(c) Biodegrades in 7 days

(d) Low risk of antibacterial resistance

(4) Antimicrobial rinse irrigation at periodontal pocket; chlorhexidine may have short-term beneficial effect

(5) Minocycline powdered microspheres (Arestin)

(a) Premixed, premeasured powder injected into periodontal pocket

(b) Effective against periodontal pathogens

(c) Microspheres are bioresorbed

XI. PERIODONTAL SURGERY—treatment alternative if nonsurgical therapy does not produce expected end results

A. Advantages or outcomes

1. Attain shallow probing depths that are easier to maintain and more conducive to microbial flora of periodontal health
2. Reestablish or regenerate form and function of bone
3. Enhance gingival anatomy to facilitate supragingival plaque removal and resist both periodontal breakdown and caries
4. Facilitate restorative procedures where clinical crown length is inadequate for prosthetic care or where restorative margins would invade biological attachment level

B. Procedures

1. *Gingivectomy*

a) Excision or removal of diseased gingiva

b) Establishes healthy gingival contour

c) Indications—fibrous gingiva, deep bony pocket, gingival enlargements, and crown lengthening

2. *Gingivoplasty*

a) Reshaping gingiva to increase physiological contours

b) Not intended to eliminate pockets

3. *Periodontal flap surgery*—provides visibility and access to root surfaces and bone
4. *Mucogingival surgery*
   a) Corrects gingival—mucous membrane relationships
   b) Creates or widens zone of attached gingiva
5. *Gingival grafts*—borrows gingival tissue from one location to be placed at a gingival defect
6. *Frenectomy*—releases or removes labial frenum that is impinging on gingival tissue
7. *Bone graft*—fills bony defect
8. *Guided tissue regeneration*
   a) Creates environment where desirable cells are allowed to grow and undesirable cells are inhibited from growing
   b) Uses a barrier membrane—polytetrafluorethylene membrane (ePTFE) and polylactic acid with citric acid membrane
9. *Osteoplasty*—reshapes bone without removing tooth supporting bone
10. *Osteoectomy*
    a) Removes tooth supporting bone
    b) Corrects exostosis, craters, and ledges

C. Healing—wound heals in series of physiological steps that are part of inflammatory process; restores integrity of injured tissue

1. Healing sequence
   a) Clot formation—initial response to tissue wound; contains platelets that initiate and regulate clot formation
   b) Granulation tissue development—highly vascular connective tissue, containing capillaries, fibroblasts, and inflammatory cells; fibroblasts create extracellular matrix on which wound repairs occur
   c) Epithelialization—epithelial cells cover wound, allowing underlying granulation tissue to mature to connective tissue
   d) Collagen formation—strengthens wound
   e) Regeneration—vascular granulation tissue is replaced by original cell types
   f) Maturation—wound healing is complete

XII. DENTAL IMPLANTS

A. Patient selection—factors include good oral hygiene, positive dental and medical histories including reasonable ability to heal, adequate bone for implant placement, and motivated patient

B. Implant surgery—usually accomplished in several phases with long periods of healing after each surgery before prosthesis is placed

C. Implant success

1. *Osseointegration*—biological anchorage or contact that is established between implant surface and bone; bone forming in and around implant

2. Clinical signs of success
   a) No clinical mobility
   b) Ability to bear load (have a functioning prostheses)
   c) Comfortable
   d) Intact adjacent structures
   e) No evidence of peri-implant radiolucency
   f) Minimal loss of bone height

D. Implant failure

1. Recognition of implant failure—lack of osseointegration
   a) Implant mobility
   b) Feeling of discomfort
   c) Peri-implant radiolucency
   d) Inability to support prosthesis
2. Treatment—remove implant

XIII. PERIODONTAL EMERGENCIES

A. Periodontal abscess—localized, purulent inflammatory process

1. Associated with periodontal pockets and furcation involvement
2. Involves a blocked or occluded sulcus, preventing drainage of bacteria
3. Can result in periodontal destruction
   a) Acute—sudden onset may resolve quickly
   b) Chronic—slow to develop, may be present for a long time, sometimes becomes acute
4. Signs and symptoms
   a) Pain (more common with acute)
   b) Swelling of soft tissues
   c) Tenderness to percussion
   d) Tooth extruded from socket
   e) Mobility of affected tooth
5. Treatment
   a) Establish drainage at gingival margin of pocket or at point of swelling
   b) Use warm saltwater rinses and antibiotics
   c) Eliminate pocket surgically
6. Differentiating between endodontic and periodontal abscess
   a) *Endodontic abscess* is an infection of the tooth pulp; tooth will be nonvital
   b) *Periodontal abscess* is associated with periodontal structures primarily, not pulp; tooth may be vital

B. Gingival abscess

1. Acute localized infection at marginal gingiva or interdental papilla
2. Evidence of purulent area in connective tissue
3. Etiology—wedged or embedded debris or food at gingival margin (e.g., popcorn hull)
4. Not associated with periodontal disease

C. *Pericoronitis*

1. Occurs at partially erupting or impacted tooth, often third molars; areas not easily cleaned where food or debris are wedged under gingival tissue
2. Gingival tissue (operculum) partially covering erupting tooth creates environment for bacterial growth to occur
3. Signs and symptoms
   a) Red, swollen gingival tissues at site of erupting tooth; swelling may extend to angle of jaw, ear, and cervical lymph nodes
   b) May be painful to touch
4. Treatment
   a) Establish drainage
   b) Irrigate with saline, antimicrobial rinse, or warm saltwater rinses
   c) Follow-up treatment may include tooth extraction or surgical removal of operculum

D. Necrotizing ulcerative gingivitis (NUG)—acute, destructive condition of gingival tissues (also referred to as ANUG)

1. Associated with presence of several microorganisms
2. Not considered contagious
3. Bacterial plaque is primary etiological factor—host-parasite imbalance
4. Contributing factors to development of NUG—stress, cigarette smoking, alcohol consumption, low socioeconomic status, poor nutrition, age, general debilitated state
5. Additional factors contributing to NUG—calculus, operculum, overhanging margins, improper tooth contacts, malposed teeth, and food impaction
6. Signs and symptoms
   a) Sudden severe pain of teeth or gingiva, gingival bleeding (sometimes spontaneous), and fetid breath odor
   b) Ulcerated marginal gingiva and interdental papilla—described as punched out areas or craters
   c) Ulceration may occur on other soft tissues, including tongue and lips
   d) Evidence of fever, headache, loss of appetite, and lymphadenopathy
7. Treatment
   a) Remove debris as soon as possible to reduce risk of permanent loss of papilla
   b) Use ultrasonic instrumentation for both debridement and irrigation
   c) Emphasize plaque control and home care
   d) Use antibiotics, when indicated
   e) Schedule multiple treatment visits

E. Acute herpetic gingivostomatitis—an acute, viral infection of the oral mucosa; 7- to 10-day duration

1. Etiology—herpes simplex virus

2. Signs and symptoms
   a) Clinical appearance of small yellow ulcers with raised, red margins
   b) May be present on tongue, gingiva, lips, buccal mucosa, palate, pharynx and tonsils
   c) Sore mouth, often too sore to eat or drink
3. Treatment
   a) Palliative; keep patient comfortable; use warm water rinses and soft diet
   b) Emphasize fluid intake and topical anesthetic rinses

XIV. ENDPOINT OBJECTIVES OF PERIODONTAL THERAPY

A. Specific objectives

1. Resolution of inflammation
   a) No bleeding on probing
   b) No suppuration
   c) Gingival contours—color, texture, and form are within normal limits
   d) Gingival attachment is resistant to recurrent disease

B. Supportive periodontal treatment (SPT)

1. Following definitive treatment and post-treatment evaluation, schedule patient for SPT at 3-month intervals
2. SPT visit—evaluate signs of disease activity (e.g, bleeding and/or suppuration on probing, increase in probing depths, and gingival atypia)
3. Direct therapeutic application to sites reflecting recurrence of disease or periodontal breakdown
4. Assess plaque control motivation

C. Periodontal maintenance

1. Once periodontal health has been established, goal of further care centers on maintaining periodontal health
2. Without continued periodontal maintenance, there is little value in therapeutic periodontal care

XV. DENTAL CONDITIONS IN THE PERIODONTAL PATIENT

A. Root caries

1. Prevalence
   a) Incidence is increasing as population is keeping their teeth longer
   b) Once established, may progress rapidly
2. Risk factors
   a) Periodontal disease—because of exposed root surfaces
   b) Lack of fluoridated water
   c) Dry mouth (xerostomia)
   d) Oral hygiene deficits
   e) Cariogenic diet
3. Etiology—*Actinomyces viscosus*
4. Clinical detection

a) Root caries color ranges from light yellow to dark brown/black
b) Explorer will stick
c) May be subgingival

5. Prevention
a) Fluoride therapy (including home fluoride regimen)
b) Oral hygiene improvement
c) Diet modification

B. Dentin hypersensitivity

1. Associated with periodontal disease because it frequently is related to exposed root surfaces
2. Commonly seen in individuals who have periodontal disease or who have had treatment for periodontal disease; result of root surfaces open to the oral environment
3. Most frequently found on facial surfaces of teeth at cervical margins
4. Pain transmission
a) Caused by mechanical, chemical, thermal, or bacterial stimuli to exposed dentinal tubules
b) Sweets, acids, sour substances, acidic plaque, temperature changes (especially cold), and drying or desiccation of exposed dentin can be painful
c) Pain is localized and sharp; usually disappears quickly when stimulus is removed
5. Hydrodynamic theory of hypersensitivity—current theory
a) Dentinal tubules are open channels extending from pulp chamber
b) Tubules are fluid-filled and may have odontoblasts extending from pulp into tubule
c) Fluid within dentinal tubules flows both outward and inward depending on pressure variations in surrounding tissues
d) Rapid movement of fluid in open dentinal tubules may disrupt odontoblasts eliciting transmission of pain-causing stimulus
e) Pain is detected by myelinated A-delta fibers in pulp
6. Contributing factors
a) Loss of tooth structure from occlusal wear, toothbrush abrasion, enamel erosion, and parafunctional habits
b) Exposure of root surface to oral environment because of gingival recession, aging, chronic periodontal disease, periodontal surgery, incorrect toothbrushing habits, and root surface preparation for dental restorations
7. Management—related to covering, sealing, or blocking tubules because pain is related to open dentinal tubules; tubules can also close naturally
8. Numerous products are available with variable results
a) Active ingredients include potassium nitrate, sodium citrate, potassium oxalate, strontium chloride, and fluoride
b) Varnishes, resins, sealants, glass ionomers; composite restorations can be used

review questions

DIRECTIONS Each of the questions or incomplete statements below is followed by suggested answers or completions. Select the **one** answer that is best in each case.

1. Characteristics of the outer surface of Gram-positive bacteria include all of the following EXCEPT one. Which one is the EXCEPTION?
   A. vesicles or blebs, which contain endotoxins
   B. retained crystal violet (purple) stain
   C. a slime layer or glycocalyx
   D. a thick peptidoglycan layer, which is composed of repeating amino sugar units

2. The subgingival bacteria MOST closely associated with periodontal destruction
   A. may be moving freely close to the sulcus wall, but not attached to the plaque matrix.
   B. are incorporated in the plaque's intercellular matrix.
   C. will be Gram-positive cocci, such as *Streptococcus mutans.*
   D. will have high oxygen needs for survival.

3. Of the following, which is LEAST likely to be associated with plaque bacteria found on a patient with healthy gingiva?
   A. most organisms will have fimbriae
   B. most will be aerobic or facultative anaerobic bacteria
   C. *Actinomyces* sp. is often found
   D. Gram-positive will be more prevalent than Gram-negative bacteria

4. Gram-negative rods, associated with periodontitis, include all of the following EXCEPT one. Which one is the EXCEPTION?
   A. *Porphyromonas gingivalis*
   B. *Campylobacter rectus*
   C. *Treponema denticola*
   D. *Prevotella intermedia*
   E. *Bacteroides forsythus*

5. The "attachment apparatus" includes all of the following periodontal tissues EXCEPT one. Which one is the EXCEPTION?
   A. gingiva
   B. periodontal ligament
   C. cementum
   D. alveolar bone

6. Of the following risk factors, the MOST significant in the development of periodontal disease is
   A. alcohol consumption.
   B. diet.
   C. cigarette smoking.
   D. low income.
   E. increased age.

7. Lipopolysaccharides or endotoxins associated with Gram-negative bacteria are known to
   A. cause spontaneous bleeding at the marginal gingiva.
   B. stimulate osteoclast-mediated bone resorption.
   C. stimulate corticosteroid formation.

D. decrease the production of sulcular fluid.
E. increase the quantity of albumin in the cementum.

8. The current regimen for prophylactic antibiotic premedication, before invasive dental procedures in patients at risk of endocarditis is
   A. 3 grams of penicillin 1 hour before dental procedure, then 1 gram 6 hours later.
   B. 3 grams of E.E.S. 2 hours before dental procedure; 1.5 grams of E.E.S. 2 hours after the dental procedure.
   C. 5 grams of amoxicillin 6 hours before dental procedure.
   D. 2 grams of amoxicillin 1 hour before dental procedure.
   E. 2 grams of tetracycline 1 hour before dental procedure and 1 gram 6 hours later.

9. The MOST significant periodontal pathogen based on its numeric presence is
   A. *Porphyromonas gingivalis.*
   B. *Bacteroides forsythus.*
   C. *Prevotella oralis.*
   D. *Treponema denticola.*
   E. *Actinobacillus actinomycetemcomitans.*

10. Rapid and progressive periodontal disease is more likely to occur in all of the following systemic conditions EXCEPT one. Which one is the EXCEPTION?
   A. agranulocytosis
   B. Down syndrome
   C. HIV infection
   D. neurological disorders, including epilepsy
   E. diabetes

11. Factors to be evaluated in determining a tooth's periodontal prognosis include all of the following EXCEPT one. Which one is the EXCEPTION?
   A. intrinsic stain
   B. mobility
   C. furcation involvement
   D. pocket depths
   E. root anatomy

12. Mouth rinses containing phenolic compounds are effective in reducing plaque by
   A. altering the bacterial cell wall.
   B. degrading the bacteria's genetic code.
   C. inactivating the mitochondria.
   D. nourishing the Gram-positive bacteria.
   E. prohibiting pellicle formation.

13. In gingival health, which of the following oral structures would NOT be keratinized or parakeratinized?
   A. attached gingiva
   B. palatal mucosa
   C. sulcular epithelium
   D. interdental or papillary gingiva

14. The fusion of cementum to alveolar bone occurs through
   A. cementicles.
   B. hemidesmosomes.
   C. hypercementosis.
   D. ankylosis.
   E. cementoids.

15. Clinically, the labial attached gingiva is identified coronally by the free gingival groove and apically by the
   A. lamina dura.
   B. basal lamina.
   C. junctional epithelium.
   D. mucogingival junction.
   E. lamina propria.

16. The portion of the periodontal ligament anchored in the cementum includes
   A. osteocytes.
   B. Sharpey's fibers.
   C. cementoid.
   D. cancellous bone.
   E. osteoid.

17. In the initial stage of gingivitis, the cell type MOST closely associated with the inflammatory response is
   A. fibroblast.
   B. neutrophil.
   C. plasma cell.
   D. erythrocyte.
   E. osteoclast.

18. Gingival recession is a risk factor for all of the following EXCEPT one. Which one is the EXCEPTION?
    A. occlusal caries
    B. loss of cementum
    C. tooth sensitivity
    D. increased interproximal plaque accumulation
    E. loss of tooth structure

19. An essential clinical feature in detecting the presence of periodontitis is
    A. bone loss.
    B. pocketing.
    C. bad breath.
    D. presence of calculus and plaque.
    E. presence of pain.

20. The MOST reliable clinical sign of gingival inflammation is the presence of
    A. neutrophils in the connective tissue and junctional epithelium.
    B. plasma cells infiltrating the connective tissue of the sulcus.
    C. increased production of fluid in the gingival sulcus.
    D. bleeding on probing at the gingival sulcus.
    E. subgingival plaque accumulation.

21. An oral side effect of Dilantin is
    A. gingival abscesses.
    B. squamous cell carcinoma.
    C. papilloma.
    D. pyogenic granuloma.
    E. gingival hyperplasia.

22. Periodontal tissue innervation is by the following nerve(s):
    A. Cranial VII—facial
    B. Cranial V—trigeminal
    C. Cranial III and Cranial V
    D. Cranial XII
    E. Cranial VII and Cranial VI

23. The MOST common position of the cementum in relation to the enamel is
    A. enamel overlaps cementum.
    B. cementum meets the enamel, with no overlap.
    C. enamel stops 0.5 mm short of the cementum.
    D. cementum slightly overlaps the enamel.

24. The diagnostic sign associated with localized juvenile periodontitis is
    A. bleeding on probing.
    B. pain and abscess formation.
    C. presence of diastema.
    D. vertical bone loss at molars and incisors.
    E. pocket formation and presence of calculus at affected teeth.

25. The MOST plentiful inorganic component of calculus is
    A. brushite.
    B. mucopolysaccharides.
    C. magnesium phosphate.
    D. calcium phosphate.

26. The MOST accurate method to detect furcation involvement is through
    A. interviewing the patient.
    B. radiographic examination.
    C. clinical probing.
    D. testing for fremitus.
    E. presence of suppuration.

27. Antibiotic premedication before invasive dental treatment is advised for the patient with a pathological heart murmur to reduce risk of
    A. myocardial infarction.
    B. cerebrovascular accident.
    C. bacterial endocarditis.
    D. pyogenic granuloma.

28. Increased tissue redness, associated with gingival inflammation, is caused by
    A. hyperkeratosis.
    B. fluid exudation.
    C. capillary proliferation.
    D. gingival bleeding.
    E. increased sulcular fluid.

29. A previous episode of necrotizing ulcerative gingivitis (NUG) may result in which of the following alterations of the interdental papillae?
    A. edema
    B. atrophy
    C. cratering
    D. recession
    E. hyperplasia

30. Occlusal forces on the teeth
    A. should be directed axially.
    B. should not be directed axially because the force will destroy the apical area of the socket.
    C. will result in the narrowing of the PDL if the force is excessive.
    D. will result in osteoblast activity at the area with the most pressure.
    E. causes erosion on the teeth.

31. Fetid breath odor, pseudomembranous ulceration at the marginal gingiva and interdental papillae, gingival bleeding, and the presence of spirochetes and fusiform bacteria are associated with
    A. periapical abscess.
    B. herpes simplex I.
    C. necrotizing ulcerative gingivitis (NUG).
    D. aphthous ulceration.
    E. pericoronitis.

32. The two earliest signs of gingival inflammation preceding established gingivitis are
    A. increased collagen fibers and vascularity.
    B. increased gingival fluid and bleeding on probing the sulcus.
    C. gingival recession and increased bleeding on probing the sulcus.
    D. presence of calculus and bone loss.
    E. gnawing discomfort and ulceration of the marginal gingiva.

33. The valley-like depression of the gingiva, connecting the facial and lingual interdental papillae, is the
    A. mucogingival junction.
    B. furcation.
    C. col.
    D. gingival sulcus.
    E. free gingival groove.

34. Which of the following fibers embeds in the cementum of adjacent teeth and extends over the alveolar crest?
    A. transseptal
    B. circular
    C. alveolar crest
    D. interradicular
    E. oblique

35. The removal of a periodontal pocket's gingival wall with a Gracey 11/12 curet or similar instrument with the intent of removing diseased soft tissue is known as
    A. gingivoplasty.
    B. root planing.
    C. gingival curettage.
    D. gingivectomy.

36. Most of the solid material in the composition of plaque consists of
    A. calcium phosphate.
    B. desquamated epithelial cells.
    C. bacteria.
    D. leukocytes and macrophages.
    E. intercellular matrix.

37. Which of the following provides the BEST opportunity for improved reattachment of periodontal ligament fibers to the tooth's root surface?
    A. disintegration of cementum and dentin
    B. degeneration of Sharpey's fibers
    C. presence of infection
    D. excessive tooth mobility
    E. removal of the junctional epithelium

38. Which of the following is NOT a cardinal sign of inflammation?
    A. redness
    B. heat
    C. infection
    D. swelling
    E. pain

39. A normal distance, in millimeters, between the CEJ and the alveolar crest is
    A. 0.5 to 2.0.
    B. 3.0 to 4.5.
    C. 4.5 to 6.0.
    D. 6.0 to 7.0.
    E. 7.0 to 7.5.

40. The bluish-red appearance of the gingiva with periodontitis is associated with a(n)
    A. decrease in plasma cells and an increase in neutrophils.
    B. increase in collagen destruction.
    C. endotoxin and desquamated epithelial cells in the periodontal pocket.
    D. increase in the presence of fibrous connective tissue.
    E. circulatory stagnation and deoxygenated blood.

41. Xerostomia can be associated with all of the following EXCEPT one. Which one is the EXCEPTION?
    A. antihypertensive medications
    B. antidepressant and antianxiety medication
    C. consumption of acidic foods
    D. mouth breathing
    E. vitamin A and B deficiencies

42. Chlorhexidine gluconate is effective as an antimicrobial agent against all of the following EXCEPT one. Which one is the EXCEPTION?
    A. *Streptococcus* sp.
    B. Gram-positive bacteria
    C. Gram-negative bacteria
    D. viruses

43. The antibiotic "family" that has shown much promise in the management of periodontal disease is
    A. tetracycline.
    B. sulfa drugs.
    C. erythromycin.
    D. cephalosporine.

answers & rationales

1.

A. The characteristic of vesicles or blebs is noteworthy in Gram-negative bacteria, not Gram-positive. The endotoxin that is contained within the blebs is associated with tissue damage. The retention of Gram stain, a crystal violet stain, by a bacteria's wall is an identifier for Gram-positive bacteria. Slime layer or glycocalyx and a peptidoglycan layer with repeating amino sugar units are associated with Gram-positive bacteria.

2.

A. The layers closest to the soft tissues contain large numbers of flagellated motile bacteria and spirochetes. Studies suggest that some significant periodontal pathogens are in the loosely adherent or freely movable material in the periodontal pocket, rather than being incorporated into the intercellular matrix of adherent plaque. *Streptococcus mutans* is associated with dental decay, not periodontal destruction. The bacteria associated with periodontal destruction are anaerobic.

3.

A. A significant number of bacteria considered periodontal pathogens have fimbriae or hairlike projections on their surface. "Healthy" plaque is composed of Gram-positive rods and cocci, which are aerobic or facultative anaerobes. *Actinomyces* sp. is also commonly found.

4.

C. *Treponema denticola* is a spirochete, not a rod. *Porphyromonas gingivalis, Campylobacter rectus, Prevotella intermedia,* and *Bacteriodes forsythus* are all Gram-negative rods.

5.

A. Gingiva is not considered part of the "attachment apparatus." The attachment apparatus refers to the periodontal ligament's attachment to the tooth (via the cementum) and the alveolar bone.

6.

C. Cigarette smoking has been identified as a significant risk factor in the development and progression of periodontal disease. While alcohol consumption, diet, low income, and increased age may be identified as possible risk factors, studies do not consistently identify them to be as significant as tobacco use.

7.

B. Endotoxin is known to induce tissue inflammatory response and to stimulate osteoclast-mediated bone resorption. Spontaneous bleeding at the marginal gingiva can be seen when the tissue is fragile. Corticosteroids may inhibit osteoclast activity; however, endotoxin does not stimulate its activity. The presence of plaque and its irritants results in gingival inflammation. There will be an increase, not decrease, in the production of sulcular fluid.

8.

D. The American Heart Association regimen was revised in 1997. This regimen for non-penicillin-allergic individuals calls for 2 grams of amoxicillin 1 hour before dental procedure. This current regimen does not indicate a need for a follow-up dose. The remaining regimens are not current for antibiotic prophylaxis.

9.

A. Although a number of Gram-negative microorganisms are implicated in the various periodontal diseases, *Porphyromonas gingivalis* is found in the greatest quantity. *Bacteroides forsythus, Prevotella oralis, Treponema denticola,* and *Actinobacillus actinomycetemcomitans* are all considered periodontal pathogens, but are not found in as great quantity as *Porphyromonas gingivalis.*

10.

D. Rapid and progressive periodontal disease is not associated with neurological disorders. It is seen in numerous systemic conditions including those where wound healing is limited, there is a defect in the quantity or quality of the neutrophils, and when the immune system is deficient. A defect in quantity or quality of neutrophils, such as in agranulocytosis, is associated with rapidly progressive periodontal disease. Down syndrome may have neutrophil defects or impairment secondary to the systemic disease. There is depressed immune function as a result of the invasion of the HIV virus into T-helper cells. There may also be inadequate function of PMN leukocytes, which will alter the inflammatory response. Diabetes is associated with poor wound healing, resulting in a greater risk of RPP.

11.

A. Intrinsic stain, which is incorporated into the tooth structure, does not affect the periodontal prognosis. A tooth's prognosis worsens as the mobility increases. Teeth with furcation involvement are more difficult to keep plaque- and calculus-free, worsening their prognosis. Significant increases in pocket depths worsen a tooth's prognosis, as it is harder to keep these teeth plaque-free. Longer, broad roots have more surface area to assist with securing the tooth in the socket. A short, tapered root has less surface area secured in the socket and therefore has a poorer periodontal prognosis.

12.

A. Altering the bacterial cell wall inhibits the bacteria's ability to survive. An example of a mouth rinse containing a phenol compound is Listerine. Currently, no available mouth rinses degrade the bacteria's genetic code. Cell mitochondria are not inactivated by phenolic mouth rinses. Phenolic compounds are not a source of nutrients for Gram-positive bacteria and do not prohibit pellicle formation.

13.

C. Sulcular epithelium is nonkeratinized tissue. This allows for more movement of fluids and pathogens across the sulcular wall. Attached and interdental gingiva and palatal mucosa are keratinized epithelial tissues.

14.

D. Ankylosis is the fusion of cementum to bone. The cause may be related to tooth trauma or infection. Cementicles are abnormal calcified bodies occasionally found in the periodontal ligament. Hemidesmosomes attach the junctional epithelium to the tooth surface. Hypercementosis is an excess production of cementum on a root surface. Cementoid is the uncalcified matrix that is the first step in cementum formation.

15.

D. The mucogingival junction is the terminal portion of the attached gingiva and the beginning of the alveolar mucosa. Lamina dura is the compact bone that appears as a radiopaque line surrounding the root of the tooth and the alveolar crest. Basal lamina is the amorphous material adjacent to the basal layer of epithelial cells. Junctional epithelium closely adheres to the tooth at the base of the sulcus. Lamina propria is the highly organized connective tissue component of the oral mucosa.

16.

B. Sharpey's fibers are the terminal portion of the PDL. They are the points of attachment to bone and cementum. Osteocytes are bone-forming cells. Cementoid is uncalcified cementum. Cancellous or spongy bone is located between the cortical plates. Osteoid is the uncalcified layer of intercellular substance which eventually becomes bone.

17.

B. The PMN leukocyte, known as the neutrophil, is the white blood cell associated with the acute inflammatory response. Stage I gingivitis is the initial inflammatory response of the gingival tissue to plaque. Fibroblasts are cells that form connective tissue. Plasma cells produce immunoglobulin and are more commonly seen in chronic inflammation. The erythrocyte or red blood cell (RBC) is not associated with acute inflammatory response. An osteoclast is a bone-forming cell.

18.

A. There is greater risk of root surface caries, not occlusal, with gingival recession. Loss of cementum exposes dentinal tubules, which may cause dentin hypersensitivity. Intact papillae protect the embrasure spaces from plaque accumulation. When the papillae are lost, the embrasure space is now more plaque retentive. Tooth root structure may be lost through caries, abrasion, and erosion.

19.

B. Pocketing, related to attachment loss, is a distinctive factor in evaluating periodontal disease. Pocketing can be detected clinically using a probe. Although bone loss is a distinctive factor in periodontal disease, it may not be detected clinically. Use of radiographs is a better means to detect bone loss. Not all causes of bad breath are related to periodontal disease. It is not an essential clinical feature of periodontitis. Calculus and plaque may be present when there is gingivitis and periodontitis. However, it is possible to have plaque and calculus present with no evidence of disease. Pain is not usually associated with periodontitis.

20.

D. Bleeding on probing is the most reliable clinical sign of gingival inflammation. Neutrophils and plasma cells must be seen microscopically, as they cannot be seen clinically. Gingival inflammation does not result in an increase of sulcular fluid. However, this is difficult to detect and not a reliable clinical sign of gingival inflammation. Subgingival plaque accumulation is not easily detectable and not a good indicator of gingival inflammation.

21.

E. Gingival hyperplasia can be a side effect of the medication Dilantin. This is not an inflammatory response, but an excess growth of gingival tissue. Gingival abscesses are infections and not oral side effects of Dilantin. Squamous cell carcinoma is a malignancy and not an oral side effect of Dilantin. Pyogenic granuloma is an excessive inflammatory response to an irritant often associated with hormonal imbalances.

22.

B. The trigeminal nerve is a mixed motor and sensory nerve. Its branches innervate the periodontal tissues. The facial nerve is responsible for facial expression. The oculomotor nerve is a motor nerve that sends impulses to muscles that raise the eyelid and move the eyes. The hypoglossal is a motor nerve that sends impulses to muscles that move the tongue. The abducens is a motor nerve that sends impulses to muscles that move the eyes.

23.

D. Cementum overlaps enamel 60% to 65% of the time. Enamel does not overlap the cementum. Cementum meets the enamel 30% of the time. Enamel stops 0.5 mm short of the cementum 5% to 10% of the time.

24.

D. The characteristic diagnostic sign of localized juvenile periodontitis is vertical bone loss at first molars and incisors. Bleeding on probing and diastemas are not unique signs for LJP. LJP is not painful and abscess formation is not a common feature. There is not a significant amount of calculus present in LJP.

25.

D. Calcium phosphate makes up approximately 75% of the inorganic content of calculus. Brushite is present in calculus in small quantities. Mucopolysaccharides are organic, not inorganic compounds. Magnesium phosphate is the second largest inorganic component of calculus.

26.

C. The most accurate way to detect furcation involvement is by clinical probing using a specially designed probe, such as the Nabors. A typical patient would not be aware of a furcation involvement, as furcations are not readily seen. Some furcation involvement can be viewed on radiographs. However, because of variations in film and beam placement, furcations may not routinely be detected this way. Fremitus describes the slight movement of a tooth that can be felt when a tooth experiences excess occlusal forces. Although furcations are risk factors for periodontal abscesses, not all furcations will have evidence of suppuration or purulence.

27.

C. Numerous medical conditions may put a patient at risk of bacterial endocarditis, including disease-produced heart murmur or artificial (prosthetic) heart valves and some congenital heart defects. Myocardial infarction results from an occluded coronary artery.

Antibiotic premedication will not prevent a heart attack. Cerebrovascular accident or stroke occurs when there is oxygen deprivation to a portion of the brain resulting from an occluded or damaged vessel in the brain. Antibiotic treatment will not prevent a stroke. Pyogenic granulomas are an exaggerated tissue response to a local irritant. They are associated with patients with hormone imbalances, such as occurs during pregnancy. Reducing the local irritant may manage pyogenic granulomas.

28.

C. The tissue redness seen in gingivitis is characteristic of the inflammatory process. It is related to the increase in capillary formation at the inflammatory site. Hyperkeratosis, an increase in the layer of keratinized epithelial (nonvascular) tissue, would cause tissue to have a pale appearance, not red. Exudation is clear and a sign of inflammation. Bleeding on probing will occur when the gingiva is inflamed; however bleeding does not cause inflammatory redness. The quantity of sulcular fluid increases with gingival inflammation, but it is not red.

29.

C. Tissue destruction evidenced by blunting or cratering of the interdental papillae is a distinct feature of NUG. After the episode of NUG has resolved, the affected tissue would not be edematous or swollen. The interdental papillae will be destroyed through the disease process. They do not atrophy or shrink. Recession is not a significant factor in identifying past history of NUG. Gingival hyperplasia may be associated with intake of specific medications or hereditary; however it is not associated with NUG.

30.

A. Occlusal forces directed axially result in a uniform distribution along the PDL into the surrounding bone. Forces that are not directed axially contribute to tissue destruction, including vertical bone defects. Evidence of excess occlusal forces may appear on a radiograph as widened PDL space. Osteoblast activity occurs at areas of tension in bone. Osteoclasts—cells that remove bone—are present at areas of pressure on the bone. Erosion is the loss of tooth structure that has had contact with a chemical.

31.

C. Necrotizing ulcerative gingivitis has symptoms such as fetid breath odor, gingival bleeding, presence of spirochetes and fusiform bacteria, and pseudomembranous ulcerations at the marginal gingiva and interdental papillae. This condition may be acute or chronic. A periapical abscess occurs with pulp necrosis. There would be signs of this condition at the marginal gingiva or interdental papillae. Herpes simplex I has generalized ulceration on the mucosa, not limited to the marginal gingiva. Pericoronitis is painful inflammation, with probable infection.

32.

B. Bleeding on probing and an increase in sulcular fluid are the two earliest signs of gingivitis. Collagen fibers are destroyed, not increased, in early gingivitis. Gingival recession and bone loss would be noted with periodontitis, not gingivitis. Calculus alone is not an indicator of either gingivitis or periodontitis. Gingivitis is not painful. However, there will be microulceration of the sulcular epithelium as the gingivitis progresses.

33.

C. The col is located in the proximal space between the facial and lingual papillae. The mucogingival junction is the line of demarcation between the attached gingiva and the oral mucous membrane. A furcation involves the area on a multirooted tooth where the roots separate. The gingival sulcus is the space between the root of the tooth and the sulcular wall of the marginal gingiva. The free gingival groove identifies where the marginal gingiva ends and the attached gingiva begins.

34.

A. Transseptal fibers attach from the cementum of one tooth to the cementum of an adjacent tooth. These fibers are also considered a gingival fiber group. Circular fibers are located in the marginal gingiva. Alveolar crest fibers extend obliquely from the cementum apical to the junctional epithelium to the alveolar crest. Interradicular periodontal ligament fibers are found only in multirooted teeth. They extend from the cementum at the furcation to the bone in the same area. Oblique periodontal ligament fibers extend from the cementum in a coronal direction to the bone. This is the largest and most significant fiber group.

35.

C. The intent of gingival curettage is to create a better environment for healing, by removing the diseased pocket wall. Gingivoplasty reshapes the gingiva to improve its contour. Root planing smooths root surfaces. Gingivectomy surgically removes diseased gingiva.

36.

C. The content of plaque solids is 70% to 80% bacteria. Plaque has very little inorganic material. There will be small quantities of desquamated epithelial cells present in plaque. Leukocytes and macrophages are not present in plaque in any significant quantity. Intercellular matrix holds the plaque together. Its quantity by volume is considerably less than the bacteria present in plaque.

37.

E. The position of the junctional epithelium determines the maximum height at which the PDL fibers can reattach. During the healing process, both the epithelium and the periodontal ligament fibers may heal more coronally if the junctional epithelium is removed. Periodontal ligament fibers are embedded in cementum by Sharpey's fibers. Without cementum there is no point of attachment. A nondiseased environment is required for good healing or reattachment. Tooth mobility inhibits fibers from reattaching.

38.

C. Infection describes the accumulation and proliferation of a microorganism. An infection is pathological, not physiological, and results in an inflammatory response. Redness, heat, swelling, and pain are all cardinal signs of inflammation. Inflammation is a physiological response to tissue injury.

39.

A. A distance greater than 2.0 mm between the CEJ and the crest of the alveolar bone is suggestive of bone destruction associated with periodontal disease.

40.

E. In chronic periodontitis, there is an increased amount of vasculature, but a slowed rate of circulation. The blood stagnates at the point of inflammation. Because the blood is deoxygenated, it has a dark red/purple or less than bright red appearance. The presence of plasma cells, neutrophils, collagen, products in periodontal pockets, and fibrous connective tissue do not create a bluish-red appearance of the gingiva.

41.

C. Consumption of acidic foods, such as lemons and pickles, induce rather than reduce saliva production. Numerous medications, including antihypertensive, antidepressant, and antianxiety, may cause xerostomia. Mouth breathing results in xerostomia, as do deficiencies of vitamins A and B.

42.

D. Chlorhexidine is not effective against viruses, bacterial spores, or acid-fast bacteria. However, it does possess antimicrobial properties for both Gram-positive and Gram-negative bacteria, as well as yeast.

43.

A. Tetracycline, minacycline, doxacycline, and natural or synthetic tetracycline have been used successfully in the management of several forms of periodontal disease, including juvenile periodontitis and refractory periodontitis. Sulfa drugs, erythromycin, and cephalosporine are not as effective in managing periodontal disease.

CHAPTER

13 Medical Emergencies

Patricia Nunn, RDH, MS

contents

Medical conditions occur suddenly with little or no warning. Most of these emergency medical conditions are precipitated by physiological or psychological stress like that experienced in a dental office. The dental hygienist will encounter at least one medical crisis during his or her practice lifetime. Actions taken during that time can have a direct impact on the outcome of the crisis.

I. PREVENTION

A. *Medical crisis*

1. Awareness of risk factors
2. Take and carefully evaluate thorough patient history
   a) Identify medical conditions indicative of potential emergency medical risk
   b) Identify drugs taken that are indicative of conditions that may cause potential emergency medical risk
3. Seek medical consultation if history indicates potential problems or if more information is needed
4. Take precautions to prevent life-threatening emergencies from occurring, based on the medical history
5. Avoid complacency about patient's medical risk status
   a) Patient's longevity in the practice or absence of a previous problem, resulting in a lack of a history update or precautions addressed
   b) Must be a first time for the emergency
      (1) Know potential risk of the patient
      (2) Take necessary precautions to avoid medical emergency
      (3) Know what to do to manage the emergency
6. Recognize physical signs and symptoms of *anxiety*
   a) Cold, sweaty palms or forehead
   b) Unnaturally stiff posture
   c) "White knuckle syndrome" (tightly gripping the arm of the chair or other objects)
   d) Wringing hands, playing with items in the hands
   e) Increased blood pressure and heart rate
   f) Trembling
   g) Excessive sweating
   h) Dilated pupils
7. Take precautions or actions appropriate to particular medical status
8. Reduce anxiety and stress

B. Preparation for potential emergency situations

1. Staff training—provides knowledge and skills to respond immediately and appropriately to potentially life-threatening incident
2. Victim survival is possibly dependent on first few minutes or hours
3. Know when emergency has occurred and what to do until medical assistance arrives
4. Ideally, all team members should be trained and certified in cardiopulmonary resuscitation; must know and post emergency medical assistance phone number(s)

5. Know contents of emergency kit or crash cart
6. Know roles for a given emergency scenario
7. Emergency practice drills
   a) Necessary to keep staff ready for potential emergencies
   b) Practice to keep skills updated
   c) Become comfortable with individual roles to prevent chaos in crisis situation
8. Need for emergency kit or crash cart
   a) Essential items that are readily and easily accessible
   b) Contents must be regularly checked; nothing should be out-of-date or contents are not useful
   c) Awareness of what team members can or should legally administer
   d) With most emergencies, no drugs are necessary—mainly first aid items
   e) Some emergencies require immediate use of drugs—can make the difference between life and death
   f) Commercially available
9. Considerations for a custom-designed kit
   a) Type of practice
   b) Knowledge and skill of dentist(s) in emergency medicine
   c) Type of emergencies most commonly encountered
   d) Choose only equipment and drugs for which personnel are trained
   e) Select only equipment and drugs legally allowed to be utilized
10. Primary role of auxiliary
    a) Provision of basic life support
    b) Support of dentist in administration of additional supportive therapies until medical emergency personnel arrive
11. Emergency first aid kit or crash cart basic contents
    a) Resuscitation mask or face shield with one-way valve
    b) Oxygen with positive pressure ventilation capability (e.g., demand/positive pressure valves, or a self-inflating device such as an Ambu bag)
    c) Nitroglycerin tabs 0.3 mg. (fresh and unopened) or oral nitroglycerin spray
    d) Epinephrine—at least two preloaded 1:1,000 epinephrine syringes
    e) Injectable antihistamine, such as diphenhydramine HCl 10 mg/ml or chlorpheniramine 10 mg/ml
12. Common optional additional drugs and equipment
    a) 21-gauge needle
    b) Amyl nitrate vaporole
    c) Antiasthmatic bronchodilator
    d) Aromatic ammonia vaporoles
    e) Gauze, bandages, and adhesive tape
    f) Oral sucrose
    g) Syringes
    h) Tourniquets (3)

13. Additional optional drugs and equipment—requires additional knowledge and advanced training for safe use; to be added according to ability and desire of the dentist
    a) Airways, adult and child; oropharyngeal or nasopharyngeal
    b) *Analgesic* (morphine)
    c) *Anticholinergic* (atropine)
    d) *Anticonvulsant* (midazolam)
    e) *Antihypertensive* (nifedipine)
    f) Corticosteroid (injectable)—hydrocortisone sodium succinate
    g) Cricothyrotomy needle or scalpel
    h) Endotracheal intubation equipment
    i) *Narcotic antagonist* (naloxone)
    j) Vasopressor (injectable)—methoxamine
14. *Good Samaritan statutes*
    a) Laws for legal protection of people who willingly give emergency care without accepting anything in return
    b) Vary from state to state
    c) All require individuals to act as reasonable and as prudent as another person would act under the same conditions
    d) Provides for protection of person providing emergency care from being successfully sued and found financially responsible
    e) Common sense and reasonable level of skill is expected, but not what is beyond training and legal limitations
    f) Standard of care expected is not as strict in an emergency situation as it is in a nonemergency situation

C. Emergency Management

1. Need for immediate recognition and action for acutely life-threatening conditions
    a) Purpose is to sustain life until medical attention can provide definitive treatment
    b) Recognize potential to become threat to life
    c) Take action to prevent exacerbation of condition to one of grave potential
2. Basic Medical Emergency Procedures (*BMEP*)—necessary management for most acute medical emergency conditions
    a) Terminate any dental care in progress and immediately notify dentist of emergency
    b) Place patient in supine position
        (1) UNLESS there is respiratory discomfort and/or chest pain in that position
        (2) As an alternative, patient should be placed in semisupine or upright position
    c) Check for consciousness
    d) Check for adequate breathing
        (1) If there is an airway obstruction and signs of respiratory difficulty, establish and maintain open airway
        (2) Oxygen may be administered (DO NOT administer oxygen to a person who is hyperventilating)

e) Check pulse
f) In absence of respiration or respiration and pulse, administer basic life support
g) Establish baseline vital signs—respiration, pulse, blood pressure
h) Call Emergency Medical Service (EMS) and provide information about the emergency
i) Continue to monitor vital signs
j) Do no harm
k) Provide or assist in specific supportive treatment as indicated by the condition
l) Stay calm throughout

D. Terminology

1. *Allergen*—antigen that can exhibit allergic symptoms
2. *Allergy*—hypersensitive response to allergen
3. *Anaphylactic*—life-threatening systemic allergic reaction; also called anaphylactic shock
4. *Idiosyncrasy*—peculiar or individual reaction to drugs and/or food substance
5. *Infarct*—death of tissue from lack of oxygen
6. *Pruritus*—severe itching
7. *Tachypnea*—rapid respiration
8. *Urticaria* (also called hives)—vascular reaction of skin, characterized by wheals or papules
9. *Bradycardia*—slow heart rate

II. UNCONSCIOUSNESS

A. *Vasodepressor syncope*—most common emergency in dentistry

1. Medical history findings
   a) Caused by decreased oxygen flow to brain, most frequently occurring in young adult male patients (16 to 35 years old) with unexpressed stress or fear
   b) Psychogenic factors—"fight or flight response"
      (1) Fright
      (2) Anxiety
      (3) Emotional stress
      (4) Pain
   c) Nonpsychogenic factors
      (1) Hunger
      (2) Exhaustion
      (3) Poor physical condition
      (4) Sitting/standing in upright position
      (5) Hot, humid, and/or crowded environment
2. Common symptoms
   a) Presyncope—patient reports pale cool skin, "cold sweat," feeling faint or dizzy, and seeing spots before the eyes
      (1) Vital signs—increase in respiration and heart rate

b) Syncope—irregular breathing, jerky, pupils dilate
   (1) Vital signs
      (a) Bradycardia
      (b) Decreased blood pressure
c) Postsyncope—patient feels disoriented and confused

3. Dental considerations
   a) Presyncope
      (1) Discontinue procedure as soon as symptoms are noted
      (2) Place patient in supine position—feet elevated
      (3) Pass ammonia vaporale under patient's nose
   b) Syncope—assess consciousness
   c) Postsyncope—do not continue dental treatment
4. Emergency treatment
   a) Presyncope—patient in supine position with legs elevated; move legs vigorously
   b) Syncope—loss of consciousness
      (1) Place patient in supine position
      (2) Assess ABCs (airway, breathing, circulation)
      (3) If recovery is not within 3 to 5 minutes, call EMS and perform BMEP
   c) Postsyncope—do not continue dental treatment; have a friend take the patient home

B. *Postural hypotension* (*orthostatic hypotension*)—second leading cause of loss of consciousness

1. Fall in blood pressure in which patient faints when rapidly brought to an upright position with legs elevated
   a) May be caused by drugs, varicose veins, later stages of pregnancy, prolonged periods of recumbency
   b) Results when there is a pooling of blood in lower extremities that diverts from brain and other vital organs
2. Medical history findings
   a) Medications—check for antihypertensives, antidepressants, and narcotics
3. Common symptoms upon standing or sitting
   a) Light-headedness, pallor, dizziness, sweat, blurred vision
   b) May lose consciousness
   c) Vital signs—blood pressure is low; heart rate at baseline or above
4. Dental consideration—return chair slowly to upright position
5. Emergency treatment
   a) Assess consciousness
   b) Place patient in supine position with feet elevated above the level of heart
   c) Patient may flex thigh muscles to encourage blood flow to return to the brain before raising the chair slowly
   d) Assess ABCs
   e) Monitor vital signs
   f) Administer oxygen, if necessary
   g) Elevate patient slowly and reevaluate vital signs

C. *Acute adrenal insufficiency* (*adrenal crisis*)

1. Sudden lack of sufficient circulating adrenal hormones
   a) Before glucocorticosteroid therapy, was the terminal stage of Addison's disease
   b) Hypersecretion of cortisol is referred to as Cushing's syndrome
2. Medical history findings
   a) History of Addison's disease
   b) Acute withdrawal of steroids after long term use
   c) Acute adrenal insufficiency is seen in only 0.01% to 0.7% of normal population
3. Common symptoms
   a) Mental confusion
   b) Muscle weakness
   c) Intense abdominal pain
   d) Lower back and/or leg pain
   e) Signs of hypoglycemia
   f) Extreme fatigue and weakness
   g) Episodic syncope
   h) Anorexia, weight loss
   i) Hypotension
4. Dental considerations
   a) Establish treatment plan
   b) Consult physician before beginning dental treatment
   c) Use stress-reduction protocol
   d) Within 2 to 3 months after discontinuing adrenocortical hormone therapy, patient is susceptible when undergoing trauma to subacute form of adrenal crisis
5. Emergency treatment
   a) BMEP
   b) Give oxygen
   c) Call EMS immediately
   d) Dentist should administer glucocorticosteroid from patient's kit or office emergency kit if available, or EMT will administer
   e) Transport patient to hospital

III. ALTERED CONSCIOUSNESS

A. *Cerebrovascular accident* (*CVA, stroke*)—most common form of brain disease

1. Types
   a) Hemorrhagic
   b) Occlusive
2. Medical history finding
   a) May have previously experienced transient ischemic attacks (TIA or ministroke)
   b) High blood pressure
   c) Diabetes
   d) Use of oral contraceptives
   e) Cigarette smoking

3. Common symptoms
   a) Sudden unilateral weakness and numbness or paralysis
   b) Difficulty speaking (aphasia)
   c) Pupils of unequal size
   d) Hemorrhagic CVA may also include
      (1) Sudden severe headache
      (2) Nausea
      (3) Vomiting
      (4) Chills
      (5) Sweating
      (6) Vertigo
      (7) Unconsciousness (indicates grim prognosis)
4. Dental considerations
   a) Do not schedule for elective treatment within 6 months of episode—recurrence is greater
   b) Use stress-reduction protocol
   c) Record vitals—monitor blood pressure and heart rate
   d) Assess bleeding—patients are often on aspirin or anticoagulant therapy
5. Emergency treatment
   a) Treatments to prevent or limit brain damage are time-sensitive—call EMS immediately
   b) Monitor vital signs—if blood pressure is markedly elevated, raise head and chest slightly
   c) Administer oxygen
   d) If office is equipped, an IV line should be established using 5% dextrose

B. *Hypoglycemic episode* in a diabetic patient (insulin shock)

1. Lack of adequate circulating blood sugar with acute onset of severe symptoms
   a) Can result in death
   b) May be triggered by normal insulin intake and lack of adequate food, overdose of insulin, overexercise, or other physical or emotional stress
2. Medical history findings
   a) Insulin-dependent diabetes mellitus (IDDM)—Type 1
   b) Normal insulin intake with failure to eat normally
3. Common symptoms
   a) Changes in level of consciousness including
      (1) Less spontaneity of conversation
      (2) Lethargy
      (3) Incoherence
      (4) Dizziness
      (5) Drowsiness
      (6) Confusion
   b) Personality change—(sometimes these symptoms are mistakenly assumed to be result of inebriation)
   c) Central nervous system (CNS) involvement includes

(1) Hunger
(2) Weakness
(3) Nervousness
(4) Trembling
(5) Cold sweat (symptom that helps distinguish hypoglycemia from hyperglycemia)

d) Following CNS symptoms are clinical signs of
(1) Tachycardia
(2) Pallor
(3) Sometimes paresthesia (numbness and tingling sensation)

e) Later stage—unconsciousness, tonic-clonic movements, hypotension, rapid thready pulse, hypothermia

4. Dental considerations
a) Be sure patient has tested blood sugar level
b) Patient has eaten adequate meal before dental visit
c) Schedule appointments early in day
d) Avoid use of epinephrine in local anesthesia
e) Provide stress-reduction protocol

5. Emergency treatment
a) If conscious, give patient something with sugar in it and place patient in upright position
b) If no response in approximately 5 minutes, call EMS and monitor vital signs
c) If unconscious
(1) Call EMS
(2) Monitor vital signs
(3) Give basic life support as necessary

d) If response is immediate, further action may not be necessary

IV. CHEST PAIN

A. *Myocardial infarction* (MI, heart attack)

1. Result of deficient blood supply to heart muscle, resulting in cellular death
2. Characterized by sudden severe and prolonged substernal pain
3. Medical history findings
a) Coronary heart disease
b) Hypertension
c) Obesity
d) Males (50 to 70 years)
e) Survivors are usually receiving medications, such as diuretics, digitalis, aspirin, nitrates

4. Common symptoms
a) Severe persistent crushing pain or pressure in sternum that is not relieved by change in position, rest, or nitroglycerin (if it has been previously prescribed)
b) Patient may clutch at chest with fist (Levine sign)
c) Pain or pressure may radiate to neck, jaw, and/or arms
d) Breathing difficulty

e) Pale, ashen, or cyanotic appearance
f) Profuse sweating
g) Nausea and vomiting possible when pain is severe
h) Vital signs appear as blood pressure may be low, respiration rapid and shallow, and heart rate weak, thready, and shallow

5. Dental considerations
   a) DO NOT treat patient within 6 months after MI without cardiology consult
   b) Use stress reduction protocol
   c) Nitrous oxide is highly recommended for sedation
6. Emergency treatment
   a) Call EMS—survival chances may depend on time it takes to receive definitive care (cardiac arrest may occur at any time)
   b) Help victim to rest comfortably, usually in upright or semi-upright position
   c) Monitor vital signs
   d) Oxygen may be administered; administer nitroglycerin (do not administer in presence of hypotension [i.e., systolic pressure below 100 mm Hg])
   f) Be prepared to provide CPR

B. *Angina pectoris*

1. Rapid accumulation of fluid in alveoli and interstitial tissue of lungs
2. Extreme difficulty in breathing caused by weakening or failure of left side of heart
3. Medical history finding—history of angina pectoris
4. Common symptoms
   a) Squeezing, heavy, dull chest pain lasting from 1 to 10 minutes
   b) Vital signs are normal
5. Dental considerations
   a) Use stress reduction protocol
   b) Place patient in comfortable position
6. Emergency treatment
   a) BMEP
   b) Administer vasodilator, nitroglycerin tablet(s)/spray
   c) May administer oxygen
   d) When episode is over, a decision whether or not to continue dental work is made
   e) If the episode does not abate, administer oxygen and a second dose of nitroglycerin (no more than 3 doses). If pain is not relieved within 10 minutes, treat as MI and call EMS

V. RESPIRATORY DISTRESS

A. *Hyperventilation*

1. Most common emergency situation in dental office
2. Prevalent in especially tense and nervous patients 15 to 40 years of age

3. Common findings
   a) Overbreathing (increased respirations)
   b) Feeling of a lump in the throat (globus hystericus)
   c) Lightheaded, giddy
   d) Increased apprehension
   e) Later—paresthesia of hands feet and perioral area, muscular twitching, carpopedal tetany, and unconsciousness
4. Emergency treatment
   a) Position upright, remove materials from mouth, and loosen clothing
   b) DO NOT administer oxygen
   c) If attempt is unsuccessful, have patient breathe into cupped hands or small paper bag
   d) Assist patient in reducing anxiety by allowing patient to express fears

B. *Acute pulmonary edema*

1. Rapid accumulation of fluid in alveoli and interstitial tissue of lungs
2. Results in extreme difficulty in breathing caused by weakening or failure of left side of heart
3. Medical history findings
   a) Congestive heart failure
   b) Possible history of heart disease, hypertension, and/or chronic lung disease
4. Common symptoms
   a) Extreme dyspnea (difficulty breathing)
   b) Tachypnea (rapid respiration)
   c) Cyanosis
   d) Frothy pink sputum
   e) Cold extremities
5. Emergency treatment
   a) BMEP, with patient upright to assist breathing
   b) Administer oxygen
   c) Alleviate symptoms of respiratory distress by bloodless phlebotomy (phlebostasia)
      (1) Tourniquets or blood pressure cuffs applied to extremities using just enough pressure to keep blood from entering extremity
      (2) One tourniquet is released for 5 minutes then reapplied, followed by release of another extremity, continuing this rotation until the patient has been transported by EMS to medical care facility
6. Definitive treatment
   a) Dentist or emergency personnel may administer vasodilator
   b) Patient transported to acute care facility for additional procedures

c) If office is equipped and dentist is comfortable, administration of either morphine sulfate or meperidine (Demerol) to relieve apprehension and to improve circulatory dynamics is indicated.

C. Acute asthmatic episode

1. Medical history finding
   a) *Asthma*—usually with acute asthmatic episodes requiring emergency care or hospitalization
2. Common symptoms
   a) Dyspnea (difficulty breathing)
   b) Normal inspiration with wheezing exhalation because diameter of brachial tube has decreased
   c) Tachypnea (increased rate of breathing)
   d) Cyanosis
   e) Chest distension
   f) Nasal flaring
3. Status asthmaticus
   a) Symptoms continue unabated even with treatment
   b) Patient experiences
      (1) Extreme fatigue
      (2) Dehydration
      (3) Cyanosis
      (4) Peripheral vascular shock
      (5) Drug intoxication
      (6) Rapid heart rate
4. Emergency treatment
   a) BMEP
   b) Position comfortable, usually upright with arms forward
   c) Assist patient in administering bronchodilator, if available (his/her own, or from emergency kit)
   d) Avoid using barbiturates and narcotics because they may increase risk of bronchospasms
   e) If episode continues, administer oxygen and call EMS immediately

D. *Emphysema*

1. Condition of lungs in which there is decrease in the ability to draw extra oxygen
2. Form of chronic obstructive pulmonary disease (COPD)
3. Decrease in tissue and lung elasticity
4. Common symptoms
   a) Undue breathlessness on exertion
   b) Can coexist with chronic bronchitis
   c) Bronchioles become plugged with mucus
5. Emergency treatment
   a) BMEP
   b) Sit patient in upright position
   c) Follow stress-reduction protocol
   d) Be cautious about administering oxygen—could cause patient to go into respiratory arrest

VI. CARDIAC ARREST

A. *Clinical death*

1. Heart stops beating or beats ineffectively in generating a pulse
2. Causes inadequate circulation to brain and other vital organs
3. Common causes
   a) Anaphylaxis
   b) Drowning
   c) Drug overdose
   d) Electrocution
   e) Massive trauma
   f) Suffocation or hypoxia
4. Medical history finding—cardiovascular disease
5. Common symptoms
   a) No breathing
   b) No pulse
   c) No respiration
6. Emergency treatment
   a) Follow BMEP (As a refresher, the steps in cardiopulmonary resuscitation follow—be sure to keep CPR certification current)
      (1) Assess consciousness, shake, and shout
      (2) Call for help
      (3) Position in supine position
      (4) Head tilt–chin lift
      (5) Look, listen, and feel for respiration for 5 seconds
      (6) If no breathing, pinch nose shut and give two full breaths (use one-way valve face mask if available) or use Ambu bag or positive pressure oxygen ventilation
      (7) Check carotid pulse (5 to 10 seconds)
      (8) Call for EMS
      (9) If no pulse, find the hand position by
         (a) Locating notch at lower end of sternum with two fingers
         (b) Place heel of other hand on sternum next to fingers
         (c) Remove first hand and place it on hand that is on sternum, keeping fingers off chest
      (10) Position rescuer's shoulders over hands
         (a) Compress victim's chest 1 1/2 to 2 inches
         (b) Move up and down smoothly
         (c) Always keep hand in contact with chest
      (11) Give 15 compressions
      (12) Give 2 full breaths and repeat cycle of 15 compressions and 2 breaths for 1 full minute
      (13) Reassess pulse—if no pulse continue CPR, rechecking pulse every few minutes
      (14) Do not stop
         (a) Until another trained person takes over
         (b) Until EMS personnel arrive and take over

(c) Until person's heart restarts
(d) Unless you are too exhausted to continue
(15) If pulse returns, but breathing does not—continue rescue breathing
(16) If patient is breathing and has a pulse, maintain airway and monitor vitals until EMS personnel arrive

B. *Respiratory arrest*

1. Cessation of breathing due to illness, injury, electrical shock, obstructed airway, or drowning
2. May possibly follow respiratory distress
   a) Air passages becoming narrow due to swelling
   b) As a result of swelling, adequate air exchange is blocked and respiratory arrest results
3. Common symptom—breathing ceases
4. Emergency treatment
   a) Follow BMEP (as a refresher, the steps in rescue breathing follow)
   b) Assess consciousness, shake, and shout
   c) Call for help
   d) Position in supine position (on left side in third trimester of pregnancy)
   e) Head tilt–chin lift
   f) Look, listen, and feel for respiration for 5 seconds
   g) If not breathing, pinch nose shut and give two full breaths (use one-way oxygen ventilation)
   h) Check carotid pulse (5 to 10 seconds)
   i) If pulse, continue rescue breathing once every 5 seconds for adults (every 3 seconds for child)

VII. DRUG-RELATED EMERGENCIES

A. *Anaphylactic shock*

1. Severe allergic reaction causing systemic release of histamines and other chemical mediators
2. Produces acute life-threatening changes involving circulation and bronchioles consistent with shock
3. Medical history findings—previous allergic reactions, particularly to drugs and/or materials used in or during dental procedures
4. Common symptoms—onset rapidly after contact with allergen and typically, but not always, evolve through four phases
   a) Skin reactions (such as generalized rash, intense pruritus, urticaria, flushing, edema)
   b) Smooth muscle spasm (gastrointestinal reactions such as cramping, abdominal pain, nausea, vomiting, diarrhea)
   c) Acute respiratory distress due to laryngeal edema—wheezing
   d) Cardiovascular distress and collapse (hypotension, cardiac arrhythmias, tachycardia, cyanosis, circulatory collapse, and cardiac arrest)

5. Emergency treatment—Fatalities may occur in minutes; quick action is necessary
   a) Follow BMEP
   b) Definitive treatment—Dentist or emergency personnel should determine dosage, route of administration, and administer epinephrine
      (1) Dose is generally 0.3 to 0.5 ml of 1:1,000 epinephrine intramuscular (IM), intravenous (IV), subcutaneously (SC), sublingual, or directly into tongue
      (2) Have epinephrine ready to administer in preloaded syringe
      (3) If there is no significant improvement within 5 minutes, a second dose of epinephrine is usually administered
   c) Continue to monitor vital signs
   d) Additional drugs that may be administered after clinical improvement are noted (e.g., antihistamine and corticosteroid)

VIII. SEIZURES OR CONVULSIONS

A. *Epilepsy*

1. *Grand mal* (generalized tonic-clonic)—most common form
   a) Prodromal phase
      (1) Patient experiences increase in anxiety or depression
      (2) Aura (sensory phenomena) may follow
   b) Preictal phase
      (1) Patient loses consciousness
      (2) Experiences myoclonic jerks
      (3) Epileptic cry occurs
   c) Ictal phase
      (1) Tonic
         (a) Generalized muscle contractions
         (b) Evidence of dyspnea and cyanosis
         (c) Lasts 10 to 20 seconds
      (2) Clonic
         (a) Generalized relaxation of muscles
         (b) Heavy breathing
         (c) Patient may froth at the mouth
         (d) Lasts 2 to 5 minutes
   d) Postictal phase
      (1) Tonic-clonic movements stop
      (2) Breathing returns to normal
      (3) Consciousness returns—patient may fall asleep
      (4) Full recovery within 2 hours
2. *Petit mal* (absence of seizures)
   a) Occurs shortly after awakening or during periods of inactivity
   b) Brief loss of awareness
   c) Patient may stare blankly or experience rapid blinking of eyes
   d) History of seizures

3. Common symptoms
   a) Momentary altered consciousness
   b) Loss of consciousness and bilateral jerking of extremities
   c) Sustained muscular contraction
   d) Alternating contraction (tonic contractions) and relaxation of muscles (clonic convulsions)
   e) Possible aura (sensory phenomena) experienced before seizure
4. Emergency treatment
   a) Protect victim from harm by removing objects nearby that could cause injury (do not attempt to restrain or wedge mouth open)
   b) Maintain airway if needed
   c) Summon EMS only if the following occurs
      (1) Seizure lasts longer than 5 minutes
      (2) Injury is present
      (3) Victim has no previous history of seizure
      (4) Victim is pregnant, diabetic, or does not immediately regain consciousness

review questions

DIRECTIONS Each of the questions or incomplete statements below is followed by suggested answers or completions. Select the **one** answer that is best in each case.

1. In acute adrenal insufficiency, which of the following hormones is suddenly lacking?
   A. glucocorticosteroid
   B. epinephrine
   C. insulin
   D. thyroxin

2. Which of the following conditions would contraindicate placing a patient in the supine position during the management of an acute medical emergency?
   A. unconscious respiratory distress
   B. second trimester of pregnancy
   C. syncope
   D. cerebrovascular accident in a patient with normal blood pressure

3. A 70-year-old man with a history of hypertension and congestive heart failure, suddenly experiences tachypnea, extreme dyspnea with cyanosis, and frothy pink sputum. Which of the following conditions is being experienced?
   A. hyperventilation
   B. acute asthmatic episode
   C. cerebrovascular accident
   D. acute pulmonary edema

4. Which of the following is the MOST acute diabetic problem encountered in the dental office?
   A. hypoglycemia
   B. ketoacidosis
   C. hyperglycemia
   D. hypoinsulinism
   E. infection

5. Which of the following would be the MOST appropriate treatment for a hyperventilating patient?
   A. administer epinephrine
   B. have patient breathe into a paper bag
   C. place patient in a supine position
   D. administer oxygen

6. Bloodless phlebotomy may relieve the symptoms of respiratory distress associated with acute pulmonary edema. Tourniquets are applied to extremities using enough pressure to keep blood from entering the extremity. One tourniquet is released then reapplied and another is released. This rotation is continued. All of the following are true of bloodless phlebotomy EXCEPT one. Which one is the EXCEPTION?
   A. The tourniquet is released on the extremity 10 minutes at a time.
   B. Rotations of release and reapplication of tourniquets are continued until the patient reaches a medical facility for more definitive treatment.
   C. A synonym for bloodless phlebotomy is phlebostasia.

7. The initial treatment for syncope is to
   A. administer spirits of ammonia.
   B. administer epinephrine.
   C. administer oxygen.
   D. place patient in a supine position with legs elevated.

8. A known diabetic patient states she is not feeling well. She is feeling cool, looks pale, and is beginning to slur her speech. Immediate treatment should include administration of
   A. insulin.
   B. oxygen.
   C. epinephrine.
   D. orange juice or a sugared beverage.

9. All of the following patients have an increased chance of orthostatic hypotension EXCEPT one. Which one is the EXCEPTION?
   A. those with varicose veins
   B. elderly
   C. woman in third trimester of pregnancy
   D. children

10. Angina pectoris is due to
    A. anxiety.
    B. ischemia.
    C. hyperoxia.
    D. hypercalcemia.

11. Emergency treatment of hyperventilation includes all of the following EXCEPT one. Which one is the EXCEPTION?
    A. have patient breathe into cupped hands
    B. stop treatment
    C. position client upright
    D. administer oxygen

12. In the management of the conscious CVA patient, all of the following procedures apply EXCEPT one. Which one is the EXCEPTION?
    A. administer oxygen
    B. call EMS
    C. place client in supine position
    D. monitor vital signs

13. Dyspnea refers to
    A. the inability to breathe, except in an upright position.
    B. increased rate of breathing.
    C. difficulty in breathing.
    D. no respiratory movement.

14. The MOST common breathing change observed in the dental office is
    A. airway obstruction.
    B. hyperventilation.
    C. hypoventilation.
    D. asthma.

15. All of the following are symptoms of asthma EXCEPT one. Which one is the EXCEPTION?
    A. hyperventilation
    B. dyspnea
    C. wheezing
    D. cyanosis

16. Tachycardia is characterized by an increase in
    A. pulse rate.
    B. respiration rate.
    C. body temperature.
    D. blood pressure.

17. The clinical manifestations of respiratory distress include all of the following EXCEPT one. Which one is the EXCEPTION?
    A. increased heart rate
    B. hypoventilation
    C. abnormal breathing noises
    D. coughing

18. Which of the following does NOT pertain to managing the patient experiencing a grand mal seizure?
    A. protect the patient from injury
    B. call 911
    C. patient is confused and has a headache during the postictal stage
    D. move patient to the floor for safety reasons

19. Predisposing factors of hyperventilation occur in all of the following patients EXCEPT one. Which one is the EXCEPTION?
    A. children
    B. those with acute anxiety
    C. those experiencing pain
    D. those 15 to 40 years old

20. Which of the following is a predisposing factor of acute myocardial infarction?
    A. males 70 to 80 years of age
    B. females 60 to 70 years of age
    C. obesity
    D. diet high in vitamin C

21. Dental therapy considerations for a patient with a history of angina would include all of the following EXCEPT one. Which one is the EXCEPTION?
    A. cease treatment if patient is sweating
    B. give oxygen during treatment
    C. use nitrous oxide during treatment
    D. keep patient in supine position if attack is under way

22. Destruction of the alveolar wall and loss of elastic recoil of the lungs are a result of which of the following disease processes?
    A. emphysema
    B. asthma
    C. acute pulmonary edema
    D. airway obstruction

23. The most common medical emergency in the dental office is
    A. diabetic coma.
    B. syncope.
    C. myocardial infarction.
    D. drug overdose reaction.

24. Exophthalmos, tachycardia, and nervousness are all signs of which of the following conditions?
    A. hypertension
    B. hypotension
    C. hyperthyroidism
    D. hypothyroidism

25. Which of the following conditions is NOT stress-induced?
    A. angina pectoris
    B. epilepsy
    C. orthostatic hypotension
    D. syncope

answers & rationales

1.

A. Glucocorticosteroid is the hormone lacking in acute adrenal insufficiency. The adrenal gland is made up of two glands, the cortex and the medulla. Cortisol, a glucocorticosteroid, is the most important product of the adrenal cortex and helps the body adapt to stress. Epinephrine is an adrenal hormone and a synthetic adrenergic vasoconstrictor used to treat asthmatic attacks, bronchospasm, and allergic reactions. Insulin is a hormone released by the pancreas to regulate blood glucose. Thyroxin (T_4) is a hormone of the thyroid gland that influences metabolic rate.

2.

D. A cerebrovascular accident (CVA) patient exhibiting normal blood pressure should be placed in a comfortable sitting position—upright or semiupright. An unconscious respiratory distress patient, a patient pregnant in her second trimester, and a syncope patient can be placed in a supine position.

3.

D. Patients with acute pulmonary edema usually experience symptoms such as tachypnea, extreme dyspnea with cyanosis, and pink frothy sputum. The symptoms of hyperventilation include a feeling of tightness, light-headedness, and palpation of the heart. An acute asthmatic episode is precipitated by nonallergic factors, and the patient usually experiences shortness of breath, wheezing, and coughing. A cerebrovascular accident (CVA) patient may experience the following: headache with blurred vision, aphasia, and altered consciousness.

4.

A. Hypoglycemia is the most common acute problem experienced by a diabetic. Its cause is most commonly due to a patient not eating or not eating enough after injection of insulin. Ketoacidosis, a complication of diabetes, results from an accumulation of ketone bodies as a result of an inadequate carbohydrate metabolism. It is characterized by acetone breath and mental confusion. Diabetics (hyperglycemics) are more prone to infections. Hypoinsulinism is a result of too little insulin.

5.

B. When a patient is hyperventilating, the most appropriate form of treatment is having the patient breathe into a paper bag or cupped hands. Epinephrine is contraindicated; the drug of choice is diazepam. It is also recommended to bring the patient to an upright position. Do not administer oxygen, because the patient needs more carbon dioxide to balance the system.

6.

A. The tourniquets, which are applied to the extremities, should be released 5 minutes at a time—not 10. Rotations of release and reapplication of tourniquets are continued until the patient has reached a medical facility. Phlebostasia is a synonym for bloodless phlebotomy.

7.

D. The initial treatment for syncope is to place the patient in a supine position. The next step is to place ammonia spirits under the patient's nose. Oxygen may be administered, but epinephrine is not recommended.

If bradycardia persists, an anticholinergic (atropine) may be administered.

8.

D. The diabetic patient is experiencing signs of hypoglycemia and should be given a substance containing sugar, such as orange juice. A patient should be given insulin when there is evidence of hyperglycemia. Oxygen and epinephrine are not recommended for the treatment of hypoglycemia. The patient will already be experiencing an increase in epinephrine and anxiety activities during the hypoglycemic state.

9.

D. Children usually do not experience orthostatic hypotension. Most generally, causes include prolonged periods of recumbency and convalescence, increased age, varicose veins, and the third trimester of pregnancy.

10.

B. Angina pectoris is due to an insufficient blood supply to the heart muscle. Coronary arteries are not providing the myocardium with an adequate supply of oxygen, causing myocardial ischemia. In treating this patient, the healthcare provider needs to practice stress-reduction protocol to minimize anxiety. Hyperoxia is a condition with abnormally high oxygen tension in the blood. Hypercalcemia refers to a greater amount of calcium in the blood.

11.

D. It is not recommended to administer oxygen to a hyperventilating patient. The patient needs to breathe in a gaseous mixture (7% CO_2 + 93% O_2) instead. As this is not available in most practices, it would be more likely to have the patient breathe into a paper bag or cupped hands. Always stop treatment first and place the patient in an upright position before continuing with the proper management steps.

12.

C. The conscious CVA patient should be placed in a comfortable position—upright or semiupright—instead of in a supine position. Then the vital signs should be taken. It would be appropriate to call the EMS and be ready to administer oxygen.

13.

C. Dyspnea refers to difficulty in breathing. Tachypnea refers to an increased respiratory rate. Orthopnea refers to the inability to breathe, except in an upright position, and apnea refers to no respiratory movement.

14.

B. Hyperventilation is an increase in frequency or depth of respiration. It is a common emergency situation experienced in dentistry because it is triggered as a result of extreme anxiety. With airway obstruction, patients with good airflow may experience a forceful cough, wheezing between coughs, and the ability to breathe. Individuals with poor air exchange may experience a weak cough and absent voice sounds. Hypoventilation does not meet metabolic demands and is common in acute asthmatic attacks.

15.

A. Hyperventilation is not a common symptom for asthmatics. However, they do experience dyspnea, wheezing, coughing, and cyanosis.

16.

A. Tachycardia is an increase in pulse rate. Tachypnea is an increase in respiratory rate. An increase in body temperature and blood pressure result in fever and hypertension, respectively.

17.

B. Hyperventilation, not hypoventilation, is a generalized problem associated with respiratory distress. Wheezing, coughing, and an increased heart rate are also clinical manifestations of respiratory distress.

18.

D. If the seizure occurs while the patient is in the dental chair, do not move the patient—place the chair in a supine position. Moving the patient could be difficult. However, if the patient is not seated and seizure develops, place the patient on the floor in a supine position. If the seizure continues longer than 5 minutes, summon medical assistance. In the meantime, it is important to protect the patient from injury. It is common for the patient to be confused and have a headache in the postictal stage.

19.

A. Hyperventilation rarely occurs in children, because they usually do not hide their fears. However, it can occur from acute anxiety and in individuals experiencing pain, metabolic acidosis, and drug intoxication. It is most generally experienced in adults between the ages of 15 and 40 years.

20.

C. Obesity is a prediposing factor of acute myocardial infarction. Other risk factors include coronary artery disease, being male (especially those in their 50s to 70s), and undue stress. A diet including vitamin C does not cause myocardial infarction.

21.

D. The patient experiencing angina should be placed in an upright position, not supine. If there is evidence of the patient sweating, treatment should cease. It is protocol to use nitrous oxide and oxygen during treatment.

22.

A. With emphysema, there is destruction of the alveolar wall and loss of elastic recoil of the lungs. With asthma, the lungs overdistend. The mucous plugs occlude the smaller bronchi, which results in a decreased size of the airway lumen. In acute pulmonary edema, fluid fills the alveolar spaces of the lungs from the pulmonary capillary bed. With complete airway obstruction, sympathetic outflow increases, causing an increase in blood pressure, heart rate, and respiratory rate.

23.

B. Fainting—a sudden loss of consciousness—is the most common medical emergency that occurs in the dental office. Diabetic coma, myocardial infarction, and drug overdose reaction are not the most frequently occurring medical emergencies in the dental office.

24.

C. Exophthalmos (bug-eyed), tachycardia, and nervousness are common characteristics found in individuals with hyperthyroidism. With hypothyroidism, common characteristics include apathy, fatigue, weak skeletal muscles, and decreased appetite, heart rate, and blood pressure. Hypertension involves an increase and hypotension a decrease in blood pressure.

25.

C. Orthostatic hypotension is a disorder of the autonomic nervous system in which the patient faints when assuming an upright position. It can be caused by prolonged periods of recumbency. Angina pectoris, epilepsy, and syncope are all stressed-induced conditions. Therefore, using a stressed-reduction protocol when dealing with these patients in the office is mandatory.

CHAPTER

14 Dental Materials

Jeffrey A. Platt, DDS, MS

contents

The science of dental materials encompasses substances used to restore or replace missing tooth structure, oral bone, and soft tissue.

I. INTRODUCTION

A. Difficulties of the oral environment

1. Physical demands—exceeds those typically required for construction
   a) Produce high stresses
   b) Create large temperature variations and pH changes
   c) Provide saline environment
2. Biological demands
   a) Require little or no toxic or allergenic potential
   b) Require little or no pulpal response because of high thermal and electrical conductivity
   c) Require no postoperative sensitivity and secondary decay through marginal leakage

B. Regulatory involvement—provides criteria for material performance

1. Food and Drug Administration (FDA)—regulates safety and efficacy of medical and dental materials and devices
2. Americal Dental Associaton (ADA)—Council on Scientific Affairs provides a certification program for materials, which is not required for a material to be marketed
   a) ADA Seal Acceptance Program
   b) ADA Specification Program
3. International bodies include International Standards Organization (ISO) and Fédération Dentaire Internationale (FDI)—provide guidelines for international standards
4. Occupational Safety and Health Administration (OSHA)—provides guidelines for safety and welfare of those in the workplace
   a) ADA Regulatory Compliance Manual
   b) Materials Safety Data Sheet (MSDS)

C. Dental restorations

1. Direct restorations—fabricated directly in oral cavity
2. Indirect restorations—fabricated using cast replica of oral structures involved
   a) Inlay—replaces intracoronal tooth structure and is cemented to tooth structure
   b) Crown—replaces extracoronal tooth structure and is cemented to tooth structure or an implant
   c) Fixed partial denture (bridge)—replaces missing tooth or teeth and is cemented to adjacent teeth or implants
   d) Removable partial denture—replaces missing teeth and is often retained with aid of clasps
   e) Complete denture—replaces fully edentulous arch

II. STRUCTURES AND PROPERTIES OF DENTAL MATERIALS

A. Characteristics of *solids*

1. Definition—matter that occupies definite volume of space and whose shape does not depend on a container
2. Types
   a) *Crystalline solids*—regularly arranged atoms in a lattice configuration (rigid); (e.g., metals and gypsum products)
   b) *Amorphous solids* (literally means without form)—randomly arranged atoms that have some liquid characteristics (e.g., glass)

B. Bonding and adhesion

1. Mechanical bonding (retention)
   a) Responsible for retention of most dental restorations, therefore used frequently in dentistry
      (1) Dental amalgam restorations
      (2) Zinc phosphate cement
      (3) Micromechanical retention of bonded restorations
   b) Involves secondary bonding forces because no primary bonds are formed
2. Adhesion and cohesion
   a) Definitions
      (1) *Adhesion*—creates force that causes *unlike* molecules to attach to one another; examples include resin to enamel and plaque to tooth structure
      (2) *Cohesion*—creates force that causes *like* molecules to attach to one another; examples include welding and direct gold restorations
   b) Types of molecular interaction
      (1) Primary—result of forming chemical bonds; systems based on polyacrylic acid demonstrate primary bonding
         (a) Zinc polycarboxylate cements
         (b) Glass ionomer cements
      (2) Secondary
         (a) Involves physical forces with no chemical union
         (b) Most common type
         (c) Examples include van der Waals forces and hydrogen bonding
3. *Wetting*—required for an adhesive to function well with a given adherend
   a) *Contact angle*—ability of an adhesive to wet an adherend; internal angle formed when an adhesive is placed on an adherend
   b) Good adhesive has a contact angle that approaches 0

C. Stress and strain

1. Definitions
   a) *Stress*—internal force developed within an object when an external load is applied = Force/Area (lb/in^2 or MN/m^2)

b) *Strain*—change in shape caused by a given stress; has no dimensions $(L-L_0)/(L_0)$

2. Types of stress and strain
   a) Compressive stress occurs when structure is compressed
   b) Tensile stress occurs when structure is stretched or elongated
   c) Shear stress occurs when one portion of structure is forced to slide by another portion
   d) Complex stresses and strains are combinations of compressive, tensile, and shear
      (1) Torsion
      (2) Flexion
      (3) Diametral tensile
   e) Elastic strain disappears when stress is removed
3. *Proportional limit*
   a) Stress and strain are directly proportional until proportional limit is reached
   b) Stresses above proportional limit create plastic strain or permanent deformation
   c) Essentially equal to elastic limit
4. *Modulus of elasticity* (MOE)—also known as *Elastic modulus* or *Young's modulus*
   a) Defines rigidity of material under stresses at or below proportional limit
   b) Equal to stress divided by strain at or below proportional limit
5. *Toughness*
   a) Describes ability of material to resist fracture
   b) Defined by area under entire stress-strain curve
6. *Resilience*
   a) Describes ability of material to resist permanent deformation
   b) Defined by area under stress-strain curve up to the proportional limit
7. *Strength*
   a) Defined as greatest stress that can be withstood without rupture
   b) Determined by using compressive, tensile, or shear stresses

D. Ductility and malleability

1. *Ductility*—ability of material to withstand deformation under tension without fracturing
   a) Measurement of ductility—Percentage of elongation is used to communicate ductility and equals increase in length ÷ original length × 100 when a wire is fractured under tension
   b) May be determined by reduction in a cross-sectional area at fractured ends of a wire broken under tension
   c) Low ductility indicates brittleness in a material
2. *Malleability*—ability of a material to withstand deformation under compression

E. Flow and creep

1. *Flow*—continual permanent deformation under load of an amorphous or noncrystalline solid

2. *Creep*—tendency of crystalline solid to deform under a constantly applied load

F. Hardness and *abrasion resistance*

1. *Hardness*—ability of material to resist penetration
2. Restorative materials with high hardness tend to resist abrasion

G. Rheology—study of the flow of liquids

1. *Viscosity*—resistance of a liquid to flow
2. *Thixotropic* materials experience a lowering of viscosity (thinning) with mechanical stimulation (mixing)

H. Thermophysical properties

1. *Thermal conductivity*—ability to transmit heat
   a) Metals, such as gold alloys and dental amalgam, are good thermal conductors
   b) Human enamel, dentin, dental cements, and composite resins are insulators and poor thermal conductors
2. *Linear coefficient of thermal expansion*
   a) Expansion or contraction of a material per unit length when experiencing a temperature change of 1°C
   b) Ideally, restorative material has linear coefficient of thermal expansion equal to that of tooth structure
   c) Differences in linear coefficient of thermal expansion may cause microleakage between restoration and tooth structure

I. Color

1. Dimensions
   a) *Hue*—predominant wavelengths present (e.g., color of an object—red or blue)
   b) *Chroma*—strength (saturation) of hue or how much of wavelength is being seen
   c) *Value*—luminance or how bright or dark object is
2. Definitions
   a) *Metamerism*—colors that look different under different light sources
   b) *Fluorescence*—absorption of nonvisible light released by material as visible light
   c) *Opacity*—degree to which passage of light is prevented
   d) *Translucency*—dispersion of light through a material such that objects cannot be seen through it
   e) *Transparent*—passage of minimally distorted light through a material such that objects may be clearly seen through it
3. Shade guides are used to communicate color between practitioners, technicians, and patients

J. Solidification reactions

1. Physical reaction—solidification through change in physical state by cooling or drying with no chemical reaction
2. Chemical reaction—solidification through formation of new chemical bonds within structure

III. GYPSUM PRODUCTS—gypsum is a common sulfate material

A. Chemical component—consists of calcium sulfate dihydrate ($CaSO_4 \cdot 2H_2O$)

B. Setting mechanism

1. Manufacturer makes calcium sulfate hemihydrate $(CaSO_4)_2 \cdot H_2O$
   a) Mineral is first mined
   b) Then it is heated and water is driven off; method of driving off water determines gypsum type
      (1) *Plaster*—result of heating gypsum at atmospheric pressure
      (2) *Dental stone*—result of heating gypsum under steam pressure
      (3) *Die stone*—result of dehydrating gypsum in calcium chloride
2. User adds water to calcium sulfate hemihydrate to recreate calcium sulfate dihydrate—an exothermic reaction
3. Definitions
   a) *Exothermic reaction*—gives off heat as components react
   b) *Endothermic reaction*—absorbs heat as components react
   c) *Models*—replicate tissues used for study
   d) *Casts*—produce accurate replicas used for fabrication of appliances or restorations
   e) *Dies*—produce casts of one or more teeth used for fabrication of restoration
4. Setting of hemihydrate
   a) Calcium sulfate hemihydrate (plaster/stone) + water → calcium sulfate dihydrate (gypsum) + heat
   b) Crystals form from center—nucleus of crystallization
   c) Branches from crystal growth intertwine to form solid mass

C. Effect of water properties

1. Improper amount of water will adversely affect strength and setting expansion
2. Lower water/powder ratio (within limits) gives increased physical properties

D. Types and classification

1. Type I: Impression plaster—W/P ratio = 0.50–0.75 ml/g
2. Type II: Laboratory or model plaster—W/P ratio = 0.45–0.50 ml/g
3. Type III: Laboratory stone—W/P ratio = 0.28–0.30 ml/g
4. Type IV: Die stone—W/P ratio = 0.22–0.24 ml/g
5. Type V: High-strength, high expansion die stone—W/P ratio = 0.18–0.22 ml/g

E. Handling issues (manipulation)

1. Proportioning—use proportioned powder and water; important for accuracy
2. Mixing—add powder to water; use vibration or vacuum to minimize porosity
3. Control of setting time
   a) Manufacturer methods of control

(1) Decreasing setting time
(a) Leave more dihydrate crystals (nuclei of crystallization) in the powder
(b) Use accelerators (e.g., potassium sulfate)
(2) Increasing setting time—use retarders (e.g., borax)
b) Operator methods of control
(1) Decreasing setting time—use longer and more rapid mixing or slurry water
(2) Increasing setting time—increase water/powder ratio (more water)
4. Care of powder and set products
a) Store powder in airtight, dry containers
b) Lose detail of set cast under running water
5. Properties
a) Dental stones are stronger and harder than plaster
b) More water required in mix yields less interaction of dihydrate crystals and therefore lowers strength and hardness
c) Excess water (free water) is needed to mix gypsum and decreases strength and hardness
d) *Dry strength* (free water evaporated) is two to three times greater than wet strength (free water present)

IV. DENTAL IMPRESSION MATERIALS

A. *Inelastic materials*—used in edentulous areas and primary dentition

1. Impression compound
a) *Thermoplastic*—made soft and moldable by increasing its temperature and hardened by lowering temperature
b) Supplied as plates or sticks
c) Accomplish uniform heating in a water bath and with adequate time because of a low thermal conductivity; heating above 45°C to 50°C will damage oral tissues
d) Disinfect by immersing 10 to 30 minutes in a glutaraldehyde or an iodophor
2. Zinc oxide-eugenol (ZOE) impression paste
a) ZnO (base paste) + eugenol (catalyst paste) → Zinc eugenolate + unreacted ZnO
(1) Catalyst contains 12% to 15% eugenol
(2) Eugenol—main component of oil of cloves
b) Mix paste on oil-impervious surface
c) Heat and moisture decrease setting time
d) Coat patient's lips with petroleum jelly before impression is made
e) Accomplish clean up with orange solvent
f) Disinfect by immersing 10 to 30 minutes in glutaraldehyde or an iodophor

B. *Elastic materials*—appropriate for areas with tooth or bony undercuts

1. Definition—material assumes its original form after load is removed

2. Aqueous materials
   a) *Hydrocolloids*—fine-sized particles (< 1 μm) dispersed in water
      (1) Dimensinal stability—depends on fluid content
         (a) Syneresis—results in shrinkage due to exuding and evaporation of fluid
         (b) Imbibition—results in swelling when water is absorbed
   b) *Alginate* (irreversible hydrocolloid)—solution transfers to gel
      (1) Major components—potassium alginate and calcium sulfate
      (2) Minor components—zinc oxide, potassium titanium fluoride, diatomaceous earth, trisodium phosphate, antimicrobials
      (3) Chemical setting reaction—potassium alginate + calcium sulfate → potassium sulfate + calcium alginate
      (4) Shelf life—approximately 1 year, shortened by exposure to heat or moisture
      (5) ADA types
         (a) Type I (fast-setting)—1 to 2 minutes
         (b) Type II (normal setting)—2 to 4.5 minutes
      (6) Handling concerns
         (a) Increase gelation time by using cool water
         (b) Pour soon after making impression
      (7) Common uses—study models, primary impressions, bleaching trays, athletic mouthguards, orthodontic retainers
      (8) Advantages—low cost, ease of manipulation, adequate accuracy for many uses
      (9) Disadvantages—does not reproduce fine detail and unable to store for prolonged periods
      (10) Disinfect by spraying with glutaraldehyde or iodophor and place in sealed plastic bag for 10 minutes
   c) Agar-agar (reversible hydrocolloid)—hydrocolloid, water-based impression material
      (1) Components—include 8% to 15% agar, 85% water, borax and potassium sulfate
      (2) Advantages—inexpensive material, easy clean up, hydrophilic
      (3) Disadvantages—expensive start-up costs and not dimensionally stable for long periods
      (4) Preparation of material—requires boiling to create a sol, which is stored at an elevated temperature until use
      (5) Handling—tray material must be conditioned and syringe material is used straight from storage
      (6) Material gels when cooled—thermoplastic (physical) reaction
      (7) Clinical applications—produce accurate impressions for indirect restorations
      (8) Disinfect by spraying with glutaraldehyde, iodophor, or hypochlorite solution and placing in a sealed plastic bag for 10 minutes

3. Nonaqueous elastomers (rubber impression materials)
   a) Various viscosities available—include low, medium, high, and very high
   b) Tray adhesives are type-specific
   c) Clinical applications—any type of indirect restoration, bite registration, or whenever accuracy is desired
   d) Set by chemical reaction called polymerization
      (1) *Condensation polymerization* forms by-products and is less dimensionally stable
      (2) *Addition polymerization* forms no by-products and is more dimensionally stable
   e) Disinfect by
      (1) Immersing in glutaraldahyde or iodophor solution for 10 minutes (2 to 3 minutes in a chlorine solution for polyethers)
      (2) Spray with solution and place in sealed bag for 10 minutes
   f) Types
      (1) *Polysulfide rubber*
         (a) Composition—low-molecular-weight mercaptan polymer, sulfur, lead dioxide, copper hydroxide, and peroxides
         (b) Advantages—high flexibility and tear strength
         (c) Disadvantages—long working and setting times; high shrinkage on setting and stains
         (d) Forms water as a by-product
      (2) Condensation silicone rubber (polysiloxane)
         (a) Composition—silicone polymer (polysiloxane), silica, alkyl silicate, and tin octoate
         (b) Advantages—shorter setting time and has easy cleanup
         (c) Disadvantages—poor dimensional stability and wettability by gypsum
         (d) Forms ethyl alcohol as a by-product
      (3) Addition polymerizing silicone (polyvinyl siloxane)
         (a) Composition—vinyl siloxane, hydrogen siloxane, chloroplatinic acid and fillers
         (b) Advantages—excellent dimensional stability, easy cleanup, short setting time
         (c) Disadvantages—low flexibility and poor tear resistance and wettability by gypsum
         (d) Forms no by-product
         (e) May release hydrogen gas—pour should be delayed 45 to 60 minutes
         (f) Available in a gun and cartridge self-mixing system
         (g) Setting may be inhibited by contact with other impression materials or latex
      (4) Polyether rubber
         (a) Composition—polyether, sulfonic acid ester, and a body modifier to reduce stiffness

(b) Advantages—short working and setting times,excellent dimensional stability and good wettability by gypsum

(c) Disadvantages—low flexibility and poor tear resistance

V. DENTAL POLYMERS

A. Definitions

1. *Thermoplastic*—molded without chemical reaction taking place; change is able to occur owing to temperature changes
2. *Thermosetting*—chemical change takes place during molding
3. *Polymerization*—conversion of low-molecular weight compounds (monomers) to high-molecular weight compounds (polymers)
4. *Cross-linking*—forms a network through joining of adjacent polymer chains
5. *Copolymer*—contains two or more different monomers
6. *Composite*—physical mixture of insoluble materials; properties are superior or intermediate to those of component materials

B. Methods of polymerization induction—addition of energy to a monomer

1. Heat-activated through activating benzoyl peroxide
2. Chemically activated—often benzoyl peroxide activated by a tertiary amine
3. Light-activated through activating camphoroquinone or amines
4. Microwave activated

C. *Acrylic*—includes family of compounds derived from acrylic acid

1. Polymethylmethacrylate (PMMA)—monomer is methyl methacrylate
   - a) Characteristics
     - (1) Polymerization shrinkage—6% to 7%
     - (2) Water absorption—causes slight swelling of material
       - (a) Drying material will cause it to shrink
       - (b) Acrylic appliances should be stored in water
     - (3) Thermal insulator—inhibits patient perception of hot and cold
     - (4) High coefficient of thermal expansion and contraction
   - b) Clinical applications—involve denture bases, artificial teeth, orthodontic retainers, and removable appliances
   - c) Handling considerations
     - (1) Distorts at higher temperatures; appliances should not be cleaned in hot water
     - (2) Low abrasion resistance requires use of a soft brush when cleaning acrylic appliances
     - (3) Residual monomer may cause soft tissue irritation or allergic reaction
   - d) Denture liners
     - (1) Used for patients with soft tissue irritations
     - (2) Long-term liners (soft liners) may function for a prolonged time in patients with severe bony undercuts or sore ridges

(3) Short-term liners (tissue conditioners) are used to aid in healing of soft tissue over a period of days
(4) Composition
(a) Soft liners—plasticized acrylic copolymers, silicone rubber or fluoroelastomers
(b) Tissue conditioners—PMMA with high levels of plasticizers such as alcohol
(5) Properties
(a) Liners flow under low pressure
(b) Hardness is low initially but may increase as plasticizers are leached out during use
(c) Resilience and elasticity are high initially, but may decrease as plasticizers are leached out during use

D. Direct esthetic materials

1. Clinical indications
   a) Anterior restorations
   b) Conservative posterior restorations
   c) Veneers
   d) Cores for cast restorations
2. Composition of dental composites
   a) Resin matrix—includes BIS-GMA or UDMA (urethane dimethacrylate) with low-molecular-weight diluents such as TEGDMA
   b) *Fillers*—components used to reinforce matrix; quartz, glasses (lithium, barium, strontium are radiopaque), colloidal silica
   c) *Coupling agent*—organosilane in which silane bonds to filler and organic portion bonds to matrix
3. Classification
   a) Polymerization systems
      (1) *Chemically activated resins*—benzoyl peroxide initiator and tertiary amine activator in two pastes
      (2) *Visible light-activated resins*—peroxide or diketone initiator and amine accelerator in one paste
      (3) *Dual-activated resins*—chemical and visible light-activated components present in two-paste system
   b) Filler particle size
      (1) *Conventional or macrofill composite*—quartz or glass (range of 1 to 100 μm and an average of 8 to 12 μm)
      (2) *Microfilled composite*—silica or prepolymerized resin fillers (range of 0.01 to 0.1 μm and an average of 0.04 μm)
      (3) *Small-particle composite*—medium-sized particles (range of 0.1 to 10 μm and an average of 1.0 to 3.0 μm)
      (4) *Hybrid composite*—cross between the small particle and microfilled (range of 0.01 to 3 μm with an average of 0.5 to 1 μm)
      (5) *Flowable*—maintains decreased level of filler to allow for improved flow properties (average filler size of 0.7 to 1.5 μm)

c) Matrix includes
   (1) BIS-GMA
   (2) UDMA (urethane dimethacrylate)
   (3) TEGDMA—used as a matrix diluent

4. Advantages and disadvantages of different classes—choice of material is dependent on need for strength or esthetics
   a) Conventional
      (1) Physical and mechanical properties are significantly improved over unfilled resin
      (2) Surface roughness and wear are high
   b) Microfilled
      (1) Surface roughness is very low; esthetics are good
      (2) Physical and mechanical properties are lower than other composites
   c) Small-particle—physical and mechanical properties are the best of any composite
   d) Hybrid
      (1) Often referred to as all-purpose resins
      (2) Physical and mechanical properties are between conventional and small-particle composite resins
      (3) Surface roughness approaches microfilled
   e) *Compomers*
      (1) Contain composite resins with fluoride-releasing glasses
      (2) Used for Class III and V restorations and pediatric lesions
5. Acid etch—conditioning agents
   a) Enamel
      (1) Apply 37% phosphoric acid for 15 to 60 seconds
         (a) Deciduous teeth and highly fluoridated enamel require more etch time
         (b) Manufacturer's instructions may vary
      (2) Produces pitting due to partial demineralization of surface
   b) Dentin
      (1) Use phosphoric acid, ethylenediamine tetraacetic acid (EDTA), polyacrylic acid, citric acid, maleic acid, or nitric acid
      (2) Acid removes smear layer and demineralizes surface leaving exposed collagen
      (3) Allows for formation of hybrid layer
6. Bonding agents
   a) Definitions
      (1) *Smear layer*—adhered debris formed on the dentin surface by a dental instrument during cavity preparation
      (2) Bonding—forms resin layer that connects prepared tooth surface to overlying restoration
      (3) *Hydrophobic*—water "hating," which characterizes restorative resins
      (4) *Hydrophilic*—water "loving," which characterizes a portion of dentin primers

b) Enamel
   (1) Use unfilled or lightly filled resin
   (2) Use is common in orthodontic bonding systems and in repairing fractured composite restorations
c) Dentin
   (1) Vital dentin is a moist substrate; hydrophobic resins will not bond to it
   (2) Hydrophilic/hydrophobic primer wets dentinal collagen to form a hybrid layer
   (3) Bonding resin interacts with hydrophobic portion of primer and restorative composite resin
   (4) Primer and bonding resin may be combined in one bottle
d) Amalgam bonding agents bond to enamel, dentin, and dental amalgam during placement of amalgam restorations
e) Primer components include
   (1) Hydrophobic monomers
   (2) Hydrophilic monomers such as hydroxyethyl methacrylate (HEMA)
f) Bonding agent components include
   (1) BIS-GMA or UDMA
   (2) Often a hydrophilic monomer such as HEMA is added
g) Retention is primarily due to micromechanical interaction
h) If demineralized collagen is not thoroughly surrounded by bonding agent, hydrolysis of collagen can occur
i) Biological concerns
   (1) Conditioners can be irritating to soft tissues if placed in direct contact
   (2) Some uncured priming monomers, such as HEMA, are allergens for some people

7. Pit and fissure sealants
   a) Applications include
      (1) Deep pits and fissures of newly erupted posterior teeth
      (2) Lingual fissures of anterior teeth
      (3) Patients with active *Streptococcus mutans*
      (4) Combining with composite resins as a preventive resin restoration
   b) Polymerization
      (1) Self-cure (amine accelerator)
      (2) Light-cured (light accelerator)
   c) Composition includes
      (1) Unfilled or lightly filled composite resin matrix; matrix is BIS-GMA or UDMA with diluent such as TEGDMA
      (2) Initiator—benzoyl peroxide in self-cured and diketone in light-cured
      (3) Accelerator—an amine
      (4) Opaque filler—makes material detectable on tooth surfaces
      (5) Filler—may be added in small amounts
      (6) Fluoride may be present

- d) Physical and mechanical properties
  - (1) Wetting of enamel is best accomplished with low-viscosity resins
  - (2) Low-wear resistance allows loss of material from self-cleansing areas
  - (3) Cleaning with air abrasion units can cause rapid destruction of sealants
  - (4) Retention of sealant is result of mechanical bonding
- e) Clinical efficacy
  - (1) 100% caries prevention may be achieved if retention occurs
  - (2) Regular 6- or 12-month evaluations are needed to evaluate retention of sealant
  - (3) Lost sealant should be reapplied

E. Mouth protectors

1. Types
   - a) *Stock*—provides least protection
   - b) *Mouth-formed*—fits better than stock trays
   - c) *Custom-made*—best-fitting and most comfortable of all choices
2. Properties
   - a) Include semirigid, soft plastics such as polyvinylacetate or polyethylene
   - b) Thermoplastic inserts—can soften and mold after heating
   - c) Maintain minimal strength and tear resistance
3. Steps in fabrication of custom mouth protectors
   - a) Make maxillary impression with alginate impression material
   - b) Fabricate cast from gypsum product
   - c) Heated polymer is vacuum-adapted to cast
   - d) Remove from cast and trim 1/8-inch short of labial fold
4. Care of mouth protectors
   - a) Rinse after each use
   - b) Occasionally clean with soap and cool water
   - c) Do not use alcohol solutions or denture cleansers
   - d) Avoid chewing, clenching, or grinding during wear—shortens lifetime of appliance

VI. METALS

A. Definitions

1. *Pure metal*—any chemical element that forms a positive ion in chemical reaction or in solution (e.g., gold)
2. *Alloy*—combination of pure metals that are mutually soluble in molten state
3. *Freezing temperature*—temperature at which liquid metal becomes solid
4. *Melting temperature*—temperature at which solid metal becomes liquid; if temperature change is slow, freezing temperature equals melting temperature
5. *Latent heat of solidification*—heat loss during freezing; equals calories of heat liberated from 1 gram of substance changing from liquid to solid

6. *Latent heat of fusion*—absorbed heat as solid changes to liquid
7. *Grains*—individual crystals of solid metal
8. *Grain boundaries*—edges of crystals in metal
9. *Grain size*—determines strength and ductility of metal; fine-grained alloys are generally stronger and more ductile
10. *As cast*—metal or alloy that has been allowed to solidify after melting
11. *Wrought metal*—as-cast metal that is worked or shaped
12. *Strain hardening*—produces increase in strength and hardness when proportional limit is exceeded

B. Direct filling gold

1. Pure gold is condensed directly into a cavity preparation to create cohesive bonding within the gold
2. Functions as a wrought metal; strength comes from strain hardening
3. Of all metals, gold is most resistant to corrosion and most ductile and malleable

C. *Corrosion*—involves loss of surface caused by chemical attack

1. Most corrosion is electrochemical and requires
   a) Corroding metal surface
   b) Electrical conductor to carry electrons
   c) Second surface for reduction reaction
   d) Electrolyte that bathes system
2. Variations in oxygen concentration on different areas of restoration can increase corrosion activity
3. Methods of providing corrosion resistance include
   a) Polishing metal surfaces
   b) Preventing dissimilar metal contact
   c) Noble metal (gold, platinum, palladium) in alloy
   d) Metal that passivates—forms an oxide layer (aluminum, chromium, titanium)—in the alloy

VII. DENTAL AMALGAM

A. Definition

1. Amalgam—alloy that contains mercury
2. Amalgam alloy—formulated as powder particles containing silver, tin, copper, zinc
3. Dental amalgam—dental alloy containing mercury that has reacted with an amalgam alloy

B. Use—confined to replacement of posterior tooth structure and as retrofill material in endodontic surgery

C. Classification

1. Copper content—increased amount of copper increases strength, hardness, setting expansion, and corrosion resistance of amalgam alloy
   a) Traditional (low-copper) alloy—contains less than 6% copper in alloy powder

(1) Contents
(a) Silver—68%–70%
(b) Tin—26%–27%
(c) Copper—4%–5%
(d) Zinc—0%–1%

b) *High-copper amalgam*—contains greater than 6% copper in alloy powder (enough copper to suppress the gamma-2 phase)
(1) Contents
(a) Silver—40%–70%
(b) Tin—22%–30%
(c) Copper—13%–30%
(d) Zinc—0%–1%

2. By-powder particles
a) *Lathe-cut alloy*—powder produced by grinding or cutting alloy into small particles
b) *Spherical alloy*—powder produced by spraying molten alloy and allowing it to solidify as tiny spheres
c) *Admixed high-copper (dispersion) alloy*—mixes a low-copper lathe-cut powder with second, copper-rich spherical powder
d) *Single composition high-copper alloy*—contains single copper-rich powder

D. Structure

1. Setting reactions
a) Low-copper alloy consists of mercury + silver-tin → silver-tin + silver-mercury + tin-mercury
b) High-copper alloy
(1) Types
(a) Single composition alloy consists of mercury + silver-tin-copper → silver-tin-copper + silver-mercury + silver-copper
(b) Admixed alloy consists of mercury + silver-tin + silver-copper → silver-tin + silver-copper + silver-mercury + copper-tin

2. Phases
a) Gamma—original alloy; strongest and most corrosion-resistant
b) Gamma-1—silver-mercury portion of set amalgam
c) Gamma-2—tin-mercury portion of low-copper amalgams; weakest, most corrosive of phases
d) Eta—copper-tin, replaces gamma-2 in matrix of high-copper amalgams; improves strength and corrosion resistance

E. Properties

1. Dimensional change owing to hardening of amalgam
a) High setting expansion can cause postoperative pain
b) High mercury alloy ratios create increased setting expansion
c) Increased trituration (amalgamation) reduces amount of setting expansion

2. Strength
   a) Requires several days to achieve maximum strength
   b) Compressive strength—45,000 to 70,000 psi
   c) Low early strength leads to bulk fracture
   d) Spherical high-copper amalgams have higher early strength than others
   e) Strength is decreased with increased mercury content and porosity
   f) Patient should not chew on new restorations for several hours
3. Creep—result of metal (under fixed stress) undergoing continual plastic deformation
   a) Values greater than 1% correlate to increased marginal breakdown
   b) Associated with gamma-2 phase
   c) High-copper amalgams have less than 1% creep
4. Corrosion
   a) Slows marginal leakage of restorations
   b) Low-copper amalgams corrode more than high-copper amalgams

F. Manipulation

1. Alloy selection
   a) Alloy must meet clinical requirements for strength
   b) Handling preferences play large role in selection
2. Proportioning alloy and mercury
   a) Preproportioned capsules standardize technique
   b) Convenient capsules eliminate bulk mercury in dental office
   c) Disposable capsules are not infection-control problem
3. *Trituration* (mixing of dental amalgam)
   a) Mechanical amalgamators
      (1) Allow for miminum amount of mercury in mix
      (2) Possess variable time and speed settings
      (3) Settings dependent on product
   b) Length of trituration
      (1) Low-copper—10 to 20 seconds
      (2) High-copper—5 to 10 seconds
      (3) Overtriturated amalgam is difficult to remove from capsule and has little tendency to hold its form
      (4) Undertriturated amalgam is dull in appearance and crumbly
4. Condensation
   a) Objectives
      (1) Adapt amalgam to prepared cavity walls, matrix, and margins
      (2) Develop uniform, compact mass with minimum voids
      (3) Reduce residual mercury content in final restoration
   b) Requirements
      (1) Place and condense amalgam in small increments
      (2) Place force with hand condenser as great as clinical situation allows
      (3) Use larger tipped condensers with spherical amalgams because they are more fluid
      (4) Apply within 3 minutes after trituration

5. Moisture contamination—avoid by using a dry-field technique; causes
   a) Delayed expansion in zinc-containing alloys
   b) Loss of strength in some spherical high-copper alloys
6. Finishing and polishing
   a) Perform carving and burnishing at time of placement
   b) Delay polishing for 24 hours
      (1) Produces a more corrosion-resistant restoration
      (2) Accomplish during dental prophylaxis by using rubber points and abrasives
      (3) Avoid heat generation because mercury is released above 60°C (140°F)

G. Mercury

1. Function of mercury in dental amalgam
   a) Provides moldable mass because it is liquid at room temperature
   b) Decreases strength of restoration if there is too much or too little; required amount is ≤ 50%
2. Toxicity
   a) Pathways of entry into human body
      (1) Absorbs through skin
      (2) Inhalation of mercury vapor and airborne particles is of greatest concern
      (3) Through food, water, air, dental, or medical sources; amount of mercury entering from dental restoration has been shown to be small compared with other sources
   b) Lethal forms—methyl and ethyl (organic) mercury; metallic mercury is least toxic
   c) Maximum safe environmental concentration of mercury vapor in air is noted to be 50 μg (0.05 mg) Hg/m^3 on average over a 40-hour work week
   d) Patient's allergic reaction is small, but possible risk
3. Handling precautions
   a) AVOID handling with bare skin
   b) Clean spills with an Hg absorbing kit, not a vacuum cleaner, to avoid vaporization
   c) AVOID heating mercury or teeth with amalgam restorations owing to generation of high levels of mercury vapor
      (1) Do not sterilize in an autoclave
   d) Mix in single-use, tightly sealed capsules
   e) Store spent amalgam under water or fixer in tightly sealed container
   f) Use amalgamators with covers

VIII. DENTAL CASTING ALLOYS

A. Definitions

1. *Precious metal*—possesses intrinsic monetary value; includes gold, silver, platinum, and palladium
2. *Noble metal*—precious metals resistant to corrosion

3. Base metal—alloys that are reactive or corrosive
4. Passivation—forms an oxide layer on base metal that provides corrosion resistance
5. *Karat*—parts of pure gold in 24 parts of alloy; 75% gold alloy is 18 karat
6. *Fineness*—parts of pure gold in 1000 parts of alloy; 75% gold alloy is 750 fine

B. Noble metal alloy

1. Classification (ADA Specification No. 5)
   a) Type I—83% noble metals (used for small inlays with low stress)
   b) Type II—78% noble metals (used for inlays)
   c) Type III—78% noble metals (used for onlays, crowns, and bridges)
   d) Type IV—75% noble metals (used for long span bridges and partial dentures)
2. Components
   a) Gold—provides corrosion resistance
   b) Copper—strengthens and reddens alloy
   c) Silver—counteracts copper reddening
   d) Platinum—raises melting point and whitens alloy
   e) Palladium—raises melting point and reduces silver tarnish
   f) Zinc—deoxidizes and cleanses during melting and casting process

C. Base metal partial denture casting alloys

1. Composition contains not less than 85% of nickel, cobalt, and chromium
2. Components
   a) Chromium provides passivation and corrosion resistance
   b) Cobalt increases rigidity of alloy
   c) Nickel increases ductility of alloy
   d) Beryllium decreases melting temperature of alloy
   e) Molybdenum strengthens alloy
   f) Silicon and manganese aid in castability of alloy
3. Considerations
   a) More difficult to cast, finish, and polish than noble metal alloys
   b) Density is approximately half that of Type IV gold alloys so partial denture frameworks can be thinner and lighter
   c) Up to 10% of population may have nickel sensitivity
   d) Beryllium is toxic and can be released with grinding
   e) Work hardening leads to clasp fracture
   f) Chlorine causes a rapid corrosive attack; therefore these alloys should not be immersed in chlorine solutions such as bleach

D. Metal-ceramic alloy (MC)—also termed porcelain-fused-to-metal (PFM)

1. Used as substructure for dental porcelain in crowns and bridges
2. Requirements
   a) Must have melting point higher than porcelain-fusing temperature to allow addition of porcelain to alloy

b) Thermal coefficient of expansion must be compatible with porcelain to avoid fracture of porcelain
c) Must provide mechanism for chemically bonding to porcelain
d) Must be biocompatible

3. Components
   a) High-gold alloys
      (1) 98% gold, platinum, and palladium
      (2) 2% iron, tin, and indium
   b) Palladium-silver alloys
      (1) 50% to 60% palladium
      (2) 30% to 40% silver
      (3) Lower percentage of base metals for hardening
   c) Nickel-chromium
      (1) 70% to 80% nickel
      (2) 15% chromium
      (3) 5% to 15% aluminum, beryllium, molybdenum, and manganese

E. Alternative casting alloys

1. Low-gold alloys have < 75% gold and physical properties comparable to ADA Type III and IV gold alloys
2. Silver-palladium alloys are "white" and have properties comparable to ADA Type III and IV gold alloys

F. Dental solders

1. Terminology
   a) *Soldering*—joining metal components together by fusion with alloy that melts below 500°C
   b) *Brazing*—joining metal components together by fusion with alloy that melts above 500°C
   c) *Welding*—melting and alloying of pieces to be joined
   d) *Flux*—low melting compound that removes and prevents oxidation
2. Technical considerations
   a) Solder must melt below melting temperature of components being joined
   b) Solder used to fabricate porcelain-fused-to-metal restorations must not soften during firing of porcelain
   c) Gold solders are identified with two numbers (e.g., 16-650 is a 650 fine solder to be used with a 16 karat gold alloy)
   d) Silver solders are used to join wires and other components in fabrication of orthodontic appliances

IX. WAXES

A. Types

1. Pattern waxes—use inlay, casting, and baseplate in fabrication of inlays, onlays, crowns, pontics, bridges, partial dentures, and bases for setting denture teeth
2. Processing waxes—use boxing, utility, sticky, and carding as auxiliary materials to aid in production of casts, extension of impression trays, and temporary attachment of solid objects

3. Impression waxes—use corrective impression and bite registration to register tooth or soft tissue positions

B. Components

1. Base waxes—possess high-molecular-weight esters and alcohols such as paraffin
2. Modifying waxes—use carnauba, gum dammar, beeswax, ceresin, and synthetic to modify handling properties
3. Additives—produce desired color for wax

C. Properties

1. Thermoplastic
2. Possess high coefficient of thermal expansion
3. Degrade (burn) into CO_2 and H_2O
4. Possess flow, brittleness, stiffness, hardness, and strength depending on modifying waxes

X. INDIRECT ESTHETIC RESTORATIONS

A. Terminology

1. *Ceramic*—material composed of metal bonded to nonmetal
2. *Porcelain*—ceramic commonly used in dentistry
3. *Fusion temperature*—temperature at which grains of porcelain powder fuse to form ceramic mass
4. *Sinter*—process of fusing particles together without completely melting them
5. *Frit*—consists of fine porcelain powder provided by manufacturer
6. *Glaze*—creates smooth, translucent surface similar to enamel in appearance

B. Dental porcelain

1. Classification
   a) High-fusing porcelain (used for denture teeth)
   b) Medium-fusing porcelain (used for all ceramic restorations)
   c) Low-fusing porcelain (used for metal-ceramic restorations)
2. Components
   a) Primary components include quartz and feldspar
   b) Metal oxides are added to control color, opacity, and fluorescence
   c) Aluminous porcelain has part of quartz replaced by alumina
3. Properties
   a) Excellent electrical and thermal insulator
   b) Low coefficient of thermal expansion
   c) Excellent esthetic value
   d) Low tensile strength
   e) High compressive strength
   f) Not resistant to acids
   g) Harder than tooth structure and can cause wear of opposing teeth
4. Manipulation
   a) Porcelain frit is mixed with water, condensed into position, and fired in a vacuum furnace to reduce porosity

b) Shrinkage is high, requiring multiple firings
c) Surface may be stained and is glazed on completion

C. Metal-ceramic (porcelain-fused-to-metal) restorations

1. Advantages
   a) Reinforce porcelain to avoid brittle fracture
   b) Evidence shows years of clinical success
2. Disadvantages
   a) Limited esthetics primarily owing to opacity of metal substrate
   b) Involves time-consuming and expensive construction
   c) Appropriate tooth reduction may cause pulp problems, particularly in younger patient
   d) Porcelain is susceptible to attack by topical applications of acidulated phosphate fluoride (APF)

D. All-ceramic restorations

1. Classification by mode of fabrication
   a) *Porcelain jacket crown/porcelain inlay* is hand condensed on platinum foil or refractory die
   b) *Pressed ceramic* is pressed into mold to form crown substructure
   c) *Castable ceramic* is cast using lost wax technique
   d) *CAD-CAM* (Computer aided design-computer aided machining)—restoration is designed and milled by computer
2. Advantages
   a) Produces superior esthetics
   b) Aluminous core material—provides high strength values and reinforces overlying feldspathic porcelain
   c) Metal-free and very biocompatible
   d) CAD-CAM restorations fabricated in one appointment
3. Disadvantages
   a) High cost of fabrication
   b) Difficult to make endodontic access preparation
   c) Adaptation of margins is not as good as metal

E. Indirect resin restorations

1. Composition is similar to that of direct posterior composite restorations
2. Consists of light-cured and heat-processed composites
   a) Make an impression and die
   b) Form and process restoration using light and/or heat
   c) Place restoration using dual-cure or self-cure resin cement
3. Advantages
   a) Reduces marginal leakage because of reduced polymerization shrinkage at cementation
   b) Improves mechanical properties
4. Disadvantages
   a) Requires removal of more tooth structure
   b) May require a second appointment
   c) Requires use of more materials
   d) More expensive than direct resin-matrix composite restorations

F. Veneers

1. Classification
   a) Laminate veneer—place PMMA shell on enamel surface
   b) Direct composite resin veneer
   c) Indirect composite resin veneer (laboratory processed)
   d) Porcelain veneer
   e) Pressed ceramic veneer
   f) CAD-CAM ceramic veneer
2. Advantages
   a) Provides good esthetics
   b) Porcelain and ceramic veneers provide good abrasion resistance
   c) PMMA and composite veneers are acid resistant
3. Disadvantages
   a) Luting cement may affect color
   b) Marginal leakage may cause discoloration with time
   c) PMMA and composite veneers are subject to scratching
   d) Veneers are degraded by acids such as APF

XI. DENTAL CEMENTS

A. Restorative cements

1. Uses
   a) Class V restorations—glass ionomers and resin-modified glass ionomers
   b) Class II restorations—resin-modified glass and metal-reinforced glass ionomers used in deciduous teeth
   c) Class III restorations—glass and resin-modified glass ionomers
   d) Temporary restorations—zinc oxide-eugenol, improved zinc oxide-eugenol, and zinc phosphate
2. Glass ionomer cements
   a) Components
      (1) Powder—calcium fluoroaluminosilicate glass
      (2) Liquid—aqueous (water) solution copolymers (acrylic acid with maleic, itaconic, and tartaric acids)
      (3) Resin-modified glass ionomer liquid also contains water-soluble monomers such as HEMA
      (4) Metal-modified glass ionomers have silver or silver alloy added to powder
   b) Glass ionomer reaction
      (1) Acid-base reaction releases ions including fluoride
      (2) Cross-linking with calcium occurs
      (3) Protection from saliva is required for 24 hours
   c) Resin-modified glass ionomer reaction
      (1) Acid-base glass ionomer reaction is present
      (2) Polymerization occurs via carbon-carbon double bonds of water-soluble monomers; can be self- or light-cure
   d) Properties
      (1) Good thermal and electrical insulators
      (2) Good radiopacity
      (3) Linear coefficient of thermal expansion of glass ionomer closely resembles tooth structure

(4) Good esthetics for resin-modified glass ionomers
(5) Chemical bonding to tooth structure through reactive acid side groups
(6) Compressive strength of resin-modified glass ionomers is higher than for glass ionomers
(7) Fluoride release decreases acid solubility of surrounding enamel

e) Advantages
(1) Bonds to tooth structure and requires no mechanical retention in cavity preparation
(2) Rapid placement and setting of light-cured, resin-modified glass ionomers

f) Disadvantages
(1) Long setting time of glass ionomers
(2) Poor esthetic qualities of glass ionomers
(3) Difficult handling of glass ionomers and resin-modified glass ionomers

3. Zinc oxide-eugenol cements
a) Composition
(1) Powder is zinc oxide and PMMA, resin, or alumina
(2) Liquid is eugenol (may have ethoxybenzoic acid [EBA])
(3) Oil of cloves may be substituted for eugenol because it contains 70% to 85% eugenol

b) Properties
(1) Produces obtundent responses
(2) Low mechanical properties prohibit use in high-stress areas

B. Varnishes

1. Indications for placement
a) Dentin under amalgam restorations
b) Dentin under cast restorations placed with nonadhesive cements
c) Surface of moisture-sensitive materials during setting
d) Surface of a recently placed metallic restoration exhibiting galvanism

2. Composition
a) Solvent—acetone, chloroform, or ether
b) Solute—copal resin, rosin, cellulose, or synthetic resin

C. Liners

1. Used to prevent penetration of irritating substances into dentin
2. Composition
a) Suspension of calcium hydroxide
b) Low-viscosity zinc oxide-eugenol

3. Clinical properties
a) Calcium hydroxide stimulates formation of reparative dentin
b) Zinc oxide—eugenol acts as pulp obtundent

D. Bases

1. Indications
a) Use as thermal insulation below restoration
b) Block out undercuts and contribute to core for cast restorations

2. Classifications
   a) Zinc phosphate cement
   b) Polycarboxylate cement
   c) Hard-setting calcium hydroxide cement
   d) Zinc oxide-eugenol cement
   e) Glass ionomer cement
   f) Resin-modified glass ionomer cement
3. Properties
   a) Excellent thermal and electrical insulation
   b) Solubility is lower than liners
   c) Resin-modified glass ionomers are strongest
   d) Zinc oxide-eugenol is weakest

E. Luting Cements

1. Involves bonding by mechanical interlocking of surfaces
2. Components of liquid-powder systems—powder is chemically basic and liquid is chemically acidic
3. Classification
   a) Zinc phosphate cement
      (1) Maintains long history of clinical use
      (2) Manufactured as powder (zinc oxide) and liquid (phosphoric acid and water)
   b) Improved zinc oxide-eugenol cement
      (1) Used to minimize postoperative sensitivity
      (2) Manufactured as powder (zinc oxide) and liquid (eugenol)
   c) Zinc polycarboxylate cement
      (1) Used to minimize postoperative sensitivity and has largely replaced zinc oxide-eugenol for this purpose
      (2) Manufactured as powder (zinc oxide) and liquid (polyacrylic acid and water)
   d) Glass ionomer cement
      (1) Popular choice because of fluoride-release property
      (2) Manufactured as powder (calcium fluoraluminosilicate glass) and liquid (polyacrylic acid or other polyalkenoic acids)
   e) Resin cement
      (1) Used for resin-retained bridges, orthodontic brackets, all-ceremic restorations, and indirect resin restorations
      (2) May react as light-, self-, or dual-cured polymerization
      (3) Advantage—maintains low or no solubility
   f) Resin-modified glass ionomer cement
      (1) Combines glass ionomer chemistry and resin cement chemistry in attempt to gain advantages of both cements
      (2) Manufactured as powder (calcium fluoroaluminosilicate glass) and liquid (copolymer acid in water, water-soluble monomers)
   g) Temporary luting cements
      (1) Used for cementing temporary restorations
      (2) Include zinc oxide-eugenol, noneugenol, and resin

XII. DENTAL IMPLANTS

A. Types

1. Subperiosteal
   a) Casting is placed between bone and periosteum
   b) Used for fully edentulous arches
2. Endosseous (root form)
   a) Place cylinders within bone
   b) Most commonly placed implant
   c) Used for single tooth to full arch replacement
3. Transosseous
   a) Include mandibular systems that are placed through mandible
   b) Used for fully edentulous arches
4. Bone substitutes
   a) Creates bone to support other implants
   b) Used in periodontal defects
5. Temperomandibular joint prosthesis
6. Osseointegrated—closely associated with bone

B. Materials

1. Metallic—titanium, titanium-aluminum-vanadium alloy, stainless steel, and chromium-cobalt
2. Polymeric—PMMA
3. Ceramic—hydroxyapatite and carbon

C. Mode of attachment

1. Bioactive surface that osseointegrates
2. Nonactive porous surface for micromechanical retention by osseointegration
3. Nonactive, nonporous surface for ankylosis by osseointegration
4. Fibrointegration by formation of fibrous tissue capsule

D. Properties

1. Must be abrasion- and corrision-resistant
2. Must have a high elastic modulus
3. Must be resistant to scratching and abrasion during hygiene procedures

XIII. CUTTING, ABRASION, AND POLISHING

A. Cutting—removal of material by blade in regular pattern

B. Abrasion—wear of surface caused by multiple randomly acting blades

1. Factors affecting abrasion
   a) Abrasive must be harder than material being abraded
   b) Abrasive must maintain edge sharpness
   c) Increased speed of application increases rate of abrasion
   d) Increased pressure increases rate of abrasion
   e) Larger abrasive particle size increases rate of abrasion

C. Polishing

1. Creates smooth surface on material being treated
2. Technique
   a) Requires following specific sequence of abrasives

b) Moves from coarse abrasives to fine abrasives
c) Avoid heat generation—can cause pulp damage

D. Abrasive agents

1. Order of abrasion resistance: diamond > emery > cuttle > quartz > tin oxide, porcelain > tripoli > pumice > composite resin > enamel > rouge > amalgam > gold alloy > dentin > acrylic
2. Polymeric restorative materials are subject to abrasion while polishing

XIV. BLEACHING AGENTS

A. Composition

1. In-office systems—30% to 35% hydrogen peroxide
2. Home systems—10% to 15% carbamide peroxide

B. Technique

1. In-office—agent is applied and activated by heat or light
2. Home—custom-made application tray holds bleach and is placed by patient

review questions

DIRECTIONS Each of the questions or incomplete statements below is followed by suggested answers or completions. Select the **one** answer that is best in each case.

1. In the United States, which of the following organizations must provide approval before a material can be marketed for dental use?
   A. International Standards Organization
   B. American Dental Association
   C. Occupational Safety and Health Administration
   D. Food and Drug Administration

2. For an adhesive to work on a given adherend, it must wet the surface well. All of the following aid wetting EXCEPT one. Which one is the EXCEPTION?
   A. a clean surface
   B. fluoride
   C. high surface energy
   D. a smooth surface

3. Which of the following properties can be determined if an applied stress is proportional to a resulting strain for a given material?
   A. modulus of elasticity
   B. toughness
   C. ductility
   D. ultimate strength

4. All of the following increase the rate of abrasion EXCEPT one. Which one is the EXCEPTION?
   A. increased pressure
   B. abrasive harder than the surface being abraded
   C. decreased speed of abrasive application
   D. larger abrasive particle

5. Which physical property of an amalgam restoration is LIKELY to cause hot and cold sensitivity following its placement?
   A. thermal conductivity
   B. modulus of elasticity
   C. toughness
   D. creep

6. All of the following are dimensions of color EXCEPT one. Which one is the EXCEPTION?
   A. hue
   B. value
   C. shade
   D. chroma

7. Increased water/powder ratios (more water) will affect gypsum by
   A. increasing its strength.
   B. decreasing its strength.
   C. increasing its abrasion resistance.
   D. decreasing its setting time.

8. Alginate (irreversible hydrocolloid) impressions are used to fabricate all of the following EXCEPT one. Which one is the EXCEPTION?
   A. bleach tray
   B. 3-unit fixed bridge
   C. custom mouthguard
   D. study cast

9. All of the following methods supply energy to a monomer (resulting in polymerization) EXCEPT one. Which one is the EXCEPTION?
   A. heat activation
   B. chemical activation
   C. light activation
   D. copolymerization

10. Which of the following materials is used to prepare the enamel for sealant and bonded orthodontic bracket applications?
    A. 10% hydrofluoric acid
    B. 10% citric acid
    C. 30% to 50% phosphoric acid
    D. EDTA

11. Which of the following cements provides chemical adhesion to tooth structure?
    A. glass ionomer
    B. zinc phosphate
    C. zinc-oxide eugenol
    D. resin

12. The combination of metals, which are mutually soluble in the molten state, is referred to as a(n)
    A. composite resin.
    B. polymer.
    C. cement.
    D. alloy.

13. Metals can be protected from corrosion in the oral environment by all of the following EXCEPT one. Which one is the EXCEPTION?
    A. polishing the surface
    B. including a noble metal in the alloy
    C. including a metal that passivates in the alloy
    D. placing the metal in contact with a dissimilar metal

14. Which form of mercury is of MOST concern for the dental professional?
    A. vapor
    B. droplets
    C. combined with a dental amalgam alloy
    D. metallic mercury

15. Materials used to protect the pulp from thermal stimulation, often experienced with metallic restorations, are classified as
    A. varnishes.
    B. low-strength bases.
    C. high-strength bases.
    D. liners.

16. During an amalgam polishing procedure, which of the following factors can produce the largest biological effect?
    A. odor
    B. heat
    C. debris
    D. tin oxide

17. For a material to be considered a posterior restorative, all of the following criteria must be included EXCEPT one. Which one is the EXCEPTION?
    A. ability to withstand high stresses
    B. ability to withstand large temperature changes with no detrimental effects
    C. minimal toxic or allergenic potential
    D. ability to replicate the color of the tooth structure

18. Which of the following is an advantage of indirect restoration?
    A. allows for optimum development of the form of a restoration
    B. minimizes patient visits
    C. less costly than direct restorations
    D. requires fewer materials

19. A composite resin material that fails to release absorbed light lacks
    A. metamerism.
    B. opacity.
    C. translucency.
    D. fluorescence.

20. Which of the following is NOT an inelastic impression material?
    A. impression compound
    B. ZOE impression paste
    C. alginate
    D. impression plaster

21. What can be done to increase working time when using a mix of reversible hydrocolloid (alginate) impression material?
    A. increase the water/powder ratio
    B. decrease the water/powder ratio
    C. use cooler water
    D. use warmer water

22. Which of the following is an acceptable method of disinfecting alginate impressions?
    A. immerse in sodium hypochlorite for 30 minutes
    B. immerse in alcohol for 30 minutes
    C. spray with a glutaraldehyde or an iodophor and place in a sealed plastic bag for 10 minutes
    D. immerse in sodium hypochlorite for 10 minutes

23. Which of the following is NOT a common component of a dental composite resin matrix?
    A. silane
    B. BIS-GMA
    C. UDMA (urethane dimethacrylate)
    D. TEGDMA

24. Which of the following restorative materials releases significant amounts of fluoride?
    A. dental amalgam
    B. glass ionomer cement
    C. gold alloys
    D. dental porcelain

25. Which of the following materials has the greatest ultimate tensile strength?
    A. composite resin
    B. zinc phosphate cement
    C. gold alloy
    D. dental amalgam

26. Which of the following is the primary monomer used in fabricating denture bases?
    A. methyl methacrylate
    B. TEGDMA
    C. BIS-GMA
    D. UDMA

answers & rationales

1.

D. Since May 1976, the FDA has had regulatory jurisdiction over the safety and efficacy of medical and dental materials and devices. The ISO provides guidelines for international standards. The ADA provides a certification program for materials, which meet minimum standards. A certification is not required for a material to be marketed. OSHA is responsible for the safety and welfare of people in the workplace.

2.

B. The addition of a halogen atom, such as fluorine, reduces the surface energy and makes it more difficult to wet. A Teflon pan is an example of this. A clean or smooth surface is easier to wet than a dirty one. Also, a surface with a high surface energy wets easier than a surface with a low surface energy.

3.

A. Stress divided by strain below the proportional limit is equal to the modulus of elasticity for the material. Toughness is the energy required to cause fracture of a material. Ductility is the ability of a material to resist deformation under tension. Ultimate strength is the greatest stress that can be withstood without fracture.

4.

C. The rate of abrasion is decreased when the speed of application is decreased. Increased pressure, an abrasive harder than the surface being abraded, and larger particle sizes increase the rate of abrasion.

5.

A. Thermal conductivity describes the ability of a material to transmit heat. Metals, such as dental amalgam, typically have a high thermal conductivity and increase the likelihood of postoperative temperature sensitivity. The modulus of elasticity describes the stiffness of a material. Toughness is the energy required to cause fracture of a material. Creep is the gradual flow of a material under an applied stress, usually at temperatures approaching the melting point.

6.

C. Shade is commonly used to communicate and describe a color through the use of a shade guide. It includes all the dimensions: hue, value, and chroma. Hue describes the predominant wavelength of a color. Value describes the brightness or darkness of a color. Chroma describes the strength of the hue or how much of a wavelength is being seen.

7.

B. Increasing the water/powder ratio of a gypsum product will decrease its strength, hardness, and abrasion resistance, but increase its setting time.

8.

B. Alginate does not reproduce the detail needed for the fabrication of fixed prostheses such as a 3-unit bridge. Alginate is often used in the fabrication of bleach trays, custom mouthguards, and study casts.

9.

D. Copolymerization is the process of combining two or more monomers when creating a polymer. Methods of polymerization induction in dentistry include the use of heat, chemical, light, and/or microwave activation or a combination of these.

10.

C. Enamel acid etching is effectively accomplished with 30% to 50% phosphoric acid. Hydrofluoric acid is a strong acid that has been used to etch porcelain. Ten percent citric acid is a weak acid and does not predictably etch enamel. EDTA effectively removes the dentin smear layer, but does not effectively etch dentin.

11.

A. Materials based on polyacrylic or polycarboxylic acids create chemical adhesion to tooth structure. These include glass ionomer, zinc polycarboxylate, and resin-modified glass ionomer cements. Zinc phosphate and zinc-oxide eugenol cements provide mechanical retention. Resin cements also provide mechanical retention.

12.

D. An alloy is a combination of metals that are mutually soluble in the molten stage. Dental composite resins are composed of a polymer matrix with glass or ceramic fillers. Polymers are high molecular weight compounds resulting from the linking of low-molecular-weight compounds. Cements are generally hard, brittle materials formed by mixing a powder oxide with a liquid.

13.

D. Placing dissimilar metals in contact with another metal can increase corrosion. This combination can also cause a galvanic reaction and tooth sensitivity. Polishing reduces metal corrosion. Noble metals and metals that passivate reduce corrosion activity.

14.

A. Mercury vapor is available for inhalation, the most effective portal of entry to the human bloodstream. Therefore, precautions should be taken to prevent the vaporization of mercury. Droplets of mercury are less of a risk than mercury vapor. Mercury bound in dental amalgam presents a very low risk. Mercury is an occupational hazard and requires proper handling.

15.

C. A high-strength base with a minimum thickness of 0.5 mm is capable of providing thermal insulation for pulp tissue. Varnishes are used to decrease initial marginal leakage with dental amalgam and to diminish the movement of corrosion products through the dentin. Low-strength bases function as a barrier to irritating chemicals and provide a therapeutic benefit to the pulp. They are not thick enough to provide thermal protection. A suspension of calcium hydroxide is used to neutralize acids.

16.

B. The heat generated during polishing can cause pulp damage and release mercury vapor. Efforts should be taken to minimize these effects. An odor may be produced during polishing, but is not a significant biological threat. Debris produced during polishing should not cause any long-term biological effects. Tin oxide is often used to produce a polish layer when polishing dental amalgams.

17.

D. Although creating tooth-colored restorations is often desirable, it is not a requirement for a functioning restoration. Molar regions may experience stresses of 28,000 psi. Large temperature changes are common when eating. Restorative materials must be biologically compatible.

18.

A. An indirect restorative technique replicates a patient's oral structures. This allows for improved access in creating optimum contour and occlusal form of dental restorations. Indirect restorative techniques usually require more materials and multiple visits and are typically more costly than direct procedures.

19.

D. Fluorescence describes the ability of a material to absorb a nonvisible energy and then release visible light with longer wavelengths. This property adds to the vital appearance of esthetic restorations. Metamerism causes a material to have a different color under different light sources. Opacity describes the degree to which the passage of light through a material is inhibited. Translucency describes the dispersion of light through a material such that objects cannot be seen through it.

20.

C. Alginate is an elastic material and therefore is useful in making impressions of structures that contain undercuts. Impression compound and plaster and ZOE impression paste are inelastic.

21.

C. Cooler water will prolong gelation of alginate and provide more working time. The water/powder ratio of the material should not be changed. Increasing the water/powder ratio should not be used to increase working time. Decreasing the water/powder ratio does not increase working time. However, using warmer water does decrease working time.

22.

C. Immersion of alginate materials can cause imbibition (swelling) and significant dimensional change. They should be sprayed with a glutaraldehyde or an iodophor and sealed in a plastic bag for 10 minutes.

23.

A. Silane is used as a coupling agent between the matrix and the filler particles of a dental composite resin. BIS-GMA, UDMA, and TEGDMA are all common components of the matrix.

24.

B. Glass ionomer cements release fluoride over time. They contain fluoroaluminosilicate glasses. Dental amalgam, gold alloys, and dental porcelain do not release fluoride.

25.

C. The casting alloys are among the strongest materials used in dentistry. Of the materials given, the gold alloy would be expected to have the highest ultimate tensile strength. Composite resin and dental amalgam have intermediate strength values. Zinc phosphate cement has low strength values.

26.

A. Methyl methacrylate is the primary monomer in denture bases and forms poly(methyl methacrylate) on polymerization. TEGDMA, BIS-GMA, and UDMA are components in composite resins.

CHAPTER

15 Community Dental Health

Elizabeth C. Reynolds, RDH, MS

contents

Dental hygienists play a crucial role in dental public health by becoming educators, directors of community-based prevention programs, members of epidemiological survey teams, and active participants in programs for the dentally neglected. With increased emphasis on improving public access to oral healthcare, the opportunities of dental hygienists to promote oral health in the community are numerous.

I. PUBLIC HEALTH DENTISTRY AND DENTAL HYGIENE

A. *Dental public health* is one of eight specialties of dentistry in the United States. The American Dental Association (ADA) defines the specialty as follows:

1. Dental public health is the science and art of preventing and controlling dental diseases and promoting dental health through organized community efforts
2. It is that form of dental practice which serves the *community* as a patient rather than the individual
3. It is concerned with the dental health education of the public, with applied dental research, and with the administration of group dental care programs as well as the prevention and control of dental diseases on a community basis

B. Specialist Skills—inherent in the definition is that the specialist possesses broad knowledge and skills in

1. Program administration
2. Research methods
3. Assessment, prevention, and control of oral diseases
4. Methods of financing dental care services

C. For dental professionals to become specialists

1. Be employed full-time with the administration of public health programs (which can include health promotion, community preventive services, and provision of dental care to specified groups in need)

Comparisons of Private Dental Practice and Community Health Care

The procedures in public health practice parallel those of private dental practice even though dental public health programs treat the community as a patient versus the individual seeking care in a dental office setting. The similarities can be summarized as follows:

Public Health Practice	Private Practice
Survey and needs assessment	Health history and examination
Data analysis	Diagnosis
Program planning	Treatment planning
Program operation	Treatment
Program funding	Payment
Program appraisal	Evaluation

2. Become faculty members in departments dealing with community oral health planning and practice
3. Become researchers in epidemiology, prevention, or provision of health services
4. Dentists become recognized specialists when, combined with full-time employment in these fields, they achieve diplomate status with the American Board of Dental Public Health
5. Dental hygienists can obtain advanced educational degrees in a variety of public health-minded programs enabling them to pursue careers as community healthcare providers and educators.

II. CRITERIA FOR DEFINING A PUBLIC DENTAL HEALTH PROBLEM—a dental health problem must meet two criteria to be considered a public dental health problem

A. A condition or situation that is a widespread actual or potential cause of morbidity or mortality

1. *Morbidity*—relative incidence of a disease
2. *Mortality*—incidence of death or loss; in dentistry, tooth loss is considered mortality as a result of disease or injury

B. Existing perception that condition is public health problem on part of the public, government, or public health authorities

III. FOUR GOVERNMENTAL LEVELS OF DENTAL PUBLIC HEALTH

A. International—World Health Organization (WHO)

1. Coordinates programs for underdeveloped nations and gathers epidemiological data for comparison across nations
2. Establishes principles of primary healthcare to maintain health
3. Develops means to summarize treatment needs of international populations utilizing minimal equipment (e.g., Community Periodontal Index of Treatment Needs [CPITN])

B. Federal

1. Acts on oral health problems of national significance
2. Funds research endeavors
3. Primarily within the jurisdiction of the Department of Health and Human Services (DHHS)
4. Examples of federally funded dental activities
   a) Biological research
   b) Disease prevention and control
   c) Planning and development programs in dental labor
   d) Education and services research
   e) Regulation and compliance functions (quality assessment)
   f) Programs concerned with provision of dental services

C. State

1. Provides consultation services to local health departments
2. Directly administers some programs (especially those in rural areas)
3. Allocates prevention block grant funds
4. Example—many states report spending a portion of their Maternal and Child Health Services funds in dental-related services

D. Local

1. People-to-people level of public health that provides direct services
2. Directly administers county and city programs
3. Initiates dental health legislative measures (such as fluoridation)
4. Although the division of responsibilities in delivering oral health programs to the community is delineated, it is clear that budget constraints are hampering program development and implementation at all levels
5. Evidence suggests that dental health care programs that are part of neighborhood, rural, migrant, and homeless health centers—founded largely through federal dollars—have experienced extreme difficulties in recent years owing to budget constraints
6. Examples of local dental activities
   a) Classroom presentations to grade school children on home care techniques by a dental hygienist
   b) Local dental hygiene component sponsorship of oral cancer screenings during a city-wide health fair

V. EPIDEMIOLOGY

A. Multifactorial study of health and disease in populations

B. Seeks to examine effects of host factors, biology, physical environment, and lifestyle on health

C. Epidemiological studies require that disease be measured quantitatively

D. Host factors

1. Age
2. Gender
3. Race
4. Immunity

E. Biological causes

1. Bacteria
2. Virus
3. Protozoa

F. Physical environmental factors

1. Sun
2. Industrial pollutants
3. Radiation

G. Lifestyle considerations

1. Education
2. Socioeconomic status
3. Drug and alcohol consumption
4. Diet

H. Research methods

1. Descriptive studies
   a) Examine data collected without specific hypothesis to be tested and are designed to describe disease or condition within a

population and relationships between it and other variables without establishing causality

b) Classified as either incidence or prevalence studies
   (1) *Incidence study*—describes the number of new cases of a disease within a specified time period
   (2) *Prevalence study*—describes total number of cases of disease at a point in time (termed "point prevalence") or during a period of time (known as "period prevalence")

c) Increase understanding of disease by
   (1) Describing normal biological processes
   (2) Observing natural history of diseases
   (3) Providing distribution statistics of disease in the population
   (4) Identifying determinants of disease
   (5) Testing hypotheses for disease prevention and control
   (6) Planning and evaluating healthcare services

2. Experimental studies
   a) Longitudinal and prospective and test hypotheses designed to answer a particular question to establish causality
   b) Characteristics of an experimental study include
      (1) Manipulation of one or more independent variables (IV)
      (2) Measurement of one or more dependent variables (DV)
      (3) Occurrence of IV before measurement of DV
      (4) Concept of control group
   c) Example of an experimental study—clinical trial tests the efficacy of an agent or procedure
      (1) Controlled experimental study of group comparison based on epidemiological principles and designed to test hypothesis that a particular agent or procedure favorably alters the natural history of the disease
      (2) Overall aim is to ensure the only difference between the groups is that the test group receives the agent under study and control group does not
      (3) Clinical trials require specific considerations such as
         (a) Choice of study population (should be determined by the purpose of the trial)
         (b) Adequate numbers of test subjects
         (c) Comparability of study and control groups
         (d) Placebo use in control group
         (e) Control of operational procedure
         (f) Reliability in diagnosis
         (g) Duration of the trial
         (h) Statistical analysis
         (i) Ethical considerations

3. Other types of studies used frequently in epidemiological endeavors
   a) *Analytical study*
      (1) Descriptive study analyzing the occurrence of a disease or condition relative to characteristics within the population or environment

(2) Seeks to analyze relationships between and among variables

b) *Longitudinal study*—study approach used in either descriptive or experimental protocols in which repeated measures are used while observing a sample over time

c) *Prospective study*—longitudinal study that can be either descriptive or experimental in which subjects are observed and data collected over time to determine if a disease or condition develops

d) *Retrospective study*—a descriptive study that investigates previously collected data

e) *Developmental study*—descriptive study that examines progression or development of disease, condition, or program over a period of time using a longitudinal or cross-sectional approach

(1) Cohort study—one group (cohort) of subjects is followed over a period of time to observe development of disease (prospective)

(2) Case history—group with disease or condition is compared to a group without the disease or condition to determine variables or factors that relate to its occurrence (retrospective); also known as ex post facto study

(3) Cross-sectional—representative cross section of a population is observed at one point in time to determine occurrence of disease or condition and relate its occurrence to other variables or factors within the population

4. Considerations when designing an epidemiological study

a) Validity of the measure

(1) Internal validity

(a) Degree to which change in IV actually brought about the change in DV

(b) Influenced by control of extraneous variables and group equivalency

(2) External validity

(a) Degree to which the results of the study can be generalized from sample to population

(b) Influenced by type and size of sample

(3) Components of validity

(a) *Sensitivity*—measure is sensitive if it will test positive when the disease or condition is present

(b) *Specificity*—measure is specific if it will test negative when the disease or condition is absent

(c) *Predictive value*—ability of a measure to identify presence and absence of a disease or condition

(4) Increasing validity

(a) Correct theoretical assumption relative to the hypothesis

(b) Bias elimination

(c) Extraneous variable control

(d) Representative sample

(e) Equivalent groups

(f) Reliable measurement instruments, methods, and examiners
(g) Length of study must produce meaningful results

b) Reliability
(1) Measure reliability
(a) Instrument reliability
i) Consistent
ii) Reproducible
(b) Examiner reliability
i) *Intraexaminer reliability*—within one examiner
ii) *Interexaminer reliability*—between two or more examiners
(2) Increasing reliability
(a) Standardization of study conditions
(b) Examiner calibration
(c) Use of established reliable measures
(d) Conduction of pretest questionnaires and interviews designed for the study
(e) Careful administration of study

c) Sampling
(1) Types of samples
(a) Random sample
(b) Stratified random sample—most representative type of sample
(c) Systematic sample—every *n*th person is selected from the population for membership in the sample
(d) Convenience sample—least valid type of sample
(2) Sample size
(a) Large enough to provide "power" (the ability to detect a difference if one exists)
(b) Allow for attrition
(3) Minimize sampling error (sample is never 100% accurate in terms of representing entire population)

d) Group assignment
(1) Randomization (random assignment to groups)
(2) Matching of groups in process of randomization

e) Methods of measuring disease
(1) Count—not a useful measure as disease prevalence increases
(2) Proportion—e.g., prevalence
(3) Rates—e.g., incidence
(4) Indexes

V. METHODS OF MEASURING ORAL DISEASES

A. Counts

1. Simplest form of measuring any disease
2. Involves counting the number of cases of particular disease state
3. Most useful with unusual conditions of low prevalence

B. Proportions

1. Count can be turned into a proportion by adding a denominator
2. Determines prevalence

3. Proportions DO NOT include time dimension
4. Example: The count of caries-free children aged 3 to 5 years can be divided by the population of the group to give the prevalence:
   a) Total sample size = 400
   b) Number of caries-free children in sample population = 20
   c) Prevalence = number of caries-free children ÷ Total sample size
   d) Prevalence = 20 ÷ 400
   e) Prevalence of caries-free children = 0.05 or 5% of the total sample population

C. Rates

1. Proportion that uses standardized denominator and a time dimension
2. Not often used in oral disease measures

D. Indexes (or indices)

1. Graduated, numerical scale with upper and lower limits
2. Scores on the scale correspond to specific criteria
3. Index scores can be expressed for an individual or group
4. Determines degrees of intensity
5. Characteristics of ideal index
   a) *Validity*—measures what it is intended to measure
   b) *Reliability*—must be reproducible when used by the same or different examiners
   c) Clarity, simplicity, and objectivity—criteria should be clear and unambiguous; examiners should be able to readily memorize criteria after some practice
   d) *Quantifiability*—must lend itself to statistical analysis to express status of a group in terms of distribution, mean, median, or other statistical measure
   e) Sensitivity—should be able to detect clinically relevant changes in the condition
   f) Acceptability—should be painless and nondemeaning to the patient
   g) Quick to use—should use minimal equipment in a simple manner
6. An index may be reversible or irreversible
   a) *Irreversible index* measures cumulative conditions that cannot be reversed (such as caries)
   b) *Reversible index* measures condition that may resolve (e.g., gingivitis index)
7. Purposes and uses of indexes
   a) Individual assessment for treatment planning
   b) Research endeavors
   c) Community needs assessment for program planning
8. Types of dental indexes
   a) Dental caries indexes
      (1) Conventional method of defining caries evidence in a given population

DMFT and DMFS Indexes

Scoring

1. Based on 28 permanent teeth only
2. Not included are third molars, unerupted, congentially missing, supernumerary or retained primary teeth

D recordings

1. Used for restorable, decayed permanent teeth (or surfaces)
2. When both dental caries and a restoration are present, the tooth is listed as a "D"
3. The "D" refers to the morbidity of the disease and represents treatment needs

M recordings

1. Teeth (or surfaces) missing or indicated for extraction due to caries only are assigned an "M"
2. "M" refers to the mortality or fatality of the disease

F recordings

1. Restored ("filled") teeth or surfaces are listed as "F"
2. Used only for restorative work that is an outcome of carious lesions; cosmetic restorations, bridge abutments, sealants and fracture repairs are not recorded as "F"
3. Tooth with a defective filling but without evidence of dental caries is recorded as "F"

Once the teeth have been categorized, individual and group scores can be calculated to determine either the DMFT or DMFS.

---

(2) DMFT/DMFS—measures the number of permanent teeth (DMFT) or tooth surfaces (DMFS) decayed, missing or filled
- (a) Can be used to determine specific treatment needs of individual or group
- (b) Utilizes minimal equipment and time
- (c) Each tooth is examined visually with a mirror, light, and explorers of same design and with standardized dimensions of working ends
- (d) Calibrated clinicians examine only questionable small lesions

(3) dft/dfs—applies to deciduous dentition
- (a) Twenty teeth are evaluated to determine the dft index and 88 surfaces (based on 8 deciduous molars and 12 anterior teeth) are used to calculate dfs index
- (b) Supernumerary, unerupted, and congenitally missing teeth are not scored
- (c) Teeth restored for reasons other than dental caries are not counted as filled ("f")

DMFT Calculations

Individual

Each component is totaled separately and the following equation used:

DMFT = D + M + T

Sample problem:

D = 3, M = 5, and F = 10

DMFT = 3 + 5 + 10

DMFT = 18

Group of Subjects

DMFs for individual totaled and divided by number in group.

1. Based on *gender* and *age*:

   Sample problem:

   40 individuals in the population

   Total DMF = 240

   Group DMF = 240 ÷ 40

   Group DMF = 6.0

2. Based on restoration needs of the group:

   Sample problem:

   D = 150, M = 38 and F = 112

   DMFT= 150 + 38 + 112

   DMFT = 300

   D = 150

   Percentage of population needing restorations = 150 ÷ 300

   Percentage of population needing restorations = 0.50 or 50%

DMFS Calculations

1. DMFS determines past and present caries by tooth surfaces.
2. 28 teeth of permanent dentition have 128 surfaces
   - 16 posterior teeth have 5 surfaces (facial, lingual, mesial, distal, occlusal)
   - 12 anterior teeth have 4 surfaces (facial, lingual, mesial, distal)

Sample Problem:

D (surfaces) = 3, M (surfaces) = 5 (one molar is missing), F (surfaces) = 12

DMFS = D + M + F

DMFS = 20

---

dft/dfs Calculations

1. dft/dfs indexes determine the dental caries experience for primary teeth

   Sample problem:

   Total teeth present in individual = 18

   d = 10, f = 2

   dft = d + f

   dft = 12

   Total percentage of restored and carious teeth in subject = dft ÷ number of teeth present

   Total percentage of restored and carious teeth in subject = 12 ÷ 18

   Total percentage of restored and carious teeth in subject = 0.66 or 66.6%

2. To calculate the percent of surfaces in need of dental treatment, the dfs is divided by the number of surfaces present.

   Sample problem:

   d surfaces = 10, f = 0

   dfs = dtf

   dfs = 10

   Percent of surfaces in need of dental treatment = dfs ÷ # of teeth present.

   Percent of surfaces in need of dental treatment = 10 ÷ 88

   Percent of surfaces in need of dental treatment = 0.11 or 11%.

(d) Armamentarium and examination procedures are same as those described for DMFT/DMFS

(e) Following descriptions are used to assign designation for teeth being examined

i) d recordings = number of primary teeth or surfaces with dental caries but not restored

ii) f recordings = number of filled primary teeth on surfaces that do not have dental caries

b) Dental fluorosis

(1) Definition—a condition of hypomineralization of dental enamel caused by excessive ingestion of fluoride during tooth development

(2) Clinical appearance of fluorosis can range from barely noticeable to severe brown stain with pitting enamel

(3) Types of indexes

(a) Current fluorosis index, developed by H. Trendley Dean, has a 6-point scale (Table 15-1)

(b) The Tooth Surface Index of Fluorosis (TSIF)—developed in 1980 (Table 15-2)

TABLE 15-1 CRITERIA FOR DEAN'S FLUOROSIS INDEX

Diagnosis	Criteria
Normal	The enamel represents the usual translucent semivitriform type of structure. The surface is smooth, glossy, and usually of a pale creamy white color.
Questionable	The enamel discloses slight aberrations from the translucency of normal enamel, ranging from a few white flecks to occasional white spots. This classification is utilized in those instances where a definite diagnosis of the mildest form of fluorosis is not warranted and a classification of "normal" not justified.
Very mild	Small, opaque, paper white area scattered irregularly over the tooth but not involving as much as approximately 25% of the tooth surface. Frequently included in this classification are teeth showing no more than about 1 to 2 mm of white opacity at the tip of the summit of the cusps of the bicuspids or second molars.
Mild	The white opaque areas in the enamel of the teeth are more extensive but do not involve as much as 50% of the tooth.
Moderate	All enamel surfaces of the teeth are affected, and surfaces subject to attrition show marked wear. Brown stain is frequently a disfiguring feature.
Severe	Includes teeth formerly classified as "moderately severe" and "severe." All enamel surfaces are affected, and hypoplasia is so marked that the general form of the tooth may be altered. The major diagnostic sign of this classification is the discrete or confluent pitting. Brown stains are widespread, and teeth often present a corroded appearance.

From Dean HT. The investigation of physiological effects by the epidemiological method. In: Moulton FR, ed: Fluorine and dental health. Washington DC: American Association for the Advancement of Science, 1942: 23–71.

i) TSIF assigns a score on 0-to-7 scale to each tooth in the mouth
ii) TSIF is more sensitive than Dean's index for the mildest forms of fluorosis
iii) Fluorosis Risk Index (FRI)—designed for analytical studies seeking to identify risk factors for dental fluorosis

c) Periodontal disease indexes
  (1) The Periodontal Index (PI)
    (a) Described by Russell as a composite index scoring both gingivitis and periodontitis on same weighted scale
    (b) PI is invalid because it did not measure loss of attachment and graded all pockets of 3 mm or more equally
  (2) The Periodontal Disease Index (PDI)
    (a) indirectly measures the loss of periodontal attachment (LPA) described by Ramfjord
    (b) PDI identified concept of examining 6 teeth (the so-called "Ramfjord teeth") as representative of the whole mouth

TABLE 15-2 CLINICAL CRITERIA AND SCORING SYSTEM FOR THE TOOTH SURFACE INDEX OF FLUOROSIS (TSIF)

Score	Criteria
0:	Enamel shows no evidence of fluorosis.
1:	Enamel shows definite evidence of fluorosis, namely areas with parchment-white color that total less than one-third of the visible enamel surface. This category includes fluorosis confined only to incisal edges of anterior teeth and cusp tips of posterior teeth ("snowcapping").
2:	Parchment-white fluorosis totals at least one-third of the visible surface, but less than two-thirds.
3:	Parchment-white fluorosis totals at least two-thirds of the visible surface.
4:	Enamel shows staining in conjunction with any of the preceding levels of fluorosis. Staining is defined as an area of definite discoloration that may range from light to very dark brown.
5:	Discrete pitting of the enamel exists, unaccompanied by evidence of staining of intact enamel. A pit is defined as a definite physical defect in the enamel surface with a rough floor that is surrounded by a wall of intact enamel. The pitted area is usually stained or differs in color from the surrounding enamel.
6:	Both discrete pitting and staining of the intact enamel exist.
7:	Confluent pitting of the enamel surface exists. Large areas of enamel may be missing and the anatomy of the tooth may be altered. Dark-brown stain is usually present.

From Horowitz HS, Driscoll WS, Meyers RJ, et al. A new method for assessing the prevalence of dental fluorosis—the Tooth Surface Index of Fluorosis. J Am Dent Assoc. 1984; 109: 37–41.

i) Maxillary right first molar
ii) Maxillary left central
iii) Maxillary left first premolar
iv) Mandibular left first molar
v) Mandibular right central
vi) Mandibular right first premolar

(3) The Community Periodontal Index of Treatment Needs (CPITN)
   (a) First described in 1982 by WHO as an index for scoring periodontal treatment needs rather than periodontal status
   (b) Pocket depth is measured with special probe with markings of 3.5 mm and 5.5 mm with a 0.5 mm ball on the end of the probe
   (c) Individuals' treatment needs are categorized by code ranging from 0 to 4 according to results of the probing (Table 15-3)
   (d) CPITN data are presented in categorical form rather than as mean values
   (e) Current PSR clinical screening method is based on this index

TABLE 15-3 CODES AND CRITERIA USED IN THE CPITN (COMMUNITY PERIODONTAL INDEX OF TREATMENT NEEDS)	
0:	Healthy gingiva.
1:	Bleeding observed, directly or by using the mouth mirror, after "sensing" (i.e., gentle probing).
2:	Calculus felt during probing but all the black area of the probe visible (3.5–5.5 mm from ball tip).
3:	Pocket 4 or 5 mm (gingival margin situated on black area of probe, i.e., 3.5–5.5 mm from probe tip).
4:	Pocket >6 mm (black area of probe not visible).
X:	Excluded segment (fewer than two teeth present).
9:	Not recorded.

From World Health Organization. Oral health surveys: Basic methods. 4th ed. Geneva: WHO, 1997.

d) Oral hygiene indexes
   (1) The Plaque Index (PII)
      (a) Developed by Silness and Loe and is used with their Gingival Index (GI).
      (b) Same surfaces of same teeth are scored as in GI
      (c) 0-to-3 ordinal scale is used
      (d) The PII scores plaque according to its thickness at gingival margin
      (e) Most commonly used index to score plaque in use today
   (2) The Simplified Oral Hygiene Index (OHI-S)
      (a) Quick approach to measuring subgingival and supragingival plaque and calculus (Table 15-4)
      (b) Design lacks sensitivity when examining individual patients
      (c) Better serves group evaluations
   (3) The Patient Hygiene Performance Index (PHP)
      (a) Scores the same 6 teeth as the OHI-S

TABLE 15-4 CRITERIA FOR USE OF THE PLAQUE INDEX	
0:	No plaque in the gingival area.
1:	A film of plaque adhering to the free gingival margin and adjacent area of the tooth. The plaque may be recognized only by running a probe across the tooth surface.
2:	Moderate accumulation of soft deposits within the gingival pocket, on the gingival margin and/or adjacent tooth surface, which can be seen by the naked eye.
3:	Abundance of soft matter within the gingival pocket and/or on the gingival margin and adjacent tooth surface.

From Löe H. The Gingival Index, the Plaque Index, and the Retention Index Systems. *J Periodontol,* part II, 1967; 38 (Suppl): 610–6.

TABLE 15-5 SCORING OF THE OHI-S

Score	Debris	Calculus
0	No debris or stain present	No calculus present
1	Not more than gingival one-third covered and/or extrinsic stain	Supragingival, not more than one-third covered
2	One-third to two-thirds covered	One-third to two-thirds covered and/or presence of individual flecks of subgingival calculus
3	Two-thirds or more covered	Two-thirds or more covered and/or a solid band of subgingival calculus

(b) Uses disclosing solution and scores facial and lingual surfaces in five sections

(c) Useful for studies testing interproximal plaque removal, but is not frequently used

(4) Volpe-Manhold Index (VMI)

(a) Has been widely used to test agents for plaque control and calculus inhibition

(b) Designed to score new deposits of supragingival calculus following a prophylaxis

(c) Measures only supragingival calculus on gingival, distal, and mesial planes of lingual surfaces of mandibular anterior teeth

(d) Extent of calculus on lingual surfaces is measured with a probe in 0.5-mm increments up to 5 mm

(e) Scores on the three planes are summed for each tooth and then added together to generate total calculus score for individual

Gingival Index (GI)

This is based on the severity of inflammation instead of the extent and is more commonly used.

Scoring Criteria

0 = Normal gingiva
1 = Mild inflammation: slight change in color, slight edema, no bleeding on probing
2 = Moderate inflammation: redness, edema, glazing, bleeding on probing
3 = Severe inflammation: marked redness, edema, ulceration, tendency to spontaneous bleeding

Gingiva is scored around all the teeth. The individual's GI score is the average of the tooth GI scores. Individuals' scores are averaged for the population GI score. The possible range of scores is 0 to 3.

e) Gingivitis indexes
   (1) Papillary-marginal-attached (PMA)
      (a) Index assesses extent of inflammation in these three areas of the gingiva
      (b) Not commonly used
   (2) The gingival index (GI) of Loe and Silness, developed in the 1960s, is more commonly used today
      (a) GI grades gingiva on mesial, distal, facial, lingual surfaces of teeth
      (b) Each area is scored on a 0 to 3 ordinal scale according to specific criteria
      (c) GI is sensitive to distinguish between little and severe gingivitis
      (d) Bleeding on probing is more sensitive, which lends validity to GI

VI. DISTRIBUTION OF ORAL DISEASES AND CONDITIONS—an understanding of the distribution and determinants of oral diseases within populations is necessary for dental practitioners to provide expert guidance to the community on public health matters related to oral health. The following epidemiological findings provide the basis for that understanding

A. Prevalence of dental caries

1. Ancient humans
   a) Low caries
   b) High attrition rate
   c) Coarse diet
2. Modern humans
   a) High caries prevalence rate in United States
   b) Current decrease in caries prevalence due to
      (1) Water fluoridation
      (2) Fluorides
      (3) Fluoride toothpaste
      (4) Dental sealant placement
      (5) Emphasis on caries prevention
3. Underdeveloped countries—low prevalence associated with dietary patterns (less processed foods, refined carbohydrates, and sugar)

B. Factors associated with dental caries

1. Susceptibility of teeth
   a) Molars are attacked before premolars
   b) Mandibular molars are attacked before maxillary molars
   c) Higher incidence in pits and fissures than on smooth surface caries
2. Age
   a) Two specific types of caries are associated with age

(1) Nursing bottle caries (rampant caries in 1- to 3-year olds)—more prevalent in lower socioeconomic status (SES) and Hispanic populations
(2) Root caries (caries of the cemental root surfaces)
(a) Higher prevalence in developed countries, in elderly, and in lower SES groups
(b) Xerostomia is a risk factor

3. Gender
   a) Males have lower DMF scores than females
   b) Females seek out dental care more often than males
   c) Females have earlier eruption patterns than males
4. Race and ethnicity
   a) Higher caries prevalence in African Americans
   b) More untreated caries in Hispanics and African Americans owing to lower SES rather than inherent tendency to develop caries
5. Diet (total oral intake of substances that provides nourishment and/or calories)—frequency of sugar intake increases caries risk in susceptible individuals
6. Nutrition (absorption of nutrients)—no association between nutritional deficiency in infancy and caries development
7. Familial influence
   a) Genetics have limited influence
   b) Family environment is strong factor
   c) Intrafamilial transmission of cariogenic flora can occur
8. SES status (income, education, occupation, attitudes, and values)—most powerful determinant of dental caries in United States

C. Prevention of dental caries

1. Host factors
   a) Easiest to address with public health measures
   b) Examples
      (1) Fluorides
      (2) Pit and fissure sealants
2. Oral hygiene
   a) Difficult to control in public health programs
   b) Not well correlated to caries incidence
3. Control of dietary sugar is difficult

D. Prevalence of periodontal diseases

1. 70% of adults in all countries are affected by some type, form, and level of periodontal disease
2. Low rate of severe periodontal disease in US population
3. Higher rate of mild to moderate periodontal disease
4. Higher rate of mild gingivitis versus moderate to severe cases

E. Factors associated with periodontal disease

1. Plaque
   a) Etiological factor
   b) Risk depends on type of bacteria and host response

2. Age
   a) Greater prevalence and severity of periodontal diseases in elderly
      (1) Not a natural consequence of aging
      (2) Due to accumulation and progression of disease
   b) Greater prevalence of gingivitis in children
      (1) Due in part to inflammatory response associated with eruption
      (2) Oral hygiene may be inadequate in children
3. Caries—extraction of teeth and subsequent drifting is associated with periodontal breakdown

F. Prevention of periodontal disease

1. Oral hygiene
2. Regular periodontal maintenance
3. Adjunctive aids (antimicrobial administration)

G. Oral cancer frequency of occurrence by location

1. Pharynx
2. Tongue
3. Floor of the mouth
4. Lip
5. Buccal mucosa

H. Percentages

1. 3.1% of new cases of cancer are oral
2. Oral cancer accounts for 1.8% of cancer deaths

I. Associated risk factors with oral cancer

1. Gender
   a) Twice as prevalent in males
   b) Twice as many deaths in males
2. Age—higher prevalence in elderly
3. Tobacco use—greatest risk factor for oral cancer
4. Alcohol consumption
5. Sun exposure—dramatically increases risk of lip cancer
6. Poorly fitted dentures

J. Cleft lip and palate occurrence

1. 6000 children born with clefts annually
2. Associated risk factors
   a) Heredity
   b) Maternal drug consumption during first trimester
   c) Influenza and fever in first trimester

K. Malocclusion—associated risk factors

1. Oral habits such as thumb sucking
2. Early extraction of teeth
3. Heredity

L. Edentulism

1. Prevalence
   a) Higher prevalence in elderly
   b) Prevalence is decreasing

2. Associated risk factors
   a) Fluoride use has decreased incidence
   b) Prevention and control of periodontal diseases have increased retention of teeth

VII. BASIC BIOSTATISTICAL CONCEPTS

A. *Biostatistics*—seeks to collect, organize, and interpret numeric data related to living organisms

B. Uses for dental health practitioner

1. Acts as aid in design of healthcare program or facility
2. Use as an evaluation tool in determining effectiveness of ongoing program
3. Identifies needs of specific population
4. Evaluates scientific accuracy of journal articles

C. Familiarities required of practitioner

1. Measurement methods
2. Types of data
3. Descriptive statistics
4. Hypothesis testing

D. Measurement methods

1. Designed to gauge amount of characteristic through systematic assignment of numbers
2. Validity
3. Reliability
4. Scales of measurement
   a) Nominal scale
      (1) Mutually exclusive data categories or classifications
      (2) Examples—race, gender
   b) Ordinal scale
      (1) Ranked data categories of unequal or unknown intervals
      (2) Example—rating system of excellent, good, fair, poor
   c) Interval scale
      (1) Ranked data with equal intervals and no absolute zero point
      (2) Examples—height and weight

E. Types of data

1. *Baseline data*—collected during needs assessment phase of community programming, oral health education process, or pretest of experimental study
2. *Raw data*—data collected but not organized
3. *Array*—data organized in ascending or descending order
4. Continuous data—capable of any degree of measurement along linear scale such as age, height, weight
5. *Discrete data*—counted only in terms of whole numbers such as gender, marital status, number of patients

D. Descriptive statistics

1. Used to describe and summarize data
2. Measures of central tendencies
   a) Mean
      (1) Arithmetic average

Calculating Mean, Median, and Mode

Ages for sample population are: 4, 6, 2, 3, 5, 6, 6, 3, 4, 4, 3, 4, 4
Calculate the mean, median and mode for the sample.

- Mean = Total of sample ages ÷ Number of subjects
  Mean = 54 ÷ 12
  Mean = 4.5
- Median = Midpoint in distribution array
  Arrangement of scores in ascending order = 2, 3, 4, 5, 6
  Median = 4
- Mode = Most frequently occurring score in distribution
  Age 2 occurs 1 time
  Age 3 occurs 3 times
  Age 4 occurs 5 times
  Age 5 occurs 2 times
  Age 6 occurs 3 times
  Mode = 4

---

(2) Reliable for symmetrical or normal distributions
(3) Sensitive to extreme values ("skewed distribution")
(4) Can be used only with interval and ratio data

b) Median
(1) Point of distribution with 50% of the scores falling above it and 50% of the scores falling below it
(2) Arrange scores in ascending order of magnitude and locate midpoint to determine median
(3) Most reliable measure of central tendency for nonsymmetrical distribution
(4) Not affected by extreme scores
(5) Appropriate for use with ordinal data

c) Mode
(1) Most frequently occurring score in a distribution
(2) May not adequately represent central tendency for interval and ratio data
(3) Appropriate for use with nominal data

3. Measures of dispersion

a) Range
(1) Spread between highest and lowest scores in distribution
(2) Ordinal statistic
(3) Determined by only two scores of distribution
(4) Not very reliable

b) Variance—measure of average deviation or spread of scores around mean

c) Standard deviation
(1) Used to analyze descriptively spread of scores in distribution

(2) Most commonly used measure of dispersion in oral health research
(3) Small standard deviation indicates that distribution of scores is clustered around mean
(4) Large standard deviation means scores are dispersed widely around mean

4. Correlation
   a) Statistical measure for determining the strength of linear relationship between variables
   b) Correlation coefficient is calculation outcome
      (1) Values from −1.0 to +1.0
      (2) The "−" and "+" signs indicate direction of correlation
      (3) Number indicates strength of correlation
   c) Types of correlation
      (1) Positive correlation
         (a) Value of one variable increases as value of second variable also increases
         (b) Perfect positive correlation is a +1.0
      (2) Negative correlation
         (a) Inverse relationship between two variables
         (b) Perfect negative correlation is −1.0
      (3) Does not establish causality—e.g., fluorosis and low prevalence of caries: although correlated, neither was the cause of the other because fluoride content of water was cause for both

5. Graphs
   a) General rule for constructing graphs along x and y axes
      (1) Vertical y axis usually represents frequency of scores occurring along scale of measurement
      (2) Horizontal x axis represents scale that measures variable of most interest
   b) Types of graphs
      (1) Bar graph—two-dimensional pictorial display of data that is discrete
      (2) Histogram
         (a) Graphic representation formed directly from frequency distribution
         (b) Consists of set of rectangles whose base is on horizontal x axis and which extends in height along vertical y axis proportional to frequency
         (c) Similar to bar graph except rectangles touch one another in a histogram
      (3) Frequency polygon
         (a) Constructed by placing point at center of each rectangle found in histogram and connecting each point with straight line
         (b) Often superimposed on line graph to display two or more distributions in one figure
         (c) Used to depict the continuous nature of data
         (d) Most frequently used graph

E. Hypothesis testing

1. May involve
   a) Testing of theories
   b) Evaluation of effects of program interventions
   c) Randomized controlled trials
   d) Laboratory studies (e.g. Food and Drug Administration studies)
   e) Practical comparison of various strategies and methods of dental treatment
2. Types of hypotheses
   a) *Null hypothesis*—no statistical difference exists between the two variables being tested
   b) *Alternative (research) hypothesis*
      (1) Statistical significant difference exists between test variables
      (2) Example—in a study to test retention of two brands of sealants, one group of subjects received Brand A and the other group received Brand B
         (a) Null hypothesis—both groups have same rate of sealant retention
         (b) Alternative hypothesis—Brand A has statistically higher retention rate than Brand B
3. *Inferential statistics*—used to test hypothesis
   a) Parametric statistics
      (1) Data must meet certain criteria (such as large enough sample and interval or ratio scale data)
      (2) t-*test*—used to test the difference between two mean scores
         (a) t-*test for independent samples*—tests the difference between means of two groups of subjects
         (b) t-*test for correlated samples*
            i) Tests difference between two means in the same group
            ii) Example—pretest/post-test
   b) *Nonparametric statistics*
      (1) Used when data do not meet assumptions of parametric statistics
      (2) χ^2(chi square)—used to test the difference between frequency distributions
         (a) Determines whether significant difference exists between observed number of cases within designated categories and expected number predicted in null hypothesis
         (b) Tests independence of categorical variables to compare two or more distributions—especially useful for analyzing nominal data
      (2) Mann-Whitney U-test
         (a) Nonparametric counterpart to *t*-test for independent samples—used with ordinal data
      (3) Sign test
         (a) Nonparametric counterpart to *t*-test for correlated samples—used with ordinal data

VIII. PLANNING AND IMPLEMENTATION OF COMMUNITY DENTAL HEALTH PROGRAMS

A. Process

1. Problem identification
2. Priority determinations
3. Identification of goals and objectives
4. Identification of resources and constraints
5. Consideration of alternative implementation strategies

B. Steps

1. Needs assessment
   a) Definition—an organized, systemic approach it identify the target group to define programming needs
   b) Needs assessment evaluates population by identifying its
      (1) Health status
      (2) Community profile
      (3) Demographics
      (4) Income
      (5) Funding availability
      (6) Community and financial leaders
      (7) Facilities
      (8) Manpower
      (9) Current and ongoing programs and projects
   c) Needs assessment is vital part of planning a community dental health program
      (1) Defines problems and determines severity
      (2) Identifies target groups for programming
      (3) Collects necessary data for planning
      (4) Collects baseline data for program evaluation
   d) Needs assessment is always conducted before planning a community dental health program. Data collection methods used to conduct needs assessment include
      (1) Surveys
      (2) Dental indexes
      (3) Direct observation with checklists and evaluation forms
      (4) Questionnaires
      (5) Interviews
      (6) Records and documents from census bureau and county agencies
      (7) Health department and agency data
2. Planning the community program
   a) Prioritizing needs
      (1) Identification of primary health problem
      (2) Target group with greatest need
   b) Setting program goals—broad statements
   c) Establishing program objectives
      (1) Specific, measurable statements of what will be accomplished
      (2) Statement indicates what, extent, who, where, and when—e.g., by 2010, 10% or less of the population in Community X will have had teeth extracted as a result of dental caries

- d) Identifying resources and constraints
  - (1) Personnel
  - (2) Equipment
  - (3) Facilities
  - (4) Finances
  - (5) Transportation
  - (6) State practice act
- e) Identifying alternative strategies to accomplish goals and objectives
- f) Choosing activities that have been tested and shown to be effective
- g) Developing implementation strategies

3. Implementation
   - a) Follow implementation strategies developed in planning stage
   - b) Obtain approval from authorities (examples include the health department, school district health director, school principal, and nursing home director)
   - c) Introduce program to dental and dental hygiene profession
   - d) Establish rules, regulations, limitations, and other program protocol with contact person for program site or organization
   - e) Organize project
   - f) Gather supplies
   - g) Conduct the project
4. Program Evaluation
   - a) Serves as basis for necessary program revisions
   - b) Types of evaluations
     - (1) *Process evaluation*—occurs during project for effectiveness evaluation
     - (2) *Product evaluation*
       - (a) Also known as "outcome evaluation"
       - (b) Occurs at the end of the project
       - (c) Measures impact of program by determining if objectives were met
   - c) Data
     - (1) Collected in a manner similar to that used in assessment phase for comparison to baseline data
     - (2) Requires compatible data for comparison
     - (3) Statistical concepts and research methods are used to interpret and analyze data

IX. LANDMARK RESEARCH STUDIES

A. The research endeavors of some early investigators continue to provide modern researchers with valuable historical perspective and a base on which current studies can be designed.

B. Major landmark epidemiological studies on diet and dental caries include

1. Vilpeholm study (Sweden)
   - a) One of the best known attempts to study effect of diet on dental decay in humans
   - b) Study conclusions

(1) Sugar consumption increases caries activity
(2) Risk of increased caries activity is greater if sugar form is sticky
(3) Risk is greatest if sugar is taken between meals in a sticky form
(4) Increase in caries disappears on withdrawal of sticky foodstuffs from diet
(5) Caries can still occur in absence of refined sugar, natural sugars, and total dietary carbohydrates

2. Tristan da Cunha
   a) Processed food was introduced; inhabitants were dentally examined in 1932 and 1937
   b) Prevalence of caries in first molars of 6- to 19-year-olds was 0
   c) Increased to 50% in 1962 and to 80% in 1966
3. Hopewood House
   a) Australian orphanage where residents lived basically on vegetarian diets with severely restricted sucrose intake
   b) Conclusions suggested strong link between diet and dental caries incidence
4. Turku study
   a) Large-scale experiment on caries in human subjects was conducted in Turku, Finland in 1970s
   b) Aim of study was to compare cariogenicity of sucrose, fructose, and xylitol
   c) Basis for study was that xylitol is sweet substance not metabolized by plaque organisms
   d) Xylitol was shown to be either noncariogenic or anticariogenic because of numerous areas of demineralization of white spot lesions
5. Fluorosis Study
   a) Dr. McKay identified "blotching" that local inhabitants called "Colorado brown Stain."
   b) McKay teamed up with G. V. Black in 1916 to report and describe "mottled enamel"

Calculating DMFT

Sample problem

Patient A exhibits evidence of decay on occlusal surfaces of teeth #3, 4, 19, and 30. Patient had #1 and 16 removed due to impaction. Following amalgam restorations are present: #2-MO, 3-DO, 14-MOD, 15-MO, and 18-MO. Calculate DMFT for this patient.

Solution

DMFT = 8 (D = 4, M = 0, and F = 4)

Problem hints

- Restored teeth with active caries are classified as "D"
- Teeth are classified as "M" only if extracted due to caries

c) In 1931, McKay tested the water samples which were found to contain fluoride in concentrations up to 14 ppm
d) H. Trendly Dean was appointed to the NIDR to investigate and define the fluoride–mottled enamel relationships.
e) Dean coined the term fluorosis and determined that 1.0 ppm in water supplies was the "minimal threshold" and that levels below that were "of no public health significance"
f) From this information, Dean developed the Dean's Fluorosis Index to classify the extent of fluorosis

DIRECTIONS Each of the questions or incomplete statements below is followed by suggested answers or completions. Select the **one** answer that is best in each case.

➤ TESTLET 1

A high school health class has 40 students, 14 to 16 years of age. Two public health dental hygienists are asked to assess the oral health of the students. Before gathering any data, the hygienists meet to select examination procedures and review indexes to be used. Both agree to use the DMFT examination. The hygienists then conduct DMFT examinations on 10 volunteer patients at the public health facility and compare and calibrate their results. When their clinical techniques produce the same clinical findings within the volunteer patient pool, the public health hygienists conduct DMFT evaluations on the health class students. The total DMFT of the class is 160.

1. The DMFT examinations conducted by the public health dental hygienists on the volunteers before examining the health class students will increase
   A. sampling error.
   B. interexaminer reliability.
   C. sensitivity.
   D. predicative value.

2. What is the group DMFT?
   A. 1.6
   B. 8.0
   C. 4.0
   D. 16

3. If D = 40, M = 44, and F = 76, what percent of the teeth have untreated caries?
   A. 40%
   B. 25%
   C. 16%
   D. 4%

4. The relatively high F value (76) would indicate that this population
   A. has no access to dental care.
   B. has a high incidence of tooth extractions.
   C. is in need of aggressive periodontal therapy.
   D. has access to restorative dental care.

5. The amount of untreated caries in this population at the time of the examination is known as the
   A. caries incidence.
   B. caries prevalence.
   C. hidden caries.
   D. primary caries.

6. The public health hygienists agree to conduct annual DMFTs on these 40 students for 10 years. This type of study is
   A. retrospective.
   B. cross-sectional.
   C. longitudinal.
   D. experimental.

7. The M component of the group DMFT in this population assumes that missing teeth have been lost as a result of

A. caries.
B. periodontal involvement.
C. congenital defects.
D. poor oral hygiene.

8. What percentage of the examined teeth has received dental treatment?
   A. 76%
   B. 75%
   C. 40%
   D. 44%

9. When considering DMFTs 5 years after the initial examinations, the test population consists of 21 former students. This is an example of
   A. sampling error.
   B. a probability sample.
   C. quantifiability.
   D. sample attrition.

10. The DMFTs for the 21 test subjects are D = 20, M = 5, and F = 25. How does the data of unmet dental needs compare with the initial findings?
    A. There is a much greater need for dental treatment within the test population 5 years after the first examination.
    B. The sample population has maintained the same decay rate over the last 5 years.
    C. The need for dental treatment in the test population is much lower 5 years after the initial examination.
    D. Decay rates and extractions have markedly decreased since the first DMFT was conducted 5 years ago.

➤ TESTLET 2

The nursing supervisor at the tenth district health department contacted the Boulder County Dental Hygiene Component (BCDHC) with dental concerns for students in the district. During routine checkups, the supervisor had noticed a high incidence of dental neglect within the Jackson Senior High School (JSHS) student population as evidenced by severe decay, poor dietary habits, and inadequate home care. The BCDHC then sent surveys to the parents in the school district regarding dietary conditions in the home, socioeconomic status of the household, dental home care procedures, and access to routine dental care. Oral hygiene and caries status of the JSHS students were assessed in the classrooms with the use of the plaque index (PI) and DMF index. The group PI average was 2.5 and the group DMFT was as follows: D = 250, M = 5, and F = 25.

1. The use of surveys and classroom examination are integral components of
   A. conducting a needs assessment.
   B. prioritizing needs.
   C. setting program goals.
   D. developing implementation strategies.

2. The BCDHC analyzed data gathered from questionnaires and surveys. They voted unanimously "to increase access to dental care for low-income families." This is an example of a(n)
   A. program objective
   B. process evaluation.
   C. implementation strategy.
   D. program goal.

3. A task force appointed by the BCDHC to obtain approval for a school-wide dental screening and treatment day contacts the district school superintendent. This is an example of a(n)
   A. needs assessment.
   B. program objective.
   C. implementation strategy.
   D. program planning.

4. A special committee is appointed by the BCDHC to review program objectives and evaluate if they are being met. This is part of an ongoing process known as
   A. resource identification.
   B. program evaluation.
   C. community profiling.
   D. definition of needs.

5. The BCDHC agrees to sponsor a "Jackson Senior High School Day of Smiles" event where area dentists, assistants, and hygienists donate their time to treat 100% of the JSHS stridence requiring care. This is an example of a
   A. program objective.
   B. process evaluation.
   C. implementation strategy.
   D. program goal.

6. The BEST way to address this population's needs during this 1-day event is by
   A. placing sealants on permanent molars.
   B. performing thorough teeth cleaning on the students.
   C. having volunteer dentist restore or extract the carious teeth.
   D. providing fluoride treatments.

7. A PI average of 2.5 indicates that this population
   A. has severe periodontitis.
   B. has poor plaque control skills.
   C. needs dietary counseling.
   D. has generalized fluorosis.

8. When analyzing the DMFT data, the high group D value and relatively low group M and F values probably indicates that this population
   A. does not have regular access to dental care.
   B. has demonstrated an ability to control plaque.
   C. needs periodontal therapy.
   D. demonstrates the most calculus on the lingual surfaces.

9. Obtaining DMFTs on the students before the "Day of Smiles" is an example of
   A. establishing program objectives.
   B. obtaining baseline data.
   C. identifying a chief complaint.
   D. investigating surveys.

10. Comparing the group DMFT data obtained before the "JSHS Day of Smiles" to the group DMFT data obtained on the participants 90 days after the Day of Smiles is an example of
   A. process evaluation.
   B. product evaluation.
   C. program revision.
   D. identifying constraints.

➤ TESTLET 3*

A State Board of Health has just hired a veteran dental hygienist with 25 years of experience who must now begin to think on the group level rather than the individual patient level. She has been asked to assess the dental status of all second graders in a non-fluoridated school district. Dental hygiene students are available to help with screenings and gain experience with gathering data through various indices.

1. In a private practice setting, the dental status of a client is determined by an examination. In the public health setting, the examination would MOST closely parallel
   A. a survey.
   B. program planning.
   C. goal setting.
   D. program operation.

2. After information is collected, the next step is to
   A. establish goals.
   B. develop a strategic plan.
   C. conduct program appraisal.
   D. establish program funding.

3. Water testing has been completed. Due to a minimal amount of fluoride in the water, approval has been obtained from the school board for a school water fluoridation program. What is the recommended concentration of fluoride for school water supplies?
   A. 1 ppm
   B. 2 ppm
   C. 3.5 ppm
   D. 4.5 ppm

---

*Prepared by Nancy Mann, RDH, MS.

4. The socioeconomic status of the second graders receiving the MOST benefit from classroom dental health presentations would be which one of the following?
   A. high
   B. middle
   C. low
   D. all

5. Which of the following approaches would be BEST to insure that the entire school community of children are taught dental health?
   A. Have dental hygiene students teach oral health as part of their public health practicum.
   B. Have volunteer dental hygienists from the local dental hygiene component teach oral health to the school community.
   C. Teach the school nurse methods of oral hygiene.
   D. Train the teachers in methods of oral hygiene.

➤ TESTLET 4*

A new dental hygiene graduate accepts a position in a migrant worker camp as part of a loan-forgiveness program. There are 56 adults and 92 children who need to be screened and be on a prevention program. Over half of the adults smoke.

1. The first thing to be done is
   A. test the water for fluoride content.
   B. teach dental health education in group settings.
   C. assess the needs of the group.
   D. begin oral prophylaxis as soon as possible.

2. Which of the following indices will be MOST helpful for the hygienist to use in assessing the periodontal treatment needs of the adults?
   A. CPITN
   B. FRI
   C. EIB
   D. PII

3. Which of the following indices is MOST appropriate to determine the caries experience of the preschool children in the camp?
   A. DMFT
   B. DMF
   C. deft
   D. DMFS

4. The “e” in the deft index stands for
   A. erupted.
   B. exfoliated.
   C. primary teeth indicated for extraction.
   D. extracted.

5. Which of the following would be an example of a risk factor in the migrant camp group?
   A. age
   B. gender
   C. race
   D. smoking

---

*Prepared by Nancy Mann, RDH, MS.

➤ TESTLET 1

1.

B. Reaching agreement between two or more examiners is termed interexaminer reliability. It requires initial agreement on interpretation of diagnostic criteria followed by a period of training with repeated patient examinations to ensure that examiners are comparable. Sampling error results from the research sample not perfectly representing the base population. Sensitivity describes the ability of a measuring instrument to detect clinically relevant changes in the condition being measured. Predictive value refers to the ability of a diagnostic test to predict the probability that a person who tests positive will have the disease or condition (positive predictive value) or who tests negative will not have the disease or condition (negative predictive value).

2.

C. The total DMFT is divided by the number of individuals examined to calculate the group DMFT. The calculation is as follows: $160 \div 40 = 4.0$ (group DMFT). Based on the calculation used to determine the group DMFT of a study population, 1.6, 8.0, and 16 are incorrect values.

3.

B. To determine the percentage of untreated caries, divide the "D" component total by the total DMFT. The calculation is:

Total DMFT = D + M + F = 40 + 44 + 76 = 160

D ÷ total DMFT = 40 ÷ 160 = 0.25

0.25 × 100% = 25% (of teeth examined have untreated caries)

Based on the calculations used to determine the percent of the group DMFT needing restorative care, 40%, 16%, and 4% are incorrect values.

4.

D. The "F" value in a DMFT examination refers to those teeth that have been filled. Filled teeth are assumed to have decayed before restoration. Because teeth must be diagnosed as carious and restored in the dental setting, access to care must be in place.

5.

B. The prevalence of a disease in a population is the proportion of existing cases of the disease in the population at one point in time or during a specified period of time. Incidence is the proportion of a new condition or disease within a population during a specified period of time. Hidden caries is the term used to describe dentinal caries found radiographically beneath an apparently sound occlusal surface, and primary caries are those carious lesions occurring on unrestored teeth.

6.

C. Longitudinal studies require at least two series of measurements among the same population at different times to determine the progress of the condition over a specified time period. A retrospective study is descriptive in nature and investigates previously collected data. In cross-sectional study, the health conditions in a representative cross section of a population are assessed at one time. An experimental study is designed to test the efficacy or effectiveness of a therapeutic drug, preventive material, or a treatment protocol by manipulating conditions.

7.

A. Only those teeth that are missing as a result of unrestorable caries are considered in the "M" category. Teeth extracted for orthodontic reasons are not considered in the "M" category. The DMFT is an index that measures caries experience, is not used to evaluate periodontal health, and does not include congenitally missing teeth or poor oral hygiene.

8.

B. To calculate what percentage of the examined teeth have received dental treatment, the "M" and "F" values are totaled and divided by the group DMFT. A percentage of then calculated as follows:

M + F = 120

120 ÷ 160 = 0.75

0.75 × 100% = 75% (the percentage of teeth that have received dental treatment)

Based on the calculations used to determine the percentage of teeth that have received dental treatment from this group's DMFT score, 76%, 40%, and 44% are incorrect answers.

9.

D. Sample attrition refers to the decrease in number of subjects over the course of the study owing to such things as relocation, health issues, or loss of interest. Efforts to minimize sample attrition help to increase the validity of a study. Sampling error refers to the error that results from the sample not representing the base population. A probability sample is one in which the chance if each person being chosen in the sample is known. Quantifiability refers to the ability of an index to be analyzed statistically so that the status of a group can be expressed by a distribution, mean, median, or other statistical measure.

10.

A. To calculate the percentage of unmet dental needs in a DMFT score, the "D" value is divided by the total DMFT and converted to a percentage. The unmet dental needs of the sample population, examined 5 years after the initial DMFT examinations were performed, can be calculated as follows:

D = 20

Total DMFT = D + M + F = 20 + 5 + 25 = 50

D ÷ Total DMFT = 20 ÷ 50 = 0.4

0.4 × 100% = 40% (unmet dental needs of the sample population 5 years after the initial DMFT examinations were performed)

The initial DMFT examination findings conducted on the 40 high school students can be used to calculate the unmet dental needs of the sample population in a like manner. The calculations in this case are as follows:

D = 40

Total DMFT = D + M + F = 40 + 44 + 76 = 160

D ÷ Total DMFT = 40 ÷ 160 = 0.25

0.25 × 100% = 25% (unmet dental needs of the sample population at the initial DMFT examination)

Therefore, 40% of the sample population demonstrates unmet dental needs 5 years after the initial examinations compared with 25% needing restorative care initially.

➤ TESTLET 2

1.

A. A needs assessment, the first step in community planning, is used to obtain a profile of the community to ascertain the causes of the problem and helps in developing appropriate program goals and objectives in problem solving. A needs assessment identifies such things as community health status, population demographics, availability of manpower and facilities, and current ongoing programs and projects. Only after the needs assessment has been completed for the community are priorities for dealing with the identified problem(s) considered. Program goals can be established only after conduction of a needs assessment identifies areas of greatest concern. After a program plan based on analysis of the survey data, priorities and alternatives, community attitudes, and available resources has been developed, it must be approved by the community. Then, the program implementation begins.

2.

D. A program goal is a general statement about the overall purpose of a program to meet a defined problem. Program objectives are more specific than goals and describe the desired end result in a measurable way. Evaluation of a program is ongoing and occurs during program planning and implementation. Revisions to the program are based on evaluation results.

3.

C. Implementation strategies involve obtaining approval from appropriate personnel within the agency to determine rules, regulations, and possible limitations. Implementation strategies also include acquainting dental and dental hygiene professionals with the planned program, organizing the project, gathering necessary supplies, and identifying dental health education as it relates to the program. The needs assessment identifies the target group and defines programming needs. The assessment may utilize a variety of data collection methods such as surveys, dental indices, direct observations, questionnaires, interviews, and records from federal and state agencies. Program objectives are specific, measurable statements of what will be accomplished. Program planning within the community is much like developing a treatment plan to meet the dental needs of a patient in the private practice setting.

4.

B. Program evaluation is an ongoing process based on objectives serving as the standard of comparison to determine success or failure of the program. Resource identification is done during the needs assessment phase of program planning. Manpower, financial, and transportation considerations must be identified before program implementation. Community profiling is done during the needs assessment phase of program planning. The community profile of a population may include such characteristics as ethnic makeup, diet, socioeconomics status, education, and age. Defining the need of a population occurs during the needs assessment phase of program planning.

5.

A. A program objective is a specific, measurable statement of what will be accomplished. In this case, 100% of the students needing dental care (the percentage is specific and measurable) will receive it. Evaluation of a program is ongoing and occurs during program planning and implementation. Revisions to the program are based on evaluation results. Implementation strategies are developed during the planning stage of program development. A program goal is a broad general statement on the overall purpose of a program to meet a defined problem toward which program efforts are then directed.

6.

C. Because caries incidence is a nonreversible problem, preventive measures would not be effective in eliminating the existing caries. Restorative treatment is needed to optimize the dental health of the students. Placing sealants, performing cleanings, and providing fluoride treatments are preventive measures.

7.

B. The PI (plaque index) is designed to measure plaque removal based on the amount of plaque present at the time of evaluation. The possible range of scores is 0 to 3. An average PI of 2.5 indicates that there is a moderate to heavy accumulation of soft deposits within the gingival pocket and/or on the gingival margin that can be seen with the naked eye. The amount of debris indicates that plaque control is inadequate. Because the PI is designed to measure oral hygiene effectiveness based on the presence or absence of plaque and debris, it does not measure disease conditions of supporting structures of the teeth, dietary habits, or presence or extent of fluorosis.

8.

A. The high group D value represents a large percentage of carious lesions within the population. Because the group M and F values represent dental care rendered, their low values in this population suggest that dental care was not sought or obtained on a regular basis. The DMFT measures an individual's or group's caries experience and does not measure the amount of plaque, periodontal status, or presence or absence of calculus in a population.

9.

B. Baseline data are collected before program implementation. It is used to evaluate the success or failure of a given program by comparing baseline findings to program results. Program objectives are specific, measurable statements of what a program will accomplish. A survey is often initiated in response to a community's chief complaint. Investigation of surveys previously conducted by other researchers may help planners design new programs.

10.

B. Also known as "outcome evaluation," this process takes place at the end of the project and measures the impact of the program based on whether the program objectives were met. Process evaluation occurs during the project to evaluate procedures used to obtain data. Revisions to the program are based on the process evaluation. Program revisions are made during the course of the program and are based on evaluation results. Constraints may include such things as lack of manpower, inadequate financing, poor equipment, and anything else that impairs program operation.

➤ TESTLET 3

1.

A. A needs assessment, which should occur first in an examination, most closely parallels a survey. Program planning parallels treatment planning. Goal setting does not come first and program operation parallels treatment.

2.

A. Develop a goal to meet each need. Goals must be developed before strategic planning can occur. Program appraisal is the evaluation stage, and program funding cannot be established until the program is determined.

3.

D. 4.5 ppm is the amount that has been shown to reduce caries up to 40%. Levels are at this concentration since ingestion is only taking place during the school hours. 1 ppm is the optimum level for community drinking water; 2 ppm and 3.5 ppm are not recommended for school water supplies.

4.

C. The low socioeconomic group has seen the least decline in caries according to the Surgeon General's Report, Healthy People 2000, and NHANES III. The high socioeconomic group has seen the sharpest decline in caries, so the lower the SES, the more they benefit from the classroom presentations on dental health.

5.

D. Training the teachers is the best method of ensuring that the entire school community has been reached with dental health. They are present with the children every day to reinforce health habits and incorporate dental units in health and in science. Dental hygiene students and volunteer hygienists will do a great job presenting, but are only there once. The school nurse is not on a one to one with the second grade classes daily.

➤ TESTLET 4

1.

C. Assessment of needs and program planning come first. Teaching brushing and flossing are part of program implementation. Oral prophylaxis is part of program operation, and testing the water for fluoride content would take place after needs assessment.

2.

A. CPITN will assess periodontal treatment needs of a large group. FRI index is designed to identify tisk factors for fluorosis. EIB index measures bleeding with an interdental stimulator. The PII will give us plaque scores; however, treatment information is needed first.

3.

C. deft will count decayed and filled primary teeth, as well as primary teeth indicated for extraction. DMFT counts permanent decayed, missing, and filled teeth. DMFS is decayed, missing, and filled permanent surfaces. For mixed dentitions, two indices must be used, one for the deciduous dentition and one for the permanent dentition.

4.

C. "e" in deft stands for primary teeth *indicated* for extraction. deft does not measure erupted, exfoliated, or extracted teeth.

5.

D. Smoking is the risk factor that can be modified. Age, race, and gender cannot be modified, but it is possible to stop smoking.

CHAPTER

16 Case Studies

contents

review questions

DIRECTIONS Each of the questions or incomplete statements below is followed by suggested answers or completions. Select the **one** answer that is best in each case.

➤ CASE 1 (see I-2 to I-3)

1. What is the clinical significance of the reported past use of the weight reduction medication, Redux™?
   A. There is no clinical significance.
   B. A common side effect is esophageal spasms.
   C. It is known to cause valvular spasms.
   D. It causes renal damage.
   E. It produces a painless enlargement of the liver.

2. All of the following procedures are indicated for this client before treatment EXCEPT one. Which one is the EXCEPTION?
   A. The clinician should consult a pharmacological reference.
   B. A medical consultation should be obtained.
   C. Premedicate the patient with 2 grams of Cephalexin® 1 hour before treatment.
   D. Inform the client about the diastolic blood pressure reading.
   E. Conclude there is no health condition that would contraindicate treatment.

3. On examining the intraoral images, which of the following classifications BEST describes the client's occlusion?
   A. Class I ideal occlusion
   B. Class I malocclusion
   C. Class II, division 1
   D. Class II, division 2
   E. Class III occlusion

4. Which of the following is NOT an accurate description of tooth mobility?
   A. Tooth mobility is typically graded on a scale of 0 through 3.
   B. Only an ankylosed tooth would have a score of 0 tooth mobility.
   C. Radiographs do not accurately represent the degree of tooth mobility.
   D. Bidigital evaluation with instrument handles is the conventional method of measurement.
   E. This patient has tooth mobility readings consistent with normal physiological movement.

5. Examine the panoramic radiograph and intraoral camera image of the mandibular arch. What, MOST likely, is the identity of the mass located in the right and left premolar regions of the mandible?
   A. condensing osteitis
   B. primary molar root tips
   C. bilateral mandibular tori
   D. salivary stones at the duct orifices
   E. chronic focal sclerosing osteomyelitis

6. Considering the clinical and radiographic information, which of the following Case Types BEST classifies this client's disease progression?

A. I
B. II
C. III
D. IV
E. V

7. Of the following, which one MOST likely accounts for the client's reported sensitivity to cold?
   A. exposed cementum
   B. teeth clenching
   C. recurrent caries
   D. tooth mobility

8. Which of the following descriptions is NOT accurate regarding furcation involvement?
   A. A Shepherd's hook explorer and Nabors probe are instruments used to determine the degree of involvement.
   B. Furcation occurs when the loss of attachment extends into the bifurcation or trifurcation of multirooted teeth.
   C. Class I involvement indicates an early lesion in which the concavity of the furcation is detected.
   D. The interradicular bone is resorbed, exposing a through-and-through tunnel in Class II involvement.
   E. Class III involvement is indicated when the radiographs demonstrate an obvious radiolucency within the furcation.

9. Examine the molar bitewings. What correction is necessary to minimize the overlapping of the interproximal surfaces of the molar teeth?
   A. Decrease the positive vertical angulation.
   B. Direct the central ray to the center of the film.
   C. Move the horizontal angulation more forward.
   D. Align the PID in a negative vertical angulation.
   E. Direct the horizontal angulation more posterior.

10. Which of the following observations is NOT demonstrated on the bitewing radiographs?
   A. root caries on 5, 11, 13, 19
   B. generalized mild to moderate horizontal bone loss
   C. Class II amalgam restorations on 2, 5, and 14
   D. 3 and 30 have been endodontically treated with gutta percha
   E. occlusal amalgams on 1, 2, 15, 16, 17, 18, 31, 32

11. In many clients, oral contraceptives may cause a condition mimicking pregnancy gingivitis. What bacteria would predominate in this condition?
   A. *Mutans streptococcus*
   B. *Streptococcus salivarius*
   C. *Prevotella intermedia*
   D. *Porphymonas gingivalis*

12. What is the correct description of the structure identified by the arrows on the panoramic photo?
   A. fracture of the zygomatic process of the temporal bone
   B. space between the maxilla and the lateral pterygoid plate
   C. suture between the processes that form the zygoma
   D. fine posterior boundary of the infraorbital canal
   E. posterior wall of the maxillary sinus cavity

➤ CASE 2 (see I-4 to I-5)

1. Since this client has no bleeding on probing and a few areas of 3-mm pocket readings, which of the following bacteria would be more prevalent in her plaque?
   A. spirochetes
   B. cocci and rods
   C. *Fusobacterium*
   D. *Mutans streptococcus*

2. The radiolucent diagonal lines on the mandibular right molar periapical are a result of
   A. overlapped films.
   B. light leakage.
   C. film bending.
   D. overdevelopment.

review questions

3. Which of the following types of professional topical fluoride treatments is MOST appropriate for this client?
   A. stannous
   B. acidulated phosphate
   C. sodium monofluorophosphate
   D. sodium

4. Which of the following materials was MOST likely used to restore the maxillary left lateral incisor?
   A. dental amalgam
   B. composite resin
   C. gold alloy
   D. glass ionomer cement

5. Ferrous sulfate is a type of
   A. vitamin B.
   B. calcium.
   C. hormone.
   D. iron.

6. Which of the following is a good anticariogenic snack to recommend to this client?
   A. crackers
   B. pretzels
   C. carrots
   D. cheese

7. In evaluating the diet history, this client is likely to have poor intakes of all the following nutrients EXCEPT one. Which one is the EXCEPTION?
   A. calcium
   B. vitamin D
   C. vitamin C
   D. thiamin

8. Which of the following oral manifestations would be evident with folate and vitamin B_{12} deficiencies?
   A. angular cheilosis
   B. dysgeusia
   C. dysphagia
   D. oral candidiasis

9. The clinician determined that the density of the bitewing radiographs was lower than desired. Of the following, which one would NOT have caused the problem?
   A. underestimation of the client's size and stature
   B. exposure time was at too high of a setting
   C. weak or exhausted developer chemicals
   D. processing temperature was too low
   E. exposure button was released too soon

10. Ferrous sulfate is being taken
    A. as needed.
    B. before meals.
    C. twice a day.
    D. three times a day.

11. Folate and vitamin B_{12} are important for the integrity of the oral mucosa because they are involved in DNA synthesis, cell growth, and maintenance.
    A. Both statement and reason are correct and related.
    B. Both statement and reason are correct, but not related.
    C. The statement is correct, but the reason is not.
    D. The statement is not correct, but the reason is.
    E. Neither the statement nor the reason is correct.

12. The MOST appropriate recommendation for this client is to see a(n)
    A. high school counselor.
    B. school psychologist.
    C. oral surgeon.
    D. dietitian.

➤ CASE 3 (see I-6 to I-7)

1. During treatment, the client starts experiencing dyspnea and wheezing on exhalation—characteristic of an acute asthmatic attack. The first step to be taken after seating the client in the most comfortable position is to
   A. administer oxygen.
   B. prepare a cortocosteroid injection for the dentist to administer.
   C. assist the client in use of her own bronchodilator.
   D. administer sedation.

2. All of the following are side effects of Proventil EXCEPT one. Which one is the EXCEPTION?
   A. taste changes
   B. xerostomia
   C. ecchymoses
   D. tooth discoloration

3. The radiographic survey demonstrates that the maxillary left first molar has undergone endodontic therapy. Close examination reveals a difference in radiodensity between the two buccal and palatal canals. Why is that difference observed?
   A. The canals were likely obstructed at different times.
   B. Gold posts are present in the buccal canals.
   C. Gutta percha is present in the buccal canals and a silver point in the palatal canal.
   D. Gutta percha is present in the palatal canal and silver points in the buccal canals.

4. By using the photograhic and radiographic surveys, it can be determined that the mandibular first molar has been restored. Which of the following types of restoration is present?
   A. all-ceramic
   B. porcelain fused to metal (metal ceramic)
   C. indirect composite full coverage crown
   D. 3/4-gold crown

5. In evaluating the client's blood pressure, which of the following considerations would be MOST appropriate before treatment is rendered?
   A. Dental treatment can be rendered with no further consideration.
   B. A medical referral is recommended before treatment is provided.
   C. A medical referral is required before treatment is provided.
   D. Blood pressure measurement should be retaken before treatment is provided.

6. The restoration on the maxillary left first molar was fabricated using an indirect technique. Which of the following restorations is identified on this tooth?
   A. full coverage crown
   B. 3/4-coverage crown
   C. mesial-occlusal-distal onlay
   D. mesial-occlusal-distal inlay

7. The restoration on tooth #7 shows discoloration along its edges. Which of the following is the MOST likely cause?
   A. marginal leakage (percolation)
   B. overpolymerization of the restorative material
   C. improper flossing technique
   D. improper brushing technique

8. The drugs, which she takes at bedtime, require which of the following abbreviations?
   A. qid
   B. bid
   C. PRN
   D. HS

9. The maxillary right central incisor has a Class II fracture of the mesial incisal angle. Which of the following materials would NOT be an appropriate choice for restoring this fracture?
   A. glass ionomer cement
   B. composite restoration
   C. aluminous porcelain
   D. gold alloy

10. Since there is a history of dental caries activity, presence of secondary decay, and multiple restorations, which of the following topical fluoride applications would be MOST appropriate for this client?
    A. stannous fluoride
    B. neutral sodium fluoride
    C. APF gel
    D. sodium monofluorophosphate

11. Oral contraceptives may cause a condition mimicking pregnancy gingivitis. Which of the following bacteria would predominate in this condition?
    A. *Mutans streptococcus*
    B. *Streptococcus salivarius*
    C. *Provotella intermedia*
    D. *Porphyromonas gingivalis*

12. The clinical examination reveals that tooth #3 requires a full-cast crown. To anesthetize the mesial buccal root, which of the following alveolar nerves must be innervated?
    A. anterior superior
    B. middle superior
    C. posterior superior
    D. inferior

➤ CASE 4 (see I-8 to I-9)

1. During the appointment, the client complains of an intense headache at the right temple and then leans over to vomit. In a slurred manner, he states the left side of his body has gone numb, then loses consciousness. Which of the following medical emergencies has occurred?
    A. myxedema coma
    B. acute adrenal insufficiency
    C. hemorrhagic CVA
    D. thyroid storm
2. Which of the following nerves primarily innervates muscles of facial expression?
    A. V
    B. III
    C. VII
    D. IX
3. Since the client has not brushed his teeth today, which of the following bacteria would be first to aggregate on his teeth?
    A. *Mutans streptococcus*
    B. *Streptococcus sanguis*
    C. *Streptococcus salivarius*
    D. *Provotella intermedia*
4. The drug class of Catapres is
    A. antihyperlipidemic.
    B. antihypertensive.
    C. nonsteriodal ovulatory stimulant.
    D. urinary tract antibacterial.
5. Which of the following terminology describes the lesion in the photograph?
    A. diffuse leukoplakia
    B. nodular leukoplakia
    C. diffuse erythema
    D. nodular erythema
    E. speckled leukoplakia
6. Which of the following would be considered high-risk factors for this lesion?
    A. tobacco use
    B. spicy food consumption
    C. breath mint abuse
    D. alcohol consumption
    E. oral tongue habits
7. Which of the following dictates the next course of treatment?
    A. observation for 1 year
    B. incisional biopsy
    C. excisional biopsy
    D. antibiotics
    E. antifungal medication
8. Histological examination reveals top to bottom dysplastic epithelium with invasion of the basement membrane. Which of the following is the MOST likely diagnosis?
    A. mild dysplasia
    B. moderate dysplasia
    C. severe dysplasia
    D. carcinoma in situ
    E. invasive carcinoma
9. Which of the following is the MOST likely explanation for the palpable cervical node?
    A. drainage of an infection
    B. drainage of the gingival inflammation
    C. inflammation from spicy food consumption
    D. metastasis of the oropharyngeal lesion
10. The MOST likely etiology for the minor carious lesions in the facial areas of gingival recession is
    A. tobacco use.
    B. chronic sugar exposure.
    C. mouth breathing.
    D. toothpick habit.

➤ CASE 5 (see I-10 to I-11)

1. The status of this client's periodontal health would be described as
    A. healthy.
    B. acute gingivitis.

C. active periodontitis.
D. healthy, with a past history of periodontitis.

2. According to G.V. Black's classification, what class of restoration is present on teeth #s 2, 3, 13, and 14?
   A. A
   B. I
   C. II
   D. C
   E. V

3. What impact does this client's restorations have on her periodontal condition?
   A. The overhanging margins are plaque retentive and contribute to the inflammatory disease.
   B. The restorative material is known to contribute to periodontal disease.
   C. The restorations are of little concern. They do not contribute to the periodontal disease.
   D. The restorations are the cause of the periodontal disease.

4. A significant risk factor for the development and progression of this client's condition is
   A. tobacco use.
   B. diabetes.
   C. hypertension.
   D. past history of orthodontic care.

5. There is purulence present on the facial of #24. Its cause is
   A. occlusal trauma.
   B. pulp infection.
   C. periodontal infection.
   D. physical injury.

6. Diabetes increases the risk of periodontal disease. Periodontal disease complicates the management of diabetes.
   A. The first statement is TRUE, the second statement is FALSE.
   B. The first statement is FALSE, the second statement is TRUE.
   C. Both statements are TRUE.
   D. Both statements are FALSE.

7. Referring to the clinical and radiographic findings, the client's AAP Case Type is MOST likely
   A. I.
   B. II.
   C. III.
   D. IV.
   E. V.

8. Compare the radiographic appearance of the bone at the mesial of #7 with the mesial of #19. Which of the following suggests active periodontal disease at #7?
   A. There is more bone loss at #7 than #19.
   B. There is calculus present at #7 and not at #19.
   C. There is a deeper pocket at #7 than #19.
   D. The lamina dura does not appear at #7, but does at #19.

9. Tooth #7 has been recommended for extraction. The MOST appropriate referral for this client is to a(n)
   A. oral surgeon.
   B. dietitian.
   C. physician.
   D. periodontist.

10. The masseter muscle plays an active role during bruxism. Which of the following structures represent the origin and insertion of the masseter muscle?
    A. temporal fossa; coronoid process
    B. greater wing of the sphenoid; anterior surface of the temperomandibular joint (TMJ) disc
    C. zygomatic arch; angle of mandible, lateral surface
    D. lateral surface of pterygoid plate; neck of the condyle

11. Which of the following would MOST likely correct the distortion that appears on the maxillary left molar radiograph?
    A. increase vertical angulation
    B. decrease vertical angulation
    C. redirect the PID more posteriorly
    D. place the film more inferior to the occlusal surfaces

12. Which of the following muscles is primarily responsible for the client's difficulty in tilting and rotating her head?
   A. digastric
   B. sternohyoid
   C. mylohyoid
   D. sternocleidomastoid

➤ CASE 6 (see I-12 to I-13)

1. The white patches in this client's mouth are MOST likely
   A. "snuff" leukoplakia.
   B. candidiasis.
   C. hyperkeratosis.
   D. linea alba.

2. To BEST diagnose this client's medical condition, which of the following medical tests should be performed?
   A. prothrombin time
   B. antibody assay test
   C. liver enzyme test
   D. partial prothrombin time

3. The symptoms displayed by this client are MOST likely due to which of the following conditions?
   A. tuberculosis
   B. hepatitis B
   C. HIV
   D. hepatitis C

4. The blood cell type MOST likely to be affected by this client's disease is
   A. thrombocytes.
   B. B lymphocytes.
   C. CD4 lymphocytes.
   D. neutrophils.

5. What modifiable risk factor, noted in this client's history, is MOST significant in the progression of periodontal disease?
   A. high stress job
   B. hypertension
   C. long working hours
   D. tobacco use

6. All of the following auxiliary aids could be used to clean the proximal surfaces of #s 10 and 11 EXCEPT one. Which one is the EXCEPTION?
   A. dental tape
   B. interdental brush
   C. interdental wood stimulator
   D. Bass method of toothbrushing

7. Which of the following factors could contribute to plaque retention at tooth #14?
   A. porcelain-fused-to-metal crown
   B. a large MOD amalgam restoration
   C. exposed furcation
   D. extrinsic stain

8. Which of the following Gracey curets could be utilized on the distolinguals of teeth #s 30 and 31?
   A. 11
   B. 12
   C. 13
   D. 14

9. Referral to his physician is indicated for this client to
   A. identify the cause of his tooth sensitivity.
   B. provide antibiotics for treatment of his periodontal disease.
   C. identify the cause of his breath odor.
   D. evaluate his significant weight loss.

10. What AAP Case Type would classify this client?
   A. I
   B. II
   C. III
   D. IV

11. Which of the following techniques was MOST likely used to palpate the cervical lymph nodes?
   A. bimanual
   B. bilateral
   C. digital
   D. inspection

12. To prepare for treatment of this client, the dental hygienist should
   A. double glove.
   B. use barriers as appropriate.
   C. sterilize all instruments twice.
   D. use a special "isolation" room.

The case studies in this section will be used to answer the questions in Chapter 16.

client history synopsis

CASE 1

Age: 36

Gender: Female

Height: 5′4″

Weight: 180 lbs

VITAL SIGNS

Blood pressure: 130/90

Pulse rate: 77

Respiratory rate: 18

MEDICAL HISTORY

A year ago, the client lost 75 lbs. while taking Redux™ (dexfenfluramine hydrochloride) for a period of 6 months. The client reports she is allergic to penicillin.

MEDICATIONS

The client is taking the contraceptive Ortho-Novum® 1/50.

DENTAL HISTORY

Five years ago, the client received periodontal treatment and since, maintenance therapy. The client reports brushing and flossing her teeth at least twice daily. She also clenches her teeth occasionally. Her last dental visit was 6 months ago for a recall appointment.

SOCIAL HISTORY

The client reports a history of weight problems throughout adulthood and a family history of hypertension.

CHIEF COMPLAINTS

"Some of my teeth are stained and sensitive to cold. Besides that, it is time for my 6-month check-up."

ADDITIONAL FINDINGS

Class I furcation involvement is noted on teeth #s 2, 16, 17–19, and 30–32.

SUPPLEMENTAL DENTAL FINDINGS

Tooth mobility is noted on teeth #s 23–26.

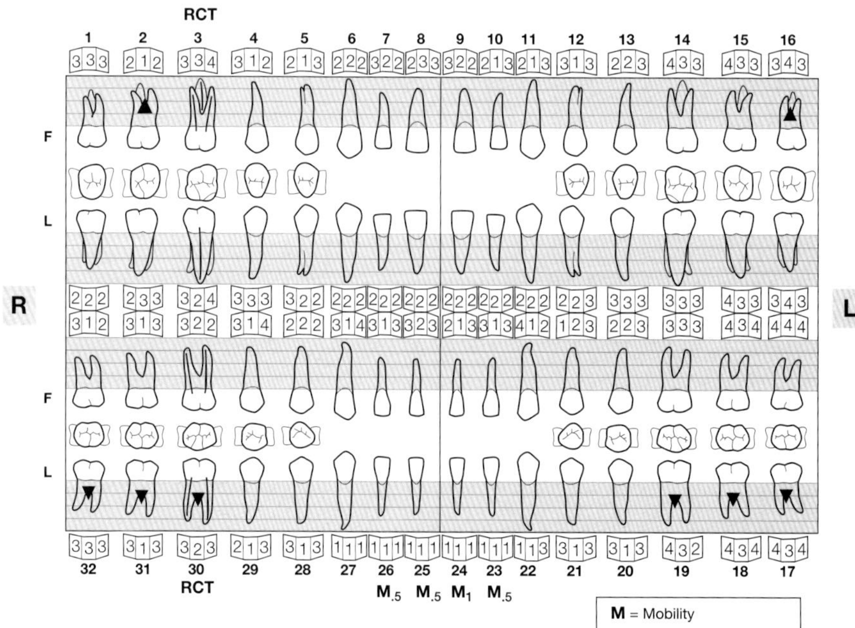

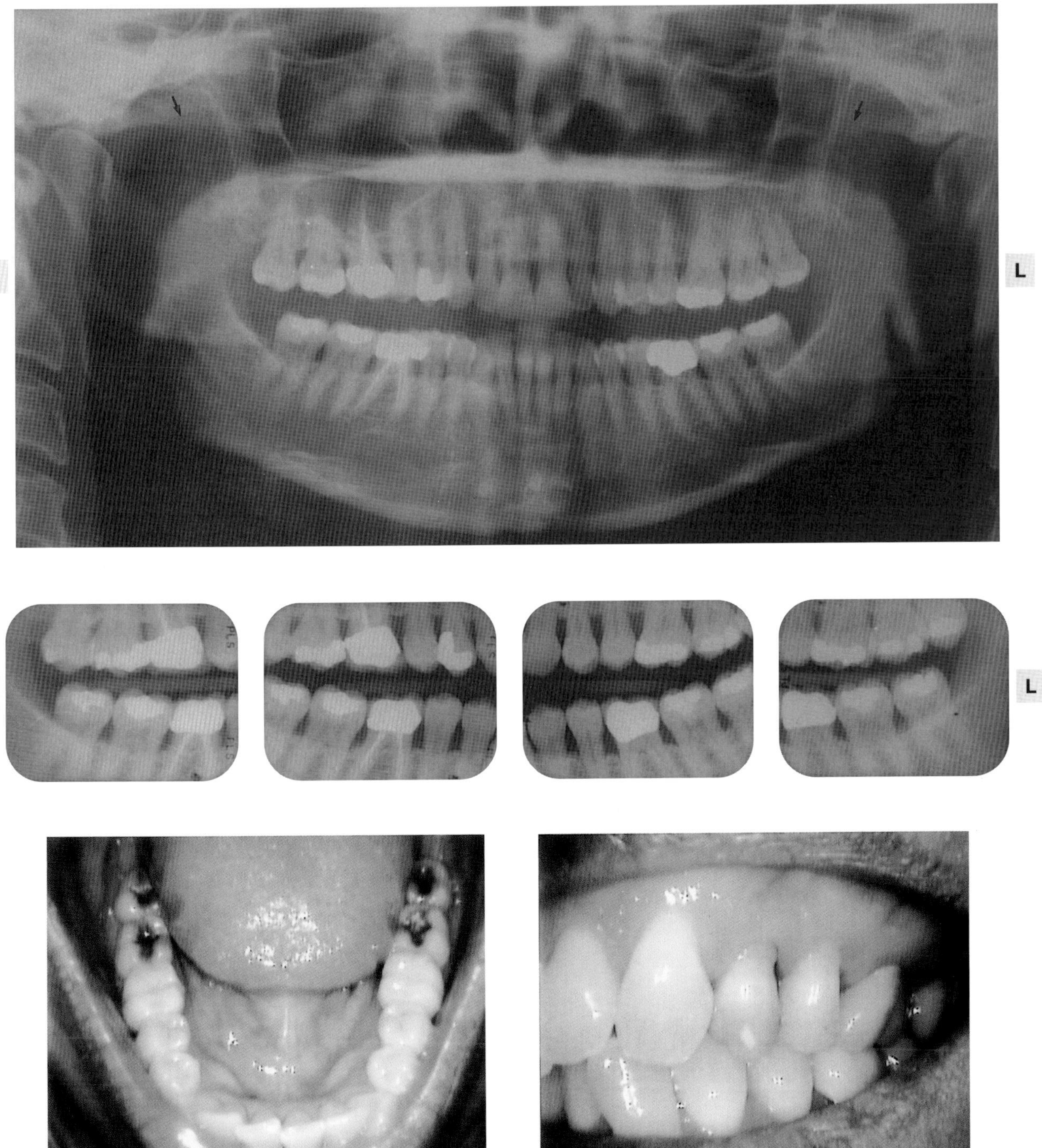
R
L
R
L

client history synopsis

CASE 2

Age: 16

Gender: Female

Height: 5′4″

Weight: 165 lbs

VITAL SIGNS

Blood pressure: 140/85

Pulse rate: 80

Respiratory rate: 20

MEDICAL HISTORY

This client has a history of morbid obesity. Two years ago she weighed 200 lbs. Repeated weight loss attempts with fad diets have failed. The client has multiple chronic nutrient deficiencies, including folate and vitamin B_{12}.

MEDICATIONS

She has been advised to take 400 to 1000 μg of folate and 30 mg of ferrous sulfate tid, but often forgets to take her medications. The client has vitamin B_{12} injections monthly.

DENTAL HISTORY

The client's radiographs indicate extensive interproximal caries, with one tooth requiring endodontic therapy. She brushes twice a day and flosses once a day.

SOCIAL HISTORY

This client is a sophomore in high school and lives at home.

CHIEF COMPLAINTS

"My teeth hurt."

ADDITIONAL FINDINGS

This client's diet consists mainly of pasta, bread, crackers, and sweets.

SUPPLEMENTAL DENTAL FINDINGS

Plaque scores are below 20%. Periodontal data reveal all pocket depths are 3 mm or less.

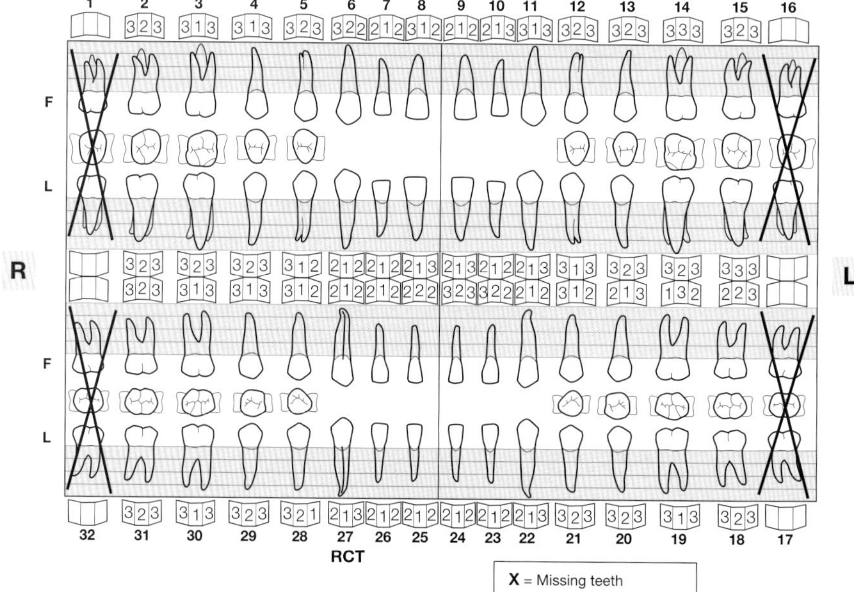

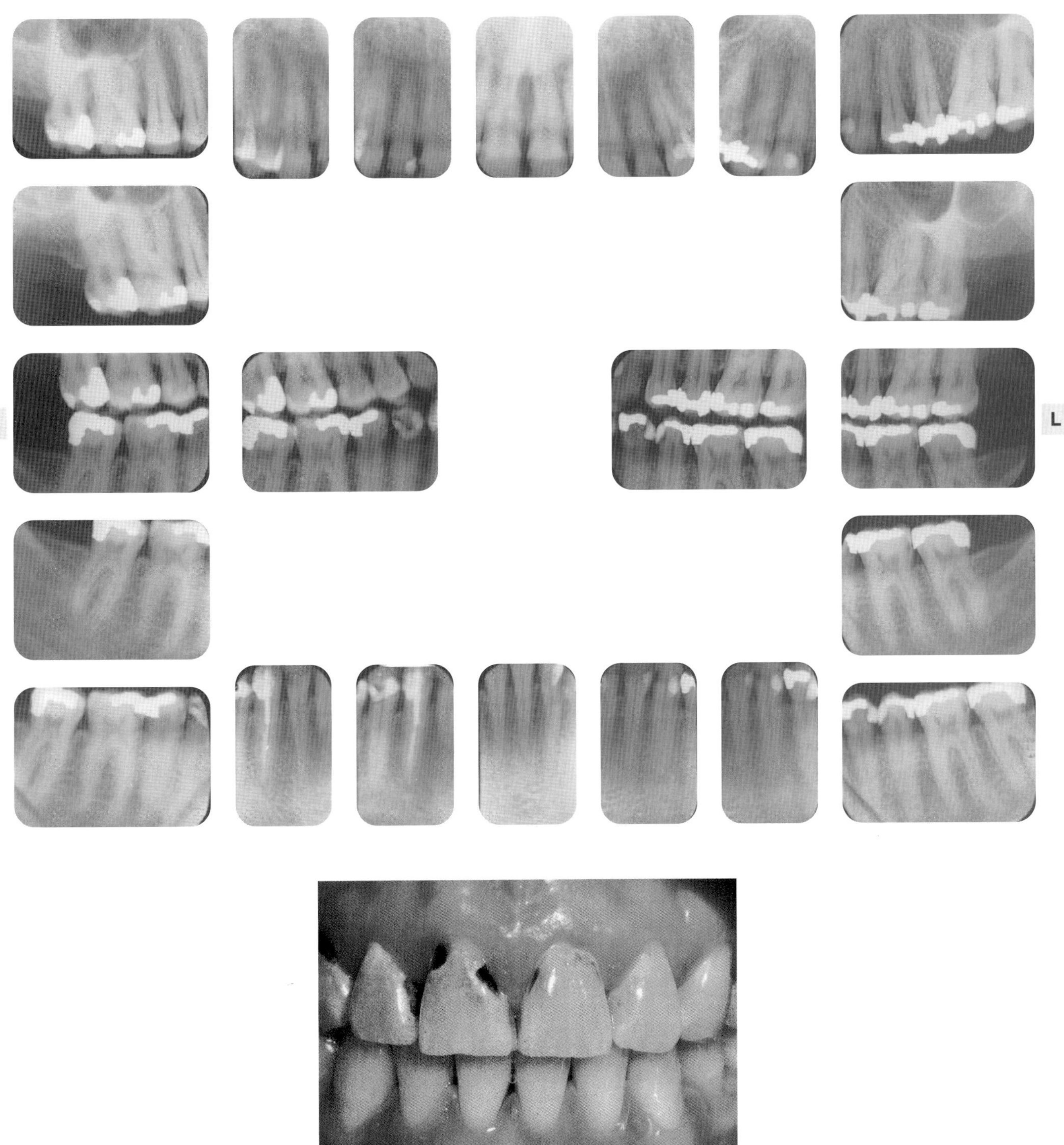
R
L

client history synopsis

CASE 3	VITAL SIGNS
Age: 32	Blood pressure: 145/90
Gender: Female	Pulse rate: 90
Height: 5′7″	Respiratory rate: 18
Weight: 145 lbs	

MEDICAL HISTORY

The client has been diagnosed with asthma and clinical depression. She states her mother was a diabetic and her father died of a heart attack at the age of 45.

MEDICATIONS

She reports taking Prozac and oral contraceptives at bedtime and Proventil 3–4 times/day.

DENTAL HISTORY

She has had routine dental treatment throughout her life and received a dental prophylaxis 9 months ago. She reports that she brushes her teeth twice a day and flosses once a day.

SOCIAL HISTORY

The client has earned a Master's degree in computer science, manages the computer networks of a major regional bank, and is the wife of an insurance executive.

CHIEF COMPLAINTS

"I am unhappy with the way my front teeth look."

ADDITIONAL FINDINGS

None.

SUPPLEMENTAL DENTAL FINDINGS

Evidence of slight gingivitis.

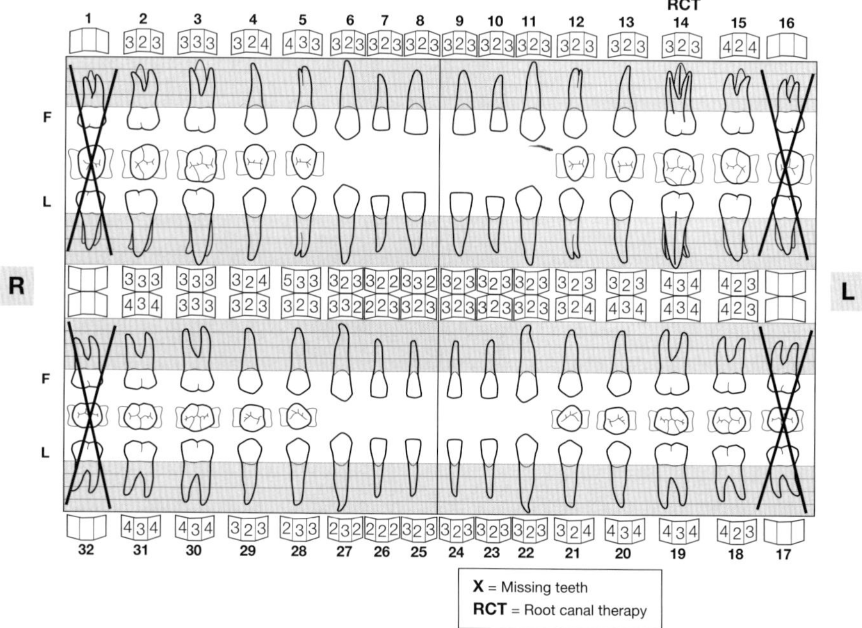

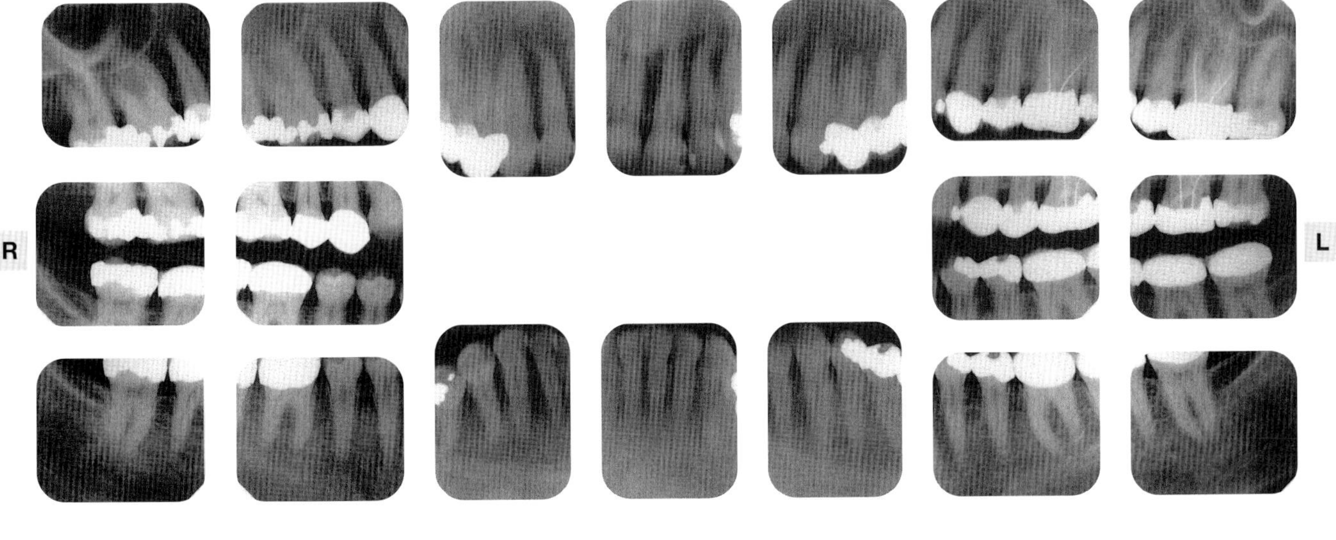
R
L

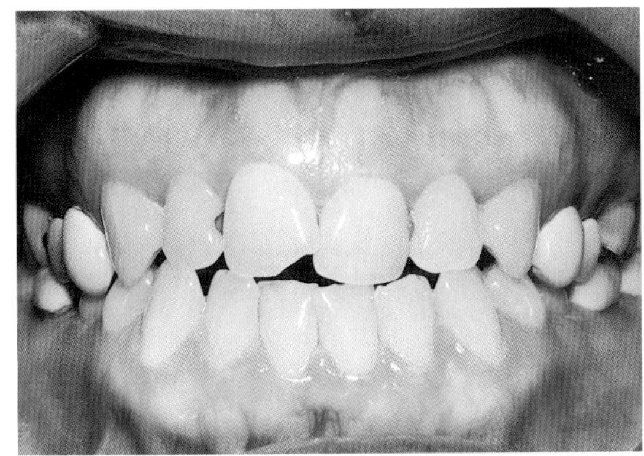

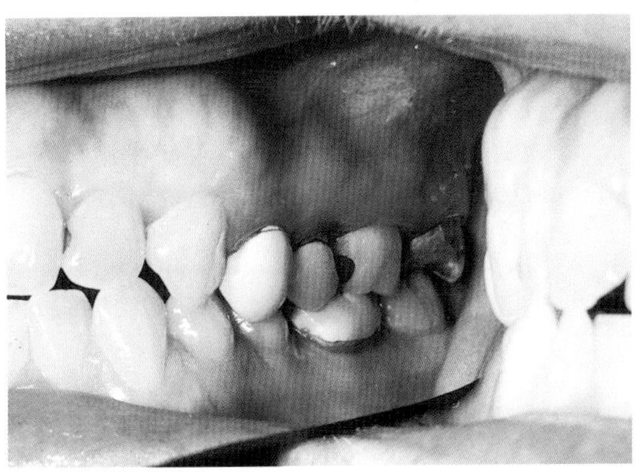

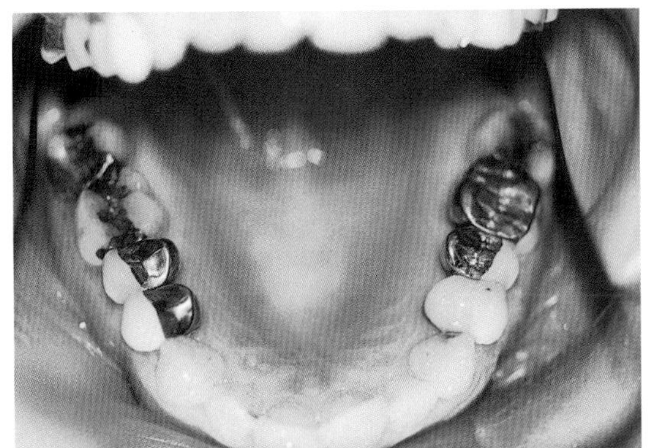

client history synopsis

CASE 4

Age: 50

Gender: Male

Height: 5′10″

Weight: 185 lbs

VITAL SIGNS

Blood pressure: 140/85

Pulse rate: 74

Respiratory rate: 20

MEDICAL HISTORY

The client has recently developed a sore throat that seems to "hang on." He presents with a hacking cough that he relates to his pipe smoking habit of 20 years. He enjoys hot, spicy oriental cuisine. After meals, he likes to suck on candy breath mints, which he holds in the buccal vestibule.

MEDICATIONS

The client takes Catapres.

DENTAL HISTORY

Minor decay exists in facial areas of gingival recession. The client states he hasn't brushed today due to his recent sore throat. The client's last dental appointment was 2 years ago.

SOCIAL HISTORY

The client is married and works as a car salesman.

CHIEF COMPLAINTS

None.

ADDITIONAL FINDINGS

The client has a nervous facial tic and several moles that he states have been present since childhood without change. A fixed, firm, nontender, left anterior node was palpable. Class I furcation involvement is noted on tooth #19.

SUPPLEMENTAL DENTAL FINDINGS

Client has white patches on his palate.

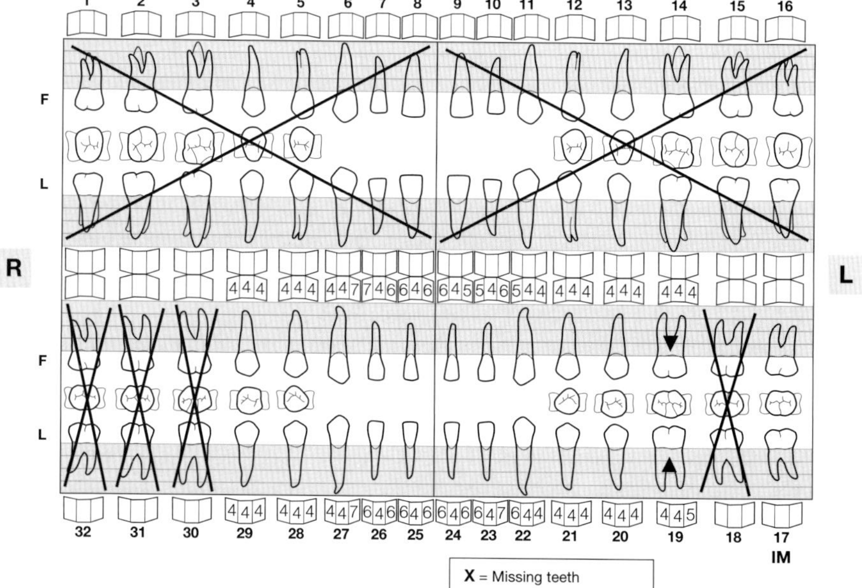

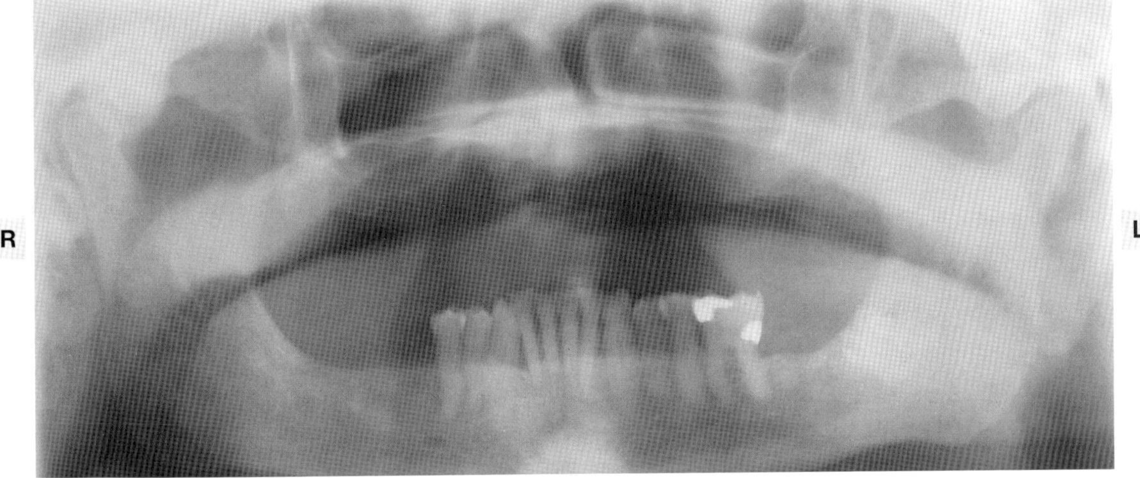
R
L

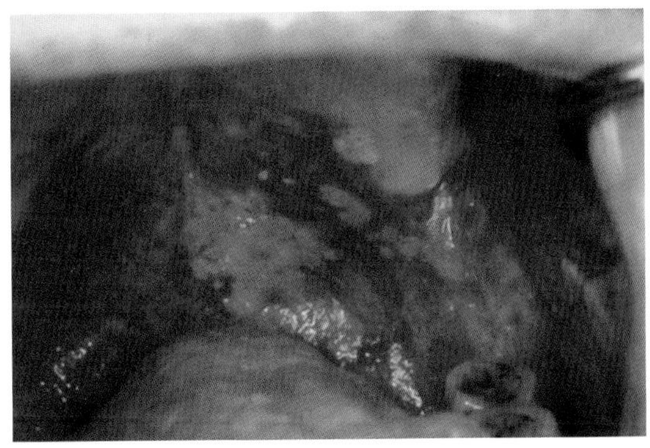

client history synopsis

CASE 5

Age: 43

Gender: Female

Height: 5′1″

Weight: 175 lbs

VITAL SIGNS

Blood pressure: 128/108

Pulse rate: 80

Respiratory rate: 16

MEDICAL HISTORY

The client has adult-onset diabetes and hypertension. She is currently under the care of a physician for her diabetes, which was diagnosed 5 months ago. The initial attempt to manage the diabetes with diet modification was unsuccessful. The patient does not smoke. She did have knee surgery for a sports injury when she was in high school with no complications.

MEDICATIONS

The client takes Glucaphase 500 mg daily.

DENTAL HISTORY

The client had her premolars and third molars removed. When she was in high school, she wore braces for 2 1/2 years. However, her dental care has been limited the past 10 years. She bruxes at night and has a habit of biting her nails. She brushes twice a day using a soft toothbrush, but does not floss. She exhibits evidence of periodontal disease, but has not been informed of her condition.

SOCIAL HISTORY

The client is divorced and currently holds a receptionist position.

CHIEF COMPLAINTS

"My gums bleed." In addition, she complains of bad breath, dry mouth, and that some of her teeth ache.

ADDITIONAL FINDINGS

While taking the radiographs, the hygienist notes the client is having difficulty positioning her head.

SUPPLEMENTAL DENTAL FINDINGS

There is evidence of generalized bleeding on probing throughout the mouth. Purulence is found at the facial of #24. The gingiva is red, with rolled margins and blunted papillae. There is Grade I mobility with tooth #s 7, 23, 24, and 25. There is also evidence of clefts at the facials of #s 8 and 24.

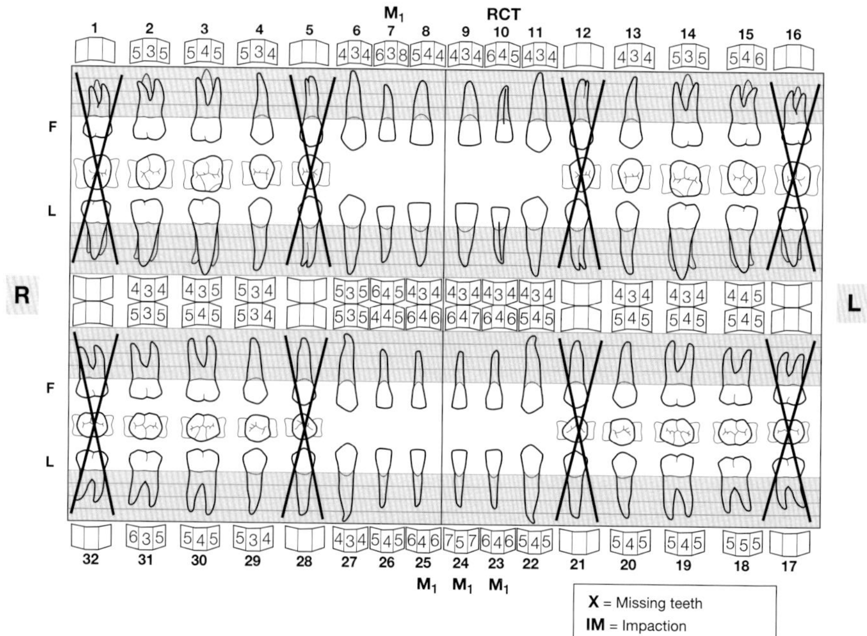

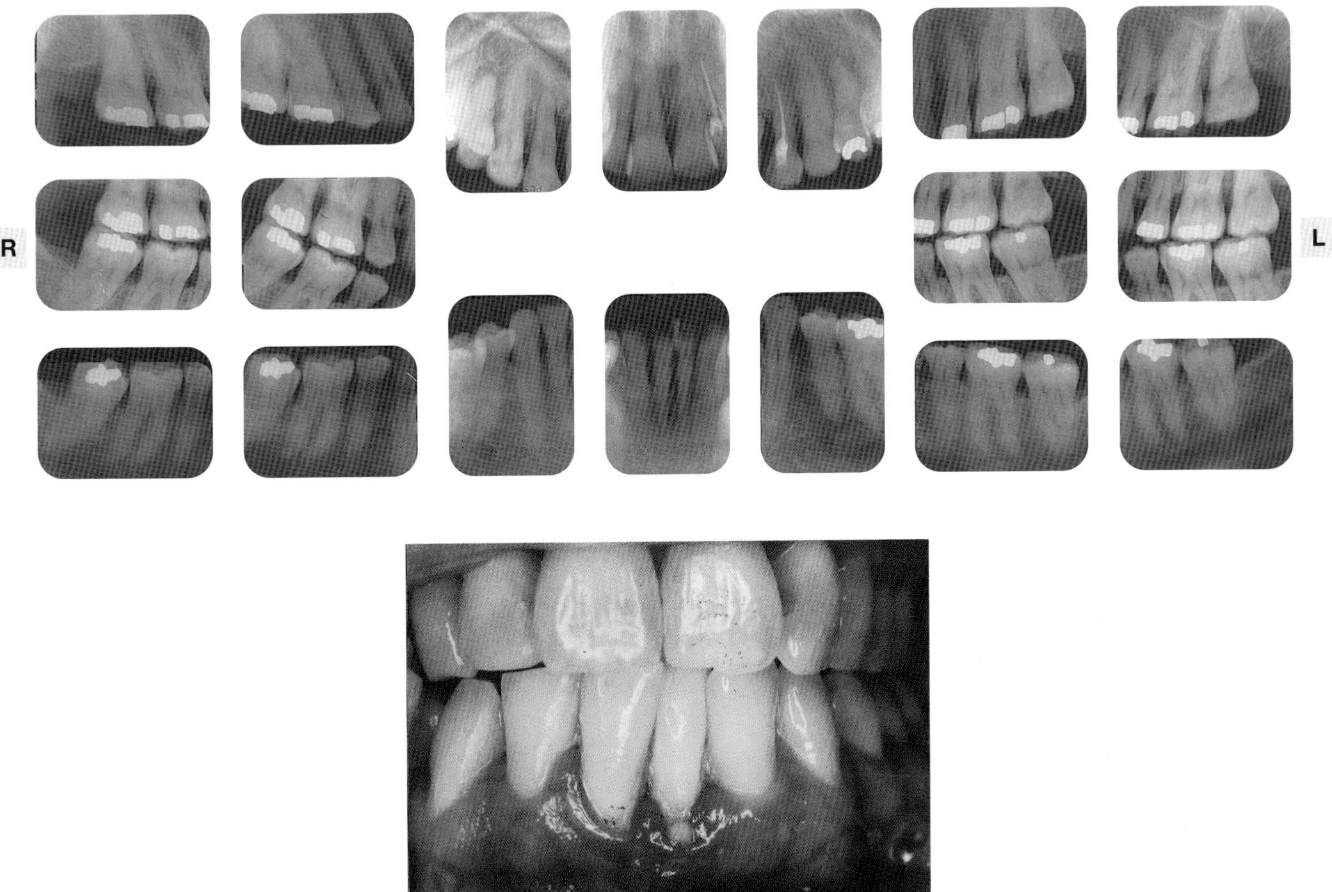
R
L

client history synopsis

CASE 6

Age: 37

Gender: Male

Height: 6′

Weight: 160 lbs

VITAL SIGNS

Blood pressure: 145/90

Pulse rate: 80

Respiratory rate: 17

MEDICAL HISTORY

The client has had a significant weight loss and complains of being tired. He does have a physician of record. He also smokes 2 packs a day.

MEDICATIONS

None.

DENTAL HISTORY

The reason for this visit is to have his teeth cleaned. The client's last visit to the dentist was 3 years ago. He routinely brushes once a day, but sometimes twice daily. He does not floss.

SOCIAL HISTORY

The client owns his own business and works many hours. He notes he has a stressful job and has 3 children who keep him busy with their outside activities.

CHIEF COMPLAINTS

"White patches in my mouth bleed when I try to scrape them off." His teeth are also cold sensitive.

ADDITIONAL FINDINGS

It is noted from his oral examination that the client has moderate plaque and calculus accumulation.

SUPPLEMENTAL DENTAL FINDINGS

The client has pronounced breath odor. There is evidence of moderate gingival inflammation, as well as color and texture change. The gingiva has been bleeding. He also has palpable cervical lymph nodes.

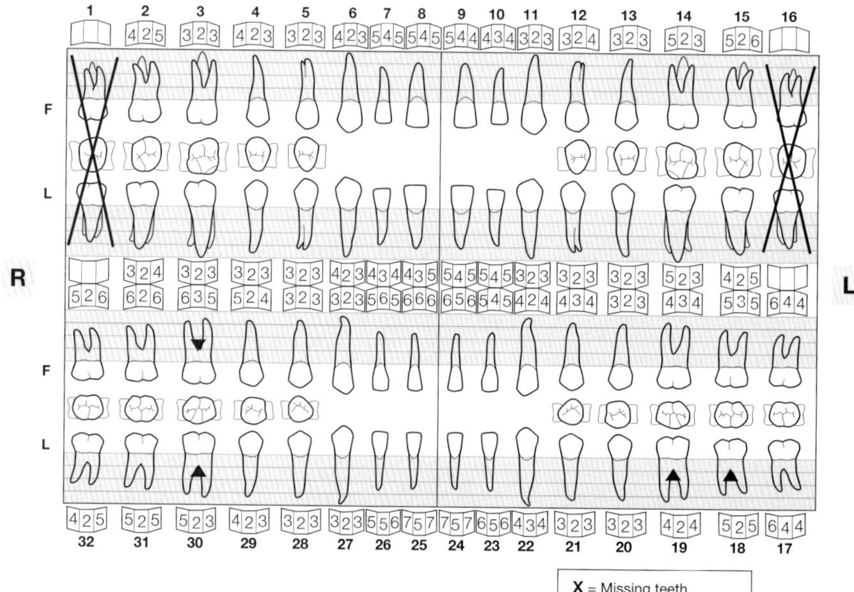

R

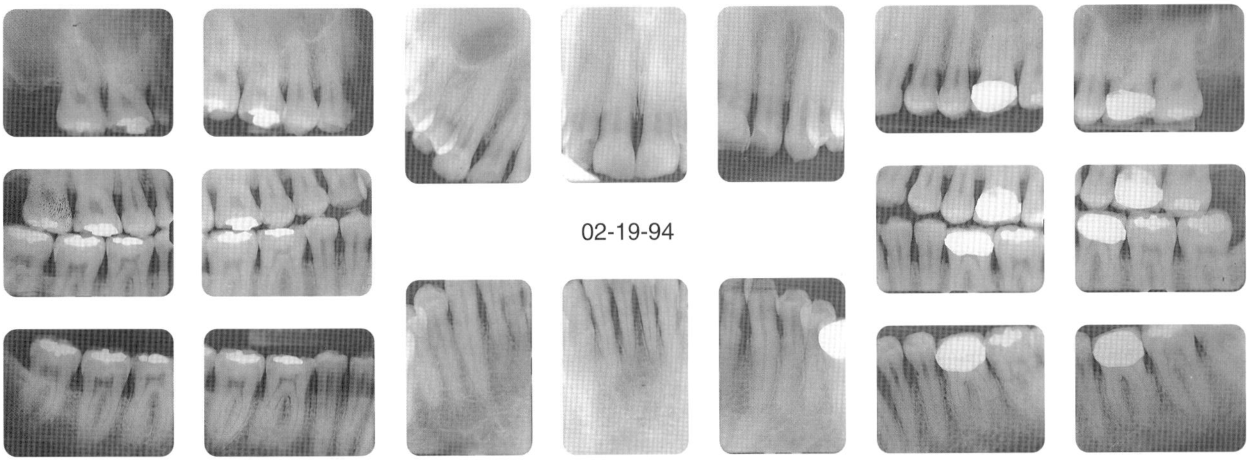

02-19-94

L

R

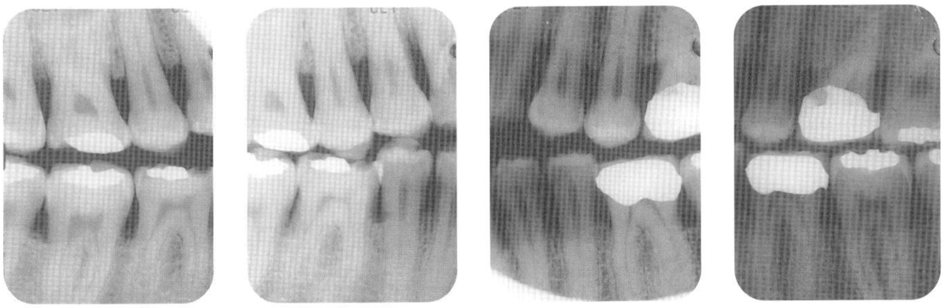

L

11-14-97

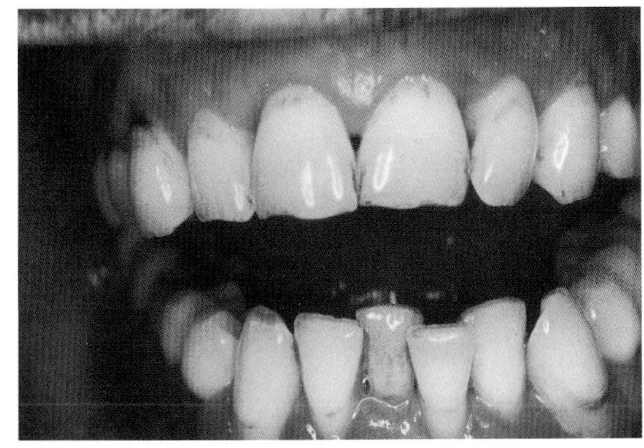

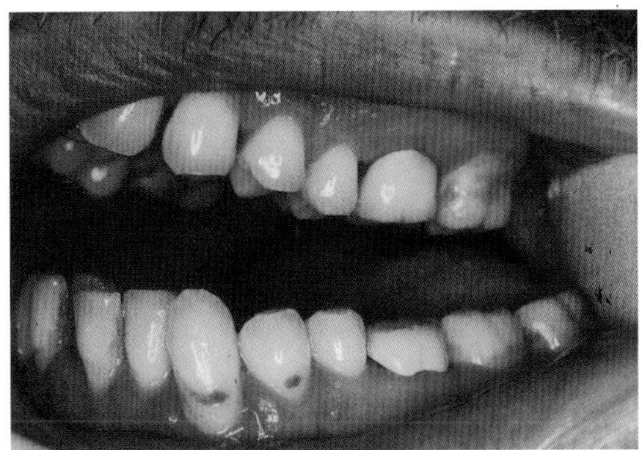

client history synopsis

CASE 7

Age: 71
Gender: Male
Height: 6′
Weight: 190 lbs

VITAL SIGNS

Blood pressure: 130/80
Pulse rate: 64
Respiratory rate: 18

MEDICAL HISTORY

The client has Type 1 diabetes. His last complete physical examination was 2 years ago at a Family Health Center. The client has no past history of surgeries except for skin grafts on his neck and chest due to a scalding burn when he was a toddler.

MEDICATIONS

Insulin.

DENTAL HISTORY

A year ago the client came to the dental office for a routine prophylaxis appointment. It had been years since his last visit. His chief complaint at that time was " bleeding gums." There is evidence of existing restorations and missing teeth. The client does not floss regularly.

SOCIAL HISTORY

The client is the oldest of 5 brothers and is the only member of his family living in the state. He is on a fixed income and cannot afford extensive dental treatment. He is currently working part-time.

CHIEF COMPLAINTS

"Food gets stuck in my cheeks. I'm also in a hurry to get to work, so I hope this doesn't take too long. I do want to keep my teeth."

ADDITIONAL FINDINGS

None.

SUPPLEMENTAL DENTAL FINDINGS

Radiographs present with bone loss typical of periodontal disease. Calculus and tooth mobility are present as well as exudate around tooth #30.

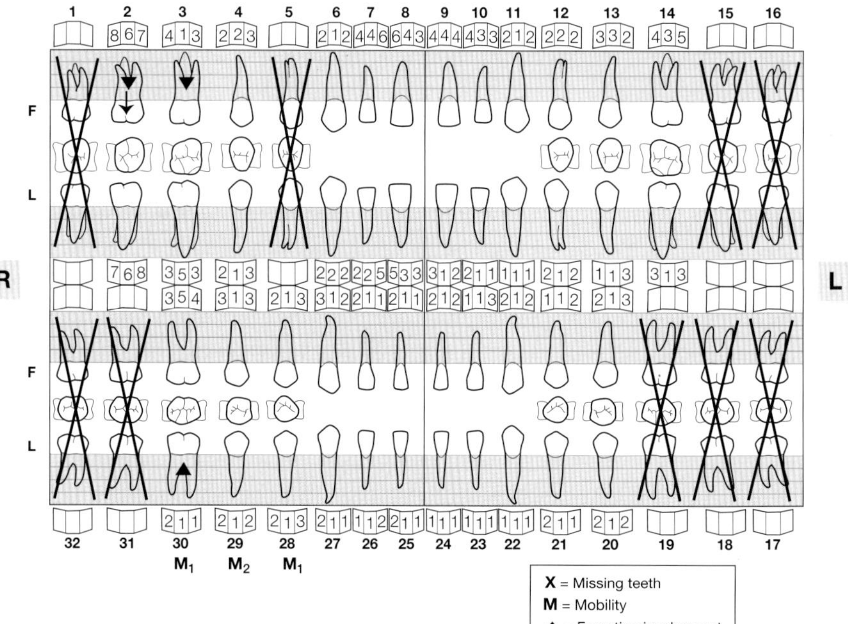

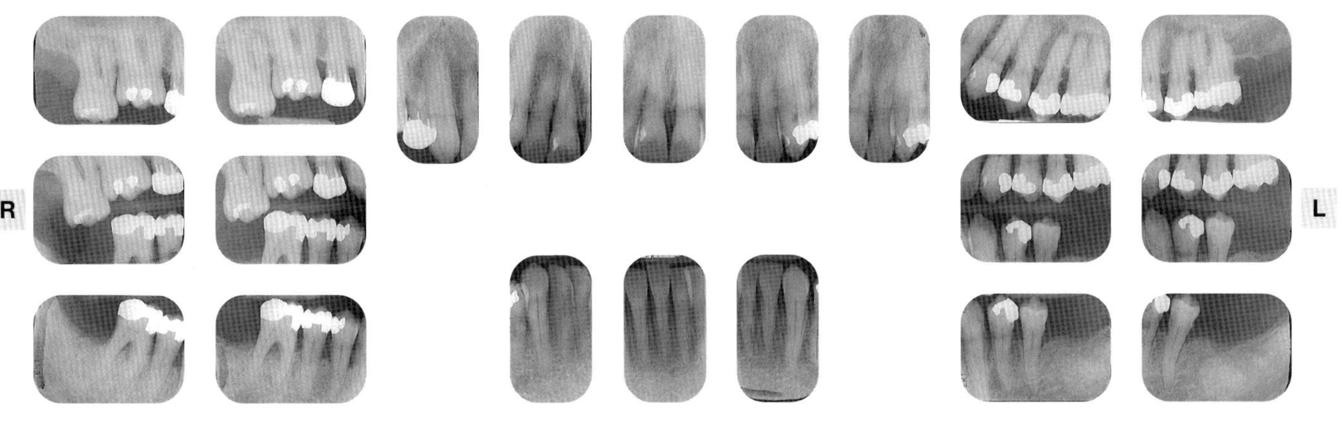
R
L

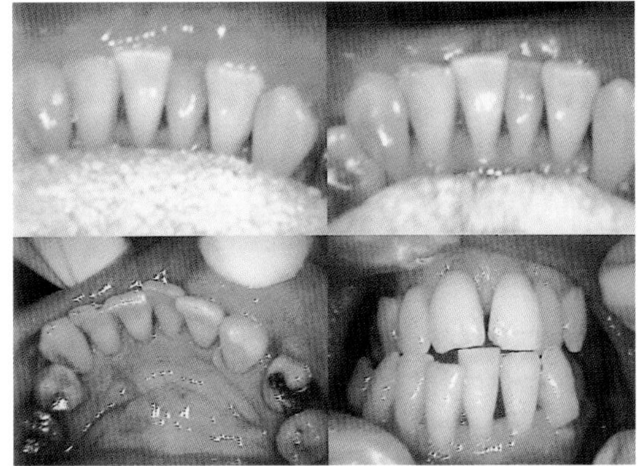

client history synopsis

CASE 8	VITAL SIGNS
Age: 68	Blood pressure: 142/86
Gender: Female	Pulse rate: 84
Height: 5′7″	Respiratory rate: 16
Weight: 180 lbs	

MEDICAL HISTORY

The client notes that she has heart problems (a fast heartbeat). She complains of shortness of breath and states she has been treated for ulcers.

MEDICATIONS

Diltiazem, Estratest, Atenolol, and Medroxyprophyl.

DENTAL HISTORY

The client has a full upper denture that was placed at age 40. Her lower removable partial was placed at age 53. She cleans her teeth with baking soda 3 times a week, but does not use an auxiliary aid to clean under the mandibular bar since it is too time-consuming. She realizes the importance of removing plaque and states she does clean her denture and partial every night.

SOCIAL HISTORY

The client currently works part-time as a secretary for a law firm.

CHIEF COMPLAINTS

At the initial appointment, the patient wants to have her lower partial adjusted. "Food also gets trapped under my partial."

ADDITIONAL FINDINGS

When the client returned for a 1-month evaluation after her prophylaxis, the tissues around #s 22, 27, and 28 were inflamed with rolled margins and covered with heavy calculus. She states she would rely on the hygienist to maintain the health of her oral cavity.

SUPPLEMENTAL DENTAL FINDINGS

During the extraoral examination, crepitance is noted on her left TMJ.

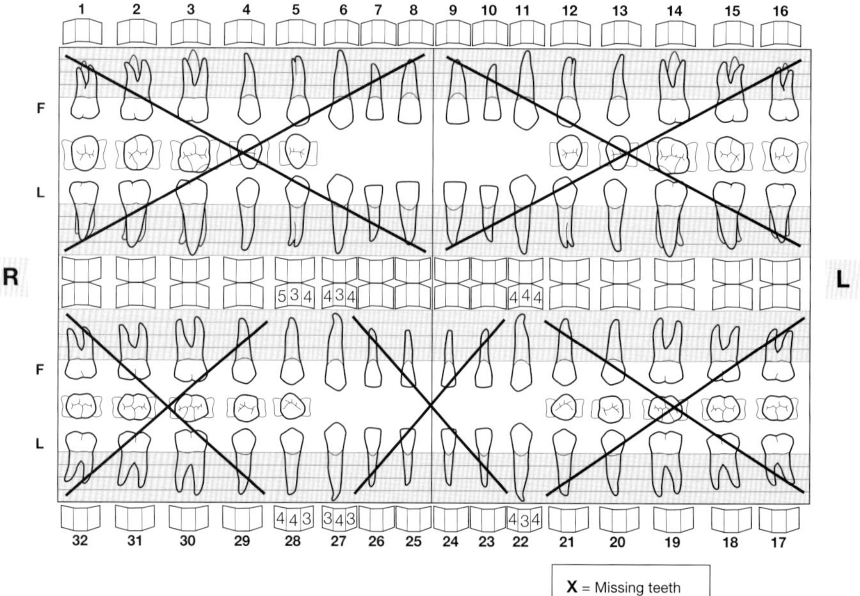

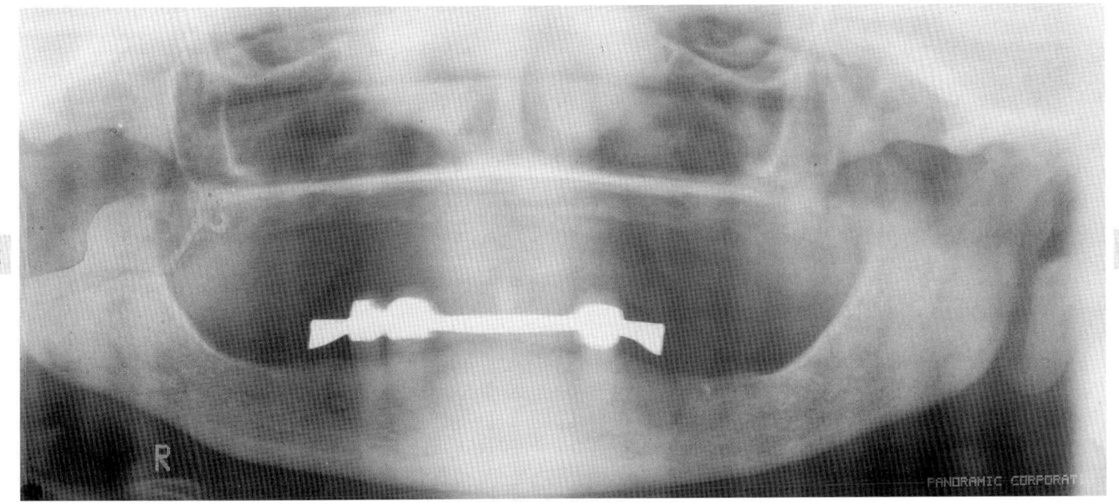
R
L
R
PANORAMIC CORPORAT

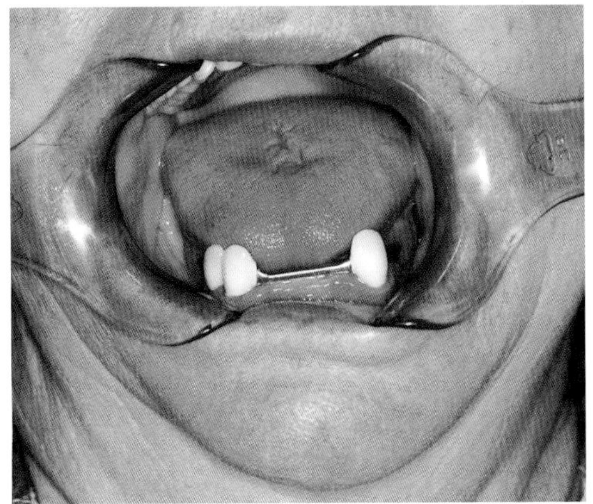

client history synopsis

CASE 9

Age: 42

Gender: Female

Height: 5′7″

Weight: 135 lbs

VITAL SIGNS

Blood pressure: 122/78

Pulse rate: 80

Respiratory rate: 16

MEDICAL HISTORY

The client has a history of rheumatic fever and numbness on her extremities. She has been hospitalized for multiple childbirths. She denies having been told of the presence of a heart murmur and has never taken antibiotics before dental treatment. She is allergic to Bactrim.

MEDICATIONS

Calen.

DENTAL HISTORY

The patient reports receiving regular dental care throughout her life. She has multiple restorations. She has had no problems with her previous treatment. Her last visit was 6 months ago.

SOCIAL HISTORY

The client is a mother of 5 children.

CHIEF COMPLAINTS

None.

ADDITIONAL FINDINGS

None.

SUPPLEMENTAL DENTAL FINDINGS

None.

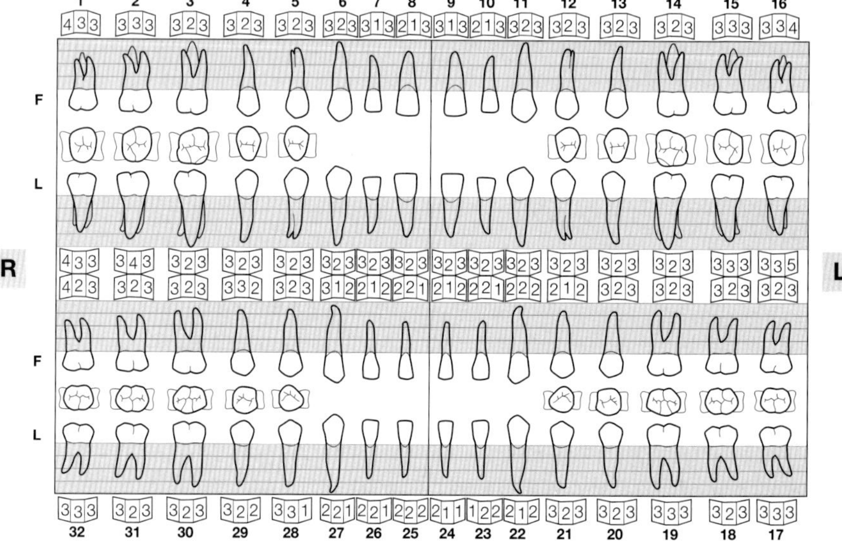

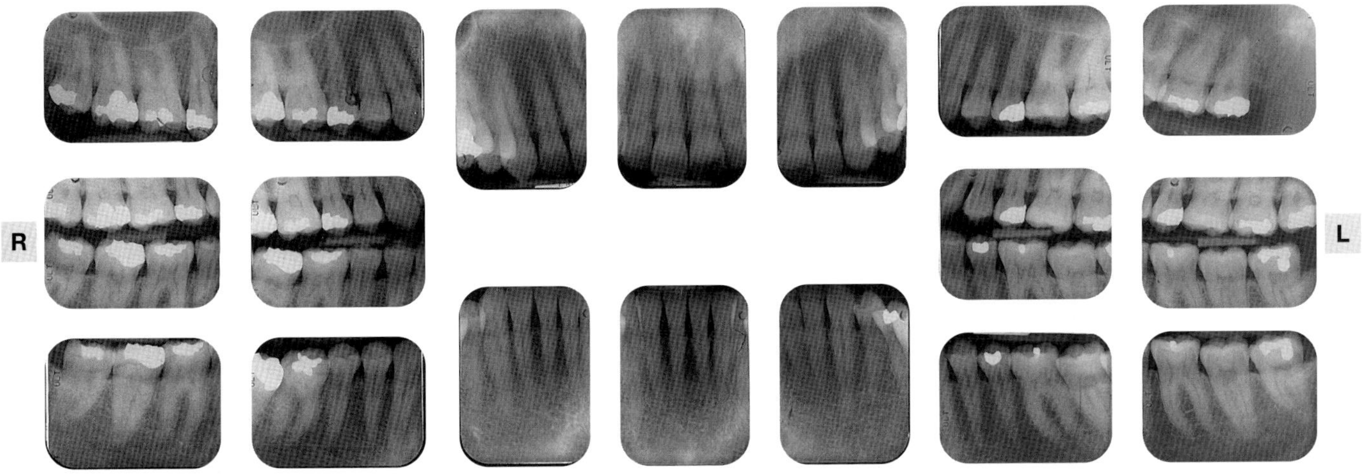

R

L

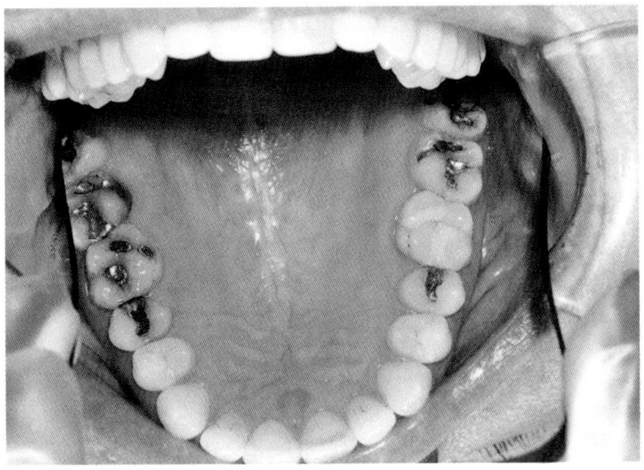

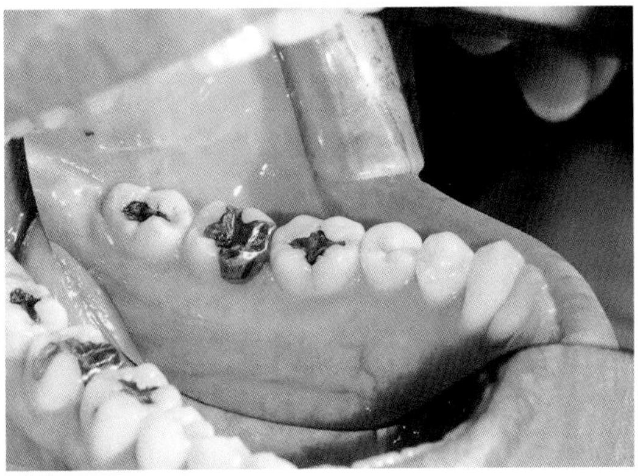

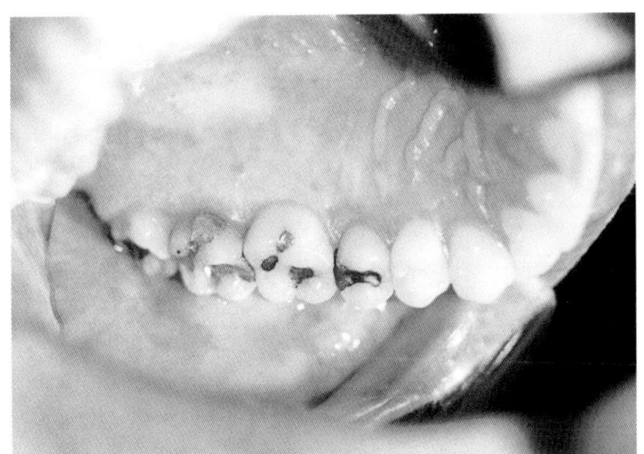

client history synopsis

CASE 10		VITAL SIGNS	
Age:	49	Blood pressure:	121/64
Gender:	Male	Pulse rate:	80
Height:	5′8″	Respiratory rate:	14
Weight:	177 lbs		

MEDICAL HISTORY

The client has not been under the care of a physician for the past 5 years, but reports recent symptoms of abdominal discomfort, nausea, and vomiting. He is allergic to penicillin.

MEDICATIONS

None.

DENTAL HISTORY

The client's last dental treatment was 1 year ago. A full-mouth series was taken at that time and non-surgical periodontal therapy was completed by the dental hygienist. The client states he was diagnosed with periodontal disease over 11 years ago, but has not been able to afford treatment. He has received annual cleanings and emergency extractions–#s 14 and 30. He brushes twice a day, but does not floss.

SOCIAL HISTORY

The client's occupation is construction work. He is married and has 6 children. He reports experiencing financial difficulties.

CHIEF COMPLAINTS

"My gums bleed when I brush."

ADDITIONAL FINDINGS

Class II mobility was observed on teeth #s 12, 15, and 31. Class I or II furcation involvement was noted on 4 of his remaining 6 molars. The gingiva exhibited generalized marginal redness, edema, and bleeding on probing.

SUPPLEMENTAL DENTAL FINDINGS

The client has moderate plaque, calculus, and stain. He exhibits generalized attrition and cervical abrasion, as well as localized areas of dentinal hypersensitivity.

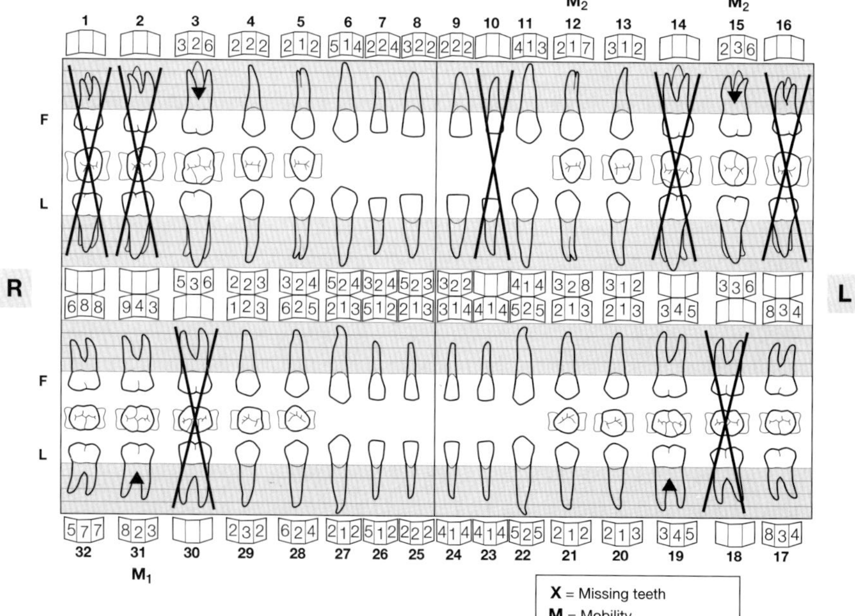

R

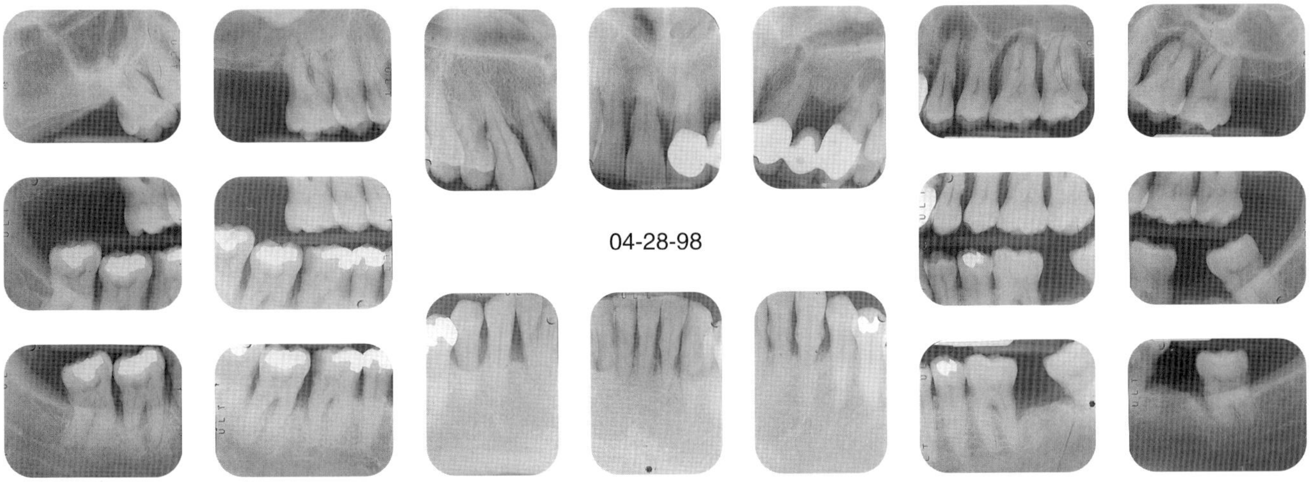

04-28-98

L

R

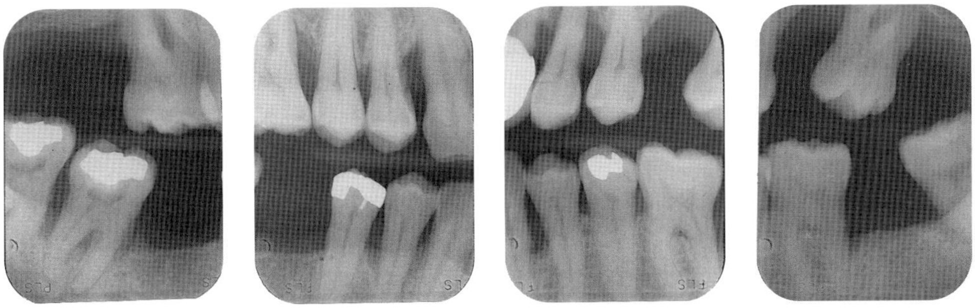

L

03-31-99

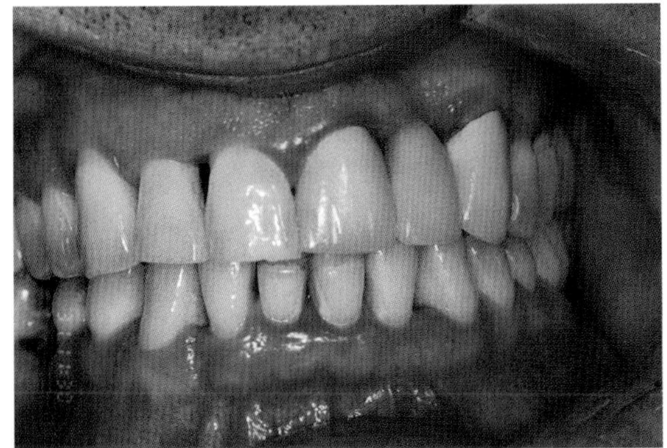

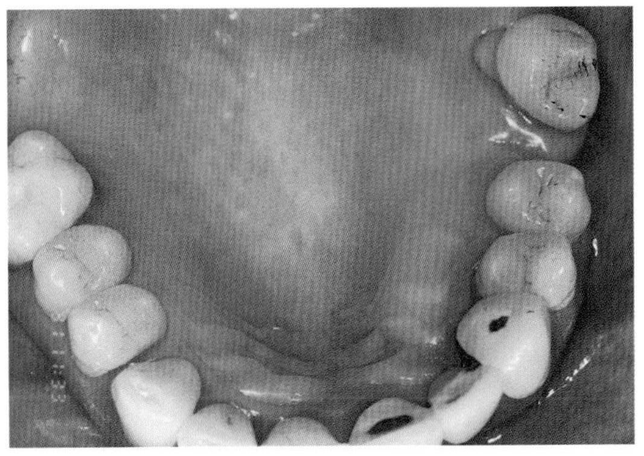

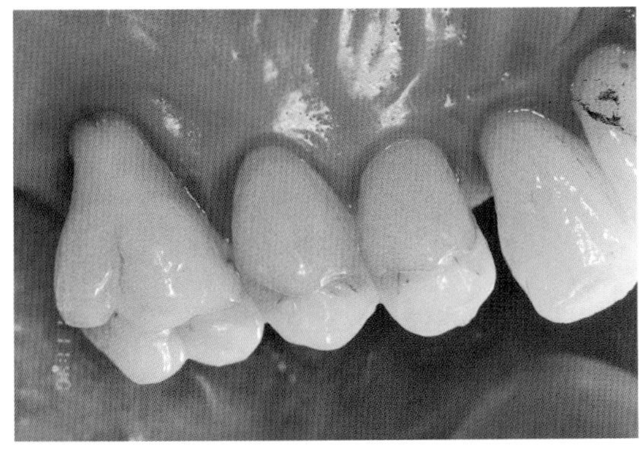

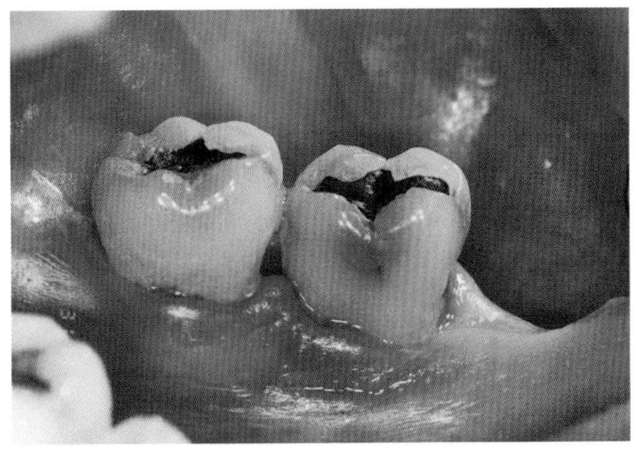

client history synopsis

CASE 11	
Age: 77	
Gender: Female	
Height: 5′2″	
Weight: 130 lbs	

VITAL SIGNS	
Blood pressure: 96/58	
Pulse rate: 80	
Respiratory rate: 18	

MEDICAL HISTORY

The client has arthritis in both hands, a functional heart murmur, and ptosis of the left eye.

MEDICATIONS

Motrin and multivitamins.

DENTAL HISTORY

The client's frequency of visits to the dental clinic is based on discomfort—she had a tooth extracted 2 years ago. Her last prophylaxis was 3 years ago. When asked about the importance of maintaining her oral health, she states she would like to keep her teeth for the rest of her life. She brushes once a day, when her arthritis is not bothering her. She does not use an interdental cleaning aid since she cannot manipulate the dental floss.

SOCIAL HISTORY

The client is retired with a high school diploma.

CHIEF COMPLAINTS

"I want to have my front tooth replaced."

ADDITIONAL FINDINGS

None.

SUPPLEMENTAL DENTAL FINDINGS

The client has generalized moderate periodontitis and pigmentation. She has bilateral mandibular and palatal tori. On examining the client's TMJ, the hygienist notes difficulty in opening.

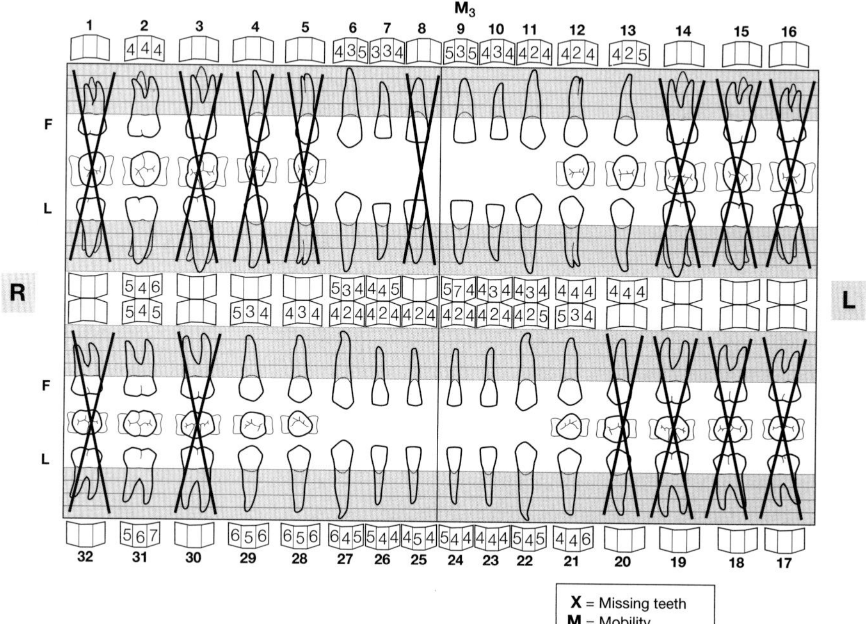

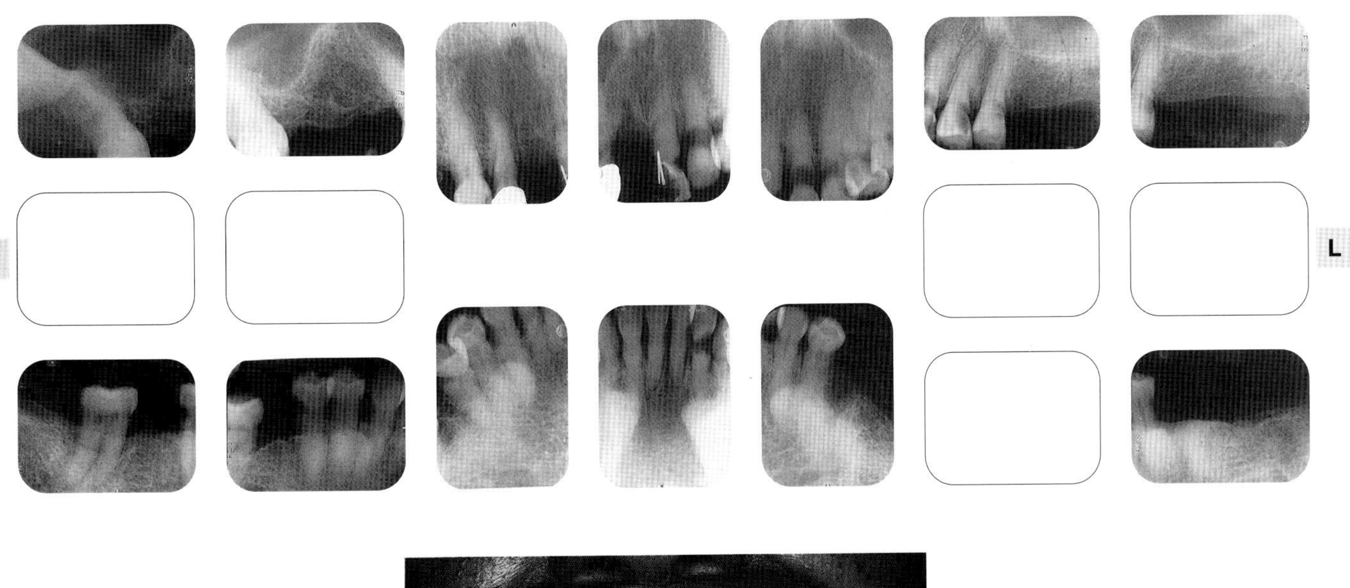
R
L

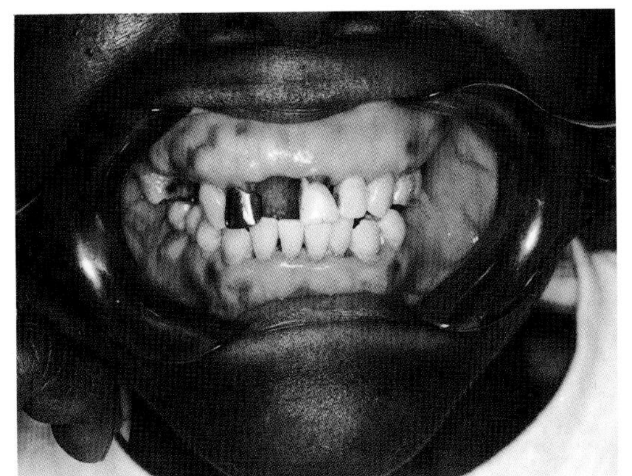

client history synopsis

CASE 12		VITAL SIGNS	
Age:	41	Blood pressure:	110/78
Gender:	Female	Pulse rate:	72
Height:	5′3″	Respiratory rate:	18
Weight:	140 lbs		

MEDICAL HISTORY

This client has seasonal allergies and hypothyroidism. She is under the care of a physician for her hypothyroidism. She smokes socially.

MEDICATIONS

Synthroid 125 mg, Levoxyl 125 mg, meclizine, Naprosyn.

DENTAL HISTORY

The client's past care has been limited to dental emergencies. She brushes her teeth twice a day, but does not floss or use any other cleaning aids.

SOCIAL HISTORY

This client cleans homes for a living. Owing to her recent move, she is worried about her two children not adjusting to their new school.

CHIEF COMPLAINTS

"My teeth hurt and sometimes my gums bleed when I brush."

ADDITIONAL FINDINGS

None.

SUPPLEMENTAL DENTAL FINDINGS

This client has generalized inflammation with bleeding on probing. There is also evidence of generalized recession and furcation involvement at teeth #s 3, 14, 15, 17, 30, and 32. Tooth #7 has grade I mobility.

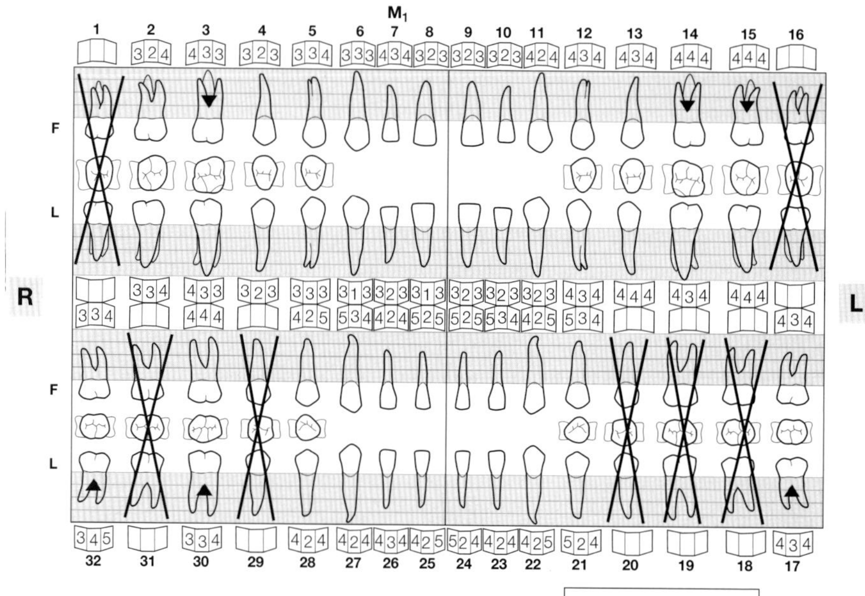

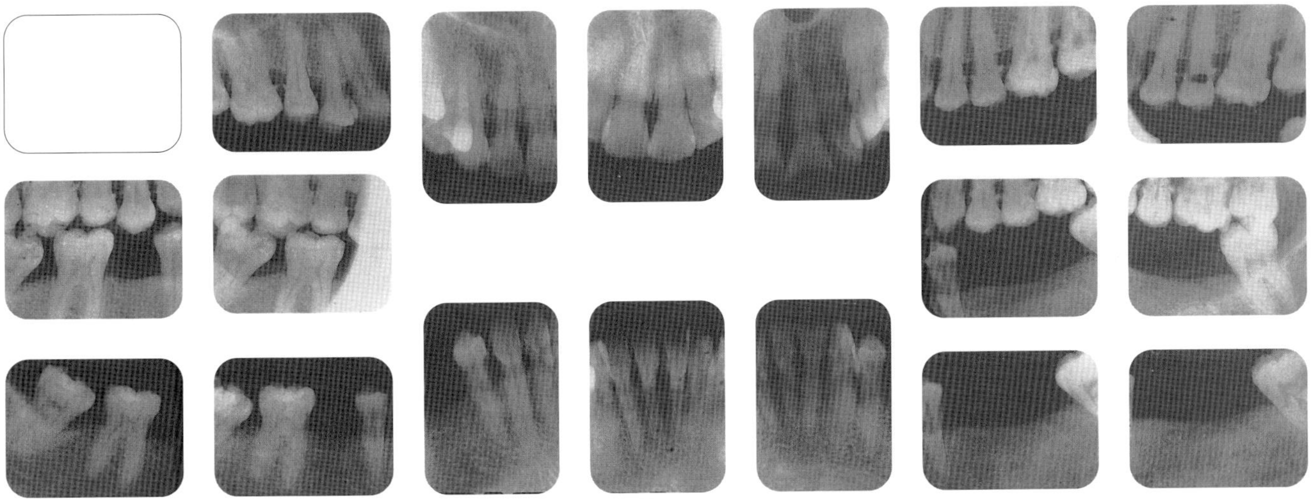

R

L

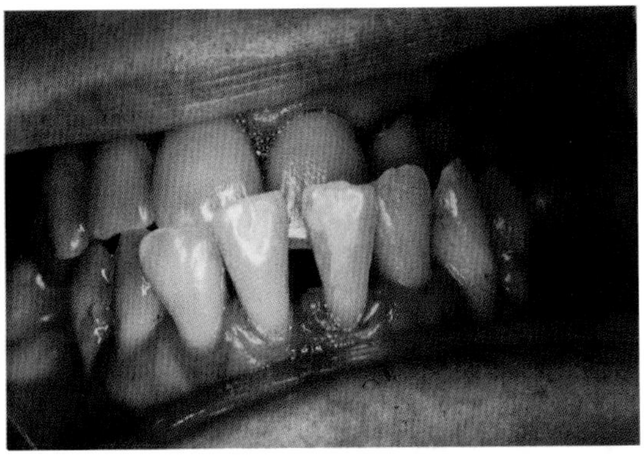

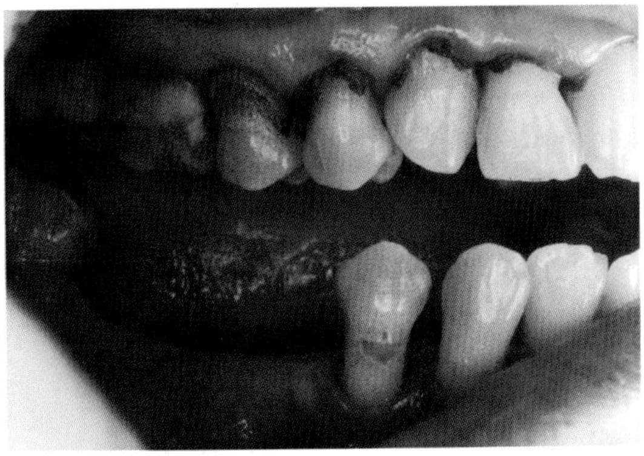

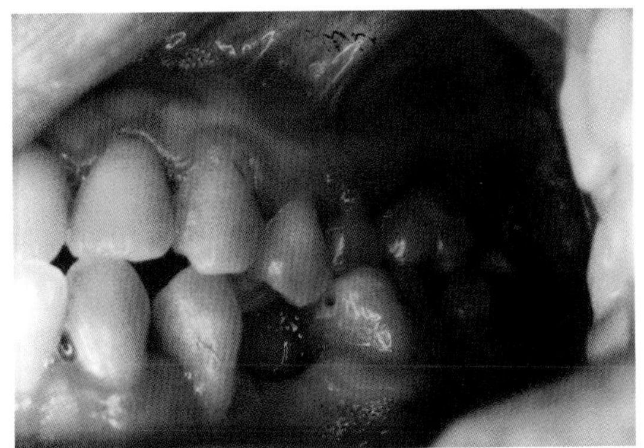

client history synopsis

CASE 13

Age: 50

Gender: Female

Height: 5′7″

Weight: 145 lbs

VITAL SIGNS

Blood pressure: 140/90

Pulse rate: 74

Respiratory rate: 16

MEDICAL HISTORY

The client had a complete hysterectomy 7 years ago due to precancerous lesion in her uterus. She also had a wrist fracture 1 year ago.

MEDICATIONS

None.

DENTAL HISTORY

The client visits the dentist every 6 months for a routine prophylaxis. She brushes at least twice a day with tartar-control toothpaste and flosses at least 5 times per week. She has not had any new carious lesions for 5 years.

SOCIAL HISTORY

The client retired as a professor from a local university. She enjoys being involved in the community and is a member of several women's groups. She frequents fast-food restaurants with her 3 young grandchildren.

CHIEF COMPLAINTS

"My tissues are tender when I brush. I'm also concerned about 'losing' bone from my mouth."

ADDITIONAL FINDINGS

On today's examination, there is little plaque found in her mouth.

SUPPLEMENTAL DENTAL FINDINGS

Slightly fissured tongue.

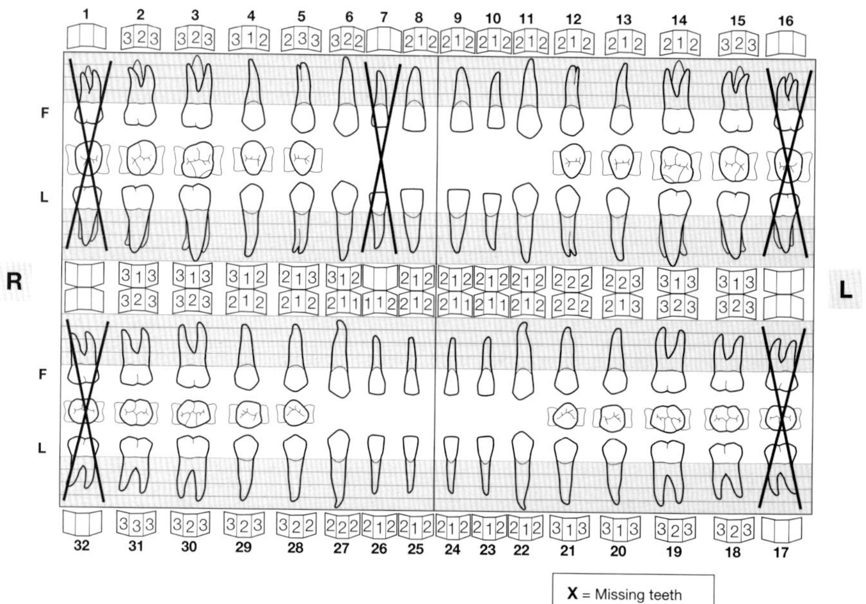

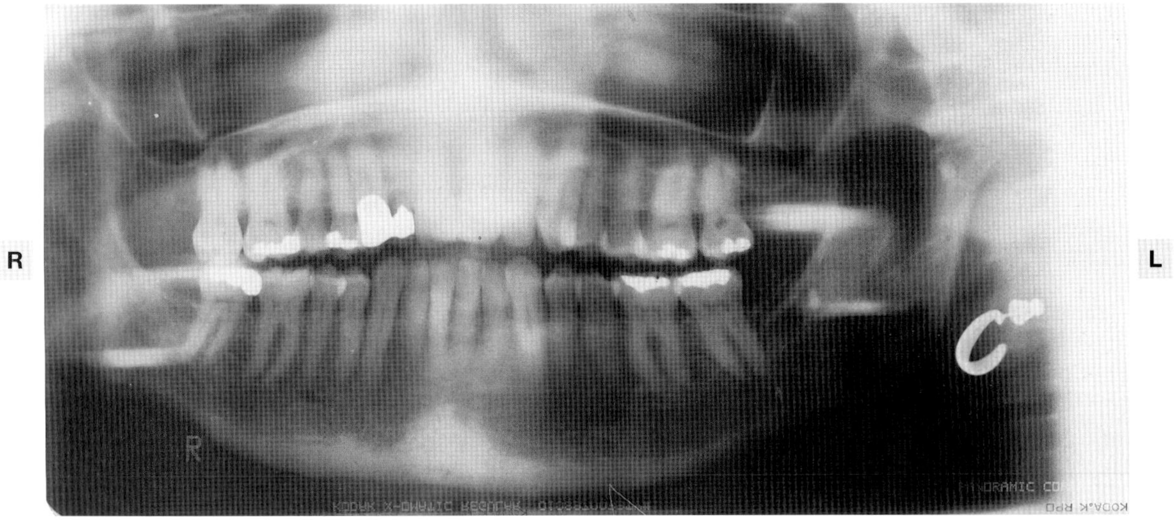
R
L

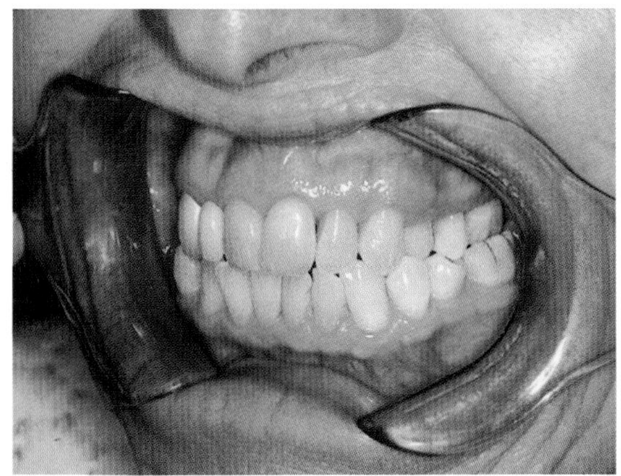

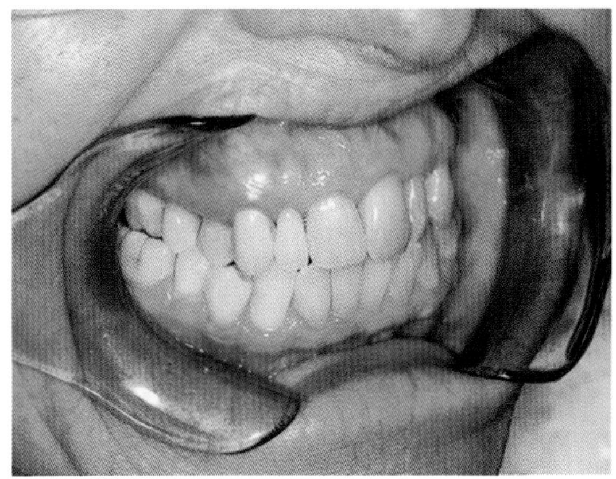

client history synopsis

CASE 14

Age: 37

Gender: Female

Height: 5′6″

Weight: 185 lbs

VITAL SIGNS

Blood pressure: 142/92

Pulse rate: 80

Respiratory rate: 16

MEDICAL HISTORY

The client has chronic allergies and sinus trouble and was recently diagnosed with multiple sclerosis. She is allergic to penicillin. She has a history of herpes labialis following sun exposure.

MEDICATIONS

The client is currently taking Phentermine HCL (Fastin) and OTC medications for allergies.

DENTAL HISTORY

The client's last dental visit was over 8 years ago. At that time she received a cleaning and examination. She brushes 2–3 times a day with a medium-hard toothbrush and experiences gingival bleeding. She never flosses and experiences chronic halitosis.

SOCIAL HISTORY

The client works as a waitress. She is a single mother of 2 children. She reports being under stress due to financial problems.

CHIEF COMPLAINTS

"I need to have my teeth cleaned."

ADDITIONAL FINDINGS

The client's jaw "pops" occasionally when opening her mouth and she grinds her teeth at night.

SUPPLEMENTAL DENTAL FINDINGS

The client has generalized 4–5 mm pockets and 1–4 mm gingival recession. She has xerostomia and generalized mobility and furcation involvement.

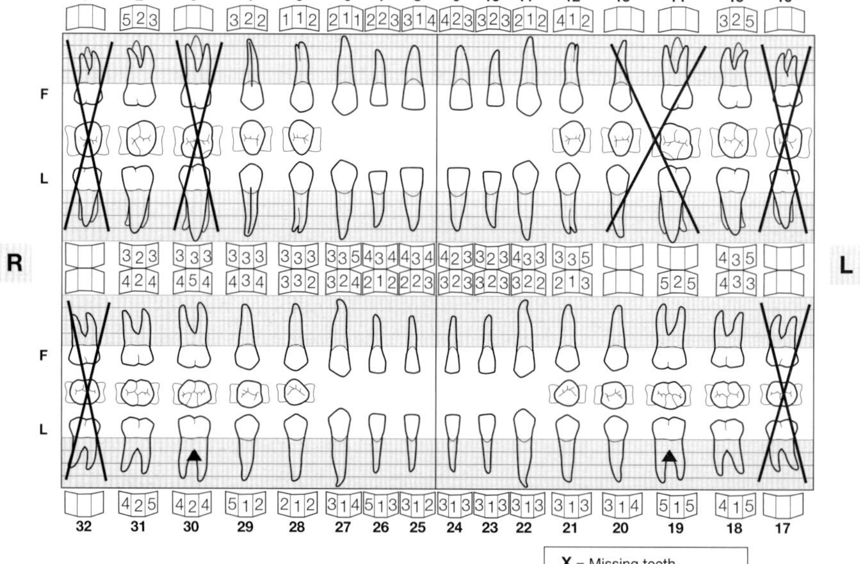

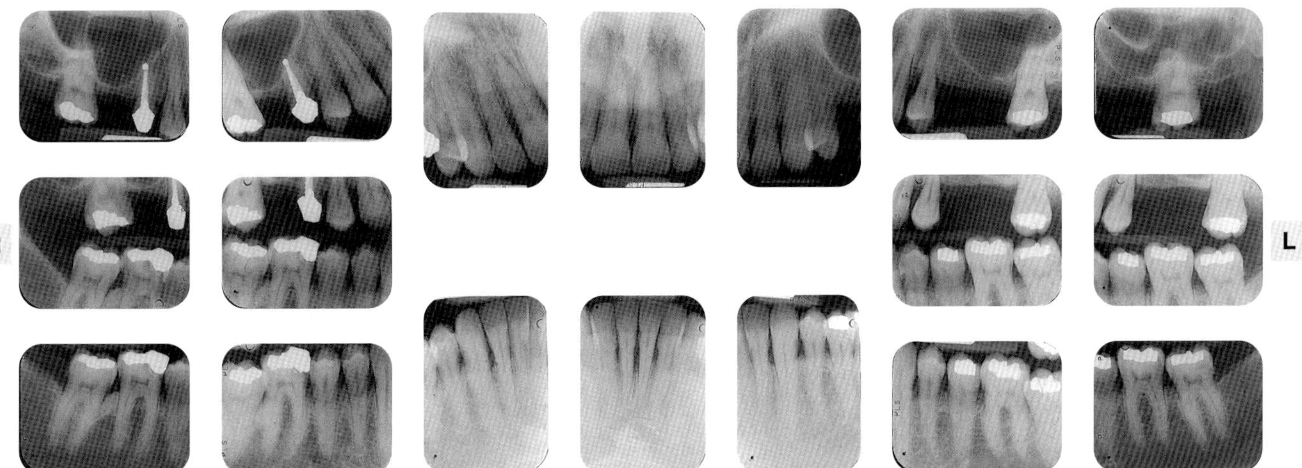
R
L

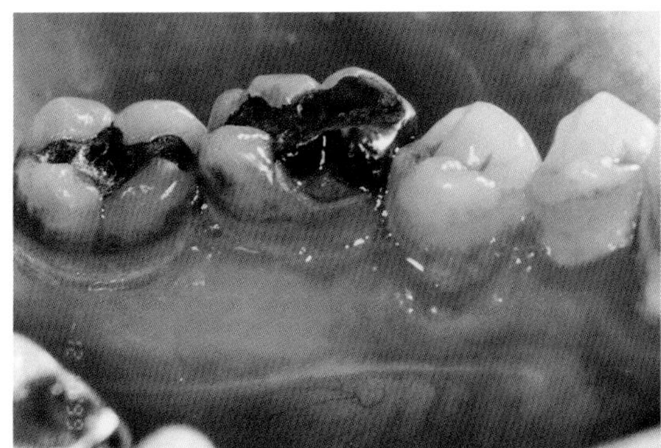

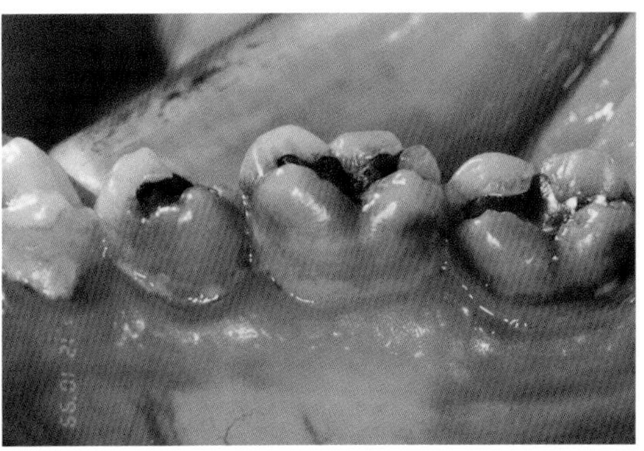

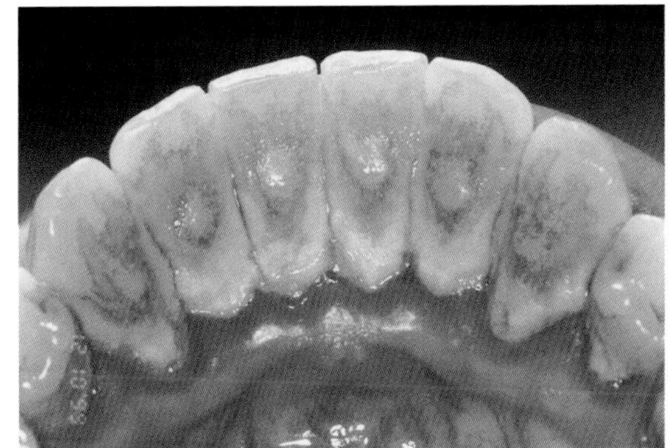

➤ CASE 7

1. The client's complaint of accumulating food in the vestibule might suggest a malfunction of which of the following muscles?
   A. risorius
   B. buccinator
   C. orbicularis oris
   D. medial pterygoid

2. Since extensive scaling and pocket debridement are to be performed on the maxillary incisors, which of the following nerves would require anesthesia?
   A. inferior alveolar and long buccal
   B. mental and inferior alveolar
   C. posterior superior alveolar and greater anterior palatine
   D. anterior superior alveolar and nasopalatine

3. Local anesthesia was administered using 2% lidocaine plus epinephrine 1:50,000. About 5 minutes after the injection, the client experiences the following symptoms: sweating, pallor, headache, dizziness, and weakness. The pulse rate is 100 and the blood pressure is 140/90. The client's symptoms are MOST likely due to
   A. drug reaction.
   B. anaphylactic allergic reaction.
   C. myocardial infarction.
   D. insulin shock.

4. To have prevented this medical emergency, the clinician should have
   A. taken the client's blood pressure reading first.
   B. maintained the client in a supine position.
   C. made certain the client was not allergic to any of the components of the local anesthesia.
   D. determined if the client had eaten and administered his medication before his appointment.

5. The initial treatment for the emergency would be to administer
   A. sugar in some form.
   B. oxygen and 15 units of insulin subcutaneously.
   C. oxygen and any available antihistamine.
   D. oxygen only.

6. What is the BEST oral hygiene aid to recommend to this client to help remove plaque from the proximal areas of the mandibular anterior teeth?
   A. tooth pick
   B. oral irrigation
   C. interdental brush
   D. child-size toothbrush

7. Radiopaque spurs, visible interproximally on the posterior films of all quadrants, are evidence of
   A. bone.
   B. calculus.
   C. fixer spots.
   D. overhanging margins.

8. Which of the following teeth clearly has a furcation involvement evident on the radiograph?
   A. maxillary right first molar
   B. maxillary left first premolar
   C. maxillary left first molar
   D. mandibular right first molar

9. What classification of restoration would be used to restore the facial fracture on tooth #9?
   A. III
   B. IV
   C. V
   D. VI

10. The mandibular left first premolar exhibits iatrogenic dentistry in the form of a(n)
    A. open contact.
    B. overhang.
    C. fracture.
    D. leaky margin.

11. The radiopaque areas on the distal of #8 and the mesial of #11 are a result of which of the following?
    A. calcium hydroxide base
    B. amalgam restorations
    C. composite restorations
    D. splashes of fixer

12. Based on the client's social, medical, and dental histories, what type of dental treatment would be MOST appropriate for him?
    A. regular six-month prophylaxis appointments
    B. referral to a periodontist for extensive treatment
    C. referral to prosthodontist for complete dentures
    D. three-month intervals for scaling and periodontal debridement

➤ CASE 8 (see I-16 to I-17)

1. Which of the following bacteria would be MOST predominant at the evaluation appointment?
   A. Gram-positive cocci
   B. Gram-negative cocci
   C. Gram-positive spirochetes
   D. Gram-negative spirochetes

2. Which of the following toothbrush techniques is MOST appropriate to recommend to this client?
   A. Fones
   B. Bass
   C. Roll
   D. Charters

3. All of the following are appropriate physiotherapy aids to recommend for this client to help clean under the mandibular bar EXCEPT one. Which one is the EXCEPTION?
   A. interdental brush
   B. oral irrigating device
   C. wooden interdental cleaner
   D. Super Floss®

4. The MOST appropriate referral for this client is to a(n)
   A. occupational therapist.
   B. psychologist.
   C. dietitian.
   D. physical therapist.

5. Which of the following numbers, taken from the client's vital signs, represents the phase of the cardiac cycle in which the heart relaxes between contractions?
   A. 142
   B. 86
   C. 84
   D. 16

6. All of the following protocol should be used to help reduce the risk of a medical emergency EXCEPT one. Which one is the EXCEPTION?
   A. Call the physician.
   B. Use stress reduction.
   C. Have the patient sit in a supine position for at least 2 minutes before releasing.
   D. Schedule longer appointment times.

7. When using a periodontal probe to determine the clinical attachment level of tooth #27, what is the reference point on the tooth to begin measurement readings?
   A. marginal ridge
   B. CEJ
   C. apical margin of the crown
   D. mandibular bar

8. What is the MOST likely cause of bleeding at probing the mesial of #28?
   A. heavy plaque
   B. heavy pressure while exploring
   C. poorly contoured crown margin
   D. diseased gingival tissue

9. At which stage of the learning ladder is this client regarding plaque removal?
   A. unawareness
   B. awareness
   C. self-interest
   D. involvement

10. All of the following factors could lower the client's blood pressure EXCEPT one. Which one is the EXCEPTION?
    A. exercise
    B. ulcers
    C. use of Atenolol
    D. use of Diltiazem

➤ CASE 9 (see I-18 to I-19)

1. A gingivectomy is indicated for the mandibular right third molar. After reviewing the client's medical history, which of the

following assessments should be made prior to treatment?
A. A history of rheumatic fever requires antibiotic prophylactic therapy for all dental treatment.
B. A history of rheumatic fever requires antibiotic prophylactic therapy for some dental treatment, but not for minor surgical procedures.
C. The client has never been premedicated with antibiotics for dental treatment and therefore does not need it.
D. A medical consultation is required to determine the cardiac status of this client.

2. The classification of restoration on the maxillary right second premolar is
A. I.
B. II.
C. III.
D. IV.

3. Which of the following materials was MOST likely used to restore the maxillary right second premolar?
A. dental amalgam
B. composite resin
C. gold alloy
D. glass ionomer cement

4. The probable cause of the overhang on the maxillary left second premolar may be due to improper
A. condensation of the amalgam.
B. polishing of the restoration.
C. placement of the matrix band and wedge.
D. burnishing of the restoration.

5. Since this client has healthy tissue, all of the following microorganisms would be found EXCEPT one. Which one is the EXCEPTION?
A. predominately Gram-positive
B. aerobic cocci
C. anaerobic spirochetes
D. predominately Gram-negative

6. The client has several occlusal restorations. Which one of the following bacteria is primarily associated with coronal caries?
A. *Mutans streptococcus*
B. *Lactobacillus*
C. *Actinomyces*
D. *Staphylococcus*

7. The dental amalgam on the mandibular right first molar is to be polished. Which of the following is NOT a reason for minimizing heat during this procedure?
A. pulp damage
B. weakened marginal areas by adversely affecting mercury concentration
C. release of mercury vapor
D. discoloration of the tooth

8. The mandibular right second molar has an existing restoration fabricated by an indirect technique. What material was MOST likely used to restore this tooth?
A. dental amalgam
B. composite resin
C. gold alloy
D. glass ionomer

9. What is the radiolucent band visible on the radiograph at the neck of tooth #9?
A. an artifact
B. caries
C. cervical burnout
D. incisive foramen

10. Side effects of antihypersensitive drugs are MOST likely to include all of the following EXCEPT one. Which one is the EXCEPTION?
A. postural hypotension
B. gingival hyperplasia
C. xerostomia
D. increased gag reflex

➤ CASE 10 (see I-20 to I-21)

1. Which of the following procedures would be contraindicated for this client?
A. phase microscope
B. air polishing
C. oral irrigation
D. local anesthesia

review questions

2. This client represents which of the following AAP Case Types?
   A. I
   B. II
   C. III
   D. IV
   E. V

3. Which of the following ultrasonic instrument tips would be BEST to use for debridement on the lingual aspect of tooth #31?
   A. modified (thin) straight ultrasonic
   B. modified (thin) curved right
   C. modified (thin) curved left
   D. standard rigid

4. All of the following antimicrobial/antibiotic adjuncts can be considered for use with this client EXCEPT one. Which one is the EXCEPTION?
   A. tetracycline fiber placement
   B. chlorhexidine gluconate in ultrasonic unit
   C. daily stannous fluoride home irrigation
   D. oral penicillin
   E. daily phenolic compound rinses

5. The clinical attachment level on the direct lingual of tooth #3, in millimeters, is
   A. 5.
   B. 6.
   C. 8.
   D. 10.

6. All of the following conditions are evident in this client's full mouth radiographic series EXCEPT one. Which one is the EXCEPTION?
   A. calculus
   B. amalgam overhang
   C. furcation involvement
   D. vertical bone loss
   E. periapical pathology

7. All of the following home care recommendations are appropriate and address the client's chief complaint EXCEPT one. Which one is the EXCEPTION?
   A. interdental brush
   B. desensitizing dentifrice
   C. sulcular flossing
   D. antimicrobial mouth rinse
   E. perio aid (toothpick in holder)

8. Based on the data provided, what is the MOST appropriate continued care regimen for this client?
   A. 3 months
   B. 4 months
   C. 6 months
   D. 12 months

9. Which of the following terms BEST describes the lingual tissue between teeth #s 31 and 32?
   A. bulbous
   B. blunted
   C. cratered
   D. festooned
   E. flattened

10. Because of the client's periodontal condition relative to his age and length of time since a physician last examined him, a referral for medical examination may be indicated. Which of the following undiagnosed medical conditions is MOST likely suspected as a contributing factor to this client's physical symptoms?
    A. thyroid disease
    B. diabetes
    C. tuberculosis
    D. hepatitis C

11. All of the following instruments may be appropriate to debride the mesial surface of tooth #3 EXCEPT one. Which one is the EXCEPTION?
    A. Columbia 4R/4L
    B. Gracey 15/16
    C. Gracey 5/6
    D. modified (thin) curved right ultrasonic tip
    E. modified (thin) curved left ultrasonic tip

12. Which of the following Gracey curets is LEAST appropriate to use to debride the facial surface and furcation on tooth #15?
    A. 3/4
    B. 7/8

C. 11/12
D. 13/14

➤ CASE 11 (see I-22 to I-23)

1. Using G.V. Black's classification, which one of the following would accurately classify the restoration on tooth #9?
   A. II
   B. III
   C. IV
   D. V
2. All of the following oral physiotherapy aids would be appropriate for this client EXCEPT one. Which one is the EXCEPTION?
   A. automatic toothbrush
   B. floss holder
   C. oral irrigator
   D. interdental brush
3. All of the following are appropriate practices for providing fluoride to the client's dentition EXCEPT one. Which one is the EXCEPTION?
   A. dentifrice
   B. dietary supplement
   C. mouth rinse
   D. professional fluoride treatment
4. What is the total (actual) recession, in millimeters, on tooth #21?
   A. 3
   B. 4
   C. 5
   D. 6
5. Which intraoral technique was used to determine the finding on the hard palate?
   A. inspection
   B. digital
   C. bimanual
   D. bilateral
6. Which of the following radiographs shows evidence of nutrient canals?
   A. maxillary left molar
   B. mandibular right molar
   C. mandibular central incisor
   D. mandibular right canine
7. The client has decided to have a removable partial made to replace tooth #8. All of the following materials are appropriate for obtaining an impression EXCEPT one. Which one is the EXCEPTION?
   A. reversible hydrocolloid
   B. addition silicone
   C. irreversible hydrocolloid
   D. polysulfide
8. All of the following vital signs are within normal/acceptable range EXCEPT one. Which one is the EXCEPTION?
   A. blood pressure
   B. pulse
   C. respiration
   D. temperature
9. Tooth mobility may be associated with all of the following EXCEPT one. Which one is the EXCEPTION?
   A. alveolar bone loss
   B. pregnancy
   C. NSAIDs
   D. occlusal trauma
10. For this client, the MOST important reason to remove calculus from the root surface is because it
    A. alters the dentin.
    B. irritates the junctional epithelium.
    C. harbors plaque organisms.
    D. is an irritant to the gingival sulcus.
11. The client has difficulty opening her mouth. Which of the following muscles of mastication is MOST likely involved?
    A. masseter
    B. temporalis
    C. internal (medial) ptyeroid
    D. external (lateral) pterygoid
12. Which of the following cranial nerves is involved with the client's ptosis of the left eye?
    A. glossopharyngeal
    B. facial
    C. abducens
    D. oculomotor

➤ CASE 12 (see I-24 to I-25)

1. On the facial root surface of #28 there is evidence of
   A. calculus.
   B. root caries.
   C. abrasion.
   D. tobacco stain.

2. To accurately diagnose posterior bone level, which of the following radiographs would provide the MOST accurate diagnosis?
   A. pantomogram
   B. occlusal
   C. vertical bitewings
   D. horizontal bitewings

3. Teeth #s 6–10 and 22–27 show which of the following malrelationships?
   A. overjet
   B. edge-to-edge
   C. overbite
   D. crossbite

4. The MOST appropriate procedure for calculus removal on this client would be the use of
   A. ultrasonic scaling.
   B. hoes.
   C. files.
   D. sonic scaling.

5. All of the following are characteristics of hypothyroidism EXCEPT one. Which one is the EXCEPTION?
   A. myxedema
   B. cold intolerance
   C. Graves' disease
   D. glossitis

6. All of the following medications are acceptable for clients with hypothyroidism EXCEPT one. Which one is the EXCEPTION?
   A. Synthroid
   B. Levoxyl
   C. meclizine
   D. Naprosyn

7. The MOST appropriate referral for this client at this time is to a(n)
   A. school counselor.
   B. periodontist.
   C. oral surgeon.
   D. orthodontist.

8. In addition to the heavy calculus deposits on the buccal surfaces of teeth #s 9–15, there is an accumulation of calculus on the occlusal surface of #14. This is probably due to
   A. the lack of opposing teeth, resulting in a reduction of mechanical plaque removal and therefore calculus formation.
   B. medications taken by the client.
   C. the client not flossing.
   D. the salivary flow delivered through Wharton's duct causing calculus formation.

9. Which of the following BEST describes the pattern of bone loss in this client?
   A. generalized horizontal
   B. localized horizontal
   C. generalized vertical
   D. localized vertical

10. Calculus removal at the facial of the maxillary left first molar may result in tooth sensitivity owing to
    A. occlusal caries.
    B. traumatized tissue.
    C. exposed dentinal tubules.
    D. altered occlusion.

11. Nerve fibers associated with root hypersensitivity are
    A. A-delta fibers in the pulp.
    B. myelinated C fibers in the pulp.
    C. long neurons.
    D. cranial nerves III and VIII.

12. Radiographs suggest the presence of root surface caries at the distal of #14. Which of the following microorganisms is implicated in the development of root caries?
    A. *Actinomyces viscosus*
    B. *Actinobacillus actinomycetemcomitans*
    C. *Fusobacterius nucleatum*
    D. *Prevotella intermedia*
    E. *Mutans streptococcus*

➤ CASE 13 (see I-26 to I-27)

1. What is the Angle's classification for the molars on this client?
   A. Class I
   B. Class II, Division I
   C. Class II, Division II
   D. Class III
2. Which of the following teeth demonstrate a plaque-retentive factor?
   A. maxillary right first premolar
   B. maxillary right central incisor
   C. mandibular left first molar
   D. mandibular right second molar
3. What type of prosthesis is found in the maxillary right quadrant?
   A. cantilever bridge
   B. Maryland bridge
   C. 3-unit fixed partial denture
   D. laminate
4. Which of the following active ingredients is in the toothpaste this client uses?
   A. potassium nitrate
   B. triclosan
   C. acidulated phosphate fluoride
   D. pyrophosphate
5. Which of the following vital signs is NOT within normal limits?
   A. blood pressure
   B. pulse
   C. respiration
   D. temperature
6. Which of the following areas was palpated to obtain the pulse rate?
   A. side of neck
   B. side of face
   C. bend in elbow
   D. wrist
7. Using G.V. Black's classification, how would the restoration on tooth #19 be classified?
   A. I
   B. II
   C. V
   D. VI
8. When the dentition is occluded, which of the following is the correct term for the position of the molars?
   A. end-to-end
   B. open-bite
   C. crossbite
   D. edge-to-edge
9. When reviewing the client's home care regimen, at which level is she positioned on the learning ladder?
   A. awareness
   B. self-interest
   C. involvement
   D. habit
10. If a sample of this client's plaque were examined with a phase microscope, which types of bacteria would MOST likely predominate?
    A. Gram-negative rods
    B. Gram-negative spirochetes
    C. Gram-positive cocci
    D. white blood cells
11. Given the medical and social histories, the client MOST likely suffers from which of the following conditions?
    A. obesity
    B. osteoporosis
    C. depression
    D. Type 1 diabetes
12. On reviewing the client's history, total care should address all of the following EXCEPT one. Which one is the EXCEPTION?
    A. exercise
    B. caloric intake
    C. calcium intake
    D. hormone replacement therapy

➤ CASE 14 (see I-28 to I-29)

1. All of the following are oral manifestations of multiple sclerosis EXCEPT one. Which one is the EXCEPTION?
   A. TMJ dysfunction
   B. xerostomia
   C. gingival enlargement
   D. recession

2. Which of the following is a symptom of multiple sclerosis?
   A. lip and tongue tremor
   B. lordosis
   C. impaired eye-hand coordination
   D. paralysis of facial muscles

3. Which of the following antibiotic premedication regimens is appropriate for this client?
   A. 2 g Amoxicillin orally 1 hour before procedure
   B. 600 mg Clindamycin orally 1 hour before procedure
   C. 2 g Cephalexin orally 1 hour before procedure
   D. no premedication needed

4. On the initial appointment, air polishing is contraindicated owing to all of the following EXCEPT one. Which one is the EXCEPTION?
   A. gingival recession
   B. hypertension
   C. gingivitis
   D. herpes labialis

5. Which of the following instruments is LEAST appropriate to use for initial debridement of the client's mandibular anterior lingual surfaces?
   A. Gracey curet
   B. sonic scaler
   C. hoe
   D. sickle scaler

6. All of the following conditions are radiographically evident on this client's bitewings EXCEPT one. Which one is the EXCEPTION?
   A. horizontal bone loss
   B. early furcation involvement
   C. calculus
   D. Class III restoration
   E. caries

7. All of the following recommendations may be indicated for this client EXCEPT one. Which one is the EXCEPTION?
   A. toothpick in a holder (perio aid)
   B. desensitizing dentifrice
   C. fluoride rinse containing alcohol
   D. use of a soft-bristled toothbrush

8. If the clinician chose to use an ultrasonic scaler, which of the following ultrasonic tips would be MOST effective in the initial debridement of this client's mandibular lingual surfaces?
   A. modified (thin) straight
   B. modified (thin) right
   C. modified (thin) left
   D. standard (traditional)

9. The clinical attachment level on the direct facial of tooth #6, in millimeters, is
   A. 2.
   B. 3.
   C. 4.
   D. 5.

10. All of the following procedures are indicated for this client EXCEPT one. Which one is the EXCEPTION?
    A. finish and polish amalgam in #30
    B. replace prosthesis of #s 3, 13, and 14
    C. replace crown on #4
    D. place sealants on #s 5, 12, 21, and 28

11. On this client, which of the following dental implants is contraindicated for replacement of teeth #s 13 and 14?
    A. subperiosteal
    B. transosteal
    C. endosseous
    D. an implant is not indicated

12. The client's prescription medication is contributing to all of the following conditions EXCEPT one. Which one is the EXCEPTION?
    A. xerostomia
    B. periodontal disease
    C. hypertension
    D. cervical abrasion

answers & rationales

➤ CASE 1

1.

C. This diet drug causes valvular damage, increasing the risk of bacteria during oral procedures. The diet drugs Pondimin® and Redux™ were removed from the market because of potential cardiac and pulmonary side effects including valvular damage and pulmonary hypertension. Clients who have taken these drugs must be assumed to have a valvular damage until proven otherwise and precautions must be taken before undertaking procedures that are likely to induce a bacteremia. Any client who has taken these drugs in the past requires a medical consultation from his/her physician to determine any cardiac damage and the necessity of antibiotic prophylaxis before dental procedures to prevent endocarditis.

2.

E. Conclude that the client has had no health conditions that would contraindicate treatment. This client is at high risk for developing endocarditis from scaling and polishing procedures. It is best to err on the side of caution than to proceed without proper investigation, consultation, or precautions.

3.

B. The mesiobuccal cusp of the maxillary molar occludes in the buccal groove of the mandibular molar and the maxillary canine occludes between the mandibular canine and first premolar on the right and left sides. These observations are consistent with Class I occlusion, although the anterior teeth are crowded. The best classification of this dentition would be Class I malocclusion or Class I occlusion with anterior crowding.

4.

E. This client has tooth mobility readings consistent with normal physiological movement. Typically, normal physiological movement is not graded. This client has scores ranging from .5 mm to 1 mm, which indicates that the involved teeth have slightly greater mobility than normal and up to 1 mm of movement buccolingually.

5.

C. On the panoramic radiograph, areas of increased bone density are evident just inferior to the mandibular canine and premolar teeth. This is common radiographic presentation of mandibular tori. In the mandibular arch intraoral camera view, the mandibular tori appear on the lingual surface of the mandible adjacent to the canine and premolar teeth. Condensing osteitis, root tips, salivary stones, and chronic focal sclerosing osteomyelitis are not evident on the intraoral camera image.

6.

B. The client presents with mild periodontitis with probing depths measuring from 3 to 4 mm from the cementoenamel junction (CEJ). Recession is present in all sextants and furcation involvement was noted on several maxillary and mandibular molars. There is radiographic evidence of furcation involvement on teeth #s 19 and 30 and clinical evidence of .5 to 1 mm mobility of the mandibular anterior teeth. Although the client is predominantly a Case Type II, the clinical evidence of furcation involvement and tooth mobility places her into the Case Type III classification.

7.

A. The cementum is exposed as a result of gingival recession and bone loss. The exposed root surfaces tend to be more sensitive to cold air and fluids. There is no clinical evidence of recurrent caries or enough tooth mobility to warrant cold sensitivity. The client assessment does not denote tooth clenching.

8.

D. Interradicular bone is resorbed, exposing a through-and-through tunnel in Class II involvement. In Class II furcation involvement, the explorer or probe can enter the furcation but not extend through to the other side. The description in the correct answer is consistent with Class III furcation involvement rather than Class II.

9.

C. To correct horizontal overlap, the horizontal angulation needs to be directed in a more forward direction. The horizontal angle was aligned too far posterior resulting in interproximal overlap. To correct this error, move the horizontal angle forward until the horizontal angle directs the x-rays through the contacts of the molar teeth. Adjusting vertical angulation does not correct overlapping. Directing the central ray corrects conecutting, not overlapping. Redirecting the horizontal angulation more posterior would maximize rather than minimize the overlapping.

10.

A. The radiolucent areas on the interproximal root surfaces are consistent with cervical burnout but not root caries. Cervical burnout is a phenomenon of x-ray penetration of cervical tooth anatomy. The cervical tooth anatomy is thinner and thus more radiolucent than the enamel above it and alveolar crest below it.

11.

B. *Provotella intermedia* predominates in all types of hormonal gingivitis. *S. Salivarius* is not linked to development of gingivitis; it is a common inhabitant of saliva. *Porphymonas gingivalis* is common in all types of periodontal disease, but is not considered the primary etiologic agent in pregnancy gingivitis. *Mutans streptococcus* is implicated as the primary etiologic agent in human caries.

12.

C. This structure is the zygomaticotemporal suture. It is the radiolucent diagonal junction between the zygomatic process of the temporal bone and the temporal process of the zygomatic bone. Together these processes form the zygoma.

➤ CASE 2

1.

B. The client has small amounts of plaque owing to her good home care measures. Gram-positive cocci and few rods predominate at this stage. Spirochetes and vibrios are common in mature plaque. *Fusobacterium* are more common in the middle stages of plaque development.

2.

C. Film bending causes radiolucent diagonal lines on a radiograph. Films that stick together during processing will usually have the outline border of the other film and will have dark and white areas, not lines. Since x-rays are sensitive to light, the exposed areas will appear black. The entire density of the film will appear radiolucent with overdevelopment.

3.

D. The appropriate professional topical fluoride for this client is sodium because she has composite restorations. Sodium fluoride does not etch the glass particles in composite restorations. Stannous fluoride has a strong metallic taste, which should be considered when treating a patient. It also causes brown staining in carious tooth structures. Acidulated phosphate fluoride has the disadvantage of possibly etching ceramic or porcelain restorations and should be used with caution. Sodium monofluorophosphate fluoride is recognized as effective and safe for over-the-counter toothpaste use.

4.

B. Composite resin is often used as a direct esthetic material, especially in an area where significant strength of the material is required. Dental amalgam and gold alloy are not recommended for anterior restorations for esthetic reasons. Glass ionomer cement is a brittle material and not recommended for restorations that are subjected to high stress or wear.

5.

D. Ferrous pertains to iron. Ferrous sulfate is prescribed to treat iron deficiency. It does not refer to vitamin B, calcium, or hormones.

6.

D. Cheese has been found to be anticariogenic, possibly because of its high calcium and phosphate concentrations. However, crackers and pretzels are retentive polysaccharides that could promote tooth decay. Carrots are an excellent source of fiber.

7.

D. Thiamin is found in abundance in enriched crackers, breads, and pastas that this client consumes. However, she would be deficient in calcium and vitamins D and C.

8.

A. Angular cheilosis is a common oral manifestation of B-vitamin deficiencies. Dysgeusia refers to a distortion in taste. Dysphagia refers to difficulty in swallowing. Neither is an oral manifestation of B-vitamin deficiencies. Oral candidiasis is not an oral manifestation of folate and vitamin B_{12} deficiencies.

9.

B. This selection would produce a high density or dark radiograph rather than a low density radiograph. Underestimation of the client's size and stature, weak or exhausted developer chemicals, low processing temperature, and releasing the exposure button would result in a low density image.

10.

D. As stated in the client's medication listing, she is taking ferrous sulfate tid (three times a day). The abbreviations for as needed, before meals, and twice a day are PRN, AC, and bid, respectively.

11.

A. Both the statement and reason are related and correct regarding folate and vitamin B_{12}.

12.

D. Since this client has a history of morbid obesity, nutritional deficiencies, and a high decay rate, it would be highly recommended she see a dietitian for proper nutritional counseling. A school counselor or psychologist would not be qualified in the area of nutrition. It is hoped her dentition will be restored and will not require oral surgery for the removal of any teeth.

➤ CASE 3

1.

C. After the client has been placed in a comfortable position, she should use her own bronchodilator to manage an acute stage. If the episode continues after use of the bronchodilator, oxygen should be administered. The team member should then seek medical assistance. The injection of a corticosteroid may be necessary at this time. Administration of nitrous oxide would be used during the appointment if the client is fearful.

2.

C. Ecchymoses—discoloration of the mucous membranes—is not a common side effect of Proventil. However, it is not uncommon for the client to experience taste changes, xerostomia, and tooth discoloration while taking Proventil.

3.

D. Silver points were once the standard care in the obturation of canals undergoing endodontic treatment. They appear radiopaque within the canals. Timing of obturation is not significant. Gold posts are not used to obturate canals.

4.

B. The opacity on the radiograph and the metal along the lingual margin in the photograph indicate this is a porcelain fused-to-metal crown. All-ceramic and indirect composite restorations have no metal present. Three-quarter gold crowns have no tooth-colored components.

5.

D. The blood pressure should be verified before dental treatment. The client is borderline hypertensive and should be encouraged to be evaluated for hypertension by a physician. However, a consultation is not required for dental treatment.

6.

B. The restoration covers all of the lingual, interproximal, and occlusal surfaces. It extends slightly onto the facial surface and is therefore considered a 3/4-coverage crown. A full coverage crown covers all surfaces of the tooth. The palatal surface is covered and could not be an MOD inlay or onlay.

7.

A. The marginal staining is due to the ingress of fluid and its contents between the restoration and the tooth surface. This has been called microleakage or percolation. Complete, not overpolymerization, is desired. Proper brushing and flossing will not stop marginal leakage.

8.

D. HS means take at bedtime. Qid means to take four times a day. Bid and PRN means to take twice a day and "as needed," respectively.

9.

A. The only material given that would not be expected to function properly is the glass ionomer. The composite resin and aluminous porcelain are common choices for this situation. The gold alloy could be used if aesthetic desires dictate its use.

10.

C. The application of neutral sodium fluoride would be the best choice for this client. Stannous fluoride can stain pre-carious lesions. Acid-based fluoride products, such as acidulated phosphate, are contraindicated in the presence of existing composite and porcelain restorations. Sodium monofluorophosphate is used in over-the-counter dentifrices.

11.

C. *Provotella intermedia* is a common pathogen involved in hormonal gingivitis. *S. mutans* are implicated in human caries. *S. salivarius* is commonly found in saliva. *P. gingivalis* is not the primary etiological agent implicated in hormonal gingivitis.

12.

B. The middle superior alveolar nerve serves the maxillary premolar and maxillary first molars. The anterior alveolar nerve serves the maxillary central and lateral incisors, as well as maxillary canines. The posterior superior alveolar nerve serves the distobuccal and lingual roots of the maxillary first molars and the second and third molars. The inferior alveolar nerve innervates the mandibular teeth.

➤ CASE 4

1.

C. Symptoms of hemorrhagic CVA include a sudden onset of a headache, dizziness and vertigo, sweating and chills, nausea, and vomiting. Myxedema coma is a severe complication associated with hypothyroidism. Its symptoms include hypothermia, bradycardia, hypotension, and loss of consciousness. Clients with acute adrenal insufficiency (adrenal crisis) most generally exhibit lethargy, fatigue, and weakness. Thyroid storm is a result of untreated hyperthyroidism. Symptoms include an elevated body temperature, excessive sweating, vomiting, and abdominal pain.

2.

C. The trigeminal nerve is sensory via V_1 and V_2 and sensory and motor via V_3 to muscles of mastication. The oculomotor provides motor innervation to muscles of the eyeball. The glossopharyngeal provides sensory innervation to the posterior one third of the tongue and motor to selected soft palate and pharynx muscles.

3.

B. *S. sanguis* is the first "colonizer" of tooth structures. *S. mutans* competes with *S. sanguis,* but is not the first colonizer. *S. salivarius* is found in saliva. *P. intermedia* is a periodontal pathogen found in mature plaque.

4.

B. Catapres is an antihypertensive medication.

5.

E. Areas of erythema and leukoplakia are referred to as "speckled leukoplakia" owing to interspersed areas of red and white appearances. Diffuse leukoplakia is not completely white in appearance. Nodular leukoplakia and erythema are not nodular in appearance. Diffuse erythema is not completely red in appearance.

6.

A. Tobacco usage frequently results in premalignant lesions. Use of breath mints, alcohol and spicy food consumption, and oral tongue habits are not considered high-risk factors.

7.

B. Unexplained lesions imply immediate investigation and would not be observed for an extended period of time. The lesion is too large for successful, complete excision with an excisional biopsy. Antibiotics and antifungal medications are not indicated because there is no bacterial or fungal disease implicated.

8.

E. The top-to-bottom atypical proliferation of epithelium, with violation of the basement membrane, is by definition invasive carcinoma. Mild, moderate, and severe dysplasias are not defined as top-to-bottom dysplasias. Carcinoma in situ implies a top-to-bottom dysplasia, but without violation of the basement membrane.

9.

D. When the nodes are hard, fixed, and not tender, metastasis is suspicious. When the nodes are draining from an infection, they are tender and movable. Lymphadenopathy is unusual with mild gingivitis and, if present, would be tender and movable. Metastasis of the oropharyngeal lesion is not an etiology for lymphadenopathy.

10.

B. The client has a habit of sucking on breath mints, which have a high sucrose content. Smoking, mouth breathing, and a toothpick habit are not cariogenic.

➤ CASE 5

1.

C. Generalized bleeding on probing indicates active inflammatory disease. Both the clinical examination and radiographs show evidence of periodontal destruction and furcation involvement. The client's condition would not be considered healthy since there is presence of bleeding on probing. This indicates active disease. Evidence of bone loss indicates the disease has progressed from gingivitis to periodontitis.

2.

B. Class I restorations are found on the occlusal surfaces of posterior teeth. Classes A and C are not part of G.V. Black's classifications. Class II is a two-surface posterior restoration. Class V describes restorations found at the cervical one third.

3.

C. Both the clinical and radiographic appearance of these Class I amalgams suggest that they are intact, sound restorations. They do not have overhanging margins and therefore have little impact on the development or progression of periodontal disease. An intact, smooth, non-plaque-retentive amalgam restoration does not contribute to periodontal disease. Restorations do not cause periodontal disease. If the margins of a restoration are adjacent to the gingival tissue and are plaque retentive, the restoration may contribute to periodontal disease.

4.

B. Diabetes increases the incidence of periodontal disease. There may be poor wound healing, increased incidence of periodontal abscesses, xerostomia, and burning mouth. The history does not include tobacco use. Hypertension is not considered a significant risk factor for the development and progression of periodontal disease. The presence of orthodontic bands or brackets may make plaque removal more difficult; however, past history of orthodontic care is not a risk factor.

5.

C. Radiographic and clinical findings identify pocket formation, bone loss, and supragingival calculus. These factors suggest a periodontal disease state. Purulence is related to the presence of microorganisms, not occlusal trauma. The radiographs do not show evidence of pulp pathology. There is no history of physical injury, and x-ray studies do not reveal evidence.

6.

C. Uncontrolled diabetes is a risk factor for the development and progression of periodontal disease. The bacterial infections found in periodontal disease may make it more difficult to manage the diabetes. The periodontal infections place additional burden on the host's defense mechanisms.

7.

C. Case Type III, moderate periodontitis, shows evidence of increased destruction of the periodontal structure and noticeable loss of bone support, possibly accompanied by an increase in tooth mobility. There may be furcation involvement in multirooted teeth. Case Type I, gingival disease, is characterized by inflammation of the gingiva, clinical changes in color, gingival form, surface appearance, and presence of bleeding and/or exudate. Case Type II, early periodontitis, is the progression of the gingival inflammation into the deeper periodontal structures and alveolar bone crest, with slight bone loss. There is usually a slight loss of connective tissue attachment and alveolar bone. Case Type IV, advanced periodontitis, involves further progression of periodontitis, with major loss of alveolar bone support and is usually accompanied by increased tooth mobility. Furcation involvement in multirooted teeth is likely. Case Type V, refractory periodontitis, includes multiple disease sites that continue to demonstrate attachment loss after appropriate therapy. These sites continue to be infected by periodontal pathogens.

8.

D. An indicator of active disease in bone is the loss of the crestal lamina dura. The lamina dura can be clearly identified at the mesial of #19 on the bitewings. The lamina dura is not defined on the periapical x-ray at #7. Although there may be more loss of bone support at #7 than at #19, bone level itself is not an indicator of active disease. The presence of calculus is not an indicator of active disease. Radiographs are valuable to assess calcified structures, but they have little value in assessing the status of soft tissue.

9.

C. Oral surgery procedures, associated with restricted food intake, require a medical consultation and temporary cessation of the medication. Referral to the oral surgeon is appropriate after a medical consultation. A referral to a dietitian is appropriate because the client is diabetic. The client could be referred to the periodontist after the tooth is extracted.

10.

C. The origin and insertion of the temporalis muscle are the temporal bone and coronoid process, respectively. The origin and insertion for the lateral pterygoid muscle are the greater wing of the sphenoid and anterior surface of the temperomandibular joint (TMJ), respectively. The origin and insertion of the medial pterygoid muscle are the lateral surface of the pterygoid plate and the neck of the condyle, respectively.

11.

A. To decrease the distortion evident on the maxillary left molar periapical, it would be necessary to increase the vertical angulation. Decreasing the vertical angulation would cause elongation. Redirecting the PID more posteriorly would cause a cone cut to occur. Placing the film more inferior to the occlusal surfaces would cut off the apices.

12.

D. The sternocleidomastoid is a large strap muscle in the neck that rotates and tilts the head. The digastric muscle is a minor muscle of mastication that depresses the mandible. The sternohyoid muscle helps to stabilize the hyoid bone. The mylohyoid muscle forms the floor of the mouth.

➤ CASE 6

1.

B. Candidiasis classically presents as white patches that leave a bloody area when rubbed off. The client had other risk factors that made candidiasis a likely diagnosis. The client gave no history of snuff use. Hyperkeratosis is a term for extra layers of keratinization in response to trauma. This was not the most likely diagnosis because of other risk factors.

2.

B. Antibody assays are tests used to determine what disease entity is present. Prothrombin time is a blood-clotting test. A liver enzyme test would be indicated if liver damage were suspected. Partial prothrombin time is a test of blood clotting ability.

3.

C. This client is most likely suffering from HIV. He displays lymphadenopathy, oral candidiasis, weight loss, fatigue, and bleeding gingiva. These are classic symptoms of this syndrome. Weight loss and fatigue are symptoms of tuberculosis and hepatitis B and C. However, candidiasis and bleeding tissues are not associated with TB, and there are no oral manifestations associated with hepatitis B and C.

4.

C. HIV destroys the CD4 T lymphocytes, weakening the immune system. Thrombocytes, or platelets, are cells that cause blood clotting, and B lymphocytes are the cells that produce antibodies; both are not affected by HIV. The HIV virus affects neutrophils, but the cells most harmed are the CD4 T lymphocytes.

5.

D. Tobacco use, especially smoking, has been identified as a significant factor in the development and progression of periodontal disease. The client, through smoking cessation, can alter this risk factor. Stress has been identified as a possible contributor to the progression of periodontal disease. Its significance is less well defined than the changeable risk factor of tobacco use. Hypertension and working long hours have not been identified as significant risk factors in the progression of periodontal disease.

6.

D. The Bass method of toothbrushing is used to clean the facials and linguals of teeth with pocketing. The bristles of the toothbrush are placed in the sulcus for cleaning. Because of the diastema between teeth #s 10 and 11, it is acceptable to use dental tape or interdental wood stimulators.

7.

A. Because of the overhanging or defective margin of the crown on tooth #14, more plaque is likely to accumulate. A large MOD amalgam with a defective proximal margin could contribute to plaque accumulation; however, this client does not have an amalgam on tooth #14. The clinical and radiographic evidence does not identify a furcation involvement. If one existed, it could contribute to plaque accumulation. There is no extrinsic stain noted on tooth #14.

8.

C. The Gracey curet 13 is designed for application on the distolinguals of teeth #s 30 and 31. The Gracey curet 11 and 12 are designed for use on the mesial surfaces of posterior teeth. The Gracey curet 14 would be applied on the distofacials of teeth #s 30 and 31.

9.

D. Referral to this client's physician would be indicated for his severe weight loss. The dentist would most likely be able to identify the cause for his tooth sensitivity and breath odor, as well as provide antibiotics to treat his periodontal condition.

10.

D. Advanced periodontitis is identified by its major loss of bone support, increase in tooth mobility, and probable furcation involvement. This client's condition is more severe than Case I gingival disease. Early periodontitis describes the progression of gingival inflammation with slight bone and connective tissue attachment loss. Moderate periodontitis is a more advanced disease with noticeable loss of bone support, increase in tooth mobility, and probable furcation involvement.

11.

B. Using both hands at the same time to examine corresponding structures on opposite sides of the body is called the bilateral palpation technique. Use of finger(s) and thumb from each hand, applied simultaneously, is the bimanual palpation technique. Digital palpation involves using a single finger. Inspection is not a valid tool to use to evaluate the client's TMJ.

12.

B. All clients should be treated with "universal precautions" as mandated by the Americans with Disability Act. Double gloving, sterilizing instruments twice, and use of a special isolation room violates universal precautions.

➤ CASE 7

1.

B. The buccinator muscle flattens the cheek, which pushes food out of the vestibule both vertically and horizontally. The risorius muscle is responsible for widening the mouth—as when a person smiles. The orbicularis oris muscle encircles the mouth and acts to close the lips. The medial pterygoid muscle has the function of elevating the mandible.

2.

D. The anterior superior branch supplies the maxillary centrals, laterals, and canines, whereas the nasopalatine branch innervates the soft tissue of the anterior one-third of the hard palate. The inferior alveolar innervation for the mandibular teeth and the long buccal nerve serve as afferent nerves for the mandibular teeth and skin of cheek, buccal mucous membranes, and buccal gingiva of the mandibular posterior teeth, respectively. The mental nerve (afferent) serves the chin, lower lip, and labial mucosa near the mandibular anterior teeth. The posterior superior nerve serves most portions of the maxillary molar teeth and the greater anterior palatine nerve serves the posterior hard palate.

3.

D. Symptoms of insulin shock include sweating, pallor, hunger, trembling, headaches, dizziness, and weakness. The client may also experience an increase in blood pressure and pulse rate. However, the respiration rate will remain normal or depressed. An allergic response to lidocaine is extremely rare. The client would most likely experience psychogenic responses, such as hyperventilation and vasodepressor syncope. The most common symptoms of anaphylactic shock include smooth muscle spasms, cardiovascular and acute respiratory distress, and skin reactions—a generalized rash. With myocardial infarction (heart attack), the client will experience severe pain in the sternum, difficulty in breathing, profuse sweating and nausea, with possible vomiting.

4.

D. With an insulin-dependent diabetic client, it is important to determine when insulin was last administered, as well as when the last meal was consumed. Checking the client's blood pressure, keeping him in a supine position, and determining his allergic status with the local anesthetic would not have prevented insulin shock.

5.

A. When a diabetic client goes into insulin shock, the first mode of action is to administer some form of sugar such as orange juice, candy, or a sugared soft drink. It is also vital to determine when insulin was administered. The administration of oxygen and an antihistamine would not assist the client in this situation.

6.

C. Because of bone loss and missing interdental papillae, an interdental brush is recommended to assist in removing plaque. The toothpick is used to clean along the marginal gingiva. Oral irrigation does not remove plaque. A child-size toothbrush would not provide access to the proximal areas as would the proximal brush.

7.

B. Interproximal calculus is projected as radiopaque spurs on radiographs. Bone, fixer spots, and overhangs are radiopaque, but not shaped as spurs at the interproximals of the posterior teeth.

8.

D. A radiolucent area is evident in the furcation of tooth #30. Teeth #s 3, 12, and 14 do not show evidence of furcation involvement.

9.

B. A Class IV involves the proximal and incisal angles of anterior teeth. A Class III involves proximal surfaces of incisors and canines. A Class V involves the cervical one third of facial or lingual surfaces. A Class VI involves the incisal edge of anterior teeth or the cusp tips of posterior teeth.

10.

B. Improper use of the matrix band and wood wedge allowed excess amalgam to leak through onto the distal of #21. There is no evidence of an open contact, fracture, or leaky margin on tooth #21.

11.

A. Calcium hydroxide base material is more radiopaque than composite material used on anterior teeth. An amalgam restoration is even more radiopaque than calcium hydroxide and composite material. Fixer spots are not as configured as anterior restoration materials.

12.

D. Since the client is retired and on a fixed income, maintenance appointments every 3 months would be best. Because of his periodontal status, it would be more appropriate to have him on a 3-month rather than 6-month recall. Referral to a periodontist would not be feasible because of the client's limited income, and since he wants to keep his teeth, referral for complete dentures should not be recommended.

➤ CASE 8

1.

D. Gram-negative spirochetes, associated with inflammation, would be most predominant at the evaluation appointment since gingivitis is present. Gram-positive microorganisms are associated with healthy tissues and early plaque development.

2.

B. The Bass toothbrushing technique is most appropriate because it stimulates and cleans the gingival tissues along the tooth structure and adapts to the margins of the fixed partial denture. The toothbrush bristles are directed in the gingival sulcus for thorough plaque removal. Since it is easy to learn, the Fones technique could be recommended to use because the patient does not brush on a daily basis. However, it would not be a toothbrushing method of choice. The roll technique should not be considered since it does not provide gingival stimulation. The Charters technique could be considered, but it is more difficult to comprehend and apply than the Bass method.

3.

B. The oral irrigating device does not remove plaque. The interdental brush, wooden interdental cleaner, and Super Floss® would all be appropriate for use under the mandibular bar since they are capable of removing debris without causing trauma.

4.

C. Referral to a dietitian would be the most appropriate because the client is overweight. Weight reduction could benefit the client's elevated blood pressure. Referral to an occupational therapist, psychologist, or physical therapist is not appropriate for this client.

5.

B. The diastolic reading of the blood pressure represents the phase of the cardiac cycle in which the heart relaxes between contractions. This client's diastolic reading is 86. The systolic reading of the blood pressure represents the phase of the cardiac cycle in which the left ventricle of the heart contracts and blood is forced through the aorta and pulmonary artery. This client's systolic reading is 142. The client's pulse is 84, which is the intermittent throbbing sensation felt when finger(s) are pressed against an artery. The respiration rate, 16, indicates how well the body is providing oxygen to the tissues.

6.

D. Shorter appointments would be indicated to assist with stress reduction protocol and help reduce anxiety. It is appropriate to contact the physician if the clinician has questions or concerns regarding the treatment of this client. To decrease the risk of a medical emergency, it is important to use stress reduction protocol and have the client sit up at least 2 minutes before releasing.

7.

C. To determine the clinical attachment level, a fixed point on the tooth must be selected first. In this case, the fixed point is the apical margin of the crown. Although the marginal ridge is a fixed point on the occlusal surface of the tooth, it would not be a good reference point to use to determine attachment loss, since the distance would be greater than the probe readings. The cementoenamel joint (CEJ) is the point used when obtaining the clinical attachment level. In this case, the CEJ is not visible since the crown covers it. The mandibular bar is not an appropriate reference point since it is not attached to the tooth in question.

8.

D. The cause of bleeding on probing indicates diseased gingival tissues. The tissue has lacerated pocket walls, which bleed on gentle probing. Heavy plaque and a poorly contoured crown margin are causative factors of diseased gingival tissues; however, neither is the direct cause of bleeding on probing. Heavy pressure while exploring involves use of a different assessment instrument.

9.

B. The client does not use an auxiliary aid to remove plaque from under the mandibular bar because it is too "time-consuming." This indicates she is at the awareness level of the learning ladder—she has the correct information, but it does not offer any personal meaning. The patient is aware of the importance of plaque removal, establishing her at a higher level than unawareness. However, she does not have an interest to act, which demonstrates a lack of self-interest or involvement in the stages of the learning ladder.

10.

B. The client's blood pressure is slightly elevated. The client's past history of having ulcers would not affect her blood pressure. Exercise would help with weight reduction and, in turn, assist with decreasing her blood pressure. Atenolol is an antihypertensive drug. Diltiazem is a calcium channel blocker, which is also prescribed to reduce high blood pressure.

➤ CASE 9

1.

D. The presence or absence of a heart murmur should be verified. A history of rheumatic fever with no evidence of heart murmur does not require antibiotic prophylaxis. Although the client has not been premedicated for past care, her cardiac status should be determined.

2.

B. Class II restorations involve the proximal surfaces of posterior teeth. Class I restorations involve the pits and fissures of teeth. Class III and IV restorations involve the proximal surfaces and incisal edges of anterior teeth, respectively.

3.

A. The material in tooth #4 is dental amalgam. Composite resins and glass ionomers are tooth-colored restorations. Gold alloys do not typically present with evidence of corrosion.

4.

C. Improper placement of the matrix and wedge can cause overhanging restorations. The amalgam in tooth #13 appears well condensed. Polishing techniques could be used to remove the overhang. Burnishing is used to smooth the surface of an amalgam.

5.

C. Anaerobic bacteria are found predominately in diseased tissues. All the remaining bacteria can be found in healthy tissue.

6.

A. The primary bacteria associated with the initiation of coronal caries is *Mutans streptococcus. Lactobacillus* is involved with advanced smooth surface caries. *Actinomyces* has been associated with root surface caries. *Staphylococcus* is not associated with dental caries.

7.

D. Heat generated by polishing should not discolor tooth structure. Heat generation can cause pulp damage and mercury to vaporize. It can also increase the mercury concentration, decreasing the strength of the amalgam in thin marginal areas.

8.

C. Gold alloy is a metallic material used for indirect restorations. Dental amalgam and glass ionomers are used as direct restorative materials. The restoration present is too radiopaque to be a composite restoration.

9.

C. Cervical burnout appears radiolucent because of the concavities between the facial and lingual root surfaces. An artifact is a manmade error, which can be radiolucent or radiopaque. Root surface caries have a "ditched out" appearance with some degree of bone loss. Incisive foramen is an opening in the midline in the hard palate.

10.

D. Increased gag reflex is not a side effect associated with antihypertensive drugs. Gingival hyperplasia is associated with most of the calcium channel blockers used as antihypersensitives. Postural hypotension and xerostomia are associated with antihypersensitive medications.

➤ CASE 10

1.

B. The use of airpolishing is contraindicated for a patient with an anterior porcelain-fused-to-metal bridge, generalized recession, and exposed cementum and dentin. Air polishing has demonstrated pitting and wear to porcelain, erosion of dental cements, and damage to margins of dental castings. Ultrasonic scaling is indicated for calculus removal and debridement in deep pockets, furcations, and root concavities. Antimicrobial oral irrigation may be helpful in controlling the client's periodontal disease. The phase contrast microscope may help to motivate the client into more stringent homecare and treatment recommendations. Periodontal debridement may be more efficient and comfortable for the patient if local anesthesia is used.

2.

D. This client presents with AAP Case Type IV—advanced periodontitis. There is evidence of advanced loss of alveolar bone, furcations, and increased mobility, all indicators of AAP Case Type IV. This client's periodontal condition is beyond AAP Case Types I, II, and III. Owing to the client's lack of finances, he has never received the recommended periodontal surgery and therefore could not be classified as AAP Case Type V, refractory periodontitis.

3.

C. The lingual of tooth #31 has 2-mm recession, a 5-mm pocket, Class II furcation involvement, with light to moderate plaque and calculus. The modified (thin) curved left is designed for use on the mandibular right lingual. Its design is specified for removal of light to moderate calculus, plaque, and endotoxins and provides access into furcations and pockets greater than 4 mm. The modified (thin) straight tip is designed primarily for patients with AAP Case Type I, exhibiting 3 to 4 mm pockets and minimal to no bone loss. The modified (thin) right is designed for application on the mandibular facial of #31. The standard rigid tip is designed to remove heavy or tenacious calculus.

4.

D. The client is allergic to penicillin; therefore another antibiotic would need to be selected if antibiotic therapy is deemed necessary. The new paradigm in periodontal therapy includes use of antimicrobial adjuncts such as tetracycline, chlorhexidine, and daily phenolic compound rinses.

5.

D. When the gingival margin has receded apically to the CEJ, the clinical attachment level is determined by measuring the distance from the base of the pocket to the CEJ. The pocket depth of 5 mm is added to the recession measurement of 5 mm, giving the clinical attachment a measurement of 10 mm.

6.

B. Class II restorations are only evident on teeth #s 29 and 30. Neither restoration exhibits an overhang on the radiographs. Vertical bone loss, periapical pathology (#12), and furcation involvement (on most molars) are evident on the radiographs.

7.

B. While a desensitizing dentifrice is an appropriate recommendation for the client's dentinal hypersensitivity, it does not address the client's chief complaint of bleeding gingiva. Regular use of the proxy brush, sulcular flossing, antimicrobial mouth rinses, and perio aid (toothpick) would improve plaque control and reduce gingival inflammation and bleeding.

8.

A. The client has advanced periodontitis and is unable to afford definitive periodontal treatment—periodontal surgery. In addition, the client's home care is noncompliant. Therefore, a 3-month continued care interval is most appropriate for this client to debride the periodontal pockets and monitor his periodontal condition.

9.

D. The term *festooned* refers to enlargement of the marginal gingiva with the formation of a lifesaver-like gingival prominence.

10.

D. With hepatitis C, the symptoms include abdominal discomfort, nausea, and vomiting. The symptoms of thyroid disease, diabetes, and tuberculosis do not include those stated above.

11.

C. The Gracey curet 5/6 is designed for use on anterior and premolar teeth. The Columbia 4R/4L is a universal instrument that can be used on the entire dentition. The Gracey curet 15/16 is designed to provide access to the mesials of posterior teeth. The modified curved right ultrasonic tip can access the lingual aspect of #3 and the modified curved left tip can access the facial of #3.

12.

A. The Gracey curet 3/4 is designed for use on the anterior teeth and not appropriate for use on #15. The Gracey curet 7/8 and 9/10 are designed for use on the facial and lingual surfaces of posterior teeth. The Gracey curet 11/12 and 13/14 are designed for use on the mesial and distal surfaces of posterior teeth, respectively.

➤ CASE 11

1.

C. Tooth #9 exhibits a Class IV restoration involving the proximal surface and incisal edge. A Class II restoration involves the proximal surfaces of posterior teeth. A Class III restoration involves the proximal surfaces of anterior tooth. A Class V restoration involves the cervical one third of the facial or lingual surface.

2.

D. The interdental brush would be difficult to handle for this client because of her arthritis. Also, the contour of her gingival tissues does not allow for access to the proximal areas. Owing to the larger and/or longer handles, an automatic toothbrush, floss holder, and oral irrigator would be easier to grasp.

3.

B. A dietary fluoride supplement would not be beneficial for this client because she is over 16 years of age. Dietary fluoride supplements are indicated for those under 16 who use a private water supply without natural fluoride, whose water supply has less than optimum fluoride, and who live in a community where the water supply has not been fluoridated. A dentifrice and mouth rinse containing fluoride would be appropriate for this client because they both provide a low concentration of fluoride, which has a bacteriostatic effect on the bacteria. A professional fluoride treatment would be indicated because there is evidence of dental caries.

4.

C. To get the total amount of attachment loss, the probing depth must be added to the amount of recession present. The amount of attachment loss is 5 mm because the probing depth is 3 mm and the amount of recession is 2 mm.

5.

B. The finding on the hard palate is tori. When palpating the hard palate, the digital method of examination is used that involves a single finger. Inspection, the visual examination of tissues, should be used in conjunction with the digital examination. Using only the inspection method may cause the examiner to overlook significant findings. Bimanual examination involves using the finger and thumb from each hand simultaneously. The bilateral examination method involves using both hands at the same time to examine corresponding structures on opposite sides of the body.

6.

C. The mandibular central incisor radiograph shows evidence of nutrient canals. These canals are radiolucent vertical lines located between the teeth.

7.

C. Irreversible hydrocolloid does not have adequate accuracy for predictable removable partials. Reversible hydrocolloid, addition silicone, and polysulfide are appropriate choices for impression materials.

8.

A. The client's blood pressure is slightly lower than the normal range for an elderly person—systolic, 90 to 140, and diastolic, 60 to 90. All other vital signs are within normal limits.

9.

C. NSAID is an anti-inflammatory drug that would not contribute to tooth mobility. Loss of bone support, occlusal trauma, and in some instances hormone alterations are associated with increased tooth mobility.

10.

C. Calculus is a major factor in gingival inflammation and is most damaging because its rough surface allows for plaque accumulation. Calculus can cause irritation to the tissue, but that is secondary to its ability to harbor plaque. Calculus does not alter dentin.

11.

D. The external (lateral) pterygoid pulls the head of the condyle down the posterior slope of the articular eminence. The masseter, temporalis, and internal (medial) pterygoid muscles assist in closing the mandible.

12.

D. The oculomotor is a motor nerve to the levator muscle that raises the upper eyelid. The glossopharyngeal is a motor nerve to the throat muscles. The abducens and facial nerves are motor nerves, which serve the lateral rectus and muscles of facial expression, respectively.

➤ CASE 12

1.

B. Root caries is the absence of tooth structure, but calculus and tobacco stain are deposits. Abrasion is the mechanical wearing away of tooth structure and appears smooth, shiny, and hard.

2.

C. Vertical placement of bitewings, instead of horizontal, gives the necessary view to show advanced bone loss. Occlusal film technique and the pantomogram are not useful in accurately diagnosing bone level.

3.

D. Overjet occurs when the maxillary incisors are facial to the mandibular incisors with a measurable horizontal distance. Edge-to-edge occurs when the maxillary and mandibular incisal surfaces meet. The vertical overlap of the maxillary over the mandibular teeth is overbite.

4.

A. Ultrasonic scaling is superior to sonic scaling owing to the increased frequency. Hoes and files would not be instruments of choice for this client's condition.

5.

C. Graves' disease is associated with hyperthyroidism, not hypothyroidism. Myxedema is the most severe form of hypothyroidism. The client may also experience cold intolerance and glossitis.

6.

C. Meclizine is an antihistimine. Synthroid, Levoxyl, and Naprosyn are used in treating hypothyroidism.

7.

A. Because the client is concerned about her children and has limited income, the first step should be to see the school counselor.

8.

A. Masticatory forces will help clean the occlusal surfaces of plaque. Because there are no opposing teeth, the cleansing action does not occur. Medications may contribute to calculus formation, but in this client, lack of opposing teeth is the cause. Flossing is beneficial for cleansing proximal, not occlusal, surfaces. Wharton's duct is located in the mandibular region. Salivary flow from the duct would have little impact on calculus formation in the maxillary molars.

9.

A. Horizontal bone loss is relatively constant throughout the mouth. Localized horizontal bone loss would suggest one or two isolated areas. Generalized vertical bone loss would suggest vertical or angular defects throughout the mouth. Localized vertical bone loss would suggest isolated areas of angular loss. None of the three apply.

10.

C. Calculus removal at #2 will expose dentinal tubules. These exposed tubules may cause tooth sensitivity, especially to cold and sweets. Traumatized tissue does not result in tissue sensitivity. There is no evidence of occlusal caries on #14. Calculus removal on the facial will not alter the tooth's occlusion.

11.

A. The myelinated A-delta fibers are irritated because of rapid fluid movement in the open dentinal tubules. Myelinated C fibers and long neurons are not associated with dentin hypersensivity. Tooth innervation is from the trigeminal or 5th cranial nerve.

12.

A. *Actinomyces viscosis* is associated with root surface caries. *Actinobacillus actinomycemcomitans, Fusobacterium nucleatum,* and *Prevotella intermedia* are involved in the development of periodontal disease. *Streptococcus mutans* is an etiological agent in coronal caries.

➤ CASE 13

1.

A. The Angle's classification is Class I. The mesial cusp of the maxillary first molar is aligned with the buccal groove of the mandibular first molar, and the cusp of the maxillary canine is positioned to the immediate distal of the mandibular canine. Classes II and III are not choices for this client's occlusion since she has a Class I occlusion for the reasons stated previously.

2.

D. Tooth #31 has a proximal restoration, which can be a plaque-retentive factor. Bacteria will more likely adhere to a restoration.

3.

A. Tooth #7 is the pontic of the cantilever bridge, which has only one abutment. A Maryland bridge would have metal fingers extending on the linguals of teeth #s 6 and 8. A three-unit fixed bridge would have #8 as an abutment with a crown. A laminate needs to have a tooth available to be attached and tooth #7 is missing. Also, it would not be durable enough to hold a pontic.

4.

D. The active ingredient in tartar-control toothpaste is pyrophosphate. Potassium nitrate and triclosan are active ingredients in antihypersensitivity and antigingivitis dentifrices, respectively. Acidulated phosphate fluoride in the only fluoride not added to dentifrices. It is used in in-office fluoride applications.

5.

A. The client's blood pressure, 144/92, is higher than the normal average, which is systolic 90 to 140, and diastolic, 60 to 90. The remaining vital sign readings are within the normal adult limits. Normal limits for the pulse are 60 to 100 and normal limits for the respiration rate are 12 to 20.

6.

D. To obtain the radial pulse, it is necessary to palpate the radial artery, which is located on the radial side of the wrist. The carotid artery is palpated on the side of the neck. The facial artery is palpated on the side of the face, near the angle of the mandible. The brachial artery is palpated at the antecubital fossa at the bend of the elbow.

7.

A. The alloy on tooth #19 is on the occlusal surface—a Class I restoration. A Class II restoration involves the proximal surface of posterior teeth. A Class V restoration involves the cervical one third of either the facial or lingual surfaces. A Class VI restoration involves the incisal edges of anterior teeth and cusps of posterior teeth.

8.

C. The first permanent molars are in crossbite. There is no evidence that the first molars are end-to-end, open-bite, or edge-to-edge.

9.

D. The client is at the habit level of the learning ladder. She demonstrates routine oral hygiene practices with her brushing and flossing. This client has surpassed the awareness, self-interest, and involvement stages of the learning ladder.

10.

C. The bacteria most likely found in a healthy mouth would be Gram-positive cocci. The remaining three, Gram-negative rods, spirochetes, and white blood cells, are present in diseased gingival tissues.

11.

B. For the client's height, her weight is within normal body weight range. Signs of depression include withdrawal from social contact and loss of appetite, which are not evidenced by this client. The symptoms of Type 1 diabetes are abrupt weight loss, weakness, and insulin dependency, none of which are evidenced by this client.

12.

B. Because the client's weight is within normal limits, her caloric intake appears to be fine. Exercise, calcium intake, and hormone replacement therapy are recommended for an individual suffering from osteoporosis.

➤ CASE 14

1.

B. Recession is not associated with multiple sclerosis. However, TMJ dysfunction, xerostomia, and gingival enlargement are associated with multiple sclerosis.

2.

C. Lip and tongue tremor is associated with Parkinson's disease. Lordosis, an increased curvature of any part of the back, is associated with muscular dystrophy, and paralysis of facial muscles is associated with Bell's palsy.

3.

D. The client has a functional heart murmur that does NOT require antibiotic premedication.

4.

D. The client has a history of herpes labialis, which is a communicable disease and, thus, contraindicated for air polishing. However, no current herpes lesions were detected at this visit. Air polishing is contraindicated for clients with gingival recession, hypertension, and gingivitis.

5.

A. The Gracey curet is used for removal of light calculus deposits and root surface debridement. The hoe, file, and sickle scaler are used to remove heavy calculus and therefore are appropriate for initial debridement.

6.

D. A Class III restoration involves a proximal surface of an anterior tooth and does not involve the incisal angle. Horizontal bone loss and caries are evident on tooth #30, and calculus is evident on several posterior teeth.

7.

C. Because of the client's xerostomia, nonalcohol mouth rinses should be recommended. Alcohol will dry the oral mucosa. A toothpick holder (perio aid) is effective for daily plaque removal in areas of early furcation. A daily desensitizing dentifrice is indicated for areas of dentinal hypersensitivity—noted on the facials of most of the client's teeth. Use of a soft-bristled toothbrush will help decrease gingival bleeding, often caused by using a medium-hard toothbrush.

8.

D. Because the client has medium to heavy calculus deposits on the mandibular anterior, a traditional ultrasonic tip, which is designed for removal of such deposits, would be most appropriate. Modified (thin) tips are used to deplaque and remove light to moderate calculus and endotoxins.

9.

D. When the gingival margin has receded apically to the CEJ, the clinical attachment level is determined by measuring the distance from the base of the pocket to the CEJ. In this client, the pocket depth of 2 mm on the direct facial of tooth #6 is added to the recession measurement of 3 mm, resulting in a clinical attachment level of 5 mm.

10.

A. The amalgam in tooth #30 is contraindicated for finishing and polishing, as the mesiolingual cusp is broken and secondary decay is present. Prosthetic replacement should be recommended for replacing teeth #s 3, 13, and 14. The lost crown on #4 should also be replaced. Sealants are recommended on clients when they are caries-active.

11.

B. A transosteal dental implant is placed completely through the bone and is designed strictly for use on the mandible. It cannot be placed in the maxilla. A subperiosteal dental implant may be placed in the mandible or maxilla when the width or depth of the bone is insufficient for an endosseous implant. An endosseous implant is placed within the maxillary or mandibular bone to support a fixed or removable prosthetic appliance.

12.

D. The client's cervical abrasion is most likely due to overbrushing with a medium to hard toothbrush and is not related to the drug Fastin. Side effects of Fastin include xerostomia, which has an indirect effect on caries, periodontal disease, and hypertension.

References

CHAPTER 2 REFERENCES

Aqur, A.: *Grant's Atlas of Anatomy,* 10th Edition, Philadelphia, Lippincott Williams & Wilkins, 1999.

Mader, S.S.: *Understanding Human Anatomy and Physiology,* 3rd Edition, Dubuque, IA, Wm. C. Brown Publishers, 1997.

Moore, K.L. and Dalley, A.F.: *Clinically Oriented Anatomy,* 4th Edition, Philadelphia, Lippincott Williams & Wilkins, 1999.

Netter, F.: *Digestive System, Vols 1–3,* New York, Ciba, 1971.

Netter, F.: *Nervous System,* New York, Ciba, 1968.

Netter, F.: *Reproductive System,* Summit, NJ, Ciba, 1954.

Netter, F.: *Endocrine System and Selected Metabolic Diseases,* New York, Ciba, 1970.

Netter, F.: *Heart,* New York, Ciba 1971.

Netter, F.: *Kidneys, Ureters, and Urinary Bladder,* New York, Ciba, 1973.

Rosse, C. and Gaddum-Rosse, P.: *Hollinshead's Textbook of Anatomy,* 5th Edition, Philadelphia, Lippincott-Raven, 1997.

CHAPTER 3 REFERENCES

Gardner, M.: *Basic Anatomy of the Head and Neck,* 1st Edition, Philadelphia, Lea & Febiger, 1992.

Grant, J.C.: *A Method of Anatomy,* 2nd Edition, Baltimore, Williams & Wilkins, 1940.

Hiatt, J. and Gartner, L.: *Texbook of Head and Neck Anatomy,* 1st Edition, Baltimore, Williams & Wilkins, 1987.

King, B. and Showers, M.J.: *Human Anatomy and Physiology,* 6th Edition, Philadelphia, W.B. Saunders Co., 1963.

Moore, K.: *The Developing Human,* 1st Edition, Philadelphia, W.B. Saunders Co., 1973.

Reed, G. and Sheppard, V.: *Basic Structures of the Head and Neck,* 1st Edition, Philadelphia, W.B. Saunders Co., 1976.

CHAPTER 4 REFERENCES

Darby, M.: *Comprehensive Review of Dental Hygiene,* 4th Edition, St. Louis, Mosby, 1998.

Melphi, R.: *Permar's Oral Embryology and Microscopic Anatomy,* 9th Edition, Philadelphia, Lea & Febiger, 1994.

Thomas, C.: *Taber's Cyclopedia Medical Dictionary,* 16th Edition, Philadelphia, F.A. Davis Company, 1989.

Woefel, J.B. and Scheid, R.C.: *Dental Anatomy: Its Relevance to Dentistry,* 5th Edition, Baltimore, Williams & Wilkins, 1997.

CHAPTER 5 REFERENCES

Davis, J.R. and Stegeman, C.A.: *The Dental Hygienist's Guide to Nutritional Care,* 1st Edition, Philadelphia, W.B. Saunders Co., 1998.

Food and Nutrition Board: *Dietary Reference Intakes: Calcium, Phosphorus, Magnesium, Vitamin D, and Fluoride,* Washington, D.C., National Academy of Sciences, 1997.

Mahan, L.K. and Escott-Stump, S.: *Krause's Food, Nutrition, and Diet Therapy,* 9th Edition, W.B. Saunders Co., 1996.

Palmer, C.A.: *Nutrition and the Oral Condition: A Case-Based Guide for Clinicians,* Prentice Hall, in press.

CHAPTER 6 REFERENCES

Alcamo, I.E.: *Fundamentals of Microbiology*, 5th Edition, Menlo Park, CA. Addison Wesley Longman, Inc., 1997.

Black, J.G.: *Microbiology Principles & Applications*, 3rd Edition, Upper Saddle River, NJ, Prentice Hall, 1996.

Darby, M.K.: *Mosby's Comprehensive Review of Dental Hygiene*, 4th Edition, St Louis, Mosby, 1998.

Janusz, S.: *Adventures in Learning*, Periodontology Board Review, Champaign, IL, 1999.

Madigan, M.T., Martinko, J.M., and Parker, J.: *Brock Biology of Microorganisms*, 8th Edition, Upper Saddle River, NJ, Prentice Hall, 1997.

Nester, E.W., Roberts, C.E., and Nester, M.T.: *Microbiology: A Human Perspective*, Dubuque, IA, Wm. C. Brown Publishers, 1995.

Schaechter, M., Engleberg, N.C., Eisenstein, B.I., and Medoff, G.: *Mechanisms of Microbial Disease,* 3rd Edition, Baltimore, Williams & Wilkins, 1998.

Wilkens, E.M.: *Clinical Practice of the Dental Hygienist,* 8th Edition, Philadelphia, Lippincott Williams & Wilkins, 1999.

Willet, N.P, White, R.R., and Rosen, S.: *Essential Dental Microbiology,* Norwalk, CT, Appleton & Lange, 1991.

CHAPTER 7 REFERENCES

Iben, P.: *Oral Pathology for the Dental Hygienist,* 2nd Edition, Philadelphia, W.B. Saunders Co., 1996.

Neville, D. and Allen B.: *Oral and Maxillofacial Pathology,* Philadelphia, W.B. Saunders Co., 1995.

Regezi, S.: *Oral Pathology: Clinical-Pathologic Correlation,* 3rd Edition, Philadelphia, W.B. Saunders Co., 1999.

CHAPTER 8 REFERENCES

Haveles, E.B.: *Pharmacology for Dental Hygiene Practice.* Albany, NY, Delmar Publishers, 1997.

Requa-Clark, B.S. and Holroyd, S.V.: *Applied Pharmacology for the Dental Hygienist,* 3rd Edition, St Louis, Mosby, 1995.

Yagiela, J.A., Neidle, E.A., and Dowd, F.J.: *Pharmacology and Therapeutics for Dentistry,* 4th Edition, St Louis, Mosby, 1998.

Gage, T. and Pickett, F.: *Mosby's Dental Drug Reference,* 4th Edition, St Louis, Mosby, 1999.

CHAPTER 9 REFERENCES

Cochran, D., Kalkwarf, K., and Brunsvold, M.: *Plaque and Calculus Removal: Considerations for the Professional,* Chicago, Quintessence Books, 1994.

Darby, M.L. and Walsh, M.M.: *Dental Hygiene Theory and Practice,* 1st Edition, Philadelphia, W.B. Saunders Co., 1994.

Harris, N.O. and Garcia-Goday, F.: *Primary Preventive Dentistry,* 5th Edition, Stamford, CT, Appleton & Lange, 1999.

Perry, D., Beemsterboer, P., and Taggert, E.: *Periodontology for the Dental Hygienist,* Philadelphia, W.B. Saunders Co., 1996.

Wilkens, E.M.: *Clinical Practice of the Dental Hygienist,* 8th Edition, Philadelphia, Lippincott Williams &Wilkins, 1999.

CHAPTER 10 REFERENCES

Darby, M.: *Comprehensive Review of Dental Hygiene,* 4th Edition, St Louis, Mosby, 1998.

Hodges, K.: *Concepts in Nonsurgical Periodontal Therapy,* Albany, NY, Delmar, 1998.

Neild-Gehrig, J. and Houseman, G.: *Fundamentals of Periodontal Instrumentation,* Baltimore, William & Wilkins, 1996.

Wilkins, E.: *Clinical Practice of the Dental Hygienist,* 8th Edition, Baltimore, Williams & Wilkins, 1999.

Woodall, I.: *Comprehensive Dental Hygiene Care,* 4th Edition, St Louis, Mosby, 1993.

CHAPTER 11 REFERENCES

Goaz, P.W. and White S.C.: *Oral Radiology: Principles and Interpretation,* 3rd Edition. St Louis, Mosby-Yearbook, 1994.

Haring, J.I. and Lind L.J.: *Dental Radiography: Principles and Techniques,* Philadelphia, W.B. Saunders, 1996.

Hodges, K.O.: *Concepts in Nonsurgical Periodontal Therapy.* Cincinnati, Delmar Publishers, 1997.

Holm-Pedersen, P. and Loe, H.: *Textbook of Geriatric Dentistry,* 2nd Edition. Copenhagen, Munksgaard, 1996.

Papas, A.S., Niessen, L.C. and Chauncey, H.H.: *Geriatric Dentistry, Aging and Oral Health,* St Louis, Mosby-Yearbook, 1991.

Physicians' Desk Reference, 52nd Edition. Montvale, NJ, Medical Economics Company, 1998.

Razmus, T.F. and Williamson, G.F.: *Current Oral and Maxillofacial Imaging,* Philadelphia, W.B. Saunders, 1996.

Woodall, I.R.: *Comprehensive Dental Hygiene,* 4th Edition. St Louis, Mosby-Yearbook, 1993.

CHAPTER 12 REFERENCES

Carranza, F.E., Newman, M.G.: *Clinical Periodontology,* 8th Edition, Philadelphia, W.B. Saunders Co., 1996.

Carranza, F.E.: *Glickman's Clinical Periodontology,* 6th Edition, Philadelphia, W.B. Saunders, Co., 1984.

Darby, M.L. and Walsh, M.M.: *Dental Hygiene Theory and Practice,* Philadelphia, W.B. Saunders, Co., 1995.

Fedi, P.F. and Vernino, A.R.: *The Periodontal Syllabus,* 3rd Edition, Baltimore, Williams & Wilkins, 1995.

Schwartz, M., Lamster, I.B., and Fine, J.B.: *Clinical Guide to Periodontics,* Philadelphia, W.B. Saunders, Co., 1995.

CHAPTER 13 REFERENCES

American Red Cross: *First Aid – Responding to Emergencies.* St Louis: Mosby Lifeline, 1996.

Little, J.W. and Falace, D.A.: *Dental Management of the Medically Compromised Patient,* St Louis, Mosby, 1997.

Malamed, S.F.: *Medical Emergencies in the Dental Office.* St Louis, Mosby, 1993.

CHAPTER 14 REFERENCES

Craig, R.G., O'Brien, W.J., and Powers, J.M.: *Dental Materials: Properties and Manipulation,* 6th Edition, St Louis, Mosby, 1996.

Darby, M.L.: *Mosby's Comprehensive Review of Dental Hygiene,* 3rd Edition, St Louis, Mosby, 1994.

Ferracane, J.L.: *Materials in Dentistry: Principles and Applications,* Philadelphia, J.B. Lippinott Co., 1995.

Phillips, R.W. and Moore, B.K.: *Elements of Dental Materials,* 5th Edition, Philadelphia, W.B. Saunders Co., 1994.

CHAPTER 15 REFERENCES

Burt, B.A. and Eklund, S.A.: *Dentistry, Dental Practice, and the Community,* Philadelphia, W.B. Saunders Co., 1999.

Corbin, S.B. and Martin, F.R.: The future of dental public health report—preparing dental public health to meet the challenges: Opportunities of the 21st century. *J Public Health Dent* 54:80, 1994.

Dean, H.T.: The investigation of physiological effects by the epidemiological method. In: Moulton, F.R., ed: *Fluorine and Dental Health,* Washington, DC, American Association for the Advancement of Science, 1942, pp. 23–71.

Ferjerskov, H.S., et al.: A new method for assessing the prevalence of dental fluorosis—the Tooth Surface Index of Fluorosis, *J Am Dent Assoc* 109:37–41, 1984.

Fisher, F.J.: A field survey of dental caries, periodontal disease and enamel defects in Tristan da Cunha. *Br Dent J* 125:447–453, 1968.

Gluck, G.M. and Morganstein, W.M.: *Jong's Community Dental Health,* 4th Edition, St Louis, Mosby, 1998.

Greenstein, G.: The role of bleeding upon probing in the diagnosis of periodontal disease, *J Periodontol* 55:684–688, 1984.

Klein, H., Palmer, C., and Knutson, J.W.: Studies of dental caries. I. Dental status and dental needs of elementary school children. *Public Health Rep* 53:751–765, 1938

Locker, D. and Slade, G.D.: Association between clinical and subjective indicators of oral health status in older adult populations. *Gerontology* 11:108–114, 1994

Ramfjord, S.P.: Indices for prevalence and incidence of periodontal disease. *J Periodontol* 30:51–59, 1959.

Russell, A.L.: A system of scoring for prevalence surveys of periodontal disease. *J Dent Res* 35:350–359, 1956.

Takeuchi, M.: Epidemiological study on dental caries in Japanese children before, during, and after World War II. *Int Dent J* 11:443–457, 1961.

American Association of Public Health Dentistry and American Board of Public Health: Dental public health: The past, present, and future. *J Am Dent Assoc* 117:171–176, 1988.

Index